FOURTH EDITION

Learning

PRINCIPLES AND APPLICATIONS

Stephen B. Klein
Mississippi State University

Boston   Burr Ridge, IL   Dubuque, IA   Madison, WI   New York   San Francisco   St. Louis
Bangkok   Bogotá   Caracas   Kuala Lumpur   Lisbon   London   Madrid   Mexico City
Milan   Montreal   New Delhi   Santiago   Seoul   Singapore   Sydney   Taipei   Toronto

McGraw-Hill Higher Education

A Division of The **McGraw-Hill** *Companies*

LEARNING: PRINCIPLES AND APPLICATIONS
FOURTH EDITION

Published by McGraw-Hill, a business unit of The McGraw-Hill Companies, Inc., 1221 Avenue of the Americas, New York, NY 10020. Copyright © 2002, 1996, 1991, 1987 by The McGraw-Hill Companies, Inc. All rights reserved. No part of this publication may be reproduced or distributed in any form or by any means, or stored in a database or retrieval system, without the prior written consent of The McGraw-Hill Companies, Inc., including, but not limited to, in any network or other electronic storage or transmission, or broadcast for distance learning.

Some ancillaries, including electronic and print components, may not be available to customers outside the United States.

This book is printed on acid-free paper.

International 1 2 3 4 5 6 7 8 9 0 DOC/DOC 0 9 8 7 6 5 4 3 2 1
Domestic   2 3 4 5 6 7 8 9 0 DOC/DOC 0 9 8 7 6 5 4 3 2

ISBN 0–07–249046–2
ISBN 0–07–113143–4 (ISE)

Editorial director: *Jane E. Karpacz*
Senior sponsoring editor: *Melissa Mashburn*
Editorial coordinator: *Cheri Dellelo*
Senior marketing manager: *Chris Hall*
Project manager: *Christine Walker*
Production supervisor: *Sherry L. Kane*
Designer: *K. Wayne Harms*
Cover design: *Nathan Bahls*
Senior supplement producer: *Stacy A. Patch*
Media technology senior producer: *Sean Crowley*
Compositor: *GAC—Indianapolis*
Typeface: *10/12 Palatino*
Printer: *R. R. Donnelley & Sons Company/Crawfordsville, IN*

The credits section for this book begins on page 534 and is considered an extension of the copyright page.

Library of Congress Cataloging-in-Publication Data
Klein, Stephen B.
   Learning : principles and applications / Stephen B. Klein.—4th ed.
      p. cm.
   Includes bibliographical references (p.   ) and indexes.
   ISBN 0–07–249046–2 (alk. paper)
   1. Learning. 2. Conditioned response. I. Title.

   LB1060 .K59   2002
   370.15′23—dc21

                                                                            2001030711
                                                                            CIP

INTERNATIONAL EDITION ISBN 0–07–113143–4
Copyright © 2002. Exclusive rights by The McGraw-Hill Companies, Inc., for manufacture and export. This book cannot be re-exported from the country to which it is sold by McGraw-Hill. The International Edition is not available in North America.

www.mhhe.com

About the Author

STEPHEN B. KLEIN is professor and head of the psychology department at Mississippi State University. He received a B.S. degree in psychology in 1968 from Virginia Polytechnic Institute and a Ph.D. degree in psychology in 1971 from Rutgers University. Professor Klein taught at Old Dominion University for twelve years and at Fort Hays State University for seven years prior to coming to Mississippi State University in 1990. He has written numerous articles for psychological journals in the area of the biological basis of learning and memory and is the author of *Motivation: Biosocial Approaches,* published by McGraw-Hill in 1982; *Learning: Principles and Applications,* published by McGraw-Hill in 1987, 1991, 1996, and 2002; and *Biological Psychology,* published by Prentice-Hall in 2000. Dr. Klein coedited the two-volume text *Contemporary Learning Theories* in 1989 and *Handbook of Contemporary Learning Theories* in 2001, both published by Lawrence Erlbaum. His family includes his wife, Marie, and five children, Dora, David, Jason, Katherine, and William. In his spare time, he enjoys sports, most passionately baseball, and science fiction, especially Star Trek and Star Wars.

To my wife, Marie, and my daughter, Dora,
who have helped in innumerable ways
with the writing of this text.

Contents

Preface

Learning: Principles and Applications seeks to provide students with an up-to-date presentation of the current knowledge in learning. Basic principles are described and supplemented by research studies to provide validation of those principles, and both classic experiments and important contemporary studies are incorporated into the text. The fourth edition continues to uphold the same uncompromising scholarship of earlier editions. Psychologists who study the nature of the learning process have uncovered many important principles about how we acquire information about the structure of our environment and how we use this understanding to interact effectively with our environment. As in earlier editions, the fourth edition provides a thorough, up-to-date coverage of such principles and applications.

Much exciting new research in learning has occurred in the last few years, and I focus attention on these findings throughout the text. Some of the key new discoveries include the conditioning of immune system suppression, the identification of behavioral economic principles in operant conditioning, the determination of conditions that lead to a reinforcer being devalued, the recognition of processes that provide the reinforcing power of psychoactive drugs, the study of the question of whether language learning occurs in primates, and the relevance of memory reconstruction to understanding the validity of repressed memories.

As in previous editions, the text presents the important contributions of both human and nonhuman animal research, as both are crucial to our understanding of the learning process. In many instances, nonhuman animal studies and human research have yielded identical results, indicating the generality of the processes governing learning. While there are many general laws of learning, there are also instances in which species differ in their ability to learn a particular behavior. The use of different animals has shown that biological character affects learning. Furthermore, in some situations, only animal research can be ethically conducted, while in other cases, only human research can identify the learning process that is unique to people.

ORGANIZATION

Based on feedback from users of the previous edition of the book, the discussion of theories of learning has been moved to follow the presentation of the basic learning principles. This change allows the student to understand the basic principles by which behavior is learned or eliminated before the discussion of the nature of that learning. Brief descriptions of chapter coverage follow.

Chapter 1 gives a brief introduction to learning as well as a discussion of the origins of behavior theory. The student is first introduced to basic learning principles through a description of the research findings and theories of Thorndike, Pavlov, and Watson. The importance of their work will be evident throughout the text. A brief presentation of the ethics of conducting research is also included in this chapter.

Chapter 2 describes the nature of instinctive processes and how instincts govern behavior. This chapter also describes two learning processes, habituation and sensitization, by which experience can alter instinctive behaviors. Opponent process theory, which describes the affective responses both during and following an event, also is introduced in this chapter.

Chapter 3 details Pavlovian conditioning, a process that involves learning when and where events will or will not occur. This discussion first explores the factors that govern the acquisition or elimination of conditioned responses. Several procedures (higher order conditioning, sensory precondition, and vicarious conditioning) in which a conditioned response can be learned with direct CS-UCS pairings can be found in this chapter. Several of the Pavlovian conditioning principles that have been used to establish effective and eliminating impairing conditioned responses are also presented.

Chapters 4 and 5 describe instrumental or operant conditioning, a process that involves learning how to behave in order to obtain the positive aspects (reinforcers) and avoid the negative aspects (punishers) that exist in our environment. The variables influencing the development or extinction of appetitive or reinforcer-seeking behavior are described in Chapter 4, while Chapter 5 presents the determinants of escape and avoidance behavior as well as the influence of punishment on behavior. The use of reinforcement and punishment to establish appropriate and eliminate inappropriate behavior also is described in these chapters.

Chapter 6 describes traditional learning theory. The theories of Hull, Spence, Guthrie, Tolman, and Skinner are explored in this chapter. The student will be able to see the changes that have taken place in the understanding of the nature of the learning process during the first half of the 20th century.

Chapter 7 discusses the environmental control of behavior and how the stimulus environment can exert a powerful influence on how we act. A discussion of stimulus generalization and discrimination learning is the major focus of the chapter. Special attention is given to understanding the difference between the eliciting and occasion-setting functions of conditioned and discriminative stimuli.

Chapter 8 describes the cognitive processes that affect how and when we behave. This chapter examines the relative contributions of expectancies and habits to determining one's actions. The relevance of cognitive learning for understanding the causes of depression and phobias also is discussed in this chapter.

Chapter 9 describes the ideas of contemporary learning theories. This chapter discusses these contemporary views on the nature of the learning process as well as how these ideas have been shaped by the theories developed by previous generations of psychologists. These contemporary theories have focused on an examination of the nature of Pavlovian conditioning and an understanding of behavioral economic principles.

Chapter 10 discusses the biological processes that influence learning. In some instances, learning is enhanced by instinctive systems, whereas in others, learning is impaired by our biological character. This chapter also describes the biological processes that provide the pleasurable aspects of reinforcement and the negative aspects of punishment.

Chapter 11 details three complex learning processes. This chapter explores how we identify concepts, solve problems, and learn to use language. A discussion of animal cognition is an important focus of this chapter, and the issue of whether language is unique to humans is one of the key areas of this discussion.

Chapters 12 and 13 discuss memory, the process that allows us to retain the influence of a learning experience into the future. The nature of memory storage and the encoding or organization of our experiences is described in Chapter 12. The processes that allow us to retrieve some experiences or forget others are detailed in Chapter 13. Further, the biological basis of memory storage and retrieval is presented in these chapters.

PEDAGOGICAL FEATURES

Pedagogy remains a central feature of this new edition, but approaches have been reworked to enhance their impact. In addition, all-new pedagogical features have been added to promote students' understanding of the learning process and better enable them to see its relevance to their everyday lives.

Vignettes. A vignette opens each chapter, and some chapters include vignettes within the chapter as well. This pedagogical feature serves three purposes: First, it lets students know what type of material will be presented in the chapter and provides them with a frame of reference. Second, the vignette arouses the student's curiosity and enhances the impact of the text material. Third, references to the vignette have been incorporated into the text to give it a seamless quality. I have found that students like the chapter-opening vignettes, and I believe that their use solidifies the link between the text material and the students' lives.

"Before You Go On" Sections. I have included two critical thinking questions in each of the *Before You Go On* sections, which appear throughout the chapter. The *Before You Go On* questions ensure that the students understand the material and allow them to apply this knowledge in original, creative ways. My students report that the use of this pedagogy is quite helpful in understanding what can be difficult concepts.

"Application" Sections. Although applications of the text material are presented throughout, each chapter has at least one stand-alone application section. Many of the discoveries made by psychologists have been applied to solving real-world problems. These applications demonstrate that psychologists are interested in solving problems and not merely in accumulating knowledge. The application sections also enhance the relevance of the abstract ideas presented in the text, showing the student that the behaviors described do exist and are not just laboratory phenomena.

"Chapter Summaries." I have provided a review of key points at the end of each chapter, as another tool for students to check their understanding of the material that has just been covered. Once the students have read the chapter, they can easily use the review sections as a study guide to prepare for examinations.

"Critical Thinking Questions." Critical thinking questions in the form of scenarios are presented at the end of each chapter. Answering these questions requires creative application of one or more of the major concepts presented in the chapter, further assisting students in relating the principles presented in the text to situations that they may encounter in the real world.

SUPPLEMENTS

Instructor's Manual/Test Bank (0-07-2490470). This Instructor's Manual/Test Bank provides many useful tools to enhance your teaching. For each chapter, a general overview, a detailed chapter outline, teaching tips, and activities are provided. The Test Bank portion of this manual includes 50 questions for each chapter: 25 multiple choice, 15 true/false, and 10 fill-in-the-blank questions.

Custom Website (0-07-249048-9). The custom-crafted website to accompany *Learning, Fourth Edition* includes a number of resources for instructors and students to enhance their teaching and learning experience. For the instructor, this website includes an image gallery and Web links. The student portion of the site includes a Guide to Electronic Research, Web resources, Internet exercises, key terms, practice quizzes, and Web links. Visit it at www.mhhe.com/klein4.

ACKNOWLEDGMENTS

The textbook has had input from many people. I thank the students in my learning classes who read drafts of the chapters and pointed out which sections they liked, which they disliked, and which were unclear. The staff at McGraw-Hill played an important role in the creation of this edition. Melissa Mashburn and Cheri Dellelo guided the development of the text from its inception to this final product. The project manager, Christine Walker, ensured that the text was not only easy to read but also aesthetically appealing.

I also thank my colleagues who reviewed chapters of the fourth edition. I am especially grateful to John Caruso, University of Massachusetts at Dartmouth; Carl D. Cheney, Utah State University; Donna Dahlgren, Indiana University; Joel S. Freund, University of Arkansas; Michael D. Hall, University of Nevada, Las Vegas; Henry Marcucella, Boston University; Denis Mitchell, University of Southern California; and Danielle Polage, Pepperdine University for their detailed and constructive comments.

I wish to thank Barbara Butler and Brenda Lambert for their secretarial assistance and my graduate assistant, Amanda Netterville, for her technical support. Their help allowed the project to progress quite smoothly.

My family has been very supportive of my work on this edition, and I am grateful for their help and understanding.

Stephen B. Klein

Mississippi State University

CHAPTER 1

An Introduction to Learning

The Gift of Knowledge

Marcus entered college 3 years ago with the intention of studying law. His interest in the law was spurred by a course he had taken in high school. However, over the past year, he has found several of his psychology courses more exciting and challenging than his political science classes, and he now wants to obtain a degree in clinical psychology. Marcus's concern over his younger sister Yolanda's drug problems has stimulated his interest in psychology. Yolanda, an excellent student before she began to experiment with drugs several years ago, is now addicted, has quit school, and has left home. Marcus wants to understand the factors that can lead to addictive behavior, and he hopes to contribute someday to the development of an effective drug addiction therapy. Dr. Martinez, Marcus's advisor, suggested that Marcus enroll in a course on learning in order to fulfill the Psychology department's degree requirements. Spending endless hours watching rats run through mazes and analyzing pages and pages of data did not appeal to Marcus. Interested in the human aspect of psychology, Marcus wondered how this course would benefit him. However, he worried that if he did not take the course, it would adversely affect Dr. Martinez's evaluation of him for graduate school, so he enrolled in the class. Marcus soon discovered that his preconceived ideas about the learning course were incorrect. The course covered research with both human and nonhuman subjects, and the various types of experimentation complemented each other in revealing the nature of the learning processes that govern behavior. The experiments, far from boring, made the learning principles described in class seem real. Marcus soon found that learning involves developing effective methods to obtain reward and to avoid punishment, as well as an understanding of when and where these responses are appropriate. He became interested in learning how basic research has stimulated the development of behavior modification techniques and how understanding the principles of learning benefits the student of clinical psychology.

Psychology relies heavily on theory to guide its research; theory is especially important in investigations of the learning process. As Marcus discovered, many generations of psychologists have speculated on the nature of learning; and they have shown that the learning process is governed by complex, yet lawful, principles. For instance, Marcus learned that although past psychologists attempted to use a stimulus-response approach to describe the learning process, contemporary psychologists recognize that several processes are involved in the acquisition or elimination of a behavior.

Marcus now thinks that the knowledge gained from the learning class will undoubtedly help in his search for an effective treatment of addictive behavior. You will learn from this book what Marcus discovered about learning in his course. I hope your experience will be as positive as his. We begin our exploration by defining *learning*.

A DEFINITION OF LEARNING

What do we mean by the term **learning?** Learning can be defined as an experiential process resulting in a relatively permanent change in behavior that cannot be explained by temporary states, maturation, or innate response tendencies. This definition of learning has three important components. First, learning reflects a change in the potential for a behavior; it does not automatically lead to a change in behavior. We must be sufficiently motivated to translate learning into behavior. For example, although you may know the location of the campus cafeteria, you will not be motivated to go there until you are hungry. Also, we are sometimes unable to exhibit a particular behavior even though we have learned it and are sufficiently motivated to exhibit it. For example, you may learn from friends that a good movie is playing but not go because you cannot afford it.

Second, the behavior changes that learning causes are not always permanent. As a result of new experiences, previously learned behavior may no longer be exhibited. For example, you may learn a new and faster route to work and no longer take the old route. Also, we sometimes forget a previously learned behavior, and therefore are no longer able to exhibit that behavior. Forgetting the story line of a movie is one instance of the transient aspect of learning.

Third, changes in behavior can be due to processes other than learning. Our behavior can change as the result of a motivational change rather than because of learning. For example, we eat when we are hungry or study when we are worried about an upcoming exam. However, eating or studying may not necessarily be due to learning. Motivational changes, rather than learning, could trigger eating or studying. You may have already learned to eat, and your hunger motivates your eating behavior. Likewise, you may have learned to study to prevent failure, and your fear motivates studying behavior. These behavior changes are temporary; when the motivational state changes again, the behavior will also change. Therefore, you will stop eating when you are no longer hungry and quit studying when you no longer fear failing the examination. Becoming full or fatigued and ceasing to eat or study is another instance where a temporary state, rather than learning, leads to a change in behavior.

Many behavioral changes are the result of maturation. For example, a young child may fear darkness, while an adult does not show an emotional reaction to the dark. This change in emotionality reflects a maturational process and is not dependent on experiences with darkness. Another example of the impact of maturation is a child who cannot open a door at age 1, but can do so at age 2. The change in the child's behavior reflects the physical growth that allows the child to reach the doorknob.

Not all psychologists agree on the nature of the learning process. Some even argue that instinct, rather than experience, determines behavior. We begin our discussion by examining the view that instinctive processes govern human actions. Later in the chapter, we will explore the origins of behavior theory, the view that emphasizes the central role of experience in determining behavior. Throughout the rest of the text, we will discuss what we now know about the nature of learning.

HISTORICAL ORIGINS OF BEHAVIOR THEORY

Psychology has not always been interested in the role of experience in governing human behavior. Early thinking focused on the importance of instinct in human activity.

Functionalism

Functionalism was an early school of psychology that emphasized the instinctive origins and adaptive function of behavior. According to this theory, the function of behavior is to promote survival, and adaptive behaviors allow an animal to survive. However, the functionalists expressed various ideas concerning the mechanisms controlling human behavior. John Dewey (1886) suggested that the reflexive behaviors of lower animals have been replaced in humans by the mind, which has evolved as the primary mechanism for human survival. The brain enables the individual to adapt to the environment. The main idea in Dewey's functionalism was that the manner of human survival differs from that of lower animals.

In contrast to Dewey, William James, also a nineteenth-century psychologist, argued that the major difference between humans and lower animals lies in the character of their respective inborn or instinctual motives. According to James (1890), human beings possess a greater range of **instincts** that guide behavior (for example, rivalry, sympathy, fear, sociability, cleanliness, modesty, and love) than do lower animals. These social instincts directly enhance (or reduce) our successful interaction with our environment and, thus, our survival. William James also proposed that all instincts, both human and nonhuman, have a mentalistic quality, possessing both purpose and direction. Unlike Dewey, James believed that instincts motivated the behavior of both humans and lower animals.

Some psychologists (see Troland, 1928) who opposed a mentalistic concept of instinct argued that internal biochemical forces motivate behavior in all species. Concepts developed in physics and chemistry during the second half of the nineteenth century provided a framework for this mechanistic approach to motivation. Ernst Brucke stated in 1874 that "the living organism is a dynamic system in which the laws of chemistry and physics apply"—a view which led to great advances in physiology. This group of functionalists used a physiochemical approach to explain the motivation for human and animal behavior.

A number of scientists strongly criticized the instinct concept that the functionalists proposed. First, anthropologists pointed to a variety of values, beliefs, and behaviors among different cultures, an observation inconsistent with the idea of universal human instincts. Second, Watson and Morgan's (1917) observations of human infants led them to conclude that only three innate emotional responses existed—fear, rage, and love—and that only a small number of stimuli could elicit these responses. Third, some argued that the widespread and uncritical use of the instinct concept did not advance our understanding of the nature of human behavior. Bernard's (1924) analysis illustrates the weaknesses of the instinct theories of the 1920s. Bernard identified several thousand often-conflicting instincts the functionalists had proposed. For example, Bernard described one instinct as "with a glance of the eye we can estimate instinctively the age of a passerby" (page 132). With this type of proposed "instinct," it is not surprising that many psychologists reacted so negatively to the instinct concept.

BEFORE YOU GO ON

- How would Marcus explain addictive behavior using our definition of learning?
- What could Marcus learn about addiction from our discussion of functionalism?

In the 1920s, American psychology moved away from the instinct explanation of human behavior and began to emphasize the learning process. The psychologists who viewed experience as the major determinant of human actions were called behaviorists. Contemporary views suggest that behavior is traceable to both instinctive and experiential processes. We will look at instinctive processes, and how experience affects instinctive reactions, in the next chapter. In this chapter, we will examine the behaviorists' ideas concerning the nature of the learning process. We will discuss contemporary learning theories in Chapter 9, and the influence of instincts on learning in Chapter 10.

Behaviorism

The Importance of Experience

Behaviorism is a school of thought that emphasizes the role of experience in governing behavior. According to behaviorists, the important processes governing our behavior are learned. We learn both the drives that initiate behavior and the specific behaviors motivated by these drives through our interaction with the environment. A major goal of the behaviorists is to determine the laws governing learning. This concern about the nature of learning has dominated academic psychology for most of the last century. A number of ideas contributed to the behavioral view. The Greek philosopher Aristotle's concept of the association of ideas is one important origin of behaviorism.

Ex. Suppose a friend approaches you after class and remarks that your party last week was terrific. This remark causes you to recall meeting a very attractive person at your party, which in turn reminds you to ask this person for a date. This whole thought process reflects the concept of *the association of ideas:* two events become associated with each other; and thus, when you think of one event, you automatically recall the other. Aristotle proposed that in order for an **association** to develop, the two events must be contiguous (temporally paired) and either similar to or opposite from each other.

During the seventeenth and eighteenth centuries, British empiricists described the association process in greater detail. John Locke (1690) suggested that there are no innate ideas, but instead we form ideas as a result of experience. Locke distinguished simple from complex ideas. **Simple ideas** are passive impressions received by the senses, or the mind's representation of that sensory impression. In contrast, **complex ideas** represent the combination of simple ideas, or "the association of ideas." The following example illustrates the difference between simple and complex ideas. You approach a rose in a garden. Your senses detect the color, odor, and texture of the rose. Each of these sensory impressions represents a simple idea. Your mind also infers that the smell is pleasant, which also is a simple idea. The combination or association of these simple ideas creates the perception of a rose, which is a complex idea.

David Hume (1748) hypothesized that three principles connect simple ideas into a complex idea. One of these principles is **resemblance,** the second is **contiguity** in time or place, and the third is **cause and effect.** Hume's own words best illustrate these three principles, which he proposed are responsible for the association of ideas:

> A picture naturally leads our thoughts to the original [resemblance]. The mention of the apartment in a building naturally introduces an inquiry…concerning the others [contiguity]; and if we think of a wound, we can scarcely forebear reflecting on the pain which follows it [cause and effect]. (Hume, 1748/1955, p. 32)

Locke and Hume were philosophers, and it was left to later scientists to evaluate the validity of the principle of the association of ideas. The first of these scientists was Edward Thorndike, whose work we will discuss next.

Thorndike

The work of Edward Thorndike was another important influence on the development of the behaviorist view. Thorndike's 1898 publication of his studies established that animal behavior could change as a consequence of experience. Thorndike's ideas on learning and motivation developed from his research with his famous puzzle box (see **Figure 1.1**). He tested 13 kittens and young cats in *Ex.* 15 different puzzle boxes. In his studies, he placed a hungry cat in a locked box and put food within the cat's eyesight, but beyond its reach, just outside the box. The cat could escape to obtain food by exhibiting one of a number of possible behaviors. A different response or sequence of responses was required to activate a release mechanism and escape from each box. For example, two effective behaviors were pulling on a string and pressing a pedal.

Trial + Error

FIGURE 1.1. Thorndike's famous puzzle box: the hungry cat can escape, and obtain access to food, by exhibiting the appropriate response.

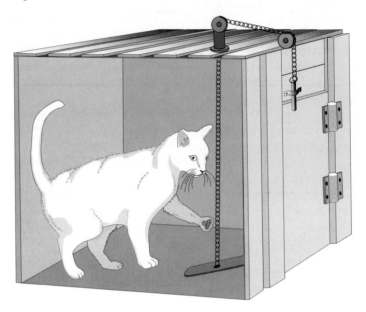

Thorndike observed that when a cat was initially placed into the puzzle box, the cat would engage in a number of behaviors, such as clawing, biting, meowing, and rubbing. Eventually, the cat would respond in a way that activated the release mechanism and opened the door to the puzzle box. The cat would then escape from the puzzle box and consume the food outside. On subsequent trials, the cat would engage in the other behaviors, but eventually would respond in the manner needed to activate the release mechanism and escape from the puzzle box. Thorndike found that not only did the cats escape, but also, with each successive trial, the time needed to activate the release decreased (see **Figure 1.2**). Further, Thorndike observed that the time the cat spent engaging in the other behaviors declined until the only behavior seen in the puzzle box was the one that activated the release mechanism.

Thorndike proposed that the cat formed an association between the stimulus (the box) and the effective response. Learning, according to Thorndike, reflects the development of an S-R (stimulus-response) association. As the result of learning, the specific stimulus elicits the appropriate response. Thorndike asserted that the animal is not conscious of this association but is instead exhibiting a mechanistic habit in response to a particular stimulus. The S-R connection developed because the cat received a **reward:** the appropriate response resulted in the ability to obtain food, which produced a satisfying state and strengthened the S-R bond. Thorndike labeled this strengthening of an S-R association by a satisfying event or reward the **law of effect.** Thus, the law of effect selects the appropriate response and connects it to the environment, thereby changing a chance act into a learned behavior.

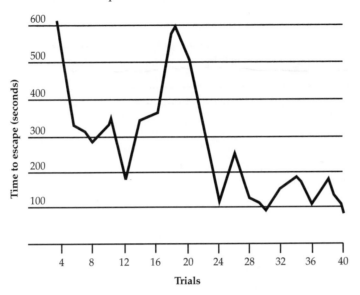

FIGURE 1.2. The median escape times of five cats over 40 trials in one of Thorndike's puzzle boxes.

Thorndike did not think that the law of effect applied only to animal behavior; he argued that it also describes the human learning process. Thorndike (1932) presented his human subjects with a concept to learn. Telling his subjects that they had responded correctly enabled the subjects to learn the appropriate response.

Reward is not the only process that strengthens a stimulus-response association. According to Thorndike's **law of exercise,** the strength of a stimulus-response connection can be increased by use, while the connection can be weakened with disuse.

Although Thorndike's views concerning the nature of the learning process were quite specific, his ideas on the motivational processes which determine behavior were more vague. According to Thorndike, learning occurs, or previously learned behavior is exhibited, only if the animal or human is "ready." Thorndike's **law of readiness** proposes that the animal or human must be motivated to develop an association or to exhibit a previously established habit. Thorndike did not hypothesize about the nature of the motivation mechanism, leaving such endeavors to future psychologists. Indeed, the motivational basis of behavior became a critical concern of the behaviorists.

Thorndike (1913) suggested a second means by which learning can occur. According to Thorndike, gradually changing the stimulus that elicited a response could result in the association of that response to a totally new stimulus. Thorndike referred to this learning process as **associative shifting.** To illustrate the associative-shifting process, consider Thorndike's example of teaching a cat to stand up on command. At first, a piece of fish is placed in front of a cat; when the cat stands to reach the fish, the trainer says "stand up." After a number of trials, the trainer omits the fish stimulus, and the verbal stimulus alone can elicit the standing response, even though this S-R association has not been rewarded. Although Thorndike believed that conditioning, or the development of a new S-R association, could occur through associative shifting, he proposed that the law of effect, rather than associative shifting, explains the learning of most S-R associations. In the next section, we will discover that Thorndike's associative shifting process bears a striking resemblance to Pavlovian conditioning.

BEFORE YOU GO ON

- **What could Marcus learn about addiction from our discussion of behaviorism?**
- **How would Marcus use Thorndike's law of effect to explain a possible cause of addiction?**

Pavlov

How did the cat choose the correct response in Thorndike's puzzle-box studies? Thorndike explained the process as one of trial and error; the cat simply performed various behaviors until it discovered a correct one. Reward then functioned to strengthen the association of the stimulus environment with that response. However, the research of Ivan Pavlov (1927) suggests that the learning process is anything but trial and error. According to Pavlov, definite rules determine which behavior occurs in the learning situation.

Behaviorists were profoundly influenced by Pavlov's work. His description of the conditioning process first appeared in English when his Huxley lecture, delivered at Charing Cross Hospital, was published in *Science* in 1906. The 1927 translation into English of his work, *Conditioned Reflexes*, provided a comprehensive description of his research. Pavlov was a physiologist, not a psychologist; his initial plan was to uncover the laws governing digestion. He observed that animals exhibit numerous reflexive responses when food is placed in their mouths (for example, salivation, gastric secretion). The function of these responses is to aid in the digestion process.

Pavlov observed during the course of his research that his dogs began to secrete stomach juices when they saw food or when it was placed in their food dishes. He concluded that the dogs had learned a new behavior, because he had not observed this response during their first exposure to the food. To explain his observation, he suggested that both humans and nonhuman animals possess innate or **unconditioned reflexes.** An unconditioned reflex consists of two components—an **unconditioned stimulus** (UCS—for example, food), which involuntarily elicits the second component, the **unconditioned response** (UCR—for example, release of saliva). A new or **conditioned reflex** develops when a neutral environmental event occurs along with the unconditioned stimulus. As conditioning progresses, the neutral stimulus becomes the **conditioned stimulus** (CS—for example, the sight of food) and is able to elicit the learned, or **conditioned response** (CR—for example, the release of saliva). The conditioned response is strengthened by increasing the number of times the conditioned stimulus and the unconditioned stimulus are paired.

The demonstration of a learned reflex in animals was an important discovery, illustrating not only an animal's ability to learn, but also the mechanism responsible for the learned behavior. According to Pavlov, any neutral stimulus paired with an unconditioned stimulus could, through conditioning, develop the capacity to elicit a CR. In his classic demonstration of the conditioning process, he first implanted a tube, called a fistula, in a dog's salivary glands to collect saliva (see **Figure 1.3**). He then presented the conditioned stimulus (the sound of a metronome) and shortly thereafter placed the unconditioned stimulus (meat powder) in the dog's mouth. On the first presentation, only the meat powder produced saliva (UCR). However, with repeated pairings of the metronome with food, the metronome sound (CS) began to elicit saliva (CR), and the strength of the conditioned response increased with increased pairings of the conditioned and unconditioned stimuli. **Figure 1.4** presents a diagram of Pavlov's classical conditioning process.

Pavlov conducted an extensive investigation of the conditioning process, identifying many procedures that influence an animal's learned behaviors; many of his ideas are still accepted today. Pavlov observed that stimuli similar to the CS can also elicit the CR through a process he called **generalization;** further, the more similar the stimulus is to the CS, the greater the generalization of the CR.

Pavlov also showed that if, after conditioning, the conditioned stimulus is presented without the unconditioned stimulus, the strength of the conditioned response diminishes. Pavlov named this process of eliminating an established conditioned response **extinction.**

FIGURE 1.3. Pavlov's salivary-conditioning apparatus. The experimenter can measure saliva output when either a conditioned stimulus (for example, the tick of a metronome) or an unconditioned stimulus (for example, meat powder) is presented to the dog. The dog is placed in a harness to minimize movement, thus ensuring an accurate measure of the salivary response.

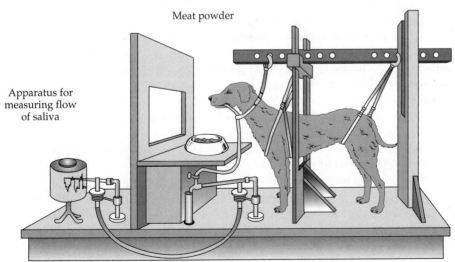

FIGURE 1.4. Schematic illustration of Pavlovian conditioning of salivation to a conditioned stimulus. Before conditioning, the novel stimulus, when presented alone, elicits no response. During conditioning, the novel stimulus is followed by the unconditioned stimulus, food, which can produce the UCR, the physiological response of salivation. After conditioning, the presentation of the NS elicits the conditioned salivation response.

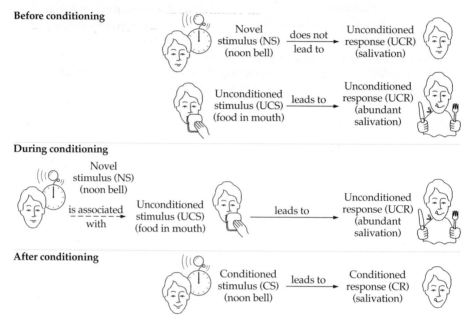

A conditioned response also can be eliminated through counterconditioning. In **counterconditioning,** the conditioned stimulus is paired with an opponent or antagonistic unconditioned stimulus. The conditioning of the opponent response causes the conditioned stimulus to no longer elicit the original conditioned response.

Pavlov's observations have profoundly influenced psychology. The conditioning process he described, often called Pavlovian conditioning, has been demonstrated in various animals, including humans. Conditioned responses have also been established to many different unconditioned stimuli, and psychologists have shown that most environmental stimuli can become conditioned stimuli.

Pavlov and Thorndike described two different learning processes—classical conditioning and instrumental conditioning. In the past, especially during the two decades following the publication of Pavlov's work, psychologists emphasized the classical conditioning process. Later, during the 1940s and 1950s, researchers focused on the instrumental conditioning process initially described by Thorndike. A renewed interest in Pavlovian conditioning has occurred during the past several decades. We will discuss the Pavlovian conditioning process in greater detail in Chapter 3 and the instrumental conditioning process in Chapters 4 and 5.

Neither Thorndike nor Pavlov was a behaviorist; each merely described the learning process. It was John B. Watson who demonstrated the importance of this process to human behavior. Although Pavlov's research excited Watson, the work of another Russian, Vladimir Bechterev, was an even greater influence. Bechterev and Pavlov conducted their research at the same time, and the 1913 American publication of Bechterev's work also contributed greatly to the popularity of behaviorism.

Whereas Pavlov used positive or pleasant UCSs, Bechterev employed aversive or unpleasant stimuli (for example, shock) to study the conditioning process. Bechterev found that a conditioned leg withdrawal response could be established in dogs by pairing a neutral stimulus with the shock. In his duplication of Bechterev's studies, Watson (1916) showed that after several pairings with electric shock, a previously neutral stimulus elicited a leg withdrawal response in dogs. Watson also was able to condition a toe or a finger withdrawal in human subjects. Further, Watson not only conditioned a toe or a finger withdrawal response, but also emotional arousal (revealed by increased breathing) as the conditioned response.

Aversive methods have same results as non-aversive

Watson believed that abnormal, as well as normal, behavior is learned. He was particularly concerned with demonstrating that human fears are acquired through Pavlovian conditioning. To illustrate this point, Watson and Rayner (1920) showed a white rat to Albert, a healthy 9-month-old infant attending a day-care center. As the child reached for the rat, he heard a loud sound (UCS) produced as Watson hit a heavy iron rail with a hammer (see **Figure 1.5**). After three CS-UCS pairings, Watson and Rayner observed that presentation of the rat (CS) alone produced a fear response in the child. The rat elicited strong emotional arousal, demonstrated by the child's attempts to escape from it, after six CS-UCS pairings. The authors observed a strong generalized response to similar objects: the child also showed fear of a white rabbit and a white fur coat.

Ex

Although Watson had intended to extinguish Albert's fear, Albert's mother withdrew him from the day-care center before Watson could eliminate the infant's fear. In 1924, Mary Cover Jones, a student working with Watson, developed an effective technique for eliminating conditioned fears. A 3-year-old boy named Peter served as the subject in her study. Jones observed that Peter was quite frightened of white rabbits. When Peter was at ease, she brought the rabbit into the same room with the child while Peter was eating, keeping enough distance between the rabbit and Peter that the child was not alarmed. She then moved the rabbit closer and closer to Peter, allowing him to grow accustomed to it in gradual steps. Eventually the child was able to touch and hold the formerly fear-inducing animal. According to Jones, this procedure had eliminated fear by conditioning a positive emotional response, produced by eating, to the rabbit. The elimination of fear by the acquisition of a fear-inhibiting emotional response occurs through the counterconditioning process. Approximately thirty years later, Jones' study played an important role in the development of an effective treatment of human phobic behavior. We will discuss this treatment, systematic desensitization, in Chapter 3.

never counterconditioned

Ex

FIGURE 1.5. While "little Albert" was playing with a white rat, Watson struck a suspended steel bar with a hammer. The loud sound disturbed the child, causing him to develop a conditioned fear of the white rat. Rosalie Rayner, Watson's assistant, distracted "little Albert" as Watson approached the bar.

BEFORE YOU GO ON

- **How might conditioning lead to addictive behavior?**
- **What could Marcus learn about a potential way to eliminate addictive behavior from the Mary Cover Jones study?**

THE ETHICS OF CONDUCTING RESEARCH

We will discuss many studies using both animals and humans in this text. There are limits to both types of research. Research must never violate principles of ethical conduct. This chapter ends by examining the research that is permissible with animals and humans.

Conducting Research with Humans

Psychological research with human subjects must be conducted in accordance with the principles published by the American Psychological Association in the book entitled *Ethical Principles in the Conduct of Research with Human Participants*. Let's briefly discuss the ethical principles a psychologist must follow when conducting research with humans.

When a psychologist plans to conduct research using human subjects, an ethics committee decides if that research is permissible under the guidelines provided by the American Psychological Association (APA, 1992). The main principle that determines whether the ethics committee will approve the research project is the demonstration that the planned study maximizes potential gain in knowledge and minimizes the costs and potential risks to human subjects. In conducting human research, the psychologist typically enters into an agreement with the subject. The subject learns the general purpose of the study and the potential risks of participating. It also is essential that no subject be coerced into participation in the study. For example, at many schools, students are required to participate in psychological experiments as a course requirement in general psychology. This requirement is permissible only if an alternative activity is available to the student. Students at other universities can volunteer to participate, but failing to volunteer cannot be counted against the student. The subject must also be free to withdraw from the study at any time.

As part of the agreement between the researcher and subject, the subject is informed that he or she will receive some tangible rewards (that is, money), personal help (that is, counseling), or information regarding the study (that is, results). The researcher must live up to this agreement, as it is a contract between the researcher and participant. After the study is completed, the subject is **debriefed** by the experimenter, who provides information about the nature of the study. Further, the anonymity and confidentiality of the subject's behavior in the study must be maintained. All of this information must be explained to the individual in a written agreement, and the subject must sign an **informed consent** agreement indicating that he or she is willing to participate in the study.

The Use of Nonhuman Animals in Research

Many of the studies described in this text used nonhuman animals as subjects, including mice, rats, birds, cats, dogs, and monkeys. Why do psychologists use nonhuman animals in their research? There are several reasons. One is the problem of documenting causal relationships. People differ greatly in terms of their behavior, which makes it difficult to obtain a representative sample. Because the behavior of animals is less variable, it is easier to show causal relationships in lower animals than in humans.

Another reason for using nonhuman animals is that some types of research cannot be ethically conducted in humans. For example, suppose that a psychologist suspects that damage to a certain area of the brain impairs memory storage. This idea may come from case histories of individuals with memory disorders who have tumors in this brain area. But these case histories cannot be used to infer causality. The only way to demonstrate causality is to damage this area of the brain and see if memory storage problems result. Obviously, we cannot do this type of research with humans; it would be unethical to expose a person to any treatment that would lead to a behavior pathology. The use of animals provides a way to show that this brain area controls memory storage and that damage to this area leads to memory disorders.

Some individuals object to the use of animals for demonstrating that a certain area of the brain controls memory storage, or for any other reason. Several

Good outcomes

arguments have been offered in defense of the use of animals for psychological research. Humans suffer from many different behavior disorders, and animal research can provide us with knowledge concerning the causes of these disorders as well as treatments that can prevent or cure behavioral problems. As the noted psychologist Neal Miller (1985) points out, animal research has led to a variety of programs, including rehabilitation treatments for neuromuscular disorders and the development of drug and behavioral treatments for phobias, depression, schizophrenia, and other behavior pathologies.

Certainly animals should not be tortured, and their discomfort should be minimized. Yet, when a great deal of human suffering may be prevented, the use of animals in studies seems appropriate (Feeney, 1987). Animal research also has led to significant advances in veterinary medicine, and far more animals are sacrificed for food, hunting, or furs than for research and education (Nichols & Russell, 1990). Currently, animal research is conducted only when approved by a committee, such as the Institutional Animal Use and Care Committee (IACUC), that acts to ensure that animals are used humanely and in strict accordance with local, state, and federal guidelines.

BEFORE YOU GO ON

- **What would Marcus need to do to conduct a study using human subjects?**
- **How would Marcus justify the use of animals to study addictive behavior?**

CHAPTER SUMMARY

We have defined learning as an experiential process resulting in a relatively permanent change in behavior that cannot be explained by temporary states, maturation, or innate response tendencies.

The twentieth century began with the functionalists emphasizing the instinctive character of human behavior. However, the functionalists could not agree on the nature of instinctive processes or the number of instincts. Many psychologists adopted the behavioral view, or the belief that most human behavior is learned.

Thorndike observed that hungry cats could learn a new behavior to obtain food. He repeatedly placed individual cats in a puzzle box and found that the cats increasingly used the behavior that enabled them to escape from the box. Thorndike believed that the effect of the food reward was to strengthen the association between the stimulus of the puzzle box and the effective response. Thorndike's law of use proposed that the S-R (stimulus-response) association was strengthened by practice, while his law of readiness proposed that motivation was necessary for learning to occur. Thorndike believed that the gradual changing of the stimulus could lead to a new S-R association through the associative-shifting process.

Pavlov demonstrated the conditioning of a new reflex. He paired a novel stimulus (the conditioned stimulus) with a biologically significant event (the unconditioned stimulus). Pavlov observed that prior to conditioning, only the unconditioned stimulus elicited the unconditioned response. After the pairing of the conditioned and unconditioned stimuli, the conditioned stimulus was able to elicit the conditioned response.

Watson showed that an emotional fear response could be conditioned in humans. He discovered that a young child would become frightened of a rat if the rat was paired with a loud noise. The child also showed fear of other white animals and objects. Mary Cover Jones discovered that pairing a feared rabbit with food could eliminate a child's fear of the rabbit through the process of counterconditioning.

Ethical principles established by the American Psychological Association govern what kind of research is permissible with humans. A researcher must demonstrate to an ethics committee that the planned study maximizes the potential gain in psychological knowledge and minimizes the costs and potential risks to human subjects.

Many psychologists use animals as subjects in their research. One reason for using animal subjects is that causal relationships can be demonstrated in animals in certain types of studies that cannot be ethically conducted with humans. The discomfort experienced by the animals should be minimized; however, a great deal of human suffering can be prevented by conducting research with animals. Animal research must be approved by a committee, such as the IACUC, which acts to ensure that animals are used in accordance with local, state, and federal guidelines.

CRITICAL THINKING QUESTIONS

1. Functionalism and behaviorism present quite different explanations for the causes of behavior. Explain the differences between functionalism and behaviorism. Select a behavior. Explain that behavior using both the functionalist and behaviorist perspectives.
2. Pavlov and Thorndike had a significant impact on our understanding of the learning process. Describe their work, and indicate why it is important for learning theory.
3. Many individuals object to the use of animals in psychological research. Discuss the basis of their objections. Is there any rationale for using animals? Explain why some psychologists use animals in their studies. Is there any way to reconcile these opposing perspectives?

KEY TERMS

association	conditioned reflex	counterconditioning
associative shifting	conditioned response	debriefing
behaviorism	(CR)	extinction
cause and effect	conditioned stimulus (CS)	functionalism
complex ideas	contiguity	generalization

informed consent
instinct
law of effect
law of exercise
law of readiness

learning
resemblance
reward
simple ideas
unconditioned reflex

unconditioned response
   (UCR)
unconditioned stimulus
   (UCS)

CHAPTER 2

The Modification of Instinctive Behavior

Do You Have a Light?

For 2 *days, Greg has resisted his urge to smoke. Having attempted to quit on more occasions than he can count, he's determined not to let his extreme nervousness and irritability keep him from succeeding this time. His family tries to distract his thoughts from cigarettes, but these attempts work only temporarily. Anticipating tonight's televised championship boxing match helped him for a while, but even this cannot prevent his recurrent, intense impulses to smoke. Greg began smoking cigarettes when he was 15. All his friends smoked, so it seemed like the natural thing to do. At first, he did not like to smoke; it made him cough and sometimes feel slightly nauseated. Greg smoked only with his friends to feel part of the group, and he pretended to inhale. However, as the unpleasant effects began to disappear, he learned to inhale and began to smoke more. By the age of 18, Greg smoked two to three packs of cigarettes each day. He never thought about stopping until he met Paula. A nonsmoker, she tried to convince him to quit. Finding himself unable to break his habit, he simply did not smoke while with Paula. After they married, Paula continued to plead with Greg to stop smoking. He has tried every now and then over the past ten years to resist cigarettes, usually avoiding his habit for a day or two. This time had to be different. At age 35, Greg felt himself in perfect health, but a routine check-up with the family physician two days ago proved him wrong. Greg learned that his extremely high blood pressure made him a prime candidate for a heart attack. The doctor told Greg that he must lower his blood pressure through special diet, medication, and no smoking. Continued smoking would undoubtedly interfere with the other treatments. The threat of a heart attack frightened Greg; he had seen his father suffer the consequences of an attack several years ago. Determined now to quit, he only hopes he can endure his withdrawal symptoms.*

Millions of people share Greg's intense desire to smoke, as well as his record of repeated attempts to stop. Their addiction, stemming from dependence on the effects of cigarettes, motivates their behavior. Evidence of this dependence includes the aversive withdrawal symptoms that many people experience when they attempt to stop smoking. When the symptoms are strong enough, the withdrawal state motivates them to resume smoking.

Cigarette smoking is just one example of addictive behavior. People become addicted to many drugs that exert quite different effects. For example, the painkilling effects of heroin contrast sharply with the arousing effects of cocaine. Although the effects of drugs may differ, the cycle of drug effects, withdrawal symptoms, and the resumption of addictive behavior characterizes all addictive behaviors.

Addictive behavior is thought to reflect the combined influence of instinctive and experiential processes. In this chapter, we will focus on the influence of instinct on addictive behavior, as well as on other behaviors. The role that experience plays in addictive behavior, as well as in other behaviors, also will be addressed in this chapter and throughout the rest of the text.

THE INSTINCTIVE BASIS OF BEHAVIOR

Konrad Lorenz (1969) suggested that instinctive systems enhance a human's or nonhuman animal's ability to adapt to the environment. Adaptation sometimes involves internal energy (or tension) aroused by a specific environmental stimulus that motivates a predetermined sequence of behaviors. In these cases, experience affects neither the eliciting stimulus nor the behavior. However, in other cases, experience can alter the eliciting environmental stimulus, the instinctive action motivated by internal tension, or both.

According to Lorenz, the ability to learn from experience and respond differentially to varied environmental circumstances is programmed into the genetic structure of a species, providing the flexibility the species needs to adapt to changing conditions. Sometimes experience alters the ability of an environmental event to elicit a specific behavior, the efficiency of instinctive behavior elicited by a particular stimulus, or both. Under other conditions, learning produces new eliciting stimuli, new behaviors, or both, which then enhance survival. Lorenz contends that learning facilitates adaptation to the environment, and that the ability to learn is innate.

The Search for Knowledge

The evolutionary process is central to an animal's or person's capacity to adapt (Lorenz, 1969). **Evolution** represents changes a species undergoes in behavioral and physical characteristics in order to survive in a new environment. The environment contains much information, and knowledge of this information provides an animal or person with adaptive capacity. Lorenz argues that knowledge represents an increased sensitivity to particular aspects of the environment. A species' ability to adapt increases as, through natural selection, it incorporates knowledge about its environment into its genetic programming. According to Lorenz, evolution occurs when a species incorporates into its genetic structure the ability to absorb specific environmental knowledge.

Lorenz and his colleague Niko Tinbergen developed their instinctive theory from years of observing animal behavior. To illustrate their model, we present one of Lorenz and Tinbergen's classic observations, followed by their analysis of the systems controlling this observed behavior.

In 1938, Lorenz and Tinbergen reported their observations of the egg-rolling behavior of the greylag goose. This species builds a shallow nest on the ground to incubate its eggs. When an egg rolls to the side of the nest, the goose reacts by stretching toward the egg and bending its neck, bringing its bill toward its breast. This action causes the bill to nudge the egg to the center of the nest. If during transit the egg begins to veer to one side, the goose adjusts the position of its bill to reverse the direction of the egg. What causes the goose to react to the rolling egg? Lorenz's energy model addresses this question.

Energy Model

According to Lorenz (1950), **action-specific energy** constantly accumulates (see **Figure 2.1**). This accumulation of energy resembles the filling of a reservoir with water; the more liquid in the reservoir, the greater the internal pressure for its release. In behavioral terms, we would say that the greater the pressure, the more motivated the animal is to behave in a specific way. The internal pressure (action-specific energy) motivates **appetitive behavior,** which enables an animal to approach and contact a specific and distinctive event called a **sign stimulus.** The presence of the sign stimulus releases the accumulated energy. In our goose example, the stretching movement and adjustment reaction are appetitive behaviors directed toward the rolling egg, which is the sign stimulus.

The goose does not exhibit the retrieving behavior until it has reached the egg. The retrieving behavior is an example of a **fixed action pattern,** an instinctive behavior triggered by the presence of a specific environmental cue, the sign stimulus. An internal block exists for each fixed action pattern, preventing the behavior from occurring until the appropriate time. The animal's appetitive behavior, motivated by the buildup of action-specific energy, allows the animal to come into contact with the appropriate releasing stimulus. According to Lorenz and Tinbergen, the sign stimulus acts to remove the block by stimulating an internal **innate releasing mechanism (IRM).** The IRM removes the block, thereby releasing the fixed action pattern. The sight of the egg stimulates the appropriate IRM, which triggers the retrieving response in the goose. After the goose has retrieved one egg and its energy reserve is dissipated, the bird will allow another egg to remain at the side of the nest until sufficient action-specific energy has accumulated to motivate the bird to return the second egg to the middle of the nest.

In some situations, a chain of fixed action patterns occurs (see **Figure 2.1**). In these cases, a block exists for each specific fixed action pattern in the sequence, and the appropriate releasing mechanism must be activated for each behavior. For example, a male Siamese fighting fish exhibits a ritualistic aggressive display when he sees another male or even when he sees a reflection of himself in a mirror. However, no actual aggressive behavior occurs until one

FIGURE 2.1. Diagram of Lorenz's energy system. The energy flows constantly from the tap T into the reservoir R. The cone valve V represents the releasing mechanism, which is open when the sign stimulus exerts pressure on the scale pan SP. The weight on the pan corresponds to the intensity of stimulation. The spring S represents inhibition from higher centers. Energy released from the reservoir R flows into the reservoirs for lower instinctive levels TR. The diagram shows the interactions of internal pressure that occur from the accumulation of action-specific energy and the external stimulation of the sign stimulus; both act to release the stored energy.

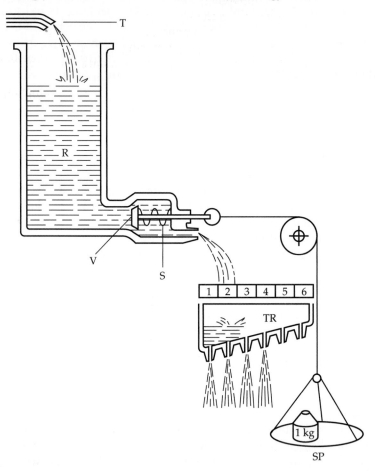

male intrudes on the other's territory. The second fixed action pattern is blocked until the two males come into close proximity. If neither fish retreats after the ritualistic display, the fish approach each other (an appetitive act) and fighting behavior is released.

Environmental Release

In some cases, the sign stimulus for a particular fixed action pattern is a simple environmental stimulus. For example, Tinbergen (1951) observed that the red belly of the male stickleback is the sign stimulus that releases fighting behavior between two male sticklebacks. An experimental dummy stickleback, which resembles the stickleback only in color, releases aggressive behavior in a real male stickleback, supporting this conclusion.

The releasing sign stimulus can be quite complex for other fixed action patterns; for example, consider the sexual pursuit of the male grayling butterfly (Tinbergen, 1951). Tinbergen found that a male grayling would pursue a female flying past. Although the color and shape of a model grayling did not influence the male's flight behavior, the darkness of the female, the distance from the male, and the pattern of movement that stimulated the male's forward and backward flight all influenced pursuit. Tinbergen noticed that the absence of one female characteristic could be compensated for by an increased value in another component. For instance, one model passing by at a certain distance from the male did not elicit a flight reaction. However, a darker model at the same distance did elicit pursuit.

The likelihood of eliciting a fixed action pattern depends upon both the accumulated level of action-specific energy and the intensity of the sign stimulus. Research (Lorenz, 1950; Tinbergen, 1951) indicates that the greater the level of accumulated energy, the weaker the sign stimulus that can still release a particular fixed action pattern. For example, Baerends, Brouwer, and Waterbolk (1955) examined the relationship between a male guppie's readiness to respond and the size of the female. They found that a large female model released courtship behavior even in a male that was typically unresponsive.

Why does reliance on external stimulation for the release of a fixed action pattern decrease as the time increases since the last response? Lorenz (1950) envisioned an IRM as a gate blocking the release of stored energy. The gate is opened either by pulling from external stimulation or by pushing from within. As the internal pressure increases, the amount of external pull needed to open the gate and release the behavior decreases.

Another view, proposed by Tinbergen (1951), suggested that sensitivity to the sign stimulus changes as a function of time passed since the occurrence of the specific behavior. According to Tinbergen, the sensitivity of the innate releasing mechanism to the sign stimulus increases when there has been no recent fixed action pattern.

Hierarchical System

Lorenz proposed that action-specific energy exists for each fixed action pattern. It is now clear, however, that the internal motivation for functionally equivalent behaviors depends on a common source. Tinbergen (1951) suggested that a central instinctive system (for example, the reproductive instinct of stickleback fish) controls the occurrence of a number of potential behaviors (refer to **Figure 2.2**). Energy accumulates in a specific brain center for each major instinct, and numerous systems can contribute energy for each instinct. Internal impulses can develop from the release of energy from a higher center following the occurrence of a fixed action pattern, from energy buildup at the level on which the animal is presently operating, or from both. Hormones or other internal stimuli as well as external forces can also generate energy. All of these factors influence the level of accumulated energy and the likelihood of additional behavior.

FIGURE 2.2. Reproductive instinct of the male stickleback fish. The diagram shows the fixed action patterns that can be released by the appropriate sign stimuli at each level of the hierarchy.

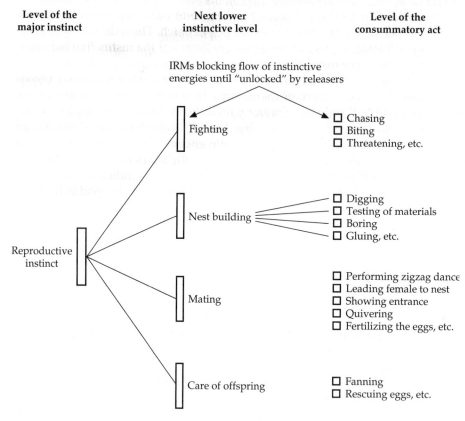

Once an effective sign stimulus releases energy, this energy flows to lower centers. The next fixed action pattern (or patterns) occurring in the chain depends on prevailing environmental conditions. Several fixed action patterns might be released, but the sign stimulus determines the specific fixed action pattern that will be exhibited.

Let's consider the reproductive instinct of the male stickleback fish to illustrate Tinbergen's hierarchical system (see **Figure 2.2**). If sufficient space exists, the reproductive instinct will be activated when a mature male is placed in an aquarium. The stimulation of the reproductive instinct causes the male to establish a territory and releases energy to lower brain systems that control specific instinctive behaviors. The presence of specific environmental events determines which of the lower center's IRMs will be activated and, therefore, which specific fixed action pattern (or patterns) will occur. Thus, the male stickleback will defend his territory and use threadlike weeds to build a nest, but the nest-building instinct is not activated if there are no weeds in the territory. Similarly, the mating and care-of-offspring instincts also depend on the presence of appropriate releasing stimuli. If a female swollen with eggs approaches the male's territory, the male displays a ritualistic courtship pattern, first exhibiting a zigzag dance, then leading the female to his nest. The male's quivering behavior causes the female to lay her eggs in his nest, and the male fertilizes them. The presence of the eggs then activates the care-of-offspring instinct and motivates the male to fan the eggs, enabling them to hatch. Thus, the presence of appropriate releasing sign stimuli determines which of the instinctive behaviors that the reproductive instinct controls will actually occur.

Von Holst and Von St. Paul in 1962 found support for Tinbergen's hierarchical theory in their study of the manner in which chickens go to sleep. A chicken exhibits a ritualistic behavior pattern before sleeping, standing on one leg and putting its head under one wing. Von Holst and Von St. Paul discovered that electrical stimulation of one brain site elicited the whole behavioral sequence; however, stimulation of other locations elicited only specific behavioral components, such as the presleeping ritual. These results indicate that different brain systems mediate the central instinctive motive and the specific fixed action patterns that this motive controls.

Conflicting Motives

An often-observed phenomenon occurs when two incompatible sign stimuli are encountered; the response is different from the fixed action patterns typically released by either sign stimuli acting alone. According to Tinbergen (1951), when a human or nonhuman animal is experiencing conflict due to the presence of two antagonistic sign stimuli, energy overflows into another motivational instinct system and releases a behavior from this other system. The process of activating a third instinct system, different from the two involved in the conflict, is called **displacement.**

Naturalistic settings are ideal for observing displacement behaviors. Tinbergen and Van Iersel (1947) reported that the stickleback, when between its own territory and the territory of another stickleback, often displays nest-building behavior. This "out-of-context" nest building is presumably due to the fish's conflict between attacking the neighbor's territory and escaping into its own. A person who whistles nervously before a date may be exhibiting displaced activity resulting from the conflict between anticipation of the date and fear of acting inappropriately.

The Importance of Experience

You might have the impression that an instinctive response is inflexible, or that the releasing sign stimulus cannot be altered. Although this view is often accurate, in some circumstances, experience can modify instinctive systems. Lorenz suggested that the instinctive processes of lower animals and human beings are programmed to change as the result of experience. The impact of an experience, referred to as learning or conditioning, can provide additional knowledge about the environment.

According to Lorenz, a conditioning experience can alter instinctive behavior, the releasing mechanism for instinctive behavior, or both. Only the consummatory response at the end of the behavior chain, according to Lorenz, is resistant to modification. Conditioning can alter the effectiveness of existing appetitive behavior or change the sensitivity of the releasing mechanism to the sign stimulus. Depending on the nature of the conditioning experience, this change can be either increased or decreased sensitivity. In addition, conditioning can establish new behaviors or new releasing stimuli. All of these modifications increase the organism's ability to adapt to the environment.

Lorenz's observations of the jackdaw's nest building illustrate his view of the importance of learning in adaptation. He discovered that the jackdaw does not instinctively know the best types of twigs to use as nesting material. This bird displays an instinctive nest-building response—stuffing twigs into a foundation—but must try different twigs until it finds one that lodges firmly and does not break. Once it has discovered a suitable type of twig, the bird selects only that type. According to Lorenz, the twig gained the ability to release instinctive behavior as the result of the bird's success.

It is important to distinguish the general theory of the Lorenz-Tinbergen instinctive approach from the specific aspects of their hypothetical energy system. Our understanding of the factors that govern a wide range of behaviors has benefitted from the instinctive approach. Further, the hypothetical energy system is an excellent way to conceptualize the processes motivating instinctive behavior. Environmental stimuli do release instinctive behaviors, and the likelihood of environmental release is dependent upon both the time since the last occurrence of the behavior and the intensity of the releaser. Animals do approach environmental releasers, and the intensity of the approach is influenced by the animal's motivation level. However, recent physiological research has raised questions concerning certain aspects of Lorenz and Tinbergen's theory. Although scientists (Friesen, 1989; Willows & Hoyle, 1969; Wine & Krasne, 1982) have identified brain systems responsible for the release of both appetitive behavior and fixed action patterns, no physiological system operates according to the structure of the energy model. Energy does not appear to accumulate in any identified brain systems, nor does it appear to flow from one system to another. Brain structures do communicate and interact, but not in accordance with Lorenz and Tinbergen's energy model. Let's examine one study that illustrates this interaction.

Willows and Hoyle (1969) examined the brain structures controlling the innate escape response of the sea slug, elicited by contact with a predatory starfish. Contact with the starfish releases a chemical from the starfish's tentacles that receptors on the sea slug's body detect. The sea slug's chemical sensory receptors then send a message through the sea slug's nervous system that elicits alternating contractions of the muscles on the sea slug's back and underside. Willows and Hoyle traced the neural circuit from the sensory receptors to the muscles (see **Figure 2.3**). The neural message is first sent to Area 1 in the slug's brain. Activity in Area 1 causes the muscles in the sea slug's back to contract, and also inhibits brain Area 2, which controls the muscles on the slug's underside. Willows and Hoyle found that activity in brain Area 1 lasted for a set period of time. When activity in brain Area 1 stopped, the inhibition of brain Area 2 was removed, thereby allowing activity in brain Area 3 to stimulate brain Area 2. (Activity in brain Area 3 began when the message reached the brain, but Area 3 could not stimulate brain Area 2 until the inhibition from brain Area 1 ended.) Activity in brain Area 2 causes the sea slug's underside to contract, as well as inhibits brain Area 1. The neural activity in brain Area 2 continues for a

FIGURE 2.3. A schematic representation of the neural network controlling the sea slug's escape behavior.

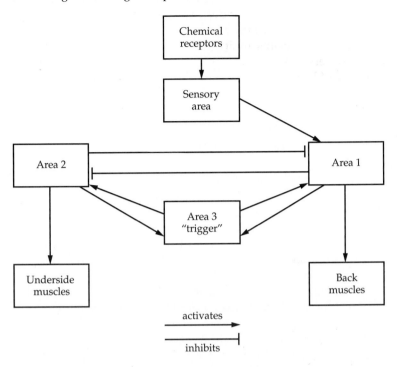

set time and then stops, removing the inhibition from brain Area 1. The removal of this inhibition allows brain Area 3 to stimulate brain Area 1. Activity in brain Areas 1 and 2 will continue to cycle, resulting in alternating contractions of the sea slug's back and underside muscles. What is the function of the alternating contractions? This innate sequence of muscle responses can propel the slug to safety away from the predatory starfish.

BEFORE YOU GO ON

- **Are any aspects of Greg's smoking explainable as instinctive?**
- **How might experience interact with these instinctive aspects of Greg's smoking?**

Lorenz believed that conditioning enhanced a species' adaptation to its environment, and that the ability to learn is programmed into each species' genetic structure. However, Lorenz did not detail the mechanism responsible for translating learning into behavior. In addition, the ethologists did not investigate the factors determining the effectiveness of conditioning.

We next examine the changes in instinctive behavior that occur with experience. In later chapters, we will discuss how new releasing stimuli or new behaviors are acquired as a result of experience.

Students who have to give speeches in a class show different reactions to their experience. Some students become less nervous with experience; yet, for others, the anxiety increases rather than declines with experience. Why do some students experience less distress after several speeches, while others find the experience more distressing? The phenomena of habituation and sensitization provide one reason.

With **habituation,** responsiveness to a specific stimulus declines with repeated experiences with that stimulus. In our example, the lessened anxiety some students feel after several experiences giving a speech may be due to habituation. **Sensitization** refers to an increased reaction to environmental events. The greater nervousness other students feel after several instances of giving a speech may be due to sensitization. It is also possible that Pavlovian conditioning leads to the increased or decreased reactions to giving a speech; for example, a change in nervousness may be the result of negative or positive aspects of giving the speech. We will look at Pavlovian conditioning in Chapter 3. There are many real-world examples of habituation and sensitization; we will examine these phenomena next.

Suppose an animal is given a new food. Most animals would only eat a little of this novel food, an avoidance referred to as **ingestional neophobia.** This neophobic response has considerable adaptive significance. Many foods in the natural environment contain poisons. If the animal eats too much of a poisoned food, it will die. To determine if the food can be safely consumed, the animal eats only a small quantity of the food on the first exposure. After repeated experiences with a nonpoisoned food, the neophobic response habituates and the animal consumes greater amounts.

Domjan's 1976 study documents the habituation of ingestional neophobia. Rats received either a 2% saccharin and water solution or just water. **Figure 2.4** shows that the rats drank very little saccharin solution when first exposed to this novel flavor. However, intake of saccharin increased with each subsequent experience with this flavor. Eventually, the animals drank as much as rats given only plain water. These results indicate that the habituation of the neophobic response led to the greater consumption of saccharin.

Animals also can show an increased neophobic response. Suppose that an animal is sick. Under this illness condition, the animal will exhibit an increased ingestional neophobia (Domjan, 1977). The greater neophobic response when animals are ill is due to the sensitization process.

The Nature of Habituation and Sensitization

Why do animals show a decreased (habituated) or increased (sensitized) reaction to environmental events? Groves and Thompson (1970) suggested that habituation reflects a decreased responsiveness of innate reflexes; that is, a stimulus becomes less able to elicit a response as a result of repeated exposure to that stimulus. In contrast, sensitization reflects an increased readiness to react

FIGURE 2.4. Animals show a reluctance to consume novel foods, but repeated exposure to a food will lead to habituation of neophobia. Animals in group S were given access each day to a 2% saccharin solution for 30 minutes, followed by 30 minutes of tap water. Over a 20-day period, the intake of saccharin in group S increased, while their consumption of tap water declined. The animals in group W received only 30 minutes of tap water each day, and their intake of water remained steady.

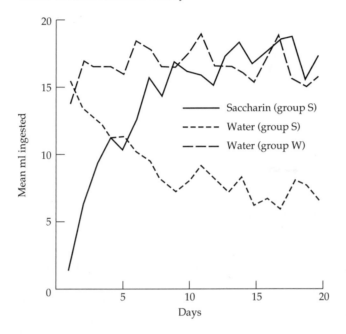

to all stimuli. This increased reactivity operates in the animal's central nervous system. According to Groves and Thompson, drugs that stimulate the central nervous system increase an animal's overall readiness to respond, while depressive drugs suppress reactivity. Emotional distress can also affect responsivity: anxiety increases reactivity; depression decreases responsiveness.

Research on the startle response (Davis, 1974) provides support for Groves and Thompson's view. When animals are exposed to an unexpected stimulus, they show a sudden jump reaction due to tensing muscles. A variety of stimuli, such as a brief tone or light, will elicit the startle response. As an example, imagine your reaction when you are working on a project and someone talks to you unexpectedly. In all likelihood, you would exhibit the startle reaction to the unexpected sound.

Repeated presentations of unexpected stimuli can lead to either a decreased or increased intensity of the startle reaction. Davis (1974) investigated habituation and sensitization of the startle reaction in rats. A brief 90-millisecond, 110-decibel (db) tone was presented to two groups of rats. For one group of rats, the unexpected tone was presented against a relatively quiet 60-db noise

FIGURE 2.5. The magnitude of the startle response to the tone declined over trials with the 60-db background noise (habituation), but increased when an 80-db background noise was used (sensitization).

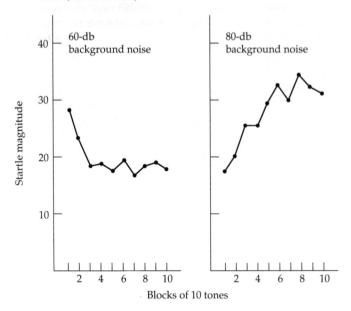

background. Davis noted that repeated presentation of the tone under this condition produced a decreased startle response (see **Figure 2.5**). The other group of rats experienced the unexpected tone against a louder 80-db noise background. In contrast to the habituation observed with the quiet background, repeated experiences with the tone against the louder background intensified the startle reaction (refer to **Figure 2.5**).

Why does the startle response habituate with a quiet background but sensitize with a loud background? A loud background is arousing and should lead to enhanced reactivity. This greater reactivity should lead to a greater startle reaction (sensitization). In contrast, in a quiet background, arousal of the central nervous system would be minimal. This should reduce the ability of the unexpected stimulus to elicit the startle reaction (habituation).

John Garcia and his associates (Garcia, 1988; Garcia, Brett, & Rusiniak, 1989) suggested that changes in animals' innate reactions to environmental events have considerable adaptiveness. For example, the reduced neophobia to safe foods allows the animal to consume nutritionally valuable foods. We will discuss the modification of innate feeding responses further when we look at biological influences on learning in Chapter 10.

The Conditions Affecting Habituation and Sensitization

Habituation or sensitization does not always occur with repeated experience. A number of variables affect the occurrence of habituation or sensitization; we will look at several important ones next.

First, research (Groves, Lee, & Thompson, 1969) indicates that more intense stimuli produce stronger sensitization than weaker ones. The opposite is true with habituation; that is, the stronger the stimulus, the weaker the habituation. In fact, habituation may not occur to very intense stimuli.

Second, greater sensitization occurs when a strong stimulus is experienced more frequently. Similarly, habituation increases with more frequent stimulus presentations, although the amount of habituation becomes progressively smaller over the course of habituation.

Third, habituation to a stimulus appears to depend upon the specific characteristics of the stimulus (refer to Thompson & Spencer, 1966). A change in any characteristic of the stimulus will result in an absence of habituation. For example, many birds become alarmed when seeing a hawklike object flying overhead (Tinbergen, 1951). This alarm reaction can be elicited by any novel object flying overhead and will habituate when the stimulus is repeatedly experienced, but the reaction will return if any quality of the object is altered. For example, in one study, Schleidt (1961) reported habituation of the alarm reaction in young turkeys when either a circular or rectangular silhouette flew overhead. However, if the shape of stimulus is changed, habituation ceases, and the alarm reaction returns.

What is the significance of these observations? There appears to be no specific sign stimulus eliciting alarm in young turkeys. In the natural environment, the birds will habituate their alarm reaction to members of their species. When a hawk approaches (or the shape changes), the turkeys experience a new shape, and their alarm reaction is elicited.

A change in the properties of the stimulus typically does not affect sensitization. The effect of stimulus specificity on habituation but not on sensitization provides further support for the view that habituation reflects changes in an innate response to a specific stimulus, while sensitization represents an increased responsiveness to many stimuli.

Finally, both habituation and sensitization can be relatively transient phenomena. When a delay intervenes between stimulus presentations, habituation weakens (Thompson & Spencer, 1966). In some instances, habituation is lost if several seconds or minutes intervene between stimuli. Yet, at other times, delay does not lead to a loss of habituation. This long-term habituation does not appear to reflect a change in an innate response to a stimulus. Instead, it seems to represent a more complex type of learning. We will look at the long-term habituation of responding to a stimulus in Chapter 9.

Sensitization is also affected by time. Sensitization is lost shortly after the sensitizing event ends. For example, Davis (1974) noted that sensitization of the startle response to a tone was absent 10 to 15 minutes after a loud noise was terminated. Unlike the long-term habituation effect, sensitization is always a temporary effect. This also points to a nonspecific increased responsivity as the cause of sensitization.

Dishabituation

You are driving to school and thinking about going to the movies tonight when suddenly a car turns into your lane. Startled by the car, you notice that you are going too fast and put your foot on the brake to slow down. Why did you notice your speed after, but not before, the car turned into your lane? The phenomenon of **dishabituation** is one likely reason.

Dishabituation refers to the recovery of a habituated response as a result of the presentation of a sensitizing stimulus (Hall & Channell, 1985; Wagner, 1981). Hall and Channell (1985) provide one study demonstrating dishabituation. In the Hall and Channell study, rats habituated to a light stimulus in one context. Habituation was demonstrated by a reduced orienting response (turning toward the light and rearing in front of it). Hall and Channell then presented the light stimulus to the rats in a context in which they had never experienced the light. The second context was either another familiar context or a novel environment. An orienting response was observed to the light stimulus in the novel context. In contrast, the orienting response was not observed in the familiar environment.

Why did exposure to the novel, but not the familiar, context lead to dishabituation? According to the Groves and Thompson dual-process theory (Groves & Thompson, 1970), the arousing effect of the sensitizing stimulus causes the habituated response to return. In the absence of a sensitizing stimulus, habituation remains. Exposure to a novel context is arousing, and this arousal caused the rats' orienting response to the light to return in the Hall and Channell study. In contrast, the orienting response did not return when the rats were exposed to a nonarousing, familiar environment. In terms of our automobile example, the car turning into your lane aroused your central nervous system, which caused you to again notice the setting on the speedometer.

Our discussion suggests that habituation and sensitization represent independent, but also interdependent, processes. Habituation will result in a stimulus that is no longer able to elicit a response, while an arousing stimulus can cause either a return to normal response in the case of dishabituation, or a heightened response in the case of sensitization. This interdependence of habituation and sensitization has clear adaptive value. Habituation allows us to ignore unimportant or irrelevant stimuli, while sensitization reinstates the response in case those stimuli have now become important. While it is not essential that you notice how fast you are going while you are just driving down the road, a car turning in front of you makes noticing your speed important again. It might just prevent you from having an accident (or getting a speeding ticket).

BEFORE YOU GO ON

- **Would habituation cause Greg to smoke less?**
- **Would sensitization cause Greg to smoke more?**

We have learned that experience can lead to either an intensification (sensitization) or diminution (habituation) of reaction to environmental events. Our discussion has focused on the response produced *during* exposure to a situation. However, responses also occur *following* an experience. Solomon and Corbit examined this aspect of the innate reaction to events. We now turn our attention to their **opponent-process theory.**

Recall Greg's addiction to cigarettes, described in the chapter-opening vignette. Why does Greg crave cigarettes and find it so difficult to stop smoking? Opponent-process theory provides us with one answer to this question.

Our Initial Reaction

Solomon and Corbit (1974) observed that all experiences (both biological and psychological) produce an initial affective reaction, the **A state** (see **Figure 2.6**), which can either be pleasant or unpleasant. For example, drinking alcohol usually produces a pleasurable A state, while taking an exam often produces an unpleasant A state. According to Solomon and Corbit's view, the strength of the A state depends upon the intensity of the experience; the stronger the event, the more intense the A state.

The A state arouses a second affective reaction, the **B state.** The B state is the opposite of the A state; if A state is positive, then B state will be negative, and vice-versa. Thus, the pleasurable A state aroused by drinking initiates an opposing, or opponent, aversive affective state. Similarly, the pain produced during the examination creates a pleasurable relief response. In Solomon and

FIGURE 2.6. Schematic diagram of the affective changes experienced during and after an environmental event during the first few exposures to that event. Notice the large initial A state reaction, the reduced A state over the course of the event, and the small opponent B state reaction that occurs after termination of the event.

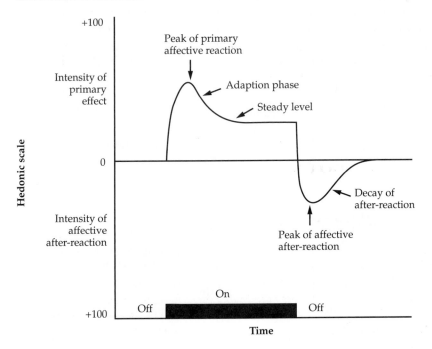

Corbit's view, our biological systems automatically initiate an opposite, or opponent, response to counter the initial effect of all events.

Several important aspects of the opponent process must be described in order to understand the system **Figure 2.6** depicts. First, the B state is initially less intense than the A state. Second, the B state intensifies more slowly than the A state. This increased strength of the B state produces the adaptation or reduced affective response seen while the event continues. Finally, after an event has terminated, the strength of the B state diminishes more slowly than the A state. As a result of the slower decline of the B state than A state, the opponent affective response will only be experienced when the event ends.

Consider Greg's addiction to smoking to illustrate how these rules operate. Smoking a cigarette activates a positive A state—pleasure. Automatic arousal of the opponent B state—pain or withdrawal—causes his initial A state (pleasure) to diminish after several puffs of the cigarette. When Greg stops smoking, the A state declines quickly, and he experiences the B state (pain or withdrawal), which will slowly diminish over time.

The Intensification of the Opponent B State

Solomon and Corbit discovered that repeated experience with a certain event often increases the strength of the opponent B state (refer to **Figure 2.7**), which in turn reduces the magnitude of the affective reaction experienced during the

FIGURE 2.7. Schematic diagram of the affective changes experienced during and after an environmental event after many presentations of that event. As a result of experiencing an event many times, there is a small A state response (tolerance) and a large and long B state reaction (withdrawal).

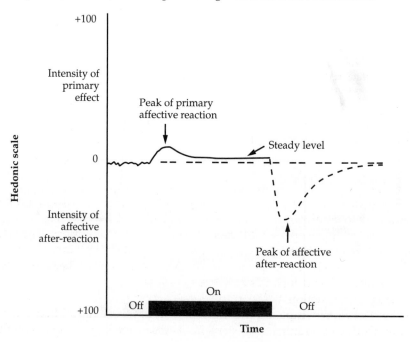

event. Thus, the strengthening of the opponent B state may well be responsible for the development of **tolerance.** Tolerance represents a decreased reactivity to an event with repeated experience. Furthermore, when the event ends, an intense opponent affective response is experienced. The strong opponent affect that is experienced in the absence of the event is called **withdrawal.**

Let's return to our example of Greg's cigarette smoking to illustrate this intensification of the B state process. Greg has smoked for many years, causing him to experience only mild pleasure from smoking. Yet, he feels intense prolonged pain or withdrawal when he stops smoking. It should be noted that the intensification of the B state does not alter the strength of the A state, but merely influences the resulting effect of the drug. Thus, the increased intensity of the B state not only produces reduced pleasure in smoking a cigarette, but it also increases withdrawal when the effects of smoking end.

Katcher, Solomon, Turner, LoLordo, Overmeir, and Rescorla's study (1969) demonstrates this process. These experimenters observed physiological reactions in dogs during and after electric shock. After the termination of shock, physiological responses (for example, heart rate) declined below preshock levels for several minutes before returning to baseline. After many presentations, the decline was greater and lasted longer. These observations show (1) a strong A state and a weak opponent B state during the first presentations of shock and (2) a diminished A state (tolerance) and an intensified B state (withdrawal) after many experiences.

The opponent process operates in many different situations (see Solomon & Corbit, 1974). Epstein's (1967) description of the emotional reactions of military parachutists is one real-world example of the opponent process. Epstein reported that during the first free fall, all the parachutists showed an intense aversive A state (terror). This A state diminished after they had landed, and they looked stunned for several minutes. Then, the parachutists began to talk enthusiastically with friends. This opponent B state (relief) lasted for about 10 minutes.

The affective response of experienced parachutists is quite different. During the free fall, experienced parachutists seemed tense, eager, or excited, reporting only a mildly aversive A state. Their opponent B state was exhilaration. Having landed safely, experienced parachutists showed (1) a high level of activity, (2) euphoria, and (3) intense social interaction. This opponent B state (exhilaration) decreased slowly, lasting for several hours.

The Addictive Process

Opponent-process theory (Solomon, 1977, 1980) offers an explanation for the development of addiction. In Solomon's view, addictive behavior is a coping response to an aversive opponent B state. Addictive behavior is an example of behavior motivated to terminate (or prevent) the unpleasant withdrawal state.

Most people who drink alcohol do not become alcoholics. Similarly, people who consume other drugs do not always become drug addicts. Solomon suggests that for addiction to develop, people must recognize that abstinence causes withdrawal symptoms and that the resumption of the addictive behavior after abstinence eliminates or prevents aversive feelings. People who think that the discomfort they experience is caused by factors other than the absence of the drug are not motivated to resume the addictive behavior. Under these circumstances, addiction does not develop.

There is another reason why addiction may not occur following repeated exposure. The number of exposures to a substance or event alone does not determine the intensification of the B state. If sufficient time intervenes between experiences, the opponent state does not intensify. And without the aversive withdrawal B state, the motivation for addiction does not exist. In support of Solomon's view, Starr (1978) discovered that young ducklings showed no distress in the absence of their mother when a 5-minute interval lapsed between separations. In contrast, with a 1- or 2-minute interval, strong withdrawal symptoms occurred. The importance of frequency in strengthening the opponent state helps explain why some people can take a drug infrequently and never experience intense withdrawal symptoms after its effect has ended.

Once an addiction is established, an addict is motivated to prevent or terminate withdrawal symptoms. One consequence of addiction is the sacrifice of potential reinforcers (for example, friends or a job). Most addicts recognize the serious consequences of their addiction and try to stop their self-destructive behavior. Let's examine why it is so difficult for addicts to break their habits.

The Influence of Other Aversive Events

Why is it so difficult for addicts to be cured? The aversive withdrawal reaction is a nonspecific unpleasant affective state. Therefore, any event which arouses the aversive state will motivate the addictive behavior. Usually, alcoholics who attempt to stop drinking face multiple problems. Inhibiting drinking while experiencing the B state is only part of the problem. Many daily stressors, such as problems at work or home, can activate the aversive motivational state, which can motivate the habitual addictive behavior.

For example, suppose that an alcoholic's mother-in-law arrives, and that her presence is a very aversive event. Under these conditions, the mother-in-law's presence will activate the aversive state, thus intensifying the pressure to drink. Solomon believes that all potential aversive events must be prevented for addicts to break their habits. Other reasons that it is so difficult to eliminate addictive behavior will be described in Chapter 3.

The Search for Pleasure

Most of us equate addictive behavior with situations in which people are motivated to terminate the aversive withdrawal state and reinstate a pleasant initial state. However, some people deliberately expose themselves to an aversive A state in order to experience the pleasant opponent B state (Solomon, 1977, 1980). The behavior of experienced parachutists is one example. Most people who anticipate parachuting from an aircraft never jump at all or quit after one jump. However, those who do jump and experience a strong reinforcing B state are often motivated to jump again. Epstein reported that some experienced jumpers become extremely depressed when bad weather cancels a jump. The behavior of these parachutists when denied the opportunity to jump resembles that of drug addicts who cannot obtain the desired drug. Other behaviors in which the positive opponent state may lead to addiction include running in marathons (Milvy, 1977) and jogging (Booth, 1980).

Craig and Siegel (1980) discovered that introductory psychology students taking a test felt apprehensive and experienced a euphoric feeling when the test ended. However, it is unlikely that students' level of positive affect after taking a test is as strong as that of an experienced parachutist after jumping. Perhaps most students are not tested often enough to develop a strong opponent reinforcing B state. You might suggest that your instructor test you more frequently to decrease your initial aversive apprehension and to intensify your positive affective relief when the test ends.

BEFORE YOU GO ON

- How would opponent-process theory explain Greg's addiction to smoking cigarettes?
- Does opponent-process theory make a prediction regarding how Greg might best quit smoking cigarettes?

CHAPTER SUMMARY

Lorenz and Tinbergen stressed the instinctive aspects of behavior. According to these ethologists, a specific internal tension (or action-specific energy) exists for each major instinct. The accumulation of internal energy motivates appetitive behavior, which continues until a specific environmental cue, called a sign stimulus, is encountered. This sign stimulus can activate an innate releasing mechanism (IRM), which releases the stored energy and activates the appropriate fixed action pattern.

A central instinctive system controls the occurrence of a number of potential behaviors. Once an effective sign stimulus releases energy for a higher structure, this energy flows to lower centers until the fixed action pattern is released.

The instinctive system is not inflexible; experience can sometimes alter the releasing stimuli, the instinctive behavior, or both. In some cases, the modification involves altering the effectiveness of the existing instinctive actions. At other times, new releasing stimuli, new behaviors, or both enable an animal or human to adapt. According to Lorenz, this adaptability is programmed into the genetic structure.

Habituation is a decreased response to a stimulus following repeated experiences with that stimulus. In contrast, sensitization reflects an increased reaction to a stimulus. Groves and Thompson suggest that habituation is the result of decreased ability of the stimulus to elicit the response (innate reflexes), while sensitization represents an increased reactivity to all stimuli (central nervous system). Dishabituation is the recovery of a habituated response as a result of the presentation of a sensitizing stimulus.

Animals exposed to a novel food show ingestional neophobia, or avoidance of the food. With repeated experience, the ingestional neophobia habituates, and the animal eats more of the food. When an animal is ill, it becomes sensitized and shows enhanced ingestional neophobia.

Solomon and Corbit suggested that all experiences produce an initial affective reaction, called the A state. The A state can either be pleasant or unpleasant. The A state arouses a second affective reaction, called the B state, which is the opposite of the A state; if the A state is positive, then the B state will be negative, and vice versa. The B state is initially less intense, develops more slowly, and declines more slowly than the A state.

When an event is experienced often, the strength of the B state increases. This increased B state reduces the affective reaction (A state) experienced during the event. Further, after the event ends, the increased B state leads to the experience of a strong opponent B state. The reduced A response to the event is called tolerance, and the intensified opponent B reaction in the absence of the event is called withdrawal.

Some people become addicted to pleasurable experiences even though arousal decreases with repeated experience. Addiction develops when these people learn that withdrawal occurs after the event ends, and that their addictive behavior terminates the aversive opponent withdrawal state. A second form of addiction occurs when a person learns that an intense pleasurable opponent state can be produced following exposure to an initial aversive state. Although early experience with the event was unpleasant, "the pleasure addict" now finds the initial affective response only mildly aversive and the opponent state very pleasurable. The anticipated pleasure motivates the addict to experience the aversive event.

CRITICAL THINKING QUESTIONS

1. Ming can usually pass a bakery without buying a donut, but sometimes she cannot resist the temptation. Using Lorenz and Tinbergen's energy model, explain Ming's behaviors.
2. Jamaal no longer notices the high pitch of his friend's voice. LaToya finds the friend's voice piercing. Explain how habituation and sensitization can be responsible for the different reactions of Jamaal and LaToya to their friend's voice.
3. Neal enjoys a few beers after work. He claims that it calms him after a hard day at the office. Using what you have learned about opponent-process theory, explain as much as you can about Neal's behavior. Focus on the conditions that cause Neal to drink, how drinking makes him feel, and how he might feel in the morning.

KEY TERMS

action-specific energy	evolution	opponent-process theory
appetitive behavior	fixed action pattern	sensitization
A state	habituation	sign stimulus
B state	ingestional neophobia	tolerance
dishabituation	innate releasing	withdrawal
displacement	mechanism (IRM)	

Principles and Applications of Pavlovian Conditioning

A Lingering Fear

Juliette is an attorney for a prestigious law firm. Although her coworkers often ask her to socialize after work, Juliette always rejects their requests; instead, driving home, she proceeds hurriedly from her car to her apartment. Once inside, Juliette locks the door and refuses to leave until the next morning. On weekends, Juliette will shop with her sister, who lives with their parents several blocks away. However, once darkness approaches, Juliette compulsively returns to her apartment. Although her sister, her parents, or close friends sometimes visit during the evening, Juliette refuses any of their invitations to go out after dark. Several men—all seemingly pleasant, sociable, and handsome—have asked Juliette for dates during the past year. Juliette has desperately wanted to socialize with them, yet she has been unable to accept any of their invitations. Juliette's fear of going out at night and her inability to accept dates began thirteen months ago. She had dined with her parents at their home and had left about 9:30 p.m. Since it was a pleasant fall evening, she decided to walk the several blocks to her apartment. Within a block of her apartment, a man grabbed her, dragging her to a nearby alley. The man kicked her several times before running away upon hearing another person approach. Since Juliette did not see her assailant, the police doubted they could apprehend him. The few friends and relatives whom Juliette told about the attack tried to support her; yet, she found no solace. Juliette still has nightmares about the attack and often wakes up terrified. On the few occasions after the attack that Juliette did go out after dark, she felt very uncomfortable and had to return home. She has become fearful even thinking about having to go out at night and arranges her schedule so she is home before dark. Juliette wants to overcome her fears, but she does not know how to do it.

Juliette's fear of darkness is a classically conditioned emotional response that she acquired as a result of the attack. This fear motivates Juliette to avoid going out at night. In this chapter, we will describe the classical conditioning process responsible for Juliette's intense fear reaction. The learning mechanism that causes Juliette to avoid darkness will be discussed in Chapters 5 and 6.

Juliette does not have to remain afraid of going out into the darkness. There are two effective behavior therapies, systematic desensitization and flooding, that employ the classical conditioning process to eliminate intense, conditioned fear reactions like Juliette's. We will discuss systematic desensitization later in this chapter, and flooding in Chapter 5.

THE ACQUISITION OF THE CONDITIONED RESPONSE

The Conditioning Paradigm

Basic Components

Four basic components make up the conditioning paradigm: (1) the **unconditioned stimulus (UCS)**, (2) the **unconditioned response (UCR)**, (3) the **conditioned stimulus (CS)**, and (4) the **conditioned response (CR).** Prior to conditioning, the UCS elicits the UCR, but the CS cannot elicit the CR. During conditioning, the CS is paired with the UCS. Following conditioning, the CS is able to elicit the CR. The strength (or intensity) of the CR increases steadily during acquisition until a maximum or **asymptotic level** is reached (see **Figure 3.1**). The UCS-UCR complex is referred to as the **unconditioned reflex;** the CS-CR complex is called the **conditioned reflex.**

Although the pairing of the CS and UCS is essential to the development of the CR, other factors determine whether conditioning occurs as well as the final asymptotic level of the CR. We will detail the conditions that influence the ability of the CS to elicit the CR later in the chapter. Let's use two examples to illustrate the basic elements of conditioning.

The Conditioning of Hunger

Suppose you become hungry when arriving home after class; the home environment at this time of day is the CS eliciting the hunger reaction (the CR). This conditioned hunger reflects the association of arriving home (CS) with

FIGURE 3.1. Acquisition and extinction of a conditioned response. The strength of the conditioned response increases during acquisition, when the CS and UCS are paired, while presentation of the CS without the UCS during extinction lowers the strength of the conditioned response. The strength of the conditioned response will spontaneously recover when a short interval follows extinction, but it will decline again with additional presentations of the CS alone.

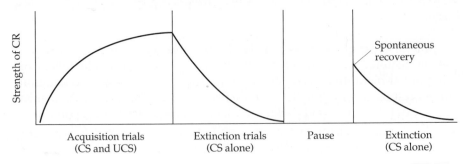

deprivation-induced hunger cues. A period of time without food is the UCS and the internal physiological changes produced by deprivation are the UCR. One probable cause of this conditioning is that you often arrive at home late in the day and have not eaten for awhile.

Your hunger undoubtedly intensifies when you go into the kitchen and see the refrigerator. Opening the refrigerator, you notice the milk and pie. Why does the sight of the refrigerator and the food increase your hunger and your motivation to obtain food? The answer lies in the association of the kitchen, the refrigerator, and the sight of food (CSs) with the taste and the smell of the food (UCSs).

When animals or people are exposed to food, they exhibit a set of unconditioned responses which prepare them to digest, metabolize, and store ingested food. These unconditioned feeding responses include the secretion of saliva, gastric juices, pancreatic enzymes, and insulin. One important action of insulin is to lower blood glucose, which in turn stimulates hunger and motivates eating (Mayer, 1953). Thus, we become hungry when we taste or smell food. The intensity of these unconditioned feeding responses is directly related to the palatability of food. The more attractive the food, the greater the unconditioned feeding responses and the more we eat.

These unconditioned feeding responses to food can be conditioned (Powley, 1977). The conditioning of these feeding responses to environmental cues plays an important role in your motivation to eat when you arrive home. Since cues such as the kitchen and the refrigerator have been associated with food, they are capable of eliciting these feeding responses. As a result of this conditioning experience, when you go to the kitchen and see the refrigerator, your body reflexively releases insulin, which lowers your blood glucose level and makes you hungry. As we will discover shortly, the strength of the conditioned response (CR) is dependent upon the intensity of the unconditioned stimulus (UCS). If you have associated the environment of the kitchen with highly palatable foods capable of eliciting an intense unconditioned feeding reaction, the stimuli in the kitchen will elicit an intense conditioned feeding response, and your hunger will be acute.

The Conditioning of Fear

For most people, experiencing turbulence in an airplane is an unpleasant event. When the plane drops suddenly and sharply (the UCS), an unconditioned pain reaction is elicited (the UCR). The psychological distress you experience when the airplane drops is one aspect of your pain reaction; the increased physiological arousal is another aspect. Although the unpleasantness may lessen as the plane continues to shake, you will most likely not experience relief until the turbulence ends.

Experiences with turbulence differ considerably in their degree of aversiveness. You respond intensely to some experiences; others elicit only a mild pain reaction. Many factors determine the level of aversiveness. The severity of the turbulence is one factor influencing how intensely you respond; a lot of air movement will elicit a stronger pain reaction than a little air movement. This is one example of the influence of the strength of the UCS on the intensity of the UCR. Another factor that often affects the aversiveness of experiencing turbulence is the number of times you have experienced it before. You may experience less distress if you have never before encountered turbulence than if you have often experienced the unsettling motion of a plane (sensitization).

Through past experiences, the cues that predict turbulence become able to elicit an anticipatory pain reaction (the CR). We typically call this anticipatory pain reaction "fear." One stimulus associated with turbulence is slight movements of the airplane. Thus, you may become frightened (CR) when the plane dips or shakes slightly (CS). Another cue may be storm clouds or a darkening sky. Each of these CSs may have been associated with sudden and sharp movement of the airplane; if so, each can become able to elicit fear. Even a forecast of bad weather might become a conditioned stimulus that elicits fear.

Psychologists have consistently observed that fear is conditioned when a novel stimulus (the CS) is associated with an aversive event. The Russian physiologist Bechterev's (1913) observation that a conditioned response (for example, withdrawal of the leg) can be established by pairing a neutral stimulus with shock, was the first experimental demonstration of fear conditioning. In 1916, John Watson showed that emotional arousal can be conditioned during the pairing of a novel stimulus with shock. Other researchers have consistently reported the development of fear through classical conditioning in animals (Miller, 1948) and humans (Staats & Staats, 1957).

Fear also motivates an escape response to an aversive event. Neal Miller's classic 1948 study demonstrates the motivational properties of fear. Miller first conditioned fear in rats by administering electric shock in the white compartment of a shuttle box apparatus (see **Figure 3.2**). After administering the shock,

FIGURE 3.2. Apparatus similar to the one Miller (1948) employed to investigate acquisition of a fear response. The rat's emotional response to the white chamber, previously paired with shock, motivates the rat to learn to turn the wheel, which raises the gate and allows escape.

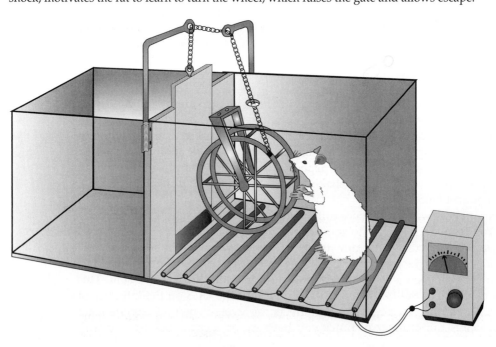

Miller allowed the rats to escape into the black compartment. After the initial pairings of the white compartment with shock, he confined the animals in the white compartment without presenting any additional shock. However, each rat could escape the white chamber by turning a wheel to open the door to the black compartment. Miller found that about half of the rats learned to turn the wheel to escape the aversive white chamber; the other half "froze" and did not learn the required response. The results show that the association of an environment (the white chamber) with an unconditioned aversive event (shock) can cause the environment to acquire motivational properties.

We learned earlier that the degree of hunger various environmental cues induce depends upon the UCS intensity; the stronger the UCS, the more intense our conditioned hunger reaction. The strength of the aversive unconditioned event also influences our conditioned fear reaction. We are more fearful of flying when the weather is bad than when the sun is shining and there are no storm clouds in the sky.

Not all people are frightened by flying in turbulent conditions, and some do not learn that driving is one way to reduce fear and avoid an unpleasant airplane ride. This chapter describes the conditions which influence the development of a conditioned fear response. Chapter 5 will detail the factors that govern avoidance acquisition.

Other Examples of Conditioned Responses

Hunger and fear are not the only examples of responses that can be conditioned. Other examples include feeling nauseous when seeing a type of food that has previously made you ill, becoming thirsty at a ball game as a result of previously consuming drinks in that setting, experiencing sexual arousal during a candlelight dinner because of previous sexual activity, and lowering your head when going down the stairs to the basement due to previously hitting your head when going down the stairs. These examples not only demonstrate four additional conditioned responses—nausea, thirst, sexual arousal, and lowering the head—but also show that stimuli other than food or shock can be involved in the conditioning process. The four unconditioned stimuli in the above examples are poison, fluid, sexual activity, and hitting your head. Of course, people encounter many more conditioned responses and unconditioned stimuli in the real world. Other examples are presented throughout the chapter.

Most of the experiments on classical conditioning have investigated the conditioning of only a single conditioned response. In most cases, several responses are conditioned during CS-UCS pairings. The conditioning of several responses has an obvious adaptive value. For example, when a CS is experienced along with food, several different digestive responses occur: the conditioned salivary reflex aids in swallowing, the conditioned gastric secretion response facilitates digestion, and the conditioned insulin release enhances food storage.

Conditioning Situations

Psychologists now use several techniques to investigate the conditioning process. Pavlov's surgical technique to measure the visceral reactions (saliva, gastric juices, insulin) to stimuli associated with food is the most familiar measure of conditioning. Other techniques that reveal the strength of conditioning include sign tracking, eyeblink conditioning, fear conditioning, and flavor-aversion learning. These measures of conditioning will be briefly described to familiarize you with the techniques; their widespread use will be evident in our discussion of Pavlovian conditioning principles and applications in this chapter.

Sign Tracking

Animals need to locate rewards (for example, food and water) in their natural environments. How do they find these rewards? Environmental events, or stimuli signaling the availability of reward, are approached and contacted by animals seeking reward. By tracking these environmental stimuli, an animal is able to obtain reward. Consider a predator tracking its prey: certain sights, movements, odors, and noises are characteristic of the prey. The predator can catch the prey only by approaching and then contacting these stimuli.

Predatory aggressive behavior reflects an instinctive species-specific response that can be improved with experience—experience increases a predatory animal's ability, for example, to aim its biting response toward the desired part of the prey (Eibl-Eibesfeldt, 1970) and to attack motionless prey (Eibl-Eibesfeldt, 1961; Fox, 1969). Predators, according to Eibl-Eibesfeldt, learn to limit their attack to the anterior part of the prey in order to avoid being bitten.

The establishment of effective predatory behavior is not the result of instrumental conditioning, or when a specific behavior is required to receive a reward, because a young predator's attack response improves even when its predatory behavior is unsuccessful. Furthermore, although nonpredatory animals can learn to kill other animals for food, they do not exhibit the instinctive species-specific responses characteristic of predatory behavior. For example, Moyer reported in 1972 that while nonpredatory rats can be trained to kill and eat mice, they never acquire the neck-biting aggressive response that predatory rats show. Pavlovian conditioning undoubtedly contributes to the enhancement of the predatory attack by causing the animal to approach and contact the stimuli characteristic of the prey.

Brown and Jenkins (1968) conducted the first **sign-tracking,** or **autoshaping,** experiment. They placed pigeons in an operant chamber; this environmental chamber contained a small circular key, which could be illuminated, and a food dispenser. [In the typical operant conditioning situation, an animal (in this case a pigeon) must respond (peck at the key) in order to receive reinforcement. A more extensive discussion of operant conditioning will be found in Chapter 4.] Hungry pigeons were fed at 15-second intervals, and the key was illuminated for 8 seconds prior to each food presentation. The pigeons did not have to do anything to obtain food. Brown and Jenkins reported that the pigeons, instead of approaching the food dish when the food was presented, started to peck at the key. The pigeons did not have to peck at the key to obtain food, but the presentation of the illuminated key prior to food was sufficient to elicit a key-pecking response. The measure of conditioning was the frequency with which the pigeons responded to the key. The acquisition of the key-pecking response was slow, and the pigeons only gradually learned to peck at the illuminated key.

Perhaps you think that the pigeons' key pecking in the Brown and Jenkins study is an instrumental response reinforced by food rather than a conditioned response elicited by the illuminated key (see the discussion of the law of effect in Chapter 1). If the key pecking is indeed an operant response, then its characteristics would not differ with the use of various reinforcers. However, if the illuminated key is producing an instinctive response, then the pigeons' response will differ with various rewards. The research on autoshaping with reinforcers other than food indicates that the key-pecking response is a conditioned response rather than an operant behavior in the autoshaping paradigm.

Jenkins and Moore (1973) used either food or water as the reinforcer in their autoshaping study. Observations of the pigeons' key-pecking responses demonstrated distinct differences between pigeons receiving the reinforcer of food and those receiving water. Pigeons autoshaped with food pecked the key sharply and vigorously; their behavior resembled their response toward food. Pigeons autoshaped with water exhibited a slower, more sustained contact with the key. Furthermore, these pigeons frequently made swallowing movements; their behavior toward the key resembled their response to water. Jenkins and Moore also autoshaped pigeons using two keys: one with food reinforcement, the other with water reinforcement. The pigeons responded with intense, short pecks to the key associated with food and with slow, sustained contact to the key paired with water.

In an interesting study of autoshaping, Rackham (1971) reported conditioned fetish behavior in pigeons. Rackham used four mated pairs of birds, housing the male and female of each pair in adjacent compartments of a large chamber with a sliding door separating the two birds. A stimulus, a light, was turned on daily just prior to the removal of the sliding door, which allowed the male to initiate courtship with the female. Rackham initially observed that when the light came on, the male pigeons began to approach the light, nodding and bowing. They then began cooing, strutting, and pirouetting. Finally, midway through the study, Rackham observed the male pigeons emitting nest calls. The male pigeons' response to the light stimulus was similar to behavior they exhibited to the female. This conditioned courtship response, like the autoshaped eating and drinking responses observed by Jenkins and Moore (1973), was directed toward the conditioned stimulus.

Eyeblink Conditioning

A puff of air is presented to a rabbit's eye. The rabbit reflexively blinks its eye. If a tone is paired with the puff of air, the rabbit will come to blink in response to the tone as well as to the puff of air. The pairing of a tone (CS) with the puff of air (UCS) leads to the establishment of an eyeblink response (CR). The process that leads to the rabbit's response is called **eyeblink conditioning** (see **Figure 3.3**).

Eyeblink conditioning is possible because the rabbit not only has an outer eyelid similar to that of humans, but also an inner eyelid called a nictitating membrane. The nictitating membrane reacts by closing whenever it detects any air movement near the eye. The closure of the nictitating membrane then causes the rabbit's eye to blink. Researchers have widely used eyeblink conditioning to investigate the nature of Pavlovian conditioning (Gormezano, Kehoe, &

FIGURE 3.3. Illustration of an apparatus used to condition an eyeblink response. The potentiometer records the closure of the eye following its exposure to a puff of air (UCS) or a tone (CS).

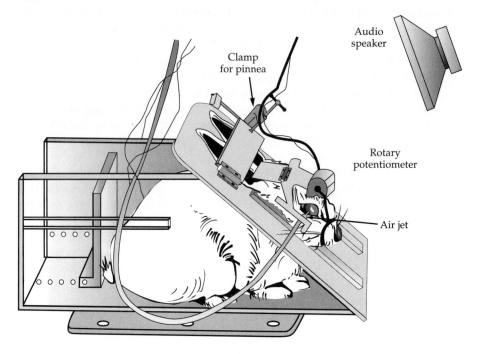

Marshall, 1983). They have also used it to study the brain mechanisms that underlie conditioning (Thompson, Hicks, & Shvyrok, 1980). While most eyeblink conditioning studies have used rabbits as subjects, eyeblink conditioning also occurs in humans.

We need to make several important points about eyeblink conditioning. A puff of air (the UCS) will elicit a rapid eyeblink response. A mild irritation of the skin below the eye with a brief electrical shock will also produce a rapid, unconditioned eyeblink response. By contrast, the CS (tone, light, or tactile stimulus) will produce a slow, gradual closure of the eye. The measure of conditioning is the percentage of trials in which the rabbit responds to the CS. Eyeblink conditioning is quite slow, taking as many as 100 CS-UCS pairings before the rabbit responds to the CS on 50% of the trials.

Fear Conditioning

We discussed several examples of **fear conditioning** earlier in the chapter. Fear can be measured in several ways. One measure is escape or avoidance behavior in response to a stimulus associated with a painful UCS. However, while avoidance behavior is highly correlated with fear, avoidance performance does not automatically provide a measure of fear. As we will discover in Chapter 6, animals show no overt evidence of fear with a well-learned avoidance behavior (Kamin, Brimer, & Black, 1963). Further, animals can fail to avoid despite being afraid (Monti & Smith, 1976).

Another measure of fear is the **conditioned emotional response (CER).**
Animals may freeze in an open environment when exposed to a feared stimulus. They will suppress operant behavior reinforced by food or water when a
feared stimulus is present. Estes and Skinner (1941) developed a CER procedure
for detecting the level of fear, and their methodology has been used often to
provide a measure of conditioned fear (Davis, 1968; Hoffman, 1969). Fear conditioning develops much more rapidly than eyeblink conditioning, and significant suppression can be found within 10 trials.

To obtain a measure of conditioned fear, researchers first have animals learn
to bar press or key peck to obtain food or water reinforcement. Following operant training, a neutral stimulus (usually a light or tone) is paired with an aversive event (usually electric shock or a loud noise). The animals are then returned
to the operant chamber, and the tone or light CS is presented during the training session. The presentation of the CS follows an equal period of time when the
CS is not present. Fear conditioned to the tone or light will lead to suppression
of operant behavior. If fear is conditioned only to the CS, the animal will exhibit
the operant behavior when the CS is not present.

To determine the level of fear conditioned to the CS, a suppression ratio is
calculated. This **suppression ratio** compares the level of response during the interval when the CS is absent to the level of response when the CS is present. To
obtain the ratio, the number of responses during the CS is divided by the total
number of responses (responses during and before the CS).

$$\text{Suppression ratio} = \frac{\text{Responses during CS}}{\text{Responses during CS} + \text{Responses without CS}}$$

How can we interpret a particular suppression ratio? A suppression ratio of
0.5 indicates that fear has not been conditioned to the CS, because the animal responds equally when the CS is on and off. For example, if the animal responds
15 times when the CS is on and 15 times when it is off, the suppression ratio will
be 0.5. A suppression ratio of 0 indicates that the animal responds only when
the CS is off; for example, an animal might respond 0 times when the CS is on
and 15 times when the CS is off. Only on rare occasions will the suppression ratio be as low as 0 or as high as 0.5. In most instances, the suppression ratio will
fall between 0 and 0.5.

Flavor Aversion Learning

I have a friend who refuses to walk down a supermarket aisle where tomato
sauce is displayed; he says that even the sight of cans of tomatoes makes him ill.
My oldest son once got sick after eating string beans, and now he refuses to touch
them. I once became nauseous several hours after eating at a local restaurant, and
I have not returned there since. Almost all of us have some food we will not eat
or a restaurant we avoid. Often, the reason for this behavior is that at some time
we experienced illness after eating a particular food or dining at a particular
place, and we associated the food or the place with the illness through classical
conditioning. Such an experience creates a conditioned **flavor aversion** to the
taste (or smell or sight) of the food or the place itself. Subsequently, we avoid it.

The classic research of John Garcia and his associates (Garcia, Kimeldorf, &
Hunt, 1957; Garcia, Kimeldorf, & Koelling, 1955) demonstrated that animals

learn to avoid a flavor associated with illness. Although rats have a strong preference for saccharin and will consume large quantities even when nondeprived, Garcia and colleagues discovered that the animals will not drink saccharin if illness follows its consumption. In their studies, rats were made ill after consuming saccharin by agents such as X-ray irradiation or lithium chloride; the rats subsequently avoided the taste of saccharin. The measure of conditioning is the amount of the fluid or food consumed. Flavor aversion learning is quite rapid, with significant avoidance observed after a single trial.

Does a person's dislike for a particular food reflect the establishment of a flavor aversion? It seems reasonable that people's aversion to a specific food often develops after they eat it and become ill. Informally questioning the students in my learning class last year, I found that many of them indeed had had an experience in which illness followed eating a certain food and that these students no longer could eat that food. If you have had a similar experience, perhaps you too can identify the cause of your aversion to some food. In a more formal investigation, Garb and Stunkard (1974) questioned 696 subjects about their food aversions, reporting that 38% of the subjects had at least one strong food aversion. The researchers found that 89% of the people reporting a strong food aversion could identify a specific instance associated with illness after eating the food. Even though most often the illness did not begin until several hours after consumption of the food, the subjects still avoided the food subsequently. Also, Garb and Stunkard's survey indicated that the subjects were more likely to develop aversions between the ages of 6 and 12 than at any other age.

More recent surveys suggest that the number of persons with flavor aversions is even higher than Garb and Stunkard reported. For example, Logue, Ophir, and Strauss (1981) found that over half of the college students they surveyed reported at least one food aversion. Further, many people have an aversion to a flavor even when they know that the flavor did not cause the illness. This observation suggests that aversions are controlled by mechanistic rather than cognitive processes; we will have more to say about the nature of flavor-aversion learning in Chapter 10.

Conditioning Paradigms

Five different paradigms have been used in conditioning studies (see **Figure 3.4**). These procedures represent the varied ways to pair a CS with a UCS. As we will discover, they are not equally effective.

Delayed Conditioning

In **delayed conditioning,** the CS onset precedes UCS onset. The termination of the CS occurs either with UCS onset or during UCS presentation. If, for instance, a darkening sky precedes a severe storm, delayed conditioning may occur. The darkening sky is the CS; its occurrence precedes the storm, and it remains present until the storm occurs. A person who has experienced this type of conditioning may be frightened whenever he or she sees a darkened sky.

Trace Conditioning

With this conditioning paradigm, the CS is presented and terminated prior to UCS onset. A parent who calls a child to dinner is using a trace conditioning

FIGURE 3.4. Schematic drawing of the five major classical conditioning paradigms. The CS occurs prior to the UCS, but remains on until the UCS is presented in delayed conditioning; the CS occurs and ends prior to the UCS in trace conditioning; the CS and the UCS occur together in simultaneous conditioning; and the CS occurs after UCS in backward conditioning. There is no explicit CS in temporal conditioning.

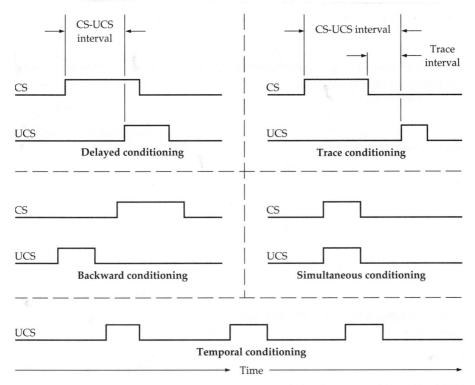

procedure. In this example, the announcement of dinner (CS) terminates prior to the presentation of food (UCS). As we will discover in the next section, the hunger that this **trace conditioning** paradigm elicits can be quite weak unless the interval between CS termination and UCS onset (the trace interval) is very short.

Simultaneous Conditioning

The CS and UCS are presented together when the **simultaneous conditioning** paradigm is used. An example of simultaneous conditioning would be walking into a fast food restaurant. In this setting, the restaurant (CS) and the smell of food (UCS) occur at the same time. The simultaneous conditioning procedure in this case would probably lead to weak hunger conditioned to the restaurant.

Backward Conditioning

In the **backward conditioning** paradigm, the UCS is presented and terminated prior to the CS. Suppose that a candlelight dinner (CS) follows sexual activity (UCS). With this example of backward conditioning, sexual arousal to the candlelight dinner may not develop. In fact, contemporary research (Tait & Saladin, 1986) indicates that the backward conditioning procedure often results in the development of another type of CR. The backward conditioning paradigm is also a conditioned inhibition procedure; that is, the CS is actually paired with the absence of the UCS. In some instances, a person would experience a conditioned inhibition rather than conditioned excitation when exposed to the CS. We will look at the factors that determine whether a backward conditioning paradigm conditions excitation or inhibition in Chapter 9.

Temporal Conditioning

There is no distinctive CS in **temporal conditioning.** Instead, the UCS is presented at regular intervals, and over time the CR will be exhibited just prior to the onset of the UCS. To show that conditioning has occurred, the UCS is omitted, and the strength of the CR assessed. What mechanism allows for temporal conditioning? In temporal conditioning, a specific biological state often provides the CS. When the same internal state precedes each UCS exposure, that state will be conditioned to elicit the CR.

Consider the following example to illustrate the temporal conditioning procedure. You set your alarm to awaken you at 7:00 A.M. for an 8:00 A.M. class. After several months, you awaken just prior to the alarm's sounding. The reason lies in the temporal conditioning process. The alarm (UCS) produces an arousal reaction (UCR), which awakens you. Your internal state every day just before the alarm rings (the CS) becomes conditioned to produce arousal; this arousal (CR) awakens you prior to the alarm's sounding.

The five different paradigms for presenting the CS and UCS are not equally effective (Keith-Lucas & Guttman, 1975). The delayed conditioning paradigm usually is the most effective; the backward conditioning, the least. The other three paradigms typically have an intermediate level of effectiveness.

BEFORE YOU GO ON

- **How might a clinical psychologist measure Juliette's fear of darkness?**
- **What conditioning paradigm was responsible for the conditioning of Juliette's fear?**

Conditions Affecting the Acquisition of a Conditioned Response

In the last section, we learned that a conditioned response develops when a novel stimulus is paired with an unconditioned stimulus. However, the pairing of a CS and a UCS does not automatically insure that the subject will acquire a conditioned response. A number of factors determine whether a CR will develop following CS-UCS pairings. Let us now look at the factors that play an important role in classical conditioning.

Contiguity

Consider the following example to illustrate the importance of contiguity to the development of a conditioned response. An 8-year-old girl hits her 6-year-old brother. The mother informs her aggressive daughter that her father will punish her when he gets home from work. Even though this father frequently punishes his daughter for aggression toward her younger brother, the mother's threat instills no fear. The failure of her threat to elicit fear renders the mother unable to curb her daughter's inappropriate behavior.

Why doesn't the girl fear her mother's threat, since it has been consistently paired with her father's punishment? The answer to this question relates to the close temporal pairing, or **contiguity,** of the CS and UCS in classical conditioning. A threat (the CS) provides information concerning future punishment and elicits the emotional state that motivates avoidance behavior. Although the mother's threat does predict future punishment, the child's fright at the time of the threat is not adaptive, since the punishment will not occur for several hours. Instead of being frightened from the time that the threat is made until the father's arrival, the girl becomes afraid only when her father arrives. This girl's fear now motivates her to avoid punishment, perhaps by crying and promising not to hit her little brother again.

THE OPTIMAL CS-UCS INTERVAL. Many studies document the importance of contiguity to the acquisition of a conditioned response. Experiments designed to evaluate the influence of contiguity on classical conditioning have varied the interval between the CS and UCS, and then evaluated the strength of the CR. The results of these studies show that the optimal **CS-UCS interval,** or interstimulus interval (ISI), is very short. Intervals even shorter than the optimal ISI produce weaker conditioning, with the strength of the CR increasing as the ISI becomes longer until the optimal CS-UCS interval is reached. An ISI longer than the optimal CS-UCS interval also leads to weaker conditioning, with the intensity of the CR decreasing as the ISI increases beyond the optimal.

The optimal CS-UCS interval is different for different responses. For example, the optimal conditioning interval is 450 milliseconds for eyeblink conditioning. This 450-millisecond ISI for the conditioning of the eyelid closure reflex has been observed in both animals (Smith, Coleman, & Gormezano, 1969) and humans (Kimble & Reynolds, 1967). **Figure 3.5** presents the CS-UCS interval gradient for eyeblink conditioning in humans. Some other optimal ISIs include 2.0 seconds for skeletal movements (Noble & Harding, 1963), 4.0 seconds for salivary reflexes (Gormezano, 1972), and 20 seconds for heart rate responses (Church & Black, 1958).

Why does the optimal CS-UCS interval vary among responses? The optimal ISI is thought to reflect the latency to respond in a particular reflex system (Hilgard & Marquis, 1940). Hilgard and Marquis suggested that the different optimal CS-UCS intervals occur because the response latency of the autonomic nervous system is longer than that of the eyeblink closure reflex. Wagner and Brandon's theory (1989) addresses the question of how response latency affects the optimal ISI; we will look at their view in Chapter 9.

A BRIDGE BETWEEN THE CS AND THE UCS. We have learned that the acquisition of the CR is impaired when the CS-UCS interval is longer than a few seconds. Several studies (Pearce, Nicholas, & Dickinson, 1981; Rescorla, 1982) have

FIGURE 3.5. An idealized interstimulus interval (ISI) gradient obtained from eyeblink conditioning data in humans. The graph shows that the level of conditioning increases with CS-UCS delays up to the optimal interval, then declines with longer intervals.

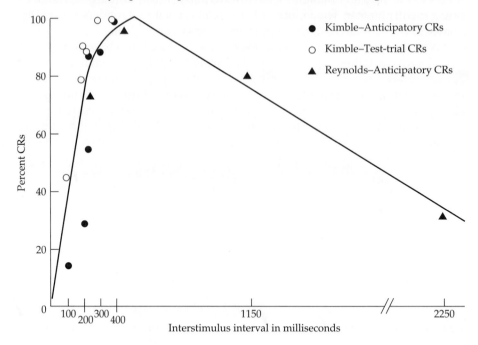

reported that the attenuation of conditioning produced by a temporal gap between the CS and UCS can be reduced if a second stimulus is presented between the CS and UCS.

Consider the Rescorla (1982) study to illustrate this phenomenon. Rescorla's subjects, pigeons, were shown a colored light, followed by food 10 seconds later. On the trials when one color—for example, red—was presented, a second stimulus, either a white light or a tone, was presented during the 10 seconds between the red light and the food. The white light or tone was not presented on trials in which a different colored light, say green, was used. Rescorla found that the level of conditioning was significantly greater to the color (in this case, the red light) followed by the white light or tone than to the color (in this case, the green light) not followed by the intermediate stimulus.

Why does the intermediate stimulus produce conditioning despite the delay between the CS and UCS? According to Rescorla (1982), the intermediate stimulus acts as a catalyst, enhancing the association of the CS and the UCS. This observation suggests that with appropriate procedures, a high level of conditioning can develop even when there is a significant delay between the CS and the UCS.

LONG-DELAY LEARNING. There is one noteworthy exception to the contiguity principle. Animals and humans are capable of associating a flavor stimulus (CS) with an illness experience (UCS) that occurs several hours later. The association of taste with illness, called **flavor-aversion learning,** contrasts sharply with the other forms of classical conditioning, in which no conditioning occurs if the CS-UCS interval is longer than several minutes. While flavor-aversion learning can occur even with long delays, a CS-UCS interval gradient does exist for it, with the strongest conditioning occurring when the flavor and illness are separated only by 30 minutes (Garcia, Clark, & Hankins, 1973). We will take a more detailed look at flavor-aversion learning in Chapter 10.

The Influence of Intensity

CS INTENSITY. Suppose that you were bitten by a dog. Would you be more afraid of the dog if it were large or small? If we assume that the pain induced by bites (the UCS) from each are equivalent, research on the intensity of the CS and the strength of conditioning indicates your fear would be equivalent only if one dog bites you. However, if you were bitten by both sizes of dogs (not necessarily at the same time), you would be more afraid of the more intense CS, the large dog, even if its bite was no more painful. Let's now look at research examining the influence of CS intensity on CR strength.

Initial research indicated that the intensity of the CS does not affect CR strength. For example, Grant and Schneider (1948, 1949) reported that CS intensity did not influence the classical conditioning of the eyeblink response in humans. Carter (1941) and Wilcott (1953) showed similar results. However, more recent research clearly demonstrates that CS intensity can affect the strength of the conditioned response. A greater CR strength, produced by a more intense CS, has been shown in dogs (Barnes, 1956), rabbits (Frey, 1969), rats (Kamin & Schaub, 1963), and humans (Grice & Hunter, 1964).

Why does a more intense CS only sometimes elicit a stronger CR? When an animal or person experiences only a single stimulus (either weak or intense), an intense CS does not produce an appreciably greater CR than a weak CS. However, if the subject experiences both the intense and the weak CS, the intense CS will produce a greater CR.

A study by Grice and Hunter (1964) shows the important influence of the type of training procedure on the magnitude of CS intensity effect. In Grice and Hunter's study, one group of human subjects received 100 eyelid conditioning trials of a loud (100-db) tone CS paired with an air puff UCS. A second group of subjects had a soft (50-db) tone CS paired with the air puff for 100 trials, and a third group was given 50 trials with the loud tone and 50 with the soft tone. Grice and Hunter's results, presented in **Figure 3.6,** show that CS intensity (loudness of tone) had a much greater effect on conditioning when a subject experienced both stimuli than when a subject was exposed to only the soft or the loud tone.

UCS INTENSITY. Recall Juliette's intense fear of darkness and men described in the chapter-opening vignette. The intensity of the attack was a critical factor in causing Juliette's extreme fear of darkness and men. Yet, not all experiences are as aversive as Juliette's attack. Suppose that you have the misfortune of being in an automobile accident. How much fear will arise the next time you get into a car? Research on UCS intensity and CR strength indicates that your level of fear will depend upon the intensity of the accident; the more severe the accident, the greater your fear of automobiles. Thus, if the accident was a minor one causing only slight discomfort, your subsequent fear will be minimal. A more severe accident will cause an intense fear.

The literature provides conclusive documentation that the strength of the CR increases with higher UCS intensity. To show the influence of UCS on eyelid response conditioning, Prokasy, Grant, and Myers (1958) gave their human subjects either a 50-, 120-, 190-, or 260-mm intensity air puff UCS paired with a light CS. They found that the strength of the CR was directly related to the UCS intensity; that is, the more intense the air puff, the stronger the eyeblink CR (see **Figure 3.7**).

The Salience of the CS

Martin Seligman (1970) suggested that animals or humans have an evolutionary predisposition or **preparedness** to associate a particular stimulus with a specific unconditioned stimulus, but that other CS-UCS associations cannot be learned. The concept of **contrapreparedness** suggests that some stimuli, despite

FIGURE 3.6. The percentage of conditioned responses during the last 60 trials is greater to a loud (100-db) tone than to a soft (50-db) tone in the two-stimuli condition, but not in the one-stimulus condition.

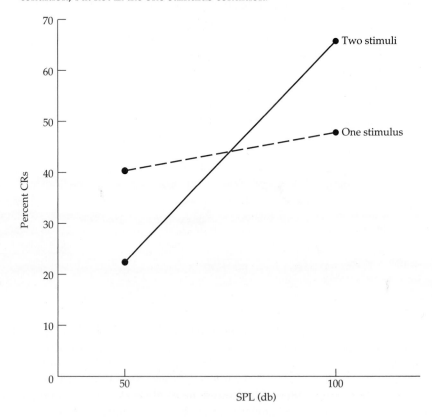

repeated CS-UCS pairings, cannot become associated with a particular UCS. The likelihood that a particular neutral stimulus will become able to elicit a conditioned response after pairing with an unconditioned stimulus reflects the **salience** of the neutral stimulus. Seligman proposed that preparedness makes a stimulus more salient. Thus, salient stimuli rapidly become associated with a particular unconditioned stimulus, while nonsalient stimuli do not, despite repeated CS-UCS pairings. Many, perhaps most, stimuli are not particularly salient or nonsalient; instead, most stimuli will gradually develop the ability to elicit a conditioned response as the result of conditioning experiences. In addition, salience is species-dependent; that is, a stimulus may be salient to one species but not to another. Chapter 10 discusses the biological significance of stimulus salience in Pavlovian conditioning; we will examine the influence of species-specific stimulus salience on the acquisition of a conditioned response in that chapter.

The Predictiveness of the CS

Robert Bolles (1972, 1979) proposed that contiguity alone is not sufficient for the development of a conditioned response. In Bolles's view, events must consistently occur together before we can acquire a conditioned response. A neutral stimulus may be simultaneously paired with a UCS, but unless the neutral stimulus reliably predicts the occurrence of the UCS, it will not elicit the CR. Additionally, when two or more stimuli are presented with the UCS, only the most reliable predictor of the UCS becomes able to elicit the CR.

FIGURE 3.7. The percentage of conditioned responses during acquisition increases with greater UCS intensity.

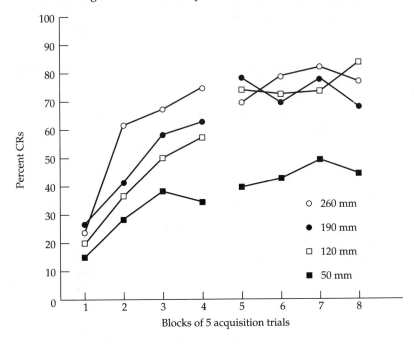

The following example illustrates the importance of **cue predictiveness** to the development of a conditioned response. Many parents threaten their children prior to punishment; yet their threats instill no fear, despite repeated threat (CS)-punishment (UCS) pairings. Why is parental threat ineffective? One likely reason is that these parents often threaten their children without punishing them. Under these circumstances, the threat is not a reliable predictor of punishment. Thus, its presentation will elicit little or no fear, even though the threat and punishment have frequently been experienced together. We will first examine evidence showing that CR acquisition is impaired if the UCS is often presented without the CS. Then we will review research which shows that presentations of the CS alone decrease the development of the CR.

UCS-ALONE PRESENTATIONS. Robert Rescorla's (1968) research demonstrates the influence of cue predictiveness in classical conditioning. After his rats learned to bar press for food, Rescorla divided the 2-hour training sessions into 2-minute segments. One of three events occurred in each segment: (1) a distinctive cue (CS; tone) was paired with a shock (UCS); (2) a shock was presented without the distinctive cue; or (3) neither tone nor shock occurred. Rescorla varied the likelihood that the shock would occur with (or without) the tone in each 2-minute segment. He found that the tone suppressed the bar-press response for food when the tone reliably predicted shock, indicating that the rats had formed an association between the tone and shock. However, the influence of the tone on the rats' behavior diminished as the frequency of the shock occurring without the tone increased. The tone had no effect on behavior when the shock occurred as frequently when the tone was absent as it did when the tone was present. **Figure 3.8** presents the results for those subjects that received a 0.4 UCS-alone probability (or UCS alone on 40% of the 2-minute segments).

One important finding from Rescorla's data is that even with only a few pairings, the presentation of the tone produced intense fear and suppressed bar pressing if the shock was administered only with the tone. However, when the shock occurred without the tone as frequently as it did with it, no conditioning appears to occur, even with a large number of tone-shock pairings. These results indicate that the predictability of a stimulus, not the number of CS-UCS pairings, determines an environmental event's ability to elicit a CR.

CS-ALONE PRESENTATIONS. The acquisition of a CR is also impaired or prevented when the CS is presented alone during conditioning. Many studies (see Hall, 1976) have documented the attenuation of conditioning when the CS is presented without, as well as with, the UCS.

The level of conditioning depends upon the percentage of trials pairing the CS with the UCS; the greater the percentage, the greater the conditioning. Hartman and Grant's (1960) study provides one example of the influence of the percentage of paired CS-UCS presentations on CR strength. All of Hartman and Grant's human subjects received 40 light (CS) and air puff (UCS) pairings. For subjects in the 25% group, the UCS occurred following 40 of the 160 CS presentations; for subjects in the 50% group, the air puff followed the tone on 40 of 80 CS presentations; for subjects in the 75% group, the UCS followed the CS on 40 of 54 trials; and for subjects in the 100% group, the air puff was presented after

FIGURE 3.8. Suppression of bar-pressing behavior during six test sessions (a low value indicates that the CS elicits fear and thereby suppresses bar pressing for food). The probability of the UCS occurring with the CS is 0.4 for all groups, and the values shown in the graph represent the probability that the UCS will occur alone in a 2-minute segment. When the two probabilities are equal, the CS does not elicit fear and, therefore, does not suppress the response. Only when the UCS occurs more frequently with than without the CS will the CS elicit fear and suppress bar pressing.

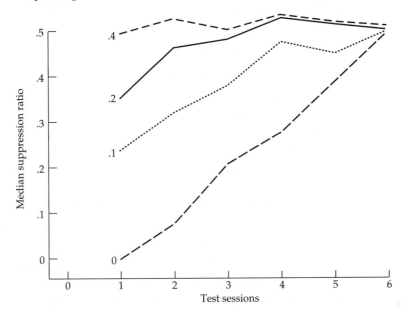

the light on 40 of 40 trials. Hartman and Grant's results showed that conditioning was strengthened as the percentage of trials that paired the CS with the UCS increased (see **Figure 3.9**).

The Redundancy of the CS

Recall from the last section the example of parental threats that fail to instill fear. In addition to a lack of predictiveness, another possible explanation for this lack of fear is that the child is already afraid when the threat is presented. Perhaps they are afraid of their parents; if so, parental presence (the CS) will interfere with the acquisition of fear to the threat, despite repeated threat-punishment pairings.

For a cue to elicit a CR, and thereby influence behavior, Bolles (1978) suggested that the cue must not only predict the occurrence of the UCS, but must also provide information not signaled by the other cues in the environment. The research of Leon Kamin (1968) suggests that the presence of a predictive cue (CS_1) will prevent, or **block,** the development of an association between a second cue (CS_2) also paired with the UCS. To demonstrate the importance of relative cue predictability, Kamin presented to all of his subjects a distinctive cue (CS_1, a

FIGURE 3.9. The percentage of conditioned responses during each block of acquisition trials decreases when the percentage of trials in which the UCS follows the CS also decreases.

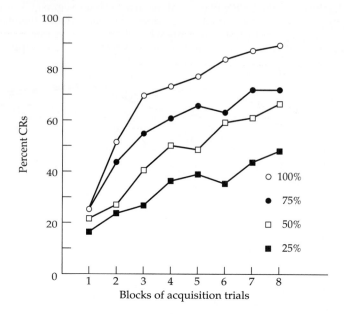

light) paired with a shock (UCS) eight times during the first phase of the study (see **Figure 3.10**). In the second phase of the study, the experimental group subjects received eight pairings of the light (CS_1), a new cue (CS_2, a tone), and shock (UCS). Kamin observed that while presentation of the light (CS_1) suppressed bar pressing, the tone cue (CS_2) alone had no influence on it. The light had become associated with the shock, while tone had apparently not. Kamin's results do not indicate that a tone cannot be associated with shock. Control group animals that received only tone (CS_2)-shock pairings during the second phase of study showed strong suppression in response to the tone (CS_2).

BEFORE YOU GO ON

- How did the intensity of the attack contribute to the conditioning of Juliette's fear of darkness?
- Was salience a factor in the conditioning of Juliette's fear? Predictiveness? Redundancy?

EXTINCTION OF THE CONDITIONED RESPONSE

Earlier in the chapter, you learned that environmental stimuli, through their association with deprivation, reward, or both, can acquire the ability to elicit hunger. Our conditioned responses typically have an adaptive function; the

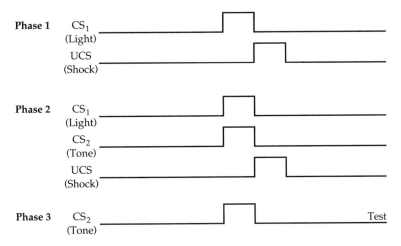

FIGURE 3.10. The design of Kamin's blocking study. In phase 1, the CS, (light) is paired with the UCS (shock); in the second phase, both the CS_1 and CS_2 (tone) are paired with the UCS (shock). The ability of the CS_2 (tone) to elicit fear is assessed during phase 3.

development of a conditioned hunger enables us to eat at regularly scheduled times. However, the conditioning of hunger can also be harmful. For example, people can eat too much and become obese.

Clinical research (Masters, Burish, Hollon, & Rimm, 1987) has revealed that overweight people eat in many situations (for example, while watching television, driving, or at the movies). In order to lose weight, overweight people must restrict their food intake to the dining room (or the room where they usually eat), a process called **stimulus narrowing.** Yet, how can those who are overweight control their intake in varied environmental circumstances? One answer is through **extinction,** a method of eliminating a conditioned response. As the person's hunger response to varied environmental circumstances has developed through the classical conditioning process, so the conditioned hunger reaction can be extinguished through it.

Extinction can also be effective for people who are extremely fearful of flying. Because fear of flying may be acquired through the classical conditioning process, extinction again represents a potentially effective method for eliminating the conditioned reaction.

In the next section, we will describe the extinction process and explain how extinction might eliminate a person's hunger reaction to an environmental event like watching television or reduce someone's fear reaction to flying in an airplane. We will also explore the reason that extinction is not always an effective method of eliminating a conditioned response. Let's begin by looking at the extinction paradigm.

Extinction Paradigm

The extinction of a conditioned response will occur when the conditioned stimulus is presented without the unconditioned stimulus. The strength of the CR decreases as the number of CS-alone experiences increases, until eventually the CS elicits no CR (refer to **Figure 3.1**).

Pavlov reported in his classic 1927 book that a classically conditioned salivation response in dogs could rapidly be extinguished by presenting the CS (tone) without the UCS (meat powder). Since Pavlov's initial observations, many psychologists have documented the extinction of a CR by using CS-alone presentations; the extinction process is definitely one of the most reliable conditioning phenomenon.

Extinction is one way to eliminate a person's hunger reaction to environmental stimuli such as watching television. In this case, the person can eliminate the hunger response by repeatedly watching television without eating food (the UCS). However, people experiencing hunger-inducing circumstances are not always able to refrain from eating. Other behavioral techniques (for example, aversive counterconditioning or reinforcement therapy) are often necessary to inhibit eating and, thereby, to extinguish the conditioned hunger response. The use of reinforcement is examined in Chapter 4; the use of punishment is discussed in Chapter 5.

Fear of flying can also be eliminated by extinction. If a person flies and does not experience extreme plane movements, the fear will be diminished. However, fear is not only an aversive emotion, it can also be an intense motivator of avoidance behavior. Thus, people who are afraid of flying may not be able to withstand the fear and inhibit their avoidance of flying. Other techniques (for example, desensitization, response prevention, and modeling) also are available to eliminate fears. Desensitization is discussed in this chapter; response prevention in Chapter 5, and modeling in Chapter 8.

How Rapidly Does a Conditioned Response Extinguish?

We have learned that many factors can facilitate or hinder the acquisition of the CR; we will next discuss the variables that determine its rate of extinction.

The Strength of the CR

Hull (1943) envisioned the extinction process as a mirror image of acquisition; that is, the stronger the CS-CR bond, the more difficult it is to extinguish the CR. Thus, Hull assumed that the stronger the CR, the slower the extinction of that response. Although many studies have found that acquisition level does influence resistance to extinction, other research shows the relationship between the strength of the CR during acquisition and the rate of the extinction of that response is not a perfect correspondence. As Hall (1976) stated, one reason for this discrepancy is that the omission of the UCS during extinction changes the subject's motivational level from that which existed during acquisition. This altered motivation level makes extinction differ from acquisition, and thereby decreases the correlation between the CR acquisition level and the resistance to extinction.

The Influence of Predictiveness

In 1939, Humphreys examined how the percentage of trials in which the UCS followed the CS during acquisition influenced resistance to extinction. To study this effect, he conditioned an eyelid response in humans. During acquisition, subjects in group 1 received 96 CS-UCS pairings and no CS-alone presentations; subjects in group 2 received 48 CS-UCS pairings and 48 CS-alone presentations; and subjects in group 3 were given 48 CS-UCS pairings and no CS-alone presentations. Humphreys discovered that in the subjects who received CS-UCS pairings on 50% of the trials (group 2), the conditioned eyeblink response extinguished significantly more slowly than in those subjects given CS-UCS pairings on 100% of the trials (groups 1 and 3). Humphrey's results, presented in **Figure 3.11,** show that the number of CS-UCS pairings during acquisition does not determine resistance to extinction; the rates of extinction were equal in animals given only 48 or 96 CS-UCS pairings. Instead, extinction was more rapid when the CS was more predictive of the UCS during acquisition.

Duration of CS Exposure

We have discovered that the strength of the conditioned response declines as the CS-alone experience increases. You might think that the number of CS-alone presentations would determine the level of extinction; that is, as the number of extinction trials increases, the strength of the CR declines. However, research

FIGURE 3.11. The extinction of the conditioned response as a function of the percentage of trials where the UCS followed the CS during acquisition. Subjects in groups 1 and 3 received CS-UCS pairings on 100% of the acquisition trials; those in group 2, on 50%. Resistance to extinction is greater with only partial pairings of CS and UCS during acquisition.

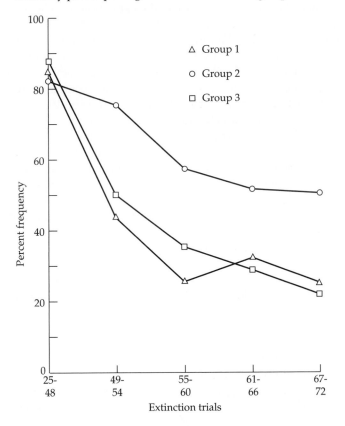

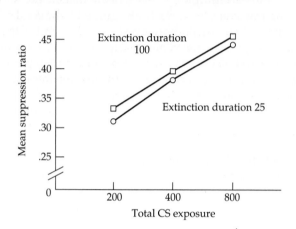

FIGURE 3.12. The suppression of the licking-for-water response to the conditioned stimulus decreases (or the suppression ratio increases) with greater duration of CS exposure during extinction.

(Monti & Smith, 1976; Shipley, 1974) clearly shows that the total duration of CS-alone exposure, not the number of extinction trials, determines the rate of extinction. These studies demonstrate that as the duration of CS-alone exposure increases, the strength of the CR weakens. Let's briefly look at Shipley's study to see the influence of CS-alone duration on the extinction of a CR.

Shipley (1974) initially trained water-deprived rats to lick a water tube to obtain liquid reinforcement. Following lick training, the animals received 20 exposures to a tone paired with electric shock. Extinction occurred following fear conditioning. Half of the animals were given 25-sec. CS-alone exposures during extinction; the other half received 100-sec. CS-alone experiences during extinction. One-third of the animals in both the 25-sec. and the 100-sec. CS duration groups were given sufficient extinction experience that they received a total of 200 sec. of CS exposure; another third received 400 sec., and the last third 800 sec. of exposure. For example, to have 200 total sec. of CS exposure, the animals given 25 sec. on each trial received 8 trials, compared to 2 trials for subjects receiving 100 sec. on each. Shipley reported that the suppression of licking the CS produced was not affected by either the number of CS-alone exposures or the duration of each exposure. Only the total duration of CS exposure during extinction determined the rate of extinction for the CR; the greater the length of the total CS exposure during extinction, the less suppression the tone produced (see **Figure 3.12**).

We have examined the variables which affect extinction rate; let's next look at the spontaneous recovery of responding following the extinction of a CR.

Spontaneous Recovery

Pavlov (1927) proposed that the extinction of a CR is caused by the **inhibition** of the CR. This inhibition develops because of the activation of a central inhibitory state that occurs when the CS is presented without the UCS. The continued presentation of the CS without the UCS strengthens this inhibitory state and acts to prevent the occurrence of the CR.

The initial inhibition of the CR during extinction is only temporary. According to Pavlov, the arousal of the inhibitory state declines following the initial extinction. As the strength of the inhibitory state diminishes, the ability of the CS to elicit the CR returns (see **Figure 3.1**). The return of the CR following extinction is called **spontaneous recovery.** The continued presentation of the CS without the UCS eventually leads to the long-term suppression of the CR. The inhibition of a CR can become permanent as the result of conditioned inhibition; we will discuss the conditioned inhibition process shortly.

Other Inhibitory Processes

We have learned that a temporary inhibition is involved in the extinction of a conditioned response. The inhibition of the CR can also become permanent, a process Pavlov called conditioned inhibition. There are also several other types of inhibition: external inhibition, latent inhibition, and inhibition of delay. Inhibition can be disrupted through a process called disinhibition.

Conditioned Inhibition

The initial inhibition of a CR can become permanent. If a new stimulus (CS−) similar to the conditioned stimulus (CS+) is presented in the absence of the unconditioned stimulus, the CS− will act to inhibit a CR to the CS+. The process of developing a permanent inhibitor is called **conditioned inhibition.** Conditioned inhibition is believed to reflect the ability of the CS− to activate the inhibitory state, which can suppress the CR.

Consider the following example to illustrate the conditioned inhibition phenomenon. Recall our discussion of conditioned hunger; because of past experiences, you became hungry when arriving home after your classes. Suppose that when you open the refrigerator, you find no food. In all likelihood, the empty refrigerator would act to inhibit your hunger. This inhibitory property of the empty refrigerator developed as a result of past pairings of the empty refrigerator with an absence of food. Many studies have shown that associating new stimuli with the absence of the UCS causes these stimuli to develop permanent inhibitory properties. Let's examine one of these studies.

Rescorla and LoLordo (1965) initially trained dogs to avoid electric shock using a Sidman avoidance schedule. With this procedure, the dogs received a shock every 10 seconds unless they jumped over a hurdle dividing the two compartments of a shuttlebox (see Chapter 5). If a dog avoided a shock, the next shock was postponed for 30 seconds. The advantage of this technique is twofold: it employs no external CS, and it allows the researcher to assess the influence of fear-inducing cues (CS+) and fear-inhibiting cues (CS−). After three days of avoidance conditioning, the dogs were locked in one compartment of the shuttlebox and exposed on some trials to a 1,200-hertz tone (CS+) and shock (UCS) and on other trials to a 400-hertz tone (CS−) without shock. Following conditioned inhibition training, the CS+ aroused fear and increased avoidance responses. In contrast, the CS− inhibited fear, causing the dogs to stop responding. These results indicate that the CS+ elicited fear and the

CS— inhibited fear, and that conditioned stimuli have an important motivational influence on instrumental behavior. We will examine that influence in Chapter 7.

External Inhibition

Pavlov (1927) suggested that inhibition could occur in situations other than extinction. In support of his theory, he observed that the presentation of a novel stimulus during conditioning reduces the strength of the conditioned response. Pavlov labeled this temporary activation of the inhibitory state **external inhibition.** The inhibition of the CR will not occur on a subsequent trial unless the novel stimulus is presented again; if the novel stimulus is not presented during the next trial, the strength of the conditioned response will return to its previous level.

Latent Inhibition

Preexposure to the CS impairs conditioning of the CR when the CS and UCS are later presented together. Lubow and Moore (1959) attributed the effect of CS preexposure to **latent inhibition;** that is, they argued that exposure to the CS prior to conditioning caused the CS to acquire inhibitory properties that subsequently interfered with excitatory conditioning when the CS and the UCS were paired.

Mackintosh (1983) believes that CS preexposure leads to learned irrelevance—the subject learns that a stimulus does not predict any significant event. The subject therefore has difficulty recognizing the correlation between the stimulus and the UCS.

A number of studies (Baker & Mackintosh, 1977; Rescorla, 1971) have examined the effect of CS preexposure on the acquisition of conditioned inhibition. If the impact of CS preexposure resulted from inhibition, then CS preexposure should enhance conditioned inhibition training. However, these studies show that preexposure to a stimulus not only retards excitatory conditioning but also interferes with inhibitory conditioning. Thus, it appears that CS preexposure does not lead to the development of latent inhibition. We will look more closely at the influence of CS preexposure on classical conditioning in Chapter 9.

Inhibition of Delay

There are many occasions when a short delay separates the CS and the UCS. For example, several minutes elapse from the time we enter a restaurant until we receive our food. Under these conditions, we inhibit our responses until just prior to receiving the food. (If we did begin to salivate as soon as we entered the restaurant, our mouths would be dry when we were served our food, and our digestive processes would be impaired.) Further, the ability to inhibit the response until the end of the CS-UCS interval improves with experience. At first, we respond immediately when a CS is presented; our ability to withhold the CR improves with increased exposure to CS-UCS pairings.

Pavlov's classic research (1927) demonstrated that the dogs developed the ability to suppress the CR until the end of the CS-UCS interval, a phenomenon he labeled **inhibition of delay.** Other experimenters (Kimmel, 1965; Sheffield, 1965) have also shown that animals and humans can inhibit the CR until just

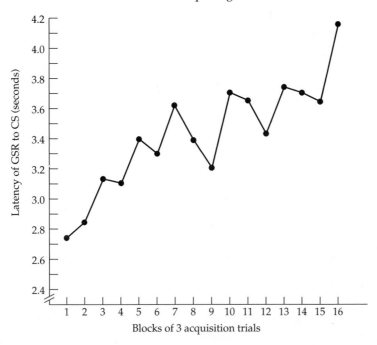

FIGURE 3.13. The average latency of GSR response to a conditioned stimulus, which preceded the unconditioned stimulus by 7.5 seconds, increases as the number of CS-UCS pairings increases.

Blocks of 3 acquisition trials

before the UCS presentation. For example, Kimmel (1965) gave human subjects 50 trials of a red light (CS) paired with shock (UCS). The red light was presented 7.5 seconds prior to shock, and both terminated simultaneously. Kimmel reported that the latency of the galvanic skin response (GSR) increased with increased training trials (see **Figure 3.13**).

Disinhibition

We have learned that the presentation of a novel stimulus during conditioning causes the CS to inhibit the elicitation of the CR. Presenting a novel stimulus during extinction also causes disruption; however, in this case, the novel stimulus causes an increase in the strength of the conditioned response. The extinction process will proceed normally on the next trial if the novel stimulus is not presented. Pavlov labeled the process of increasing the strength of the CR **disinhibition.**

Kimmel's (1965) study shows the disinhibition phenomenon in an inhibition-of-delay paradigm. Kimmel observed that a novel tone presented with the CS disrupted the ability of the subjects to withhold the CR during the 7.5-second CS-UCS interval. Whereas the subjects exhibited the CR approximately 4.0 seconds after the CS was presented following 50 acquisition trials, the latency dropped to 2.3 seconds when the novel stimulus was presented along with the CS. These results indicate that a novel stimulus can disrupt the inhibition of a CR. They also show that inhibition is responsible for the suppression of the CR observed in the inhibition-of-delay phenomenon.

- **How might Juliette's fear of darkness be extinguished?**
- **What problems might a clinical psychologist encounter trying to extinguish Juliette's fear?**

A CR WITHOUT A CS-UCS PAIRING?

Although many conditioned responses are acquired through direct experience, many stimuli develop the ability to elicit a conditioned response indirectly; that is, a stimulus which is never directly paired with the UCS nevertheless elicits a CR. For example, although many people with test anxiety have developed their fear because of the direct pairing of a test and failure, many others who have never failed an examination also fear tests. We will next discuss three ways—higher-order conditioning, sensory preconditioning, and vicarious conditioning—that a CR can develop without a CS-UCS pairing. A fourth way—stimulus generalization (see Chapter 1)—will be explored further in Chapter 7.

Higher-Order Conditioning

You did poorly last semester in Professor Jones's class. Not only do you dislike Professor Jones, but you also dislike Professor Rice, who is Professor Jones's friend. Why do you dislike Professor Rice, with whom you have never had a class? Higher-order conditioning provides one likely reason for your dislike.

The Higher-Order Conditioning Paradigm

Pavlov (1927) observed that following several CS-UCS pairings, presenting the CS with another neutral stimulus (CS_2) enabled the CS_2 to elicit the CR. In one of Pavlov's studies using dogs, a tone (the beat of a metronome) was paired with meat powder. After this first-order conditioning, the tone was presented with a black square, but the meat powder was omitted. Following the black square-tone pairings, the black square (CS_2) alone was able to elicit salivation. Pavlov called this conditioning process higher-order conditioning. (In this particular study, the higher-order conditioning was of the second-order.) **Figure 3.14** presents a diagram of the **higher-order conditioning** process.

Research on Higher-Order Conditioning

The strength of a CR acquired through higher-order conditioning is weaker than that developed through first-order conditioning. Pavlov discovered that a second-order CR is approximately 50% as strong as a first-order CR, and a third-order CR is very weak. He found it impossible to develop a fourth-order CR.

Psychologists since the time of Pavlov's original studies have not always been successful in producing a CR through higher-order conditioning. Rescorla's (Holland & Rescorla, 1975; Rescorla, 1973, 1978; Rizley & Rescorla, 1972) elegant analysis of the higher-order conditioning process demonstrates the reason for these failures. According to Rescorla, the problem with higher-order conditioning

FIGURE 3.14. The higher-order conditioning process. In phase 1, the CS_1 (light) is paired with the UCS; in phase 2, the CS_1 (light) and the CS_2 (buzzer) are presented together. The ability of the CS_2 to elicit the CR is evaluated in phase 3.

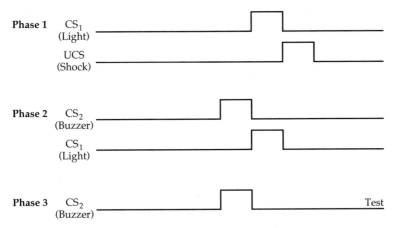

is that the pairing of CS_2-CS_1 without the UCS during the second phase of conditioning also represents a conditioned inhibition paradigm. Thus, not only are the CS_2-CS_1 pairings conditioning the excitation of the CR to the CS_2, but they are also conditioning the inhibition of the CR by pairing the compound stimulus (CS_2 & CS_1) in the absence of the UCS.

When will higher-order conditioning occur? Rescorla and his associates have discovered that conditioned excitation develops more rapidly than conditioned inhibition. Thus, with only a few pairings, a CS_2 will elicit the CR. However, as conditioned inhibition develops, CR strength declines until the CS_2 can no longer elicit the CR. At this time, the conditioned inhibition equals the conditioned excitation produced by the CS_2, and the presentation of the CS_2 will not elicit the CR.

Rizley and Rescorla's (1972) study illustrates the influence of the number of CS_2-CS_1 pairings on the strength of a higher-order conditioned fear. Rizley and Rescorla presented eight pairings of a 10-second flashing light (CS_1) paired with a 1 ma. 0.5-second electric shock (UCS). Following first-order conditioning, the light (CS_1) was paired with a 1,800-Hz tone (CS_2). Rizley and Rescorla discovered that the strength of the fear conditioned to the CS_2 increased with initial CS_2-CS_1 pairings, reaching a maximum strength after four pairings (see **Figure 3.15**). However, the intensity of fear elicited by the CS_2 declined with each additional pairing until the CS_2 produced no fear after 15 CS_2-CS_1 presentations. Holland and Rescorla (1975) obtained similar results in measuring the effects of higher-order conditioning on the development of a conditioned appetitive response.

The observation that the strength of a second-order CR diminishes after the presentation of more than a few CS_2-CS_1 pairings does not indicate that higher-order conditioning has no role in real-world settings. For example, once a CR, such as fear, is conditioned to a CS_2, such as high places, the fear the CS_2 produces will motivate avoidance behavior, resulting in only a brief exposure to the

FIGURE 3.15. The fear response to CS_2 increases with a few CS_1 and CS_2 pairings, but decreases with greater pairings of CS_1 and CS_2.

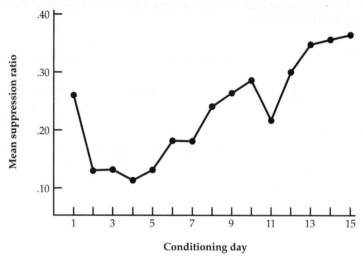

CS₂. This rapid avoidance response will result in slow development of conditioned inhibition. The slow acquisition of conditioned inhibition permits the CS_2 to elicit fear for a very long, possibly indefinite, period of time.

Sensory Preconditioning

Consider the following example to illustrate the sensory preconditioning process. Your neighbor owns a large German shepherd; you associate the neighbor with his dog. As you are walking down the street, the dog bites you, causing you to become afraid of the dog. You may also develop a dislike for your neighbor as the result of your previous association of the neighbor with the dog.

The Sensory Preconditioning Paradigm

In **sensory preconditioning,** two neutral stimuli, CS_1 and CS_2, are paired (see **Figure 3.16**). Following the association of CS_1 and CS_2 (dog and neighbor), CS_1 is presented with an unconditioned stimulus (bite). The CS_1-UCS pairing results in the ability of the CS_2, as well as the CS_1, to elicit the CR (fear). Thus, as a result of the initial CS_2-CS_1 association, the CS_2 is able to produce the CR even though it was never directly paired with the UCS.

Research on Sensory Preconditioning

Brogden's (1939) classic research represents an early successful sensory preconditioning study. In the first phase of Brogden's experiment, dogs in the experimental condition received 200 simultaneous pairings of a light and a buzzer. Control animals did not receive light-buzzer pairings. Following this initial conditioning, one of the cues (either the light or the buzzer) was presented with an electric shock to the dog's foot. Brogden reported that presentation of the cue not paired with shock elicited the CR (leg flexion) in experimental animals but not in

FIGURE 3.16. The sensory preconditioning process. In phase 1, the CS_1 (light) and CS_2 (buzzer) are paired; in phase 2, the CS_1 (light) is presented with the UCS. The ability of the CS_2 (buzzer) to elicit the CR is evaluated in phase 3.

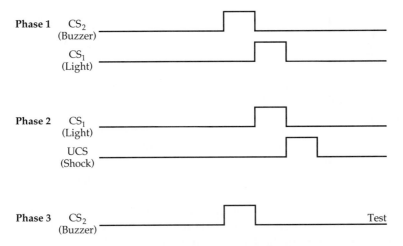

control animals. Although Brogden's results showed that a cue can develop the ability to elicit a CR through the sensory preconditioning process, the leg flexion CR to the CS_2 was weaker than the CR to the CS_1. Other researchers (see Kimble, 1961) during the 1940s and 1950s also observed that the magnitude of the sensory preconditioning effect was small.

More recent studies (Rizley & Rescorla, 1972; Tait, Marquis, Williams, Weinstein, & Suboski, 1969) indicate that the early studies did not employ the best procedures to produce a strong, reliable sensory preconditioning effect. These later studies found that the CS_2 will elicit a strong CR if, during the initial conditioning, (1) the CS_2 precedes the CS_1 by several seconds and (2) only a few CS_2-CS_1 pairings are used in order to prevent the development of learned irrelevance. Recall that when the CS is presented without the UCS prior to conditioning, it diminishes the conditioning of a CR when the CS and UCS are later paired during training.

Vicarious Conditioning

A person can develop an emotional response to a specific stimulus through direct experience; a person can also learn to respond to a particular stimulus after observing the experiences of others. For example, a person can become afraid of dogs after being bitten, or after seeing another person being bitten. The development of a CS's ability to elicit a CR following such an observation is called **vicarious conditioning.** Although many emotional responses are clearly developed through direct conditioning experience, the research (see Bandura, 1977) also demonstrates that CS-CR associations can be acquired through vicarious conditioning experiences. Let's examine several studies which show the vicarious conditioning of a CR.

Berger's study (1962) demonstrates the vicarious conditioning of a conditioned fear reaction to a neutral stimulus. Berger's subjects listened to a neutral tone and then saw another person receiving an electric shock and exhibiting pain reactions (this other person, a confederate, pretended to be shocked and hurt). Berger found that subjects who repeatedly heard the tone and then witnessed the scene developed an emotional response to the tone. Bandura and Rosenthal (1966) also observed that vicarious conditioning of fear occurred when a subject observed another person being shocked.

One can also develop an emotional reaction by observing people fail at a task (Bandura, Blanchard, & Ritter, 1969; Craig & Weinstein, 1965). In the Craig and Weinstein study, subjects watched another person either succeed or fail at a motor task. The subjects who witnessed the other person failing showed a stronger conditioned stress reaction to the task than subjects who saw the other person succeed. This indicates we can learn to fear a task merely by watching others fail at it.

Vicarious conditioning is not unique to humans. Crooks (1967) reported that monkeys can develop a fear of certain objects after viewing the experience of another monkey with these objects. In Crooks's study, the subjects heard a tape-recorded distress sound when a model monkey touched some particular objects; they did not hear the emotional reaction when the model touched other objects. Crooks discovered that subjects subsequently played with the objects not associated with distress but would not touch the objects that appeared to have hurt the other monkey. In a more recent study, Mineka, Davidson, Cook, and Keir (1984) found that monkeys learned to fear snakes after seeing another monkey react fearfully to a snake. In the absence of this experience, the monkeys showed no evidence of a fear of snakes.

The Importance of Arousal

We do not always develop a CR after watching the experiences of others. For vicarious conditioning to occur, we must respond emotionally to the scene we witness. Bandura and Rosenthal (1966) evaluated the level of vicarious CR conditioning as a function of the subject's arousal level during conditioning. They found that observers moderately aroused by seeing another person being shocked subsequently showed a strong autonomic reaction to the tone that was paired with the scene; subjects either minimally distressed or intensely upset by viewing the shock displayed only weak vicarious conditioning. The highly aroused subjects stopped attending to the person receiving the shock; Bandura and Rosenthal suggested that their altered attention reduced the association of the tone with shock. These results indicate that we must be aroused—but not too aroused—if we are to develop conditioned responses from observing the experiences of others.

We have learned that the strength of higher-order conditioning, sensory preconditioning, and vicarious conditioning is weaker than conditioning developed through the direct pairing of the CS and the UCS. Does this weaker conditioning mean that an intense CR cannot develop indirectly? The answer to this question is no. Several sources may contribute to the intensity of the conditioned response. For example, the combined influence of vicarious conditioning and sensory preconditioning may cause an intense conditioned reaction to the CS.

BEFORE YOU GO ON

69

CHAPTER 3
Principles and
Applications of
Pavlovian
Conditioning

- **How might Juliette have developed a fear of darkness through higher-order conditioning? sensory preconditioning? vicarious conditioning?**

APPLICATIONS OF PAVLOVIAN CONDITIONING

We will discuss three applications of Pavlovian conditioning in this chapter. The first involves the use of Pavlovian conditioning principles to modify phobic behavior. This procedure, called systematic desensitization, has been used to eliminate the fears of people with phobias for over forty years. The second application, which involves extinction of a person's craving for a drug, has only recently been used to treat drug addiction. The last application has not been clinically tested, but it represents a possible use of Pavlovian conditioning to correct immune system dysfunction in patients with lupus and other diseases of the immune system.

Systematic Desensitization

Suppose a person is extremely frightened of taking examinations. This fear could cause the individual to do poorly in college. What can be done to allow this student to take examinations with minimal or no fear? **Systematic desensitization,** a therapy developed by Joseph Wolpe, acts to inhibit fear and suppress phobic behavior (a phobia is an unrealistic fear of an object or situation). Wolpe's therapy can help people with extreme test anxiety. His treatment is based on Pavlovian conditioning principles and represents an important application of classical conditioning. Let's examine this technique to discover how Pavlovian conditioning can alleviate extreme fear.

Original Animal Studies

Wolpe's therapy developed from his animal research. In an initial study (Wolpe, 1958), he shocked one group of cats in their home cages after they heard a buzzer. For the other cats, he paired the buzzer with food in the home cages and then shocked them. Both groups of cats later showed extreme fear of the buzzer; one indication of their fear was their refusal to eat when hearing the buzzer. Since fear inhibited eating, Wolpe reasoned that eating could—if sufficiently intense—suppress fear. As we learned in Chapter 1, counterconditioning is the process of establishing a response that competes with a previously acquired response. Wolpe suggested that counterconditioning is a potentially effective way of treating human phobic behavior. He based this idea on three lines of evidence: (1) Sherrington's statement (1906) that an animal can only experience one emotional state at a time—a phenomenon Wolpe termed **reciprocal inhibition;** (2) Jones's report (1924) that she had successfully eliminated a young boy's conditioned fear of rabbits by presenting the feared stimulus (a rabbit) while the boy was eating (see Chapter 1); and (3) Wolpe's own research using cats. Wolpe initially placed the cats—which had developed a conditioned fear of the buzzer and the environment in which the buzzer was experienced—in a cage with food; this cage was quite dissimilar to their home cage. He used the dissimilar cage, which produced only a low fear level due to little generalization (see Chapter 1), because the home cage would produce too intense a fear and therefore inhibit eating. Wolpe observed that the cats ate in the dissimilar cage and did not appear afraid either during or after eating. Wolpe concluded that in the dissimilar environment, the eating response had replaced the fear response. Once the fear in the dissimilar cage was eliminated, the cats were less fearful in another cage more closely resembling the home cage. The reason for this reduced fear was that the inhibition of fear conditioned to the dissimilar cage generalized to the second cage. Using the counterconditioning process with this second cage, Wolpe found that presentation of food in this cage quickly reversed the cats' fear. Wolpe continued the gradual counterconditioning treatment by slowly changing the characteristics of the test cage until the cats were able to eat in their home cages without any evidence of fear. Wolpe also found that a gradual exposure of the buzzer paired with food modified the cats' fear response to the buzzer.

Clinical Treatment

Wolpe (1958) believed that human phobias could be eliminated in a manner similar to the one he used with his cats. He chose not to use eating to inhibit human fears, but instead used three classes of inhibitors: relaxation, assertion, and sexual responses. We will limit our discussion in this chapter to the use of relaxation.

Wolpe's therapy using relaxation to counter human phobic behavior is called systematic desensitization. Basically, desensitization involves relaxing while imagining anxiety-inducing scenes. To promote relaxation, Wolpe used a series of muscle exercises Jacobson developed in 1938. These exercises involve tensing a particular muscle and then releasing this tension. Presumably, tension is related to anxiety, and tension reduction is relaxing (or reinforcing). The patient tenses and relaxes each major muscle group in a specific sequence.

Masters, Burish, Hollon, and Rimm (1987) indicated that relaxation is most effective when the tension phase lasts approximately 10 seconds and is followed by 10 to 15 seconds of relaxation for each muscle group. The typical procedure requires about 30 to 40 minutes to complete; however, later in therapy, patients need less time as they become more readily able to experience relaxation. Once relaxed, patients are required to think of a specific word (for example, *calm*). This procedure, which Russell and Sipich labeled **cue-controlled relaxation** in 1973, promotes the development of a conditioned relaxation response that enables a specific stimulus to elicit relaxation promptly; the patient then uses the cue to inhibit any anxiety occurring during therapy.

The desensitization treatment consists of four separate phases: (1) the construction of the anxiety hierarchy, (2) relaxation training, (3) counterconditioning, or the pairing of relaxation with the feared stimulus, and (4) an assessment of whether the patient can successfully interact with the phobic object. In the first stage, patients are instructed to construct a graded series of anxiety-inducing scenes related to their phobia. A 10-to-15-item list of low-, moderate-, and high-anxiety scenes is typically employed. Using index cards, the patient writes descriptions of the scenes and then ranks them in a hierarchy from those that produce low to those that produce high anxiety.

Paul (1969) identified two major types of hierarchies: thematic and spatial-temporal. In **thematic hierarchies,** the scenes are related to a basic theme. **Table 3.1** presents a hierarchy detailing the anxiety an insurance salesman experienced when anticipating interactions with coworkers or clients. Each scene in the hierarchy is somewhat different, but all are related to his fear of possible failure in professional situations. In contrast, a **spatial-temporal hierarchy** is based on phobic behavior in which the intensity of fear is determined by distance (either physical or temporal) to the phobic object. The test anxiety hierarchy shown in **Table 3.2** indicates that the level of anxiety is related to the proximity to exam time.

We need to point out one important aspect of the hierarchy presented in **Table 3.2.** Perhaps contrary to your intuition, this student experienced more anxiety en route to the exam than when actually in the test area. Others may have a different hierarchy; when taking the exam, they experience the most fear. These observations indicate that each individual's phobic response is highly idiosyncratic and dependent on that person's unique learning experience. Therefore, a hierarchy must be specially constructed for each student. Some phobias require a combination of thematic and spatial-temporal hierarchies. For example, a person with a height phobia can experience varying levels of anxiety at different places and at different distances form the edges of these places.

TABLE 3.1. Thematic Hierarchy

Level	Scene
1	In your office with an agent, R. C., discussing a prospective interview. The client in question is stalling on his payment, and you must tell R. C. what to do.
2	Monday morning working in your office. In a few minutes you will attend the regularly scheduled sales meeting. You are prepared for the meeting.
3	Conducting an exploratory interview with a prospective client.
4	Sitting at home. The telephone rings.
5	Anticipating returning a call from the district director.
6	Anticipating returning a call from a stranger.
7	Entering the Monday sales meeting unprepared.
8	Anticipating a visit from the regional director.
9	Listening as a fellow agent requests a joint visit with a client.
10	On a joint visit with a fellow agent.
11	Attempting to close a sale.
12	Thinking about attending an agents' and managers' meeting.
13	Thinking of contacting a client who should have been contacted earlier.
14	Thinking about calling a prospective client.
15	Thinking about the regional director's request for names of prospective agents.
16	Alone, driving to prospective client's home.
17	Calling a prospective client.

Note: In the fear hierarchy, a higher level represents greater fear.
Source: Masters, J. C., Burish, T. G., Hollon, S. D., and Rimm, D. C. (1987). *Behavior therapy: Techniques and empirical findings* (3rd ed.). San Diego, Calif.: Harcourt Brace Jovanovich. Reprinted by permission of the publisher.

TABLE 3.2. Spatial-Temporal Hierarchy

Level	Scene
1	Four days before an examination.
2	Three days before an examination.
3	Two days before an examination.
4	One day before an examination.
5	The night before an examination.
6	The examination paper lies face down before the student.
7	Awaiting the distribution of examination papers.
8	Before the unopened doors of the examination room.
9	In the process of answering an examination paper.
10	On the way to the university on the day of the examination.

Note: In the fear hierarchy, a higher level represents greater fear.
Source: Wolpe, J. (1982). *The practice of behavior therapy* (3rd ed.). Oxford: Pergamon.

After the hierarchy is constructed, the patient learns to relax. Relaxation training follows the establishment of the hierarchy to prevent the generalization of relaxation to the hierarchical stimuli and thereby preclude an accurate assessment of the level of fear to each stimulus. The counterconditioning phase of treatment begins following relaxation training. The patient is instructed to relax and imagine as clearly as possible the lowest scene on the hierarchy. Since even this scene elicits some anxiety, Masters, Burish, Hollon, and Rimm (1987) suggested that the first exposure be quite brief (5 seconds). The duration of the imagined scene can then be slowly increased as counterconditioning progresses.

It is important that the patient not become anxious while picturing the scene; otherwise, additional anxiety, rather than relaxation, will be conditioned. The therapist instructs the patient to signal when experiencing anxiety, and the therapist terminates the scene. After a scene has ended, the patient is instructed to relax. The scene can again be visualized when relaxation has been reinstated. If the individual can imagine the first scene without any discomfort, the next scene in the hierarchy is imagined. The process of slowly counterconditioning each level of the hierarchy continues until the patient can imagine the most aversive scene without becoming anxious.

Clinical Effectiveness

The last phase of desensitization evaluates the therapy's success. To test the effectiveness of desensitization, the individual is required to encounter the feared object. The success of desensitization as a treatment for phobic behavior is quite impressive. Wolpe (1958) reported that 90% of 210 patients showed significant improvement with desensitization, compared to a 60% success rate when psychoanalysis was used. The comparison is more striking when one considers that desensitization produced a rapid extinction of phobic behavior—according to Wolpe (1976), a range of 12 to 29 sessions was effective—compared to the longer length of treatment (3 to 5 years) necessary for psychoanalysis to cure phobic behavior. Although Lazarus (1971) reported that some patients showed a relapse 1 to 3 years after therapy, the renewed anxiety could be readily reversed with additional desensitization. The range of phobias successfully treated or extinguished by desensitization is impressive: fears of heights, driving, snakes, dogs, insects, tests, water, flying, rejection by others, crowds, enclosed places, and injections are a few in a long list. In addition, desensitization apparently can be used with any behavior disorder initiated by anxiety. For instance, desensitization should help treat an alcoholic whose drinking occurs in response to anxiety. In general, research has demonstrated that systematic desensitization is a very effective way of successfully treating phobic behavior (Emmelkamp & Scholing, 1990; Nietzel, Bernstein, & Milich, 1994).

However, systematic desensitization therapy requires that patients be able to vividly imagine the fearful scene. Approximately 10% of patients cannot imagine the phobic object sufficiently to experience anxiety (Masters, Burish, Hollon, & Rimm, 1987); for these patients another form of therapy is needed. Further, Rachman (1990) observed that therapy is more effective when a patient confronts a real rather than imagined phobic object. Imagined scenes are used in the initial phase of systematic desensitization in order to control the duration of exposure and prevent the association of the phobic objects with anxiety. You might be wondering if a patient can confront a phobic object, but be able to control the duration of exposure to that object. Fortunately, modern technology appears to have made this possible. What is that technology? Perhaps you guessed: the use of a virtual reality environment.

Rothbaum, Hodges, Kooper, and Opdyke (1995) evaluated whether graded exposure to height-related stimuli in a virtual reality environment could effectively treat acrophobia. The researchers constructed a number of height-related stimuli, such as standing on a bridge, standing on a balcony, or riding in a glass elevator. The height of the stimuli varied: the bridge could be up to 80 meters above water, while the balcony or elevator could be as high as 49 floors. Rothbaum, Hodges, Kooper, and Opdyke reported that a graded virtual reality exposure to height-related stimuli was an effective treatment for acrophobia. Following treatment, patients were able to stand on a real bridge or balcony or ride in a glass elevator. Similarly, Carlin, Hoffman, and Weghorst (1997) found that a virtual reality environment can be used to treat a spider phobia. Virtual reality is a relatively new technology. As the technology improves, it seems highly likely that its use in systematic desensitization treatment will become more widespread.

Explorations for the Future

Desensitization is a well-established application of Pavlovian conditioning. Researchers are developing new applications based on current research; we will look at two of these new applications in this section.

An Intense Craving

In Chapter 2, we discovered that animals and people experience withdrawal following a drug exposure. The withdrawal from the drug can be intense, and can act to motivate continued use of the drug. An opponent withdrawal state can be conditioned to the environmental cues surrounding drug administration, and exposure to these cues can produce withdrawal as a conditioned response. The conditioned withdrawal response produces a drug craving which then motivates use of the drug. Further, the greater the intensity of the withdrawal response, the greater the craving and the higher the likelihood of continued drug use.

Can an environmental stimulus produce withdrawal symptoms? Wikler and Prescor (1967) demonstrated that the **conditioned withdrawal reaction** can be elicited even after months of abstinence. They repeatedly injected dogs with morphine when the animals were in a distinctive cage. The addicted dogs were then allowed to overcome their unconditioned withdrawal reaction in their home cages and were not injected for several months. When placed in the distinctive cages again, these dogs showed a strong withdrawal reaction, including excessive shaking, hypothermia, loss of appetite, and increased emotionality.

Why is it so difficult for an addict to quit using drugs? Whenever an addict encounters the cues associated with a drug (for example, the end of a meal for a smoker), a conditioned withdrawal will be elicited. The experience of this withdrawal may motivate the person to resume taking the drug. According to Solomon (1980), conditioned withdrawal reactions are what make eliminating addictions so difficult.

Any substance abuse treatment needs to pay attention to conditioned withdrawal reactions. To ensure a permanent cure, an addict must not only stop "cold turkey" and withstand the pain of withdrawal, he or she must also extinguish the conditioned withdrawal reactions all of the cues associated with the addictive behavior produce. Ignoring these conditioned withdrawal reactions increases the likelihood that addicts will eventually return to their addictive behavior. Consider the alcoholic who goes to a bar just to socialize. Even though this alcoholic may have abstained for weeks, the environment of the bar can produce a conditioned withdrawal reaction and motivate this person to resume drinking.

Can exposure to drug-related stimuli enhance an addict's ability to avoid relapse? Charles O'Brien and his colleagues (Childress, Ehrman, McLellan, & O'Brien, 1986; Ehrman, Robbins, Childress, & O'Brien, 1992) have addressed this issue. Childress, Ehrman, McLellan, and O'Brien (1986) repeatedly exposed cocaine addicts to the stimuli they associated with drug taking. Extinction experiences for these cocaine abusers involved watching videotapes of their "cook-up" procedure, listening to audiotapes of cocaine talk, and handling their drug paraphernalia. Childress, Ehrman, McLellan, and O'Brien reported that their patients' withdrawal responses and craving for drugs decreased as a result of exposure to drug-related cues. Further, the extinction treatment significantly reduced the resumption of drug use.

Ehrman, Robbins, Childress, and O'Brien (1992) found that when cocaine users are exposed to cocaine-related stimuli (talking about drug experiences, watching a videotape of people buying and using cocaine, pretending to freebase and smoke cocaine), these stimuli elicit increased heart rates as well as feelings of cocaine craving. Cocaine users reported no craving nor exhibited any physiological response to either heroin-related stimuli or nondrug-related stimuli. In contrast, subjects who did not use cocaine showed no psychological or physiological response to cocaine-related stimuli. The results of these studies indicate the important role the environment plays in motivating addictive behavior. In the future, we can expect this extinction procedure to play a more prominent role in the treatment of addictive disorders.

Robert Ader and Nathan Cohen (Ader & Cohen, 1981, 1985, 1993) discovered that environmental events could suppress the functioning of our immune systems. Interestingly, they made this discovery by accident. Following the pairing of saccharin-flavored water (CS) with cyclophosphamide (UCS), a drug which produces nausea, Ader and Cohen extinguished the aversion to the saccharin-flavored water. They reported that some of their animals died as a result of the presentation of the CS without the UCS.

Why would presentation of saccharin-flavored water kill some of their animals? Ader and Cohen (1981) recognized that cyclophosphamide not only produces nausea but also suppresses the immune system. Perhaps the association of saccharin and cyclophosphamide resulted in the conditioning of immune system suppression as well as of nausea.

Ader and Cohen (1981) tested the idea that conditioned immune system suppression was responsible for the deaths of animals exposed to the saccharin-flavored water CS. These researchers injected animals with red blood cells from sheep. This alien substance normally activates the animals' immune systems and produces high levels of antibodies. Following injection of the red blood cells, some animals were presented saccharin paired with cyclophosphamide. Other animals did not experience the saccharin-cyclophosphamide pairing. All animals then were placed in several extinction trials in which saccharin was presented alone. Ader and Cohen reported that the presence of saccharin during extinction produced significantly fewer antibodies in those animals that received saccharin paired with cyclophosphamide than in animals that had not experienced saccharin and cyclophosphamide. These results indicate that exposure to an environmental event (saccharin) associated with a drug (cyclophosphamide) produced immune system suppression as a CR. Other researchers (Gorczynski, 1987; O'Reilly & Exon, 1986) have also reported that a flavor paired with cyclophosphamide becomes able to suppress immune system functioning.

Cyclophosphamide is not the only immunopharmacologic agent that has been used to produce **conditioned immune system suppression.** Coussons, Dykstra, and Lysle (1992) paired a distinctive environmental stimulus with morphine, a drug that suppresses several nonspecific immune responses. Following conditioning, exposure to the environmental stimulus produced a conditioned immune system suppression. Other immunopharmacologic agents that can produce conditioned immunosuppression include corticosteroids (King, Husband, & Kusnecov, 1987) and antilymphocyte serum (Kusnecov, Sivyer, King, Husband, Cripps, & Clancy, 1983). Electric shock also can cause immune system suppression, and the stimuli associated with a shock stressor will become able to produce conditioned immune system suppression (Lysle & Maslonek, 1991; Zalcman, Irwin, & Anisman, 1991).

The conditioning of immune system functions could be used to treat diseases of the immune system. The drug cyclophosphamide is used to suppress the immune system as part of the treatment for lupus, a disorder in which the immune system causes the body to attack itself. Yet cyclophosphamide has some seriously debilitating side effects. Perhaps the dose of cyclophosphamide could be reduced and its use supplemented with a psychological treatment to suppress the immune system. Ader and Cohen (1982) provided support for this idea by showing that the conditioning of immune system suppression delayed the development of systemic lupus erythematosus in New Zealand mice. In this study, the experimental group female mice received one trial of saccharin-cyclophosphamide pairing each week. Ader and Cohen found that these experimental animals showed a slower rate of lupus progression and a lower mortality than animals that did not experience trials of saccharin paired with cyclophosphamide or than animals that experienced trials of saccharin without cyclophosphamide. Some retardation of illness was seen in animals that experienced an equal number of saccharin-cyclophosphamide and saccharin-saline pairings. **Figure 3.17** presents the results of this study.

Can Pavlovian conditioning be used in the treatment of lupus? Olness and Ader (1992) described their successful application of Pavlovian conditioning to the treatment of severe lupus in an 11-year-old girl. Their treatment consisted of six pairings of a taste (cod liver oil) and smell (rose perfume) with cyclophosphamide over a 12-month period. The pairings were given every other month. (The usual treatment would have consisted of 12 cyclophosphamide treatments.) The girl received a taste-only experience between each cyclophosphamide treatment. Olness and Ader found a significant reduction in the symptoms of lupus in the girl during the 12-month treatment period. Also, she continued to do well when evaluated 5 years after the conditioning treatment ended. While the results of a single case study must be viewed with caution, this successful application of Pavlovian conditioning suggests an important breakthrough in the treatment of this immune system disorder.

In several diseases in which the immune system is suppressed, such as acquired immune deficiency syndrome (AIDS), psychologists have attempted to condition increased immune system functioning. Several studies (Hiramoto, Hiramoto, Solvason, & Ghanta, 1987; Krank & MacQueen, 1988; Solvason, Ghanta,

FIGURE 3.17. A slowing of the progression of the immune disease lupus erythematosus in New Zealand mice is produced by conditioned immune system suppression. The development of disease and mortality rates were lower in animals in group C100, which were given one pairing of saccharin and cyclophosphamide, than in group NC50, which received unpaired saccharin and cyclophosphamide, or in control mice, which were given saccharin but no cyclophosphamide. The mice in the C50 group received two saccharin-cyclophosphamide and two saccharin-saline pairings each week. These animals showed some retardation in disease progression.

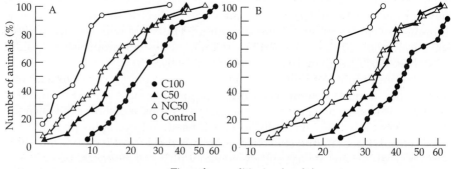

Time after conditioning (weeks)

& Hiramoto, 1988) have reported **conditioned immune system enhancement.** In a study involving human subjects, Buske-Kirschbaum, Kirschbaum, Stierle, Jabaij, and Helhammer (1994) paired a sherbet flavor with injections of adrenaline. One unconditioned response to adrenaline is increased activity of natural killer (NK) cells of the immune system. Following several sherbet-adrenaline pairings, the sherbet elicited an enhanced immune system response. While it seems clear that immune system enhancement can be conditioned, additional research is needed to determine its applicability to the treatment of AIDS and other diseases involving immune system suppression.

BEFORE YOU GO ON

- **How might systematic desensitization be used to overcome Juliette's fear of darkness?**
- **What might be the effect of Juliette's fear on her immune system?**

CHAPTER SUMMARY

Many environmental stimuli can produce internal reactions; these emotional responses often make a particular response more likely. The hunger you experience while watching a food commercial on television, or the fear you experience when anticipating an airplane flight in bad weather, are two examples of our emotional reactions to environmental stimuli. Furthermore, the hunger response may be sufficiently intense to make it more likely you will get a sandwich from the refrigerator, or the fear response may be intense enough to make you more likely to cancel your flight plans.

The ability of environmental events to produce emotional reactions which, in turn, motivate instrumental behavior develops through the classical conditioning process. Conditioning involves the pairing of a neutral environmental cue with a biologically important event. Prior to conditioning, only the biologically important stimulus, called an unconditioned stimulus, can elicit a response. This response, called the unconditioned response, consists of both an overt behavioral reaction and an internal emotional response. As the result of conditioning, the neutral environmental stimulus, now a conditioned stimulus, can also elicit a response, called the conditioned response.

There are five conditioning paradigms. With delayed conditioning, the CS remains present until the UCS begins. The CS ends prior to the onset of the UCS with trace conditioning. With simultaneous conditioning, the CS and UCS occur at the same time. Backward conditioning presents the CS following the presentation of the UCS, and temporal conditioning takes place when the UCS is presented at regular intervals of time. Delayed conditioning is usually the most efficient and backward conditioning the least.

Five factors, in addition to its pairing with the unconditioned stimulus, influence whether a stimulus develops the ability to elicit a conditioned response. One factor affecting the strength of conditioning is temporal contiguity: contiguity must exist between the CS and UCS for conditioning to occur. An aversion to a flavor cue paired with illness is an exception; it can develop despite a lack of contiguity. An intermediate stimulus between the CS and UCS can facilitate the development of a conditioned response.

The intensity of the CS and UCS is a second factor affecting the intensity of the CR. An intense stimulus typically leads to a stronger CR. A third variable conditioning is salience. Some stimuli are more salient than others and therefore are more likely to elicit a CR following pairing with a UCS. The stimulus must also be a reliable predictor of the UCS. The more often the CS occurs without the UCS, or the UCS without the CS, the weaker the CR. Redundancy is the final factor affecting the strength of the conditioned response. The presence of a conditioned stimulus can prevent or block the development of a conditioned response to a new stimulus when both stimuli are paired with the UCS.

Stimuli sometimes produce undesired conditioned emotional reactions. Extinction represents an effective method of eliminating the ability of the conditioned stimulus to elicit the conditioned response; the presentation of the CS without the UCS will cause a reduction in CR strength. With continued CS-alone presentations, the conditioned stimulus will eventually fail to elicit the conditioned response.

Extinction of a conditioned response is thought to reflect an inhibitory process. The dissipation of inhibition is believed to cause spontaneous recovery, which is the return of a CR following an interval between extinction and testing without additional CS-UCS pairings.

Other inhibitory processes that suppress conditioned responses include conditioned inhibition, external inhibition, and inhibition of delay. Conditioned inhibition develops when the CS+ is paired with the UCS and the CS− with the absence of the UCS. External inhibition occurs when a novel stimulus is experienced prior to the CS during acquisition. Inhibition of delay reflects the suppression of the CR until presentation of the UCS. These inhibitory processes can be disrupted during extinction by the presentation of a novel stimulus, causing a disinhibition effect and resulting in an increased CR strength.

A conditioned stimulus can develop the ability to elicit the conditioned response indirectly; that is, without being directly paired with the UCS. Indirect conditioning methods include higher-order conditioning, sensory preconditioning, and vicarious conditioning. Higher-order conditioning occurs when, after CS_1 and UCS pairings, a new stimulus (CS_2) is presented with the CS_1 and UCS. In contrast, the CS_1 and CS_2 occur together prior to CS_1 and UCS pairings with sensory preconditioning. In both higher-order conditioning and sensory preconditioning, the CS_2 elicits the CR even though it has never been directly paired with the UCS.

A CR can be established through vicarious conditioning when one person observes another person experiencing the pairing of CS and UCS. For vicarious conditioning to occur, the observer must be sufficiently aroused while witnessing the other person's conditioning experience.

Pavlovian conditioning principles have been successfully used to modify undesired conditioned responses. Wolpe developed a technique called systematic desensitization, a graduated counterconditioning procedure, to eliminate phobias. The patient first constructs a hierarchy of feared stimuli; relaxation is then paired with the feared stimuli. The counterconditioning process begins with imagining the least feared stimulus for a brief time. The time the patient spends imagining this stimulus is increased until the patient can imagine it without any discomfort. The next stimulus on the hierarchy is then associated with relaxation. The process of slowly counterconditioning each level continues until the patient can imagine the most aversive stimulus without becoming anxious. The success of desensitization is considerable; the elimination of fear of heights, driving, tests, flying, and enclosed places are a few examples of its successful application.

The stimuli paired with the use of drugs can elicit a conditioned withdrawal state. This withdrawal state produces a craving for the drug and motivates resumption of drug use. As part of a treatment program for addiction, exposure to the stimuli associated with drug use can extinguish the conditioned craving and reduce the likelihood of continued use.

A flavor stimulus presented prior to the administration of cyclophosphamide, a drug that suppresses the immune system, can become able to elicit a conditioned suppression of the immune system. Conditioned immune system suppression can help explain the increased susceptibility to disease associated with exposure to stressful events. It also represents a potential application of Pavlovian conditioning in the treatment of lupus and other diseases of the immune system. Immune system enhancement can also be conditioned, and may represent an application of Pavlovian conditioning in the treatment of AIDS.

CRITICAL THINKING QUESTIONS

1. Pavlovian conditioning has a significant influence on human emotions. Identify your emotional response to several environmental events. Describe the experiences that led to the establishment of these emotional responses. Indicate the CS, CR, UCS, and UCR in these examples. How have these conditioned emotional responses affected your life?
2. Tamiko becomes extremely anxious prior to giving a speech. Mia feels only slightly tense when speaking in public. Using the principles presented in the text, suggest possible explanations for the differences in fear shown by Tamiko and Mia.
3. Greg has an intense desire to smoke cigarettes. His nicotine craving occurs after a meal, a class, or a movie, as well as at other times. Describe the process responsible for Greg's craving. How might Greg eliminate his craving? What problems might Greg encounter? How can he avoid these problems?

KEY TERMS

asymptotic level	conditioned immune	conditioned response
autoshaping	system enhancement	conditioned stimulus
backward conditioning	conditioned immune	conditioned withdrawal
blocking	system suppression	reaction
conditioned emotional	conditioned inhibition	contiguity
response	conditioned reflex	contrapredaredness

CS-UCS interval
cue-controlled relaxation
cue predictiveness
delayed conditioning
disinhibition
external inhibition
extinction of conditioned
    response
eyeblink conditioning
fear conditioning
flavor-aversion learning
higher-order conditioning

inhibition
inhibition of delay
latent inhibition
preparedness
reciprocal inhibition
salience
sensory preconditioning
sign tracking
simultaneous
    conditioning
spatial-temporal
    hierarchy

spontaneous recovery
stimulus narrowing
suppression ratio
systematic desensitization
temporal conditioning
thematic hierarchy
trace conditioning
unconditioned reflex
unconditioned response
unconditioned stimulus
vicarious conditioning

Principles and Applications of Appetitive Conditioning

A Loss of Control

T raci and her husband Andre moved to Las Vegas last month. His accounting firm had asked him to move; the new position paid more and was more challenging than his old position. They discussed the move for several weeks before he agreed to the transfer. At first, Traci was upset by the move. She was a sophomore in college and would have to transfer to a new school. Andre assured her that there were good schools in Nevada. Traci was also concerned about being so far from home, but Andre promised that they would visit her family several times each year. The company took care of all the moving details, and they found a great apartment near Andre's office. As the move approached, Traci became excited. She had never been to Las Vegas and was especially looking forward to visiting the casinos. Her friends asked her if she was going to do any gambling. Traci did enjoy playing the state lottery and thought that gambling in a casino would be fun. She and Andre arrived in Las Vegas several days early and decided to stay at one of the large hotels. Arriving at the hotel, Traci was struck by the glitter of the casino. She could hardly wait to unpack and go to the casino. Andre did not seem interested in gambling. He told her to go down to the casino as he was tired. When he awoke, he would get her for dinner. Traci decided to play the $5 dollar blackjack table. To her surprise, she got a blackjack on her first hand and won $7.50. The thrill of winning was fantastic, and she bet another $5 on the next hand. She lost that hand and was disappointed. She continued to play for the next two hours, until Andre came for dinner. Traci did not want to leave. She was down $25 but felt her luck was changing. Reluctantly, she agreed to go to dinner but thought of nothing else but getting back to the blackjack table. After dinner, they returned to the casino. Andre wanted to tour the town, but Traci was insistent upon returning to the casino. Had she not been self-conscious, she would have run back to the table. She decided to try her luck at the $10 table and grew quite excited when the first card she received was an ace.

Why was Traci so anxious about returning to the blackjack table? Winning a hand of blackjack can be a very powerful reinforcer; Traci's excitement reflects the reinforcing power of winning. Other examples of potential reinforcers include getting an A on an examination, going to the movies, or dining out at one's favorite restaurant. In this chapter, we will examine the influence of reinforcement on behavior.

Gambling can become an addictive behavior. Unless Traci can limit her gambling activities, she might be headed for serious trouble. A less obvious potential problem is for a person to do little else but go to the movies. Obviously, a student who sees too many movies is unlikely to do well in school. This chapter will describe the use of reinforcement and/or nonreinforcement to alter undesired behavior.

THE ACQUISITION OF AN APPETITIVE RESPONSE

Skinner's Contribution

B. F. Skinner (1938) conducted an extensive investigation into the influence of reinforcement on behavior. His work showed that reinforcement has a significant impact on our actions. The concept of contingency is a central aspect of Skinner's theory. A **contingency** is a specified relationship between behavior and reinforcement. According to Skinner, the environment determines contingencies, and people must perform the appropriate behavior to obtain a reinforcer.

What is a **reinforcer?** We learned in Chapter 1 that Thorndike thought of a reward as a satisfying state. Skinner rejected such internal explanations of reinforcement; instead, he proposed that an event is reinforcing if it increases the frequency of the behavior that precedes the event. Thus, Skinner defined reinforcement merely by its influence on future behavior. In Skinner's view, any event that increases the probability of a behavior occurring is a reinforcer.

You might wonder why Skinner defined reinforcement this way. One reason is that the same event may be reinforcing to one person but not to another. Rather than using one's own perspective on what is satisfying, a psychologist can select a reinforcer based on its observed effect on behavior. This definition forces the psychologist to ignore preconceptions about what might be an effective reinforcer and to select one that actually works. We will have more to say about the use of reinforcement to modify behavior later.

The Distinction Between Instrumental and Operant Conditioning

Psychologists have used many different procedures to study the impact of reinforcement on behavior. Some psychologists have examined learning in a setting where the opportunity to respond is constrained; that is, the animal or person has limited opportunity to behave. For example, suppose a psychologist rewards an animal for running down an alley or turning left in a T-maze (see **Figure 4.1**). In both of these situations, the animal has a limited opportunity to gain reward. The rat can run down the alley or turn left in the maze and be rewarded, but future opportunities are determined by whether the researcher puts the rat back in the alley or maze. The rat has no control over how often it has the opportunity to obtain reward.

FIGURE 4.1. *(a)* A simple T-maze. In this maze, the rat must learn whether to turn left or right to obtain reward. *(b)* A runway or alley. In this apparatus, the rat receives a reward when it reaches the goal box; latency to run down the alley is the index of performance.

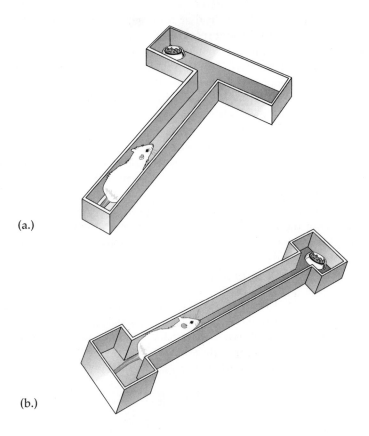

(a.)

(b.)

When the environment constrains the opportunity for reward, the researcher is investigating **instrumental conditioning.** Evidence of the acquisition of an instrumental response could be how rapidly the rat runs down the alley or how many errors the rat makes in the maze.

Consider the following example to illustrate the instrumental conditioning process. A parent is concerned about his or her child's failure to do required homework. The parent could reward the child each evening following the completion of assigned homework. The child can obtain the reward by doing homework; however, the child only has a single opportunity to gain the reward each evening.

In operant conditioning there is no constraint on the amount of reinforcement the subject can obtain. In an **operant conditioning** situation, an animal or person is able to control the frequency of response and thereby determine the amount of reinforcement obtained. The lack of response constraint allows the subject to repeat the behavior, and evidence of learning is the frequency and consistency of responding. (There often is some limit on the length of time that reinforcement is available, but within that time period, the animal or person controls the amount of reinforcement received.)

B. F. Skinner needed a simple structured environment to study operant behavior, so he invented his own. This apparatus, which Skinner called an **operant chamber,** is an enclosed environment with a small bar on the inside wall. There is a dispenser for presenting either food or liquid reinforcement when the bar is pressed. (A more elaborate version of an operant chamber has the capacity to present tones or lights in order to study generalization and discrimination.) The operant chamber has been modified to accommodate many different animal species. **Figure 4.2** presents a basic operant chamber for use with pigeons, in which an illuminated disk or a key replaces the bar press used for rats and some other species.

Skinner also developed his own methodology to study behavior. More interested in observing the rate of a behavior than the intensity of a specific response, he developed the cumulative recorder (refer to **Figure 4.2**). The pen attached to the recorder moves at a specific rate across the page; at the same time, each key-peck response produces an upward movement on the pen,

FIGURE 4.2. Operant chamber designed for pigeons. When the pigeon pecks the key, reinforcement (a food pellet) is delivered. Each peck produces an upward deflection on the cumulative recorder, providing a permanent record of the pigeon's behavior.

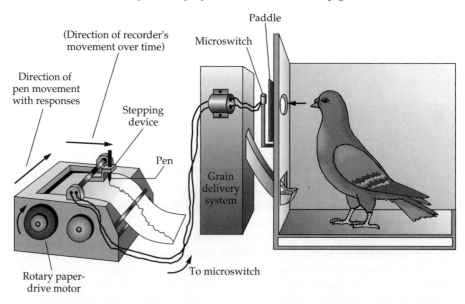

Cumulative recorder   **Operant chamber**

enabling the experimenter to determine the rate of behavior. Modern technology has replaced the cumulative recorder with a computer able to generate sophisticated graphics that show the animal's behavior.

There are many real-world examples of operant conditioning. Traci, in the chapter opening vignette, was being reinforced in an operant conditioning situation. There were no constraints on the number of reinforcers she could earn, and the amount of reinforcement she received was partly determined by the number of times she played blackjack. Other instances of operant conditioning include fishing—where a person can freely cast—or dating—where an individual can ask out one or many different people.

Skinner believed that operant behavior is not elicited by a stimulus. Instead, he believed that an animal or person voluntarily emits a specific behavior in order to gain reinforcement. Yet, environmental stimuli do affect operant responding. According to Skinner, environmental events set the occasion for operant behavior; that is, they inform the animal or person when reinforcement is available. Thus, environmental stimuli act to motivate operant responding. We will examine the occasion-setting function of environmental stimuli in Chapter 7.

Instrumental behavior is also influenced by environmental circumstance. Thorndike proposed that stimulus-response connections develop as a result of reward (see Chapter 1). Conditioned stimuli have a powerful influence over instrumental activity; we will see how this influence works in Chapter 7.

In the next three sections, we will examine several processes that affect instrumental and operant behavior. We will discover that these processes have a comparable influence on both instrumental and operant conditioning. Thus, important similarities as well as differences exist between instrumental and operant conditioning.

One further point deserves mention. Reward and reinforcer are two concepts frequently referred to in psychology. For our purposes, there is no distinction between the two. However, the concept of reward is typically used in instrumental conditioning situations, while a reinforcer usually refers to operant conditioning. We will maintain this distinction between reward and reinforcer to help distinguish instrumental and operant conditioning.

Types of Reinforcers

Skinner (1938) identified several different categories of reinforcers. A **primary reinforcer** has innate reinforcing properties; a **secondary reinforcer** has developed its reinforcing properties through its association with primary reinforcers. For example, food is a primary reinforcer, while money is a secondary reinforcer.

A number of variables affect the strength of a secondary reinforcer. First, the magnitude of the primary reinforcer paired with the secondary reinforcing stimulus influences the reinforcing power of the secondary reinforcer. Butter and Thomas (1958) presented a click prior to either an 8% sucrose solution or a 24% solution. These investigators found that rats made significantly more responses to the cue associated with the larger reinforcer. This indicates that a stimulus paired with a larger reinforcer acquires more reinforcing properties than a cue associated with a smaller reinforcer.

FIGURE 4.3. The strength of a secondary reinforcer increases as a function of the number of secondary and primary reinforcer pairings during acquisition. The measure of the power of the secondary reinforcer is the number of responses emitted during the first 10 minutes of testing.

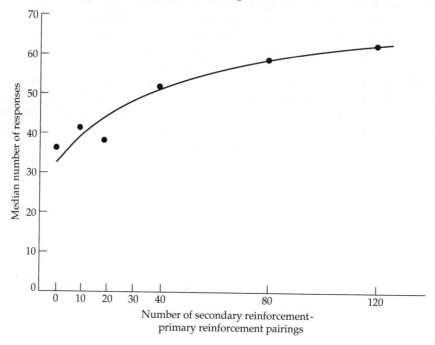

Second, the number of pairings of the secondary stimulus and primary reinforcer affects the strength of the secondary reinforcer. Many experiments (Bersh, 1951; Miles, 1956) have found that the greater the number of secondary reinforcing stimulus-primary reinforcer pairings, the stronger the reinforcing power of the secondary reinforcer. For example, Bersh (1951) presented a 3-second light cue prior to either 10, 20, 40, 80, or 120 reinforcements (food pellets) for bar pressing. After training, primary reinforcement was discontinued and the bar press response extinguished; this procedure equated the bar press response strength for all subjects. The testing phase consisted of the presentation of the light following a bar press response. As **Figure 4.3** shows, the number of responses emitted to produce the light increased as a function of light-food pairings. These results point out that the reinforcing power of a secondary reinforcer increases with a greater number of pairings of the secondary reinforcer and the primary reinforcer.

Third, the time elapsing between the presentation of a secondary reinforcer and the primary reinforcer affects the strength of the secondary reinforcer. Bersh (1951) varied the interval between light and food reinforcement in an operant chamber; the food followed the light stimulus by either .5, 1.0, 2.0, 4.0, or 10.0 seconds. Bersh observed that the number of responses emitted to obtain the light cue decreased as the interval between the secondary and the primary reinforcer increased. Bersh's results indicate that the power of a secondary reinforcer decreases as the interval between the secondary reinforcer and the primary reinforcer increases.

We have learned that the value of the primary reinforcer, the number of pairings, and the temporal delay affects the reinforcing strength of a secondary reinforcer. The influence of these variables is not surprising: secondary reinforcers acquire their reinforcing ability through the Pavlovian conditioning process. As we learned in Chapter 3, these variables influence the association of a conditioned stimulus and an unconditioned stimulus.

Skinner also distinguished between positive and negative reinforcers. A **positive reinforcer** is an event added to the environment that increases the frequency of the behavior that produces it. Examples of positive reinforcers include food and money. The termination of an aversive event can also be reinforcing. When the reinforcer is the termination of an aversive event, the reinforcer is referred to as a **negative reinforcer.**

In an experimental demonstration of a negative reinforcer, Skinner (1938) observed that rats learned to bar press to turn off electric shock. For a real-world example, suppose that a teacher is standing over a child who is doing schoolwork, encouraging the child to complete the assignment. As a result of the teacher's presence, the child rapidly finishes the work. When the child completes the homework, the teacher leaves. In our example, the child considers the teacher's presence aversive, and the child's completion of his or her assignment is reinforced by the teacher's departure.

Shaping

The environment usually specifies the behavior necessary to obtain reinforcement. However, many operant behaviors occur infrequently or not at all, making it unlikely that the behavior-reinforcement contingency will be experienced. Under such conditions, the result is either no change or a slow change in the frequency of the behavior. Skinner (1938) developed a procedure called **shaping,** also known as the **successive approximation procedure,** to increase the rate at which an operant behavior is learned. During shaping, a behavior with a higher baseline rate of response than the desired behavior is selected and reinforced. When this behavior increases in frequency, the contingency is then changed and a closer approximation to the desired final behavior is reinforced. The contingency is slowly changed until the only way that the animal can obtain reinforcement is by performing the appropriate behavior.

Training a Rat to Bar Press

Many scientists have demonstrated that the successive approximation technique effectively and quickly modifies behavior. This technique has been used, for example, to train a rat to bar press to obtain reinforcement. A rat's initial rate of bar pressing is not necessarily zero, since an animal exploring a small operant chamber may occasionally hit the bar. Therefore, the rat might learn the association between pressing the bar and obtaining food on its own. However, this self-training procedure is often slow, and the rate of learning varies considerably between animals. Shaping of bar pressing helps to ensure a rapid acquisition of desired behavior.

The first stage of the shaping procedure involves reinforcing the rat for eating out of the food dispenser (refer to **Figure 4.4**). When this feeding response occurs consistently (which will be only a short time after training begins), the contingency must be changed to a closer approximation of the final bar press response. The second stage of shaping consists of reinforcing the rat when it is moving away from the food dispenser. The moving-away response continues to be reinforced until this behavior occurs consistently; then the contingency is changed again.

In the third phase of shaping, the rat is reinforced only for moving away from the dispenser in the direction of the bar. The change in contingency at first causes the rat to move in a number of directions. The experimenter must wait, reinforcing only movement toward the bar. The shaping procedure is continued, with closer and closer approximations reinforced until the rat presses the bar. At this point, shaping is complete. The use of shaping to develop a bar press response is a reliable technique that can be used to train most rats to bar press in approximately an hour. Let's next consider a real-world application of the shaping technique.

Shaping Social Discourse

Many parents struggle to teach their children social skills. Even simple social skills like talking with company can be difficult for many children. Many parents undoubtedly use reinforcement (probably praise) as well as punishment (probably scolding) to try to teach their children social skills. Yet, parents typically reinforce only the final response. Since children need considerable practice to learn effective social skills, children may experience much frustration and give up.

Parents can employ the shaping technique to teach social skills to their children. Beginning by reinforcing a behavior that their children can readily

FIGURE 4.4. Shaping a bar press response in rats. In the initial phase, the rat is reinforced for eating out of the pellet dispenser (scene 1). During the second phase of shaping (scenes 2, 3, 4, and 5), the rat must move away from the dispenser to receive reinforcement. Later in the shaping process (scenes 6 and 7), the rat must move toward the bar to receive the food reinforcer.

perform (for example, opening the door for company), parents should then gradually change the contingencies to train more complex behaviors. Now the child must say "hello" to company in order to be reinforced. Next, a question such as "How are you today?" or "Would you like something to drink?" would yield reinforcement. By successively reinforcing behaviors that more and more closely resemble the final desired behavior, parents can teach their children to converse with others.

BEFORE YOU GO ON

- **What does Traci find so reinforcing about playing blackjack?**
- **How might the shaping process explain why Traci plays blackjack and Andre does not?**

We have learned that the contingency between behavior and reinforcement influences how we act. Our discussion has focused on situations in which a single behavior produces reinforcement. However, reinforcement typically is not programmed to occur like this: usually, we must not only learn how to act to be reinforced, but also how often and/or when to act. Skinner's research (see Ferster & Skinner, 1957) called this aspect of the contingency the **schedule of reinforcement,** and the schedule specifies how often or when we must act to receive reinforcement.

Schedules of Reinforcement

Reinforcement can be programmed using two basic methods. First, behavior can be reinforced based on the number of responses emitted. Skinner (1938) labeled a situation in which the contingency requires a certain number of responses to produce reinforcement a **ratio schedule of reinforcement.**

Reinforcement also can be scheduled on a time basis; Skinner called the timed programming of reinforcement an **interval schedule of reinforcement.** With an interval schedule, reinforcement becomes available at a certain period of time after the last reinforcement. Any behavior occurring during the interval receives no reinforcement, while the first response occurring at the end of the interval is reinforced. In an interval schedule, reinforcement must be obtained before another interval begins.

There are two classes of both ratio and interval schedules: fixed- and variable-reinforcement schedules. With a fixed-ratio (FR) schedule, a constant number of responses is necessary to produce reinforcement. In contrast, with a variable-ratio (VR) schedule, an average number of responses produces reinforcement; that is, the number of responses needed to obtain reinforcement varies from one reinforcer to the next. Similarly, reinforcement can be programmed on a fixed-interval (FI) schedule of reinforcement, in which the same interval always separates available reinforcements, or it can become available after a varying interval of time. With a variable-interval (VI) schedule, there is an average interval between available reinforcements, but the exact interval differs.

We have discussed four types of reinforcement schedules that have an important influence on our behavior. The pattern and rate of behavior is very different depending on the type of reinforcement schedule. Let's now briefly examine the behavioral characteristics of these reinforcement schedules. The interested reader should refer to Ferster and Skinner (1957) for a detailed discussion of schedules of reinforcement.

Fixed-Ratio Schedules

On a fixed-ratio schedule, a specific number of responses is necessary to produce reinforcement. With an FR-1 (or continuous) schedule, reinforcement is given after a single response. Likewise, 10 responses must occur to receive reinforcement on an FR-10 schedule. As an example of a **fixed-ratio schedule,** a rat may be reinforced after every 10 bar presses. This would be an FR-10 schedule. Two real-world examples of a fixed-ratio schedule are an adult earning a free round-trip ticket for travel within the United States after getting 25,000 frequent flyer miles or a child receiving a toy from a company for sending in five cereal box tops.

Fixed-ratio schedules produce a consistent response rate; that is, an animal or person responds at a steady rate during the entire time that reinforcement is possible or until satiation occurs (refer to **Figure 4.5**). Furthermore, the rate of responding increases with higher FR schedules. For example, Collier, Hirsch, and Hamlin (1972) noted that rats bar press at a higher rate on an FR-20 than an

FIGURE 4.5. Samples of cumulative records of bar press responding under the simple schedules of reinforcement. The slash marks on the response records indicate presentations of reinforcement. The steeper the cumulative response gradient, the higher the animal's rate of response.

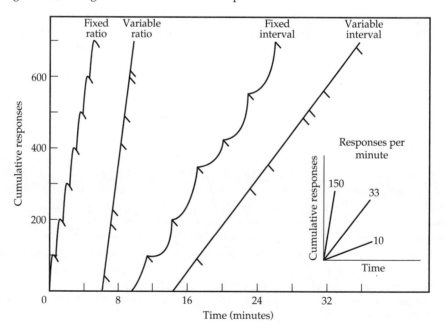

FR-10 schedule and higher still on an FR-60 than an FR-40 (see **Figure 4.6**). Similar results were obtained with pigeons (Felton & Lyon, 1966), cats (Kanarek, 1974), prairie dogs (Todd & Cogan, 1978), and children (Stephens, Pear, Wray, & Jackson, 1975).

Fixed-ratio schedules have another distinctive characteristic. Following reinforcement, responding will temporarily stop. The pause after reinforcement is called a **postreinforcement pause.** After the pause, responding resumes at the rate present before reinforcement. Therefore, the animal or person on a fixed-ratio schedule either responds at the intensity characteristic of that ratio or does not respond at all.

A postreinforcement pause is not observed with all fixed-ratio schedules. The higher the number of responses needed to obtain reinforcement, the more likely a pause will follow reinforcement. As **Figure 4.6** shows, there is no pause after reinforcement on an FR-100 schedule, but a pause does follow reinforcement on an FR-200 schedule. The length of the pause also varies; the higher the ratio schedule, the longer the pause (Todd & Cogan, 1978). Other researchers (for example, Collier, Hirsch, & Hamlin, 1972) have noted that the greater the effort necessary to obtain reinforcement, the longer the pause after receiving reinforcement. The length of the pause also depends upon satiation (Sidman & Stebbins, 1954). Sidman and Stebbins found that the greater the satiation, the longer the pause following reinforcement.

Variable-Ratio Schedules

On a variable-ratio schedule, an average number of responses produces reinforcement, but the actual number of responses required to produce reinforcement

FIGURE 4.6. Cumulative response records on various fixed-ratio schedules. Behavior is affected by the fixed ratio used during conditioning. The rate of response increases with higher fixed ratios, and the postreinforcement pause occurs only at the highest FR schedules.

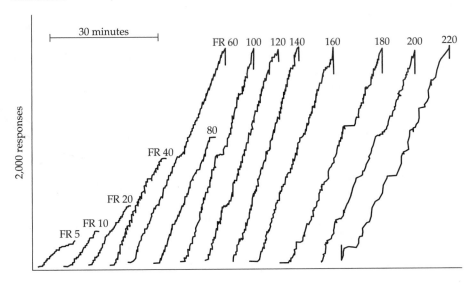

varies over the course of training. Suppose that a rat is reinforced for bar pressing on a VR-20 schedule. While the rat must bar press twenty times on the average to receive reinforcement, the rat may press the bar 10 times to get the reinforcer one time, but have to respond 30 times to obtain the next reinforcer. Two real-world examples of a **variable-ratio schedule** are a door-to-door salesperson who makes two consecutive sales and then has to knock on fifty doors before making another sale, or a child who receives a star card in the first baseball pack opened, but then has to open five packs before getting another star card.

Like the FR schedules, VR schedules produce a consistent response rate (refer to **Figure 4.5**). Furthermore, the greater the average number of responses necessary to produce reinforcement, the higher the response rate. For example, Felton and Lyon (1966) found that rats bar press at a higher rate on a VR-200 than a VR-50. Similarly, Ferster and Skinner (1957) observed that the rate at which pigeons key peck is higher on a VR-100 than a VR-50, and still higher on a VR-200 schedule of reinforcement.

In contrast to the pause after reinforcement on a fixed-ratio schedule, postreinforcement pauses occur only occasionally on variable-ratio schedules (see Felton & Lyon, 1966 or Ferster & Skinner, 1957). The relative absence of pause behavior after reinforcement on VR schedules results in a higher response rate on a VR than a comparable FR schedule. Thus, rats bar press more times during an hour-long session with a VR-50 than an FR-50 schedule (see **Figure 4.5**).

The high response rate that occurs with VR schedules can explain the persistent and vigorous behavior characteristic of gambling. For example, a slot machine is programmed to pay off after an average number of operations. However, the exact number of operations necessary to obtain reinforcement is unpredictable. People who play a slot machine for hours, constantly putting money into it, do so because of the variable-ratio programming of the slot machines.

Fixed-Interval Schedule

With a fixed-interval schedule, reinforcement depends upon both the passage of time and the exhibition of the appropriate behavior. Reinforcement is available only after a specified period of time, and the first response emitted after the interval has elapsed is reinforced. Therefore, a rat on an FI-1 minute schedule is reinforced for the first bar press after the minute interval has elapsed; in contrast, a rat on an FI-2 minute schedule must wait 2 minutes before its response is reinforced.

One example of a fixed-interval schedule is having the mail delivered at about the same time every day. Making gelatin is another real-world example of a **fixed-interval schedule.** After it is mixed and dissolved, gelatin is placed in the refrigerator to set. After a few hours, the gelatin is ready to be eaten. However, while the cook may eat the gelatin as soon as it is ready, a few hours or even a few days may elapse before the cook actually goes to the refrigerator and obtains the gelatin reinforcement.

Have you ever seen the behavior of a child waiting for gelatin to set? The child will go to the refrigerator, shake the dish, recognize the gelatin is not ready, and place it back in the refrigerator. The child will repeat this action every once in awhile. A similar behavior occurs when someone is waiting for an important piece of mail. With each check, the gelatin is closer to being ready or the mail nearer to being delivered. These behaviors illustrate one aspect of a fixed-interval schedule. After receiving reinforcement on a fixed-interval schedule, an animal or person stops responding; then the rate of response slowly increases as the time approaches when reinforcement will once more become available (refer to **Figure 4.5**). This characteristic response pattern produced by an FI schedule was referred to as the **scallop effect** by Ferster and Skinner. The scallop effect has been observed with a number of species, including pigeons (Catania & Reynolds, 1968), rats (Innis, 1979), and humans (Shimoff, Catania, & Matthews, 1981).

Two variables affect the length of the pause on FI schedules. First, the ability to withhold responding until close to the end of the interval increases with experience (Cruser & Klein, 1984). Second, the pause is longer with longer FI schedules (Gentry, Weiss, & Laties, 1983).

While a considerable amount of research has investigated fixed-interval schedules, there are not many real-world situations in which behavior is reinforced on a fixed-interval schedule. Consider the example of a person being paid once a week, a situation often used to illustrate behavior reinforced on a fixed-interval schedule. In reality, being paid weekly is not an example of an FI schedule. If it were, the paycheck would not only become available at the end of the week, but a specific behavior would be required to receive the pay (reinforcer). Further, the contingent behavior could occur any time after the end of the week and still be reinforced. Instead of being an example of a fixed interval schedule, a weekly paycheck reflects the operation of response-cost or negative punishment (refer to Chapter 5). In a response-cost situation, a person receives reinforcement (money) without having to perform a specific behavior, but can lose money or be fired for failing to perform the appropriate behavior. Thus, the weekly paycheck will continue unless the person no longer behaves in an acceptable manner.

Variable-Interval Schedules

On a variable-interval schedule, an average interval of time elapses between available reinforcements; however, the interval of time varies from one reinforcement to the next. For example, the average interval is 2 minutes on a VI-2 minute schedule; yet, one time, the rat may wait only 1 minute between reinforcements, and the next time, 5 minutes. Consider the following illustration of a **variable-interval schedule.** Suppose you go fishing. How successful will your fishing trip be? The number of times you cast is not important. Instead, when the fish swims by the bait is critical. You may have to wait only a few minutes between catches on one occasion, but wait many minutes on another.

VI schedules are characterized by a steady rate of responding (see **Figure 4.5**). Furthermore, the rate of responding is affected by VI length; the longer the average interval between reinforcements, the lower the response rate. For example, Catania and Reynolds (1968) discovered that pigeons responded 60 to 100 times per minute on a VI-.2 minute schedule, but only 20 to 70 times per minute on a VI-7.1 minute schedule. Nevin (1973) obtained similar results with rats, as did Todd and Cogan (1978) with prairie dogs.

The scallop effect characteristic of FI schedules does not occur on VI schedules: there is no pause following reinforcement on a VI schedule. However, Catania and Reynolds (1968) reported that the maximum rate of response on VI schedules occurred just prior to reinforcement.

Differential Reinforcement Schedules.

In many situations, a specific number of behaviors must occur or not occur within a specified amount of time to produce reinforcement. When reinforcement depends on both time and the number of responses, the contingency is a **differential reinforcement schedule.** For example, students required to complete an assignment during a semester are being reinforced on a differential reinforcement schedule. Why isn't this an example of a fixed-interval schedule? A fixed-interval schedule imposes no time limit on the occurrence of the appropriate behavior; with a differential reinforcement schedule, if the behavior does not occur within the time limit, no reinforcement is provided. We will now discuss three important types of differential reinforcement schedules.

DIFFERENTIAL REINFORCEMENT OF HIGH RESPONDING SCHEDULES. Reinforcement can be made contingent on a high rate of responding; such a schedule is called a **differential reinforcement of high responding (DRH) schedule.** Consider the following example of a DRH schedule. Your instructor assigns a paper due in 2 weeks. It must be at least 10 typed pages. In this situation, a substantial amount of effort must be exerted in a short time to complete the assignment. Although you may not enjoy it, you are likely to work hard to complete the assignment if your behavior is controlled by the DRH schedule of reinforcement.

DRH schedules are extremely effective. Animals exhibit a consistently high rate of responding when reinforcement is provided on a DRH schedule (Catania, 1979). For example, a pigeon on such a schedule can learn to peck a key more than 10 times per second. However, DRH schedules contain an inherent danger. If the high level of responding needed to produce reinforcement cannot be maintained, the animal will receive less reinforcement. This lowered reinforcement further decreases the response rate. In a vicious cycle, the response rate and the obtained reinforcement decline until no responses are performed. Therefore, to ensure consistent responding, the response rate of the DRH schedule must be high, but not too high.

Interestingly, people often respond to a DRH schedule as if it were an FI schedule. For example, a series of exams scheduled for a semester is a DRH schedule; that is, a high rate of responding (studying) is necessary to obtain a good grade. However, most students treat exams as they would an FI: They stop responding after an exam and slowly increase their response rate until they are "cramming" for the next test. By limiting studying to the times just prior to examinations, students are not likely to respond enough to do well. The more effective strategy would be to respond consistently throughout the interval, which is the response pattern characteristic of DRH schedules. Several ways exist to increase the likelihood that students will respond appropriately. For example, the interval between tests could be shortened to reduce pause behavior, or papers due shortly after their assignment could replace exams.

DIFFERENTIAL REINFORCEMENT OF LOW RESPONDING SCHEDULES. Rein-

95

CHAPTER 4
*Principles and
Applications of
Appetitive
Conditioning*

forcement can also be scheduled contingent upon a low rate of responding; this schedule is a **differential reinforcement of low responding (DRL) schedule.** With this schedule, a certain interval of time must elapse without a response, then the first response at the end of the interval is reinforced. If an animal responds during the interval, the interval is reset and the response withheld for the length of time specified in the contingency. The following example illustrates the DRL schedule. As you attempt to start your car, you flood the engine. If you try to start it before waiting several minutes, it will flood again, and you will have to wait a few more minutes before it will start. Thus, to start your engine after flooding it, you must withhold your starting behavior for several minutes.

DRH schedules produce high rates of responding. By contrast, DRL schedules limit the response rate. DRL schedules, like DRH schedules, effectively control behavior; that is, individuals learn to respond according to the schedule of reinforcement. However, DRL schedules, unlike DRH schedules, require time to become effective (Reynolds, 1968). The effect of reinforcement is an increase in the response rate, which subsequently acts to prevent reinforcement. The absence of reinforcement lowers the response rate. Eventually, the influence of the schedule appears, and the individual is able to withhold responding until the end of the interval (see **Figure 4.7**).

DIFFERENTIAL REINFORCEMENT OF OTHER BEHAVIORS SCHEDULE. Providing reinforcement only in the absence of a particular response in a specified period

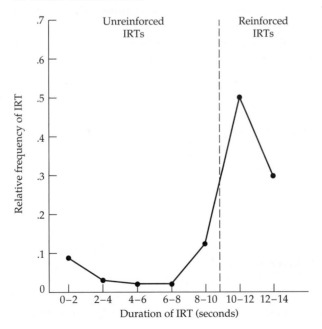

FIGURE 4.7. Relative frequency distribution of interresponse times in rats receiving reinforcement on a 10-second DRL schedule.

of time is called a **differential reinforcement of other behaviors (DRO) schedule.** The DRO schedule is unique because it reinforces the failure to exhibit a
specific behavior during a particular time period. Suppose that a parent informs
his or her child that hitting a younger sibling again before dinner will result in
no television viewing that evening. In this situation, the parent is using a DRO
schedule; that is, in order for the child to watch television (obtain reinforcement), no aggressive responses can occur prior to dinner. DRO schedules are
widely used in the treatment of problem behaviors, such as the aggressiveness
of the child just mentioned.

Compound Schedules

The contingency between behavior and reinforcement sometimes involves
more than one schedule. With a **compound schedule,** two or more schedules
are combined. As an example of a compound schedule, consider the rat who
must bar press 10 times (FR-10) and wait 1 minute after the last bar press (FI =
1 minute) until another bar press will produce reinforcement. The rat must complete both schedules in the appropriate sequence in order to obtain reinforcement. Animals and humans are sensitive to the complexities of schedules and
can learn to respond appropriately. An extensive discussion of compound
schedules of reinforcement is beyond the scope of this text. Interested readers
should consult D'Amato (1970) for a detailed discussion of the varied compound schedules of reinforcement.

BEFORE YOU GO ON

- **What schedule of reinforcement was responsible for Traci's high level of
  playing blackjack?**
- **What might the casino do to cause Traci to wager more on each hand of
  blackjack?**

We have learned that in order to obtain reinforcement, animals or people must
discover the contingency that exists between behavior and reinforcement. A
number of variables affect the acquisition of instrumental or operant behavior.
Let's now turn our attention to the factors which influence whether we respond
according to the contingency and thus obtain reinforcement.

How Readily Is an Instrumental
or Operant Response Learned?

Although many variables affect the development of instrumental or operant
behavior, we will look at two factors that play a significant role in determining
the strength of conditioning.

The Importance of Contiguity

You help a friend change a tire on his or her car; you're thanked for your assistance. The effect of the social reward is to increase your likelihood of future

helping behavior. However, if your friend waits several days before thanking you, the impact of the reward is reduced. This observation points to the importance of contiguity in instrumental or operant conditioning: reward can lead to the acquisition of an instrumental or operant response if it immediately follows the behavior, while learning is impaired if reward is delayed. Furthermore, the longer the delay between the response and reward, the less conditioning that occurs. Many studies have documented the effect of delay on the acquisition of an instrumental or operant behavior; we will discuss several of them next.

THE EFFECT OF DELAY. In a classic study, Grice (1948) investigated the role of reward delay on the rat's learning to go into a black chamber instead of a white one. Grice varied the delay between the correct response and reward. In his study, the delay interval was either 0, .5, 1.2, 2, 5, or 10 seconds. As **Figure 4.8** indicates, there is a very steep delay gradient: little conditioning occurred with delay intervals as short as 1.2 seconds.

However, not all experiments (Logan, 1952; Perin, 1943) have reported a delay gradient comparable to Grice's data. For example, Perin (1943) found moderate levels of conditioning of bar press responses even with a 10-second delay, while with a delay of 30 seconds or more, rats were unable to learn to bar press to obtain reinforcement.

FIGURE 4.8. The level of learning decreases with an increased delay between the instrumental response and reward. The measure of learning is the reciprocal × 1,000 of the number of trials to reach 75% correct choices; thus, the higher the value, the greater the level of learning.

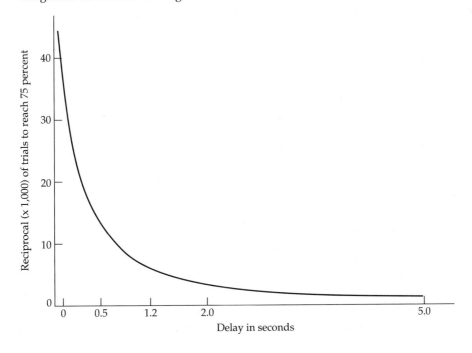

Why do the delay gradients differ in Grice's and Perin's experiments? The presence or absence of secondary reward cues is important. The presence of a secondary reward during the interval can strengthen the instrumental behavior and lessen the influence of delay. In contrast, when cues associated with reward are not present during the interval, even a very short delay produces little conditioning. In support of this view, animals in Grice's study spent the delay interval in an environment not associated with reward. In contrast, the rats in Perin's experiment remained in the conditioning environment (the operant chamber) associated with reinforcement during the interval between responding and primary reinforcement. If this analysis is correct, the presence of a secondary reward should reduce the effects of a delay of reward. As expected, Williams (1991) found that the presence of a secondary reward could "bridge" the interval and reduce the effect of a delayed primary reward.

DELAY OF REWARD AND CONDITIONING IN HUMANS. The importance of reward delay has also been demonstrated by studies using children as subjects. These studies (see Hall, 1976) consistently show that the longer the delay between the instrumental behavior and reward, the poorer the conditioning of the instrumental response. **Table 4.1** presents a sample of these delay-of-reward studies; let's examine one of them more closely.

Terrell and Ware (1961) gave kindergarten and first-grade children two easy problems to solve. The children received immediate reward for responding correctly to one of the problems; a 7-second delay of reward followed the correct solution for the other problem. Terrell and Ware reported that the children required approximately 7 trials with immediate reward to learn to solve the problems, compared with an average of 17 trials when reward was delayed. These observations indicate that a delay between the correct response and the reward interferes with the acquisition of that response.

The Impact of Reward Magnitude

THE ACQUISITION OF AN INSTRUMENTAL OR OPERANT RESPONSE. Suppose that parents decide to reward their children for learning vocabulary words. The rate of acquisition of the vocabulary words depends upon the magnitude of the reward provided; the larger the reward magnitude, the faster the vocabulary words will be acquired. Many studies (Hall, 1976) show that the magnitude of reward affects the rate of acquisition of an instrumental or operant response; let's look at several of these studies.

Crespi's 1942 study demonstrates the influence of reward magnitude on the acquisition of an instrumental running response in an alley. Upon reaching the goal box, Crespi's rats received either 1, 4, 16, 64, or 256 units of food. Crespi observed that the greater the reward magnitude, the faster the animals ran down the alley.

Researchers have also shown that reinforcer magnitude affects the acquisition of a bar press response in an operant chamber. For example, Guttman (1953) varied the amount of reinforcement rats received for bar pressing; animals were given either a 4%, 8%, 16%, or 32% sucrose solution following the operant response. Guttman discovered that the greater the reinforcer

TABLE 4.1. Some Studies Investigating Delay of Reward with Normal and Retarded Children

Students	Task	Delay intervals	Response measure	Results	Investigators
Preschool children	2-stimulus, 1-choice apparatus, with reward delivered immediately to one stimulus and after 7 seconds to the other	0 and 7 seconds	Response speed and preference for one of the two stimuli	Subjects preferred to respond to immediately rewarded stimulus; no difference in response speed.	Lipsitt and Castaneda (1958)
Fourth-grade children	Simultaneous and successive discrimination tasks	0, 3, or 6 seconds	Number correct	No delay-of-reinforcement gradient obtained, although 6-second group performed most poorly.	Erickson and Lipsitt (1960)
Fourth-grade children	2-stimulus (easy) and 3-stimulus (difficult) successive discrimination problems	0, 10, or 30 seconds	Number correct	Increasing delay had progressively deleterious effect on difficult discrimination; no difference among groups with easy task.	Hockman and Lipsitt (1961)
Kindergarten and first-grade children	(1) Discrimination learning with subjects required to learn a size and form problem concurrently (2) 3-stimulus size and form problem learned concurrently	In both (1) and (2), one problem learned with 0-second delay, other problem with 7-second delay	Number correct	Both (1) and (2) revealed delay resulted in poorer learning.	Terrell and Ware (1961)
Moderately and severely retarded children; also normal first graders	2-choice discrimination problem	0, 1.5, 6, or 12 seconds	Errors and trials to criterion	12-second delay significantly increased errors and trials to criterion for all groups. No difference among other delay intervals.	Hetherington, Ross, and Pick (1964)
Mental retardates	Discrimination of geometric forms e.g., square, subjects required to solve 10 problems (1 problem per day)	0 or 5 seconds	Errors	Delay increased difficulty of problem. Effect appeared to be limited to initial trials on each problem.	Schoelkopf and Orlando (1965)

TABLE 4.1. Continued

Students	Task	Delay intervals	Response measure	Results	Investigators
Mental retardates	2-choice discrimination problem; chosen stimulus was visible or not visible during delay	0, 12, or 18 seconds	Errors and trials to criterion	Zero-second delay significantly superior to 12- or 18-second groups for both conditions.	Ross, Hetherington, and Wray (1965)
Normal and moderately retarded children	Simple discrimination	0 or 12 seconds	Errors and trials to criterion	12-second delay increased errors for retardates; no difference between 0- and 12-second delay for normal children.	Hetherington and Ross (1967)
Mental retardates	2-choice discrimination problem	0 or 15 seconds	Number of correct responses	Zero-second delay significantly superior to 15 seconds.	Keeley and Sprague (1969)

Source: Hall, J. F. (1976). *Classical conditioning and instrumental learning: A contemporary approach.* Philadelphia: Lippincott.

magnitude, the faster the animals learned to bar press to obtain reinforcement (refer to **Figure 4.9**).

THE PERFORMANCE OF AN INSTRUMENTAL OR OPERANT RESPONSE. A while back, my middle son informed me that ten dollars was no longer enough money for mowing the yard; he now wanted twenty dollars to do the job. His behavior indicates the critical influence that the magnitude of reward has on the performance of an instrumental behavior. The likelihood and intensity of an instrumental or operant response depends upon the magnitude of reward provided following a particular response. In many instances, the magnitude of reward must be of a sufficient level to cause the behavior to occur; thus, my son's mowing response would occur only if the payment was sufficiently high. At other times, the instrumental or operant behavior may occur and the intensity of the response will depend upon the reward magnitude. Under these circumstances, the greater the reward magnitude, the higher the level of performance of the instrumental response. The literature (Pubols, 1960) consistently shows that reward magnitude affects performance. This section examines several studies documenting this influence.

Crespi's 1942 study also evaluated the level of instrumental performance as a function of reward magnitude. Crespi discovered that the greater the magnitude, the faster the rats ran down the alley to obtain reward, an observation that indicates that the magnitude of reward influences the level of

101

CHAPTER 4
Principles and
Applications of
Appetitive
Conditioning

FIGURE 4.9. A rat's rate of responding, or the number of bar press responses per minute, increases with the magnitude of reinforcement—in this case, higher concentrations of sucrose in the water.

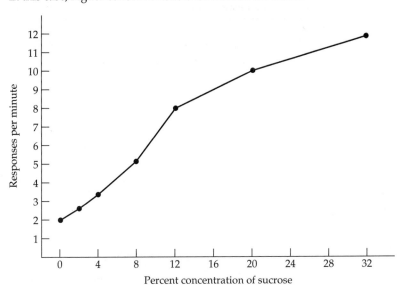

instrumental behavior. Other studies also show that reward magnitude determines the level of performance in the runway situation (Mellgren, 1972) and in the operant chamber (Gutman, Sutterer, & Brush, 1975).

You may have the impression that the magnitude of reward influences the level of conditioning. However, evidence indicates that the differences in performance reflect motivational rather than learning differences. According to this view, the greater the reward magnitude, the greater the motivation to obtain the reward. How can this approach be validated? To assess the relative contributions of learning and motivation, the reward value must be shifted to a higher (or lower) level. If the reward magnitude shift causes a gradual alteration in behavior, the change in responding is thought to reflect a learning influence, since learning changes are thought to occur slowly; if the alteration in behavior following the shift is rapid, the inference is that motivational processes are causing the behavior change.

Many studies (Crespi, 1942; Zeaman, 1949) report a rapid change in behavior when reward magnitude is shifted, which suggests that motivational differences are responsible for the performance differences associated with differences in reward magnitude (refer to **Figure 4.10**). For example, Crespi (1942) shifted some animals from a high reward magnitude (256 units) to a moderate reward level (16 units) on trial 20; other animals were shifted from a low (1 unit) to the moderate reward magnitude. The animals showed a rapid change in behavior on the trial following the shift in reward magnitude: the high-to-moderate-shift animals exhibited a significantly lowered response time on trial 21, while the low-to-moderate-shift subjects ran significantly faster on trial 21 than on the preceding trial.

FIGURE 4.10. A higher level of performance occurs with a larger reward magnitude during the preshift phase. Not only does the level of responding decline following a shift from high to low reward magnitude, but it is even lower than it would be if the level of reward had always been low (a depression or negative contrast effect). By contrast, a shift from low to high reward magnitude not only leads to a higher level of responding, but it also produces a response level that is greater than it would be if the level of reward had always been high (an elation or positive contrast effect). The contrast effects last for only a few trials; then responding returns to the level appropriate for that reward magnitude.

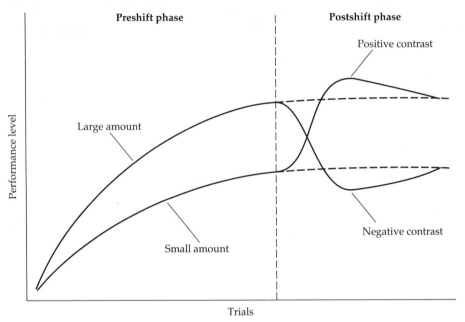

THE IMPORTANCE OF PAST EXPERIENCE. Suppose that your boss's marginal profits cause you to take a cut in salary. Under these conditions, your behavior will be less efficient as the result of the lowered magnitude of reward. How much will your output decline? Research (Crespi, 1942) indicates that you will exhibit less output now than if your salary had always been low (see **Figure 4.10**). This process—in which a shift from a high to a low reward magnitude produces a level of performance that is lower than it would be if the level of reward had always been low—is called the **depression effect.**

Perhaps your boss's profits increase and you receive a raise. Under these conditions, your behavior will become more efficient as a result of the higher magnitude of reward. In contrast to the depression effect, a shift from low to high reward magnitude produces a level of performance greater than it would be if the higher reward level had always been used. The heightened performance produced by a shift from low to high reward is called an **elation effect.**

Zeaman (1949) suggested replacing the terms *elation* and *depression effects* with **positive** and **negative contrast effects** to indicate that the specific context in which a stimulus is experienced can produce exaggerated or reduced effects.

Thus, experience with low reward heightens the influence of a high reward (positive contrast effect); that is, a large reward is more effective than it normally would be because of previous experience with a smaller reward. In contrast, experience exaggerates the impact of a low-reward magnitude (negative contrast effect); that is, a small reward is less effective than it would normally be because of experience with a larger reward.

103

CHAPTER 4
Principles and
Applications of
Appetitive
Conditioning

Investigations (Flaherty, 1982) since Crespi's original study have consistently produced a negative contrast effect; yet, research conducted during the 1960s seemed to indicate that the positive contrast effect could not be induced (Black, 1968). However, Bower (1981) suggested that a ceiling effect was responsible for the inability to produce a positive contrast effect; that is, high reward magnitude alone was causing maximum responding, and therefore the shift from low to high could not raise performance. Studies (Mellgren, 1972; Shanab, Sanders, & Premack, 1969) conducted in the late 1960s and early 1970s demonstrated that a positive contrast effect can be induced if animals are initially responding at a level below the upper limit.

We should note that the contrast effects last for only short periods of time. Thus, animals shifted from high to low (or low to high) reward respond at a lower (or higher) level than animals always experiencing the low (or high) reward magnitude for only a few trials.

Why do the contrast effects occur? The emotion of frustration seems to play an important role in the negative contrast effect. According to Flaherty (1985), an animal establishes an expected level of reward during initial acquisition training. The presentation of a lower-than-expected level of reward in the second phase causes frustration, which interferes with instrumental activity and thereby produces a response level lower than it would have been for the expected reward. The observation that drugs that reduce anxiety in humans eliminate the negative contrast effect supports this view; this result has been found with the tranquilizer Librium (Becker & Flaherty, 1983), with alcohol (Becker & Flaherty, 1982), and with barbiturates (Flaherty & Driscoll, 1980). Flaherty suggests that the emotional response of elation produced by receiving a reward greater than the expected magnitude may explain the positive contrast effect; however, evidence validating this view is not available.

THE INFLUENCE OF REWARD MAGNITUDE IN HUMANS. Although most of the research on reward magnitude has used animals as subjects, some research with people has indicated that reward value affects the performance of an instrumental or operant response. Research with young children (see Hall, 1976) has shown that the magnitude of reward does affect the development of an instrumental or operant response. For example, Siegel and Andrews (1962) found that 4- and 5-year-old children responded correctly more often on a task when given a large reward (for example, a small prize) rather than a small reward (a button). Studies have also shown that reward magnitude influences instrumental or operant behavior in adults. For example, Atkinson's research (Atkinson, 1958) found that the amount of money paid for successful performance influences the level of achievement behavior.

BEFORE YOU GO ON

- **How does knowing right away whether a hand of blackjack is a winner or loser contribute to Traci's gambling behavior?**
- **What would happen if Traci increased the amount of a wager and then won that hand of blackjack? What if she lost?**

EXTINCTION OF AN OPERANT OR INSTRUMENTAL RESPONSE

An operant or instrumental response, acquired when reinforcement follows the occurrence of a specific behavior, can be extinguished when the reinforcer no longer follows the response. Continued failure of the operant or instrumental behavior to produce reinforcement causes the strength of the response to diminish until eventually the subject no longer performs the operant or instrumental response.

Consider the following examples to illustrate the **extinction** of an operant or instrumental response: (1) A hungry rat has received food reinforcement for bar pressing, which has resulted in the development of an operant bar press response. During extinction, food reinforcement is no longer presented, and the rate of bar pressing declines until the rat stops pressing the bar. (2) A child shopping with his or her mother sees a favorite candy bar and discovers that a temper tantrum persuades his mother to buy the candy. The contingency between the temper tantrum and candy teaches the child to have a tantrum every time he wants a candy bar. The child's mother, tired of being manipulated, decides to no longer submit to her child's unruly behavior. The mother no longer reinforces the child's tantrums with candy, and the incidence of tantrums declines slowly until the child learns to enter a store and behave when candy is refused. (3) A man eats in a specific restaurant nightly; it is not the quality of the food that draws him there, but the attractive waitress. Arriving at the restaurant one night, he finds that the waitress has quit. Although the man continues to eat at the restaurant infrequently for a while, he eventually stops. Many studies have shown that when reinforcement is no longer provided, the operant or instrumental behavior ceases to be performed. Let's examine several experiments demonstrating the extinction of an operant or instrumental response when reinforcement is discontinued.

The Discontinuance of Reinforcement

In 1938, Skinner observed that the failure to reinforce a previously acquired bar press response in rats caused the extinction of that response. When reinforcement is first discontinued, the rate of responding remains high (see **Figure 4.11**), or under some conditions, actually increases. Consider the child whose temper tantrums are no longer reinforced by a parent. Anyone who has spent some time with a young child has certainly observed the increased intensity of temper tantrums once they are no longer reinforced. The continued failure of the

105

CHAPTER 4
Principles and
Applications of
Appetitive
Conditioning

FIGURE 4.11. Cumulative response record during the extinction of a bar press response. The rate of responding is initially high, but responding declines until the rat stops bar pressing when reinforcement is discontinued.

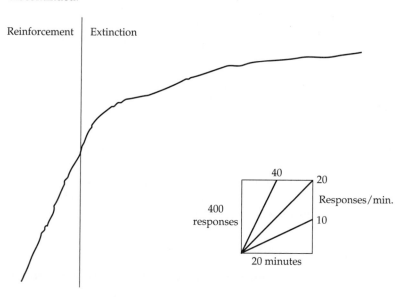

response to produce reinforcement causes the rate of responding to then decline until the behavior stops. Thus, the rat eventually stops bar pressing, and the child eventually stops having temper tantrums.

Responding is erratic during extinction; there are periods of high response rates and times when no responding occurs. Other psychologists (Perin, 1942; Williams, 1938) also have reported that animals cease bar pressing when reinforcement is no longer provided following an operant bar press response. Furthermore, researchers have found that extinction of a previously rewarded instrumental response occurs when reward is no longer presented in a runway apparatus (Hill & Spear, 1963).

Extinction of a previously reinforced behavior has also been documented in humans. For example, Lewis and Duncan (1958) reinforced college students for pulling the lever of a slot machine. When reinforcement (a disk exchangeable for 5 cents) was discontinued, the students eventually stopped pulling the lever. Lewis (1952) noted a similar extinction pattern in 6- and 7-year-old children who were no longer reinforced with toys for pressing a button.

Spontaneous Recovery

In Chapter 3, we learned that when a CS is presented without the UCS, a temporary inhibition suppresses all responding due to fatigue. When fatigue dissipates, the conditioned response reappears. This increase in response shortly after extinction is called **spontaneous recovery** (see Chapter 3). A similar recovery of an instrumental or operant behavior occurs when an interval of time follows the extinction of that behavior.

We also learned that if the CS continues to occur in the absence of the UCS, a permanent conditioned inhibition develops specifically to the CS. The conditioning of inhibition to the CS leads to a loss of spontaneous recovery. The loss of spontaneous recovery is also seen in instrumental or operant conditioning if the response continues to be unrewarded. According to Hull (1943), the conditioned inhibition of a response occurs because the environmental events that are present during the nonrewarded behavior become associated with the inhibitory nonreward state. When these cues are experienced again, the inhibitory state is aroused and the behavior suppressed, leading to a loss of spontaneous recovery.

Consider the following example to illustrate Hull's view of extinction. A rat runs down an alley but is not rewarded; nonreward elicits an inhibition response which, in turn, becomes associated with the alley through the classical conditioning process. When the rat is again placed in the alley, inhibition is elicited as a conditioned response, and the rat's running response is suppressed. Inhibition is not the only cause of the suppression of undesired behavior; the influence of the aversive quality of nonreward is examined next.

The Aversive Quality of Nonreward

Abram Amsel (1958) suggested that nonreward elicits an aversive internal frustration state. Stimuli associated with nonreward become able to elicit frustration as a conditioned response, and escape from this aversive situation is rewarded. Adelman and Maatsch (1956) provided evidence of the aversiveness of frustration and the rewarding quality of escaping from a frustrating situation. They found that animals would jump out of a box previously associated with reward and up onto a ledge within 5 seconds if they were not rewarded. In contrast, animals that had been rewarded with food for jumping onto the ledge took 20 seconds to jump. Further, while the rewarded animals stopped jumping after about 60 extinction trials, the frustrated animals did not quit responding after 100 trials, even though their only reward was escape from a frustrating situation.

Other researchers (Brooks, 1980; Daly, 1974) have shown that the cues associated with nonreward develop aversive qualities. Let's briefly examine Daly's study to demonstrate the aversive quality of cues associated with nonreward. Daly presented a cue (either a distinctive box or a light) during nonrewarded trials in the first phase of her study; during the second part of the experiment, the rats learned a response—jumping a hurdle—that enabled them to turn off the light or to escape from the box. Apparently, the cues (distinctive box or light) had acquired aversive qualities during nonrewarded trials; the presence of these cues subsequently motivated the escape response. Termination of these cues rewarded the acquisition of the hurdle jump response.

Activation of an Instrumental or Operant Behavior

One additional point about the influence of nonreward on instrumental or operant behavior deserves our attention. Nonreward sometimes increases rather than decreases the intensity of the behavior. Nonreward will motivate appeti-

107

CHAPTER 4
*Principles and
Applications of
Appetitive
Conditioning*

tive responding when frustration cues have been conditioned to elicit appetitive instead of avoidance behavior. An animal's behavior on a single alternation task illustrates that nonreward can become conditioned to motivate an appetitive response (Flaherty & Davenport, 1972). In the single alternation situation, reward and nonreward trials alternate. Studies using the single alternation task report that the intensity of responding increases following a nonrewarded trial but declines after a rewarded trial.

Why does response latency decrease after nonreward but increase after reward in the single alternation task? E. J. Capaldi's sequential theory (Capaldi, 1971, 1994) explains this conditioning process. According to Capaldi, at the beginning of each trial, a subject remembers whether reward or nonreward occurred on the last trial; Capaldi labels the memory of reward S^R and the memory of nonreward S^N. When reward follows a nonrewarded trial, the memory of the nonreward (S^N) becomes associated with the appetitive response. The conditioning of the memory of nonreward (S^N) to the appetitive response leads to an increase in responding following nonreward. Furthermore, since nonreward always follows a rewarded trial, the memory of reward (S^R) is associated with nonreward, which results in the conditioning of an avoidance response to S^R. Thus, the memory of reward elicits avoidance behavior; the decreased intensity of the appetitive response after rewarded trials provides support for Capaldi's approach.

Resistance to Extinction

Three factors appear to contribute to the resistance to extinction of an instrumental or operant response. We will examine these factors next.

The Influence of Reward Magnitude

D'Amato (1970) suggested that the influence of reward magnitude on resistance to extinction depends upon the amount of acquisition training. As **Figure 4.12** demonstrates, when the level of acquisition training is low, a large reward produces a greater resistance to extinction than does a small reward. However, the opposite effect is observed with extended acquisition: a small reward in acquisition produces more resistance to extinction of the instrumental behavior than a larger reward magnitude.

The literature provides support for D'Amato's suggestion. Hill and Spear (1963), giving their subjects only a few acquisition trials in the runway and providing either a small or large reward in the goal box, found that the large reward was associated with more resistance to extinction than the small reward. Armus (1959) and Hulse (1958) used a large number of acquisition trials in the runway and presented either a small or large reward magnitude in the goal box. Both studies observed that resistance to extinction was greater for the animals given the small rather than large reward during extended acquisition. Furthermore, several other studies (Senkowski, 1978; Traupman, 1972) varied both the acquisition reward magnitude and the number of acquisition trials; the results of the studies support the relationship **Figure 4.12** depicts.

Why does the influence of reward magnitude on resistance to extinction depend on the amount of acquisition training? According to D'Amato (1970),

FIGURE 4.12. Hypothesized resistance to extinction of an instrumental response as a function of level of acquisition training and magnitude of reinforcement.

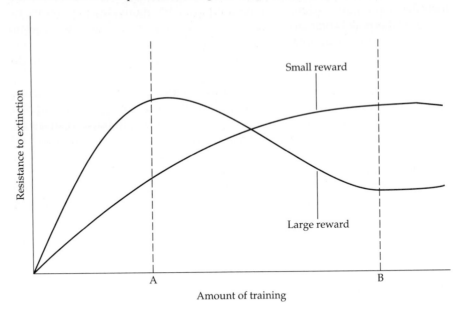

when a small reward magnitude is provided during acquisition, an anticipatory goal response (a conditioned anticipation of impending reward) develops very slowly. (A detailed discussion of the anticipatory goal concept, originally proposed by Kenneth Spence, will be presented in Chapter 6.) During extinction, substantial differences in the level of the anticipatory goal response will not occur, and, therefore, the frustration produced during extinction will be small. (This conclusion is based on the view that frustration is not produced until a reward is anticipated and that the amount of frustration produced is dependent upon the strength of the anticipatory goal response.) Since frustration is minimal, resistance to extinction should depend only on the amount of acquisition training. The results of studies using a small reward magnitude support this prediction; the greater the level of acquisition training with a small reward magnitude, the more resistant the appetitive behavior is to extinction.

In contrast, the anticipatory goal response is conditioned rapidly when a large reward is provided during acquisition. Frustration will not be elicited if extinction occurs following low levels of training; however, resistance to extinction will increase as the anticipation of reward is conditioned. Once the anticipatory goal response is strong enough to produce frustration, increases in the strength of the anticipatory goal response should lead to higher levels of frustration during extinction. These increases in frustration, produced as a result of extended training with a large reward, lead to a more rapid extinction of the appetitive response. Researchers employing a large reward magnitude have observed that increased acquisition training first leads to an increase and then to a decrease in resistance to extinction.

The Influence of Delay of Reward

109

CHAPTER *4*
*Principles and
Applications of
Appetitive
Conditioning*

The effect of delay of reward on resistance to extinction depends upon the consistency of the delay. When a constant delay is used in acquisition, delay has no effect on resistance to extinction. In contrast, inconsistent delay of reward in acquisition increases resistance to extinction.

Consider Tombaugh's 1966 study to illustrate the influence of consistent delay of acquisition reward on later resistance to extinction. Tombaugh's rats were given 70 acquisition trials in a runway apparatus, with reward in the goal box delayed for periods of 0, 5, 10, or 20 seconds. During the 60 extinction trials, the rats were confined to the goal box for a period of delay equivalent to that experienced during acquisition. Controlling for terminal acquisition performance levels, Tombaugh found no differences in resistance to extinction as a function of the delay of reward used in acquisition.

By comparing varied and constant delay of reward in acquisition, it is clear that inconsistent delay of reinforcement does influence resistance to extinction. A number of researchers (Logan, 1960; Shanab & Birnbaum, 1974) reported a greater resistance to extinction when reward was sometimes delayed as compared to when reward was never delayed. However, varied delay only increases resistance to extinction if the delay is substantial (20 to 30 seconds).

The Importance of Consistency of Reinforcement

Earlier in the chapter, we described an example of a mother extinguishing her child's temper tantrums in a grocery store. Suppose that after several nonrewarded trips to the store, and a reduction in the duration and intensity of the temper tantrums, the mother, on the next trip to the store, has a headache when the child starts to cry. The headache seems to intensify the unpleasantness of the tantrum; thus, she decides to buy her child candy to stop the crying. If the mother has headaches infrequently but rewards a tantrum whenever she does have a headache, this mother is now intermittently rather than continuously rewarding her child's temper tantrums. This intermittent reward causes the intensity of the temper tantrum to return to its original strength. Further, the intensity of the child's behavior will soon exceed the intensity produced when the response was continuously rewarded. Despite how she feels, in all likelihood, the mother will eventually become so annoyed that she decides to no longer tolerate her child's temper tantrums; unfortunately, extinguishing this behavior will be extremely difficult since she has intermittently rewarded the child's temper tantrums.

The previous example illustrates the influence of consistency of reinforcement on the extinction of an instrumental or operant behavior: extinction is slower following partial rather than continuous reinforcement. The greater resistance to extinction which occurs with intermittent rather than continuous reinforcement is referred to as the **partial reinforcement effect,** or **PRE.** Humphreys (1939) and Skinner (1938) were the first to describe this greater resistance to extinction with partial rather than continuous reinforcement. Many subsequent studies have demonstrated a partial reinforcement effect; this effect is one of the most reliable phenomena in psychology. Several studies document the effect of consistency of reinforcement during acquisition on resistance to extinction.

Jenkins, McFann, and Clayton (1950) trained rats to bar press for food reinforcement. Half of the rats were reinforced on a VI schedule; the others, on a continuous schedule. As **Figure 4.13** shows, rats receiving intermittent reinforcement emitted five times as many responses during extinction as rats given continuous reinforcement.

Much research on the partial reinforcement effect has used the runway apparatus; the results of these studies have consistently demonstrated the PRE effect. Consider Weinstock's 1958 study. Weinstock's rats received 108 acquisition trials with reward occurring on either 16.7%, 33.5%, 50.0%, 66.7%, 83.3%, or 100% of the trials; each rat was then given 60 extinction trials. Weinstock found an inverse relationship between resistance to extinction and the percentage of rewarded trials. These results indicate that as the likelihood that an instrumental response will produce rewards during acquisition decreases, resistance to extinction increases. Many other experiments have demonstrated that intermittent reward during acquisition increases resistance to extinction in the runway; see Robbins (1971) for a review of this literature.

The partial reinforcement effect has also been demonstrated with human adults (Lewis & Duncan, 1958) and children (Lewis, 1952). To illustrate the impact of partial reinforcement on humans, let's examine the Lewis and Duncan (1958) study. College students were given reinforcement (a disk exchangeable for $.05) for pulling the arm of a slot machine. The percentage of reinforced lever-pull responses varied: subjects received reinforcement after either 33%, 67%, or 100% of the responses. Lewis and Duncan allowed subjects to play the slot machine as long as they liked during extinction, reporting that the lower the percentage of responses reinforced during acquisition, the greater the resistance to extinction.

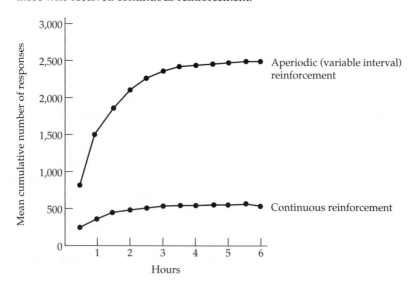

FIGURE 4.13. The mean cumulative number of bar press responses during extinction is higher in rats who received intermittent reinforcement than in those who received continuous reinforcement.

Still, the percentage of reinforced trials cannot be too low (Lewis, 1960) or learning will be minimal and extinction rapid. Different percentages of reinforced trials generally produce a U-shaped relationship between the percentage of reinforced responses and resistance to extinction, with a low or high percentage of reinforcement producing a more rapid extinction.

111

CHAPTER 4
*Principles and
Applications of
Appetitive
Conditioning*

Psychologists have proposed many explanations of the partial reinforcement effect since Humphreys's and Skinner's initial observations. Abram Amsel's frustration theory (Amsel, 1967, 1994) and E. J. Capaldi's sequential theory (Capaldi, 1971, 1994) seem best able to describe the processes responsible for increased resistance to extinction following intermittent rather than continuous reinforcement. A brief summary of each view is provided here; the interested reader should see Amsel (1994) or Capaldi (1994) for a more detailed description of these theories.

Amsel (1967, 1994) proposed a frustration-based theory for the partial reinforcement effect. According to Amsel, the elicitation of an anticipatory frustration response during extinction in animals that received continuous rewards leads to a rapid suppression of response (a more detailed discussion of the anticipatory frustration concept will be presented in Chapter 6). The effect of anticipatory frustration in animals that received intermittent reward is quite different. Early in acquisition, the anticipation of nonreward does not produce sufficient frustration to suppress behavior due to the low associative strength of the instrumental or operant response, which causes continued responding on subsequent trials. When reward then follows nonreward during acquisition, the anticipatory frustration response becomes associated with responding. The conditioning of the anticipatory frustration response to the operant or instrumental behavior causes the nonreward experienced during extinction to elicit rather than suppress responding. In other words, animals receiving intermittent reward learn to persist when they experience frustration. As a result of this conditioned persistence, the anticipation of nonreward elicits responding, rather than inhibiting it, during the early stages of extinction. Eventually, continued nonreward leads to a suppression of responding, but the intermittently rewarded animal responds for longer periods of time during extinction than the continuously reinforced animal.

Evidence for Amsel's frustration theory can be found in studies varying the amount of reward experienced prior to nonreward during acquisition. For example, Hulse (1958) provided rats with either a large (1.0 gram) or small (0.08 gram) reward during acquisition in the runway. Half of the animals in each reward magnitude condition received either continuous (100 percent) or intermittent (46 percent) reward. Hulse found greater resistance to extinction in the intermittent than in the continuous reward groups (see **Figure 4.14**). He also observed significantly greater resistance to extinction in intermittently rewarded animals receiving a large rather than a small reward, but no difference as a function of reward magnitude in animals given continuous reward. Why did reward magnitude affect resistance to extinction in intermittently but not continuously rewarded animals? A large reward followed by nonreward elicits greater frustration than a small reward followed by nonreward. The greater anticipatory frustration response produced by the removal of the large reward leads to a stronger association of the anticipatory frustration response to the

FIGURE 4.14. This figure presents the latency of running
(1/running time × 100) during extinction as a function of the
percentage of reward (46 or 100%) and the magnitude of reward
(0.08 or 1.0 gram). The reference point contains the latency from
the first training trial and the first extinction trial.

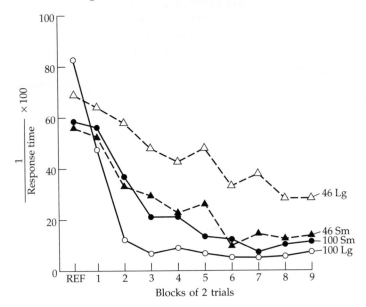

instrumental response. This greater conditioning produces more persistence
and slower extinction in animals receiving a large rather than a small reward.
However, the conditioning of the anticipatory frustration response only occurs
in intermittently rewarded animals because continuously rewarded animals
never experience reward following nonreward.

Capaldi (1971, 1994) presents a quite different view of the partial reinforcement effect. According to Capaldi, if reward follows a nonrewarded trial, the
animal will then associate the memory of the nonrewarded experience (S^N) with
the operant or instrumental response. Capaldi suggests that the conditioning of
the S^N to the operant or instrumental behavior is responsible for the increased
resistance to extinction with partial reward. During extinction, the only memory
present after the first nonrewarded experience is S^N. Animals receiving continuous reward do not experience S^N during acquisition; therefore, they do not associate S^N with the operant or instrumental response. The presence of S^N in
continuously rewarded animals during extinction changes the stimulus context
from that present during acquisition. This change produces a reduction in response strength because of a generalization decrement, a reduced intensity of a
response when the stimulus present is dissimilar to the stimulus conditioned to
the response (see Chapter 7 for a discussion of generalization). The loss of response strength because of generalization decrement, combined with the inhibition developed during extinction, produces a rapid extinction of the operant
or instrumental response in animals receiving continuous reward in acquisition.
However, a different process occurs in animals receiving partial reward in

113

CHAPTER 4
Principles and
Applications of
Appetitive
Conditioning

acquisition: these animals associate S^N with the operant or instrumental response during acquisition and, therefore, no generalization decrement occurs during extinction. The absence of the generalization decrement causes the strength of the operant or instrumental response at the beginning of extinction to remain at the level conditioned during acquisition. Thus, the inhibition developed during extinction only slowly suppresses the operant or instrumental response, and extinction is slower with partial than with continuous reward.

Capaldi and his associates (Capaldi, Hart, & Stanley, 1963; Capaldi & Spivey, 1964) conducted several studies to demonstrate the influence of S^N experienced during a rewarded trial on resistance to extinction. In these studies, during the interval between the nonrewarded and the rewarded trials, reward was given in an environmental other than the runway. The effect of this intertrial reward procedure is the replacement of the memory of nonreward (S^N) with a memory of reward (S^R) and thus a reduced resistance to extinction. Rats given intertrial reward showed a faster extinction of the instrumental response than control animals receiving only partial reward.

We have presented two views of the partial reinforcement effect. While these two views seem opposite, it is possible that both are valid. The partial reinforcement effect could result from both conditioned persistence and the conditioning of the memory of nonreward to the instrumental or operant response.

What is the significance of the partial reinforcement effect? According to Flaherty (1985), observations of animals in their natural environments indicate that an animal's attempts to attain a desired goal are sometimes successful, at other times not. Flaherty asserts that the PRE effect is adaptive because it motivates animals not to give up too easily and thus lose the opportunity to succeed. Yet, animals receiving partial reward do not continue to respond indefinitely without reward; this observation indicates that animals will not persist forever in the face of continued frustration.

BEFORE YOU GO ON

- **What might cause Traci to stop playing blackjack?**
- **Does the partial reinforcement effect have anything to say about the likelihood that Traci will no longer gamble?**

In this chapter, we have learned that the way we behave is affected by the reward and nonreward. The importance of reward and nonreward on instrumental or operant behavior has impressed many psychologists, who have designed conditioning procedures to control human behavior. These psychologists have used reward to institute more effective patterns of behavior, and nonreward to eliminate inappropriate behavior patterns. We end our discussion of appetitive conditioning by examining its use in controlling human behavior.

APPLICATION: CONTINGENCY MANAGEMENT

In 1953, B. F. Skinner suggested that poorly arranged reinforcer contingencies are sometimes responsible for people's behavior problems. In many instances, effective instrumental or operant responding does not occur because reinforcement is unavailable. At other times, reinforcing people's behavior problems sustains their occurrence. Skinner believed that rearranging reinforcement contingencies could eliminate behavior pathology and increase the occurrence of more effective ways of responding. Many psychologists (for example, Ullman & Krasner, 1965) accepted Skinner's view, and the restructuring of reinforcement contingencies emerged as an effective way of altering human behavior. The use of reinforcement and nonreinforcement to control people's behavior was initially labeled **behavior modification.** However, behavior modification refers to all types of behavioral treatments; thus, behavior therapists (Masters, Burish, Hollon, & Rimm, 1987) now use the term **contingency management** to indicate that contingent reinforcement and nonreinforcement are being used to increase the frequency of appropriate behaviors and to eliminate or reduce inappropriate responses. We begin by examining the procedures required to effectively use reinforcement and nonreinforcement to alter instrumental or operant behavior. Evidence for the effectiveness of contingency management is described later in this section.

There are three main stages in the effective implementation of a contingency management program (see Masters, Burish, Hollon, & Rimm, 1987, for a more detailed discussion of these procedures). The initial stage of therapy assesses the frequency of appropriate and inappropriate behaviors and determines the situations in which these behaviors occur. In addition, the reinforcement maintaining the inappropriate response, as well as potential reinforcers for the appropriate behavior, are determined in the assessment phase. The second phase of therapy, the contingency contracting stage of treatment, specifies the relationship between responding and reinforcement. Also, the therapist determines the method of administering the reinforcement contingent upon the appropriate behaviors. During the next stage of contingency management, the treatment is implemented. The changes in responding during and following treatment are evaluated in the last phase of contingency management: this ensures that (1) the therapy program produces behavioral changes and (2) these changes continue after the termination of formal treatment. As we will discover shortly, contingency management is an effective way to alter behavior; if the treatment fails to change behavior, it often means that the program was not developed and/or implemented correctly, and changes are needed to ensure behavioral change.

The Assessment Phase

The therapist must first define the behavior problem and determine the situations in which it does or does not occur. Discussions with the client, others who are familiar with the client, or both, are the initial source of information concerning the problem behavior. However, the therapist cannot rely solely on this subjective reporting, which merely provides the therapist with an impression of the problem. Direct observations are necessary to establish the precise baseline level of the target behaviors. These observations may be made by the staff of an institution, other people around the client, or the client. Regardless of who

115

CHAPTER 4
*Principles and
Applications of
Appetitive
Conditioning*

TABLE 4.2. Instances of Tantrum Behavior and Parental Reaction to Tantrums During 7-Day Baseline Assessment Period

Day	Tantrums	Duration (minutes)	Response
1	1	4	Comforted child when he slipped and banged head during crying
2	1	5	Told child to be quiet but finally gave cookie to quiet him down
	2	6	Ignored until couldn't stand it; gave cookie
3	1	5	Ignored
	2	6	Ignored
	3	8	Ignored until child took cookie himself; spanked child
4	1	4	Ignored; child stopped spontaneously
5	1	4	Company present; gave child cookie to quiet him
	2	5	Ignored; finally gave in
6	1	8	Ignored; went into bathroom, had cigarette, read magazine until child quieted himself
	2	4	Ignored; just as about to give in, child stopped
7	1	3	Ignored; child stopped, began to play

Source: Behavior Therapy: Techniques and Empirical Findings by J. C. Masters, T. G. Burish, S. D. Hollon, and D. C. Rimm. Copyright 1987 by Harcourt Brace Jovanovich. Reprinted by permission of the publisher.

observes the target behavior, accurate observations are essential, and training is needed to ensure reliable data recording.

Consider the following example to illustrate the observational training process. Parents complain to a behavior therapist that their child frequently has temper tantrums, which they have tried but failed to eliminate. The therapist instructs the parents to fill in a chart (see **Table 4.2**) indicating both the number and duration of tantrums occurring each day for a week, as well as their response to each tantrum. The parents' observation provides a relatively accurate recording of the frequency and intensity of the problem behavior.

The parents' observations also indicate the reinforcement of the problem behavior. As **Table 4.2** shows, a parental response to the tantrum increased the frequency of the behavior; when parents ignored the behavior, the temper tantrums decreased in frequency. It is essential in the assessment phase to record the events following the target behavior; this information identifies the reinforcer of the problem behavior.

The assessment must also indicate when and where the target behavior occurs. For example, the child may be having tantrums at home every day after school but not at school. This information about the target behavior shows the extent of the behavior problem, as well as the stimulus conditions which precipitate the response.

Based on information obtained in the assessment phase, the therapist can determine the reinforcer to be used during therapy. In some cases, the behavioral recording indicates an effective reinforcer for appropriate behavior; in other instances, the therapist must discover what works. Behavior therapists

(Masters, Burish, Hollon, & Rimm, 1987)) have developed a number of reinforcer assessment techniques. For example, the Mediation-Reinforcer Incomplete Blank (MRB), a modified incomplete sentence test developed by Tharp and Wetzel (1969), reveals the client's view of a reinforcer. A client's response to the question "I will do almost anything to get _____" shows what the client considers a reinforcer.

The Contingency Contracting Phase

In this phase, the therapist and client specify the desired instrumental or operant response and establish the precise relationship between that response and reinforcement. This involves deciding the schedule of reinforcement necessary to establish the desired response. In addition, if a shaping procedure is needed, the contract will detail the changes in contingency to occur at various stages of treatment. Furthermore, because an inappropriate instrumental or operant response has often elicited reinforcement in the past, the contingency will indicate that this inappropriate response will no longer be reinforced.

Who will administer the reinforcer? In the traditional application of contingency management, people other than the client (for example, a nurse in a mental hospital, a teacher in a school setting, or a parent in the home) provide reinforcement contingent upon the appropriate behavior. During the contracting stage, the individuals administering reinforcement are trained to identify and reinforce appropriate behavior.

Enlisting people around the client to provide reinforcement is ideally suited to many types of situations. However, in some circumstances, this technique is not feasible. This is especially true for adults seeking to change their behavior by using outpatient therapy; the use of the self-reinforcement procedure has often proven effective in these situations. Although psychologists (see Skinner, 1953) were initially skeptical of the efficacy of self-reinforcement in behavioral management, Bandura and Perloff (1967) demonstrated that the self-reinforcement technique is as effective in changing behavior as the typical reinforcement procedure. In their study, 7- to 10-year-old children received reinforcement for exerting effort on a wheel-turning task. At the beginning of the experiment, some children were given a supply of tokens they could exchange for prizes. They then used the tokens to provide their own reinforcement for attaining a high level of performance. Other children attaining a high level of performance received tokens from the experimenter. Bandura and Perloff reported that both the self-imposed reinforcement groups and the externally imposed reinforcement groups showed an equivalent level of performance, responding at a higher level than children receiving reinforcement prior to the task or no reinforcement. Self-reinforcement procedures have effectively modified a number of undesired behaviors, including impulsive overspending (Paulsen, Rimm, Woodburn, & Rimm, 1977), depression (Fuchs & Rehm, 1977), inadequate study habits (Greiner & Karoly, 1976), and overeating (Stuart, 1971).

Contingency management programs in which other people provide reward have yielded impressive results for changing a wide variety of behaviors. A brief discussion of the effectiveness of such programs completes our examination of contingency management.

The Implementation of the Contingency
Management Program

117

CHAPTER 4
*Principles and
Applications of
Appetitive
Conditioning*

Skinner's idea that reinforcement could be systematically employed to modify behavior was empirically tested in the early 1960s by Ayllon and Azrin at Anna State Hospital in Illinois (see Ayllon & Azrin, 1965, 1968). Ayllon and Azrin established a contingency management program for institutionalized adult female psychotic clients. These clients received tokens, which they could later exchange for desired primary reinforcers, when they engaged in instrumental or operant responses they would need for effective adjustment outside of the hospital. Two classes of instrumental or operant behaviors were reinforced: (1) self-care activities such as grooming and bathing; and (2) job activities such as washing dishes and serving food. Ayllon and Azrin reported that the frequency of appropriate responding significantly increased as the result of their contingency management program (see **Figure 4.15**). (Their approach is often called a token economy program because of the use of tokens as secondary reinforcers.)

Ayllon and Azrin's treatment shows that psychiatric patients can develop the behaviors necessary for successful adjustment when they are reinforced for

FIGURE 4.15. The presentation of reinforcement contingent upon target behaviors increases the frequency of appropriate responding. The frequency of the target behaviors declined when reinforcement was discontinued but increased when contingent reinforcement was restored.

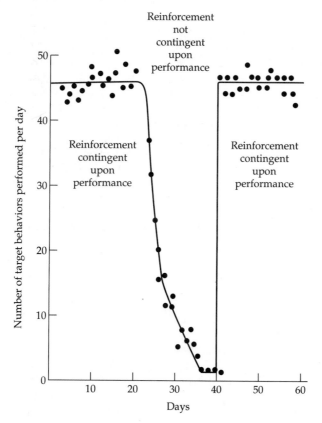

those behaviors. In fact, many studies (Fairweather, Sanders, Maynard, & Cressler, 1969; Paul & Lentz, 1977) have found that psychotic patients receiving a contingency management treatment exhibit a significantly better adjustment to daily living than patients given standard hospital treatment programs. The efficacy of instrumental or operant conditioning in altering the behavior of hospitalized psychotic clients appears to be well established.

Contingency management programs have been successfully used to alter behavior in a wide variety of settings. A sample of these programs are shown in **Table 4.3.** Contingency management appears to be an effective treatment for a

Table 4.3. Sample of Behaviors Influenced by a Contingency Management Program

Target Behavior/competency	Population	Outcome	Source of report
Social			
Social and emotional behaviors	Handicapped children	Increased	Cook and Apolloni (1976)
Prosocial verbal behavior	Delinquent adolescent	Increased	Emshoff, Redd, and Davidson (1976)
Social interaction	Chronically psychotic adults	Increased	Fichter, Wallace, Liberman, and Davis (1976)
Social interaction	Retarded adolescents	Increased	L. Williams, Martin, McDonald, Hardy, and Lambert (1975)
Sharing, praising	Children	Increased	Rogers-Warren and Baer (1976)
Social speech	Retarded children	Increased	Mithaug and Wolfe (1976)
Social greeting	Retarded children	Increased	Stokes, Baer, and Jackson (1974)
Social skills	Predelinquent adolescents	Increased	D. M. Maloney, Harper, Braukmann, Fixsen, Phillips, and Wolf (1976)
Extreme withdrawal	Children	Improved	Allen, Hart, Buell, Harris, and Wolf (1964); Brawley, Harris, Allen, Fleming, and Peterson (1969)
Extreme passivity	Children	Improved	Johnston, Kelley, Harris, and Wolf (1966)
Sharing	Children	Increased	Warren, Rogers-Warren, and Baer (1976)
Social disruption	Children	Decreased	MacPherson, Candee, and Hohman (1974)
Self-control			
Hyperactivity/ attention span	Retarded children	Decreased/ increased	Alabiso (1975)
Hyperactivity	Children	Decreased	Wulbert and Dries (1977)
Obesity	Children	Decreased	Epstein, Parker, McCoy, and McGee (1976)
Classroom disruption	Children	Decreased	Todd, Scott, Bostow, and Alexander (1976)
Family interaction	Mother and adolescent	Improved responsibility	Blechman, Olson, Schornagle, Halsdorf, and Turner (1976)
Enuresis	Adolescent	Eliminated	Popler (1976)

Table 4.3. Continued

Target Behavior/competency	Population	Outcome	Source of report
Rumination	Infant	Eliminated	Linscheid and Cunningham (1977)
Classroom disruption	Children	Decreased	Robertson, DeReus, and Drabman (1976)
Classroom disruption	Children	Decreased	Ayllon, Garber, and Pisor (1975)
Classroom task attention	Children	Increased	Hay, Hay, and Nelson (1977b)
Classroom task attention	Children	Increased	Marholin and Steinman (1977)
Homework	Children	Improved	Harris and Shermann (1974)
School attendance	Predelinquent	Improved	Alexander, Corbett, and Smigel (1976)
Curfew obedience	Adolescents	Improved	Alexander, Corbett, and Smigel (1976)
Writer's block	Adult	Eliminated	Passman (1976)
Stuttering	Adults	Eliminated	Ingham and Andrews (1973)
Cognitive-emotional			
Complex language	Autistic child	Acquired	Stevens-Long and Rasmussen (1974)
Creativity	Children	Increased	Henson (1975)
Intelligence score	Handicapped children	Increased	Smeets and Striefel (1975)
Intelligence/vocabulary	Normal children	Increased	Clingman and Fowler (1976)
Creativity	Normal children	Increased	Glover and Gary (1976)
School performance	Adolescent	Improved	Schumaker, Hovell, and Sherman (1977)
Reading/comprehension	Autistic child	Improved	Rosenbaum and Breiling (1976)
Arithmetic competence	Children	Improved	Hundert (1976)
Autisticlike behavior	Child	Eliminated	Moore and Bailey (1973)
Anxiety and depression	Adult	Eliminated	Vasta (1975)
Phobia	Adults	Eliminated	Marshall, Boutilier, and Minnes (1974)
Conversion reaction	Adult	Eliminated	Kallman, Hersen, and O'Toole (1975)
Autism	Children	Improved	Lovaas (1968); Wetzel, Baker, Rooney, and Martin (1966)
Mutism	Adults	Improved	Sherman (1965); Straughan (1968)
School phobia	Children	Eliminated	G. R. Patterson (1965)
Psychogenic seizures			Gardner (1967)
Pain	Adult	Eliminated	Cautela (1971)
Stuttering	Adults	Reduced	Ingham and Andrews (1973)

Source: Behavior Therapy: Techniques and Empirical Findings by J. C. Masters, T. G. Burish, S. D. Hollon, D. C. Rimm. Copyright 1987 by Harcourt Brace Jovanovich. Reprinted by permission of the publisher.

number of behavior pathologies other than lack of living skills. Depression is one behavior problem that has been modified by contingent reinforcement (Lieberman & Raskin, 1971). Contingency management has also been employed in the treatment of anxiety (Marshall, Boutilier, & Minnes, 1974) and pain (Kallman, Hersen, & O'Toole, 1975). In these studies, reinforcement occurred when the clients showed decreases in anxiety, depression, or pain and increases in responses incompatible with the behavior problem.

Token economy systems have been established at a number of residential treatment centers for delinquent and predelinquent children and adolescents.

The aim of these contingency management programs is to establish appropriate social and lawful behavior as well as academic competencies. These programs (Emshoff, Redd, & Davidson, 1976; Maloney, Harper, Braukmann, Fixsen, Phillips, & Wolf, 1976) have shown that contingent reinforcement can decrease the incidence of inappropriate social behaviors and increase the occurrence of desired social and academic responses.

A contingency management program can also increase effective responding in retarded children and adults. For example, contingent reinforcement has been used with retarded children to teach toilet training (Azrin, Sneed, & Foxx, 1973), personal grooming (Horner & Keilitz, 1975), and mealtime behavior (Plummer, Baer, & LeBlanc, 1977). Furthermore, contingency management can suppress several behaviors characteristic of some retarded children; for example, the incidence of self-injurious behavior (Solnick, Rincover, & Peterson, 1977), aggressive and disruptive behavior (Plummer, Baer, & LeBlanc, 1977), and self-stimulation (Wells, Forehand, Hickey, & Green, 1977) will decrease when reinforcement is made contingent upon the suppression of these behaviors.

The academic performance of normal children and adults is also responsive to contingency management treatment. For example, Lovitt, Guppy, and Blattner (1969) found that contingent free time and permission to listen to the radio increased spelling accuracy in fourth-grade children. Other studies have also found that contingency management procedures can increase academic competency in children; refer to Harris and Sherman (1973) or Rapport and Bosow (1976) for other examples. Also, contingent reinforcement has been shown to increase the studying behavior of college students; however, this procedure appears to be effective only with students of below-average ability (Bristol & Sloane, 1974) or students with low or medium grade averages (DuNann & Weber, 1976). Most likely, the other students are already exhibiting effective studying behavior and, therefore, are not likely to increase their responding even with reinforcement. Thus, contingent reinforcement will increase academic performance only for those students not already responding effectively.

Businesses have found contingency management programs to reduce tardiness, decrease theft by employees, improve worker safety, and enhance employee productivity (Martin & Pear, 1992). Effective reinforcers that have successfully modified employee behavior include pay bonuses, time off, and being mentioned in the company newsletter. Businesses also have used contingency management to change the behavior of their customers: my 6-year-old son wants to eat at the fast food restaurant offering the best kid's meal toy, and I try to fly on one particular airline to accumulate frequent flyer miles. I would imagine you can think of several examples of purchases you have made based on the reinforcement that company offers.

Contingency management can be used not only to change the behavior of individuals but is also effective with large groups of people. For example, Hayes and Cone (1977) found that direct payments to efficient energy users produced large reductions in energy consumption, while Seaver and Patterson (1976) discovered that informational feedback and a decal for efficient energy use resulted in a significant decrease in home fuel consumption. Also, McCalden and Davis (1972) discovered that reserving a special lane of the Oakland-San Francisco Bay Bridge for cars with several passengers increased car

121

CHAPTER 4
Principles and
Applications of
Appetitive
Conditioning

pooling and improved traffic flow. Finally, Geller and Hahn (1984) reported that seatbelt use increased at a large industrial plant when the opportunity to obtain reinforcement was made contingent upon the use of seatbelts.

We have learned that contingency management programs are quite effective in establishing appropriate behaviors and eliminating inappropriate behaviors. Given the effectiveness of the contingency management approach, you might expect that it would be widely used. Kazdin (1982) reports that contingency management is widely applied in classrooms and on psychiatric wards. Yet, does every school have a store, and does every major highway have a car pool lane? Surprisingly, the success of contingency management programs does not always lead to widespread use. The failure to adopt contingency management programs is nowhere more evident than in the treatment of psychiatric patients at Veterans Administration Medical Centers (Davidson & Neale, 1994). Boudewyns, Fry, and Nightingale (1986) reported that in 1983, only 20 of 152 VA Medical Centers used token economy programs in their treatment of psychiatric patients. Some reasons the centers gave for the lack of more widespread implementation of this effective treatment were that they were under pressure to reduce the time patients were hospitalized and that poorly paid staff resisted taking on additional responsibilities. Paul and Menditto (1992) surveyed VA Medical Centers almost a decade later and found that the use of token economies had not changed much.

BEFORE YOU GO ON

- Could a contingency management program help Traci minimize the losses she is likely to experience at the blackjack table?
- If so, how would you design such a program?

CHAPTER SUMMARY

Reinforcers have a powerful influence on human behavior. According to Skinner, a reinforcer is an event that increases the frequency of the behavior that produces it. A contingency specifies the behavior needed to produce reinforcement.

In instrumental conditioning, constraints are placed on the opportunity to gain reward; operant conditioning has no constraints, and the animal or person can freely respond to obtain reinforcement.

Primary reinforcers possess innate reinforcing ability, while secondary reinforcers develop the capacity to reinforce operant or instrumental behavior. The reinforcing property of a secondary reinforcer is determined by (1) the strength of the primary reinforcer it is associated with, (2) the number of pairings of the primary and secondary reinforcers, and (3) the delay between primary and secondary reinforcement. A positive reinforcer is an event, such as food or money, that has reinforcing properties; in contrast, a negative reinforcer is the termination of an aversive event.

The environment specifies the relationship between the appropriate response and reinforcement; however, when the level of responding is zero, the operant response will not increase in frequency despite the contingency between reinforcement and the operant response. Furthermore, learning is slow if the rate of response is low.

The shaping procedure can be used to ensure rapid conditioning. Shaping involves reinforcing a response that occurs at a high rate and then changing the contingency so that closer and closer approximations to the final behavior are required to produce reinforcement.

A contingency not only specifies the response that will lead to reinforcement, but also the manner in which the behavior must occur. On fixed-ratio (FR) schedules, a fixed number of responses are necessary to produce reinforcement, while with variable-ratio (VR) schedules, an average number of responses leads to reinforcement. The first response occurring after a specified interval of time produces reinforcement on an interval schedule of reinforcement; while the interval remains constant with a fixed-interval (FI) schedule, it varies from reinforcement to reinforcement on a variable-interval (VI) schedule.

A differential reinforcement schedule requires a specified number of responses within a specified amount of time. The response requirement is high with a differential reinforcement of high responding (DRH) schedule and low with a differential reinforcement of low responding (DRL) schedule. A differential reinforcement of other behaviors (DRO) schedule requires an absence of response during the specified time period. Compound schedules are a combination of two (or more) schedules of reinforcement.

Contiguity between the appropriate response and the reward influences conditioning: the subject will acquire the instrumental or operant response rapidly if reward immediately follows the response. The magnitude of reward also affects instrumental or operant conditioning. Performance of the instrumental or operant response is higher with a larger rather than smaller reward. This performance difference between large and small rewards is due to the greater motivational impact of a large reward.

A shift from large to small reward magnitude leads to a rapid decrease in response, while a shift from small to large reward magnitude causes a significant increase in responding. The negative contrast (or depression) effect is a lower level of performance when the reward magnitude is shifted from high to low than when the reward magnitude is always low; the positive contrast (or elation) effect is a higher level of performance when the reward magnitude is shifted from low to high than when the reward magnitude is always high.

Extinction of an instrumental or operant response occurs when that behavior no longer produces reward. The frequency and intensity of the behavior declines during extinction. However, nonreward sometimes increases the intensity of instrumental or operant behavior when the memory of nonreward has been conditioned to elicit the instrumental or operant response.

Nonreward of the instrumental or operant response leads to an inhibition of that response, as well as elicitation of an escape response from the frustration the nonreward state induces. Further, the environmental cues present during nonreward develop aversive properties, which motivates escape from situations associated with nonreward.

A large reward magnitude produces greater resistance to extinction than does a small reward magnitude when the amount of acquisition training is low,

123

CHAPTER 4
*Principles and
Applications of
Appetitive
Conditioning*

but the opposite is true with extended acquisition training. Also, resistance to extinction is greater when reward delay is varied rather than constant. Furthermore, partial rather than continuous reward leads to a slower extinction of the instrumental or operant behavior.

Contingent reinforcement has been useful in many real-world situations to increase appropriate behaviors and decrease inappropriate behaviors. The application of the operant conditioning process to alter human behavior is called contingency management.

There are three phases of contingency management: assessment, contracting, and implementation. In the assessment phase, the levels of appropriate and inappropriate behavior are determined as well as the situations in which these behaviors occur and the potential reinforcers of the appropriate response. The precise relationship between the instrumental or operant response and the reinforcement is decided during the contracting phase. Implementation of the contingency contract involves providing reinforcement contingent upon the appropriate response or upon the absence of the inappropriate behavior, or both.

Contingency management has been used to successfully modify many different behaviors, including inadequate living skills, depression, poor study habits, antisocial responses, and energy consumption.

CRITICAL THINKING QUESTIONS

1. Tyrone's roommate never does his share of the household chores, such as washing the dishes, vacuuming the carpet, or taking out the garbage. Tyrone finds his roommate's lack of cooperation unpleasant. Using what you know about reinforcement, suggest several reasons for the roommate's lack of cooperation. How might Tyrone shape his roommate to change his behavior and help out with the household chores?
2. Elizabeth has made the mistake of intermittently reinforcing her son's temper tantrums. Why is her use of intermittent reinforcement a mistake? How might she now extinguish the boy's temper tantrums? What problems might Elizabeth encounter, and how might she overcome these problems?
3. You are a school psychologist working with a child who seems disinterested in school. The child refuses to do homework, and her classroom performance is poor. Develop a contingency management program to improve the child's homework performance. Indicate why you are using each specific procedure to modify her behavior.

KEY TERMS

compound schedule
contingency
contingency management
depression effect
differential reinforcement
   of high responding
   (DRH) schedule

differential reinforcement
   of low responding
   (DRL) schedule
differential reinforcement
   of other behaviors
   (DRO)

differential reinforcement
   schedule
elation effect
extinction
fixed-interval schedule
   (FI)

fixed-ratio schedule
(FR)
instrumental
conditioning
interval schedule of
reinforcement
negative contrast effect
negative reinforcer
operant chamber
operant conditioning

partial reinforcement
effect (PRE)
positive contrast effect
positive reinforcer
postreinforcement pause
primary reinforcer
ratio schedule of
reinforcement
reinforcer
scallop effect

schedule of reinforcement
secondary reinforcer
shaping
spontaneous recovery
successive approximation
procedure
variable-interval schedule
(VI)
variable-ratio
schedule (VR)

Principles and Applications of Aversive Conditioning

The Pain of Failure

Edmond dreaded next week. He had a major project due at work, and he was not anywhere near being finished. His boss gave him the assignment three weeks ago. It was a difficult task that required a lot of effort. But Edmond has not been able to focus his attention on the project. Much of his time he spent worrying about being fired. Edmond had joined the accounting firm three months ago, just after graduating from college. He was very excited about working after four years of school. Edmond had enjoyed the first few weeks at work. Everything was new, and people willingly answered all of his questions. Edmond was pleased with his job until last month. Edmond's anxiety began when he made a major mistake on a report. The error was caught by a senior officer at the firm, who was furious with Edmond. He received a very strong criticism from his boss, which had an extremely adverse effect on Edmond. He did not sleep well that night and was anxious the next day at work. Edmond tried to stay away from his boss, but he could not avoid him. His boss looked angry even a week after the reprimand. By the end of each day, Edmond was so nervous that he began frequenting a bar on his way home. Several beers eased his pain. Edmond was anxious again by the time he got home, so he had several more beers before dinner and a few more while watching television. He did not like to drink a lot, but at least he could sleep. When his boss gave him the new project three weeks ago, Edmond knew he was in trouble. The boss told him that the project was extremely important and that he had better not make any mistakes. This threat made him extremely nervous, and he got really drunk that night. As the time approached when the project was due, his nervousness increased, as did his drinking. Edmond was sure he was going to get fired next week, when his boss would find out the project was not completed. His world was falling apart, and he did not know what to do to prevent its collapse.

Edmond's fear represents a reaction to his boss's reprimand (see Chapter 3 for a discussion of the conditioning of fear). Edmond responded to the situation by drinking. The alcohol dulled his nervousness, and his increased drinking has become a habitual way to cope with fear. Some people who find themselves in unpleasant circumstances may drink to reduce their distress; others may respond in more constructive ways. This chapter details the principles that determine whether a person learns to avoid aversive events as well as how rapidly he or she learns that behavior. We will describe how people learn to avoid aversive events in Chapter 6.

Edmond does not have to be scared to death of his boss and drink the night away. Systematic desensitization, described in Chapter 3, is one behavioral technique available to eliminate avoidance behavior. Other techniques include flooding and participant modeling. This chapter describes the use of flooding to eliminate avoidance behavior. Chapter 8 will discuss the modeling treatment.

THE AVERSIVE EVENTS AROUND US

Throughout life, we encounter many unpleasant events. No one is immune from experiencing them; each of us experiences an unpleasant circumstance from time to time. Unless we learn how to cope with aversive events, our lives can be quite miserable.

Some aversive events can be escaped but not avoided. We cannot anticipate these circumstances, but we must be prepared to respond to terminate them. For example, walking to the store, you are attacked by a thief who wants your money. You might be able to end the mugging by counterattacking. You will escape if your aggressive response is effective; however, if it is not, your counterattack probably will lead to even more aversive events.

Other aversive events are avoidable. To prevent aversive events, you must learn when the aversive event will occur and how you can act to prevent it. For example, many elderly people know they may be mugged if they go out at night; therefore, they do not leave their homes after dark, allowing them to avoid muggings. This chapter describes the factors that affect whether a person learns to avoid an aversive event.

Suppose a parent punishes his or her child after receiving a teacher's note about the child's poor behavior. The punishment is intended to inhibit future misbehavior in the classroom. If punishment is effective, the child will no longer misbehave in school. The factors that determine whether punishment suppresses inappropriate behavior will be detailed later in the chapter.

You might think that a parent punishing a child for misbehaving has no relationship to an elderly person remaining inside at night to avoid being mugged. Yet, punishment and avoidance conditioning typically deal with two aspects of the same process: the child can avoid punishment by not misbehaving in school, and the elderly person can avoid being mugged by not going out at night. Thus, for punishment to be effective, it must motivate the inhibition of an inappropriate response. However, in some circumstances, a person or an animal learns to prevent punishment—but with a response other than the inappropriate behavior. For example, a child may be able to prevent punishment by crying after misbehavior, rather than by not misbehaving. Although we will describe punishment and avoidance behavior separately in this chapter, it is important to realize that punishment will only be successful if inhibition of the inappropriate behavior is the only response that will prevent punishment.

Some aversive events cannot be escaped or avoided. For example, a child who is abused by a parent cannot escape or prevent the abuse. In Chapter 8, we will discover that helplessness can develop when a person or animal learns that aversive events can neither be escaped nor avoided. We begin this chapter by examining escape conditioning; then we discuss avoidance learning and punishment.

127

CHAPTER 5
Principles and
Applications of
Aversive
Conditioning

ESCAPE CONDITIONING

Many people close their eyes during a scary scene in a horror movie, opening them when they believe the unpleasant scene has ended. This behavior is one example of an **escape response,** which is a behavior motivated by an aversive event (for example, the scary scene) and rewarded by the termination of the aversive event.

Many studies (Brush, 1970; Campbell & Church, 1969) show that people and animals will try to escape aversive events. Let's examine two of these experiments. Miller's classic 1948 study (see Chapter 3) showed that rats could learn to escape painful electric shock. Miller placed rats in the white compartment of a shuttlebox and exposed them to electric shock. The rats could escape the shock by turning a wheel that opened a door and then running into the black compartment; Miller reported that the rats rapidly learned to use this escape route. In a similar study using human subjects, Hiroto (1974) exposed college students to an unpleasant noise; they could terminate it by moving their finger from one side of a shuttlebox to the other. Hiroto found that his subjects quickly learned how to escape the noise.

The Escape from Aversive Events

Several factors play an important role in determining whether a person or animal learns to escape aversive events as well as the efficiency of the escape response. We will look at these factors next.

The Intensity of the Aversive Event

Walking to class, you see a student stumble and fall. Will you stop to help? A number of variables affect helping behavior. One critical factor is the aversiveness of the emergency. According to Jane Piliavin and her associates (Piliavin, Dovidio, Gaertner, & Clark, 1981), the more unpleasant the situation, the higher the cost of helping, and therefore, the greater the motive to escape from the emergency. Thus, the more serious the injury, the less likely you are to help.

Many studies have supported this cost analysis of helping. For example, Piliavin, Piliavin, and Roden (1975) simulated an emergency on subway cars in New York City. A confederate acting as a victim would moan and then "faint." The experimenters increased the discomfort of some bystanders by having the victim expose an ugly birthmark just before fainting. The victim did not expose the unpleasant birthmark to other bystanders. Piliavin, Piliavin, and Roden's results indicate that the bystanders who saw the ugly birthmark helped the victim less often than those who did not. As the cost of helping increases—in this case,

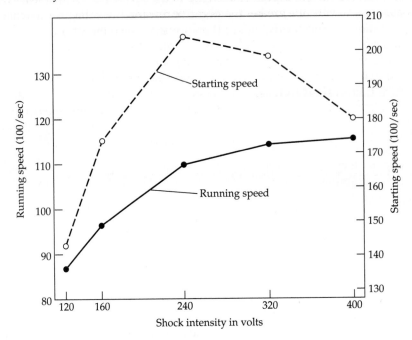

FIGURE 5.1. The mean escape performance for both starting and running speed increases over the last eight training trials with a higher shock intensity.

the cost included enduring the sight of an ugly birthmark—the likelihood of helping behavior decreases.

The escape response when anticipating failure on a task provides another illustration of the influence of the intensity of the aversive event. The more unpleasant the task, the greater the expectation of failure, the higher the motivation to escape, and, therefore, the less persistence the subjects exhibit (Atkinson, 1964; Feather, 1967).

Research with animals has also documented the effect of the intensity of the aversive event on escape behavior. Most studies have used electric shock as the aversive event. For example, Trapold and Fowler (1960) trained rats to escape electric shock in the start box of an alley by running to an uncharged goal box. The rats received either 120, 160, 240, 300, or 400 volts of electric shock in the start box. Trapold and Fowler reported that the greater the shock intensity, the shorter the latency to escape from the start box (see **Figure 5.1**). Other research has shown that the intensity of a loud noise (Masterson, 1969) or of light (Kaplan, Jackson, & Sparer, 1965) influences escape latency.

The Absence of Reward

Many people experience unsatisfying social relationships but remain in those relationships. Why do these people fail to escape from their unpleasant social relationships? One likely reason is that past escape reactions from other unpleasant social relationships did not lead to positive ones, and these individuals have therefore not learned to escape from these aversive situations. Many studies have shown that the intensity of escape behavior depends on the amount of negative reward (or the degree of decrease in the severity of an aversive event). In these experiments, the greater the negative reward, the higher the asymptotic level of escape performance. Let's now examine one of these studies.

129

CHAPTER 5
Principles and
Applications of
Aversive
Conditioning

Campbell and Kraeling (1953) exposed rats to a 400-volt electric shock in the start box of an alley. Upon reaching the goal box, the shock was reduced to either 0, 100, 200, or 300 volts. Campbell and Kraeling reported that the greater the reduction in shock intensity, the faster the rats escaped from the 400-volt electric shock. Other experiments (Bower, Fowler, & Trapold, 1959) have reported that the level of escape behavior directly relates to the level of shock reduction the escape response induces. The positive influence of negative reward magnitude on the asymptotic level of escape performance also is evident with cold water as the aversive stimulus (Woods, Davidson, & Peters, 1964).

The Impact of Delayed Reward

Research has indicated that escape behavior also depends on the delay of reward. The longer reward is delayed after an escape response, the slower the acquisition of the escape behavior, and the lower the final level of escape performance.

Fowler and Trapold's (1962) study illustrates the impact of reward delay on escape conditioning. In their study, the termination of electric shock was delayed either 0, 1, 2, 4, 8, or 16 seconds after the rats entered the goal box of the alley. Fowler and Trapold reported that the time it took the rats to reach the goal box was a direct function of reward delay: the longer the delay, the slower the speed of the escape response (see **Figure 5.2**). Furthermore, the maximum

FIGURE 5.2. The mean escape performance declines with a longer delay in shock termination.

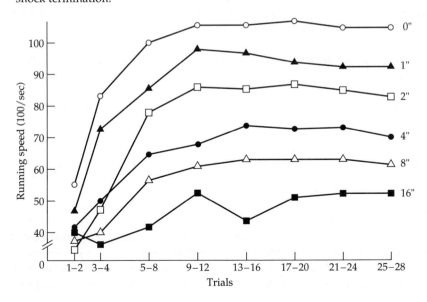

escape speed depended on the reward delay; the longer the delay, the lower the final level of escape performance. Other studies using animals (Tarpy & Koster, 1970) and humans (Penney, 1967) have also found that a delay of negative reward impairs escape conditioning.

However, some researchers report that a delay of even three seconds eliminates escape conditioning. According to Tarpy and Sawabini (1974), differences in delay gradients reflect the presence or absence of cues associated with negative reward (termination of an aversive event). The experiments showing very short delay gradients have used the operant chamber, with bar pressing as the escape response to terminate shock. Since no cues are typically associated with shock termination in the bar press situation, no secondary reinforcement cues can enhance performance when reinforcement is delayed. If cues are presented following a bar press response, these stimuli will be associated with shock termination, and some escape conditioning will occur despite a short delay in reinforcement. Recall from Chapter 4 that cues associated with reinforcers have a similar influence when positive reinforcement is delayed. Thus, one significant influence of secondary reinforcers is to counter the effect of a delay of the primary reinforcer and, therefore, to promote the conditioning of an escape response.

The Elimination of an Escape Response

A rat shocked in the start box of an alley learns to escape by running into the goal box. A researcher can train the rat to no longer escape the start box. An escape response can be eliminated by no longer presenting the aversive event or by no longer terminating the aversive event following the escape response.

The Removal of Negative Reward

An escape response is eliminated when the aversive event continues despite the escape response. However, an animal or person will continue to respond for some time; the aversive event continues to motivate the escape response until an animal or person learns that the escape response no longer terminates the aversive event.

The strength of the escape response during acquisition affects resistance to extinction: the greater the acquisition training, the slower the extinction of the escape behavior. To illustrate the influence of the acquisition level on resistance to extinction, Fazzaro and D'Amato (1969) trained rats to bar press to terminate electric shock. Rats received either 200, 400, 800, or 1,600 training trials prior to extinction. Fazzaro and D'Amato found that the number of bar press responses emitted during extinction increased with greater numbers of acquisition trials (see **Figure 5.3**).

The Absence of Aversive Events

Elimination of an escape response also occurs when the aversive event is no longer experienced; yet an animal or person exhibits a number of escape responses even when the aversive event no longer occurs. Why do escape responses occur when the aversive event is not present?

D'Amato (1970) suggested an explanation. According to D'Amato, the cues present when the aversive event occurred become able to elicit an anticipatory

131

CHAPTER 5
Principles and
Applications of
Aversive
Conditioning

FIGURE 5.3. The mean number of escape responses during extinction increases with the number of acquisition trials.

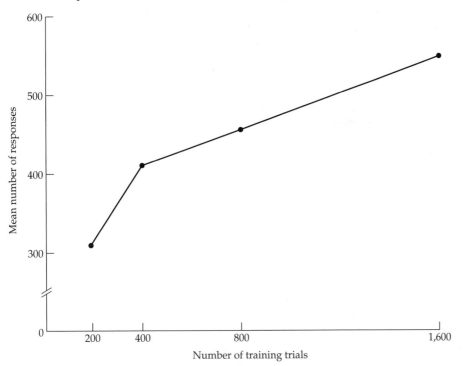

pain response (a conditioned anticipation of an impending aversive event; we will discuss the anticipatory pain concept further in Chapter 6). The physiological aftereffects of the anticipatory pain response motivate the escape response even though the aversive event is no longer presented. Escape responses will continue until the anticipatory pain response is extinguished.

Vicious-Circle Behavior

Judson Brown and his associates observed that punishment does not always eliminate escape behavior. In the Brown, Martin, and Morrow (1964) study, three groups of rats were initially placed in a 6-foot alley that was electrified except for the goal box. All of these animals learned to run to the goal box to escape the shock. For some animals, shock was eliminated in the second phase of study. As **Figure 5.4** shows, the speed of their escape response declined quickly when shock was stopped. The animals in the long-shock group continued to receive shock in the alley but not in the start box; the rats in the short-shock group received shock only in the final 2-foot segment before the goal box. Brown, Martin, and Morrow observed that the escape response continued despite punishment of the escape response in both the long-shock and short-shock groups (refer to **Figure 5.4**). Brown, Martin, and Morrow referred to these animals' actions as self-punitive or **vicious-circle behavior.**

Vicious-circle behavior has also been observed in human subjects. Renner and Tinsley (1976) trained human subjects to key press to escape shock in reaction

FIGURE 5.4. The mean escape latency during extinction for animals receiving either no shock in the alley, shock in the entire 6-foot alley (long-shock condition), or shock only in the last 2 feet of alley before the goal box (short-shock condition). The resistance to extinction is higher in the long- and short-shock conditions than in the no-shock condition.

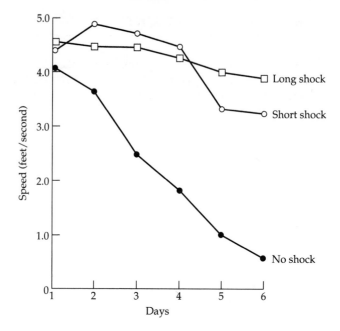

to a warning light. These subjects stopped responding when the shock was discontinued. Other subjects only received shock on their first key press on each trial. These subjects failed to stop key pressing.

Why do animals engage in vicious-circle behavior? Brown, Martin, and Morrow (1964) suggested that fear motivates running, and the conditioning of fear to the start box maintained the escape response. In contrast, Renner and Tinsley (1976) argued that vicious-circle behavior occurs because the animals or people fail to recognize that punishment will not occur if they do not respond. Renner and Tinsley observed that human subjects in a vicious-circle condition stop responding when they are told that key pressing will be shocked. This indicates that the subjects' behavior is affected by their perception of behavior-outcome contingencies. We will discuss the importance of contingency learning in Chapter 8.

BEFORE YOU GO ON

- **Will the aversiveness of Edmond's job lead him to quit?**
- **What might prevent him from quitting?**

133

CHAPTER 5
*Principles and
Applications of
Aversive
Conditioning*

Our discussion indicates that we can learn how to escape from aversive situations. However, it is more desirable, when possible, to avoid rather than escape an aversive event. In the next section, we will examine the development of responses that allow us to prevent aversive events.

THE AVOIDANCE OF AVERSIVE EVENTS

A teenage girl is invited to a party by a boy she does not like. Not wanting to hurt his feelings, she says that she would like to go, but she can't because she must study for a test. This girl is exhibiting an avoidance response: her "little white lie" allowed her to prevent an unpleasant evening.

Types of Avoidance Behavior

There are two classes of avoidance behavior: active and passive avoidance responses. Under some circumstances, an overt response, or an **active avoidance response,** is necessary to avoid the aversive event. The teenage girl exhibited an active avoidance response: she formulated an excuse in order to prevent an aversive event. In other circumstances, simply not responding, or a **passive avoidance response,** will prevent an aversive event. Suppose you receive a note from your dentist indicating it is time for your six-month checkup. Since you do not like going to the dentist, you ignore the note. This is an example of passive avoidance behavior: you avoid the dentist by not responding to the note.

Active Avoidance Learning

O. H. Mowrer's classic research (Mowrer, 1938, 1939) showed that rats could learn to exhibit an overt response to avoid electric shock. In these studies, a cue (for example, a light) was paired with painful electric shock in one chamber of a shuttlebox (see **Figure 5.5**). The rats could avoid shock by jumping across a barrier between the two compartments when the cue (CS) was presented but before the shock (UCS) onset. The animals in Mowrer's studies learned to exhibit the active avoidance hurdle-jumping response when exposed to the CS and, therefore, they avoided the electric shock. Many other psychologists since Mowrer have observed that rats can learn to cross a barrier to avoid electric shock in the shuttle box apparatus (Bower, Starr, & Lazarovitz, 1965; Theios, Lynch, & Lowe, 1966). The shuttlebox apparatus has also been used to train other animal species to avoid an aversive event. This research indicates that to avoid shock, dogs (Moscovitch & LoLordo, 1968), cats (Steinbrecher & Lockhart, 1966), and rabbits (Flakus & Steinbrecher, 1964) can learn to jump over the hurdle in a shuttlebox.

The hurdle-jumping response is one of many behaviors animals can learn in order to avoid aversive events. Miller (1941, 1948) discovered that rats could learn to turn a wheel to avoid electric shock. Other psychologists have reported that rats can learn to press a bar in an operant chamber (Biederman, D'Amato, & Keller, 1964) or even rear up on their hind legs (Bolles & Tuttle, 1967) to prevent shock.

FIGURE 5.5. A shuttle box used to study avoidance learning. When the conditioned stimulus (a light) is presented in one side of the box, the animal must jump to the other compartment to avoid the electric shock.

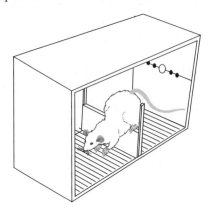

People learn many different responses that enable them to avoid aversive events. A person opening an umbrella in order to stay dry, a child doing homework to avoid failing, or an adult paying the mortgage to avoid foreclosure are three examples of humans responding to avoid unpleasant events.

Many, perhaps most, of our avoidance responses are acquired during childhood. Research with children shows that they are very adept in learning to avoid aversive events. Several studies (Penney & Kirwin, 1965; Robinson & Robinson, 1961) using loud tones as the unpleasant event reported that preschool-aged children can learn to press a lever to prevent the noise.

Passive Avoidance Learning

Psychologists have also shown that animals can learn to avoid aversive events passively. In one setting, an animal placed on top of a ledge above a grid floor receives an electric shock upon stepping down. Researchers (Hines & Paolino, 1970; McGaugh & Landfield, 1970) reported that rats refuse to leave the platform after a single training trial. Other studies demonstrated that animals readily learn to avoid shock by not entering an environment where they received shock the previous day (Baron, 1965), or by failing to bar press after being shocked for bar pressing (Camp, Raymond, & Church, 1967).

How Readily Is Avoidance Behavior Learned?

Two variables appear to have an important influence on avoidance learning. We will look at them next.

The Severity of the Aversive Event

You might suspect that the more aversive an event, the more likely it is the situation will be avoided. This relationship is true in most avoidance situations; that is, the greater the severity of the aversive event, the more readily the subject will learn the avoidance response and the higher the final level of avoidance performance will be. However, the opposite relationship is true in a two-way active avoidance task. In this type of task, the greater the severity of aversive event, the more slowly the subject will acquire the avoidance response and the lower the final level of avoidance performance will be. We will first examine evidence of the influence of the severity of the aversive event on avoidance learning, and then we will discuss why severity influences two-way avoidance behavior differently than it does other avoidance responses.

PASSIVE AVOIDANCE BEHAVIOR. Investigators (Camp, Raymond, & Church, 1967; Seligman & Campbell, 1965) have evaluated the effect of shock severity on the acquisition of a passive avoidance response. In these studies, rats were initially trained to bar press for food. After learning to bar press, the animals were shocked following a bar press response; each rat could avoid shock by not bar pressing. The severity of shock was either low, moderate, or high. The results showed that the higher the shock severity, the faster the acquisition of the passive avoidance response and the higher the final performance level of the passive avoidance behavior.

ONE-WAY ACTIVE AVOIDANCE BEHAVIOR. Shock severity also has an important influence on the acquisition and performance of a one-way active avoidance response. In this situation, the animal is shocked in one chamber of a shuttle box and can avoid shock by running to the other chamber. The shocked chamber is painted one color (for example, white), while the goal box is another color (for example, black). Many studies (McAllister, McAllister, & Douglass 1971; Moyer & Korn, 1966) have found that increasing the severity of the shock leads to faster acquisition of the one-way active avoidance response, as well as a higher level of asymptotic avoidance performance. Let's examine the Moyer and Korn (1966) study to document the role of shock intensity on a one-way active avoidance response.

Moyer and Korn placed rats on one side of a shuttle box, shocking them if they did not run to the other compartment within 5 seconds. Each rat remained in the "safe" chamber for 15 seconds and was then placed in the "dangerous" chamber to begin another trial. Animals received either .5, 1.5, 2.5, or 3.5 ma. of shock during acquisition training, and each subject was given 50 acquisition trials on a single day. Moyer and Korn reported that the greater the severity of shock, the faster the animals learned to avoid the shock (see **Figure 5.6**). Furthermore, the higher the intensity of shock, the more rapidly the animals ran from the dangerous to the safe compartment of the shuttle box.

TWO-WAY ACTIVE AVOIDANCE BEHAVIOR. In a two-way active avoidance situation, the animal is placed in one chamber (side A) of the shuttle box and exposed to a specific stimulus (for example, a light) prior to the presentation of shock. To avoid the shock, the animal must run to the other chamber (side B) before the electric shock is presented. After this trial, the animal remains in side B for a short time (for example, 60 seconds). At the end of this intertrial interval (ITI), the stimulus is again presented, and the animal must run from side B to side A to avoid being shocked; thus, the animal avoids the aversive event only by returning to the place where it was previously shocked. Learning a two-way

FIGURE 5.6. The influence of shock intensity on the acquisition of a one-way and a
two-way active avoidance response. Increases in shock intensity facilitate one-way
avoidance learning but impair two-way avoidance acquisition.

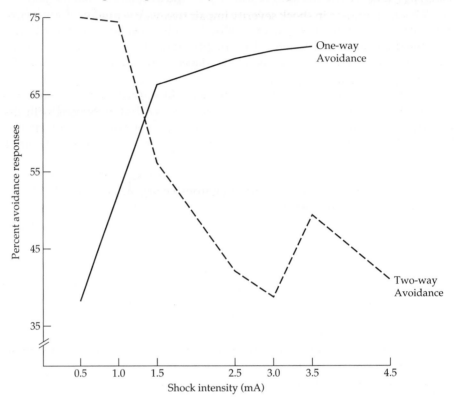

active avoidance response requires an animal to ignore situational cues (the
place where the shock was presented) and attend to a specific cue (for example,
the light). The two-way active avoidance training continues until the animal responds consistently to the specific cue (CS) and avoids the aversive electric
shock.

We learned earlier that increases in the aversiveness of an event facilitate
the acquisition of a passive avoidance response and a one-way active avoidance
behavior. In contrast, the literature (Moyer & Korn, 1964; Theios, Lynch, &
Lowe, 1966) clearly shows that a severe aversive event impairs rather than enhances the acquisition and the asymptotic performance level of a two-way active avoidance response. Let's examine one study to illustrate the influence of
aversive event severity on two-way active avoidance learning.

Moyer and Korn (1964) gave rats two-way active avoidance response training in periods of 30 trials a day for 4 days. In their study, after the CS (a tone)
was presented in one chamber, the rats had 5 seconds to run to the other chamber to avoid being shocked. Rats failing to respond within the 5-second interval
received either a .5-, 1.0-, 1.5-, or 2.5-ma. shock. Moyer and Korn found that as
shock intensity increased, the percentage of avoidance responses made during

electric shock impair an animal's ability to avoid shock in a two-way active
avoidance task.

Why do increases in shock severity impair two-way active avoidance learning, yet facilitate other forms of avoidance learning? Theios, Lynch, and Lowe (1966) suggested that in a two-way active avoidance task, the animal experiences conflict between running away from the feared stimulus and running into an environment where the aversive event occurred on the previous trial. According to Theios, Lynch, and Lowe, the more severe the aversive event, the greater the animal's reluctance to enter the environment associated with the aversive event and, therefore, the poorer the acquisition of an avoidance response. Many studies (Tarpy & Mayer, 1978) support Theios, Lynch, and Lowe's view; let's examine one of them.

Freedman, Hennessy, and Groner (1974) compared the efficiency of avoidance behavior when animals were running from a compartment associated with a high level of aversiveness into a compartment associated with less aversiveness to avoidance performance when both compartments were associated with equal shock severity. Freedman, Hennessy, and Groner theorized that the reluctance to avoid shock would decrease if animals were required to run to a less aversive compartment rather than an equally aversive compartment. In support of this view, they found that avoidance performance was enhanced if an animal was required to run into a chamber associated with a lower shock intensity.

The Delay Interval Between the CS and the UCS

We learned in Chapter 3 that the level of fear conditioning depends upon the CS-UCS interval; the longer the interval, the weaker the conditioning of the fear response. The interval between the CS and the UCS also affects the acquisition of an avoidance response. The literature (Hall, 1979) shows that the longer the CS-UCS interval, the slower the acquisition of the avoidance behavior. It seems reasonable to assume that the influence of the CS-UCS interval on fear conditioning is also responsible for its effect on avoidance learning; as the level of fear diminishes with longer CS-UCS intervals, motivation to escape the feared stimulus weakens and, therefore, the opportunity to learn to avoid it lessens. Let's next consider one study which examined the influence of the CS-UCS interval on avoidance behavior.

Kamin (1954) trained dogs to avoid shock by jumping over a barrier in a two-way active avoidance situation. The CS, a 2-second buzzer, preceded the shock UCS. The interval between the CS-UCS varied: subjects received either a 5-, 10-, 20-, or 40-second CS-UCS interval. Kamin reported that the shorter the interval between the CS and UCS, the quicker the acquisition of the avoidance response.

Application: Response Prevention or Flooding

Some psychologists, beginning with Watson, have hypothesized that phobias are learned avoidance behaviors. On the basis of this belief, techniques that are effective in eliminating avoidance behaviors in animals should be effective in eliminating phobic behaviors in humans. The problem with trying to extinguish phobic behavior is that because fear motivates avoidance of the phobic stimulus, the person will not experience the CS long enough to associate the CS with the absence of the UCS. Two treatments of phobic behavior, flooding and systematic desensitization, have been used to overcome this problem. We learned in Chapter 3 that systematic desensitization works by conditioning a relaxation response antagonistic to fear of the phobic object. Flooding forces the person to experience the feared stimulus and associate the CS with the absence of the UCS, thereby eliminating the avoidance behavior.

Flooding differs from the typical extinction procedure because the feared stimulus cannot be escaped. Otherwise, the two procedures are identical: the animal or human is exposed to the conditioned fear stimulus without an aversive consequence. Research investigating **response prevention,** or **flooding,** has demonstrated it to be an effective technique for eliminating avoidance behavior in animals (Baum, 1970). Baum found that the effectiveness of flooding increased with longer exposure to the fear stimulus. In addition, Coulter, Riccio, and Page (1969) found that flooding suppressed an avoidance response faster than a typical extinction procedure did.

Can flooding successfully eliminate avoidance behavior in humans? Malleson (1959) first reported the successful use of flooding to treat avoidance behavior in humans. Since Malleson's experiment, a large number of studies have demonstrated the effectiveness of flooding in treating a wide variety of behavior disorders, including phobias (Yule, Sacks, & Hersov, 1974), anxiety and neurosis (Girodo, 1974), and obsessive-compulsive behavior (Riggs & Foa, 1993; Steketee, 1993).

The following case history, which Meyer, Robertson, and Tatlovy reported in 1975, provides an example of the technique and its success in treating obsessive-compulsive disorder. An adult female client had become extremely disturbed about anything associated with death—even the newspaper obituary column elicited anxiety. When anxious, she compulsively washed herself and changed her clothes. Treatment began by identifying anxiety-inducing stimuli. The most aversive stimulus was dead bodies. Thus, the therapist and the patient handled a corpse at a local hospital mortuary. Treatment also involved exposure to other aversive stimuli—for example, a picture of a dead man. To prevent her ritualistic compulsive behavior, the therapist remained with her following her exposures to the feared stimuli. The authors reported that on the second treatment day, the patient was completely able to suppress the rituals. Eight months after the therapy, the woman had no inclination to perform ritualistic behaviors and demonstrated only a low level of anxiety to death-related stimuli.

Flooding appears to eliminate fear quite readily (Abramowitz, 1997). For example, Marks (1987) reported that an agorophobic's fear of a specific situation (e.g., going to a crowded shopping mall) can be eliminated in as few as three sessions. Further, the elimination of fear seems to be long lasting. Emmelkamp, van der Helm, van Zanten, and Plochg (1980) used flooding to treat a compulsive behavior. The level of the client's anxiety was measured before exposure to the feared stimulus, immediately afterwards, and 1 and 6 months later. Emmelkamp, van der Helm, van Zanten, and Plochg reported that the level of anxiety decreased significantly following exposure to the feared stimulus (see **Figure 5.7**). Most importantly, the client's decreased anxiety level persisted for

139

CHAPTER 5
Principles and
Applications of
Aversive
Conditioning

FIGURE 5.7. The client's perceived level of anxiety prior to flooding, immediately after flooding, and 1 and 6 months after flooding.

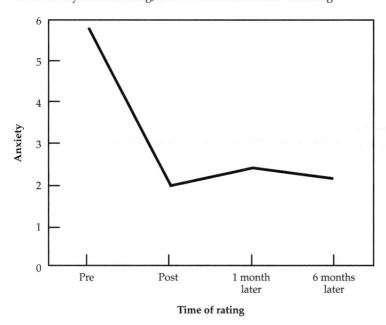

at least 6 months following treatment. While flooding has been shown to produce a faster decrease in anxiety than systematic desensitization (see Chapter 3), many patients have difficulty tolerating flooding (Gelder, 1991). In fact, many individuals will not participate in flooding because the initial anxiety is so great.

BEFORE YOU GO ON

- **Why did Edmond fail to avoid his boss's criticism?**
- **How could Edmond prevent future criticism?**

PUNISHMENT

A parent takes away a child's television privileges for hitting a younger sibling. A teacher sends a disruptive student to the principal to be suspended for three days from school. A soldier absent without leave is ordered to the stockade by the military police. An employee who is late for work faces a reprimand from the boss. Each of these situations is an example of punishment. **Punishment** is defined as the use of an aversive event contingent upon the occurrence of an inappropriate behavior. The intent of punishment is to suppress an undesired behavior; if punishment is effective, the frequency and intensity, or both, of the punished behavior will decline. For example, the parent who takes away a child's television privileges for hitting a younger sibling is using punishment to decrease the occurrence of the child's aggressive behavior. The loss of television is an effective punishment if, after being punished, the youngster hits the sibling less frequently.

Types of Punishers

We have defined punishment as the response-contingent presentation of an aversive event. There are two types of punishment: positive and negative. **Positive punishment** refers to the use of a physically or psychologically painful event as the punishment. A spanking is one example of a positive punisher; verbal criticism is another. In **negative punishment,** reinforcement is lost or unavailable as the consequence of an inappropriate behavior. The term **omission training** often is used in place of *negative punishment.* In omission training, reinforcement is provided when the undesired response does not occur, while the inappropriate behavior leads to no reinforcement.

There are two categories of negative punishment. One of these is **response cost,** in which an undesired response results in either the withdrawal of or failure to obtain reinforcement. In laboratory settings, a response cost contingency means that an undesired response will cause an animal or person to lose or not obtain either a primary reinforcer (i.e., candy or food) or a secondary reinforcer (i.e., chips, tokens, or points). Real-world examples of response cost punishment include the withdrawal or failure to obtain material reinforcers (i.e., money) or social reinforcers (i.e., approval). Losing television privileges for hitting a sibling is one example of response cost; being fined by an employer for being late for work is another.

The other kind of negative punishment is called **time-out from reinforcement** (or time-out). Time-out from reinforcement is a period of time during which reinforcement is unavailable. A child who is sent to his or her room after misbehaving is enduring time-out; so is the soldier going to the stockade for being AWOL.

Is punishment effective? Its extensive use in our society suggests that we believe punishment is an effective technique to suppress inappropriate behavior. However, psychology's view of the effectiveness of punishment has changed dramatically during the past 50 years. In the next section, we will examine how psychologists have viewed the effectiveness of punishment as a method of suppressing behavior.

The Effectiveness of Punishment

Skinner (1953) believed that punishment could only *temporarily* suppress behavior. The classic Skinner study (1938) supports this view. In his experiment, two rats were trained to bar press for food reinforcement. The rats' bar press response was then extinguished by discontinuing reinforcement. One rat was also punished for bar pressing by having his paw slapped when it touched the bar during the first few responses during extinction. The other rat did not receive punishment. Skinner observed that the initial effect of punishment was that the punished rat showed a lower response rate than that of the unpunished rat (see

141

CHAPTER 5
*Principles and
Applications of
Aversive
Conditioning*

Figure 5.8). However, the suppressive effect of punishment was short-lived; bar pressing was equivalent in the punished and the nonpunished rats within 30 minutes after punishment. Skinner also noted that the punished rat continued to respond at a high rate even after the nonpunished rat had slowed down. When both rats had finally stopped responding, both had made the same total number of responses. Skinner's observations show that punishment may temporarily suppress responding, but it does not eliminate it. Skinner suggested that extinction instead of punishment should be used to permanently suppress an inappropriate response. His conclusion certainly conflicts with our society's belief that punishment is an effective method of suppressing inappropriate behavior.

Research evaluating the influence of punishment on behavior during the 1950s and 1960s shows that under some conditions, punishment does permanently suppress inappropriate behavior (Campbell & Church, 1969). However, in other circumstances, punishment either has no effect on behavior or will only temporarily suppress behavior.

A number of variables determine whether punishment will suppress behavior, as well as how long the punished behavior will be inhibited. We will next discuss the conditions necessary for effective punishment and the circumstances in which punishment does not suppress inappropriate behavior.

When Is Punishment Effective?

Three factors have an important influence on the effectiveness of punishment. We will examine them next.

FIGURE 5.8. The effect of punishment on the extinction of the bar press response. Punishment produced a temporary reduction in bar pressing, but by the end of the second day, punishment no longer had any effect.

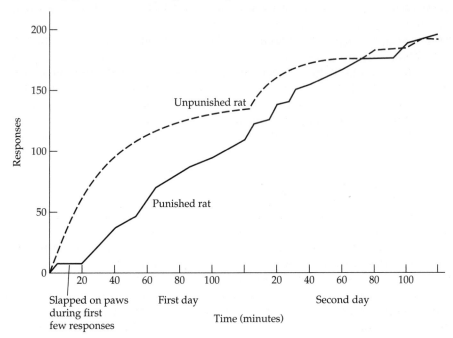

The Severity of Punishment

Most people in our society recognize the dangers of driving under the influence of alcohol. Local newspapers routinely report traffic fatalities caused by drunken drivers. Almost 41,000 persons were killed in 1999 in all traffic accidents in the United States. Of these 41,000 people, about 16,000 (or 38%) were alcohol-related crashes (National Highway Traffic Safety Board, 2000). Yet people continue to drive while intoxicated, and thousands of drunk drivers are ticketed each year. These drivers, though punished when apprehended, are most likely to drink and drive again. About 17% of fatally injured drivers in 1998 had a previous DUI conviction (National Highway Traffic Safety Board, 2000). Why are the punishments ineffective? One reason may be that the punishments are too mild to suppress drunk driving effectively. In most cases, the first offense is punished with participation in an alcohol treatment program rather than a jail sentence. Even repeat offenders rarely spend more than one year in prison.

Research has consistently shown that mild punishment produces little if any suppression of the punished response. Moreover, if any suppression does occur, it will be short-lived. The effectiveness of punishment also has been found to increase as its severity increases (Campbell & Church, 1969). Thus, a moderately severe punishment produces more suppression of an inappropriate behavior than a mild punishment, while a strong punishment is more likely to produce complete suppression of the punished behavior. Also, the more severe the punishment, the longer the punished behavior is inhibited. In fact, a severe punishment may lead to a permanent suppression of the punished response. We will examine several studies showing that the effectiveness of punishment depends upon the severity of the punishment next.

Numerous studies using animal subjects have reported that the greater the intensity of punishment, the more complete the suppression of the punished behavior (Church, 1969). Camp, Raymond, and Church's 1967 study provides an excellent example of the influence of the intensity of punishment on the degree of suppression of an operant behavior. In their study, 48 rats initially were given 8 training sessions to bar press for food reinforcement on a VI 1-minute schedule. Following initial training, the rats were divided into six groups and given either 0-, 0.1-, 0.2-, 0.3-, 0.5-, or 2.0-ma. shock punishments lasting for 2.0 seconds. An animal was punished if its response rate had not changed within the minute since it had last received punishment. As can be seen in **Figure 5.9,** the higher the intensity of shock, the greater the suppression of the operant response. These results indicate that the more severe the punisher, the more effective the shock will be in suppressing the punished response. The effect of shock intensity on the suppression of an operant response has been shown in a number of animal species, including monkeys (Hake, Azrin, & Oxford, 1967), pigeons (Azrin & Holz, 1966), and rats (Storms, Boroczi, & Broen, 1962).

Research conducted with human subjects has also demonstrated that the severity of punishment affects its effectiveness. A number of studies (Cheyne, Goyeche, & Walters, 1969; Parke & Walters, 1967) have evaluated the effect of the intensity of punishment on the suppression of playing with a forbidden toy. In these studies, children were punished with a loud noise for selecting one of a

143

CHAPTER 5
Principles and
Applications of
Aversive
Conditioning

FIGURE 5.9. The mean suppression ratio decreases, or the level of suppression increases, with higher intensities of electric shock during punishment training.

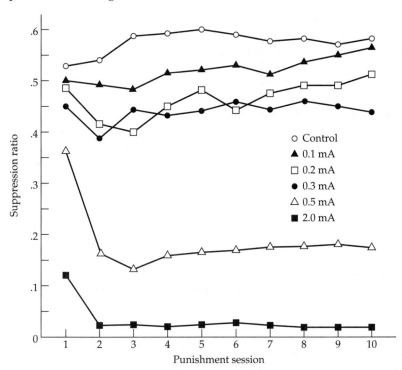

pair of toys. The noises ranged from 52 to 96 decibels, with 60 decibels being the loudness of normal conversation. After punishment, each child was isolated with toys that were either identical or similar to the toys presented at the beginning of the experiment. The studies recorded the latency for each child to touch the "wrong" toy as well as the length of time the child played with this toy. The results of these experiments show that the more intense the punishment, the greater the suppression of the child's play with the toy associated with punishment.

The severity of punishment also affects the level of response suppression in adults. Powell and Azrin (1968) punished their subjects for smoking cigarettes by using a specially designed cigarette case which delivers an electric shock when opened. Powell and Azrin reported that the smoking rate decreased as the intensity of shock increased. Similarly, Davidson (1972) found that as electric shock intensity increased, the rate of an alcoholic client's pressing a lever to obtain alcohol declined.

Addiction to smoking cigarettes generally begins in adolescence. The cigarette companies have been criticized for targeting advertising campaigns to children; and laws have been passed to prevent the sale of cigarettes to minors. Do these laws work? The answer depends upon whether the punishment for selling to minors is severe. Leonard Jason and his colleagues (Jason, Ji, Anes, & Birkhead, 1991; Jason, Ji, Anes, & Xaverious, 1992) have evaluated the influence of the severity of punishment on a store's compliance with laws prohibiting the sale of cigarettes to minors. Jason, Ji, Anes, and Birkhead (1991) measured the percentage of stores selling cigarettes to minors both before and after the Woodbridge, Illinois Town Council passed a local ordinance banning the sale of cigarettes to minors. Minors were sent into stores that sold cigarettes and the sale of (or refusal to sell) cigarettes to these minors was recorded. Prior to the ordinance, 70% of the stores sold cigarettes to minors. The ordinance provided a warning for the first offense. A $400 fine and a one-day suspension of the ability to sell cigarettes was the punishment for the second offense. Jason, Ji, Anes, and Birkhead reported that the percentage of stores selling to minors dropped to 33% after the ordinance was instituted. Many of the merchants who received a warning continued to sell to minors, but after receiving a $400 fine and one-day suspension, the percentage of these stores selling to minors dropped to 0% and remained at that level for the remainder of the 2-year study.

The Consistency of Punishment

In the last section, we learned that punishment must be severe to eliminate an undesired behavior, such as drunken driving. However, a severe punishment may not always be an effective method of suppressing this behavior. The literature shows that punishment must be consistently administered if it is to successfully eliminate inappropriate behavior. Thus, punishment should be given every time a person drives while intoxicated. Unfortunately, the odds of a drunken driver being caught are 1 in 2,000 (*Newsweek*, 1982). Rigorous observation of drivers is essential to detecting drunken drivers because a higher probability of being caught leads to a greater deterrence (Ross, 1981). In New South Wales, Australia, the likelihood of detection is high and the incidence of drunk driving low (Homel, McKay, & Henstridge, 1995). However, a high level of recording is not always feasible, and therefore drunken driving probably will continue despite the institution of severe penalties.

Numerous studies (Walters & Grusec, 1977) have demonstrated the importance of administering punishment consistently. In one of these studies, Azrin, Holz, and Hake (1963) trained rats to bar press for food reinforcement on a 3-minute VI schedule. A 240-volt shock was delivered following the response on FR punishment schedules ranging from FR-1 to FR-1,000. As **Figure 5.10** indicates, the level of suppression decreases as the punishment schedule increases. These results indicate that the less consistently the punishment is administered, the less effective the punishment is.

Research (Walters & Grusec, 1977) also points out that consistency influences the effectiveness of punishment in humans. For example, Parke and Deur (1972) reinforced 6- to 9-year-old boys with marbles for hitting a life-size Bobo doll. Then, without informing the subjects, Parke and Deur began punishing half of them with a loud buzzer every time they hit the doll; the other half were punished only 50% of the time they hit the doll and were reinforced the other 50% of the time. Parke and Deur found that the boys who received consistent punishment stopped hitting the doll sooner than those boys who were

145

CHAPTER 5
Principles and
Applications of
Aversive
Conditioning

FIGURE 5.10. This graph shows that the rate of bar press responding for food reinforcement delivered on a 3-minute variable-interval schedule increases with higher fixed-ratio schedules of punishment. The short, oblique lines indicate when punishment was delivered.

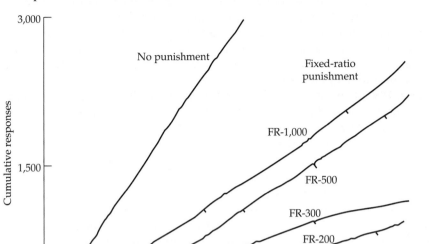

punished intermittently. In another experiment, Leff (1969) demonstrated that continuous punishment, compared with intermittent punishment, more effectively caused children to stop choosing an attractive toy and to select an unattractive toy instead.

Several correlational studies have evaluated the relationship between delinquency and the consistency of parental punishment. This research (Glueck & Glueck, 1950; McCord, McCord, & Zola, 1959) reported that delinquent boys were more likely to have received inconsistent parental discipline than nondelinquent boys. These findings suggest that parents who want to suppress their children's socially inappropriate behavior should be consistent in punishing that behavior.

Delay of Punishment

We have learned that in order for punishment to suppress undesired behavior such as drunken driving, the punishment must be severe and consistently administered. In this section, we will discover that punishment must also be immediate. The literature shows that the longer the delay between the inappropriate response and punishment, the less effective the punishment will be in suppressing the punished behavior. In our society, there is usually a long delay between a person's apprehension for drunken driving and the administration of a fine or jail sentence. Research on the delay of punishment shows this method is ineffective, suggesting that a shorter interval between the time of the offense and the time of sentencing should be implemented in order to maximize the effects of punishment.

The literature using animal subjects (Church, 1969) consistently demonstrates that immediate punishment is more effective than delayed punishment. The Camp, Raymond, and Church (1967) study provides an excellent example of this observation. After being trained to bar press for food reinforcement, rats in the Camp, Raymond, and Church experiment received a .25-ma. 1-second shock punishment either immediately, 2.0, 7.5, or 30 seconds after a bar press response. Camp, Raymond, and Church reported greatest suppression of the bar press response when shock occurred immediately after responding (see **Figure 5.11**).

Banks and Vogel-Sprott (1965) investigated the influence of delay of punishment (electric shock) on the level of suppression of their human subjects' reaction to a tone. These authors reported that although an immediate punishment inhibited responding, delayed punishment (for either 30, 60, or 120 seconds) did not affect response levels. Trenholme and Baron (1975) found a similar lack of effectiveness of delayed punishment in college students, and Abramowitz and O'Leary (1990) found the same in children. In the Abramowitz and O'Leary (1990) study, children were scolded in a classroom setting. A

FIGURE 5.11. The mean percentage of responses increases with greater delay of punishment (in seconds). The control group did not receive electric shock, and the NC group was given noncontingent shock.

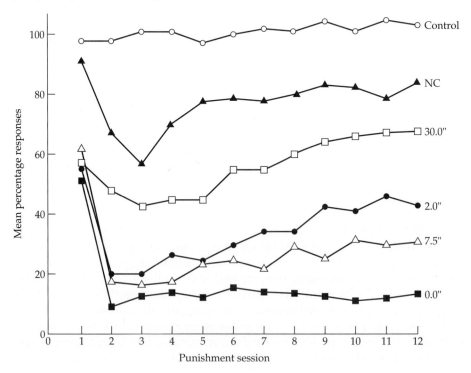

teacher's scolding was most effective when the punishment immediately followed the misbehavior.

147

CHAPTER 5
Principles and
Applications of
Aversive
Conditioning

BEFORE YOU GO ON

- **What behavior was Edmond's boss punishing?**
- **Did the punishment have the desired effect? Why or why not?**

The Negative Consequences of Punishment

The use of punishment has a number of negative consequences. In this section, we will examine some of these undesirable effects.

Pain-Induced Aggression

When animals or people are punished, they experience pain. This pain response may elicit the emotion of anger which, in turn, may arouse aggressive behavior. This discussion begins by looking at evidence that pain can produce aggression, followed by a review of studies that show why punishment can lead to aggression.

Azrin, Hutchinson, and Sallery (1964) observed that when primates are shocked, they attack other monkeys, rats, or mice. In addition, monkeys who are shocked will attack a toy tiger (Plotnick, Mir, & Delgado, 1971) or a ball (Azrin, 1964). Shock-induced aggressive attack has also been reported in cats (Ulrich, Wolff, & Azrin, 1964).

Leon Berkowitz and his associates (Berkowitz, 1971, 1978) have provided considerable support for the theory that anger induced by exposure to painful events can lead to aggression in humans. In one of these studies (Berkowitz & LePage, 1967), subjects were to list, within a period of 5 minutes, ideas a publicity agent could use to increase sales of a product. A confederate then rated some subjects' performance as poor by giving these subjects 7 electric shocks; this confederate shocked other subjects only once, to indicate a positive evaluation. According to Berkowitz and LePage, the 7-shock evaluation angered subjects, but the 1-shock evaluation did not. Next, all the subjects evaluated the confederate's performance by giving the confederate from 1 to 7 shocks. Subjects who had received 7 shocks retaliated by giving the confederate significantly more shocks than did the other subjects. These results indicate that painful events can motivate aggressive behavior.

We have seen that anger can result in aggressive behavior. However, this aggressive reaction is not motivated by the expectation of avoiding punishment; rather, it reflects an impulsive act energized by the emotional arousal characteristic of anger. Furthermore, the expression of aggressive behavior in angry animals or people appears to be highly reinforcing. Many studies show that annoyed animals will learn a behavior that gives them the opportunity to be aggressive. For example, Azrin, Hutchinson, and McLaughlin (1965) found that squirrel monkeys bit inanimate objects (for example, balls) after being shocked. However, if no object was present, they learned to pull a chain that provided them with a ball to bite.

Punishment does not always elicit aggressive behavior. Hokanson (1970) reported that people's previous experiences influence their reaction to painful events. If individuals have been reinforced for nonaggressive reactions to aversive events, punished for aggressive responses to painful events, or both, the likelihood that punishment will elicit aggression diminishes. Furthermore, the level of anger pain produces differs among individuals (Klein, 2000). Some people react intensely to an aversive event that only elicits mild anger in others. Since the probability that painful events will motivate aggression depends upon the level of anger the aversive circumstance induces, individuals who respond strongly to aversive events are much more likely to become aggressive than are people who are not very angered by aversive events.

The Modeling of Aggression

A child who has received a spanking for misbehaving may suppress the inappropriate behavior, may become aggressive, or may imitate the parent's aggressive behavior. The behavior we learn not by receiving explicit reinforcement but by observing another person's actions is called **modeling** (Bandura, 1971).

Bandura, Ross, and Ross's (1963) classic experiment illustrates the influence of a model on aggressive behavior. In this study, children saw an adult model act aggressively toward a life-sized plastic doll called a Bobo doll. The model sat on this doll, punched it, hit it with a mallet, kicked it, and tossed it up and down (see **Figure 5.12**). Other children in the study did not watch a model behave in this manner. After the initial phase of the study, all children were allowed to play with attractive toys, and then were frustrated by being required to leave these attractive toys for less attractive ones, including a Bobo doll. Bandura, Ross, and Ross recorded the level of imitative aggression (attacking the Bobo doll) and nonimitative aggression (aggressive behaviors the model had not performed). They found that while all the children exhibited nonimitative forms of aggression when they were frustrated, only the children who had watched the model showed the imitative patterns of aggression. These findings indicate that we can learn how to perform a particular behavior merely by watching others.

Other studies (Hanratty, Liebert, Morris, & Fernandez, 1969; Steuer, Applefield, & Smith, 1971) have also reported that children will imitate a model's aggressive behavior. For example, Steuer, Applefield, and Smith (1971) discovered that children who had viewed cartoons depicting aggressive behavior became more aggressive toward other children than children who had not seen the cartoons. The imitated aggression included hitting, pushing, kicking, squeezing, choking, or throwing objects at the other children. Furthermore, Hanratty, Liebert, Morris, and Fernandez (1969) reported that as the result of a modeling experience, children may even act aggressively toward an adult. In their study, young boys, after watching an aggressive model, attacked an adult dressed as a clown.

Do children who are physically punished, in turn, model this aggressive behavior? Two types of evidence support the view that they do. First, experimental research shows that children punished during a study use the same method of punishment when attempting to control the actions of other children. In one study, Mischel and Grusec (1966) verbally punished preschool-aged children for certain actions during a game; the children, in turn, employed verbal abuse toward other children playing the game. Similarly, Gelfand, Hartmann, Lamb, Smith, Mahan, and Paul (1974) found that children who had been penalized for incorrect responses during a game used this form of punishment when teaching another child to play.

149

*CHAPTER 5
Principles and
Applications of
Aversive
Conditioning*

Second, correlational studies report a strong relationship between parental use of punishment and the level of aggressive behavior in their children. Many parents use aggression in the form of a spanking or paddling to punish their children's behavior. Numerous studies (Larzelere, Schneider, Larson, & Pike, 1996; Weiss, Dodge, Bates, & Pettit, 1992) show that the use of aggression in the form of punishment leads to aggressive behavior in the child, both at school and at home. And not surprisingly, the more physical punishment parents use, the more aggressively their children act. Furthermore, many studies (Rohner, 1985; Straus & Kantor, 1994) have found that parents who abuse their children were themselves likely to have been abused by their parents. This observation suggests that children will imitate the abusive behavior of their parents and in turn may abuse their own children.

The Aversive Quality of a Punisher

We learned in Chapter 3 that environmental events present during an aversive event will become classically conditioned to elicit fear. In addition, we saw

FIGURE 5.12. The impact of observational learning (or modeling) of aggressive behavior. The children first watched the adult attack the Bobo doll (top panel). When later frustrated, the children imitated the model's aggressive response toward the Bobo doll (middle and bottom panels). These children also exhibited this form of aggressive behavior toward other children or adults. (Courtesy of Albert Bandura, Stanford University.)

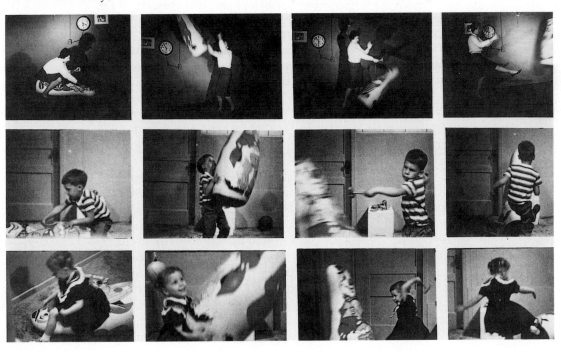

earlier in this chapter that fear motivates escape behavior. On the basis of these two observations, we should expect that because punishment is a painful event, the person providing the punishment, or the punisher, will become a conditioned stimulus capable of eliciting fear, which in turn should motivate the individual to escape from the punisher.

Azrin, Hake, Holz, and Hutchinson's study (1965) provides evidence that escape behavior occurs as the result of punishment. These psychologists first trained pigeons to key peck for food reinforcement on a fixed-ratio schedule and then punished each key peck response with electric shock. A distinctive stimulus was present during the punishment period, and the pigeons could peck at another key to terminate the cue that signaled punishment. The escape response also produced another stimulus that indicated that the original reinforcement-punishment key could be pecked safely. After the pigeons pecked the original key and received reinforcement, the safe cue was terminated and the dangerous stimulus reintroduced. Azrin, Hake, Holz, and Hutchinson reported that although the pigeons emitted few escape responses if the punishment was mild, the frequency of the escape response increased as the intensity of punishment increased until the pigeons spent the entire punishment period escaping from the cues associated with punishment.

A study by Redd, Morris, and Martin (1975) illustrates the aversive quality of a punisher in humans. In their study, 5-year-old children performed a task in the presence of an adult who made either positive comments ("You're doing well") or negative comments ("Stop throwing the tokens around" or "Don't play with the chair"). Redd, Morris, and Martin reported that although the punitive person was more effective in keeping the children on task, the children preferred working with the complimentary person.

However, little evidence supports the idea that clients escape punitive behavior therapists (Walters & Grusec, 1977). For example, Risley (1968) discovered that punishing autistic children's undesirable behavior with electric shock did not alter the children's eye contact with the therapist, who also reinforced the children's desirable responses. Other studies (Lovaas & Simmons, 1969) have also reported the absence of fear of and escape behavior from a punitive therapist. Walters and Grusec (1977) suggested that the therapist's use of reinforcement as well as punishment prevented the therapist and the therapy situation from becoming aversive and motivating escape behavior.

Additional Negative Effects of Punishment

There are two additional negative effects of punishment. First, the suppressive effects of punishment may generalize to similar behaviors; and the inhibition of these responses may be undesirable. For example, if a parent punishes a child for fighting with other children in the neighborhood, the punishment may generalize, causing the child to stop playing with these children. However, the effects of punishment do not always generalize to similar behaviors. Chapter 7 discusses the circumstances under which punishment does or does not generalize to other responses. A second negative effect of punishment is that the subject may not recognize the contingency between punishment and the undesired behavior; the aversive events may be perceived as being independent of behavior. In Chapter 8, we will discover that experiencing noncontingent aversive events can lead to helplessness and depression. Punishment is most likely to be perceived as being noncontingent when a delay occurs between the undesirable behavior and the punishment. The interval between a response and punishment makes it difficult for an animal or person to recognize that the behavior is responsible for the punishment. People must be informed of the relationship between their actions and punishment so that helplessness does not result from seemingly noncontingent aversive events.

151

CHAPTER 5
*Principles and
Applications of
Aversive
Conditioning*

Application: The Use of Punishment

The use of punishment to control human behavior is widespread in our society. The literature shows that most parents historically used punishment to govern the actions of their children. For example, Sears, Maccoby, and Levin (1957) reported that 99% of the parents of 379 kindergarten children used spanking as a form of punishment. Furthermore, Lefkowitz, Walder, and Eron (1963) reported that 57% of the parents of third-grade children in their study used physical punishment to control their children's actions. Concerns over the negative effects of punishment led many professionals in the 1970s and 1980s to discourage the use of spanking as a means of behavioral control (Rosellini, 1998). Yet, many of my students report having been spanked by a parent for some misconduct. Has any irreparable harm been done to my students? Probably not. An occasional spanking, as long as it is combined with other forms of discipline and the use of positive reinforcement for desired behavior, has not been found to be detrimental to a child's development (Larzelere, 1996).

Teachers have also traditionally employed negative events to modify students' disruptive actions. White's analysis (1975) of teacher-pupil interactions reported that while teachers showed approval of good academic performance, they also expected appropriate social behavior. Any disruptive behavior by a student produced strong disapproval from teachers. Also, Madsen, Madsen, Saudargas, Hammond, and Edgar (1970) found that 77 percent of elementary school teachers' interactions with their students were punitive.

Other individuals in our culture also employ punishment to control behavior. Police officers ticket traffic violators, the IRS jails tax evaders, the army court-martials AWOL soldiers, and employers fire employees who are habitually late for work. The following section examines several punishment procedures that psychologists report are successful in modifying undesired human activity.

Positive Punishment

We learned earlier in this chapter that positive punishment is the presentation of a painful event contingent upon the occurrence of an undesired behavior. We also learned that punishment will be effective when it is severe, occurs immediately after the undesired response, and is consistently presented. But how effective is positive punishment in altering problem behaviors in humans? The literature (Masters, Burish, Hollon, & Rimm, 1987) shows that punishment can be quite successful in suppressing human behavior. Let's examine the evidence.

Lang and Melamed (1969) described the use of punishment to suppress the persistent vomiting of a 12-pound, 9-month-old child (see **Figure 5.13**). The child

FIGURE 5.13. The photo on the left shows a 12-pound, 9-month-old child whose persistent vomiting left him seriously ill. The use of punishment suppressed vomiting within 6 sessions (1 per day) and, as the photo on the right shows, enabled the child to regain normal health. (Courtesy of Peter Lang.)

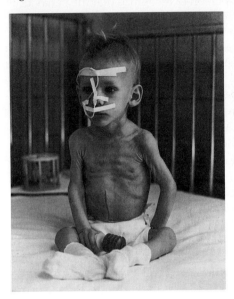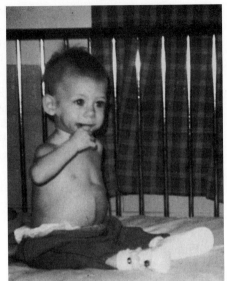

vomited most of his food within 10 minutes after eating, despite the use of various treatments (e.g., dietary changes, use of antinauseants, and frequent small feedings). Lang and Melamed detected the beginning of vomiting with an electromygram (EMG), which measures muscle activity. When the EMG indicated vomiting had begun, the child received an electric shock to the leg; the shock stopped when the child ceased vomiting. After the child had received 6 punishment sessions (1 per day), he no longer vomited after eating. Six months following treatment, the child showed no further vomiting and was of normal weight. Cunningham and Linscheid (1976) and Toister, Condron, Worley, and Arthur (1975) have also found punishment an effective way to suppress life-threatening vomiting in very young children. Furthermore, Galbraith, Byrick, and Rutledge (1970) successfully used punishment to curtail the vomiting of a 13-year-old retarded boy, while Kohlenberg (1970) reported that punishment suppressed the vomiting of a 21-year-old retarded adult.

Many other behaviors have also been successfully modified through response-contingent punishment. Behaviors reported to have been suppressed by punishment include obsessive ideation (Kenny, Solyom, & Solyom, 1973), the self-mutilating behavior and tantrum activity of autistic and retarded children (Lovaas, Koegel, Simmons, & Long, 1973), chronic cough (Creer, Chai, & Hoffman, 1977), and gagging (Glasscock, Friman, O'Brien, & Christopherson, 1986).

Although positive punishment has been effectively used to suppress a wide variety of undesired behaviors, one problem that sometimes arises with punishment therapy is the patient's difficulty generalizing suppression from the therapy situation to the real world. The Risley (1968) study provides evidence that the suppression of a punished behavior can be generalized. Risley used electric shock punishment to treat the continual climbing behavior of a 6-year-old hyperactive girl. Although Risley's treatment suppressed the climbing during the therapy situation, no change occurred in the frequency of this behavior at home. Risley then visited the home and showed the mother how to use the electric shock device. When the mother punished her daughter's climbing, the frequency of this behavior declined from 29 to 2 instances a day within 4 days and disappeared completely within a few weeks. You might feel this procedure is barbaric. However, the mother had attempted to control the climbing by spanking the child, and believed the spanking to be more unpleasant and "brutalizing" for both herself and her daughter, as well as less effective, than the shock. As Masters, Burish, Hollon, and Rimm (1987) point out, "many therapists feel that a minimal number of mild shocks is more humane than the continual but ineffective spanking or shaming of a child."

153

CHAPTER 5
*Principles and
Applications of
Aversive
Conditioning*

Response Cost

A colleague recently told me of a problem with his daughter, who was having trouble seeing the blackboard at school. When he suggested that she move to the front row of her classes, she informed him that she was already sitting there. An optometrist examined her and discovered that her eyesight was extremely poor; she was to wear glasses all of the time. Despite choosing a pair of glasses she liked, she indicated an extreme dislike for wearing them. After waiting a reasonable adjustment period and discovering that encouragement and praise were ineffective in persuading his daughter to wear the glasses, the father informed her that she would lose 50 cents of her weekly allowance every time he saw her without them. Although she was not pleased with this arrangement, she did not lose any of her allowance and no longer expresses unhappiness about wearing her glasses.

My colleague was able to modify his daughter's behavior by using a response cost procedure, which is a form of negative punishment. As we discovered earlier in the chapter, response cost refers to a penalty or fine contingent upon the occurrence of an undesired behavior. Thus, my colleague's daughter was to be fined when she did not wear her glasses. Psychologists (Kalish, 1981) have consistently observed that response cost is an effective technique for suppressing inappropriate behavior. Let's look at one study which has examined the use of response cost to alter behavior.

Peterson and Peterson's study (1968) illustrates the effectiveness of response cost in suppressing self-injurious behavior. The subject was a 6-year-old boy who had been severely mutilating himself; the experimenters reinforced him with a small amount of food when he refrained from self-injurious behavior during a 3- to 5-second period. However, if the boy exhibited self-injurious behavior, the reinforcer did not occur. Peterson and Peterson reported that they completely eliminated the boy's self-injurious behavior with the response cost procedure.

A wide range of other undesired behaviors have been successfully eliminated by using a response cost procedure. In an extensive investigation of the application of response cost, Kazdin (1972) discovered that response cost has been used to inhibit smoking, overeating, stuttering, psychotic speech, aggressiveness, and tardiness. In addition, response cost eliminated perseverative speech (Reichle, Brubakken, & Tetrault, 1976) and hyperactive behavior (Wolf, Hanley, King, Lachowicz, & Giles, 1970).

Time-Out from Reinforcement

Time-out from reinforcement, another form of negative punishment, refers to a program in which the occurrence of an inappropriate behavior results in a loss of access to reinforcement for a specified period of time. In time-out, the individual can either be removed from a reinforcing environment or from the reinforcement itself. For example, a child who hits a sibling while watching television and is sent to his or her room for a half an hour, and an overweight person who decides he cannot dine out for a week for violating his diet, are both using time-out.

It is important that if a time-out area is employed, it must not be reinforcing. Thus, sending a disruptive child to his or her room as a time-out may not stop the disruptive behavior if the room contains attractive toys and the child finds it pleasurable to be there. In fact, the frequency of disruptive behavior may actually increase if the time-out area is reinforcing. Solnick, Rincover, and Peterson's (1977) study illustrates this. They established a time-out contingent upon tantrum behavior in the treatment of a 6-year-old autistic child. Exposure to a sterile time-out environment was contingent upon the occurrence of self-stimulating behavior, and presentation of this environment increased rather than decreased the occurrence of tantrum behavior. When the investigators made physical restraint contingent upon tantrum behavior, the frequency of tantrums rapidly declined.

A wide variety of behaviors have been suppressed using time-out from reinforcement. For example, Drabman and Spitalnik (1973) reported that time-out suppressed disruptive behavior of male adolescents in a psychiatric hospital. Initial recordings showed that the adolescents exhibited very high rates of several disruptive behaviors, including physical aggression, verbal abuse, and disregard of rules. The researchers instituted a time-out procedure that placed the boys in a small room for 10 minutes if they had been physically aggressive or had left their seats without permission. The verbal abuse was not a target of intervention and, therefore, its occurrence did not result in time-out. Drabman and Spitalnik found that the level of physical aggression and disregard of rules decreased significantly after the time-out procedure had been established. In contrast, the unpunished verbal abuse did not decline. These observations demonstrate that time-out from reinforcement produces a specific reduction of behaviors contingent upon it but does not affect unpunished activity.

Elementary school children often exhibit disruptive behavior during gym class. White and Bailey (1990) punished disruptive behavior in a gym class by having the misbehaving child go sit on the side of the room, where he or she remained until all the sand had flowed through a large hourglass (which took about three minutes). Following the institution of this time-out procedure, the level of misbehavior during gym class dropped by 95%. MacPherson, Candee, and Hohman (1974) found that time-out could inhibit disruptive lunchroom activity in elementary school children, while Barton, Guess, Garcia, and Baer

(1970) observed that the disruptive behavior of retarded children during meals could be suppressed by the use of a time-out reinforcement procedure. Other behaviors that time-out has suppressed include thumb sucking (Baer, 1962) and tantrum behavior in autistic children (Wolf, Risley, & Mees, 1964) and in normal children (Wahler, Winkel, Peterson, & Morrison, 1965).

155

CHAPTER 5
*Principles and
Applications of
Aversive
Conditioning*

The Ethical Use of Punishment

When is the use of punishment permissible? The Eighth Amendment of the Constitution of the United States mandates: "Excessive bail shall not be required, nor excessive fines imposed, nor cruel and unusual punishments inflicted." What constitutes cruel and unusual punishment? When can a teacher use punishment to discipline a disruptive student, or a psychologist use punishment in therapy? The federal courts have indicated that some use of aversive remedial treatment is permissible. However, the treatment may be considered unconstitutional if it "violates minimal standards of decency, is wholly dispropriate to the alleged offense, or goes beyond what is necessary" (Schwitzgebel & Schwitzgebel, 1980).

Many unjustified uses of punishment have been used in our society. For example, the courts ruled in *Wright versus McMann* (1972) that punishing an inmate in a "psychiatric observation cell" by forcing him to sleep nude on a concrete floor in cold temperatures without soap, towels, or toilet paper constituted cruel and unusual punishment. Similarly, the courts found that it is cruel and unusual punishment to administer apormorphine (to induce vomiting) to nonconsenting mental patients (*Knecht versus Gillman*, 1973) or to forcefully administer an intramuscular injection of a tranquilizer to a juvenile inmate for a rules infraction (*Nelson versus Heyne*, 1974).

Do these abuses mean that aversive punishment procedures may never be employed? Punishment can be used to eliminate undesired behavior; however, the rights of the individual must be safeguarded. The preamble to the American Psychological Association's *Ethical Principles of Psychologists* (1992) clearly states that "psychologists respect the dignity and worth of the individual and strive for the presentation and protection of fundamental human rights. They are committed to increasing knowledge of human behavior and of people's understanding of themselves and others and to the utilization of such knowledge for the promotion of human welfare. While pursuing these objectives, they make every effort to protect the welfare of those who seek their skills."

The welfare of the individual has been safeguarded in a number of ways (see Schwitzgebel & Schwitzgebel, 1980). For example, the doctrine of "the least restrictive alternative" dictates that less severe methods of punishment must be tried before severe treatments are used. For example, Ohio Law (1977) allows "aversive stimuli" to be used for seriously disruptive behavior only after other forms of therapy have been attempted. Further, an institutional review board or human rights committee must evaluate whether the use of punishment is justified. According to Stapleton (1975), justification should be based on "the guiding principle that the procedure should entail a relatively small amount of pain and discomfort relative to a large amount of pain and discomfort if left untreated."

Concern for the individual should not be limited to the institutional use of punishment. The ethical concerns the American Psychological Association outlines should apply to all instances in which punishment is used. Certainly abuse by parents, family, and peers is of as great or greater concern than punishment administered by psychologists in the treatment of behavior disorders. A child has as much right to protection from cruel and unusual punishment at the hands of a parent as a patient does with a therapist. Adherence to ethical standards in administering punishment ensures an effective yet humane method of altering inappropriate behavior.

BEFORE YOU GO ON

- **What were the negative consequences of Edmond's boss's criticism?**
- **How could these negative consequences of punishment have been prevented?**

CHAPTER SUMMARY

Animals and people can learn to escape from an aversive event. Three variables affect the rate of acquisition of a behavior that terminates an aversive event. First, the more intense the aversive event, the faster the acquisition of an escape response. Second, the greater the decrease in the severity of the aversive event following the escape behavior, the more rapid the learning of the escape response. Third, the shorter the delay of reward following the escape behavior, the faster the acquisition of the escape response.

An escape response can also be extinguished. An animal or person may stop responding if the aversive event is no longer presented; however, fear conditioned during escape learning may impair the extinction of the escape response. Extinction typically occurs if the escape response is punished. The exception is in vicious-circle behavior, in which termination of the aversive event follows punishment of the escape response. In vicious-circle behavior, the escape response continues despite the fact that the failure to escape is not punished.

Some unpleasant circumstances can be prevented, and in these cases, a specific overt behavior can be used to avoid aversive events; in other instances, the suppression of response will prevent the aversive event. The severity of the aversive event influences the acquisition of the avoidance response. In some tasks (passive avoidance learning and one-way active avoidance learning), increases in the severity of the aversive event lead to faster avoidance learning. In other tasks (two-way active avoidance learning), an increase in the intensity of the aversive event produces slower acquisition. The CS-UCS interval also influences the rate of avoidance acquisition; the longer the interval between the CS and UCS, the slower the acquisition of the avoidance response.

157

CHAPTER 5
*Principles and
Applications of
Aversive
Conditioning*

Flooding is one viable option for treating human phobias and obsessive-compulsive behaviors. With the flooding technique, the person is prevented from exhibiting the avoidance response. The success of flooding depends upon providing sufficient exposure to the feared stimulus to extinguish the avoidance response.

Punishment is the presentation of an aversive event contingent on the occurrence of an undesired response. There are two classes of punishment. Positive punishment represents the presentation of a painful event after the occurrence of an undesired response. Negative punishment is the loss of reinforcement (response cost) or the inability to obtain reinforcement for a specified period of time (time-out), which is contingent on the occurrence of an inappropriate behavior.

Although Skinner assumed that punishment only temporarily suppresses the punished response, in some circumstances, punishment can permanently suppress undesired behavior. The effectiveness of punishment depends on three factors: the more severe the aversive event, the greater the behavioral suppression; the more consistent the punishment, the more suppression of the behavior; and the shorter the delay between punishment and the undesired behavior, the more suppression of the punished response.

Punishment has a number of potential negative effects. It can elicit aggressive behavior. The punished individual may model the use of punishment as a means of behavioral control. The environment in which punishment occurs may become aversive, thereby motivating escape behavior. The effects of punishment may generalize to other nonpunished behavior. And the contingency between behavior and punishment may go unrecognized, leading to learned helplessness.

Aversive events have been successfully used to alter undesired human behavior. However, safeguards must be established to protect individuals from cruel and unusual punishment. Adherence to ethical standards of conduct should allow the use of punishment as a method of influencing behavior while ensuring that those punished will experience less discomfort than they would if the treatment had not been employed.

CRITICAL THINKING QUESTIONS

1. Raul immediately drops a class as soon as he earns a poor grade. Suggest several reasons for Raul's behavior. How might Raul's parents persuade him not to withdraw from classes?
2. Vivica has a fear of heights. Describe how a psychologist might use flooding to eliminate Vivica's fear of heights. What problems might Vivica encounter during flooding? How can these problems be prevented?
3. Jane constantly bites her nails, and her parents have decided to punish her nail biting. Describe a psychologically sound punishment procedure that Jane's parents can use to suppress her nail biting. Why did you use the procedure that you selected? Discuss any problems that might be expected and how you would prevent these problems.

KEY TERMS

active avoidance response
escape response
flooding
modeling
negative punishment
omission training

pain-induced aggression
passive avoidance
   response
positive punishment
punishment
response cost

response prevention
time-out from
   reinforcement
vicious-circle behavior

CHAPTER 6

Traditional Learning Theories

The Oldies but Goodies

Justin goes to the movies every Friday night. The Cinema Theater shows classic movies like On the Waterfront *and* To Kill a Mockingbird. *Although he has not missed a show in almost a year, Justin was not always a fan of the classics. Before going to college, his favorite kind of movies were science fiction and adventure films. Justin especially enjoyed the* Star Wars *movies; he probably saw each* Star Wars *movie at least three times. Some of his friends are not as avid about movies, but Justin enjoys them so much that he often goes by himself. His new preference developed in his first semester at school. He met with his advisor during enrollment to discuss the courses he should take. Four courses were required, but he could enroll in one course of his choosing. His advisor gave him a list of courses that would fulfill the University's General Education program. As he looked over the list, he spotted a course entitled* "Introduction to Motion Pictures" *offered by the Theatre Department. Since he liked movies so much, Justin decided to take the course. At the first class, he received a list of 15 movies the class would see that semester. Justin had not seen most of the movies on the list, and several of the films were not familiar to him. His instructor informed the class that they would discuss each film's strengths and weaknesses after seeing it. The first movie the class saw was* High Noon. *Justin had seen many Western movies, but none compared with this one. It was not only action packed, but it revealed well-defined characters. The next week, he saw* Grapes of Wrath. *He could not believe he would like a black-and-white movie, but it was wonderful. Every week, he saw a new and exciting movie. Justin started going to the theatre in town every Friday night around the middle of the semester. The theater showed a Humphrey Bogart film festival, and several students in the class asked Justin to go. The Bogart movies were great, and he had a super time. He is now hooked on classic movies.*

Why does Justin go to the movies every Friday night? It seems his past enjoyable experiences are responsible for his present behavior. Yet how have Justin's experiences been translated into actions? Many psychologists have speculated on the nature of the learning process. Some theories attempt to explain the basis of all human actions, while others focus on specific aspects of the learning process. Some theories would attempt to describe both why Justin likes movies and why he goes to the theater every Friday. In contrast, other theories would tell us either why Justin enjoyed movies or why he went on Friday night.

In this chapter, we will examine several different global theories of learning; that is, several views that attempt to explain all aspects of behavior. Global theories emerged in the 1930s and were especially popular into the late 1960s. These global views have provided us with considerable knowledge concerning the nature of learning. Over the past 30 years, psychologists have focused on more specific aspects of the learning process. In Chapter 9, we will describe the reasons for the shift from global to more specific learning theories. We also will discuss what these theories have to say about the nature of specific learning processes.

TRADITIONAL LEARNING THEORIES

Two major theoretical approaches have been proposed to explain the nature of the learning process. The **S-R (stimulus-response) associative theorists** advocate a mechanistic view of the learning process. Learning, according to the S-R approach, occurs when an originally neutral environmental stimulus develops the ability to elicit a specific response through association with another stimulus that innately elicits the response. In contrast, the **cognitive theorists** advocate a mentalistic view of the learning process. Learning, according to the cognitive approach, involves a recognition of when important events, such as reward and punishment, are likely to occur and an understanding of how to attain reward and avoid punishment. Cognitive theorists propose a flexible view of behavior, which contrasts with the inflexible approach of the S-R theorists.

The S-R approach assumes that the stimulus environment controls behavior, while the cognitive approach proposes that mental processes control behavior. We begin by describing the S-R theories and then discuss the cognitive theories. In Chapter 7, we will further examine the stimulus environment's control of behavior. A detailed discussion of the cognitive control of behavior will follow in Chapter 8.

S-R ASSOCIATIVE THEORIES

Two very different S-R associative theories exist: one proposes that reward is necessary in order to learn an S-R association, while the other proposes that the only necessity is for the response to occur in the stimulus context. We begin by looking at the view that reward is necessary to learn an S-R association, followed by a discussion of the theory that contiguity is sufficient for S-R learning.

Hull's Drive Theory

Clark Hull (1943, 1952) developed the theory that drive motivates behavior and that drive reduction is responsible for S-R associative learning. Hull incorporated Woodworth's concept of drive into his S-R associative theory. In 1918, Robert S. Woodworth introduced the concept of **drive** to psychology. He defined drive as an intense internal force that motivates behavior. But how is drive translated into behavior? Hull provided us with many important insights into the nature of the learning process.

Hull thought that the combined influence of several factors determines the intensity of instrumental activity. In addition to drive (or D), Hull thought that the **incentive motivation** for reward (or K), the **habit strength,** or strength of the S-R association (H), and the level of inhibition (or I) control the likelihood of behavior occurring. Hull also developed a mathematical equation to express how these variables jointly determine the intensity of a response. According to Hull:

excitatory Potential

Behavioral potential ($_sE_R$) = drive (D) × incentive motivation (K) ×

event |
behavior habit strength (H) − inhibition (I)

The behavioral potential reflects the likelihood that a specific event (S) will cause the occurrence of a specific behavior (R). Hull assumed that the behavioral potential level is determined by the intensity of (1) drive (D), or the internal arousal state produced by deprivation, the presence of intense environmental events, or stimuli associated with deprivation or intense environmental events; (2) incentive motivation (K), or the internal arousal produced by reward or the stimuli associated with reward; (3) habit strength (H), or the strength of the connection between the stimulus and response produced when the response reduces drive; and (4) inhibition (I), or the suppression of a response produced when that response fails to produce reward. The factors influencing each aspect of the theory are presented in **Figure 6.1.** In Hull's view, accurate prediction of behavior is possible only when the predictor knows each factor in the mathematical relationship.

Consider the following example to illustrate Hull's theory. Imagine the "butterflies" that you experience before taking a test. The scheduled exam creates this arousal, or nervousness; the prior scheduling of the exam is an

FIGURE 6.1. Diagram of Hull's theory. The terms in the circles show the major variables influencing the likelihood of behavior. Drive (D), habit strength (H), and incentive (K) increase the excitatory potential ($_sE_R$), enhancing the likelihood that the stimulus will elicit a particular response. By contrast, inhibition (I) decreases excitatory potential. The terms in the rectangles represent the secondary processes that influence each major process.

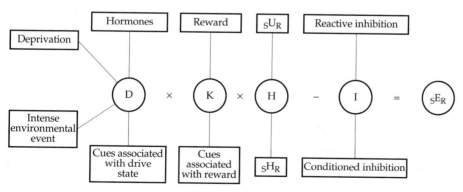

antecedent condition producing the internal drive state. Your nervousness motivates behavior that in the past reduced this drive; ideally, this behavior includes studying. We begin by examining the antecedent conditions inducing drive and motivating behavior.

Unconditioned Sources of Drive

Hull (1943) proposed that events that threaten survival (for example, failure to obtain food) activate the internal drive state. Survival requires that internal biological systems operate effectively. A deficit in these internal systems threatens survival and thus represents, according to Hull, an antecedent condition that will motivate behavior designed to restore biological systems to normal. In some cases, an internal adjustment may restore normal functioning. For instance, in the absence of food, an individual will use stored energy to maintain normal functioning. However, if the deficiency persists, behavior will be initiated to resolve the deficiency. Thus, using too much stored energy motivates the animal to obtain food.

In 1952, Hull acknowledged that events that do not threaten survival can also motivate behavior. Several types of studies forced Hull to acknowledge that an internal drive state can appear even in the absence of deprivation. First, animals show a strong preference for saccharin, consuming large quantities even when they are not hungry. Although saccharin has no caloric value, deprived animals will eat it rather than a more nutritionally valuable food. In addition, hungry rats can learn an instrumental behavior to obtain saccharin (Sheffield & Roby, 1950). Thus, instrumental behavior can occur in the absence of a biologically induced deficiency.

Several classes of nondeprivation events can induce drive and motivate behavior. Hull assumed that intense environmental events motivate behavior by activating the internal drive state. Electrical shock is one external stimulus that can induce internal arousal and motivate defensive behavior. The shock may be aversive, but it does not necessarily threaten survival.

A number of circumstances, including deprivation and intense environmental events, can produce the internal drive state that motivates behavior. These events instinctively produce drive. However, many stimuli in our environment acquire the capacity to induce the internal drive state. Let's examine how external cues develop the capacity to motivate behavior.

Acquired Drives

Hull (1943) suggested that, through Pavlovian conditioning, environmental stimuli can acquire the ability to produce an internal drive state. According to this view, the association of environmental cues with the antecedent conditions that produce an unconditioned drive state causes the development of a conditioned drive state. Once this conditioned drive state has developed, these cues can induce internal arousal and motivate behavior on subsequent occasions, even in the absence of the stimuli that induce the unconditioned drive state.

Consider the following example to illustrate Hull's **acquired drive** concept. A person goes to the ball park on a very hot day. Thirst, produced by the heat, motivates this person to go to the concession stand and consume several beers. The beers reduce the thirst, and because of this experience, the person will feel thirst even on cool days when walking past the concession stand and may well purchase a beer. This person has acquired a conditioned drive associated with the stimulus of the concession stand.

The Reinforcing Function of Drive Reduction

From the Hullian view, drive motivates behavior, but each specific behavior depends on the environment; that is, environmental events direct behavior. Which behavior does a specific stimulus elicit? Hull thought that when an animal is motivated (drive exists), the environmental cue present automatically elicits a specific response—the response with the strongest habit strength. The strength of the habit can be innate ($_sU_R$) or can be acquired through experience ($_sH_R$).

How does habit strength develop? If a response reduces the drive state, the bond between the stimulus and response is strengthened; thus, habit strength can increase as the result of drive reduction. Habit strength increases each time the behavior produces drive reduction.

Let's examine how the Hullian view of reinforcement would explain a person eating a hot dog at the ball park. This person's primary drive initially motivated behavior to reduce hunger. After a trip to the concession stand and the purchase and consumption of a hot dog, hunger was eliminated. Hull would assert that the drive reduction strengthened the bond between the concession stand and eating a hot dog. Each subsequent experience strengthens the bond until the behavior becomes habitual.

The Elimination of Unsuccessful Behavior

According to Hull, unsuccessful behavior causes drive to persist. If drive persists, all behavior is temporarily inhibited—a process referred to as **reactive inhibition.** When the reactive inhibition declines, the habitual behavior will occur again. The continued failure of the response to reduce drive leads to a permanent **conditioned inhibition.**

Conditioned inhibition is specific to a particular response, and it acts to reduce the excitatory strength of the habit. The continued failure of one behavior to reduce drive elicits the second strongest response in the **habit hierarchy.** If this behavior successfully produces drive reduction, the habit strength of this response increases. This effective habit will become the dominant habit, and will again be elicited when the animal is motivated. If the second habit in the hierarchy is ineffective, the animal will continue down the habit hierarchy until a successful response occurs.

Incentive Motivation

To suggest that a person would continue to visit the concession stand if it no longer stocked hot dogs is probably inaccurate; the behavior does reflect, to some degree, a specific desire to eat hot dogs. Hull's 1943 theory assumed that drive reduction or reward only influences the strength of the S-R bond; a more valuable reward produces greater drive reduction and, therefore, establishes a stronger habit. Once the habit is established, motivation depends on the drive level but not the reward value.

However, numerous studies have shown that the value of the reward has an important influence on motivational level. For example, Crespi (1942) found that shifts in reward magnitude produced a rapid change in rats' runway performance for food. When he increased the reward magnitude from 1 to 16 pellets on the twentieth trial, the rats' performance after just two or three trials equaled that of animals that had always received the higher reward. If reward magnitude influenced only the learning level, as Hull suggested, the change in runway speed should have been gradual. The rapid shift in the rats' behavior indicates that reward magnitude influenced their motivation; the use of a larger reward increased the rats' motivational level. A similar rapid change in behavior occurred when the reward was decreased from 256 to 16 pellets. These rats quickly decreased their running speed to a level equal to that of rats receiving the lower reward on each trial. **Figure 6.2** presents the results of Crespi's study.

The results of these experiments convinced Hull (1952) that reward magnitude affects the intensity of the motivation producing instrumental behavior. According to Hull, a large reward produces a greater arousal level, and thereby more motivation to act, than does a small reward. Furthermore, he theorized that the environmental stimuli associated with reward acquire incentive motivation properties, and that the cues present with a large reward will produce a greater conditioned incentive motivation than stimuli associated with a small reward. The importance of these acquired incentive cues is most evident when the reward cannot be seen; the cues associated with large reward elicit a greater approach to reward than do cues associated with a small reward.

FIGURE 6.2. Speed in the runway as a function of the magnitude of reinforcement. The rats received 1, 16, and 256 pellets of food. (The acquisition data for the 1-pellet group are not presented.) Sixteen pellets were given to each rat after trial 20. A shift from 1 to 16 pellets produced a rapid increase in performance, while a rapid decline in speed occurred when reward magnitude was lowered from 256 to 16 pellets.

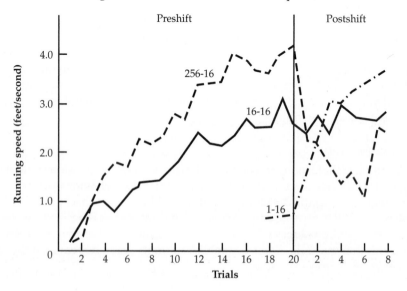

Hull's drive view represented the dominant behavioral theory from the 1930s to the 1960s. Many of Hull's ideas do accurately reflect important aspects of human behavior: (1) intense arousal can motivate behavior; (2) environmental stimuli can develop the ability to produce arousal, thereby motivating behavior; and (3) the value of reward influences the intensity of instrumental behavior. Evidence of the validity of these aspects of Hull's drive theory appears throughout the text. Although Hull's drive theory developed from research with animals, psychologists have used it to explain the basis of many human behaviors.

However, Hull's drive concept has encountered some difficulties. His concept of reward has proved to be inaccurate; that is, reward and drive reduction are not synonymous. Two types of evidence challenge the drive-reduction view of reward. First, numerous experiments—the initial study by Olds and Milner in 1943 is classic—demonstrate that direct stimulation of the brain is reinforcing. Olds and Milner placed a small wire, an electrode, into a rat's brain and passed an electrical current through the electrode. They noted that their rats learned to bar press to obtain brain stimulation. Other studies have reported that rats will learn the correct path in a maze for this reward (Mendelson & Chorover, 1965). The rewarding property of brain stimulation argues against a drive-reduction interpretation.

Sheffield (1966) argued that drive induction rather than reduction strengthens instrumental behavior. In addition, according to Sheffield, rewards produce excitement or arousal, which motivates subsequent behavior. For example, the excitement produced by the presentation of food motivates approach behavior; the food itself subsequently motivates eating. This interpretation of reward explains how secondary rewards acquire the ability to elicit behavior through association with primary rewards; this characteristic of secondary, or learned, rewards was an enigma in the Hullian view. A secondary reward (for example, money) not only rewards behavior but also motivates future behavior. The drive-induction interpretation also explains the observation that sensory-deprived animals are motivated to obtain stimulation. For example, Butler and Harlow (1954) discovered that monkeys learned an **operant response** so they could view a normal laboratory environment from their isolation chamber.

Hull's drive theory focused on the acquisition of habitual reactions. Although he did indicate that environmental stimuli associated with reward could acquire the ability to motivate behavior through the classical conditioning process, Hull did not specify the mechanism responsible for the motivational influence of these environmental stimuli. Following Hull's death in 1952, Kenneth Spence described the process responsible for the acquisition of incentive motivation. Other psychologists subsequently used the system Spence detailed to describe the conditioning of other motives. We will briefly examine their views next; their contribution is evident throughout the text.

Spence's Acquired Motive Approach

The Anticipation of Reward

To explain the influence of reward value on behavior, Hull (1952) introduced the concept of incentive motivation, or K. Although Hull indicated that an animal or human would be more motivated after receiving a large reward than a small one, Kenneth Spence (1956), Hull's colleague, detailed the transformation of K into behavior. Let's use the behavior of the person who orders a hot dog at the ball park to describe Spence's view.

Spence suggested that when a reward (the hot dog) is obtained in a goal environment, this reward elicits an unconditioned goal response (R_G). For example, when the hungry person smells and tastes the hot dog, the hot dog initiates an internal response. This internal response (for example, salivation, gastric secretion) produces an internal stimulus state (S_G) that motivates the person to eat the hot dog. The characteristics of S_G resemble those of Hull's drive state (D): they represent an internal arousal that motivates behavior. The internal response is intensified as the person eats. Until eating is inhibited, the hot dog will continue to elicit the internal goal response. The reward value determines the intensity of the goal response; the greater the reward magnitude, the stronger the goal response.

Spence thought that during the first few experiences, the environmental cues present during reward (for example, the concession stand) become associated with reward, and subsequently produce a conditioned or anticipatory goal response (r_G). This **anticipatory goal response** then causes internal stimulus changes (r_G) that motivate approach behavior. Thus, the person becomes aroused when he or she sees the ball park concession stand. The arousal motivates the person to go to the concession stand and buy a hot dog.

The reward magnitude used during conditioning determines the maximum level of responding. Since a large reward creates a more intense R_G than does a smaller reward, Spence reasoned that the environmental cues associated with the large reward produce a stronger r_G than those paired with a small reward. This idea conforms to basic Pavlovian conditioning principles: the strength of a CR depends on UCS intensity; the stronger the UCS, the greater the CR. Observations that performance level improves with greater reward (for example, Crespi, 1942) lend support to Spence's incentive motivation concept. As noted earlier, Crespi found that rats ran down an alley faster for a larger reward than for a smaller one.

Spence's theory suggests that Pavlovian conditioning is responsible for motivating the behaviors that approach reward. Other psychologists have adopted this acquired motive view to explain the motivation to avoid frustrating or painful circumstances.

Avoidance of Frustrating Events

According to Hull (1943), the absence of reward acts to inhibit behavior. Hull suggested that by inhibiting habitual behavior, nonreward allows the strengthening of other behaviors. However, this view does not completely describe the influence of nonreward on behavior. Abram Amsel's frustration theory (1958) proposes that frustration both motivates avoidance behavior and suppresses approach behavior.

Amsel proposed that the frustration state differs from the goal response. Nonreward presented in a situation that was previously rewarded produces an unconditioned frustration response (R_F). This frustration response has motivational properties: the stimulus aftereffects (S_F) energize escape behavior. The cues present during the frustration (R_F) become conditioned to produce an anticipatory frustration response (r_F). The **anticipatory frustration response** also produces distinctive internal stimuli (s_F); these stimuli (s_F) motivate the animal to avoid a potentially frustrating situation.

The following example illustrates the central aspects of Amsel's frustration model. Suppose that you have 10 minutes to reach the theater before a movie begins. You get into your car, but it will not start. The failure of your car to start is a nonreward, which in turn produces frustration (R_F). The stimulus aftereffects of frustration (S_F) motivate escape behavior; that is, you leave the car and return home. According to Amsel's view, the car becomes associated with nonreward and, therefore, produces an anticipatory frustration response (r_F). If your car continues to fail to start, you probably will sell it to avoid future frustration.

The Avoidance of Painful Events

We learned in the last chapter that animals and people can readily learn to avoid unpleasant events. What process enables animals or people to prevent aversive events? The avoidance learning research of the 1930s created problems for the Hullian drive theory. The observation that animals can act to avoid unpleasant events suggests a cognitive process; that is, behaving in order to prevent an aversive event. Yet the Hullian drive theory argued that mechanistic rather than cognitive processes govern behavior. O. H. Mowrer (1939, 1947, 1956) developed a drive-based view of avoidance behavior, an approach regarded as an accurate explanation of avoidance behavior until problems with this theory became apparent during the 1960s.

TWO-FACTOR THEORY OF AVOIDANCE LEARNING. Mowrer proposed a **two-factor theory of avoidance learning** that did not assume that avoidance behavior is a cognitive process, based on the motivation to prevent a future aversive event. According to Mowrer, we learn to avoid aversive events in two stages. In the first stage, fear is conditioned to the environmental conditions that precede such an event. In the second stage of avoidance learning, we learn an instrumental or operant behavior that successfully terminates the feared stimulus. In Mowrer's view, although it appears that we are avoiding painful events, we are actually escaping a feared stimulus. Thus, our behavior is an escape response from a feared object, not an avoidance response to future aversive events. Consider Miller's classic study (1948) to illustrate Mowrer's view of avoidance behavior.

In Miller's study, rats were shocked in a white chamber and learned to avoid shock by running from the white chamber through a doorway into a nonshocked black chamber. According to Mowrer, the rats were simply escaping the feared white compartment and were not behaving to avoid being shocked. In his view, the fear reduction that resulted from the termination of the feared stimulus (the white compartment) rewarded the rats' behavior. Mowrer believed that the rats' motivation is to escape fear, not to avoid an aversive event, and that fear reduction, not the avoidance of the aversive event, is the reward for the instrumental response.

Initial research evaluating Mowrer's theory was positive. Several studies (for example, Miller, 1948; Brown & Jacobs, 1949) reported that once fear of a distinctive cue was established, an animal learned a new response to escape from the feared stimulus. Psychologists (Miller, 1951) believed that they had discovered how avoidance behavior is learned. However, some problems with Mowrer's view became evident during the 1950s and 1960s.

CRITICISMS OF TWO-FACTOR THEORY. Several problems exist with Mowrer's two-factor theory of avoidance learning. First, although exposure to the conditioned stimulus should eliminate avoidance behavior, avoidance behavior is often extremely resistant to extinction. For example, Solomon and Wynne (1953) reported that their dogs, even after receiving over 200 extinction trials, continued to perform a previously established avoidance response. The apparent failure of extinction represents a problem for the two-factor theory: if fear is acquired through classical conditioning and is responsible for motivating the avoidance behavior, then the presentation of the CS during extinction should cause a reduction in fear, and the avoidance behavior should cease.

Levis and Boyd (1979) offered one answer to this problem: it is not the number of extinction trials, but rather the duration of exposure to the CS, that determines the fear reduction and thus the elimination of an avoidance response. Levis and Boyd found that the persistence of avoidance behavior depends on the duration of exposure to the feared stimulus: the longer the exposure, the weaker the avoidance response. Additionally, Levis (1989) suggests that a rapid avoidance response prevents the extinction of cues experienced close to the time of the UCS. Suppose that the aversive event (UCS) does not occur until ten seconds after the CS begins. If the animal avoids after two seconds, the short latency cues will extinguish but not the longer latency ones. When the avoidance response slows, the long latency cues will elicit fear, which will act to recondition fear to the short-latency cues. In support of this view, Levis (1989) found that extinction of the avoidance response is much slower if there are separate cues associated with short and long latency than if a single cue is present during the entire CS-UCS interval.

A second problem for the two-factor theory concerns the apparent absence of fear in a well-established avoidance response. For example, Kamin, Brimer, and Black (1963) observed that a CS for a well-learned avoidance behavior did not suppress an operant response for food reinforcement. The failure to suppress the response is thought to reflect an absence of fear, because one indication of fear is the suppression of appetitive behavior. However, it is possible that the absence of suppression does not indicate that an animal is experiencing no fear in response to the CS, but rather that the animal's motivation for food is stronger than the fear induced by the CS. Further, strong fear is not necessary to motivate a habitual avoidance response—an observation consistent with Hull's idea that the tendency to respond is a joint function of drive and habit strength.

The Sidman avoidance procedure represents a third problem for two-factor theory. In the **Sidman avoidance task,** an animal experiences periodic aversive events unless it responds to prevent them. The avoidance response delays the occurrence of the next aversive event for a specific period of time. The interval between aversive events is the S-S interval, while the time that the aversive event is delayed is the R-S interval. If an animal responds consistently prior to the end of the R-S interval, it will not experience an aversive event. There is no external warning stimulus in the Sidman avoidance procedure. This should prevent avoidance learning, because there is no external conditioned stimulus to arouse fear prior to the avoidance behavior, nor is there any external conditioned stimulus terminating after the avoidance response and producing fear reduction. Yet, researchers (Sidman, 1953; Weisman & Litner, 1972) have observed that animals can learn to avoid aversive events with the Sidman avoidance procedure.

Kamin's experiment (1956) demonstrating the importance of the avoidance of the aversive event during conditioning provides perhaps the most damaging evidence against Mowrer's theory. Kamin compared avoidance learning in four groups of rats: (1) rats whose response both terminated the CS and prevented the UCS (Normal condition), (2) rats shocked at a predetermined time but whose behavior terminated the CS (Terminate or Term CS condition), (3) rats that avoided the UCS while the CS remained for a short time after the response (Avoid UCS condition), and (4) rats in a control group given CS and UCS but not allowed to escape or avoid the shock (Classical Conditioning control condition). The two-factor theory predicts that subjects in the Term CS condition should learn to avoid the shock because an avoidance response terminated the CS even though that response did not prevent the aversive shock from occurring. Two-factor theory also assumes that subjects in the Avoid UCS condition should not learn because the CS remained after the avoidance response, even though the response actually prevented the shock.

The results of Kamin's study did not match these predictions. Kamin found that the level of avoidance responding was lower in both the Term CS and Avoid UCS conditions than in the Normal condition, in which the responses both terminated the CS and avoided the UCS. Also, greater avoidance responding was seen in the subjects in both the Term CS and Avoid UCS groups than in the subjects in the Classical Conditioning control condition, whose responses neither terminated the CS nor avoided the UCS. Further, the Avoid-UCS subjects responded as often as the rats in the Term CS group. **Figure 6.3** presents the results of Kamin's study, which indicate that two factors—termination of the CS and avoidance of the UCS—play an important role in avoidance learning.

D'AMATO'S VIEW OF AVOIDANCE LEARNING. Michael D'Amato (1970) developed an acquired motive view to explain why prevention of the aversive event is important in learning avoidance behavior. According to D'Amato, an aversive event such as a shock elicits an unconditioned pain response (R_P), and the stimulus consequences of the painful event (S_P) motivate escape behavior. As the result of conditioning, the environmental cues present during shock can eventually produce an anticipatory pain response (r_P). The **anticipatory pain response** also produces distinctive stimulus aftereffects (s_P), which act to motivate an escape behavior.

D'Amato's r_P-s_P mechanism motivates escape from the conditioned stimulus. The termination of an aversive event (the UCS; for example, shock) produces an unconditioned relief response (R_R). The stimulus consequences (S_R) of the relief response are rewarding. According to D'Amato, the stimuli associated with the termination of the aversive event develop the ability to elicit an anticipatory relief response (r_R). The stimulus aftereffects (s_R) of this **anticipatory relief response** are also rewarding. Furthermore, the sight of the cues associated

FIGURE 6.3. The percentage of avoidance responses as a function of the rats' ability to terminate the CS, avoid the UCS, or both. The level of avoidance behavior was greatest when the rats could both terminate the CS and avoid the UCS.

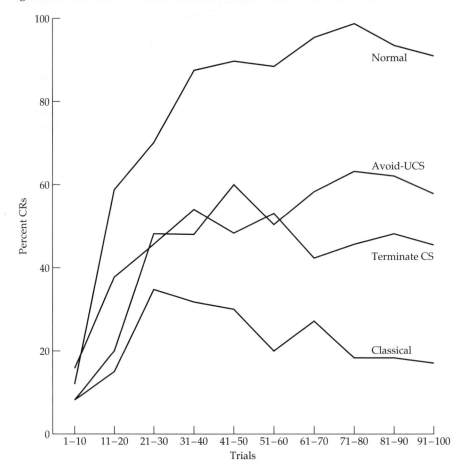

with anticipatory relief motivates approach behavior in a manner similar to Spence's description of the approach response to goal-related cues. This idea suggests a second motivational basis of avoidance behavior. The animal or human is not only escaping from an aversive situation, but also approaching a rewarding one. According to D'Amato, the avoidance of the aversive event is important because if the animal does not avoid, the r_R-s_R mechanism will not develop, and the avoidance response will not be rewarded.

Let's consider how D'Amato's theory would explain why some people avoid dogs. Being bitten by a dog is an aversive event that produces an unconditioned pain response and causes the person to associate the dog with pain. Through this conditioning, the dog produces an anticipatory pain response (r_P). The r_P-s_P mechanism motivates a person who has been bitten to get away from a dog when he or she sees one; this escape produces an unconditioned relief response. Suppose that such a person runs into a house to escape a dog. The house then becomes associated with relief and is able to produce an anticipatory relief response. Thus, if the dog is seen again, the sight of the house produces the r_R-s_R complex, which motivates the person to run into the house. Therefore, the anticipation of both pain and relief motivate the person to avoid the dog.

A number of studies support D'Amato's view of avoidance learning. D'Amato, Fazzaro, and Etkin (1968) suggested that an avoidance response is not learned when a trace-conditioning procedure is used (in this technique, the CS terminates prior to the UCS presentation) because no distinctive cue is associated with the absence of the UCS. If a cue were present when the aversive event ended, an avoidance response would be learned. To demonstrate this idea, D'Amato, Fazzaro, and Etkin presented a second cue (in addition to the CS) when their subjects exhibited an avoidance response. Although learning was slow—only reaching the level observed with the delayed-conditioning procedure (the CS and UCS terminated at the same time) after 500 trials—these subjects performed at a higher level than when the second cue was not present (see **Figure 6.4**). According to D'Amato, once the second cue was associated with the termination of shock, the r_R-s_R mechanism was acquired, and it then acted to reward avoidance behavior.

The importance of a discriminative cue signaling the absence of an aversive event can be used to explain avoidance learning with the Sidman avoidance task. Recall that there is no external warning stimulus with the Sidman avoidance task. According to Levis (1989), the periodic aversive events experienced

FIGURE 6.4. The percentage of avoidance responses during 700 trials for standard delayed-conditioning group (group C), trace-conditioning group (group T), and group receiving a cue for 5 seconds after each avoidance response (group TS). The feedback stimulus overcame the poor performance observed with the trace-conditioning procedure. The break indicates that a 24-hour interval elapsed between the fifth and sixth blocks of trials.

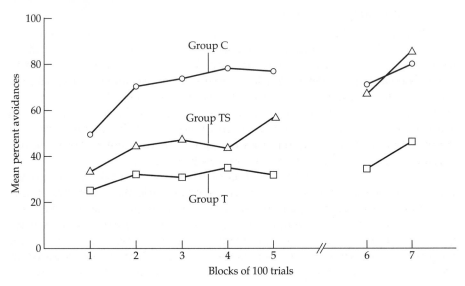

early in learning condition high levels of fear to the training environment. This fear produces high levels of activity, which motivates the avoidance response, and response-produced cues predict the absence of the aversive event. The relief experienced following the avoidance response reinforces the avoidance behavior and results in effective learning.

D'Amato's view asserts that we are motivated to approach situations associated with relief, as well as to escape events paired with aversive events. Furthermore, the relief experienced following avoidance behavior rewards that response. M. Ray Denny's research (see Denny, 1971) demonstrates the motivational and rewarding character of relief. Let's examine Denny's evidence, which validates both aspects of D'Amato's view.

Denny and Weisman (1964) demonstrated that animals anticipating pain will approach events that are associated with relief. The researchers trained rats to escape or to avoid shock in a striped shock compartment within a T-maze by turning either right into a black chamber or left into a white chamber. One of the chambers was associated with a 100-second delay before the next trials, the other chamber with only a 20-second delay. The rats learned to go to the compartment associated with the longer intertrial interval. These results suggest that when the rats anticipated experiencing an aversive event, they were motivated to seek the environment associated with the greatest relief.

Denny argues that the amount of relief depends upon the length of time between aversive events: the longer the nonshock interval (or intertrial interval, ITI), the greater the conditioned relief. In Denny's view, the greater the relief, the faster the acquisition of an avoidance habit. To test this idea, Denny and Weisman varied the time between trials from 10 to 225 seconds. They observed that acquisition of an avoidance response was directly related to the intertrial interval: animals allowed a longer interval between trials learned the avoidance response more readily than those given a shorter time between trials. These results show that the longer the period of relief after an aversive event, the more readily the rats learned to avoid the aversive event.

Nature of Anticipatory Behavior

Robert Rescorla and Richard Solomon (1967) pointed to a serious problem with the r_G-s_G mechanism that Kenneth Spence proposed. Spence envisioned the r_G to be a peripheral physiological response such as salivation. Although incentive value does influence motivation level, there are no peripheral physiological changes that are always related to instrumental behavior. Psychologists who have attempted to observe r_G directly and evaluate its influence on behavior have found that salivation might precede or follow instrumental behavior; other times, an animal might salivate without responding, or respond without salivating (Lewis, 1959; Kintsch & Witte, 1962).

Rescorla and Solomon (1967) suggested that r_G is a central rather than peripheral nervous system response. According to Rescorla and Solomon, this central nervous system response is classically conditioned, with its strength determined by reward magnitude and its effect, motivating behavior. As we will learn in Chapter 7, Rescorla and Solomon also suggested that fear, frustration, and relief reflect activity in the central rather than the peripheral nervous system.

- What S-R association did Justin learn as a result of going to the movies?
- How would changes in the level of drive, and the incentive value of the movie, influence Justin's behavior?

Guthrie's Contiguity View

Hull's drive theory proposed that reinforcement was responsible for the establishment of S-R associations. Although most psychologists during the 1930s and 1940s accepted this S-R approach, Edwin Guthrie (1935, 1942, 1959) rejected the view that reward strengthened the bond between a stimulus and a response. Instead, Guthrie proposed that **contiguity** was sufficient to establish an S-R association. According to Guthrie, if a response occurs when a particular stimulus is present, the stimulus and response will automatically become associated.

Guthrie believed that learning is a simple process governed entirely by the contiguity principle: whenever a particular stimulus and response occur simultaneously, a person reencountering that stimulus will exhibit that response. Guthrie provided many real-life examples of how a behavior could change based on his theory. Consider the following illustration of Guthrie's view of learning:

> The mother of a ten year old girl complained to a psychologist that for two years her daughter had annoyed her by habitually tossing her coat and hat on the floor as she entered the house. On a hundred occasions the mother had insisted that the girl pick up the clothing and hang it in its place. These wild ways were changed only after the mother, on advice, began to insist not only that the girl pick up the fallen garments from the floor, but that she also put them on, return to the street, and reenter the house, this time removing the coat and hat and hanging them properly. (Guthrie, 1935, page 21)

Why was this technique effective? According to Guthrie, the desired response is for the child to hang up her clothes upon entering the house; that is, to associate hanging up her clothes with entering the house. Having the child hang up the clothes after being in the house will not establish the correct association; learning, in Guthrie's view, will occur only when stimulus (entering the house) and response (hanging up the coat and hat) occur together.

Impact of Reward

Guthrie proposed that reward has an important effect on the response to a specific environmental circumstance; however, he did not believe that reward strengthens the S-R association. According to Guthrie, many responses can become conditioned to a stimulus, and the response exhibited just prior to reward will be associated with the stimulus and will occur when the stimulus is experienced again. For example, a child may draw, put together a puzzle, and study at the same desk. If her parents reward the child by allowing her to play outside after she studies but not after she draws or works on the puzzle, the next time the child sits down at the desk, she will study rather than draw or play with a puzzle. In Guthrie's view, a person must respond in a particular way (to study) in the presence of a specific stimulus (the desk) in order to obtain reward (playing outside).

Once the person exhibits the appropriate response, a reward acts to change the stimulus context (internal and/or external) that was present prior to reward. For example, suppose the child is rewarded by going outside to ride her bike. Any new actions will be conditioned to this new stimulus circumstance—being outside—and therefore they will allow the appropriate response—studying—to be produced by the original stimulus context—the desk—when it is experienced again. Thus, the reward functions to prevent further conditioning and not to strengthen an S-R association. In the example of the studying child, the reward of going outside prevents her from doing anything else at the desk; the reward does not per se strengthen the child's association between studying and the desk.

Guthrie believed that a reward must be presented immediately after the appropriate response if that response is to occur on the next stimulus exposure. If the reward is delayed, the actions occurring between the appropriate response and the reward will be exhibited when the stimulus is encountered again. For example, if the child did not go outside immediately after studying but instead watched television at the desk and then went outside, the child would watch television at the desk rather than study.

The Function of Punishment

How did Guthrie explain the influence of punishment or behavior? Guthrie suggested that punishment is an unconditioned stimulus capable of eliciting a number of responses, such as crying, pouting, or fleeing. If the response terminates the aversive event, the response will become conditioned to the stimulus context in which the punishment occurred. When the person encounters this stimulus circumstance again, the conditioned response will be elicited. If this anticipatory response is effective, punishment will not occur. However, if the response that terminates punishment does not prevent punishment, punishment cannot be avoided, only escaped.

Guthrie suggested that punishment may not always eliminate the undesired, punished behavior. Punishment will work only if the response elicited by punishment, and conditioned to the punishment situation, is incompatible with the inappropriate response. For example, suppose a child is punished for hitting a younger sibling. Punishment often acts to elicit aggression. Because the punished response—hitting a younger sibling—is not incompatible with the response elicited by punishment—aggression—punishing the child may not suppress the inappropriate behavior.

The Importance of Practice

According to Guthrie, learning occurs in a single trial; that is, the strength of an S-R association reaches its maximum value following a single pairing of the stimulus and a response. You might wonder why Guthrie believed that learning occurred on a single trial when it is obvious that the efficiency and strength of behavior improves with experience. Guthrie did not deny that behavior improves with experience; however, he rejected the Hullian view that the strength of the S-R bond slowly increases with experience.

According to Guthrie, performance gradually improves for three reasons.

First, although many potential stimuli are present during initial conditioning, the subject will attend to only some of these stimuli. The stimuli present when an animal or person responds vary from trial to trial. For a stimulus attended to the particular trial to produce a response, this stimulus must have also been attended to during a previous response. For example, suppose that in an instrumental conditioning situation, a rat is rewarded in the black compartment of a T-maze but is not attending to the color of the goal box. On a future trial, the rat does not go to the black side, even though it was rewarded in that environment on the previous trial. Although the rat's behavior may change from trial to trial, this change reflects an attentional process rather than a learning process. A second reason for improvement in performance is that many different stimuli can become conditioned to produce a particular response. As more stimuli become able to elicit a response, the strength of the response will increase. However, this increased intensity of a response is not caused by a stronger S-R association, but rather by the increased number of stimuli able to produce the response. Third, a complex behavior consists of many separate responses. For the behavior to be efficient, each response element must be conditioned to the stimulus. As each element is conditioned to the stimulus, the efficiency of the behavior will improve. According to Guthrie, the more varied the stimuli and/or the responses that must be associated to produce effective performance, the more practice is needed to make behavior efficient.

An Evaluation of Contiguity Theory

The S-R contiguity view that Guthrie proposed during the 1930s and 1940s was not accepted by many psychologists. During his career as a professor at the University of Washington, Guthrie conducted few studies to validate his approach. The lack of empirical evaluation meant that Guthrie's theory remained unrevised from its original proposal in 1935 until his final writings in 1959. More recent experiments to test Guthrie's theory have found some ideas accurate and others inaccurate.

Some parts of Guthrie's theory accurately describe aspects of the learning process. First, punishment can intensify an inappropriate behavior when punishment elicits a behavior that is compatible with the punished response; however, punishment's facilitatory influence can be offset by an intense punishment. Second, contiguity between a response and reward is critical to prevent the acquisition of competing associations. (The child must go outside immediately after studying; if she watches television first, she will associate her desk with watching television rather than with studying.) Third, only a portion of the environmental stimuli are active at a particular moment; therefore only some of the potential conditioned stimuli can become associated with the response. Later chapters will examine the evidence that supports these aspects of Guthrie's view.

Some aspects of Guthrie's theory, however, do not accurately describe the learning process. First, Guthrie rejected the law of effect, suggesting instead that reward changes the stimulus situation. However, numerous experiments (Bower & Hilgard, 1981) have disproved his concept of a reward. An experimenter can arrange for many changes to occur after a response, but if these actions do not serve as rewards the response will not be conditioned, even though substantial stimulus change followed the response. Second, Guthrie believed that recency and frequency determined which response a particular stimulus would produce. However, Noble's (1966) extensive research indicated that reward predicted response significantly better than did either frequency or recency. Third, Guthrie assumed that learning occurs on a single trial; that is, a single, simultaneous pairing of a stimulus and response results in the development of the maximum S-R associative strength. Many studies have evaluated Guthrie's view that learning occurs after a single S-R pairing. To test this view, the conditioning situation must be simple, and the trial-to-trial behavior of each subject must be assessed. In an eye-blink conditioning study using humans Voeks (1954) conducted a well-controlled evaluation of Guthrie's view. Voeks observed that most subjects showed all-or-none learning; that is, they showed no CR on one trial and an intense CR on the next trial (see **Figure 6.5**). However, other studies have not reported single-trial learning for individual subjects: instead, they have found a gradual increase in the strength of a response (Bower & Hilgard, 1981).

Spence (1956), accepting that rapid changes in responding do occur in some circumstances, indicated how an incremental learning approach could explain these results. (An incremental view holds that the strength of learned behavior increases slowly over trials.) According to Spence, although S-R habit strength increases slowly over trials, the response will not be elicited until its strength exceeds the threshold of response evocation. Spence suggested that if the threshold is near maximum strength, the learning process will appear to be of the all-or-none type. Spence's analysis allowed an incremental theory to explain the apparent single-trial learning, but more recent theories suggest that some aspects of learning can develop on a single trial, while others develop slowly. For example, we will learn in Chapter 7 that it is likely that the emotional components of a discrimination are learned slowly, while the attentional aspects of

FIGURE 6.5. The performance of six subjects on a conditioned eye blink study. The rapid change in performance of each subject from one trial to the next supports one-trial learning. Note the mean performance of all subjects slowly increases across trials, which could erroneously suggest an incremental increase in learning over trials.

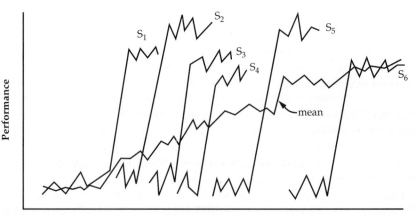

Trials

discrimination learning develop on a single trial. We will discuss this idea further when we discuss contemporaries theories of Pavlovian conditioning in Chapter 9.

BEFORE YOU GO ON

- **What competing associations could cause Justin to stop going to the movies on Friday night?**
- **How would punishment affect Justin's habit of going to the movies?**

The S-R theories propose that a mechanistic process governs our behavior. In contrast, the cognitive approach suggests that actions are guided by purpose rather than by internal and external forces. Furthermore, the cognitive approach argues that behavior is a flexible reaction rather than a habitual response. We will briefly examine the cognitive view of learning next; Chapter 8 discusses this view in greater detail.

COGNITIVE APPROACHES TO LEARNING

Tolman's Purposive Behaviorism

Edward Tolman (1932, 1959) proposed a cognitive view of learning during the 1930s and 1940s that most psychologists did not accept. Instead, Hull's mechanistic drive theory was the accepted view of learning during that period. During the 1950s, the cognitive view gained ground, and other psychologists expanded Tolman's original approach. Over the last three decades, the cognitive approach has made many important contributions to our understanding of learning. Our discussion begins with Tolman's work. Later in the chapter, we'll look at one expansion of Tolman's theory. In Chapter 8, we will examine several contemporary cognitive approaches to learning.

Flexibility of Behavior

Tolman's view conflicted in several ways with Hull's drive theory. Tolman did not believe that behavior was an automatic response to an environmental event. Instead, he proposed that our behavior has both direction and purpose. Tolman argued that behavior is goal-oriented; that is, we are motivated either to achieve a desired condition or to avoid an aversive situation. According to Tolman, certain paths lead to our goals and certain tools can help us attain these goals. In Tolman's view, we can understand the structure of our environment through experience. This knowledge allows us to reach desired goals.

Tolman proposed that not only is our behavior goal-oriented, but we also expect specific outcomes to follow specific behavior. For example, you may expect to receive an A for working hard in this class. If you do not receive an A, you will continue to work hard for the reward and will not be satisfied with a less valued goal. Thus, if you received a B on your first test, you would not be satisfied with the B and would work even harder for an A on the next test.

Tolman also believed that certain events in the environment convey information about where our goals are located. We can reach our goals only after we have learned to read the signs leading to reward or punishment in our environment. For example, you must learn the signs leading to the cafeteria to obtain food. Although Tolman believed that behavior is purposeful, he did not mean that we are always aware of either the purpose or the direction of our behavior. Tolman proposed only that we act *as if* we expect a particular behavior to lead to a specific goal.

Motivation Processes

According to Tolman, there are two types of motivations. Deprivation is one source of motivation. In Tolman's view, deprivation produces an internal drive state that increases demand for the goal object. Tolman (1959) also suggested that environmental events can acquire motivational properties through association with either a primary drive or a reward. The following example illustrates Tolman's view. A thirsty child sees a soda. According to Tolman, the ability of thirst to motivate behavior transfers to the soda. Tolman called this transference process **cathexis,** a term he borrowed from psychoanalytic theory. As a result of cathexis, the soda is now a preferred goal object, and in the future, this child—even when not thirsty—will be motivated to obtain a soda. The preference for the soda is a positive cathexis. In contrast, avoiding a certain place could reflect a negative cathexis. In Tolman's opinion, if we associate a certain place with an unpleasant experience, we will think of the place itself as an aversive object.

You might remember that Hull suggested that drives could be conditioned. Tolman's cathexis concept is very similar to Hull's view of acquired drive. And Tolman's **equivalence belief principle** is comparable to Spence's anticipatory goal concept. Animals or people react to a secondary reward (or subgoal) as they do to the original goal object; for instance, our motivation to obtain money reflects our identification of money with desired goal objects such as shelter and food.

Is Reward Necessary for Learning?

We learned in Chapter 1 that Thorndike argued that S-R associations form when the response leads to a satisfying state of affairs. Hull (1943) adopted Thorndike's law-of-effect concept and suggested that habit strength increases when a particular response decreases the drive state. In contrast to these views, Tolman (1932) proposed that reward is not necessary for learning to occur and that the simultaneous experience of two events is sufficient for learning. Thus, according to Tolman, an understanding of when events will occur can develop without reward. What is the influence of reward, in Tolman's view? He proposed that reward affects performance but not learning. The presence of a reward will motivate an animal or person to exhibit a previously learned behavior. For example, a child may have learned how to mow the yard, but he needs to be rewarded to actually do the job.

An Evaluation of Purposive Behaviorism

Tolman proposed that the expectation of future reward or punishment motivates instrumental activities. Further, knowledge of the paths and/or the tools that enable us to obtain reward or avoid punishment guides our behavior. Although the research Tolman and his students designed did not provide conclusive evidence for his cognitive approach, his work caused Hull to make major changes in his theory to accommodate Tolman's observation. For example, the idea that a conditioned anticipation of reward (r_G) motivates us to approach reward is clearly similar to Tolman's view that the expectation of reward motivates behavior intended to produce reward. Furthermore, the view that frustration can motivate both the avoidance of a less preferred reward and the continued search for the desired reward parallels the drive explanation that not just any reward will be acceptable. However, once Tolman's observations were incorporated into drive theory, most psychologists ignored Tolman's cognitive view, and continued to accept the drive view of learning. When problems developed with the drive approach during the 1960s and 1970s, the cognitive view gained wider approval. Psychologists began to use a cognitive approach to explain how behavior is learned. In the next section, we will look at one expansion of Tolman's cognitive approach.

Expectancy-Value Theory

Tolman's cognitive approach is the foundation of Julian Rotter's (1954) **expectancy-value theory.** Rotter expanded Tolman's view by describing the types of expectancies we develop.

Basic Tenets

There are three main ideas expressed in Rotter's expectancy theory. First, Rotter suggested that our preference for a particular event is determined by its reward value. According to Rotter, the value of a particular event is relative; its value is measured in comparison with other events. Thus, some of us may find an event highly rewarding because we have not experienced many rewarding events, while others who have experienced many rewarding events may not find this particular event as rewarding. Rotter also suggested that a reward can change its value when new rewards are introduced. A restaurant you have valued may lose its appeal when you compare it to a new restaurant.

The second component of Rotter's expectancy-value theory is that each person has a subjective expectation concerning the likelihood of obtaining a particular reward. We believe there is a specific probability of reaching a desired goal; these beliefs may or may not reflect reality. For example, you may feel that someone you like will not accept your dinner invitation, even though he or she would actually accept if you extended an invitation. The real probability that the event will occur does not influence your behavior; you simply will not ask because your expected probability is low. Thus, in Rotter's view, even if you are motivated, you will not behave if you do not expect reward.

The third aspect of expectancy-value theory is that our expectation of obtaining reward is determined by the situation. We may expect to receive reward in one setting but not in another. Our past experiences determine this situational dependence; we acquire the expectation that a particular goal is more likely to occur under some circumstances than others. For example, suppose that you have a strong preference for Italian food. You would then be more likely to expect reward in an Italian restaurant than in a French café. Your relative expectations act to guide your behavior; if you have to choose between these two restaurants, you are more likely to choose the Italian restaurant than the French one.

Yet, sometimes we encounter new situations that are outside of our past experience. How do we respond to these new events? According to Rotter, our generalized expectations from other past experiences guide our actions. Recall your initial feelings when you were a college freshman. You had never attended college, and therefore you had no direct experience upon which to base your expectations. Under these circumstances, your past expectations in similar situations governed your behavior.

Finally, Rotter's theory proposes that our behavior potential determines the likelihood that we will act in a particular way. Our behavioral potential represents our expectation of obtaining reward in a particular situation, as well as the value of that reward. In Rotter's view, we can predict behavior if we multiply the expectation of reward by the value of the reward. This mathematical formula has proved useful in describing and predicting behavior. Atkinson's (1964) research on achievement motivation is one example of its use. Atkinson observed that the level of a person's achievement behavior was jointly determined by the perceived probability of success and the perceived incentive value of that success; that is, achievement performance increased as the perceived probability of success and/or perceived value of success increased.

Locus of Control

Rotter (1966) is most noted for his concept of locus of control. According to Rotter, there are two significant generalized expectations—internal and external expectancies. An **internal expectancy** represents a belief that obtaining a goal depends upon one's own actions (see **Figure 6.6**). Suppose that you would like to receive a high grade on an exam next week. Your internal expectancy in this situation might be that hard work will enable you to get the good grade. And your expectation that hard work brings success will cause you to spend long hours studying for this next exam.

FIGURE 6.6. An internal expectancy reflects the belief that obtaining a goal depends upon one's own actions. In contrast, an external expectancy is the belief that the environment determines goal attainment and that attaining the goal is thus beyond one's control.

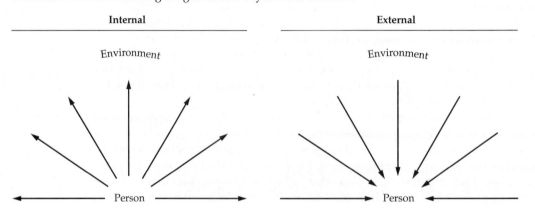

However, you will not exert much effort studying if you believe that luck will determine your grade. Rotter refers to this type of cognition as an **external expectancy.** An external expectancy reflects a belief that events are beyond your control (refer to **Figure 6.6**). Examples of external expectancies include beliefs that luck, chance, or the power of others is responsible for your attainment of desired reward. Since you believe that little or no connection exists between your behavior and the reward, you will make little or no effort to change your behavior.

There are environmental situations in which each type of expectancy is appropriate. In skill tasks, you can obtain reward by exhibiting the appropriate ability. Two examples of reinforcers obtained in skill tasks are a goal by a hockey player and a standing ovation for an actor. Chance tasks, in contrast, do not rely on any specific behavior for reward. A blackjack in gambling or a star player in a pack of baseball cards are two examples of reinforcers on chance tasks.

Many of us are aware of the distinction between external and internal expectancies and exhibit different expectations in each type of setting. We assume in skill situations that our behavior can enable us to obtain reward. When we are successful in skill tasks, we increase our expectation of future success, while failure often causes us to decrease our expectation of future reward. Our response during chance situations is quite different. Since we assume that reward occurs independently of our actions in chance tasks, we are not likely to change our expectations of future reward following either success or failure.

It is most appropriate for us to perceive each type of situation separately. We should attempt to obtain reward in skill settings, but either avoid or merely accept those situations in which success or failure occurs independently of our actions. However, many people show a generalized expectation by treating all situations as depending on either skill or chance. In Rotter's view, internally oriented persons believe that their own actions determine success or failure. Externally oriented individuals, on the other hand, believe that they have no control over their fate. Rotter coined the term **locus of control** to refer to our generalized expectation that either internal or external factors control our opportunities to reach a goal.

An Evaluation of Rotter's Expectancy-Value Theory

Rotter developed his expectancy-value theory during a period when most psychologists were advocating a drive view of behavior. In contrast to the idea that tension automatically motivates behavior, Rotter proposed that we act in a certain manner if we expect to receive a specific reward. The drive approach portrays us as responding to the environmental stimuli impinging upon us. In contrast, Rotter's expectancy view assumes that our cognitions determine our behavior. The Hullian idea that we are passive recipients of environmental forces and internal pressures contrasts sharply with Rotter's view that we play an active role in determining our actions. Although the drive approach continues to describe some aspects of the learning process, the research of Julian Rotter and his colleagues indicates that a cognitive process also plays an important role in determining our behavior. We will see further evidence of the important role cognitive processes play in determining our behavior in Chapter 8.

SKINNER'S BEHAVIORISTIC METHODOLOGY

The work of B. F. Skinner, a noted American behaviorist, spans more than half a century and has contributed greatly to our understanding of the learning process. Skinner's concept of behaviorism, often referred to as **behavior modification,** differs from theories advocated by the other behaviorists we have discussed in this chapter. In his 1938 text, *The Behavior of Organisms,* Skinner argued that the goal of behaviorism should be to identify and isolate the environmental factors that govern behavior. Skinner stated that we will understand a particular behavior only when we have learned how to predict and control the behavior. Also, Skinner suggested that the ability to predict and control a behavior depends on understanding the circumstances governing the occurrence of the behavior.

The Importance of the Environment

As we learned in Chapter 4, Skinner designed many studies to examine the factors that govern behavior. He first studied the variables responsible for a rat's behavior—pressing a lever for food reinforcement—in an operant chamber. Much of his research focused on the influence of reinforcement on operant responding. Skinner defined a **reinforcer** as an event whose occurrence increases the frequency of behavior that preceded the event. According to Skinner, the environment identifies the operant response necessary to produce reinforcement. Skinner referred to the specified relationship between the operant response and the reinforcement as a **contingency.** Skinner found that contingencies had an important impact on the rat's behavior. The rats were sensitive to contingencies and performed the behavior the contingency specified as needed to produce reinforcement.

Skinner then expanded his analysis of behavior to include other animals, humans, and situations and behaviors that differed greatly from operant chambers and bar pressing. For example, in his 1957 text, *Verbal Behavior,* Skinner argued that people do not have an instinctive capacity for expressing ideas. Instead, he believed, verbal behavior, like any other operant behavior, is controlled by differential reinforcement and punishment administered by significant others such as parents and friends. Skinner's methodology led to the development of behavior modification, an approach effective in treating behavior pathology. Chapter 4 presented evidence of Skinner's contribution to our understanding of how to establish desired behaviors and eliminate undesired behaviors.

The Role of Theory?

How does Skinner's view differ from those of the other behaviorists described in this chapter? Skinner (1938) argued that the use of "hypothetical constructs" does not contribute to our understanding of behavior. In Skinner's view, the search for evidence to validate a particular "hypothetical construct" interferes with the functional analysis of the variables controlling the behavior, and thereby limits our understanding of the circumstances that govern behavior.

Consider the following example to illustrate Skinner's approach. Many psychologists have speculated that stimulus-response associations are strengthened as the result of reinforcement, and years of research have been devoted to validating this view. According to Skinner, understanding the "theoretical construct" that underlies the effect that reinforcement has on stimulus-response associations is useful in only one respect: it points out that reinforcement is one environmental variable that can control how frequently a specific behavior occurs in a particular context.

Many psychologists do not agree with Skinner's view. These psychologists argue that theory guides research, which in turn identifies the variables that control behavior as well as explains similar results from various experiments. The work of psychologists who use theory to guide their research has contributed greatly to our understanding of learning and has increased our ability to predict and control behavior. For example, Hull's drive theory, discussed earlier, greatly influenced the development of systematic desensitization, a behavior therapy that has effectively modified phobic behavior. (We described systematic desensitization in Chapter 3.) The contribution of Hull and other theorists is also evident throughout the text.

One significant change in learning theory since the late 1960s has been a shift away from global theories (those of Hull, Spence, Guthrie, and Tolman) to a focus on more specific aspects of the learning process. We will discuss the reasons for this shift and what contemporary learning theorists have proposed and found in Chapter 9.

BEFORE YOU GO ON

- **What expectancies led Justin to go to the movies every Friday night?**
- **Does an internal or external expectancy govern Justin's movie-going behavior?**

CHAPTER SUMMARY

Hull theorized that a nonspecific intense internal arousal—drive—motivates behavior. Several classes of stimuli (deprivation and intense environmental events) are inherently capable of initiating drive, and any stimuli associated with these innate drive stimuli develop the capacity to produce drive through the classical conditioning process. Reward, and stimuli associated with reward, are also able to produce arousal and motivate behavior.

According to Hull, behavior is then directed by the specific prevailing stimulus conditions. A specific stimulus is capable of eliciting several behaviors, and the behavior with the strongest bond (or habit strength) will be repeated; the bond strengthens if the behavior produces drive reduction.

Spence suggested that the presentation of reward elicits an unconditioned goal response (R_G). The association of environmental events with reward causes the development of a conditioned anticipatory goal response (r_G). The stimuli (S_G) produced by this conditioned response motivate the approach to reward.

Amsel proposed that nonreward in a situation previously associated with reward produces an unconditioned frustration response (R_F). The anticipatory frustration response (r_F) is conditioned as a result of the association of environmental events with nonreward. The stimulus aftereffects (s_F) of this conditioned response motivate avoidance of nonreward.

Mowrer suggested that fear is conditioned during the first phase of learning. In the second stage, fear motivates any behavior that successfully terminates the fear. This effective behavior will be rewarded by fear reduction and elicited upon future exposure to the feared stimulus. According to Mowrer, the aversive event will be prevented only if the escape response to the feared stimulus also results in the avoidance of painful events.

D'Amato suggested that the classical conditioning of the anticipatory pain response mechanism (r_P-s_P) to the environmental cues associated with an aversive event motivates escape from these cues. Furthermore, the termination of pain produces an unconditioned relief response (R_R). The establishment of the anticipatory relief response mechanism (r_R-s_R) provides motivation to approach the cues associated with unconditioned relief.

Guthrie advocated a contiguity approach to S-R learning. According to Guthrie, when a stimulus and response occur together, they automatically become associated, and when the stimulus is encountered again, it will produce the response.

Guthrie proposed that reward alters the stimulus environment, thereby precluding the acquisition of any new competing S-R associations. Furthermore, Guthrie asserted that punishment suppresses an inappropriate behavior only if the response the punishment produces is incompatible with the behavior; in fact, punishment can actually increase a behavior if the response the punishment elicits is compatible with the undesired behavior. Practice increases the number of stimuli associated with a response and thereby increases the intensity of that response.

Tolman proposed a cognitive explanation of behavior in the 1930s and 1940s. In Tolman's view, behavior is goal-oriented: We are motivated to reach specific goals, and we continue to search until we attain them. Tolman further argued that expectations determine the specific behavior we perform to obtain reward or avoid punishment.

Rotter's expectancy-value theory proposes that the likelihood that a person will act in a particular way is determined jointly by the perceived expectation of reaching a goal and the perceived value of that reinforcer. According to Rotter, behavior may be inconsistent due to perceived differences in the expectancies of obtaining reward in different situations, or generalized expectancies may cause a person to behave in the same way in different settings. An internal expectancy is a belief that one's actions determine the likelihood of success or failure. In contrast, an external expectancy reflects the view that events are beyond one's control. Locus of control refers to the extent to which either internal or external expectancies guide one's actions.

Skinner argued that attempts to explain the theoretical basis of behavior interfere with the discovery of the causes of behavior. Skinner believed that psychologists should seek to identify the environmental factors governing behavior. Once these variables have been discovered, Skinner believed, we should be able to predict and control behavior.

Skinner's investigations have increased our understanding of the circumstances that influence responding; they have also contributed to a methodology that allows reliable prediction and effective control of behavior. However, the theoretical emphasis Skinner criticized has also produced important research—research that has contributed to our understanding of the common elements of various situations and behaviors, and that has produced effective procedures for controlling behaviors.

CRITICAL THINKING QUESTIONS

1. Alan drinks a couple of beers while watching sports on television. Cynthia has a glass of wine with her dinner. Using what you have learned from Hull's theory of learning, explain Alan's and Cynthia's behavior.
2. Maria becomes very nervous when she eats fattening foods, yet she impulsively eats large quantities of food before forcing herself to vomit. Discuss Maria's behavior using Mowrer's two-factor theory of avoidance behavior.
3. Some psychologists argue that environmental contingencies govern behavior. Others believe that cognitive processes determine how we act. Select a behavior and show how stimulus-response and cognitive processes could control that behavior. Use the ideas presented in the text to substantiate your statements.

KEY TERMS

acquired drive
anticipatory frustration
    response
anticipatory goal response
anticipatory pain
    response
anticipatory relief
    response
behavior modification
cathexis
cognitive theories

conditioned inhibition
contiguity
contingency
drive
equivalence belief
    principle
expectancy-value theory
external expectancy
habit hierarchy
habit strength
incentive motivation

internal expectancy
locus of control
operant response
reactive inhibition
reinforcer
Sidman avoidance task
S-R (stimulus-response)
    associative theories
two-factor theory of
    avoidance learning

CHAPTER 7

Stimulus Control of Behavior

A Case of Mistaken Identity

Walking to the grocery store, Miguel was approached by a tall man who suddenly jumped directly in front of him and drew a large knife. The stranger grabbed Miguel's arm and demanded his money. Frightened, Miguel surrendered the $25 he had planned to use to buy food. After grabbing the money, the thief bolted down the street, disappearing into an alley. Miguel began yelling, "I've been robbed! I've been robbed!" But the criminal had fled, and the several people who had witnessed the robbery had dispersed. A merchant hearing Miguel's screams did call the police, who arrived within five minutes. The police first questioned Miguel, asking him to describe the robber. The merchant, upon questioning, denied witnessing the crime, and attested only to hearing Miguel's screams. Several weeks passed before the police contacted Miguel, informing him that they had a suspect who met Miguel's description and had a record of attacks similar to the one on Miguel. The police asked Miguel to come to the police station to try to identify his assailant from a lineup. The lineup was a cinch; Miguel immediately recognized his attacker. On the basis of his criminal record and Miguel's identification, the suspect was charged with assault and robbery. However, the person Miguel identified was not his assailant. Two weeks after the lineup, another man was apprehended while attempting to rob a woman on her way home from work. During his interrogation, the man confessed not only to this crime but also to robbing Miguel.

Since Miguel had a close view of his assailant, why did he identify the wrong man? To answer, we must consider the five individuals in the lineup. Although five men were in the lineup, only two were as tall as Miguel's assailant. Of these two men, one was thin, the other, fat. Since his attacker was tall and thin, the choice seemed obvious to Miguel, and he picked the man he believed had robbed him. Miguel's behavior illustrates discrimination learning: he had recognized several important attributes of his assailant, and he used this knowledge to discriminate his assailant from the other men in the lineup. However, his discrimination was not perfect; although Miguel's assailant and the man he identified in the lineup shared two attributes—they were both thin and tall—their facial characteristics differed significantly. But Miguel had not attended to facial attributes; instead he had responded only to size characteristics.

This chapter discusses the impact of the stimulus environment on behavior. An individual can respond in the same way to similar stimuli, a process called **generalization.** In the chapter-opening vignette, Miguel responded in the same manner to both the assailant and the man in the lineup. Individuals can also learn to respond in different ways to different stimuli; the process of responding to some stimuli but not others is called **discrimination.** Miguel discriminated between his assailant and four of the five men in the lineup.

We begin our discussion of stimulus control of behavior by examining generalization, or responding to stimuli similar to the conditioning stimulus. We will address other aspects of stimulus control later in the chapter.

THE GENERALIZATION PROCESS

On February 26, 1994, a car bomb exploded in the garage beneath the 110-story World Trade Center in New York. The explosion killed 5 people and injured over 1,000 other persons. An investigation by the FBI and the New York City Police led to six Arabs who were charged with the bombing. Extensive media coverage of this and similar acts of violence has aroused the belief in some Americans that many Arab Moslems are terrorists. Why do some Americans dislike Arab Moslems? Generalization may be responsible for their strong, negatively conditioned emotional response toward Arab Moslems.

Generalization occurs frequently in the real world. Sometimes, generalization is undesirable, as when some Americans choose to dislike all Arab Moslems. Racial, ethnic, and religious prejudice are examples of undesirable generalization that occurs when someone who has had an unpleasant experience with one member of a racial, ethnic, or religious group generalizes this dislike to other members of that group.

However, generalization is often adaptive. For example, if a parent reads a book to a child and the child enjoys it, a positive emotional experience is conditioned to the book. The child then generalizes this positive emotional response to other books. The child's generalization even extends to liking books not yet read. To use another example, preschool children may enjoy playing with other neighborhood children; this enjoyment reflects a conditioned response acquired through past experience. When these children attend school, they generalize their conditioned social responses to new children and are motivated to play with them. This generalization enables children to socialize with new children; otherwise, children would have to learn to like new acquaintances before they would want to play with them. Thus, generalization allows people to respond positively to strangers. Imagine how difficult life would be if you had to have a positive experience with every person before you would talk to him or her. Clearly, generalization makes our lives much easier.

Generalization causes us to respond in basically the same way to stimuli similar to the stimulus present during training. However, different degrees of generalization occur. In some instances, we respond the same to all stimuli resembling the stimulus associated with conditioning. For example, people who become ill after eating in a specific restaurant may generalize their negative emotional experiences and avoid eating out again. In other situations, less generalization occurs as the similarity to the conditioned stimulus lessens. Suppose that a college student drinks too much vodka and becomes quite ill. This student may show an intense dislike of all white alcohol (for example, gin), experience a moderate aversion to wine, and feel only a slight dislike of beer. In this case, the greater the difference in the alcohol content of the drink, the less the generalization of dislike. Or the person might have an aversion to only straight alcohol; if so, only stimuli very similar to the conditioning stimulus (white alcohol) will elicit dislike.

To study the level of generalization, psychologists have constructed generalization gradients. A **generalization gradient** is a visual representation of the strength of each response produced by stimuli of varying degrees of similarity to the stimulus associated with training; these gradients show the level of generalization that occurs to any given stimulus similar to the one present during conditioning. A steep generalization gradient indicates that people or animals respond very little to stimuli that are not very similar to the training stimulus, while a flat generalization gradient shows that responding occurs even to stimuli quite unlike the conditioning stimulus.

Generalization Gradients

Most generalization studies have investigated the generalization of excitatory conditioning. Recall from Chapter 3 that in excitatory conditioning, a specific stimulus is presented prior to the unconditioned stimulus. Following acquisition, the stimulus (S+) that was paired with the unconditioned stimulus is presented again, along with several test stimuli varying from very similar to very dissimilar to the S+. The amount of response to the test stimulus in comparison to the amount of response to the training stimulus indicates the level of generalization of excitatory conditioning. A graph of the response to each stimulus provides a visual display of the level of excitatory generalization.

Some research has studied the generalization of inhibitory conditioning. Remember that inhibitory conditioning develops when one stimulus is presented with either reward or punishment, and another stimulus with the absence of the event (see Chapter 3). Conditioning of inhibition to the second stimulus (inhibitory stimulus, S−) will cause it to suppress the response to the first stimulus (excitatory stimulus, S+). After training, the second stimulus (S−) and several test stimuli varying from very similar to very dissimilar to the inhibitory stimulus are presented before the excitatory stimulus, which was paired with either reward or punishment (S+). The amount of suppression of the response produced by the inhibitory stimulus, compared with that produced by the test stimuli, indicates the amount of generalization of inhibition. A graph of the level of suppression produced by each stimulus can provide a visual display of the level of inhibitory generalization.

Excitatory-Conditioning Generalization Gradients

Much of the research on **excitatory generalization gradients** has been conducted using pigeons as subjects. Pigeons have excellent color vision, and it is easy to establish their generalization to stimuli similar to the color used in training. Guttman and Kalish's (1956) classic experiment trained hungry pigeons to peck a small illuminated disk to obtain food reinforcement. Four groups of pigeons were shown one of four colors (530, 550, 580, and 600 nm) ranging from yellowish-green to red as the training stimuli. During training, the key was illuminated for 60-second periods, and these periods alternated with 10-second periods of no illumination. The pigeons were reinforced on a VI 1-minute schedule of reinforcement when the key was illuminated; reinforcement was unavailable when the key was not illuminated. After acquisition training, Guttman and Kalish tested for generalization of response to similarly colored stimuli. The generalization test consisted of presenting the color illuminated during training and ten other stimuli (five were higher on the wavelength color spectrum, and five were lower). The researchers presented each stimulus randomly 12 times for a period of 30 seconds each time. The results showed that the pigeons made the maximum number of responses to the training stimuli (see **Figure 7.1**). Guttman and Kalish noted that the level of response declined as the difference between training and test stimuli increased. Note that Guttman and Kalish reported symmetrical generalization gradients. Furthermore, the general shape of each gradient was similar for all four subject groups, regardless of the training stimulus.

FIGURE 7.1. Generalization gradients obtained using four different wavelengths in separate groups of pigeons trained to key peck for food reinforcement. The results of this study showed that the amount of generalization decreased as the difference between the conditioning and the test stimuli increased.

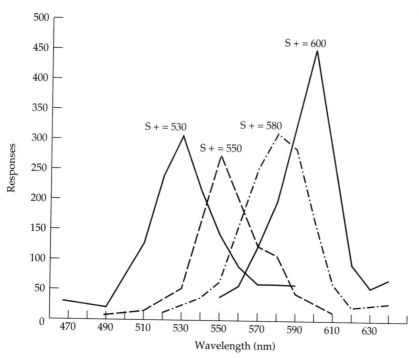

Researchers using species other than pigeons have reported generalization gradients similar to those Guttman and Kalish found in pigeons. Moore (1972) provides an illustration of this generalization gradient form in rabbits. Moore initially conditioned an eyeblink response to a 1200-Hz tone. Following conditioning, the S+ and other stimuli varying from 400 Hz to 2000 Hz were presented to the rabbits. Moore reported that the highest percentage of responding was to the 1200-Hz tone (S+) and that the rabbits' responding declined as the similarity of the test and training stimuli decreased. Razran (1949) describes the results of 54 different experiments in Pavlov's laboratory examining the generalization of salivary conditioning in dogs. The results of these experiments show a sloping-upward generalization gradient (as opposed to the sloping-downward generalization gradient **Figure 7.1** shows).

Generalization gradients like those Guttman and Kalish reported have been observed using a wide variety of stimuli and responses in humans (Bass & Hull, 1934; Hoveland, 1937; and Razran, 1949). For example, Hoveland (1937) paired a tone (S+) with electric shock and then investigated the generalization of the galvanic skin response (a measure of skin conductance that reflects autonomic nervous system arousal). Hoveland reported that less generalization occurred as the test and conditioning tones became more dissimilar (see **Figure 7.2**). Bass and Hull (1934), using a tactile stimulus (stimulation of the shoulder) as the S+ and electric shock as the UCS, presented the S+ and other tactile stimuli after conditioning of the electrodermal response (another measure of skin conductance). The form of the generalization gradient for tactile stimuli that Bass and Hull observed was similar to that found by Hoveland for auditory stimuli (refer to **Figure 7.2**). Razran (1949) examined generalization of a salivary response conditioned to words such as *style* and *urn* after pairing the training words with stimuli such as *pretzels* and *candy*. Razran noted that synonyms and homophones of the training stimuli also elicited a salivary response, and the amount of generalization increased with greater semantic similarity.

Perhaps you think the level of generalization shown in **Figure 7.1** is characteristic of all situations. Although in many circumstances an individual will respond to stimuli similar to the conditioning stimulus, in other situations, animals or people may generalize to stimuli only remotely similar to the conditioning stimulus. Consider the following example: Some people who do not interact easily with others find that being around people elicits anxiety, and, although they may be lonely, they avoid contact. These socially anxious people probably experienced some unpleasantness with another person (or persons)—perhaps another person rebuked an attempted social invitation or said something offensive. As a result of a painful social experience, a conditioned anxiety about or dislike of the other person developed. Although everyone has had an unpleasant social experience, most people limit their dislike to the person associated with the pain, or perhaps to similar individuals. Socially anxious individuals generalize their anxiety or dislike to all people, and this generalization makes all interactions difficult.

Many studies have reported flat generalization gradients; that is, an animal or person responds to stimuli quite dissimilar to the conditioning stimulus. The Jenkins and Harrison (1960) study is one example. Jenkins and Harrison trained two groups of pigeons to key peck for food reinforcement. A 1,000-Hz tone was

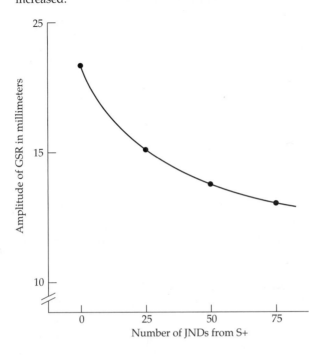

FIGURE 7.2. Amplitude of galvanic skin response (GSR) in millimeters during generalization testing as a function of the number of just noticeable differences (JNDs) from the S+. The findings revealed that the level of generalization decreased as the just noticeable difference between the conditioning and the test stimuli increased.

present during the entire conditioning phase in the control group. In contrast, animals in the experimental group received some training periods that made reinforcement contingent on key pressing, with a 1,000-Hz tone present throughout; reinforcement was unavailable despite key pecking during other training periods, and no tone was present when the reinforcement was not available. Thus, control group animals heard the 1,000-Hz tone for the entire period, while the experimental group animals heard the tone only when reinforcement was available. Generalization testing followed conditioning for both groups of pigeons. Seven tones (300, 450, 670, 1,000, 1,500, 2,250, and 3,500 Hz) were presented during generalization testing. Jenkins and Harrison's results, presented in the bottom panel of **Figure 7.3,** show that experimental animals exhibited a generalization gradient similar to the one Guttman and Kalish reported, and control animals responded to all tones equally (see top panel of **Figure 7.3**).

Inhibitory Conditioning Generalization Gradients

In all likelihood, you are apprehensive when you start dating a person. If this is your initial date with this person, you did not acquire your fear directly; your fear could be caused by one of several factors (for example, excitatory generalizations from a negative experience with another person). Suppose your

FIGURE 7.3. Percentage of total responses to S+ (1,000-Hz tone) and other stimuli (ranging in loudness from 300 to 3,500 Hz) during generalization testing for control group subjects receiving only the S+ in acquisition (top graph) and for experimental group animals given both S+ and S− in acquisition (bottom graph). A steep generalization gradient characterized the responses of experimental subjects, while a flat gradient demonstrated the behavior of control subjects.

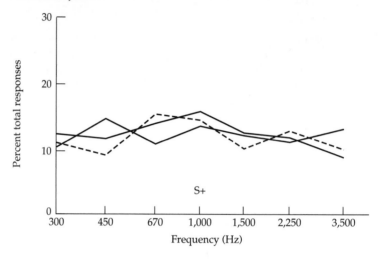

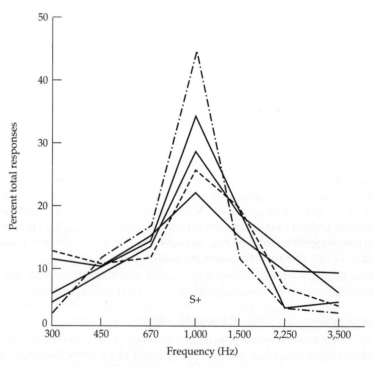

FIGURE 7.4. The inhibitory generalization gradients for five subjects receiving a vertical line as S−. The gradients show the number of responses to the test stimuli and S+. The study showed that the level of inhibition generalizing to the test stimuli increased as the difference between the training and the test stimuli decreased.

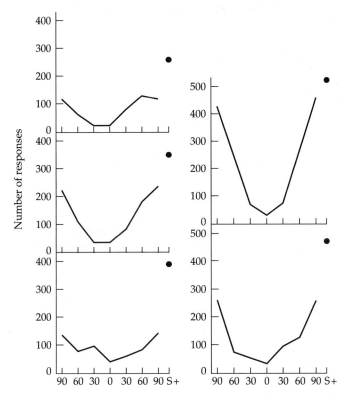

Line orientation (degrees from vertical)

fears are unfounded and you have an enjoyable time. As the result of your experience, you will associate your date with the absence of an aversive event, the occurrence of a reinforcing experience, or both. This conditioning will diminish your apprehension about dating this person again. Fortunately, the inhibition of fear not only reduces your apprehensiveness about dating this particular person but also generalizes to dating other new people. Thus, the generalization of inhibition allows you to be less fearful of dating others.

Weisman and Palmer's study (1969) illustrates the generalization of inhibition. In their study, pigeons learned to peck at a green disk (S+) to receive reinforcement on a VI 1-minute schedule. When a white vertical line (S−) was presented, the pigeons were not reinforced for disk pressing. After conditioning, the pigeons received a conditioned inhibition generalization test. In this phase of the study, the white vertical line (S−), plus six other lines that departed from the vertical line by −90, −60, −30, +30, +60, and +90 degrees were presented to the subjects. As **Figure 7.4** indicates, the presentation of the vertical line (S−) inhibited pecking. Furthermore, the amount of inhibition that generalized to other lines differed depending on the degree of similarity to the S−; the more dissimilar the line to the S−, or the extent to which the orientation of the line deviated from vertical, the less inhibition of responding.

The **inhibitory generalization gradient** shown in **Figure 7.4** is conceptually similar in form to the excitatory generalization gradient Guttman and Kalish obtained (refer to **Figure 7.1**). In both examples of generalization, maximum excitation was conditioned to the S+, or maximum inhibition was conditioned to the S−, and the degree of generalization gradually declined with decreasing similarity to the S+ or S−. As is true of excitatory generalization gradients, in certain circumstances, inhibition generalizes to stimuli quite dissimilar to the training stimulus. Even dissimilar stimuli can sometimes produce responses equivalent to those elicited by the conditioning stimulus.

The generalization of inhibition to stimuli quite dissimilar to the training stimulus is apparent in a study Hoffman (1969) did. In his study, pigeons first learned to key peck for food reinforcement. Following this initial training phase, the birds were exposed to 24 conditioning sessions. During each session, a 2-minute, 88-dB noise preceding an electric shock was presented three times, and a 2-minute, 88-dB, 1,000-Hz tone not followed by electric shock was presented three times. Hoffman's procedure established the 88-dB noise (S+) as a feared stimulus, and the presentation of the 88-dB noise suppressed key pecking. In contrast, little suppression was noted when the 88-dB, 1,000-Hz tone (S−) was presented. Furthermore, the presence of the tone inhibited fear to the noise. Generalization-of-inhibition testing consisted of presenting the noise (S+) and several test tones. The tones varied in pitch from 300 to 3,400 Hz. Hoffman reported that each tone equally inhibited the suppressive ability of the noise. Almost complete generalization of inhibition had occurred; that is, tones with very dissimilar pitches produced about as much inhibition as did the S− (1,000-Hz tone).

The Nature of the Generalization Process

Why do we generalize our response to stimuli similar to the stimulus associated with conditioning at certain times, but show no generalization to similar stimuli at other times? Many theories have been proposed to explain stimulus generalization (refer to Prokasy & Hall, 1963, for a review of these theories). We will examine the **Lashley-Wade theory** of stimulus generalization as it seems to best explain why generalization occurs on some occasions but not others.

Lashley and Wade (1946) suggested that animals and people respond to stimuli that differ from the training stimulus because they are unable to distinguish between the generalization test stimulus and the conditioning stimulus. Thus, an inability to discriminate between the training and test stimuli is responsible for stimulus generalization. For example, if people could differentiate between the conditioning stimulus and other stimuli, Lashley and Wade's view suggests that they would not show a generalized response to the other stimuli. Therefore, according to Lashley and Wade, generalization represents the failure to discriminate; discrimination prevents generalization, and a failure to discriminate leads to generalization.

Several lines of evidence support the Lashley-Wade view of stimulus generalization. First, generalization to stimuli even dissimilar to the training stimulus occurs when nondifferential reinforcement training is used. When a nondifferential reinforcement is employed, the conditioning stimulus is present during the entire training session. Thus, the only stimulus the subject experiences is the excitatory stimulus (S+). The Lashley-Wade view assumes that without experience with stimuli other than the S+, the subject will generalize to all similar stimuli. The Jenkins and Harrison study (1960) previously described provides an excellent example of the flat stimulus generalization gradient. In their study, control group animals received nondifferential training, with the 100-Hz tone present during the entire conditioning session. Following training, each subject was exposed to 7 tones ranging from 300 to 3,500 Hz and to a non-tone presentation. As the top panel of **Figure 7.3** shows, the pigeons responded equally to all tones.

The second line of evidence is that discrimination training results in generalization only to stimuli very similar to the conditioning stimulus. As discussed earlier, during discrimination training, the excitatory stimulus (S+) is present when reinforcement is available, and the inhibitory stimulus (S−) is present when reinforcement is unavailable. According to the Lashley-Wade view, an animal learns to differentiate between the S+ and other stimuli as the result of discrimination training. This knowledge produces responses that are almost always limited to the S+, with few or no responses to other stimuli; that is, little or no stimulus generalization occurs when an animal recognizes the specific stimulus associated with reinforcement.

A number of studies show that discrimination training leads to steep generalization gradients. We described a few of these experiments earlier in the chapter. The Jenkins and Harrison (1960) study also evaluated the influence of discrimination training on stimulus generalization gradients. A brief review of their experiment will document the effect of discrimination training on the level of stimulus generalization. Jenkins and Harrison trained pigeons to discriminate between a key that produced the S+ (a 100-Hz tone) and resulted in reinforcement and a key associated with the S− (no tone presented) that did not lead to reinforcement. After training, stimulus generalization testing presented seven tones ranging from 300 to 3,500 Hz. The bottom panel of **Figure 7.3** illustrates that this discrimination training produced a steep generalization gradient.

The third line of evidence, according to Lashley and Wade, is that generalization occurs when an animal cannot differentiate between the training stimulus and generalization test stimuli. An extension of this view suggests that little generalization should occur, and that discrimination should readily form, when an animal can easily differentiate between S+ and S−. The literature (see Kalish, 1969) indicates that the more able an animal is to differentiate between the S+ and S−, the easier it learns a discrimination. Furthermore, a steeper generalization gradient is observed when an animal can easily distinguish between the S+ and S−.

The final evidence supporting the Lashley-Wade theory is that perceptual experience influences the amount of stimulus generalization. The Lashley-Wade view assumes that animals learn to distinguish similarities and differences in environmental events. This perceptual learning is essential for an animal to discriminate between different stimuli, yet generalize to similar stimuli. Without this perceptual experience, different environmental events would appear similar, thereby making discrimination very difficult. For example, a person with little or no experience with varied colors might find it difficult to distinguish between green and red; this difficulty could result in failing to learn to observe traffic lights. Several studies have evaluated the influence of various levels of perceptual experience on the level of stimulus generalization (Houston, 1986); these results have shown that as perceptual experience increases, the generalization gradient becomes steeper.

Peterson's classic study (1962) illustrates the effect of perceptual experience on the amount of stimulus generalization. Peterson raised two groups of ducks under different conditions. The experimental group ducks were raised in cages illuminated by a 589-nm light and therefore experienced only a single color. In contrast, control group animals were raised in normal light and were exposed to a wide range of colors. During the initial phase of the study, Peterson trained the ducks to peck at a key illuminated by the 589-nm light. After training, both groups received generalization testing using stimuli varying from a 490-nm to 650-nm light. The top panel of **Figure 7.5** illustrates that ducklings raised in a monochromatic environment showed a flat generalization gradient. These results indicate that ducks without perceptual experience with various colors generalized their response to all colors. In contrast, the ducks raised in normal light displayed the greatest response to the S+ (the 589-nm light; see bottom panel of **Figure 7.5**). As the result of perceptual experience with various colors, animals apparently learn to differentiate between colors and are therefore less likely to generalize to similar colors. A similar influence of restricted perceptual experience on stimulus generalization was observed in rats (Walk & Walters, 1973), in monkeys (Ganz & Riesen, 1962), and in congenitally blind humans (Ganz, 1968).

BEFORE YOU GO ON

- **How would the Lashley-Wade theory explain Miguel's failure to correctly identify his assailant?**
- **What would the Lashley-Wade theory suggest might prevent Miguel from making a wrongful accusation?**

DISCRIMINATION LEARNING

We know that during some occasions, reinforcement is available and will occur contingent on an appropriate response, while during other occasions, reinforcement is unavailable and will not occur despite continued responding. To respond when reinforcement is available and not when reinforcement is unavailable, we must learn to discriminate; that is, we must not only discover the conditions indicating that reinforcement is available and respond when those conditions exist, we must also recognize the circumstances indicating that reinforcement is unavailable and not respond during these times. Skinner (1938)

FIGURE 7.5. Generalization gradients obtained with ducklings reared in monochromatic light (top graph) and in white light (bottom graph). Ducklings raised in monochromatic light exhibited flat generalization gradients, whereas those reared in white light demonstrated steep generalization gradients.

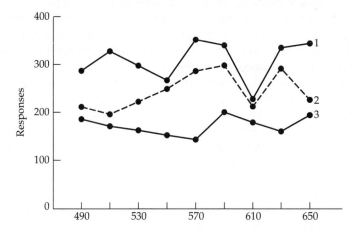

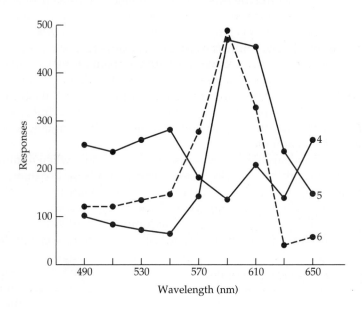

referred to a stimulus associated with reinforcement availability as an **S^D** (or S-dee) and a stimulus associated with the unavailability of reinforcement as an **S^Δ** (or an S-delta). Further, Skinner called an operant behavior under the control of a **discriminative stimulus** (either an S^D or an S^Δ) as a **discriminative operant.**

We are faced with thousands of **discrimination learning** tasks during our lives. For example, suppose that you want to see a particular movie at your local theater. In many movie theaters, you cannot just walk in; you must first get into the right line. If the line for the movie that you want to see is indicated by a blue line or specified number (S^Ds), then reinforcement (the movie) is available only if you get into the right line. You will not be able to see the movie if you get into the wrong line (S^Δ). The S^D is a stimulus signaling that the reinforcer is available, while the S^Δ is a stimulus indicating that the reinforcer is unavailable.

To interact effectively with our environment, we must learn to discriminate the conditions that indicate reinforcement availability (S^D) from the conditions that do not (S^Δ). The failure to discriminate will cause us not to respond when reinforcement is available, to respond when reinforcement is unavailable, or both. Thus, you will miss the movie that you wanted to see if you get into the wrong line at the movie theater. In most cases, the failure to discriminate will cause inconvenience. For example, you will lose time and effort if you go to the library if it's closed. Embarrassment may occur during some circumstances if you do not discriminate. If you go to the movies with friends, you will feel foolish if you usher them into the wrong line. In some cases, behavior pathology can result from discriminative failure. Consider a sociopath who fails to discriminate between the acceptability of violence on television and the unacceptability of violent behavior in real life.

The failure to discriminate need not occur. The following study illustrates that the ability to discriminate between stimuli merely reflects the use of differential reinforcement contingencies. Watanabe, Sakamoto, and Wakita (1995) reinforced pigeons for key pecking in the presence of the works of a certain painter (for example, the impressionist Claude Monet). The pigeons were not reinforced in the presence of the works of another painter (for example, the cubist Pablo Picasso). Watanabe, Sakamoto, and Wakita found that the pigeons learned to respond in the presence of Monet's paintings (S^D), but not to respond to Picasso's (S^Δ). So the next time you think you cannot discriminate between two stimuli, remember the pigeons who learned to discriminate between the paintings of Monet and Picasso.

Discrimination learning involves discovering not only when reinforcement is available or unavailable, but also when aversive events may or may not occur. For example, some conditions forecast rain, and some predict no rain. Since you will get wet (typically an aversive event) if you go out in the rain, you need to carry an umbrella when it rains to avoid becoming wet. If you fail to learn the conditions indicating impending rain, you will often become wet. Similarly, you need not carry an umbrella on a clear, sunny day. Nothing appears quite as foolish as someone carrying an umbrella when the sun is shining. However, it is difficult to learn when to carry an umbrella and when not to, because no stimuli always signal rain (the aversive event) or always indicate no rain (the absence of the aversive event). We will discuss the influence of predictiveness on discrimination learning later in the chapter.

In many circumstances, the occurrence or nonoccurrence of aversive events is easily predicted. A course outline for this class indicates that an exam is impending, but the lack of a specified prior announcement means you will have no exam. If you recognize the significance of the schedule, you will study before the next exam, but you will not study if no exam is scheduled. The failure to discriminate may cause you to study even though you have no exam, or to fail to prepare for a scheduled exam. Another example of discrimination in aversive situations involves children who misbehave for a substitute teacher but behave appropriately with their regular teacher. Their behavior is based on having learned that their regular teacher will punish them but that a substitute is not likely to do so.

You might have noticed that the abbreviations changed from S+ and S− in the generalization discussion to S^D and S^Δ in the discussion of discrimination learning. This change reflects the conventional terms used in each area of research; it does not indicate that we are talking about different stimuli, but instead that we are referring to different properties of the same stimulus. Consider the following example to illustrate that a stimulus can function as both a discriminative stimulus and a conditioned stimulus. On a hot summer day, going to the beach can be quite reinforcing. The hot summer day is a discriminative stimulus that indicates that reinforcement is available; it is also a conditioned stimulus that motivates the instrumental activity of going to the beach.

Perhaps you are still confused about the difference between a conditioned stimulus and a discrimination stimulus. A conditioned stimulus automatically elicits a conditioned response. In contrast, a discriminative stimulus "sets the occasion" for an operant or instrumental behavior. As an example, consider watching a favorite television show. As the time for the program approaches, you become excited (a conditioned response). You also turn on the television. The time of the show both elicits the involuntary conditioned response and "sets the occasion" for you to emit the voluntary operant behavior of turning on the television to the appropriate channel.

Sometimes, discrimination learning involves one stimulus as the S^D and another as the S^Δ. At other times, the same stimulus can be an S^D, while at other times, the same stimulus can be an S^Δ. In the next section, we will discuss these two types of discrimination situations.

Discrimination Paradigms

Two-Choice Discrimination Tasks

In a **two-choice discrimination learning** task, the S^D (the stimulus signaling reinforcement or punishment availability) and the S^Δ (the stimulus signaling reinforcement or punishment unavailability) are on the same stimulus dimension (for example, the S^D is a red light and the S^Δ a green light). Responding to the S^D produces reinforcement or punishment, and choosing the S^Δ leads to neither reinforcement nor punishment.

In some cases, the S^D and the S^Δ are presented simultaneously, while in other cases, the S^D and the S^Δ are presented sequentially. It also is not unusual for there to be more than one S^D and more than one S^Δ. In some situations, the choice is between just two stimuli; in other situations, the choice is between several stimuli. Two-choice discrimination occurs in a situation in which an animal or person must choose between responding to either an S^D or an S^Δ.

Consider the following example of a two-choice discrimination task. Suppose that one of a child's parents is generous, and the other parent is conservative. Asking one parent for money to go to the video arcade will be successful; a request to the other will result in failure. The first parent is an S^D since his or her presence indicates that reinforcement is available. Because reinforcement is unavailable when the other parent is asked, the presence of this parent is an S$^\Delta$.

Research evaluating two-choice discrimination learning shows that individuals begin by responding equally to the S^D and S$^\Delta$. With continued training, responding to the S^D increases and the response rate to the S$^\Delta$ declines. At the end of training, an individual is responding at a high rate to the S^D and responding little or not at all to the S$^\Delta$.

Reynolds (1961a) initially trained his pigeons to peck for food reinforcement on a multiple VI 3-minute, VI 3-minute schedule. (A multiple schedule is a compound schedule that consists of two or more independent schedules presented successively; each schedule is associated with a distinctive stimulus.) In Reynolds's study, the researchers presented a red light and a green light associated with the separate components of the multiple schedule. As **Figure 7.6** demonstrates, Reynolds's pigeons exhibited equal responses to the red and green lights during the prediscrimination phase of his study. In the discrimination stage, the schedule was changed to a multiple VI 3-minute, extinction schedule. In this schedule, the red light continued to be correlated with reinforcement and the green light was associated with the extinction (or nonreinforcement) component of the multiple schedule. During the discrimination phase of the study, Reynolds noted that the response rate to the red light (S^D) increased, and responding to the green light (S$^\Delta$) declined (refer to **Figure 7.6**). To show that the response change during the discrimination phase was due to

FIGURE 7.6. Mean number of responses per minute during discrimination learning. The pigeons' responses to the reinforced key increased as their responses to the nonreinforced key declined.

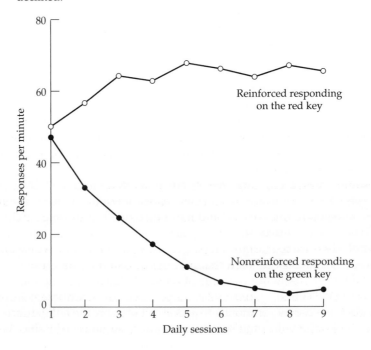

differential reinforcement, Reynolds shifted the schedule back to a multiple VI 3-minute, VI 3-minute schedule in the third phase of his study. Reynolds found that responding to the red light declined, and responding to the green light increased during the third (nondiscrimination) phase, until an equivalent response rate occurred to both stimuli. This indicates that the differential reinforcement procedure controlled responding during the discrimination phase.

Studies using human subjects indicate that people are sensitive to two-choice discrimination tasks (see Hall, 1982). Illustrating the acquisition of a two-choice discrimination in people, Terrell and Ware (1961) trained kindergarten and first-grade children to discriminate between three-dimensional geometric forms. In one discrimination, the children needed to distinguish between large and small cubed boxes; in the other discrimination, between a sphere and pyramid. A light indicated a correct response. Terrell and Ware reported that the children quickly learned to discriminate between the geometric forms. These observations indicate that positive reinforcement—in this case, a light—is a critical ingredient for discrimination learning, even with humans.

Conditional Discrimination Task

In a **conditional discrimination** task, the reinforcement contingency associated with a particular stimulus depends on the status of a second stimulus. In other words, a specific stimulus does not always signal either the availability or nonavailability of reinforcement in a conditional discrimination task. Instead, in some circumstances, a particular cue indicates that reinforcement is contingent on the occurrence of an appropriate response, whereas under other conditions, the cue does not signal reinforcement availability. As was the case with a two-choice discrimination, the stimuli may occur simultaneously or sequentially. Further, there may be two or more S^Ds and S^Δs in a conditional discrimination.

Consider the following example. Suppose that a child wants a dollar to spend at the store. The child may ask his or her parents, but knows that under most conditions the request will be denied. In contrast, when a relative is with the parents, the parents grant the child's request. This child will eventually learn to ask for money only when a relative is nearby. In this example, the parents' and relative's presence is an S^D signaling the availability of reinforcement. Thus, the child's request to the parents for money will be effective when a relative is present but ineffective when no relative is visiting (S^Δ). There are many instances of conditional discrimination in the real world. For example, a store is open at certain hours and closed at others, or a colleague is friendly sometimes but hostile at other times.

It is more difficult to learn that a particular cue signals reinforcement availability sometimes but not at other times than to learn that a specific stimulus is always associated with either reinforcer availability or nonavailability. However, we must discover when a cue signals reinforcement availability and when it does not if we are to interact effectively with our environment. Psychologists (D'Amato, 1970) have observed that both animals and humans can learn a conditional discrimination; we will look at one of these studies next.

Nissen (1951) discovered that chimpanzees can learn a conditional discrimination. In Nissen's study, large and small squares were the discriminative stimuli; the brightness of the squares was the conditional stimulus. When the squares were white, the large square was the S^D and the small square was the S^Δ; when the squares were black, the small square was the S^D and the large square was the S^Δ. Nissen reported that his chimpanzees learned to respond effectively; that is, they responded to the large square when it was white but not black, and to the small square when it was black but not white.

Behavioral Contrast

Recall our discussion of Reynolds's two-choice discrimination study in which pigeons learned to respond to a red light (S^D) and not to respond to a green light (S^Δ). Reynolds found that not only did the animals stop responding to the green light (S^Δ), but they also increased their response rate to the red light (S^D) during the discrimination phase of the study. The increased response to S^D and decreased response to S^Δ is called **behavioral contrast.** The increased response rate occurs to S^D despite the fact that the reinforcement schedule has not changed. Behavioral contrast has been consistently observed in differential reinforcement situations (Aronson, Balsam, & Gibbon, 1993; McSweeney & Melville, 1988; Williams, 1989).

Behavioral contrast also can be produced when there is a decrease or increase in reinforcement disparity (Williams, 1983). As we learned in Chapter 4, responding increases when the reinforcer magnitude changes from low to high and decreases when the reinforcer magnitude changes from high to low. Further, the level of contrast is determined by the difference in relative reinforcement contingencies: the greater the difference in reinforcement contingencies, the greater the contrast (Williams, 1983). Differences in the duration of each component of a discrimination will also produce behavioral contrast (Aronson, Balsam, & Gibbons, 1993). In this case, responding will increase when the change is from a less valued to a more valued duration, and decrease when the reinforcement duration changes from a more valued to a less valued duration. As one example, Williams (1991b) found maximum contrast with a multiple VI 3-minute, VI 10-minute contingency, with the VI-10-minute schedule being the less valued duration.

Charles Flaherty (1996) has described two important aspects of the behavioral contrast phenomenon: local contrast and sustained contrast. A change in responding (increase to the S^D and decrease to the S^Δ) that is activated by the switch from S^D to the S^Δ or vice versa is called **local contrast.** This change in responding fades with extended training and is due to the emotional reponse (elation or frustration) elicited by a change in reinforcement contingency. Thus, a pigeon becomes frustrated by the switch from S^D to S^Δ and elated by the switch from S^Δ to S^D. A change in responding that occurs due to the anticipation of the impending reinforcement contingencies is called **sustained contrast.** This change will persist as long as the differential reinforcement contingencies exist. According to Flaherty, an animal's response to S^D or to S^Δ is determined by comparing the current reinforcement with the one it just left (local contrast) and the one coming next (sustained next). If the comparison is positive (as when anticipating a shift from S^D to S^Δ), responding to the S^D will be high. In contrast, if the comparison is negative (as when anticipating a shift from S^Δ to S^D), responding to the S^Δ will be low.

Williams (1983) provides evidence that sustained contrast (which he calls **anticipatory contrast**) is due to the anticipation of a future reinforcement contingency rather than the recall of the past reinforcement contingency. Williams used a multiple VI 3-minute, VI 6-minute, VI 3-minute schedule. (In this multiple schedule, the pigeon was reinforced for key pecking on a VI 3-minute schedule for the first and third components of the schedule and on a VI 6-minute schedule for the second, middle component). A different stimulus signals each component of this schedule. Williams was most interested in the pigeons' response rate in the first and third components (or those components that preceded or followed the less valued duration). Williams found the less valued VI 6-minute second component had more influence on the pigeons' responding in the first than in the third VI 3-minute component. According to Williams, these results suggest that the level of the pigeons' responding was influenced more by the impending reinforcement contingency (VI 3-minute component to VI 6-minute component) than by the preceding reinforcement contingency (VI 6-minute to VI 3-minute component).

The behavioral contrast phenomenon points to one problem with discrimination learning: it can have negative consequences. Consider the following situation. The teacher of a disruptive child decides to extinguish the disruptive behavior by no longer reinforcing (perhaps by discontinuing attention to the child's disruptive activities). But the child's parents may continue to attend to the disruptive behavior. In this case, the child will be disruptive at home (S^D) but not at school (S^Δ). In fact, the parents will probably experience an increase in disruptive behavior at home due to behavioral contrast; that is, as the rate of disruptive behavior during school declines, the child will become more disruptive at home. Parents can deal with this situation only by discontinuing reinforcement (e.g., giving attention) of the disruptive behavior in the home. This observation points out that one consequence of extinguishing an undesired behavior in one setting is an increase in that behavior in other situations. The desired method is to extinguish an undesired behavior in all situations.

BEFORE YOU GO ON

- **What stimulus was the S^D for Miguel?**
- **Suggest an experience that led Miguel to incorrectly identify his assailant.**

Occasion Setting

You may still have difficulty understanding the difference between a conditioned stimulus that elicits (involuntarily produces) a conditioned response and a discriminative stimulus that "sets the occasion" for emitting (voluntarily producing) an operant response. One way to appreciate the difference between the eliciting function of a conditioned stimulus and the occasion-setting function of a discriminative stimulus is to examine the occasion-setting function of a conditioned stimulus.

A conditioned stimulus can have an excitatory property other than the elicitation of the conditioned response. In some circumstances, a conditioned stimulus can prepare, or "set the occasion," for an animal to respond to a second conditioned stimulus. In other words, an occasion-setting stimulus can create the conditions necessary for a conditioned stimulus to elicit the conditioned response. In the absence of the occasion-setting stimulus, the conditioned stimulus has no effect on behavior.

Perhaps a real-world example of occasion setting would be helpful. Many people smoke at the end of a meal. These people see a cigarette at this time and feel a need to smoke. Yet, at other times, the sight of a cigarette does not produce a craving to smoke. It could be argued that the end of the meal is the occasion-setter for the cigarette to elicit craving as the conditioned response. Why would the end of the meal be an occasion-setter for cigarette-induced craving? People report that smoking a cigarette is more pleasurable after a meal than at other times. Thus, a cigarette is more strongly associated with pleasure following a meal (the occasion-setter) than at other times.

Holland (1992) has referred to the ability of one stimulus to enhance the response to another stimulus as **occasion setting,** because one stimulus "sets the occasion" for another stimulus to elicit the conditioned response. Rescorla (1990) suggested that the occasion-setting stimulus facilitates responding to the conditioned stimulus.

When will a stimulus be able to facilitate responding by another stimulus? Holland (1983, 1986, 1992) and Rescorla (1985, 1986, 1990) conducted a number of studies investigating the occasion-setting ability of a stimulus. In a typical experiment, pigeons experience stimulus A (for example, a localized lighted key on the wall of operant chamber) without the unconditioned stimulus on some trials (see **Figure 7.7**). On other trials, stimulus A follows a diffuse stimulus B (for example, an 1,800-Hz tone), and both stimuli are paired with the unconditioned stimulus of food. In this research, the conditioned response is the key peck to the lighted key; that is, the pigeons' conditioned response to the lighted key is the same as their unconditioned pecking response to food (see Chapter 3). The presentation of stimulus A (the lighted key) alone elicited no responding. In contrast, the presentation of stimulus B, or the occasion-setting stimulus (a 1,800-Hz tone), prior to stimulus A (the lighted key) caused stimulus A to elicit the conditioned key peck response. In other words, the pigeons did not peck at the lighted key when it was presented alone, but the lighted key did elicit a conditioned key peck response when it followed the tone.

You might think that the response to stimulus A (lighted key) in the presence of stimulus B (tone) is merely due to excitatory conditioning to stimulus B. However, both Holland (1992) and Rescorla (1990) argue that conditioned excitation and facilitation are separate properties of a stimulus. Conditioned excitation refers to a stimulus eliciting a conditioned response, while facilitation represents a stimulus's occasion-setting function.

Several lines of evidence demonstrate the separate facilitation and excitation properties of a stimulus. Excitatory conditioning to stimulus B does not automatically lead that stimulus to facilitate a response to stimulus A (Rescorla, 1985). Also, the establishment of stimulus B as a facilitator of response to stimulus A does not result in the ability of stimulus B to elicit a conditioned response (Holland, 1983). Further, the facilitating influence of stimulus B may transfer to conditioned stimuli other than stimulus A (Rescorla, 1985). These observations provide strong support for the view that facilitation and excitation represent separate learning processes.

What process enables a conditioned stimulus to facilitate responding to other stimuli? Rescorla (1986) argued that the facilitating effect of a stimulus is produced by lowering the threshold of reaction to conditioned stimuli. He suggests that this facilitation effect is the opposite of the effect of conditioned inhibition, which raises the threshold reaction. Support for this conclusion can be found in the observation that stimulus B facilitates responding to excitatory conditioned stimuli but not to neutral stimuli (Rescorla, 1985). Thus, the facilitating effect of a stimulus seems to be limited to stimuli possessing excitatory associative strength.

An occasion-setter, however, facilitates responding to an excitatory conditioned stimulus only if that conditioned stimulus has previously served as a target stimulus for other occasion-setters (Holland, 1992; Wilson & Pearce, 1990). If the excitatory conditioned stimulus has not been associated with another occasion-setter during conditioning, the presentation of the occasion-setting stimuli will not facilitate a response to that excitatory stimulus. The fact that an occasion-setter influences the response only to those excitatory conditioning stimuli previously associated with other occasion-setting stimuli points to the important role that contingency plays in Pavlovian conditioning. The process by which contingency affects Pavlovian conditioning will be explored in the next chapter.

FIGURE 7.7. Illustration of the occasion-setting procedure. Animals receive light (stimulus A) without a food UCS on some (X) trials. On other (Y) trials, the light stimulus follows a more diffuse tone (stimulus B), which are both paired with the food UCS.

X trials
Light — Food (stimulus A) (UCS)

Y trials
Diffuse + Light + Food tone (stimulus A) (UCS) (stimulus B)

An occasion-setter can inhibit as well as facilitate responding (Holland, 1985). A stimulus will suppress rather than enhance the response to a conditioned stimulus when the occasion-setter predicts that the unconditioned stimulus will not follow the conditioned stimulus.

We have learned that one conditioned stimulus can facilitate the ability of another conditioned stimulus to elicit a conditioned response. In the next section, we will discover that a discriminative stimulus also can enhance the response to a conditioned stimulus.

The Occasion-Setting Function of a Discriminative Stimulus

Rescorla and his colleagues (Davidson, Aparicio, & Rescorla, 1988) have reported that a Pavlovian occasion-setter can increase operant behavior. In their study, a light became a Pavlovian occasion-setter after the light was presented prior to a tone (excitatory conditioned stimulus) and food (UCS) on half of the trials, with only the tone presented on the other half of the trials. After the light was established as a Pavlovian occasion-setter, the subjects, rats, were given discrimination training in which bar pressing produced food reinforcement when a white noise was present (S^D), but not when the white noise was absent (S^Δ). Following discrimination training, the researchers assessed the influence of both a Pavlovian occasion-setter and the discriminative stimulus (S^D) on bar pressing. Davidson, Aparicio, and Rescorla found that both the Pavlovian occasion-setter and the discriminative stimulus (S^D) increased bar pressing (see **Figure 7.8**).

In the Davidson, Aparicio, and Rescorla study, the Pavlovian occasion-setter signaled reinforcement. This study also examined the effect of a pseudo-facilitatory stimulus, a stimulus that did not signal reinforcement. In the pseudofacilitation control treatment, the UCS (food) followed both the light and tone pairings and the tone alone. Thus, the light pseudofacilitatory stimulus provided no information about food reinforcement. Davidson, Aparicio, and Rescorla found that the pseudofacilitatory stimulus had no effect on the operant bar pressing response (see **Figure 7.8**). This failure of the pseudofacilitatory stimulus to influence operant responding again points to the importance of contingency in the ability of a stimulus to act as an occasion-setter.

To illustrate the influence of an occasion-setter on operant behavior, let's return to a previous example—the end of a meal acting as an occasion-setter so that the sight of a cigarette elicits a conditioned craving response. Suppose that the person does not have a cigarette. He or she might ask a friend for one. The request is an operant behavior, and the end of the meal "sets the occasion" for the request.

Recall our discussion of conditional discrimination learning earlier in this chapter. We learned that the ability of a discriminative stimulus to influence operant behavior depends upon the presence or absence of a second stimulus. Arnold, Grahame, and Miller (1991) observed a similar conditional or higher-order occasion setting. In their study, rats first learned a discrimination task; a bar press response produced water reinforcement when a light was present (S^D), but not when it was absent (S^Δ). After discrimination training, a conditional occasion-setter (a click or a buzzer) was presented prior to the light S^D and the reinforcement. When a second stimulus (a buzzer or a click) was also present, the light was not associated with reinforcement. Arnold, Grahame, and Miller

FIGURE 7.8. The mean discrimination ratio to a Pavlovian occasion-setter (L), a pseudofacilitatory stimulus (L') and an operant discriminative stimulus (S^D). (In the mean discrimination ratio, A is the mean number of responses to the stimulus, and B is the mean number of responses during the time between trials.) The results show that rats bar press when presented the Pavlovian occasion-setter (L) and the operant discriminative stimulus (S^D), but not the pseudofacilitatory stimulus (L').

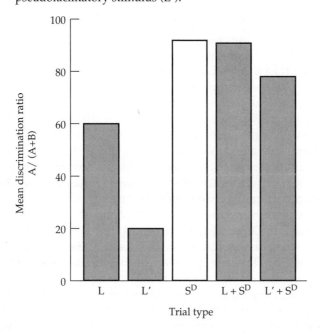

found that the rats bar pressed in the presence of the light S^D only when it followed the higher-order occasion-setter. The higher-order occasion-setter is the occasion-setting stimulus (click or buzzer) that signaled reinforcement in the presence of the light S^D.

The elicitation of a CR by an excitatory CS is influenced not only by Pavlovian occasion-setting stimuli, but also by discriminative stimuli (Davidson, Aparicio, & Rescorla, 1988). In the Davidson, Aparicio, and Rescorla study, rats initially received food reinforcement for a bar press response on a VI 30-second schedule in the presence of a light S^D, but they were not reinforced in the absence of the light. After operant conditioning, occasion-setting training occurred; a click (CS) was followed by food (UCS) only when the click was preceded by a tone (occasion-setter). Davidson, Aparico, and Rescorla reported that the presence of the light S^D enhanced the conditioned head-jerk response to the click conditioned stimulus.

These findings suggest that an S^D can facilitate the response to a CS just as an occasion-setter does. These findings also imply an interchangeability of Pavlovian occasion-setters and discriminative stimuli, with one stimulus acting on the target behaviors of the other. Perhaps Pavlovian occasion-setters and discriminative stimuli influence the same central nervous system structures. Chapter 10 will discuss the possible neural mechanisms that underlie the influence of Pavlovian occasion-setters and discriminative stimuli.

We have learned that a discriminative stimulus can "set the occasion" for a conditioned stimulus to elicit a conditioned response. Conditioned stimuli also can "set the occasion" for emitting an operant or instrumental response. The next section will discuss this additional occasion-setting influence of conditioned stimuli.

Conditioned Stimuli and Operant or Instrumental Behavior

Consider the following two situations: (1) You are in a movie theater when a fire alarm sounds. The alarm causes you to stop watching the movie and rush from the theater. (2) You are studying for tomorrow's exam when you realize it's time for your favorite television show. You stop studying to watch the show. Both examples contain a particular element (the fire alarm and the scheduled time) that suppressed one behavior and evoked another. The fire alarm motivated you to terminate watching the movie and escape from the theater; the scheduled time inhibited your studying and motivated you to turn on the television.

Rescorla and Solomon's (1967) theory offers an explanation for the behavior exhibited in the previous two examples. According to Rescorla and Solomon, two central motivational states govern behavior. Arousal of an appetitive state motivates approach behavior; activation of an aversive state arouses avoidance behavior. (One way to think of motivation is to assume that motives directly elicit behavior. Another way is to assume that motives "set the occasion" for responding. The latter is the approach adopted here.)

Two types of conditioned stimuli stimulate the appetitive state and inhibit the aversive state. Why do you stop studying to watch your favorite television show? Since you associate the scheduled time of your favorite television show with past reward, that specific time can excite the central appetitive state and suppress the aversive state as a conditioned response. Spence (1956) called this response the anticipatory goal response (see Chapter 6); Mowrer (1960) called it hope.

The other type of conditioned stimulus that activates the central appetitive state and inhibits the aversive state is associated with the absence of an aversive event. For example, if you bolted from the theater when the fire alarm sounded, you would probably reenter when the alarm stopped (if, of course, you have been reassured of safety) and resume watching the movie. Rescorla and Solomon would argue that through conditioning, the termination of a stimulus (the fire alarm) associated with the absence of an aversive event (fire) stimulated the central appetitive state and suppressed the aversive state. D'Amato (1970) labeled this response an anticipatory relief response (see Chapter 6); Mowrer (1960) labeled it relief.

Two types of conditioned stimuli also stimulate the central aversive state and inhibit the appetitive state. Because the fire alarm was associated with fire, the alarm inhibited the appetitive state and therefore suppressed the watching of the movie. In addition, the alarm activated the aversive state, which in turn motivated escape behavior. Mowrer referred to this response as fear; D'Amato called it an anticipatory pain response (see Chapter 6). When a stimulus is associated with the absence of reward, the conditioned response this stimulus produces can excite the central aversive state and inhibit the appetitive state. Amsel (1958) labeled this an anticipatory frustration response (see Chapter 6); Mowrer referred to it as disappointment.

Why does a conditioned stimulus excite one state yet inhibit the other state? Suppose that the scheduled television show aroused only the appetitive state and did not inhibit the aversive state. If this were the case, we would be unable to respond because our approach and avoidance tendencies would have equal motive strength. Judson Brown's classic research (1948) on approach-avoidance conflict shows that equivalent approach and avoidance motive strengths produce vascillation; that is, the animal or person can neither approach reward nor avoid an aversive event. Therefore, the scheduled television show must inhibit the aversive state as well as excite the appetitive state to induce you to stop studying and turn on your favorite show.

Many studies support the theory that conditioned stimuli influence operant or instrumental behavior through their effect on the two central motivational states. To validate this theory, a study must classically condition a response to a specific stimulus, establish an operant or instrumental behavior, and then evaluate how the conditioned stimulus "sets the occasion" for the operant or instrumental response. **Figure 7.9** presents a diagram of the behavioral predictions of the Rescorla-Solomon theory. The figure indicates the predicted direction of behavioral change that each type of conditioned stimulus produces. For example, hope and relief should increase appetitive behavior (cells 1 and 7) and decrease aversive behavior (cells 2 and 8). Trapold and Winokur's (1967) study shows the influence of a conditioned stimulus paired with food on bar pressing behavior. The authors found, as predicted in cell 1, that the CS previously paired with food increased bar pressing. By contrast, Trapold and Winokur observed, as predicted by cell 3, that another stimulus paired with the absence of food decreased bar pressing.

A study by Grossen, Kostensek, and Bolles (1969) illustrates how hope (cell 2) and disappointment (cell 4) influence aversive behavior. In the first phase of the study, rats were trained to postpone shock by running from one compartment of a shuttle box to a second chamber and then back to the original compartment. Following the establishment of the avoidance response, one group of rats was exposed to tone-food pairings and another group to tones with no food. Results indicated that the tone suppressed avoidance behavior among the rats that received tone-food pairings, but increased the response among the rats given tones with no food.

The emotional responses (fear and relief) acquired in aversive situations also influence operant or instrumental behavior. A study by Annau and Kamin (1961) demonstrated how fear affects an appetitive bar press response. The authors observed that a stimulus previously paired with shock suppressed rats' bar press behavior for food (as predicted in cell 5). In addition to suppressing appetitive behavior, fear also enhances avoidance behavior (cell 6). The influence of fear on avoidance behavior is exemplified in a study by Martin and Riess (1969). Following the pairing of a light with shock, the conditioned fear stimulus increased the level of a previously learned operant bar press avoidance response. Rescorla and LoLordo (1965) demonstrated that a stimulus associated

FIGURE 7.9. Matrix illustration of the interaction between conditioned stimuli and operant or instrumental behavior. Arrows indicate whether the conditioned stimulus facilitates (↑) or suppresses (↓) behavior. The terms in parentheses show the conditioned emotional response that a particular conditioned stimulus elicits.

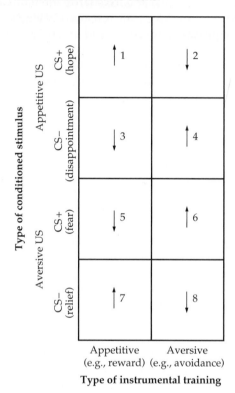

Type of instrumental training

with the absence of shock suppressed an avoidance response, as predicted in cell 8. Finally, as predicted in cell 7, Hammond (1966) showed that a stimulus paired with the absence of shock enhanced the appetitive response for food.

Our discussion indicates that emotional responses acquired through classical conditioning influence operant or instrumental behavior. It should not be surprising that an appetitive emotional response (hope or disappointment) affects appetitive behavior, or that an aversive emotional response (fear or relief) influences aversive behavior. What is surprising is the influence that appetitive conditioned responses have on aversive behavior and that aversive conditioned responses have on appetitive behavior. Why should your relief when the fire alarm terminated stimulate your return to the theater and the movie? Or why should your anticipation of a pleasant television show reduce your aversive studying behavior? In asserting the existence of two central motivational states, Rescorla and Solomon's theory provides an answer to these questions. The aversive state is activated by stimuli associated with pain and frustration; the appetitive state is stimulated by cues associated with reward and relief. An aversive conditioned response motivates avoidance behavior and suppresses approach behavior. In contrast, an appetitive conditioned response initiates approach behavior and inhibits avoidance behavior.

Chapter 10 will describe two central nervous system structures that mediate the influence of reinforcement and punishment on behavior. These same two central nervous system structures also serve the two central states in Rescorla and Solomon's theory; that is, one structure motivates us to approach reinforcers, and the other motivates us to avoid aversive events. Furthermore, reinforcers or stimuli associated with reinforcement activate the appetitive structure, and aversive events or stimuli associated with aversive events arouse the aversive structure.

BEFORE YOU GO ON

- **What Pavlovian occasion-setter might cause Miguel to pick the wrong man out of the lineup?**
- **Could this Pavlovian occasion-setter influence other aspects of Miguel's behavior?**

The Nature of Discrimination Learning

How do we learn to discriminate between the S^D and the S^Δ? Researchers have proposed several very different views of the nature of discrimination. We will start by discussing the Hull-Spence theory.

Hull–Spence Theory

Clark Hull (1943) and Kenneth Spence (1936) offered an associative explanation of discrimination learning. Although it is now believed not to be a completely accurate view of the nature of discrimination learning, the **Hull-Spence theory of discrimination learning** does describe some essential aspects of the discrimination learning process.

DEVELOPMENT OF CONDITIONED EXCITATION AND INHIBITION According to the Hull-Spence view, discrimination learning develops in three stages. First, conditioned excitation develops to the S^D as the result of reinforcement. Second, nonreinforcement in the presence of the S^Δ results in the development of conditioned inhibition to the S^Δ. As we learned earlier in the chapter, conditioned inhibition suppresses the response to the S^D. Finally, the excitation and inhibition generalize to other stimuli (see **Figure 7.10**); the combined influence of excitation and inhibition determines the level of response to each stimuli. As **Figure 7.10** indicates, the Hull-Spence model predicts a steeper generalization gradient with discrimination training than with nondiscrimination training. Also, their model assumes that maximum responding occurs not to the S^D, but rather to a stimulus other than the S^D, and in the stimulus direction opposite to that of the S^Δ. The reason for this prediction is that although the S^D (256 in the figure) has

FIGURE 7.10. Spence's theoretical view of the interaction of excitatory and inhibitory generalization gradients on discriminated behavior. During acquisition, reward is available when 256 stimulus size is present, but not when 160 stimulus size is present. Excitatory potential (solid lines) generalizes to similar stimuli, as does inhibitory potential (broken lines). The resultant reaction tendency, indicated by the value above each stimulus size, is obtained by subtracting the inhibitory from the excitatory potential.

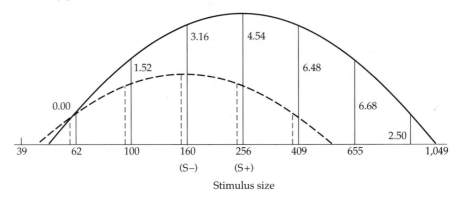

Stimulus size

the greatest excitatory strength, it also has accrued inhibitory strength. Although another stimulus (409 in the figure) may have less excitatory strength than the S^D, it also has accrued little inhibitory strength. Thus, the resultant "effective" strength of the S^D will be less than that of the other stimulus.

THE PEAK SHIFT PHENOMENON Hanson (1959) tested the assumptions of the Hull-Spence model of discrimination learning. In Hanson's study, pigeons received discrimination training using a 550-nm light as the S^D and either a 555, 560, 570, or 590-nm as the S^Δ, or nondiscrimination training using a 550-nm light present during the entire training session. Following training, both groups of pigeons were given a generalization test using stimuli ranging from 480 to 620 nm. Hanson reported three important differences between the discrimination and nondiscrimination generalization gradients (see **Figure 7.11**). First, a steeper generalization gradient appeared with discrimination than with nondiscrimination training, a prediction in accord with the Hull-Spence model. Second, the greatest responding for discrimination-training subjects was not to the 550-nm S^D, but to the 540-nm stimulus. This change, referred to as the **peak shift,** also agrees with the Hull-Spence view of discrimination training. In contrast, pigeons receiving nondiscrimination training responded maximally to the 550-nm stimulus. Finally, the overall level of responding was higher with discrimination training than with nondiscrimination training, an observation the Hull-Spence model did not predict.

The peak shift phenomenon occurs in pigeons using stimulus dimensions other than the color of the stimuli. For example, Honig and Stewart (1993) varied the number of vertical rectangles that represented the S^D and the S^Δ. In one of their studies, 18 vertical rectangles were the S^D and 25 vertical rectangles were the S^Δ. The pigeons in this study showed maximal response toward arrays

FIGURE 7.11. Mean number of responses on a generalization test (using wavelengths varying from 480 to 620 nm) for four experimental groups receiving prior discrimination training. The four groups received training with 550 nm as the S^D and either 555, 560, 570, or 590 nm as the S^Δ; the control group did not receive discrimination training. Experimental subjects showed steeper generalization gradients and a greater response to stimuli similar to S^D than did control subjects. Also, the peak shift was seen in the experimental but not in control subjects.

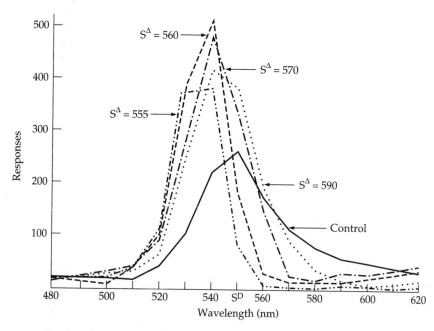

of vertical rectangles that included fewer than 18. The peak shift has also been observed in species other than pigeons, including rats (Weiss & Schindler, 1981) and humans (Thomas, Mood, Morrison, & Wiertelak, 1991).

THE AVERSIVE CHARACTER OF S^Δ Terrace (1964) suggested that behavioral contrast is responsible for the heightened responding seen with discrimination training. Terrace argued that exposure to the S^Δ is an aversive event, and that the "emotional effects of nonreinforced responding," or frustration, produced during S^Δ periods increase the intensity of the response to other stimuli. Recall from Chapter 4 that nonreinforcement and stimuli associated with nonreinforcement are aversive, and exposure to either of these can increase the intensity of response for reinforcement. Terrace's view that behavioral contrast is responsible for the heightened responding with discrimination training is consistent with the literature presented earlier in this chapter.

Several other types of research support Terrace's approach. A number of drugs (e.g., chlorpromazine and imipramine) appear to reduce the aversive effects of nonreinforcing events. Evidence of this effect is the elimination of frustration-induced behavior (e.g., aggressive behavior) with their use. Another influence of these drugs is the disruption of performance on a discrimination task (Bloomfield, 1972; Terrace, 1963c). Animals receiving chlorpromazine (an antipsychotic drug) or imipramine (an antidepressant drug) exhibit a high level of response to the S^Δ. It is thought that the reduced aversiveness of the S^Δ is responsible for the lack of inhibition of response to the S^Δ. These drugs not only caused an increased response to the S^Δ, but they also eliminated both behavioral contrast and the peak shift. Thus, the heightened response to the S^D and the maximum responding to a stimulus other than the S^D, both of which are characteristic of discrimination learning, are not seen when either chlorpromazine or imipramine is administered. These observations suggest that (1) S^Δ must be an aversive event to inhibit responding, and (2) the aversiveness of S^Δ causes both behavioral contrast and the peak shift.

The Hull-Spence model of discrimination learning suggests that conditioned excitation and inhibition lead to a steep excitatory generalization gradient and the peak shift. Hanson's (1959) research supports the Hull-Spence model. However, his study and Terrace's research indicate that nonreinforcement leads not only to the development of conditioned inhibition, but also to the development of aversive properties to the S^Δ. This aversive character of the S^Δ contributes to the heightened responding to the S^D (behavioral contrast) and maximum responding to a stimulus other than the S^D (peak shift).

The Transposition Effect

Although the peak shift phenomenon appears to support the Hull-Spence view, the noted Gestalt psychologist Wolfgang Kohler (1939) provides an alternative view of discrimination learning that can also explain the peak shift. According to Kohler, we do not evaluate stimuli in absolute terms, but instead in relation to other stimuli. For example, a 75-dB tone may seem loud in a quiet room but soft in a noisy room. Thus, when we say that a noise is loud or soft, the perceived loudness depends on the context in which the noise is heard.

Kohler's view is important when applied to discrimination learning. For example, suppose that a rat learns to discriminate between an 80-dB S^D and a 60-dB S^Δ. Has the rat learned to respond to the 80-dB tone and not to the 60-dB tone? In Kohler's view, the animal has merely learned to respond to the louder of the two tones. How would the rat react to a 90-dB tone? Since the rat learned to respond to the louder tone, Kohler's theory predicts that the rat would react more intensely to the 90-dB than the 80-dB tone. Kohler evaluated his view by training chickens and chimpanzees to respond to the brighter of two stimuli (the S^D). When he tested his subjects with the S^D and a still brighter light stimulus, the animals chose the brighter of the two lights. Kohler called this phenomenon **transposition,** a term drawn from the idea that the relation among notes comprising musical compositions does not change when the melodies are transposed to a different key.

Which view of discrimination learning is accurate: the Hull-Spence absolute view or the Kohler relational view? According to Schwartz and Reisberg (1991), there is evidence supporting both views. Studies that give animals the choice between two stimuli support the relational or transposition view; that is, the animals respond to the relative rather than absolute qualities of the stimuli. One study providing support for the relational view was conducted by Lawrence and DeRivera (1954). Lawrence and DeRivera initially exposed rats to cards that were divided in half. During training, the bottom half of the card was always an intermediate shade of gray, and the top half was one of three lighter or one of the three darker shades of gray. A darker top half meant that the rats needed to turn left to obtain reward; a lighter top half signaled a right turn for reward. **Figure 7.12** presents a diagram of this procedure. During testing, the researchers no longer presented the intermediate shade of gray; instead, two of the six shades of gray presented on top during training were shown (one on the top, the other on the bottom). Although a number of combinations of these six shades were used, only one combination is described to illustrate how this study supports a relational view. On some test trials, two of the darker shades were used, with the lighter of the two on top (refer to **Figure 7.12**). If the animals had learned based on absolute values, they would turn left, since the dark shade on the top in training meant "turn left." However, if the animals had learned based on the relation between stimuli, they would turn right during testing, since the darker stimulus was still on the bottom. Lawrence and DeRivera reported that on the overwhelming majority of such test trials, the animals' responses were based on the relation between stimuli rather than on the

FIGURE 7.12. Diagram showing the procedure used by Lawrence and DeRivera (1954) in their analysis of the absolute versus the relational view of discrimination learning. The numbers indicate darkness of gray used in the study. A left turn in response to the test stimulus shown in this illustration indicates absolute control of responding, and a right turn indicates relational control of responding.

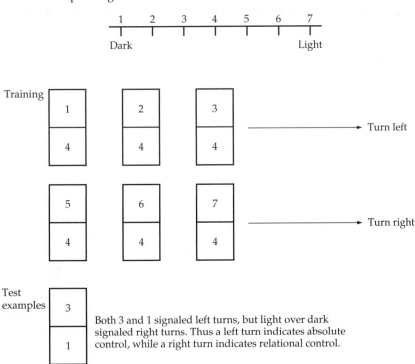

absolute value of the stimuli. Thus, in our example, most of the animals turned right because the darker shade of gray was on the bottom half of the card.

Although some studies support a relational view of discrimination, other experiments support the Hull-Spence absolute stimulus view. Hanson's study (1959) provides support for the Hull-Spence theory. Hanson trained pigeons to peck at a 550-nm (S^D) lighted key to receive reinforcement; pecking at a 590-nm (S^Δ) light yielded no reinforcement. On generalization tests, the pigeons were presented a range of lighted keys varying from 480 to 620 nm. According to the Hull-Spence view, at a point on the stimulus continuum below the S^D, the inhibitory generalization gradient does not affect excitatory responding. At this point on the gradient, response to the S^D should be greater than the response occurring at the lower wavelength test stimuli. In contrast, the relational view suggests that a lower wavelength of light will always produce a response greater than the S^D does. Hanson's results showed that while greater responding did occur to the 540-nm test light than to the 550-nm S^D, less responding occurred to the 530-nm light than to the S^D (refer to **Figure 7.12**). Thus, on generalization tests, greater responding occurs only to stimuli close to the S^D.

You might wonder why some results support the Hull-Spence absolute-value view and others suggest that Kohler's relational approach is true. As Schwartz and Reisberg (1991) point out, the relational view is supported on a choice test; that is, subjects must choose to respond to one of two stimuli. In contrast, on a generalization test where a subject responds to one stimulus, results support the Hull-Spence approach. In Schwartz and Reisberg's view, it is not unreasonable for both approaches to be valid; animals could learn both about the relation between stimuli and the absolute characteristics of the stimuli. In choice situations, the relation between stimuli is important, and the animal responds to the relational aspects it has learned. In contrast, when only a single stimulus is presented, the absolute character of a stimulus determines the level of responding.

Errorless Discrimination Training

Can an animal acquire a discrimination without ever responding to the S^Δ? Although you might not think so, psychologists have discovered that a discrimination can be learned with few or no errors. Several studies conducted during the 1930s and 1940s (Schlosberg & Solomon, 1943; Skinner, 1938) showed that with sufficient care, an animal could learn a discrimination with few errors. However, the significance of these studies was not recognized until Terrace (1963a, 1963b, 1963c, 1964, 1966) conducted a detailed examination of **errorless discrimination learning.** Terrace examined the characteristics of an errorless discrimination and developed a technique for establishing a discrimination without errors. His research also points out that one must follow specific procedures to learn a discrimination without errors.

TRAINING PROCEDURE   Terrace (1963a) trained pigeons on a red-green (S^D-S^Δ) discrimination. Each pigeon was trained to peck at a red illuminated key (S^D) to receive food reinforcement on a VI 1-minute schedule. The pigeons were divided into four groups, and each group received a different combination of procedures to introduce the S^Δ. Two groups of pigeons received a progressive S^Δ introduction. During the first phase of this procedure, the presentation of the S^Δ, a dark key, lasted 5 seconds and then increased by 5 seconds with each trial until reaching 30 seconds. In the second phase of S^Δ introduction, the duration of the S^Δ was kept at 30 seconds, and the intensity of the S^Δ was increased until it became a green light. During the final phase of the study, the duration of the S^D was slowly increased from 30 seconds to 3 minutes. (Note that the duration of the S^Δ was 3 minutes during all three phases.) By contrast, for pigeons receiving constant training, the S^Δ was initially presented at full intensity and full duration. One progressive training group and one constant training group were given an early introduction to S^Δ; the S^Δ was presented during the first session that a pigeon was placed in the training chamber. The other two groups (one progressive, one constant) received late S^Δ introduction; the S^Δ was introduced following 14 sessions of key pecking with the S^D present.

Figure 7.13 presents the results of Terrace's study. Terrace reported that pigeons receiving early progressive training did not emit many errors (a range of two to eight during the entire experiment). By contrast, the animals in the other three groups emitted many errors during S^Δ periods. Furthermore, the errors the early progressive subjects made occurred at either the beginning or the end of the S^Δ period, whereas the errors of the other three groups of pigeons occurred throughout S^Δ exposure and often came in bursts. These results show that an animal can learn a discrimination with few errors only when the S^Δ has

FIGURE 7.13. Number of responses each bird emitted during 28 trials of training as a function of discrimination-training procedure.

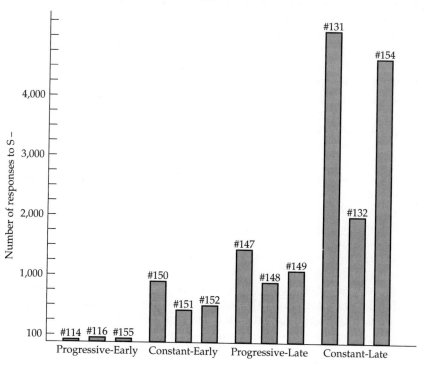

been gradually introduced early in training. In later articles, Terrace reported completely errorless discrimination training with the use of slight variations in the early progressive procedure.

Some discriminations are more difficult to acquire than others. For example, pigeons learn a color (red-green) discrimination more readily than a line-tilt (horizontal-vertical) discrimination. Furthermore, not only are pigeons slow to acquire a horizontal-vertical discrimination, but they also make many errors in response to the S^Δ. Terrace (1963b) found that pigeons can learn this difficult line-tilt discrimination without errors. To accomplish this goal, Terrace first trained pigeons on a red-green color discrimination task using the early progressive errorless training technique. After training, the vertical and horizontal lines were superimposed on the colors to form compound stimuli (the red vertical line was the S^D; the green horizontal line, the S^Δ). During this segment of training, the intensity of the colors was reduced until they were no longer visible. Terrace found that this "fading" procedure helped the pigeons to learn the horizontal-vertical discrimination quickly and without making any errors. In contrast, if colors were quickly removed or never presented with the horizontal-vertical lines, the pigeons made many errors before learning the line-tilt discrimination. Terrace's observations show that the fading technique is an effective way to teach a difficult discrimination.

APPLICATION: ERRORLESS DISCRIMINATION TRAINING IN HUMANS Errorless discrimination training also is possible with humans. Gollin and Savoy (1968) taught preschool children a shape discrimination using the fading technique; Moore and Goldiamond (1964) used this procedure to teach a pattern match; and Corey and Shamov (1972) used it to teach oral reading. In each of these studies, the children given the faded series of S^Δ stimuli made few errors, while other subjects that received standard discrimination training made many incorrect responses to the S^Δ.

The fading technique has been especially helpful in teaching discriminations to mentally handicapped individuals. For example, Sidman and Stoddard (1967) compared the effectiveness of both errorless and standard discrimination training in 9- to 14-year-old mentally impaired children trying to learn a circle-ellipse discrimination. These experimenters found that although the mentally handicapped children could not learn the discrimination using the standard training procedure, many did learn with the errorless procedure. Furthermore, Sidman and Stoddard argued that the instructional procedure was responsible for the failure of some of the mentally handicapped children to learn the discrimination using the errorless technique. Because of the design of the training procedure, a child who persevered in choosing an answer that was correct on the first trial continued to be rewarded only 50 percent of the time, hindering the child's learning of the discrimination even with the errorless procedure. Touchette (1969) taught 9- to 16-year-old children with mental handicaps a simple discrimination using either a trial-and-error or a fading procedure. He reported that the children did not learn the discrimination using the standard discrimination training, while all but one acquired the discrimination with the fading procedure.

The significance of Terrace's fading procedure is best seen in the research of Dorry and Zeaman (1973, 1975). Using the fading procedure, they trained mentally handicapped children to identify vocabulary words. In their studies, the children initially learned picture discriminations. After picture discrimination training, words were presented with the pictures; the pictures were then slowly faded out. Dorry and Zeaman compared the effectiveness of the fading procedure with that of normal discrimination training. They reported that the children taught with the fading procedure learned more words than did children given standard discrimination training.

Programs for mentally handicapped children have successfully incorporated errorless procedures into the teaching of discriminations (Conners, 1992; Zygmont, Lazar, Dube, & McIlvane, 1992). However, not all errorless procedures have worked. Jones and Eayrs (1992) reported that mentally handicapped children have difficulty generalizing their discrimination learning to new situations, while McIlvane, Kledaras, Iennaco, McDonald, and Stoddard (1995) found that such children have difficulty learning discrimination reversals in which the consequences of the S^D and S^Δ are reversed.

The errorless discrimination procedure has also been used successfully with children who have difficulty detecting speech sounds. Merzenich, Jenkins, William, Johnston, Schreiner, Miller, and Tallal (1996) first presented sounds that had certain components exaggerated by making the sounds longer or louder. For example, the word banana became baaaanana. As the children with difficulty detecting sounds correctly identified a sound, the sound was gradually made normal. Merzenich and his colleagues reported that these children correctly learned the sounds with few errors.

NONAVERSIVE S^Δ Remember from earlier in the chapter that there are three important behavioral characteristics of excitatory-generalization gradients obtained after standard discrimination training. First, maximum responding is to a stimulus other than the S^Δ; this phenomenon is called peak shift. Also, a steeper excitatory-generalization gradient and a higher level of response are obtained with standard discrimination training than with nondiscrimination training. Finally, presentation of the S^Δ, but not other stimuli, inhibits responding, but the administration of drugs that reduce frustration (for example, chlorpromazine or imipramine) disrupts effective discrimination performance by increasing the response to the S^Δ. These results demonstrate that the S^Δ is aversive, and that this aversiveness is responsible for the inhibitory properties of the S^Δ. These observations are consistent with the Hull-Spence approach to discrimination learning.

However, the behavioral characteristics found with standard discrimination training are not observed with errorless discrimination training (Terrace, 1964). The peak shift does not appear in errorless discrimination training. Errorless discrimination training produces the same level of response to the S^D as nondiscrimination training does. Furthermore, the presentation of the S^Δ, as well as stimuli other than the S^D, inhibits responding in subjects receiving errorless discrimination training. Finally, the administration of chlorpromazine or imipramine does not disrupt discrimination performance; that is, the individual continues to respond to the S^D, but not to the S^Δ.

Terrace's observations have important implications for our understanding of the nature of discrimination learning. These data indicate that with errorless discrimination training, the S^Δ is not aversive. Also, Terrace argues that with errorless discrimination, the S^Δ does not develop inhibitory control; instead, individuals learn to respond only to the S^D. These results suggest that excitatory and inhibitory control are not the only responses acquired during discrimination training. In fact, inhibitory control does not seem to be essential for effective discrimination performance. How can a pigeon or person learn not to respond to the S^Δ with errorless discrimination training? Perhaps the pigeon or person learns to expect that no reinforcement will occur during S^Δ, and this expectancy leads the pigeon or person to not respond to the S^Δ. The next chapter will examine the evidence that expectancies, as well as emotions, affect behavior.

Sutherland and Mackintosh's Attentional View

Sutherland and Mackintosh (1971) suggested that discrimination learning occurs in two stages. During the first stage, an individual's attention to the relevant dimension strengthens. The second phase involves the association of a particular response to the relevant stimulus.

THE RECOGNITION OF THE RELEVANT DIMENSION Suppose that the S^D and the S^Δ are multidimensional; that is, each consists of several different stimulus dimensions. For example, perhaps the S^D is a bright, green, striped light, while the S^Δ is a dull, red, solid light. How would a pigeon respond in this situation? When a stimulus consists of more than one dimension, one of the stimulus dimensions generally gains control of responding. Why? According to Sutherland and Mackintosh, each stimulus dimension can activate an **analyzer.** The analyzer detects the presence of the salient or relevant aspect of a stimulus, and the arousal of a particular analyzer causes an animal to attend to that dimension. Thus, the presentation of a compound stimulus arouses the analyzer of the relevant dimension, but not the analyzers of the other stimulus dimensions.

Consider the following example to illustrate the **Sutherland-Mackintosh attentional theory.** A person viewing a 5-inch red horizontal bar projected onto a gray background could attend to several dimensions—for example, the color, brightness, length, or orientation of the bar. However, this person notices only the color of the bar. In Sutherland and Mackintosh's view, the reason for this phenomenon is that the analyzer for the color dimension is aroused, but the analyzers for the other dimensions are not.

What determines which analyzer will be aroused? Initially, the level of arousal of a particular analyzer is related to the intensity and salience of the stimulus dimension; the greater the strength and salience of a particular stimulus dimension, the more likely that dimension will activate the analyzer sufficiently to arouse attention. With certain types of experiences, the ability of analyzers to attract attention changes. According to Sutherland and Mackintosh, the predictive value of a particular stimulus dimension influences the amount of attention the analyzer of that stimulus dimension arouses. The analyzer will arouse more attention if the stimulus dimension predicts important events. However, an analyzer will arouse less attention if the stimulus dimension for that analyzer is not predictive of future events.

In the second phase of discrimination learning, the output from the analyzer is attached to a particular response. The connection between the analyzer output and the response strengthens as the result of reinforcement. Thus, in Sutherland and Mackintosh's view, reinforcement increases both the attention to a particular dimension and the ability of a particular stimulus to elicit the response.

PREDICTIVE VALUE OF DISCRIMINATIVE STIMULI Research indicates that predictiveness has an important influence on discrimination learning. Recall from Chapter 3 that the predictive value of the CS determines whether it becomes able to elicit a CR. Similarly, the ability of the S^D to predict reinforcement is important; the predictiveness of the S^D determines whether it will gain control over responding. If the S^D is predictive of reinforcement, it will control responding. Conversely, the S^D will not control responding if it does not reliably predict the reinforcement.

Wagner, Logan, Haberlandt, and Price (1968) investigated the influence of the S^D's predictiveness on its control of operant responding. Two groups of rats were trained to bar press for reinforcement. Subjects in the first group were reinforced on 50% of the trials in which the light-with-the-first-tone compound stimulus was presented, and on 50% of the trials in which the light-with-the-second-tone compound stimulus was presented (see **Figure 7.14**). The rats in the second group received the light-with-the-first-tone stimulus paired with reinforcement 100% of the time; the light-with-the-second-tone stimulus was presented 0% of the time. These investigators were interested in the degree of control the light cue would gain. For subjects in the first group, the light cue was present when reinforcement was available on 50% of the trials. For the second group, the first tone was much more predictive of reinforcement than the light cue; for these subjects, the first tone was present 100% of the trials on which reinforcement was available, but the light was paired with reinforcement on only 50% of the trials. Although the light was paired with reinforcement availability on 50% of the trials in both groups, the light was a better predictor in the first group than in the second: no cue in the first group predicted reinforcement more reliably than did the light, whereas in the second group, the first tone predicted reinforcement better than the light. Wagner, Logan, Haberlandt, and Price reported that the light better controlled responding for subjects in the first group than in the second group. These results indicate that it is the relative predictiveness of an S^D—not the percentage of trials in which the S^D is associated with reinforcement—that determines its ability to control responding.

Continuity versus Discontinuity

The Hull-Spence view asserts that excitation and inhibition gradually increase during the acquisition of a discrimination. This position is referred to as a **continuity theory of discrimination learning** because it assumes that the development of a discrimination is a continuous and gradual acquisition of excitation to the S^D and inhibition to the S^Δ. Krechevsky (1932) and Lashley (1929) presented a view of discrimination learning that differs substantially from the Hull-Spence approach. According to Krechevsky and Lashley, the learning of a

FIGURE 7.14. Two treatment conditions in the Wagner, Logan, Haberlandt, and Price (1968) study. For subjects in group 1, the light was equally predictive of reinforcement as either tone, but for group 2, the light was a worse predictor than tone 1 and a better predictor than tone 2.

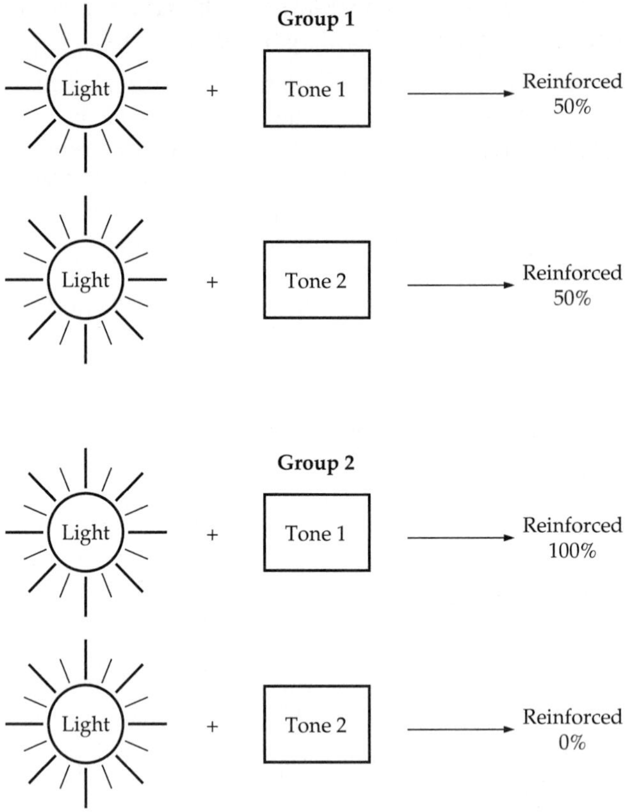

discrimination is not a gradual, continuous process. Instead, they believe that an animal or person acquires a discrimination by establishing a "hypothesis" about which stimulus is associated with reinforcement. While testing this hypothesis, the animal attends to the stimulus relevant to its hypothesis and learns nothing about other stimuli. The view is referred to as a **noncontinuity theory of discrimination learning** because it assumes that once an animal focuses its attention on the relevant stimuli, it will rapidly acquire the discrimination.

A considerable amount of research has attempted to evaluate the continuity and noncontinuity views. Some studies support the continuity approach of Hull and Spence, and other research has agreed with the noncontinuity approach Krechevsky and Lashley take. It is not surprising that research exists to validate both points of view, since discrimination learning reflects both the acquisition of excitatory and inhibitory strength and the development of attention to predictive events in the environment. It seems reasonable that continuity theory explains how the emotional components of a discrimination are learned and that noncontinuity theory describes the attentional aspects of discrimination learning.

- How would the Hull-Spence theory explain Miguel's failure to correctly identify his assailant?
- How would the Sutherland-Mackintosh attentional view explain Miguel's failure to correctly identify his assailant?

CHAPTER SUMMARY

Generalization is a process in which animals or people respond in the same way to similar stimuli; discrimination is a process in which animals or people learn to respond in different ways to different stimuli. Generalization enables us to respond to unfamiliar stimuli without having to directly discover their significance, and discrimination allows us to know when to respond and when not to respond.

In excitatory generalization, a cue is associated with reinforcement or punishment, and stimuli similar to the S+ will elicit the response. In contrast, in inhibitory generalization, a cue is associated with the absence of reinforcement or punishment, and stimuli similar to the S− will inhibit responding.

A steep generalization gradient occurs when an animal or person only responds to stimuli very similar to the S+ or the S−. A flat generalization gradient occurs when the animal or person exhibits the same amount of excitation or inhibition to any stimuli resembling S+ or S−.

According to the Lashley-Wade view, animals and people generalize to stimuli quite dissimilar to the conditioning stimulus when they fail to distinguish between the S+ and other stimuli. In contrast, learning to differentiate between the S+ and other stimuli results in little or no generalization.

Reinforcement is available in some circumstances and unavailable in others. In discrimination learning, an individual discovers the stimuli (S^D) signaling reinforcement availability and the events (S^Δ) indicating that reinforcement is unavailable. Learning the discrimination results in responding when the S^D, but not the S^Δ, is present. Individuals must also learn to discriminate between occasions when punishment will occur and when it will not.

There is an increased response to S^D and a decreased response to S^Δ during discrimination learning, an effect called behavioral contrast. The switch from the S^D to the S^Δ, or vice versa, causes an emotional response and a temporary change in responding called local contrast. The anticipation of a change in reinforcement contingencies causes a long-lasting change in responding called sustained contrast.

When a stimulus signals the occurrence of a conditioned stimulus and the unconditioned stimulus, the presence of the first stimulus enhances responding to the conditioned stimulus. A stimulus develops occasion-setting properties when the conditioned stimulus and the UCS follow the occasion-setting stimulus and the conditioned stimulus occurs without the UCS when the occasion-setting stimulus is not present. Rescorla suggests that a stimulus facilitates the response to another stimulus by lowering the elicitation threshold of the conditioned response to the second stimulus.

Pavlovian occasion-setters also have an influence on operant behavior; the presence of a Pavlovian occasion-setter has the same effect on an operant response as an S^D. By the same token, an operant S^D has the same facilitatory influence on an excitatory conditioned stimulus to elicit a conditioned response as a Pavlovian occasion-setter.

Stimuli paired with reward or with the absence of an aversive event motivate appetitive behavior and suppress avoidance responding. Other stimuli that occur with aversive events or with the absence of reward motivate avoidance behavior and suppress appetitive behavior. Rescorla and Solomon suggested that the central appetitive and aversive motivational states mediate the influence of conditioned stimuli on operant or instrumental behavior.

The Hull-Spence view assumes that conditioned excitation develops to the S^D as the result of reward; this conditioned excitation allows the S^D to produce the instrumental or operant response. After conditioned excitation is established, nonreward in the presence of the S^Δ results in the development of conditioned inhibition to the S^Δ; this decreases the response to the S^Δ.

Discrimination training causes a steeper generalization gradient than nondiscrimination training. The greatest responding for discrimination-training subjects is not to the S^D, but to a similar stimulus, a phenomenon referred to as the peak shift. Terrace assumed that exposure to the S^Δ is an aversive event and that the "emotional effects of nonreinforced responding," or frustration, produced during S^Δ periods increase the intensity of responding to other stimuli.

Kohler's relational or transposition view assumes that animals or people learn the relative relationship between the S^D and the S^Δ. Rather than just responding to a particular stimulus, they learn, for example, to choose the larger or smaller stimulus, or the louder or softer stimulus.

A discrimination can be learned without responding to the S^Δ in a procedure called errorless discrimination training. The peak shift does not occur using errorless discrimination training. Errorless discrimination training produces the same level of response to the S^D as is found with nondiscrimination training. The presentation of the S^Δ, as well as stimuli other than the S^D, inhibits responding in subjects receiving errorless discrimination training. For a discrimination to be learned without errors, the S^Δ must be introduced using an early progressive treatment.

Sutherland and Mackintosh suggest that during discrimination learning, an animal's attention to relevant dimensions strengthens. The ability of a stimulus analyzer to attract attention enables the individual to respond appropriately to the discriminative stimuli. According to the Sutherland-Mackintosh view, after an animal is attending to the relevant dimension, the association between the instrumental or operant response and the relevant stimulus is strengthened.

The continuity view of discrimination learning assumes that excitation and inhibition gradually increase during the acquisition of a discrimination; this approach appears to describe the development of the emotional components of discrimination learning. In contrast, the noncontinuity approach asserts that there is an abrupt recognition of the salient features of a discrimination; this approach seems to describe the attentional aspects of discrimination learning.

1. Generalization can lead to effective coping, or it can cause behavioral problems. Discuss the positive and negative aspects of the generalization process. What can be done to prevent unwanted generalization?
2. Shameca is very selective about the clothes she buys. She will shop in some stores, but not in others. Explain one possible basis for Shameca's selectivity.
3. Natalie becomes sexually aroused by her husband when they are alone with the lights dimmed and soft music playing. By contrast, she is not physically aroused by him when they are shopping in a mall. Describe how occasion setting can explain Natalie's different responses to her husband.

KEY TERMS

analyzer
anticipatory contrast
behavioral contrast
conditional
   discrimination
continuity theory of
   discrimination learning
discrimination
discrimination learning
discriminative stimulus
discriminative operant
errorless discrimination
   learning

excitatory generalization
   gradient
generalization
generalization gradient
Hull-Spence theory
   of discrimination
   learning
inhibitory generalization
   gradient
Lashley-Wade theory of
   generalization
local contrast
noncontinuity theory of
   discrimination learning

occasion setting
peak shift
S^D
S^Δ
sustained contrast
Sutherland-Mackintosh
   attentional theory
transposition
two-choice discrimination
   learning

CHAPTER EIGHT

Cognitive Control of Behavior

The Insurmountable Barrier

*M*ath *has always been an obstacle for Martha. Her distaste for arithmetic was evident even in elementary school. She dreaded working with numbers, and her lowest grade was always in math. Martha's high marks in her other classes came without much effort, but she always had to struggle to earn an acceptable grade in her math courses. In college, she avoided the high-level math courses and chose only the ones other students said were easy. She did well in these courses because they resembled her high school math classes. During the summer before her junior year in college, Martha decided to major in psychology. Two Bs in college math were the only marks to mar her superior grade record. To earn her psychology degree, Martha should have completed a statistics course during the fall semester of her junior year, but she did not. The hour was not right that fall, and she did not like the professor the following spring. Determined to complete her degree, Martha enrolled in the statistics course this past fall—only to drop out three weeks later. She could not comprehend the material and had failed the first exam. Martha knows that she cannot finish her psychology degree without the statistics class, and now only one semester remains until she is scheduled to graduate. However, she does not believe she can pass the course. She has discussed her problem with her parents and friends, and they regularly offer encouragement. Unfortunately, their good wishes could not make her problem go away. Yesterday, Martha learned from a friend that he had a similar problem with chemistry and that a psychologist at the University Counseling Center helped him overcome his "chemistry phobia." This friend suggested to Martha that the center might help her, too. Martha has never considered her math aversion a psychological problem and is reluctant to acknowledge any need for clinical treatment. She knows that she must decide before next week's registration whether to seek help at the center.*

If Martha goes for help, she may learn several things: Her fear of the statistics course results from her belief that her past failures are attributable to a lack of ability in math and her feeling that she cannot endure taking another statistics course. On the basis of these beliefs, Martha expects to fail the course. Later in the chapter, we suggest a cognitive explanation for Martha's math phobia, as well as a treatment that has successfully modified the expectations that maintain the phobic behavior of people like Martha.

The term **cognition** refers to an animal's or person's knowledge of the environment. Psychologists investigating cognitive processes have focused on two distinctively different areas of inquiry. Many psychologists have evaluated an individual's understanding of the structure of the psychological environment (i.e., when events occur, and what has to be done to obtain reward or avoid punishment) and how this understanding, referred to as an expectancy, acts to control responding. We will discuss the role of cognition in governing behavior in this chapter. Other psychologists have evaluated the processes that enable an individual to acquire knowledge of the environment. This research has investigated learning processes such as concept formation, problem solving, language acquisition, and memory. These processes provide the mental structure for thinking; we will discuss them in later chapters.

TOLMAN'S PURPOSIVE BEHAVIORISM

Edward Tolman proposed a cognitive view of learning during the 1930s and 1940s. At this time, this approach was unacceptable to most psychologists. The S-R associative approach was the accepted view of learning during that period. As we discussed in Chapter 6, the cognitive view gained some acceptance during the 1950s and 1960s as other psychologists expanded Tolman's original cognitive approach, but only in the past few decades have psychologists recognized the important contribution of cognitions in the learning process. We briefly discussed Tolman's view in Chapter 6. Our discussion in this chapter begins with a more detailed look at Tolman's work; later in the chapter, we'll look at the ideas and research of the contemporary cognitive psychologists.

Learning Principles

Edward Tolman's (1932, 1959) view of learning contrasts with the associative view described in Chapter 6. Tolman did not envision that behavior reflects an automatic response to an environmental event (due to an S-R association); rather, he thought that human behavior has both direction and purpose. According to Tolman, our behavior is goal-oriented because we are motivated either to approach a particular reward or to avoid a specific aversive event. In addition, we are capable of understanding the structure of our environment. There are paths leading to our goals, and tools we can employ to reach these goals. Through experience, we gain an expectation of how to use these paths and tools. Although Tolman used the terms *purpose* and *expectation* to describe the process that motivates our behavior, he did not mean that we are aware of either the purpose or the direction of our behavior. He theorized that we act *as if* we expect a particular action to lead to a specific goal.

According to Tolman, not only is our behavior goal-oriented, but we also expect specific outcomes to follow specific behaviors. For example, we expect that going to a favorite restaurant will result in a great meal. If we do not obtain our goal, we will continue to search for the reward and will not be satisfied with a less valued goal object. If our favorite restaurant is closed, we will not accept just any restaurant, but will choose only a suitable alternative. Also, certain events in the environment convey information about where our goals are located. According to Tolman, we are able to reach our goals only after we have learned to recognize the signs leading to reward or punishment in our environment. Thus, we know where our favorite restaurant is located, and we use this information to guide us to that restaurant.

Tolman suggests that we do not have to be reinforced to learn. However, our expectations will not be translated into behavior unless we are motivated. Tolman proposed that motivation has two functions: (1) it produces a state of internal tension that creates a demand for the goal object, and (2) it determines the environmental features we will attend to. For example, if we are not hungry, we are less likely to learn where food is located than if we are starving. However, tension does not possess the mechanistic quality it did in Hull's theory. According to Tolman, our expectations control the direction of our drives. Therefore, when we are motivated, we do not respond in a fixed, automatic, or stereotyped way to reduce our drive; rather, our behavior will remain flexible enough to enable us to reach our goal.

While much research has been conducted to evaluate the validity of Hull's mechanistic approach, the research effort to validate Tolman's cognitive view has been meager, although Tolman and his students conducted several key studies that provide support for his approach. The next sections will examine these studies and describe what they tell us about learning.

Place-Learning Studies

Tolman suggested that people expect reward in a certain place, and they follow the paths leading to that place. In contrast, Hull proposed that environmental cues elicit specific motor responses that have led to reward in the past. How do we know which view is valid? Under normal conditions, we cannot determine whether our expectations or our habits will lead us to reward. Tolman designed his place-learning studies to provide us with an answer.

T-Maze Experiments

Tolman, Ritchie, and Kalish (1946) designed several experiments to distinguish behavior based on S-R associations from behavior based on spatial expectations. In their studies, rats were placed for half of the trials in place S_1 in the apparatus shown in **Figure 8.1.** For the other half of the trials, the rats began in place S_2. For the place-learning condition, reward was always in the same location (e.g., F_1), but the turning response needed to reach the reward differed for each trial, depending on whether the rat started at S_1 or S_2. In contrast, although in the response-learning condition the rats received reward in both places, only one response—either right or left—produced reward. Tolman, Ritchie, and Kalish found that all the place-condition animals learned within eight trials and continued to behave without errors for the next ten trials. None of the rats in the response-learning condition learned this rapidly; even after responding correctly, they continued to make errors. Tolman, Ritchie, and Kalish's results illustrate that superior learning occurs when we can obtain reward in a certain place rather than by using a certain response.

FIGURE 8.1. Schematic diagram of typical apparatus for a place-learning study. Rats can start at either S_1 or S_2 and receive reward in either F_1 or F_2.

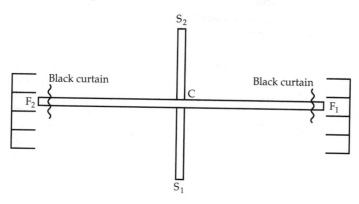

A second study by Tolman, Ritchie, and Kalish (1946) demonstrates that a rat will go to a place associated with reward even when an entirely new motor response is required to reach the place. During the first phase of their study, they always put their rats in location S_1 and placed the reward in F_1. For these rats, both a habit (right turn) and an expectation of where food will be located (F_1) produce reward. During the second phase of their study, the researchers placed the rats at location S_2. In this stage, the rats reached the goal only by turning left toward F_1; the habitual right response led to an empty goal box. Tolman, Ritchie, and Kalish reported that their subjects turned left and went to F_1, the place associated with reward. These results suggest that expectancies, not S-R associations, controlled behavior in this study.

Numerous studies have compared place versus response learning. However, the results of some indicate that response learning is superior to place learning. Fortunately, there are several likely explanations for these different results. One cause of the conflicting results is the presence of cues to guide behavior (Blodgett & McCutchan, 1947, 1948). For example, place learning is superior to response learning when extra maze cues (for example, the ceiling lights in the laboratory) are present, allowing a spatial orientation to guide the rats to the correct location. Without extra maze cues, the animals are forced to rely on motor responses to produce reward.

The degree of experience with the task is another reason for the different results. I have sometimes experienced the following situation while driving home. Instead of turning from my typical path to run a planned errand, I continue past the turn and arrive home. Why did I drive my usual route home rather than turn off on the route necessary to do my errand? One likely answer is that I have driven home so often that the response has become the habitual route home. Kendler and Gasser's (1948) study indicates that well-learned behavior is typically under the control of mechanistic rather than cognitive processes. They found that with fewer than twenty trials, animals responded to place cues, whereas with greater training, the rats exhibited the appropriate motor response.

Examine the map in **Figure 8.2**. Pretend that these paths represents routes to school. While path would you choose? In all likelihood, you would use path A, the shortest. However, what would you do if path A were blocked at point Y? If you were behaving according to your spatial knowledge, you would choose path C. Even though path C is longer than B, your cognitive map, or your spatial representation of the physical environment, would produce the expectation that B is also blocked and thus would motivate you to choose C. In contrast, an S-R associative interpretation predicts that you would choose B since it represents the second strongest habit. Path C is your choice if you behave like the rats did in Tolman and Honzik's (1930a, 1930b) study. In their study, animals were familiar with the maze but usually chose path A to reach the goal. If path A were blocked at point Y, however, most rats chose path C. These results point out that knowledge of our environment, rather than "blind habit," often influences our behavior.

Other psychologists have attempted to replicate the results of Tolman and Honzik's study (e.g., Caldwell & Jones, 1954). However, animals in these studies have not always chosen path C. For example, Keller and Hull (1936) discovered that changing the width of the alleys caused their rats to respond according to habit and choose the blocked path. Unfortunately, there has been no definitive evaluation of why the rats sometimes choose the blocked path. We can conclude from our prior discussion that the salience of cues leading to the

FIGURE 8.2. Apparatus used in Tolman and Honzik's alternative-path experiment. Obstacle Y blocks not only the shortest path (A), but also the middle-length path (B). With paths A and B blocked, the only available route to the goal is the longest route, path C.

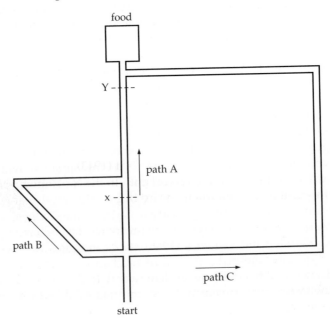

goal and the degree of experience with the paths probably determine the processes controlling behavior. Thus, if we attend to paths leading to reward and the paths have not been employed frequently, our expectations rather than our habits will determine our action.

Is Reward Necessary for Learning?

Recall our discussion of the law of effect in Chapter 1. According to Thorndike, S-R associations are established when the response leads to a satisfying state of affairs. As we discussed in Chapter 6, Hull (1943) expanded Thorndike's early view and asserted that associative or habit strength increases when a particular response decreases the drive state. Tolman (1932) thought that reward is not necessary for learning to occur, that the simultaneous experience of two events is sufficient. The incentive motivation process, which we explored in Chapter 6, was initially detailed by Hull in 1952 and then later described by Spence in 1956. The research of Tolman and his students strongly influenced the nature of the incentive motivation concept.

Latent-Learning Studies

Tolman believed that we can acquire knowledge of the spatial characteristics of a specific environment merely by exploring the environment. Reward is not necessary for us to develop a cognitive map; reward influences behavior only when we must use that information to obtain reward. Tolman distinguished between learning and performance by asserting that reward motivates behavior but does not affect learning.

Tolman and Honzik's (1930a) classic study directly assessed the importance of reward in learning and performance. Tolman and Honzik assigned their subjects to one of three conditions: (1) hungry rats in the R group always received reward (food) in the goal box of a 22-unit maze; (2) rats in the NR group were hungry but never received reward in the goal box; and (3) hungry rats in the NR-R group did not receive reward on the first ten days of conditioning, but did for the last ten days. Tolman and Honzik found that the animals that received reward on each trial (R group) showed a steady decrease in number of errors during training, whereas animals not given reward (NR group) showed little improvement in their performance (see **Figure 8.3**). Does this failure of the unrewarded rats to perform indicate a failure to learn? Or have the nonrewarded rats developed a cognitive map that they are not motivated to use? The behavior of those animals that did not receive reward in the goal box until the eleventh trial answers this question. Since Hull (1943) had envisioned the development of a habit as a slow process, animals in the NR-R group should have shown a slow decline in errors when reward began. However, if learning has already occurred by the eleventh trial and all these rats needed was to be motivated, they should have performed well on the twelfth trial. The results indicate that on the twelfth day and all subsequent days, animals in the R group (which were always rewarded) performed no differently from those in the NR-R group (which were only rewarded beginning with trial 11). These results suggest that NR-R animals were learning during the initial trials even though they did not receive any food reward.

FIGURE 8.3. Results of Tolman and Honzik's latent-learning study. Animals in the NR group received no reward during the experiment; those in the R group received reward throughout the study; those in the NR-R group received reward from day 11 to day 20. The results show that adding reward on day 11 led to a rapid decline in the number of errors subjects in group NR-R made to the level seen in animals receiving reward from the first trial (group R).

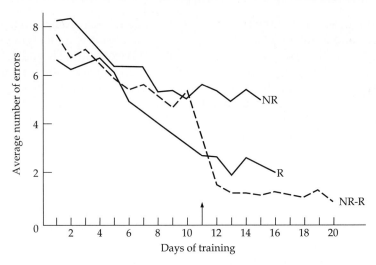

While Tolman and Honzik's results suggest that learning can occur without reward, not all studies have supported the idea of latent learning. MacCorquodale and Meehl (1954) reported that 30 of 48 studies were able to replicate the latent-learning effect. Although latent learning appears to be a real phenomenon, under some conditions it is likely, and in other circumstances it is not. MacCorquodale and Meehl observed that in studies where reward was present for nondeprived animals during the initial trials and motivation was introduced during later experience with the same reward, latent learning was typically found. However, latent learning did not typically appear in studies in which the rewards present during the initial trials were irrelevant to the motivation existing at that time, and reward only became relevant during later trials. (The presence of water in a hungry rat's goal box would be an example of an irrelevant reward.) These results suggest that a motivated animal will ignore the presence of a potent but irrelevant reward; this agrees with Tolman's belief that motivation narrows an animal's attention to those cues which are salient to its motivational state.

Johnson's (1952) study provides direct support for this interpretation. Johnson varied the level of deprivation during initial exploration in a T-maze and found that as deprivation increased, the likelihood of observing latent learning decreased. Apparently, we learn about the general aspects of our environment unless our motivation restricts our attention to some specific part of the environment.

The most consistent observation of latent learning occurs when animals are not deprived when initially exposed to reward. The anticipatory goal response (r_G-s_G) mechanism described in Chapter 6 was developed to explain the results of these latent-learning studies. The r_G-s_G develops during initial exposure to reward but is not apparent until the motivating influence of deprivation is added. However, some latent-learning studies—the original Tolman and Honzik study is one example—employ no obvious reward, yet the nonrewarded animals in those studies do show a slight improvement in their performance. This indicates, according to drive-view advocates (Kimble, 1961), that these animals did experience some reward. These advocates suggest that handling or removing the animals from the strange maze to the familiar home cage sometimes represented sufficient reward to establish the r_G-s_G during initial nonreward. Although the strength of the r_G-s_G was not intense enough to motivate behavior, additional arousal produced by the introduction of reward resulted in rapid improvement in performance.

BEFORE YOU GO ON

- **What expectancies might have caused Martha's math phobia?**
- **Could these expectancies have been learned many years earlier, remaining latent until she enrolled in the statistics class?**

THE CONCEPT OF AN EXPECTANCY

A Mental Representation of Events

What is an **expectancy?** Several psychologists have suggested than expectancy is a mental representation of event contingencies (Dickinson, 1989; Wasserman, 1993). According to this view, an internal or mental representation of an experience develops when an animal or person experiences an event. This representation contains information about the relations among previously experienced events and about the relations between behavior and the consequences of this behavior.

Types of Mental Representations

Anthony Dickinson (1989) suggested that there are two main classes of declarative knowledge or factual information contained in an expectancy. First, the contiguity between two events establishes an expectancy that contains an associative link representation of two events. The establishment of an **associative-link expectancy** allows one event to excite or inhibit the representation of the other event. For example, suppose a person eats a great steak in a particular restaurant. In Dickinson's view, the person's expectancy would contain knowledge of the restaurant and the steak. Seeing the restaurant would cause the person to expect a great steak. According to Dickinson, associative link representations mediate the impact of Pavlovian conditioning experiences. An excitatory link representation of the CS and the UCS allows the CS to activate the representation of the UCS and, thereby, elicit the conditioned response. In terms of our example, seeing the restaurant would excite the representation of the great steak and, thereby, elicit hunger. In contrast, inhibitory-link representations allow a conditioned stimulus to inhibit a conditioned response.

The second type of declarative knowledge contained in an expectancy involves an understanding of the consequences of a specific action. This knowledge is represented in propositional form as a belief that action A causes reinforcer B. For example, the person in our example would undoubtedly learn to go back to the restaurant serving the great steak. According to Dickinson's view, this individual's expectancy would contain the knowledge that going to that restaurant yields a great steak. Dickinson suggests that the representation of behavior and outcomes controls instrumental or operant activity. The intent of an animal's behavior is to obtain desired reinforcement, and activation of the relevant **behavior-reinforcer belief** enables the animal to obtain reinforcement.

In Dickinson's view, the existence of two classes of mental representations explains some important differences between Pavlovian and instrumental or operant conditioning. As we discovered in Chapter 3, Pavlovian conditioning involves the acquisition of CS-UCS associations. Dickinson suggests that CS-UCS associative link expectancies operate mechanistically; this mechanistic expectancy process causes the CS to involuntarily elicit the CR. In contrast, operant or instrumental conditioning involves the acquisition of behavior-outcome beliefs. According to Dickinson, intentionality is a property of belief expectancies. An animal engages in operant or instrumental behavior based on inferences about the consequences of specific actions.

Dickinson suggests that expectancies contain knowledge of environmental circumstance. How can the idea that expectancies contain representation of stimuli, actions, and reinforcers be validated? According to Dickinson, research must show that a representation of the training stimulus and reinforcer is stored during Pavlovian conditioning. Research also must demonstrate that during operant or instrumental conditioning, knowledge contained in the expectancy stands in declarative relation to the conditioning contingency; that is, the knowledge in the expectancy represents a belief about the impact of a behavior on the environment. Dickinson presents a number of studies supporting an expectancy view; we will examine several of them next.

Associative-Link Expectancies

Suppose that one group of thirsty rats were trained to bar press for a sodium solution and another group of thirsty rats were reinforced with a potassium solution. After this initial training, both groups of rats were sodium deprived as their operant response was extinguished. How would these two groups of rats act if the drive state was switched from water deprivation to sodium deprivation during extinction? Dickinson and Nicholas (1983) conducted such a study. They found that the rats initially reinforced for bar pressing with sodium showed a higher response rate during extinction than did the animals initially reinforced with potassium. Dickinson and Nicholas also reported there were no extinction differences between animals if the animals were extinguished either when satiated or water deprived (see **Figure 8.4**). These results show that rats reinforced with sodium during training responded at a higher level during extinction than rats reinforced with potassium, but only when the motivational state was more relevant to sodium than potassium.

What process was responsible for the **irrelevant incentive effect,** or the higher rate of responding in animals deprived of water during training and reinforced with sodium than in animals reinforced with potassium during extinction in the sodium drive state? According to Dickinson, an excitatory-link association developed during training between the contextual cues and the irrelevant incentive (either sodium or potassium). When the animals were later deprived of sodium, activation of this excitatory-link association led to a general enhancement of responding, but only when the expectancy contained knowledge that the incentive was relevant. In other words, arousing the associative-link expectancy in sodium-deprived animals increased responding for sodium because the incentive was relevant to the drive, while the responding was low in the animals previously reinforced with potassium because the incentive experienced during training was irrelevant to the drive state experienced during extinction. Since both groups received equivalent training, and the response rate during extinction under a water deprivation condition (where

FIGURE 8.4. Graph illustrating the mean rate of bar pressing during excitation for animals reinforced for bar pressing with either sodium or potassium and tested while sodium deprived, water deprived, or satiated for water. The results show that animals receiving sodium during training exhibited a higher response rate when deprivation was shifted from water to sodium than did animals given potassium during training.

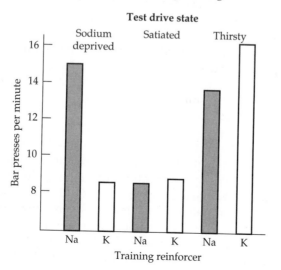

the drive state was the same for both groups) was also equal for both groups, Dickinson concluded that the animals gained declarative knowledge about the incentive experienced during initial training. Further, knowledge of the incentive was contained in an excitatory-link association; activation of this association under relevant drive conditions enhanced responding.

Dickinson suggested the existence of two types of mental representations: an excitatory-link association and a behavior-reinforcer belief. Perhaps the greater response during extinction among the sodium-reinforced rather than potassium-reinforced animals under sodium deprivation conditions was due to a behavior-reinforcer belief rather than an excitatory-link association; that is, perhaps animals developed an expectancy that responding produced sodium or potassium rather than an association that sodium or potassium was experienced in a particular environment.

Dickinson and Dawson (1987) conducted a study to determine if the irrelevant incentive effect was due to the development of a Pavlovian excitatory-link association or an operant behavior-reinforcer belief. The irrelevant incentive effect caused the increased responding in animals reinforced with sodium during training. All animals received four experiences during initial training in the hunger state. Two experiences involved Pavlovian conditioning: cue A was paired with a sucrose solution, and cue B was paired with food. Animals also received two operant conditioning experiences: they were reinforced with sucrose with cue C present, and with food with cue D present. The drive state was then switched from hunger to thirst during extinction. Dickinson and Dawson found that responding during extinction was greater to cues A and C than to cues B and D (see **Figure 8.5**). This means that responding was higher to stimuli paired with sucrose than stimuli paired with food. Since these animals were now thirsty, only an expectancy containing knowledge of sucrose would be relevant to the thirst state. The researchers also found equal responding to cues A and C. This indicates that a Pavlovian excitatory-link representation controlled responding since cue A was paired with sucrose in a Pavlovian conditioning paradigm, but was not associated with any operant contingency.

Behavior-Reinforcer Beliefs

According to Dickinson, animals also develop **behavior-reinforcer beliefs;** that is, an expectancy can contain declarative knowledge that emitting a specific behavior will result in the occurrence of a specific reinforcer. How can we validate the existence of a behavior-reinforcer belief? Dickinson uses the **reinforcer devaluation effect** to demonstrate such an expectancy.

Suppose that animals are first trained to bar press for sucrose reinforcement, and then the value of the sucrose reinforcer is devalued by pairing sucrose with illness. How would an animal respond following reinforcer devaluation? Adams and Dickinson (1981) investigated the effects of reinforcer devaluation. They presented sucrose and food to two groups of animals. One group received sucrose for bar pressing and food no matter what the response; the other group had to bar press for food but received sucrose noncontingently. Adams and Dickinson observed that bar pressing during extinction was significantly lower for animals receiving behavior-contingent sucrose devaluation than behavior-noncontingent

FIGURE 8.5. Graph illustrating the mean rate of bar pressing during extinction under water deprivation (1) in the presence of a Pavlovian-conditioned stimulus paired with sucrose solution or food pellets during training, or (2) in the presence of an operant discriminative stimulus signaling either sucrose or food availability during training. The results show that the level of responding during extinction under water deprivation was equal for both a Pavlovian-conditioned stimulus associated with sucrose and a discriminative stimulus for sucrose availability.

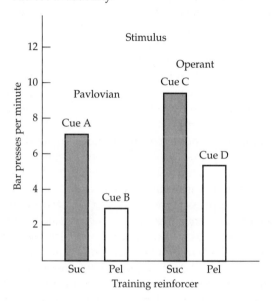

sucrose devaluation. In other words, the animals whose reinforcer was devalued responded much less during extinction than animals whose reinforcer was not devalued. This observation indicates that animals develop a belief that a specific behavior yields a specific reinforcer, and this expectancy will control responding unless the reinforcer is no longer valued.

We have discovered that reinforcer devaluation can lead to a reduction in operant responding. Garcia (1989) proposed that while flavor aversion alters the incentive value of a fluid, this learning remains latent until the animal reexperiences the flavor stimulus. In Garcia's view, flavor aversion learning establishes an association between the flavor and the gastric effects of illness. When the animal reexperiences the flavor, certain gastric reactions are elicited, and the incentive value of the flavor changes.

The idea that reexperience is necessary to alter incentive value suggests that reexposure to the flavor should be necessary to produce the reinforcer devaluation effect. Balleine and Dickinson (1991) tested this prediction by reexposing some animals to the devalued flavor. Other animals were not reexposed to the devalued flavor. Balleine and Dickinson reported that operant performance declined in those subjects reexposed to the devalued reinforcer, but not in those that did not reexperience the devalued reinforcer. These results support the idea that the incentive for a flavor paired with illness will only diminish if the animal reexperiences the flavor.

How does associating a flavor with illness cause a decrease in the level of operant behavior for that flavor? Bernard Balleine and Anthony Dickinson (Balleine, 2001; Dickinson & Balleine, 1994, 1995) provide an answer to this important question. According to Dickinson and Balleine, pairing the flavor and illness causes a representation of the sensory properties of the flavor to become associated with a mental "structure" sensitive to the effects of illness. Dickinson and Balleine refer to this structure as disgust. Subsequently experiencing the flavor activates the disgust structure. When the flavor is reexperienced in the operant setting, the mental representation of the flavor is activated, which stimulates the disgust structure. Activity in the disgust structure leads to a devalued evaluation of the outcome (flavor) of the operant response. And it is the devaluation of the outcome that leads to a reduced operant behavior.

Balleine, Garner, and Dickinson (1995) provide evidence that devaluation is a two-stage process. First, the representation of the flavor is associated with activity in the disgust system; and second, activity in the disgust system is activated when the subject reexperiences the flavor, causing the subject to devalue the outcome in the operant setting. These researchers first administered ondansetron to rats prior to pairing with either sucrose (or saline) and LiCl, an illness-inducing drug. Ondansetron, a drug with strong antiemetic, or antivomiting, effects, should suppress activity in the disgust system. Animals then received the other flavor (either saline or sucrose) and LiCl without ondansetron. Despite the fact that both flavors were paired with LiCl, the animals preferred the flavor paired with LiCl under ondansetron. Why? According to Balleine, Garner, and Dickinson, the disgust system must be active to establish an association between the representation of the flavor and the disgust system. Since ondansetron suppresses the disgust system, the association between the representation of the flavor and the disgust system does not form, despite the pairing of the flavor and LiCl. These rats will subsequently consume the poisoned flavor.

Suppose an aversion to a flavor was established, but ondansetron was given prior to reexposure to that flavor in the operant setting? Would the flavor be devalued in the operant setting? Balleine, Garner, and Dickinson (1995) conducted such an experiment. In their study, performing one behavior (pressing a lever) produced one outcome (sucrose or saline), while performing another behavior (pulling a chain) produced the other outcome. Both flavors were then paired with LiCl. Ondansetron was injected before the rats reexperienced one flavor, but not the other. During subsequent extinction testing, the rats showed a higher level of the operant behavior correlated with the flavor reexperienced under ondansetron. According to Balleine, Garner, and Dickinson, reexperiencing the flavor under ondansetron caused the suppression of the disgust system, which prevented the devaluation of the outcome. If the outcome is not devalued, the rat will continue to perform the operant behavior.

Some illness-inducing treatments also produce somatic discomfort. Somatic discomfort following an illness-inducing treatment is immediate, rather than delayed. Balleine and Dickinson (1992) observed that reexposure is not necessary for reinforcer devaluation when illness-inducing treatments also lead to somatic discomfort. According to Balleine and Dickinson, the ability of the flavor to predict somatic discomfort is merely dependent upon the pairing of the flavor and somatic discomfort, and reexperiencing the flavor is not necessary for operant performance to be suppressed. These results also suggest that avoidance of a flavor can be based either on its perceived unpalatability or on anticipated discomfort. Perceived unpalatability can only be established with reexposure, while anticipated discomfort does not depend upon reexperience of the flavor. However, in both cases, a perceived unpalatability and anticipated discomfort can lead to a devalued reinforcer.

The Importance of Habits

Some learning theorists (Levis, 1976; Rescorla & Wagner, 1972) reject the idea that subjective representations of event contingencies form. Instead, they argue that stimulus-response associations rather than expectancies form as the result of experience, and that concrete environmental events rather than subjective representations motivate behavior.

Dickinson (1989) does not reject the idea that habits exist; instead, he argues that habits as well as expectancies can control responding. In Dickinson's view, continued training leads habits rather than expectancies to govern behavior. Two lines of evidence demonstrate that habits can control behavior. First, Adams (1982) trained two groups of rats to bar press for sucrose reinforcement on a FR-1 schedule. One group received 100 reinforcements (50/day); the other group received 500 reinforcements (50/day). A third group of animals had to bar press 500 times to receive 100 reinforcements (FR-5 schedule; 50 reinforcements/day). After training, the sucrose was devalued for half of the animals in each group. Adams found that devaluation reduced responding in the groups receiving 100 reinforcements but had no effect on animals who received 500 reinforcements. According to Dickinson, operant behavior initially is under the control of behavior-reinforcer beliefs. With more training, S-R habits develop, and behavior can be controlled by habits rather than expectancies. The behavior of the animals receiving 500 reinforcements supports this view; that is, these animals continued to respond despite the fact that their actions produced a devalued reinforcer. Second, Colwill and Rescorla (1985) observed that reinforcer devaluation does not lead to a total absence of response; that is, animals respond to some degree despite reinforcer devaluation. This observation further supports the suggestion that habits develop even when expectancies are controlling responding. When the influence of expectancies is eliminated by reinforcer devaluation, responding continues to some degree due to the control of S-R habits. We saw a similar dual of behavior when we discussed place learning earlier in the chapter. Dickinson refers to the control of responding by habit rather than expectancy as **behavioral autonomy.**

Behavioral autonomy leads an animal or human to respond to a devalued reinforcer. Consider the following example to illustrate the power of behavioral autonomy. Many people collect baseball cards. One might imagine that a child (or an adult) could find obtaining the baseball card of a star player to be a valued reinforcer. Yet, many people just collect cards, often never opening a pack or box of cards. The packs or boxes are put away with the other packs or boxes. It is highly likely that this hoarding behavior is caused by behavioral autonomy; that is, they collect the cards out of habit rather than from the expectancy of obtaining a valued reinforcer.

BEFORE YOU GO ON

- **What associative-link expectancy was responsible for Martha's feelings toward math in high school?**
- **What behavior-reinforcer beliefs might have been operative when Martha took math in high school?**

What happens when an animal or person discovers that behavior and outcomes are unrelated? In the next section, we will discover that the acquisition of a belief that events are unrelated can lead to the behavior pathology of depression. We will discuss helplessness at length: it represents an area where expectancies developed through experience can lead to depression.

A COGNITIVE VIEW OF DEPRESSION

Martin Seligman (1975) described depression as the "common cold of psychopathology." No one is immune to the sense of despair indicative of depression; each of us has at some time become depressed following a disappointment or failure. For most, this unhappiness quickly wanes, and normal activity resumes. For others, the feelings of sadness last for a long time and impair the ability to interact effectively with the environment.

Why do people become depressed? According to Seligman, depression is learned. It occurs when individuals believe their failures are due to uncontrollable events and expect to continue to fail as long as these events are beyond their control. Depression develops because these persons believe that they are helpless to control their own destinies. Seligman's learned helplessness theory forms the basis for his view of depression.

Learned Helplessness Theory

Imagine that none of the medical schools to which you applied admitted you. Given that your dream since childhood has been to be a physician, you certainly would feel distressed for a while. If you are like most who are at first rejected, you might decide to enroll in some additional courses, study harder, and apply again. Or you could search for an alternative future occupation. However, these rejections might also cause you to become severely depressed. According to Seligman, if you fall prey to this last alternative, you might believe you are capable of succeeding in medical school, but think that continued rejection is inevitable. You believe that no matter how well you perform in school, you will be rejected. The belief that there is nothing you can do to be accepted leads you to become depressed. Depression, according to Seligman, occurs when individuals learn that events will happen independent of their behavior. Seligman labeled the expectation that events are uncontrollable **learned helplessness.**

Original Animal Research

Seligman developed his learned helplessness theory of depression from his animal studies (see Maier & Seligman, 1976, for a review of this literature). The original studies (Overmier & Seligman, 1967; Seligman & Maier, 1967) used dogs as subjects. Some of these dogs were strapped in hammocks and then exposed to a series of 64 intense, inescapable shocks. Other dogs received a series of 64 escapable shocks; the shocks terminated when the dogs pressed a panel with their heads. The amount of shock the dogs received in both the inescapable and escapable condition was equal: the shocks ended for the dogs that received inescapable shock when the dogs in the escapable treatment successfully terminated their shock. A third group of dogs did not receive any shock during the initial stage of these studies. The experimenters placed each of the dogs in the three groups into a shuttle box 24 hours after the first stage. In the shuttle box, each dog received 10 trials of signaled escape-avoidance training (see Chapter 5). Once the CS was presented, each dog had 10 seconds to jump over the hurdle to avoid shock. At the end of the 10-second interval, the shock was presented, and the dogs could terminate (escape) the shock by jumping the hurdle. The shock remained on for 50 seconds, or until the dog escaped. The experimenters reported that two-thirds of the animals that had received inescapable shocks 24 hours earlier did not learn either to escape or to avoid the intense electrical shock in the shuttle box (refer to **Figure 8.6**). The dogs appeared helpless: They sat in the box and endured the intense shock for the entire 50-second interval. A few of the helpless dogs occasionally jumped the hurdle and either escaped or avoided shock. However, these dogs again acted helpless on the next trial; apparently, they did not benefit from their successful experiences. In contrast, the dogs that had been given either escapable shock or no shock in the earlier phase quickly escaped shock during their initial trials in the shuttle box, and in their later trials, they learned to respond to the signal and avoid shock altogether.

A wide range of animal species is susceptible to the negative impact of uncontrollable experiences. Psychologists have observed the helplessness phenomenon in cats (Thomas & DeWald, 1977), rats (Jackson, Alexander, & Maier, 1980), and humans (Hiroto & Seligman, 1975; Roth & Kubal, 1975). Although the human studies have demonstrated that uncontrollable experiences do have an influence, the effects are small when compared to those found in lower animals. These results are not surprising; the aversive stimuli used are considerably less unpleasant in the human than in the nonhuman studies. Exposing humans to a treatment sufficiently intense to induce helplessness is unethical. Thus, human experiments in this area are primarily intended to demonstrate that uncontrollable experiences exert a similar influence in animals and humans.

Helplessness in Human Subjects

Hiroto's (1974) experiment with human subjects provides a good approximation of the original helplessness studies with dogs. Hiroto also employed a

FIGURE 8.6. Percentage of trials in which dogs failed to escape shock in the shuttle box after receiving escapable shock, inescapable shock, or no shock. The mean percent failures to escape were significantly greater for animals exposed to inescapable shock than either escapable or no shock.

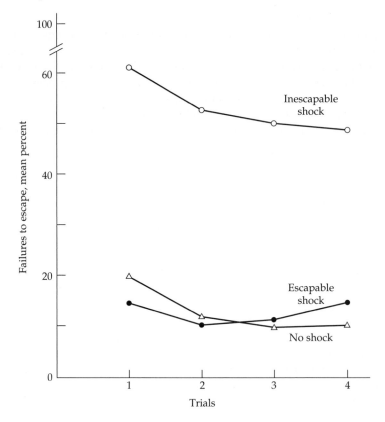

three-group design. Let's briefly examine his study to illustrate the influence of uncontrollable experiences on human subjects.

College students who volunteered to participate in the study were assigned to one of three treatment groups. Some could terminate an unpleasant noise by pushing a button four times. Although subjects in the uncontrollable group were told that their correct response would end the noise, there was actually no response that would terminate the noise. Parallel to the animal studies, the noise ended for the uncontrollable condition subjects when a comparable subject in the controllable-condition group successfully terminated the noise. A third group of subjects did not receive either of the noise treatments during the first stage of the study. Following the initial part of the study, Hiroto trained all subjects to avoid or escape noise in a finger shuttle box. The noise ended when a subject moved his or her finger from one side of the shuttle box to the other. Hiroto reported that subjects in the uncontrollable-noise condition failed to learn either to escape or avoid the noise in the shuttle box and listened passively until the noise terminated at the end of a trial. In contrast, the group that received the controllable noise, as well as the group that did not receive any initial trials, quickly learned to escape and then to avoid noise in the shuttle box. These results suggest that uncontrollable experiences produce similar negative effects on learning in both animals and humans.

Characteristics of Helplessness

Seligman (1975) proposed that exposure to uncontrollable events produces helplessness because the animal or person develops an expectation that these events are independent of behavior. Once individuals acquire the belief that they cannot influence the occurrence of aversive events, helplessness ensues. Thus, the behavioral symptoms characteristic of helplessness are caused, according to Seligman, by the expectation of a lack of control. In Seligman's view, three major behavior components make up helplessness: (1) motivational deficits, (2) cognitive deficits, and (3) emotional disturbance.

MOTIVATIONAL IMPAIRMENTS. After the establishment of helplessness, animals are unable to initiate voluntary behavior. The passivity of dogs or humans following uncontrollable events may reflect an inability to initiate instrumental behavior. Many different behaviors appear susceptible to the influence of uncontrollable events. For example, Braud, Wepman, and Russo (1969) observed that mice exposed to uncontrollable shock later were significantly slower to escape from a water maze than were mice that had received controllable shock. Rosellini and Seligman (1975) found that rats that had previously received inescapable shock did not escape from a frustrating experience; these rats sat passively in a situation formerly associated with reward. In contrast, rats that had received either escapable shock or no shock readily learned to escape from the frustrating situation.

Hiroto and Seligman's (1975) study exhibits the nonspecific character of helplessness. Human subjects received uncontrollable experiences in either a cognitive task (insoluble problems) or an instrumental task (inescapable noise). Hiroto and Seligman evaluated the effect of these uncontrollable events by using either a cognitive task (unscrambling anagrams) or an instrumental task (finger shuttle box). Results indicated that poorer performance followed uncontrollable rather than controllable events; this effect was found regardless of the nature of the uncontrollable events or the type of test situation. In addition, Hiroto and Seligman found that the uncontrollable experience and test situation did not need to be similar. For example, subjects who received uncontrollable experience in a cognitive task (insoluble problems) performed an instrumental task (finger shuttle box) more poorly than did subjects exposed to solvable problems.

INTELLECTUAL IMPAIRMENTS. Cognitive deficits also characterize helplessness. The expectation that an individual has no control over environmental events renders this person incapable of benefiting from future experiences. When individuals do not expect their lack of control to change, successful experiences fail to influence subsequent behavior. Overmier and Seligman (1967) and Seligman and Maier (1967) reported that their helpless dogs occasionally jumped over the hurdle and either escaped or avoided the electric shock. Despite this successful experience, these dogs did not change their behavior on subsequent trials; instead, they remained on the shock side of the shuttle box on the next trial. However, dogs in the escapable or no shock condition learned from success; after a successful avoidance response, they were more likely to respond correctly on the next trial. In addition, normal dogs changed their ineffective behavior; helpless dogs continued to fail to respond even though they had received punishment on each trial.

The Miller and Seligman (1975) study shows (1) a similar failure to change behavior in human subjects who were previously exposed to uncontrollable event and (2) that the reason for this failure is that the individual expects future events to be uncontrollable. The first phase of this study exposed college students to a series of escapable, inescapable, or no noise treatments. The experimenters then required all subjects to sort 15 cards into 10 categories within 15 seconds and told them that the rapidity of sorting depended on their skill. In reality, the experimenters controlled the subjects' success or failure on the sorting task; all subjects succeeded on 50 percent of the trials and failed on 50 percent of them. The experimenters determined success or failure by controlling the length of each trial so that the subjects experienced a predetermined sequence of successes and failures. They asked all subjects at the end of each trial to rate (on a scale of 0 to 10) their expectation of success on the next trial. Miller and Seligman discovered that subjects who received the inescapable noise treatment showed little expectancy change after either success or failure; these subjects did not believe their behavior influenced future events. In contrast, the subjects who were given either the escapable or no noise treatments displayed large expectancy changes after each trial; a successful trial increased their expectation of future success, and a failure on a trial decreased it. These results suggest that our expectations of future events depend on our belief that we control present and past experiences. It is the perceived ability to control events that is important, since none of Miller and Seligman's subjects actually controlled their success or failure.

EMOTIONAL TRAUMA. The expectation that events are uncontrollable, according to Seligman (1975), produces emotional disturbance. Animals exposed to uncontrollable events are obviously experiencing a traumatic emotional state. For example, the dogs in the original helplessness studies sat in a corner of the shuttle box and whined until the shock ended. Human helplessness studies show a similar emotional response. For example, Roth and Kubal (1975) administered questionnaires to their human subjects following uncontrollable experiences and reported increases in feelings of helplessness, incompetence, frustration, and depression. In addition, Gatchel and Proctor (1976) found that helplessness training lowered electrodermal activity; this lowered activity is thought to be correlated with lowered motivational level (Malmo, 1965) and occurs with clinical depression (McCarron, 1973).

Similarities of Helplessness and Depression

The importance of the learned helplessness phenomenon lies in its proposed relation to the clinical disorder of depression. Although no one can ethically conduct a direct causal test, the correlational evidence supports Seligman's statement that the expectation of an inability to control events produces human depression. These comparisons show that depressed people display the cognitive characteristics of learned helplessness.

Nondepressed individuals exposed to uncontrollable events and depressed persons show similar motivational deficits. For example, college students who had previously received uncontrollable noise failed to learn to escape noise in the finger shuttle box (Hiroto, 1974). Klein and Seligman's (1976) depressed subjects similarly failed to escape noise in the shuttle box. Their studies contained four groups of subjects: One group contained individuals who were classified as depressed according to the Beck Depression Inventory, and the other three groups contained nondepressed subjects. Klein and Seligman exposed one group of nondepressed subjects to uncontrollable noise—a procedure that produces helplessness. The second nondepressed group received escapable noise; the last nondepressed group and the depressed group received no noise treatment. The study's results indicated that the nondepressed subjects who were exposed to inescapable noise (the helpless group) and the depressed subjects escaped more slowly than did nondepressed subjects who received either the escapable noise or no noise treatment (see **Figure 8.7**). Evidently, these nondepressed individuals, as a result of uncontrollable laboratory experiences, behaved as the clinically depressed persons did. We should not assume that this treatment produced clinical depression, but rather that both groups expected they would not be able to control laboratory noise. People suffering from depression have a generalized expectation of no control; their failure to escape in the study merely reflects this generalized expectancy.

Our prior discussion indicates that subjects exposed to uncontrollable events do not benefit from their experiences; these subjects do not change their expectations for future success after experiencing either success or failure. Depressives show a similar failure to change their expectations after a successful experience (Miller & Seligman, 1973). Miller and Seligman classified college students as either depressed or nondepressed and then exposed them to one of two tasks. The first task, involving a test of skill, required the subjects to move a platform upward to prevent a steel ball from falling. The second task, a game of chance, required the subjects to guess which of two slides would be presented on a given trial. Since the presentation of slides was random, success on this task was simply due to chance. All subjects estimated after each trial whether they expected to be successful on the next trial. Miller and Seligman reported that success in the skill task increased the nondepressed subjects' expectation of future success, but depressed individuals showed significantly less expectancy change after having performed a successful skill task (see **Figure 8.8**). Thus, the depressed subjects behaved in the same manner as individuals exposed to uncontrollable events: neither changed their expectation of success much after success. Why don't depressed and helpless subjects increase their expectation of success as much as others do after a successful experience? The answer lies in the chance task behavior of both depressed and nondepressed subjects. After a successful trial on the chance task, neither depressed nor nondepressed subjects increased their expectation of future success. There was no reason to increase it, since all the subjects in this task knew their success was due to chance and was therefore beyond their control. Depressed and helpless subjects, in Seligman's

FIGURE 8.7. Escape latency to terminate noise for four groups. Group D-NN includes depressed subjects (on Beck Depression Inventory) who were not previously exposed to noise; group ND-NN contains nondepressed subjects who were not previously exposed to noise; group ND-IN contains nondepressed subjects who were previously exposed to inescapable noise; and group ND-EN includes nondepressed subjects who were previously exposed to escapable noise. The escape latency was greater for nondepressed subjects exposed to inescapable noise (ND-IN) and depressed subjects not exposed to noise (D-NN) than for nondepressed subjects exposed to escapable noise (ND-EN) or nondepressed subjects exposed to no noise (ND-NN).

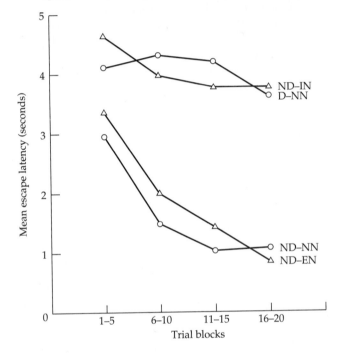

view, also credited chance for their successful skill experiences, since they believed these events were uncontrollable.

Criticism of the Learned Helplessness Approach

Seligman's original learned helplessness model generated interest in the role of the cognitive processes involved in depression. However, his theory encountered difficulties; it was too simplistic and did not precisely reflect the process that produces depression. We will next look at these problems with the original helplessness theory.

Recall from the prior description of Seligman's theory that human subjects, following exposure to uncontrollable events, did not change their future expectations in a skill task even after having success. These results suggest that the helpless subjects believed their success was due to chance. During the experiment, helpless subjects behaved as if skill tasks were chance tasks; however,

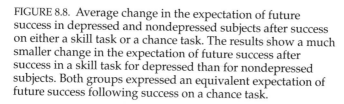

FIGURE 8.8. Average change in the expectation of future success in depressed and nondepressed subjects after success on either a skill task or a chance task. The results show a much smaller change in the expectation of future success after success in a skill task for depressed than for nondepressed subjects. Both groups expressed an equivalent expectation of future success following success on a chance task.

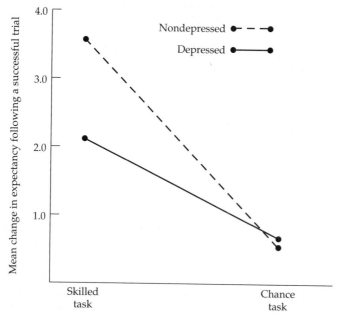

when questioned after the experiment, helplessness subjects described the situation as a skill test. The original helplessness model cannot explain why helpless subjects responded as if they had no control over events when they were aware that other people were able to control these same events.

A second problem with the original helplessness model is that some other studies have not observed performance deficits following uncontrollable experiences. In fact, several studies (Roth & Kubal, 1975; Tennen & Eller, 1977) have demonstrated improved subject performance after exposure to insoluble problems; their human subjects exposed to insoluble problems actually scored higher on subsequent tasks than did those who were exposed to solvable problems. This facilitation of performance after exposure to uncontrollable tasks is inconsistent with Seligman's original model of helplessness, which maintains that uncontrollable experiences should create expectations that impair—not improve—later behavior.

Rizley's study (1978, experiment 1) illustrates a final problem with Seligman's original helplessness theory. Rizley presented depressed and nondepressed subjects with a series of 50 numbers (either 0 or 1) and then instructed the subjects to guess the next number. Although there was no pattern to the numbers, Rizley told his subjects that there were number-order trends and tendencies and that their score would be above chance if they were aware of these trends. The subjects were told after the number presentations whether they had succeeded (passed the test) by scoring 26 or more or had failed by scoring 25 or less. (Since there were only two choices, a score of 25 meant chance-level performance.) The subjects then indicated the reason for their score from a list of several possibilities—luck, task difficulty, effort, or ability. Rizley's results demonstrated that depressed people attributed their success to the external factors of luck and task ease and their failure to internal factors of lack of effort and ability. In contrast, nondepressed people thought that internal factors accounted for their success, and that external factors caused their failure. Thus, people who are depressed attribute their failure to internal processes, but they also feel helpless because they can do nothing to prevent future failures. Seligman's learned helplessness theory could not explain Rizley's observations. Responding to such difficulties, Seligman developed the attributional model of helplessness. This model provides answers to the problems inherent in the original learned helplessness theory.

An Attributional Model

Seligman and his associates (Abramson, Garber, & Seligman, 1980; Abramson, Seligman, & Teasdale, 1978) proposed that the attributions people make for their failures determine whether they become depressed. An attribution is the perceived cause of an event. Causal attributions of failure can be made on three dimensions: personal-universal (internal-external), global-specific, and stable-unstable. An **internal attribution** is the belief that internal characteristics cause the outcome; an **external attribution** is the view that environmental forces determine success (reward) or failure (aversive event). A **stable attribution** is the belief that the perceived cause of past success or failure will determine future outcomes; an **unstable attribution** represents the belief that new factors may determine success or failure in the future. A **specific attribution** reflects the view that the cause of an outcome relates only to a specific task; a **global attribution** is the belief that the cause of the outcome in this task will determine outcomes in diverse situations. The combination of these three dimensions produces eight possible attributional outcomes (see **Table 8.1**). The specific attribution will determine whether (1) depression occurs, (2) depression generalizes to other

TABLE 8.1. The Attributional Model of Depression: A Woman Rejected

| Dimension | Internal | | External | |
	Stable	Unstable	Stable	Unstable
Global	I'm unattractive to men.	My conversation sometimes bores men.	Men are overly competitive with intelligent women.	Men get into rejecting moods.
Specific	I'm unattractive to him.	My conversation bores him.	He's overly competitive with women.	He was in a rejecting mood.

Note: The attribution of uncontrollability to internal causes produced personal helplessness, whereas an external causal attribution results in universal helplessness.
Source: Abramson, L. Y., Seligman, M. E. P., & Teasdale, J. D. (1978). Learned helplessness in humans: Critique and reformulation. *Journal of Abnormal Psychology, 87,* 49–74. Copyright 1978 by the American Psychological Association. Reprinted by permission.

situations, and (3) the depression is temporary or ongoing. Consider the examples **Table 8.1** presents. If the woman attributes her rejection to an internal, stable, global factor ("I'm unattractive to all men"), she will become depressed. In contrast, the woman will not become depressed if she attributes rejection to an external, unstable, specific factor ("He was in a rejecting mood"). This attributional model, while complex, provides us with an explanation for people's varied responses to uncontrollable experiences.

Personal versus Universal Helplessness

Consider the two following examples: (1) The economy is depressed, and the automobile industry's failure to sell enough cars forces several plants to close. An automobile worker loses her job and becomes depressed. (2) A 16-year-old who wants to play for the high school basketball team has diligently practiced all summer and fall; he is not selected for the team and becomes depressed. In both examples, depression has occurred, according to Seligman, because of each individual's perceived inability to control events: the automobile worker could not get a job, and the student could not be on the team. However, the types of helplessness the automobile worker and student feel are quite different.

The attributional model proposes two kinds of helplessness: personal and universal. The student's failure to be picked for the team is an example of **personal helplessness:** this student's inability caused failure, but other, more competent students were selected for the team. **Universal helplessness** occurs when the environment is structured so that no one can control future events: the automobile worker could not control the economy, and therefore attributes her lack of control to external forces.

Abramson (1977) ascertained from her experiments that both personal and universal helplessness produced the cognitions (expectations of future inability to control events) and motivational deficits (lack of ability to initiate voluntary behavior) characteristic of depression. In addition, Abramson and Sackeim (1977) examined the attributions of depressed people and found that those who were personally depressed made internal attributions for failure, whereas those who were universally depressed made external attributions.

The nature of the helplessness determines whether loss of esteem occurs. People who attribute their failure to external forces—universal helplessness—experience no loss of self-esteem, since they do not consider themselves responsible for their failure. However, the attribution of failure to internal factors—personal helplessness—causes a loss of self-esteem; these individuals believe their incompetency causes their failure. In support of this view, Abramson (1977) found that lowered self-esteem only occurs with personal helplessness.

Global versus Specific Causal Attributions

People exposed to uncontrollable events may not become depressed; they could make a specific attribution for their failure, and thus not experience helplessness in other circumstances. Others might make a global attribution, believing their failure will happen at other times, and become depressed. For instance, the automobile worker may come to believe that no jobs are available in any other company and stop searching for a job. In contrast, the student who failed to make the team might change schools and try again next year. Thus, the attribution of a lack of control to global factors will produce helplessness that will generalize to new situations, but the attribution to a specific situation will limit helplessness to that situation.

Roth and Kubal's (1975) experiment supports the idea that global-specific attributions are important in determining whether people feel helpless in new situations. First-year college students volunteered to participate in the Roth and Kubal study in two separate, very different experiments on the same day and in the same building. The first experiment was designed to fail all students. Subjects in one group (important condition) of this first experiment were told that the failed task was a "good predictor of college grades"; those in the other group (unimportant condition) were informed that they were participating in "an experiment in learning." Following the first experiment, all subjects proceeded to the second study. Since both groups experienced failure on the first experiment, the original helplessness model would predict that both groups would fail to perform well in the second study. However, the subjects who were told that the first test was a learning experiment did significantly better on the second test than the subjects who thought the first experiment was a predictor of future success. According to the attributional model, the subjects in the important condition attributed their failure to a more global factor, a lack of ability to succeed in college, while subjects in the unimportant condition attributed their failure to a single task. As a result, the helplessness generalized to the new situation for subjects in the important condition, but not for the subjects in the unimportant condition.

Stable versus Unstable Causal Attributions

Seligman proposed that a person's attribution of helplessness to a stable or unstable factor also influences the effect an uncontrollable experience has on behavior. Ability is considered a stable factor; effort, an unstable one. If someone attributes failure in an uncontrollable experience to lack of effort, this attribution will increase this person's subsequent effort. However, the attribution of failure to the stable factor of lack of ability will lead to helplessness, since people can change their effort but not their innate ability. Consider what would happen if the high school basketball player, rather than having attributed his failure to a lack of control, felt he had not exerted enough effort. Under this condition, failure might increase rather than decrease behavior. Thus, the facilitation that follows uncontrollable experiences in some studies probably results from the subjects' belief that increased effort will lead to success. However, continued failure will eventually cause the subject to expect no control over failure. A test of this view appears in Roth and Kubal's study (1975). Roth and Kubal gave their subjects one or two learned helplessness training tasks and found that those who failed at one task showed more motivation than control subjects, but those who failed at two tasks exhibited helplessness.

The idea that the stability or instability of the perceived cause influences helplessness also explains why depression is temporary in some situations and more enduring in others. For example, with our automobile worker, the attribution to the external factor of the poor economy caused depression, which will persist if the economy remains down. However, the depression will be temporary if the economy recovers and the worker gets a job. (If the economy improves but the worker fails to find employment, the worker may then at-tribute that failure to personal, stable factors and continue to be depressed.)

Severity of Depression

Helplessness can apparently follow several different types of uncontrollable experiences. However, severe depression typically appears when individuals attribute their failure to internal, global, and stable factors (Peterson & Selig-man, 1984). Their depression is intense because they perceive themselves as incompetent (internal attribution) in many situations (global attribution), and they believe their incompetence is unlikely to change (stable attribution). In support of this notion, Hammen and Krantz (1976) found that depressed women attributed interpersonal failure (for example, being alone on a Friday night) to internal, global, and stable factors. In contrast, nondepressed women blamed their failure on external, specific, and unstable factors. Other re-searchers (Robins, 1988; Sweeney, Anderson, & Bailey, 1986) have observed a similar difference in the attribution of failure between depressed and nonde-pressed people.

Hopelessness

Abramson, Metalsky, and Alloy (1989) have suggested a further revision of the helplessness theory. According to these researchers, some cases of depression, called **hopelessness depression,** are caused by a state of hopelessness. They de-fine **hopelessness** as the expectation that desired outcomes will not occur, or that the person has no control over undesired outcomes. The belief that one has no control over undesired outcomes is the postulated cause of depression in previous helplessness theories, while this theory focuses on the proposition that depression also can result from a belief that positive outcomes will not occur.

Why the need to again revise the helplessness theory? Alloy, Kelly, Mineka, and Clements (1990) recognized that while anxiety without depression is com-mon, depression without anxiety is rare. According to these researchers, anxiety is elicited by the possibility that a person may have no control over negative events. When the person is certain he or she is helpless, the person experiences both anxiety and hopelessness. The fact that anxiety typically precedes depres-sion supports this view of depression (Rohde, Lewinsohn, & Seeley, 1991). Abramson, Metalsky, and Alloy (1989) suggest that hopelessness is only one cause of depression. We will discuss another likely cause shortly.

A Pessimistic Explanatory Style and Depression

The attributional model suggests that **attributional** (or explanatory) **style** is causally related to depression. Metalsky, Abramson, Seligman, Semmel, and Peterson (1982) provide more direct support of the attributional model. They found that knowledge of a person's attributional style enabled them to predict susceptibility to depression following failure. In their study, the attributional style of college students was measured at the beginning of a semester. The re-sults demonstrated that those students who attributed past failures to internal, global, and stable factors were more likely to become depressed after earning a poor grade (in the student's view) on a midsemester exam than were students who attributed their past failures to external, specific, and unstable factors. This study suggests that a person's attributional style influences the likelihood of becoming depressed when facing failure. Would a change in attributional style influence depression? As predicted from the attributional model, Hollon, Evans, and DeRubeis (1990) found that changing a person's attributional style made cognitive therapy for depression more effective.

Ellen Langer (1983) suggests that "perceived control is basic to human functioning." According to Langer, individuals strive to acquire feelings of competency and to be able to master life's circumstances. Optimists feel they are able to control external events; pessimists believe they have no control. An optimistic explanatory style leads to greater successes than a pessimistic explanatory style. For example, Seligman and Schulman (1986) reported that new insurance salespersons who were optimists sold more policies and were 50% less likely to quit within one year than salespersons who habitually explained failures as uncontrollable ("I always fail," or "This is impossible"). Also, Maddux and Stanley (1986) observed that students who felt competent were less anxious and depressed and more academically successful than other students.

However, it is not clear whether attributional style causes depression in response to negative life events or whether depression changes a person's attributional style (Clark, Watson, & Mineka, 1994). Coyne and Wiffen (1995) found that the pessimistic explanatory style depressed persons use is generally an accurate reflection of their unfortunate life experiences; that is, negative life events often happened to depressed persons with a pessimistic explanatory style. Further, Haaga (1995) observed that attributional style was more strongly related to depressives who think a lot about the causes of the negative events in their lives than those who do not, while Nolen-Hoeksema, Morrow, and Fredickson (1993) reported that depressed people who ruminate about negative events and about why those negative events occur were more likely to become more depressed. Further research is needed to determine whether a pessimistic explanatory style is a symptom or a cause of depression.

Biological Influences on Learned Helplessness

Although our discussion indicates that cognitions influence the development of depressive behavior, it is important to recognize that other factors are involved in depression. Several lines of research suggest that biology, either alone or in combination with pessimistic expectancies, produces depression.

Disturbances in the functioning of the brain's noradrenergic (norepinephrine) chemical transmitter system appear to be related to the development of depression. Numerous studies (see Klein, 2000) have shown that a deficiency in norepinephrine is correlated with depression, and an elevation of norepinephrine reverses depression. The research of Jay Weiss and his associates (Weiss, Goodman, Losito, Corrigan, Charry, & Bailey, 1981; Weiss, Simpson, Ambrose, Webster, & Hoffman, 1985) has suggested that repeated exposure to uncontrollable events may produce the biochemical, as well as the behavioral, changes observed in people who are depressed. This research has found that when rats are exposed to a series of inescapable shocks, they show a pattern of behavior that includes early-morning wakefulness, decreased feeding and sex drive, decreased grooming, and a lack of voluntary response in a variety of situations, all symptoms of clinical depression.

What are the biochemical changes that occur following uncontrollable stress such as that experienced by the rats in Weiss's experiment? Several studies (Hughes, Kent, Campbell, Oke, Croskill, & Preskorn, 1984; Lehnert, Reinstein, Strowbridge, & Wurtman, 1984) have observed isolated decreases in norepinephrine in the locus coeruleus following prolonged exposure to inescapable shocks. (The locus coeruleus is a central nervous system structure that has widespread connections throughout the brain and that plays a key role in arousal and wakefulness.) According to Weiss, Simpson, Hoffman, Ambrose, Cooper, and Webster (1986), a localized decrease in norepinephrine increases locus coeruleus activity (because of the inhibitory effect of the norepinephrine-containing neurons on the activity of the locus coeruleus); that is, a decrease in norepinephrine releases the inhibitory action of these neurons, which increases overall neural activity in the locus coeruleus and thereby produces depression. In support of this view, Weiss and Simpson (1986) reported that administration of antidepressant drugs decreased locus coeruleus activity and eliminated the behavioral deficits evident following exposure to inescapable shock. These results suggest that uncontrollable events produce heightened activity in the locus coeruleus, which then produces the behavioral changes associated with depression.

It may be premature to generalize from studies of biochemical changes in animals exposed to uncontrollable events to humans affected by depression. One reason is that there is no perfect correspondence between neurochemical transmitter levels and depression. While antidepressant drugs alter neurochemical transmission in less than a day, it typically takes at least 2 weeks for the depressive mood to improve. Furthermore, Bright and Everitt (1992) reported that antihypertensive drugs that alter noradrenergic activity do not produce depression. Research continues to be conducted with the aim of identifying the precise role brain chemistry plays in depression.

A COGNITIVE VIEW OF PHOBIC BEHAVIOR

All of us have fears. In most cases, these fears are realistic and enable us to avoid aversive events. For example, people are afraid to cross a street when cars are approaching; their fear motivates them to avoid walking in front of moving cars, thereby avoiding injury or death. However, some people's fears are unrealistic. These individuals have a phobia, a fear that was once appropriate (because an aversive event did occur) but is no longer realistic. This fear motivates avoidance behavior, which prevents the person from learning that the phobia is unrealistic. In many situations, the original aversive event may not be readily apparent. An individual may have forgotten the unpleasant event, or the phobic response may have developed through high-order conditioning or vicarious conditioning (see Chapter 3). The phobic response also may result from stimulus generalization; for example, a child attacked by a peer may generalize this fear to all children. We will next examine research indicating that cognitive processes affect the development of phobias.

Phobias and Expectations

Recall our description of Martha's math phobia from the chapter's opening vignette. Albert Bandura (1977, 1982, 1986) presented a cognitive theory of phobias in which two classes of expectations—outcome and efficacy—maintain Martha's phobia. Outcome expectations reflect the perceived consequences of either a behavior and/or an event. Martha expects a statistics class to be aversive—a **stimulus-outcome expectancy**—and she believes she cannot pass the course—a **response-outcome expectancy.** Also, Martha knows she can prevent the aversive experience by not enrolling in the statistics course; this response-outcome expectancy motivates her behavior.

Martha's phobia presents her with a dilemma typical of phobic situations. Although her phobic behavior enables her to avoid the course, her phobic actions have definite negative consequences. She realizes she must pass this course to graduate, but her phobic behavior prevents her from obtaining her desired goal. Thus, she continues to avoid the course even though she cannot graduate without it.

Bandura's theory suggests that a second type of expectancy is involved in motivating Martha's phobic behavior. According to Bandura's approach, Martha feels incapable of enduring the aversive experience. Bandura labeled this belief that one can or cannot execute a particular action an **efficacy expectancy.** In Bandura's view, Martha's lack of self-efficacy causes her either to fail to register for the course or to withdraw from the course shortly after it begins.

The Importance of Our Experiences

What factors account for Martha's outcome and efficacy expectations? Martha's outcome expectation that she will fail the statistics course could have developed through direct personal experience, through observations of the experiences of other people, or through information others have provided. Since Martha has not failed this course or any other course, her outcome expectations cannot reflect any direct personal experience. Possibly Martha has observed others, whom she perceived as similar to herself, fail the course. In addition, she probably has received information from other people that the course is difficult.

Bandura (1977, 1986) suggested that we use several types of information to establish an efficacy expectation. Personal accomplishments indicate our degree of self-efficacy. Successful experiences generally increase our expectations of mastery, and failure usually decreases our sense of self-efficacy (Bandura, Jeffrey, & Gajdos, 1975). These authors discovered that the influence of success or failure on efficacy expectations depends on task difficulty, amount of effort expended, and the pattern and rate of success. We are more apt to feel competent if we usually succeed at a difficult task that requires considerable effort than if we succeed without trying.

Our sense of self-efficacy is influenced by observing the successes or failures of other people whom we perceive as similar to ourselves. Seeing others successfully cope with perceived aversive events enhances our belief that we can also be effective, while observing others fail decreases our belief that we can succeed. Several factors determine the effectiveness of a vicarious modeling experience. The success of the other person's behavior, or the model's behavior, must be clear; we cannot develop a sense of self-efficacy if the outcome of this other person's behavior is ambiguous (Kazdin, 1974a). Also, we acquire a stronger mastery expectation when we see several people rather than a single person cope with an aversive situation (Kazdin, 1974b). Furthermore, we develop greater self-efficacy when we see other people initially struggle with aversive events and slowly become more effective rather than succeed the first time we see them (Meichenbaum, 1972).

Emotional arousal also influences our sense of competence; we feel less able to cope with an aversive event when we are agitated or tense. Although Bandura suggests that emotional arousal plays a part in motivating phobic behavior, his view certainly differs from the drive approach outlined in Chapter 6. Bandura does not believe that fear directly causes avoidance behavior. Rather, he suggests that fear and defensive action are correlated, but not in a causal relationship. We are more likely to display avoidance behavior when we are afraid—but only because fear makes us feel less effective. However, because emotional arousal is only one source of information we use when developing a sense of self-efficacy, other information may enable us to feel competent even when we are afraid. Under these conditions, we will interact with feared objects even though we are still afraid because we believe we will be able to cope with aversive events. Our emotional arousal extinguishes after we have interacted with an aversive event.

Bandura and Adam's (1977) study demonstrates how efficacy expectations play a role in phobic behavior. Snake-phobic clients received the systematic desensitization therapy described in Chapter 3. Bandura and Adams discovered that even when patients no longer became emotionally disturbed by an imagined aversive scene, differences still existed in their ability to approach a snake. In contrast, the clients' self-efficacy expectation corresponded closely with their ability to interact with the snake: the greater the patients' perceived efficacy, the more able they were to inhibit phobic behavior and approach the snake (**Figure 8.9**). Thus, these clients believed they could hold the snake, and this belief allowed them to overcome their phobia. This relation between self-efficacy and an absence of phobic behavior held true even after therapy, when a new snake, different from the one used before the pretherapy and during desensitization training, was employed. These results demonstrate that if we believe we are competent, we will generalize our self-efficacy expectations to new situations.

Application: A Modeling Treatment for Phobias

Our discussion points to the critical role of outcome and efficacy expectations in motivating phobic behavior. These expectations develop both through our experiences and through our observations of the experiences of others. Over the past 30 years, behavior therapists have employed models to interact with feared objects to treat clients with phobias. The aim of this **modeling** treatment is to alter the clients' phobic behavior by vicariously modifying their expectations.

FIGURE 8.9. Influence of desensitization therapy on the subject's level of self-efficacy and his or her ability to approach a snake. The success of therapy on the posttest was evaluated using both the same snake used in therapy ("similar threat") and a different snake ("dissimilar threat"). The results of this study showed that desensitization therapy increased a person's perceived self-efficacy and interaction with either the same or a different snake.

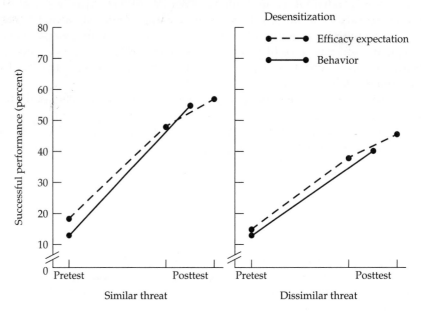

In a modeling treatment for phobias, clients see the model move closer and closer until the model encounters the feared object. A study by Bandura, Grusec, and Menlove (1967) shows the effectiveness of modeling in treating phobic behavior. These psychologists allowed children who feared dogs to watch a peer model interact with a dog. The children received eight 10-minute therapy sessions during a four-day period. At first, the children saw the model pat the dog while it was in a pen. During later observations, the children watched the model walk the dog around the room. In the final sessions, the model climbed into the pen and played with the dog. Other children did not see the model but saw only the dog, which occupied the pen for the first therapy session and was leashed in the later sessions. Bandura, Grusec, and Menlove assessed the effectiveness of modeling by determining if the children who initially feared dogs could approach and play with either the dog seen in the therapy sessions or a new dog. The results indicated that modeling reduced the children's phobic behavior and increased their interaction with the dog used in the study as well as with a new dog.

According to Bandura, the success of modeling therapy must be attributed to the vicarious modifications of a client's expectations. Support for this view is evident in a study by Bandura, Adams, and Beyer (1977). They exposed adults with a snake phobia to models interacting with a snake and assessed the influence of this modeling treatment on the subjects' approach response to the snake and their efficacy expectation—that is, their expectation of being able to interact fearlessly with the snake. Bandura, Adams, and Beyer found that the degree of success corresponded to the increase in the self-efficacy expectation; the more the model's action altered the client's efficacy expectation, the greater the client's approach to the snake. In other words, the individuals who felt most capable of handling the snake were the most likely to do so. Other studies have also demonstrated that modeling is an effective way to reduce unrealistic fears. For example, Melamed and Siegel (1975) and Shaw and Thoresen (1974) reported that children's and adult's fear of going to the dentist was reduced, in both adults and children, by watching a model. Similarly, Jaffe and Carlson (1972) found modeling effective in reducing test anxiety.

The effectiveness of modeling to reduce fears appears to be long-lasting. Ost (1989) treated 20 phobic patients with a variety of phobias including fears of dogs, cats, rats, spiders, and hypodermic needles. Not only did a two-hour modeling session reduce the phobic patients' fears and increase their interaction with a feared stimulus immediately after the modeling treatment, but Ost reported that 90% of the phobic patients maintained their improved behavior on a four-year follow-up study.

An Alternative View

Not all psychologists have accepted Bandura's view of the role of anxiety in motivating avoidance behavior. Some psychologists (Eysenck, 1978; Wolpe, 1978) have continued to advocate a drive-based view of avoidance behavior (see Chapter 6). According to these psychologists, cognitions are elicited by anxiety, but they do not affect the occurrence of avoidance responding. Eysenck considers efficacy expectations to be merely "epiphenomenological" by-products of anxiety. Other psychologists (Borkovec, 1976; Lang, 1978) suggest that three types of anxiety exist: cognitive, physiological, and behavioral. Cognitive anxiety involves the effect of anxiety on self-efficacy, physiological anxiety affects the physiological state, and behavioral anxiety directly influences behavior. In this view, cognitions or physiological state can mediate the influence of anxiety on behavior, or anxiety can directly influence behavior. According to Lang (1978), the relative contribution of each type of anxiety differs depending on the individual's learning history and type of situation. Sometimes cognitions will mediate the effect of anxiety on behavior, under other conditions, anxiety will directly affect behavior.

Our discussion suggests that both cognitive and noncognitive processes motivate avoidance behavior. A study by Feltz (1982) supports this view. Feltz examined the variables controlling whether female college students would execute a difficult back dive. Feltz discovered that self-efficacy predicted whether the subjects executed or avoided the task on the first trial; however, the influence of self-efficacy diminished on subsequent trials, indicating an influence other than cognitive anxiety. Feltz discovered that physiological arousal also influenced whether the subjects avoided the back dive; that is, physiological measures of anxiety (i.e., heart rate) predicted behavior on trials 1 and 3. Furthermore, Feltz's research demonstrates that anxiety can directly affect behavior. On trial 2, the subjects' self-reported anxiety level was the only predictor of whether they completed the back dive or avoided it. Interestingly, self-efficacy and heart rate did correlate with self-reported anxiety prior to the first dive; however, self-reported anxiety did not correlate with either efficacy or heart rate on subsequent dives. On the basis of her research, Feltz suggested that anxiety can either directly or indirectly affect behavior by altering cognitive or physiological processes. Her study also supports the idea that both cognitive and noncognitive processes motivate avoidance behavior.

BEFORE YOU GO ON

- **What outcome expectancies cause Martha's math phobia?**
- **Could Martha successfully complete a math course, yet still be afraid of taking another one?**

CHAPTER SUMMARY

Tolman proposed that our behavior is goal-oriented; we are motivated to reach specific goals and continue to search until we obtain them. Rather than viewing behavior as an inflexible habit, Tolman proposed that our behavior remains flexible enough to allow us to reach our goals. Our expectations determine the specific behavior we use to obtain reward or avoid punishment. According to Tolman, we expect that behaving in a particular way will enable us to obtain reward or avoid aversive events.

In addition to understanding the means needed to reach goals, Tolman proposed that environmental events guide us to our goals. Tolman theorized that although we may know both how to obtain our goals and where these goals are located, we will not behave unless we are motivated.

Dickinson suggested that mental representations called expectancies contain declarative knowledge gained through experience and that these expectancies guide an animal's behavior. According to Dickinson, there are two main classes of declarative knowledge that expectancies contain. First, an expectancy contains associative representations of two events. This associative-line expectancy allows one event to excite or inhibit the representation of the other event. In Dickinson's view, associative representations mediate the impact of Pavlovian conditioning experiences.

The second type of declarative knowledge an expectancy can contain involves an understanding of the consequences of a specific action. This knowledge is represented in propositional form as a belief that action A causes reinforcer B. According to Dickinson, the mental representation of behavior and outcomes controls instrumental or operant activity.

According to Dickinson, instrumental or operant behavior is initially under the control of behavior-reinforcer beliefs. With more training, S-R habits develop, and behavior can fall under the control of habit rather than expectancy. Dickinson refers to the control of responding by habit rather than expectancy as behavioral autonomy.

In some circumstances, individuals perceive no relationship between behavior and outcomes. According to Seligman, an expectation of no control of events leads to helplessness. There appear to be two types of helplessness: personal helplessness, which occurs when people consider themselves incapable of obtaining reward or avoiding punishment, and universal helplessness, which occurs when people consider the attainment of reward or the avoidance of punishment to be impossible.

The duration of helplessness depends on whether people make a stable attribution, which leads to long-lasting helplessness, or an unstable causal attribution, which results in short-lived helplessness. The extent of helplessness depends on whether a person makes a global or specific attribution; when a person makes a specific attribution, helplessness is restricted to a particular circumstance, but a global attribution leads to helplessness and depression in many situations. Hopelessness depression occurs when a person expects that either positive outcomes will not occur or that negative outcomes cannot be controlled.

Optimism is a belief in one's control of events, and optimists appear to be less anxious and depressed and more successful than pessimists. A pessimistic explanatory style is correlated with negative life events and depression. However, it is not clear whether a pessimistic explanatory style is a symptom or a cause of depression.

Phobic behavior occurs when individuals expect that (1) an aversive event will occur, (2) an avoidance behavior is the only way to prevent the aversive event, and (3) they cannot interact with the phobic object. Modeling has been found to be an effective means to change expectancies and eliminate phobic behavior.

CRITICAL THINKING QUESTIONS

1. Kai Leng is going to New Orleans next week. She loves drinking coffee and eating beignets at Cafè du Monde. Kai Leng will assuredly stop there several times while she is in New Orleans. Identify the associative-link and behavior-reinforcer expectancies responsible for Kai Leng's behavior.
2. Eric believes he will do well in his learning class, while Sidney is not so sure he will get a good grade. Using an attributional approach, suggest how Eric and Sidney might react to a poor performance on the first exam. What might be the effect of a poor outcome on the second or third exams?
3. Kasha is fearful of driving in a large city. How would Bandura's model explain Kasha's fearfulness? What approach might she take to eliminate her fear?

KEY TERMS

associative-link
  expectancy
attributional style
behavioral autonomy
behavior-belief
  representation
behavior-reinforcer
  expectancy
cognition
efficacy expectancy

expectancy
external attribution
global attribution
hopelessness
hopelessness depression
internal attribution
irrelevant incentive effect
learned helplessness
modeling
personal helplessness

reinforcer devaluation
  effect
response-outcome
  expectancy
specific attribution
stable attribution
stimulus-outcome
  expectancy
universal helplessness
unstable attribution

CHAPTER NINE

Contemporary Theories of Learning

He Never Saw It Coming

Clarence started dating Felicia several weeks ago. Their very different personalities—Clarence is quiet and shy, and Felicia is outgoing and social—did not keep them from becoming close. Felicia introduced Clarence to a social life he had never before experienced; they enjoyed romantic dinners and exciting parties. Felicia was an excellent dancer, which made dancing fun. Clarence was not used to partying until late. He had to get up early for work and felt drained the entire day after a late night out. Yet, the late nights did not seem to bother Felicia, and she was wide awake the next day, even with only a few hours of sleep. Last month, Felicia started to drink a lot of alcohol. Clarence rarely drinks more than a beer or two, and he was quite concerned about Felicia's drinking. She called him a lightweight for only having one or two drinks. Clarence did not mind the teasing, but he really did not want to drink much. He thought he was in love with Felicia; however, he was troubled by some of her actions toward him. The last several times they were out, Felicia became angry and verbally abusive toward him for no apparent reason. The verbal comments were very harsh, and Clarence was hurt. The next day, Felicia apologized for her behavior and promised not to be nasty again. Yet, the next time that they went out, Felicia again became angry and abusive. Clarence could not figure out why she became hostile, and was considering breaking off their relationship. He mentioned his concerns to his friend Jared. To Clarence's surprise, Jared said he knew why Felicia became hostile; he felt the alcohol was to blame. Jared also said he felt frightened when Felicia started to drink. Clarence was not sure that Jared was right, but he decided he would pay close attention to the amount Felicia drank and whether she became hostile afterwards. He was hopeful this was the reason for her hostility, but he was not sure what he would do if it was.

Why did Clarence fail to see the relationship between Felicia's drinking and her hostility? The answer may lie in a phenomenon called the CS preexposure effect. When a stimulus is first presented without a UCS, subsequent conditioning is impaired when that stimulus is presented with the UCS. Clarence had seen people drinking without becoming aggressive, and this experience may have caused him to fail to recognize the relationship between Felicia's drinking and her hostility. We examine the CS preexposure effect later in the chapter; our discussion may tell us what caused Clarence to fail to associate the sight of Felicia's drinking (CS) with her hostility toward him (UCS).

Clarence's friend Jared recognized the relationship between Felicia's drinking and her hostility. As a result of this recognition, Jared became frightened when he saw Felicia drinking. One of the main questions we will address in this chapter is why Jared was able to associate Felicia's drinking and her hostility. We will answer this question by examining the nature of Pavlovian conditioning. Before we begin our exploration, we need to discuss why psychologists stopped developing global theories of learning and started thinking about the nature of Pavlovian conditioning.

CONTEMPORARY DIRECTIONS FOR LEARNING THEORIES

One significant change in learning theory since the late 1960s has been the shift away from global theories of learning to focus on more specific aspects of the learning process. For example, a contemporary learning theorist might attempt to describe the nature of the conditioned response, or the conditions that determine whether an event is reinforcing.

Why have psychologists abandoned their search for a global explanation of the learning process? Mowrer and Klein (2001) identified three main reasons for the current emphasis on specific learning principles. First, global theories of learning primarily deal with the instrumental conditioning process. Global learning theories assume that Pavlovian conditioning is a simple, reflective type of learning that applies to only a few situations. Also, they assume that most responses are not classically conditioned. However, contemporary research has shown that Pavlovian conditioning is not a simple, reflexive form of learning, and that conditioned responses have a wide impact on human behavior. Further, the study of Pavlovian conditioning has revealed underlying processes that differ from those involved in instrumental conditioning. The recognition of two distinct learning processes makes it difficult to develop a single, unitary theory to explain all behavior.

Traditional learning theories also assume that some general laws of learning apply to all species. This view has led to a generalization of results of studies using various human and nonhuman subjects. However, considerable research indicates that an animal's biological character influences whether or not it will learn, as well as how rapidly it learns a specific behavior. The recognition that biological character affects learning has led to the development of psychobiological accounts of learning. This increased examination of the psychobiology of learning has been a second reason for the shift away from global theories of learning.

Finally, a greater acceptance of cognitive views of learning has also resulted in a greater focus on specific learning principles. For example, the relative contributions of associative and cognitive processes in Pavlovian conditioning have

been the topic of much research. The realization that both cognitive and associative principles may be involved in learning has made it difficult to develop a
single global learning theory.

We will discuss contemporary theories regarding the nature of Pavlovian
and operant conditioning in this chapter. In the next chapter, we will explore the
view that biological character influences learning.

THEORIES OF PAVLOVIAN CONDITIONING

Pavlov (1927) conducted an extensive investigation of the principles governing
the acquisition and extinction of a conditioned response. During the past thirty
years, many studies have examined both how conditioned responses are acquired and whether the CR is similar or different from the UCR. This research
has challenged Pavlov's assumptions regarding both the nature of conditioning
and the conditioned response. New theories have emerged to explain these recent research findings.

The Nature of the Conditioned Response

One important question in Pavlovian conditioning concerns the nature of the
conditioned response. Is the CR just the UCR elicited by the CS? Or is the CR a
behavior distinctively different from the UCR?

The Stimulus-Substitution Theory

Pavlov (1927) suggested that as a result of conditioning, the conditioned
stimulus becomes able to elicit the same response as the unconditioned stimulus.
Why would Pavlov assume that the CR and UCR were the same response?
Pavlov was observing the same digestive responses (e.g., saliva, gastric juices, insulin) as both the CR and UCR. The fact that both the CS and UCS elicit similar
responses logically leads to the conclusion that the CR and UCR are the same.

How does the CS become able to elicit the same response as the UCS? According to Pavlov, the presentation of the UCS activates one area of the brain.
Stimulation of the neural area responsible for processing the UCS leads to the
activation of a brain center responsible for generating the UCR. In Pavlov's
view, an innate, direct connection exists between the UCS brain center and the
brain center controlling the UCR; this neural connection allows the UCS to elicit
the UCR.

How might the connection between the CS and CR develop? When the
conditioned stimulus is presented, it excites a distinct brain area. When the UCS
follows the CS, the brain centers responsible for processing the CS and UCS are
active at the same time. According to Pavlov, the simultaneous activity in two
neural centers leads to a new functional neural pathway between the active centers. The establishment of this neural connection causes the CS to activate the
neural center processing the CS, which then arouses the UCS neural center. Activity in the UCS center leads to activation in the response center for the UCR,
which then allows the CS to elicit the CR. In other words, Pavlov is suggesting

FIGURE 9.1. Pavlov's stimulus-substitution view of classical conditioning. (a) The UCS activates the UCS brain center, which elicits the UCR; (b) the CS arouses the area of the brain responsible for processing it; (c) a connection develops between the CS and UCS brain centers with contiguous presentation of CS and UCS; and (d) the CS elicits the CR as a result of its ability to activate the UCS brain center.

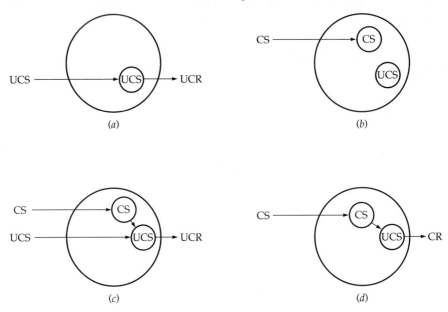

that the CS becomes a substitute for the UCS and elicits the same response as the UCS; that is, the CR is the UCR, only elicited by the CS instead of the UCS. **Figure 9.1** provides an illustration of Pavlov's stimulus-substitution view of conditioning.

Pavlov's **stimulus-substitution theory** proposes that the CS elicits the CR by way of the UCS. Holland and Rescorla's (1975) study provides strong support for this view. In their study, two groups of food-deprived rats received tone CS and food UCS pairings. After conditioning, one group of rats was satiated, while the other group remained food-deprived. The animals then received a series of CS-alone extinction trials. Holland and Rescorla reported that the CS elicited a weaker CR in the satiated than in the hungry rats. Why did the removal of food deprivation reduce the strength of the CR? According to Holland and Rescorla, food satiation reduces the value of food and thereby reduces the ability of the UCS to elicit the UCR. The reduced value of the UCS causes the CS to elicit a weaker CR.

The Conditioning of an Opponent Response

While the conditioned and unconditioned responses are often similar, in many cases, they seem dissimilar. For example, the conditioned response of fear differs in many ways from the unconditioned response of pain. While both involve internal arousal, the sensory aspects of the two responses are not the same. Warner's 1932 statement that "whatever response is grafted onto the CS, it is not snipped from the UCS" indicates a recognition of CR and UCR differences.

The research of Shepard Siegel and his colleagues (Siegel, 1975, 1984, 1989, 1991; Siegel, Hinson, Krank, & McCully, 1982; Siegel, Sherman, & Mitchell, 1980) represents the most impressive accumulation of evidence suggesting that the conditioned and unconditioned responses are different. In several of their studies, Siegel and his associates (Siegel, 1976, 1978; Siegel, Hinson, & Krank, 1978) used morphine as the unconditioned stimulus. **Analgesia,** or reduced sensitivity to pain, is one unconditioned response to morphine. Siegel reported that the conditioned response to stimuli such as lights or tones that have been paired with morphine is **hyperalgesia,** or an increased sensitivity to pain.

How did Siegel know that a conditioned stimulus associated with morphine makes an event more unpleasant? To illustrate both the analgesic effect of morphine and the hyperalgesic effect of a stimulus paired with morphine, Siegel placed a rat's paw on a hot plate and measured how long it took the rat to remove its paw. He observed that rats injected with morphine (the UCS) took longer to remove their paws from the heated plate than did animals that had not received the morphine injection. The light or tone paired with morphine, by contrast, caused the rats to remove their paws more quickly than animals that had been presented a stimulus not paired with the morphine (UCS).

Siegel (1975) also found that while the UCR to insulin is hypoglycemia, the CR to a stimulus paired with insulin is hyperglycemia. Additional studies (Crowell, Hinson, & Siegel, 1981; Le, Poulos, & Cappell, 1979) reported that the UCR to alcohol is hypothermia, while the CR to a stimulus associated with alcohol is hyperthermia.

This research suggests not only that the CR can be the opposite of the UCR, but also that conditioning is responsible, at least in part, for the phenomenon of drug tolerance. Tolerance to a drug develops when, with repeated use of a drug, the effectiveness of the drug declines and larger doses are necessary to achieve the same pharmacological effect (see Chapter 2). According to Siegel, tolerance represents the conditioning of a response that is opposite to the unconditioned drug effects. Thus, the environmental cues present during drug administration antagonize the drug's action and result in a lower pharmacological reaction to the drug.

Two lines of evidence support the idea that conditioning plays a role in drug tolerance. First, Siegel (1977) found that exposure to the CS (environment) without the UCS (drug), once the association has been conditioned, results in the extinction of the opponent CR; the elimination of the response to the CS produces a stronger reaction to the drug itself (see **Figure 9.2**). Second, Siegel, Hinson, and Krank (1978) reported an increased response to the drug can also be induced by changing the stimulus context in which the drug is administered. The novel environment does not elicit a CR opposite to the drug's unconditioned effect; in turn, the absence of the opposing CR results in a stronger unconditioned drug effect. Other researchers (Tiffany & Baker, 1981) have also discovered that a change in context leads to reduced drug tolerance. A heightened drug response in a new environment is not limited to animals. Siegel (1984) reported that 7 out of 10 victims of a drug overdose recalled that a change in environment was associated with the drug overdose, while Siegel, Hinson, Krank, and McCully (1982) observed that a drug overdose typically occurs when an addict takes his or her usual drug dose, but in an unfamiliar environment. Without the protective opposing response, the effect of the drug is increased, resulting in the overdose.

FIGURE 9.2. Tolerance develops to morphine injection (as indicated by lowered pain threshold) during first 6 injection sessions. The presentation of 12 placebo sessions (injections without morphine) in M-P-M (morphine-placebo-morphine) group animals extinguished the conditioned opponent response and reduced tolerance (as indicated by an increased pain threshold). Animals given a 12-day rest period between morphine injections (M-Rest-M group) showed no change in pain threshold from the sixth to the seventh session.

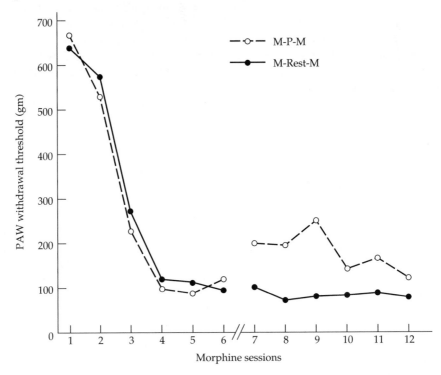

Why is the CR sometimes similar and sometimes dissimilar to the UCR? Allan Wagner's **sometimes opponent-process (SOP) theory** provides one answer to this question; we will look at his view next.

Sometimes Opponent-Process (SOP) Theory

Recall our discussion of Solomon and Corbit's opponent-process theory in Chapter 2. We learned that an event not only elicits a primary affective response, but also a secondary opponent affective reaction. Wagner's SOP theory (Brandon & Wagner, 1991; Donegan & Wagner, 1987; Wagner, 1981; Wagner & Brandon, 1989) is an extension of opponent-process theory that can explain why the CR sometimes seems the same as and sometimes different from the UCR. According to Wagner, the UCS elicits two unconditioned responses—a primary A1 component and a secondary A2 component. The primary A1 component is elicited rapidly by the UCS and decays quickly after the UCS ends. In contrast, both the onset and decay of the secondary A2 component are very gradual.

FIGURE 9.3. Wagner's SOP theory. (a) The UCS elicits the A1 and A2 components of the UCR. (b) The pairing of the CS and UCS leads to the CS being able to elicit the A2 component of the UCR.

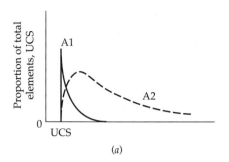
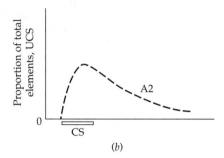

(*a*)　　　　　　　　　　　　　　　(*b*)

THE IMPORTANCE OF THE NATURE OF THE A2 RESPONSE. The secondary A2 component of the UCR can be the same as the A1 component, or the A1 and A2 components can differ. Whether A1 and A2 are the same or different is important. A key aspect of Wagner's view is that conditioning only occurs to the secondary A2 component; that is, the CR is always the secondary A2 reaction (see **Figure 9.3**). The CR and UCR will appear to be the same when the A1 and A2 components are the same. Different A1 and A2 components will yield a CR and UR that look different; however, the CR and UCR are really the same in this case. This is true because the A1 component is the response we associate with the UCR. When the A2 reaction is opponent to the A1, it looks as if the CR (A2) and UCR (A1 and A2) are different. Yet, the CR is merely the secondary A2 component of the UCR. Perhaps several examples would clarify this aspect of SOP theory.

Suppose an animal receives a brief electric shock. The initial reaction to shock is agitated hyperactivity. This initial increased reactivity is followed by a long-lasting hypoactivity or "freezing" response (Blanchard & Blanchard, 1969; Bolles & Riley, 1973). The freezing response, or **conditioned emotional reaction,** is the response conditioned to a stimulus paired with electric shock.

Paletta and Wagner (1986) demonstrated the two-phase reaction of an animal to a morphine injection. The initial A1 reaction to morphine is sedation or hypoactivity. **Figure 9.4** shows that the initial activity level is lower in rats given morphine rather than saline. However, 2 hours after the injection, the morphine-receiving rats are significantly more active than the control rats who received saline.

What is the conditioned reaction to an environmental stimulus paired with morphine? As **Figure 9.4** shows, the morphine animals were hyperactive when tested in the environment where they received morphine. Testing the morphine animals in their home cages produced a level of activity comparable to that of control animals not receiving morphine injections. These observations indicate that the conditioned reaction morphine produces is hyperactivity, which is the A2 secondary component of the UCR.

FIGURE 9.4. Illustration of activity levels following injections of morphine or saline. Activity first decreases, then increases above normal after morphine injections. Animals given morphine in a distinctive environment show increased activity, or a conditioned A2 response, when placed in that environment without morphine (shown in bar graph).

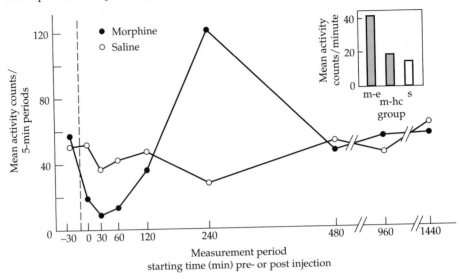

We have looked at two examples in which the A1 and A2 components of the UCR were opposite. In other cases, A1 and A2 are the same. Grau (1987) observed that the unconditioned response to radiant heat consisted of an initial short-duration **hypoalgesia,** or decreased sensitivity to pain, followed by a more persistent hypoalgesia. How do we know that both A1 and A2 reactions to a painful stimulus such as radiant heat are hypoalgesia? The use of the opiate antagonist naloxone can demonstrate this similarity of A1 and A2 response. Naloxone blocks the long-term, persistent hypoalgesia (A2) but has no effect on the short-term, immediate hypoalgesia (A1). This differential effect means that the A1 hypoalgesic response is nonopioid, while the A2 hypoalgesia involved the opioid system. Furthermore, Fanselow and his colleagues (Fanselow & Baackes, 1982; Fanselow & Bolles, 1979) showed that it is the A2 opioid hypoalgesia reaction that is conditioned to environmental stimuli paired with a painful unconditioned stimulus such as radiant heat. These researchers observed that administration of naloxone prior to conditioning prevented the conditioning of the hypoalgesic response to environmental cues that were paired with a painful event.

A study by Thompson, Clark, Donegan, Lavond, Lincoln, Madden, Mamounas, Mauk, McCormick, and Thompson (1984) provides perhaps the most impressive support for SOP theory. These researchers investigated the conditioning of an eyeblink response to a tone paired with a corneal air puff to a rabbit's eye. They found that two neural circuits mediate the rabbits' unconditioned eyeblink response (see **Figure 9.5**). A fast-acting A1 response is controlled by a relatively direct path from the area of UCS application on the fifth sensory nucleus to the sixth and seventh motor nuclei controlling the eyeblink response. Stimulation of this neural circuit produces a fast-acting and rapid-decay eyeblink response. A secondary A2 circuit begins at the fifth nucleus and goes through the inferior olive nucleus, several cerebellar structures, and red nucleus before reaching the motor nuclei. Activation of this A2 circuit produces a slow-acting eyeblink response. Thompson and his colleagues also found that destruction of the indirect pathway eliminated a previously conditioned eyeblink response but did not affect the short-latency, unconditioned eyeblink response. Destruction of the indirect A2 pathways also precluded any reconditioning of the eyeblink response.

BACKWARD CONDITIONING OF AN EXCITATORY CR. We learned in Chapter 3 that a forward conditioning paradigm produces a more reliable acquisition of the CR than a backward conditioning paradigm. While this statement is generally correct, Wagner's SOP theory indicates that backward conditioning can

FIGURE 9.5. The two neural circuits that mediate the influence of tone (CS) and corneal air puff (UCS) on the nictitating membrane response. The UCS activates a direct route between sensory (trigeminal nucleus) and motor (accessory abducens nucleus) neurons and an indirect route through the inferior olive nucleus, cerebellum (interpositus and dendrites of Purkinje cell), and red nucleus before reaching the motor nuclei controlling the nictitating membrane response. The pairing of CS and UCS produces simultaneous activity in the pontine nucleus and the inferior olive nucleus and allows the CS to activate the longer neural circuit, eliciting the nictitating membrane response.

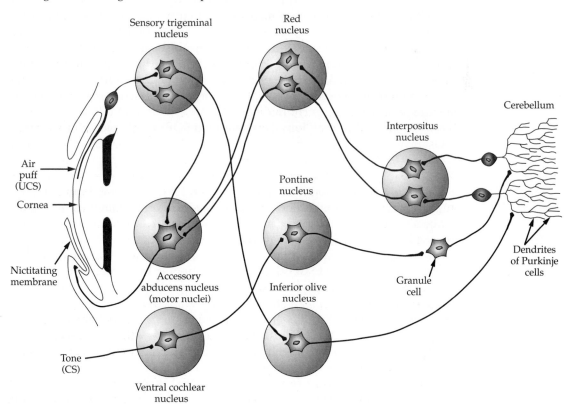

yield an excitatory CR if the CS is presented just prior to the peak of the A2 unconditioned response.

Larew (1986) provided strong support for this aspect of Wagner's SOP theory. In Larew's study, rats received a 2-second footshock UCS followed by a 30-second tone. The tone occurred either 1 second, 31 seconds, or 60 seconds after the UCS. Control rats received no UCS-CS pairings. Larew observed an excitatory conditioned response with the 31-second UCS-CS backward conditioning procedure, but no excitatory conditioning with either a 1-second UCS-CS interval or a 60-second UCS-CS interval. These results suggest that excitatory conditioning occurs with a backward procedure when the CS immediately precedes the A2 response.

PROBLEMS WITH SOP THEORY. Allan Wagner and Susan Brandon (Brandon & Wagner, 1991; Wagner & Brandon, 1989) commented that despite the strong support for SOP theory, some research seems to be inconsistent with this view. One significant problem concerns divergent results obtained from different measures of conditioning. SOP theory suggests that all response measures should yield a comparable indication of conditioning, and that variations in the training conditions should have a similar effect on all response measures. Suppose that heart rate and eyeblink response are recorded during conditioning. Since both responses are assumed to reflect A2 neural activity, the optimal CS-UCS interval should be equal for both response measures. Yet, Vandercar and Schneiderman (1967) found maximum heart rate conditioning with a 2.25-second CS-UCS interval, while the strongest eyeblink response occurred with a 7.5-second CS-UCS interval.

Recall our earlier discussion of the Thompson, et al. study. We learned that destruction of the indirect inferior olive-cerebellar-red nucleus pathway eliminated the conditioned eyeblink response. However, the authors reported that this same surgical procedure had no effect on a conditioned heart rate response. To address these inconsistent findings, Wagner and Brandon (Brandon & Wagner, 1991; Wagner & Brandon, 1989) modified SOP theory; we will look at this revision next.

Affective Extension of SOP, or AESOP

Wagner and Brandon (Brandon & Wagner, 1991; Wagner & Brandon, 1989) suggested there are two distinct unconditioned response sequences—a sensory sequence and an emotive one. The sensory and emotive attributes of an unconditioned stimulus activate separate sequences of A1 and A2 activity. Further, the latency of the sensory and emotive activity sequences (A1 & A2) can differ; that is, A2 may take longer to develop for one component than the other. This difference leads to different optimal CS-UCS intervals for the emotive and sensory components. For example, a shorter-latency A2 activity for the sensory than emotive component of a UCS causes a shorter optimal CS-UCS interval for the sensory than the emotive CR. The differences in latencies between sensory and emotive A2 responses can result in one CS eliciting an emotive CR, and another CS eliciting a sensory CR (see **Figure 9.6**).

Affective extension of SOP Theory (AESOP) has several additional aspects. A conditioned stimulus may activate a strong sensory conditioned reponse but

FIGURE 9.6. A UCS elicits separate sequences of sensory and emotive reactions. The differential optimal CS-UCS intervals for sensory and emotive A2 components can lead one stimulus (CS_A) to elicit an emotive CR and another stimulus (CS_X) to produce the sensory CR.

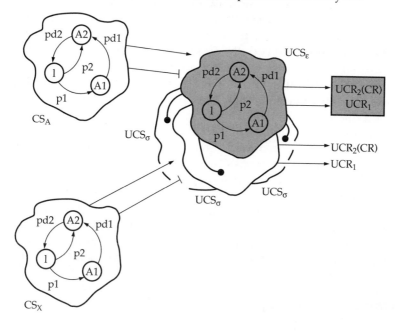

only a weak emotive CR, or vice versa. This difference would explain the lack of correspondence between response measures of conditioning. Further, while the sensory A2 neural activity elicits a discrete response, the emotive A2 neural activity produces a diffuse reaction. For example, the sensory CR might be an eyeblink response, while the emotive CR could be a startle response. Finally, two unconditioned stimuli might activate the same emotive A2 activity but different sensory A2 activities. This would lead to both similarities and differences in the responses that separate UCSs condition.

Two studies are presented that support AESOP theory. Tait and Saladin (1986) trained rabbits to respond to a 1,000-msec tone CS by presenting the tone 5,000-msec after a 100-msec shock UCS to the rabbits' eyes. Two conditioned response measures were taken in this study: the tendency of the CS to (1) suppress ongoing drinking behavior (emotive CR) and (2) elicit the eyeblink response (sensory CR). Tait and Saladin found a strong emotive CR; that is, the CS suppressed drinking. In contrast, the CS did not elicit the eyeblink response. In fact, the CS was capable of inhibiting an eyeblink response to another CS, a common result with backward conditioning. These results show a divergence of the conditioning of the sensory and emotive components of an unconditioned stimulus. Why did the rabbits acquire an emotive CR, but not a sensory CR, in the Tait and Saladin study? AESOP theory proposes that the CS occurred prior to the emotive A2 response but after the sensory A2 response.

Betts, Brandon, and Wagner (1996) provided additional support for AESOP theory. These researchers paired a vibratory stimulus with a shock UCS in the first phase of an eyeblink conditioning study in rabbits. In the second phase, the researchers presented a tone, the vibratory stimulus used in the first stage, and a shock UCS. (Recall from Chapter 3 that this is using a blocking paradigm and that the presence of the vibratory stimulus should block conditioning to the tone.) The key variable in this study was whether the UCS presented in the second phase went to the same or to a different eye than was used in the first phase. Betts, Brandon, and Wagner reported that both a reduced startle reaction and a reduced eyeblink response were conditioned to the tone when the UCS was presented to the same eye in both phases of the study. In contrast, when the UCS was presented to different eyes in each phase, the startle response to the tone was reduced, but the eyeblink response was equal to that elicited by the vibratory stimulus. Why did blocking occur to the startle response even when the location of the UCS changed, while changing the UCS location eliminated the blocking of the eyeblink response? According to Betts, Brandon, and Wagner, the startle response reflects the association of a stimulus and its emotional aspects, while the eyeblink response reflects an association between a stimulus and its sensory aspects. Changing the location of the UCS eliminated blocking of the eyeblink response because the sensory aspects of the UCS change with a change in UCS location, but this change had no effect on the startle response because the emotive aspects of the UCS do not change with a change in location.

BEFORE YOU GO ON

- **Was Jared's response to Felicia's drinking different from or similar to his response to her hostility?**
- **Would Clarence become fearful of Felicia's drinking if it followed her hostility?**

The Nature of the Pavlovian Conditioning Process

In Chapter 3, we learned that the predictiveness of the conditioned stimulus influences how readily a subject acquires a conditioned response. We also discovered that the predictive value of other stimuli also affects conditioning to the CS. How does an animal or person judge the relative predictiveness of a stimulus? Psychologists have developed several different views to explain the mechanism by which predictiveness affects classical conditioning (see **Table 9.1**). The Rescorla-Wagner associative view suggests that the availability of associative strength determines whether a CR develops to a CS paired with the UCS; comparator theory argues that performance of a conditioned response involves a comparison of the response strength to the CS and to competing stimuli; Mackintosh's attentional theory proposes that the relevance of and attention to a stimulus determine whether that stimulus will become associated with the UCS; and Baker's retrospective processing approach suggests that conditioning involves the continuous monitoring of contingencies between a CS and UCS, with the recognition of a lack of predictiveness diminishing the value of the CS.

The Rescorla-Wagner theory was developed to explain the influence of predictiveness on conditioning. We begin our discussion of the nature of classical

TABLE 9.1. Explanation of Three Conditioning Phenomena by Four Models of Pavlovian Conditioning

	Overshadowing	Blocking	Predictiveness
Rescorla-Wagner Model	Salient stimulus acquires associative strength more readily than nonsalient stimulus	Associative strength to blocking stimulus prevents conditioning to blocked stimulus	Context associations prevent conditioning to conditioned stimulus
Comparator Theory	Conditioning to salient stimulus is stronger than to nonsalient stimulus	Conditioning stronger for blocking stimulus than for blocked stimulus	Context associations stronger than conditioning to conditioned stimulus
Attentional Theory	Salient stimulus is more associable than nonsalient stimulus	Absence of surprise prevents conditioning to blocked stimulus	Animals learn that conditioned stimulus does not reliably predict unconditioned stimulus
Retrospective Processing Theory	Animals recognize the salience of different stimuli	Animals recognize greater contingency between blocking and unconditioned stimuli	Animals recognize the lack of contingency between conditioned stimulus and unconditioned stimulus

conditioning with a description of this theory. We will then examine several Pavlovian conditioning phenomena that have been used to test the validity of the **Rescorla-Wagner associative model.** Some of this research has supported this theory, while other studies have pointed to its weaknesses. We will then look at alternatives to the Rescorla-Wagner associative model of conditioning.

Rescorla-Wagner Associative Model

The associative model of Pavlovian conditioning that Robert Rescorla and Allan Wagner (1927) developed expresses four main ideas. First, there is a maximum associative strength that can develop between a CS and UCS. The UCS determines the limit of associative strength, or asymptote level of conditioning; different UCSs support different maximum levels of conditioning, and therefore have different asymptotic values. Second, while the associative strength increases with each training trial, the amount of associative strength gained on a particular training trial depends on the level of prior training. Since the typical learning curve in Pavlovian conditioning is negatively accelerating (refer to **Figure 9.7**), more associative strength will accrue on early training trials than on later trials. In fact, as **Figure 9.7** indicates, the increment on each conditioning trial declines with each CS-UCS pairing. Third, the rate of conditioning varies depending on the CS and the UCS used. Associative strength accrues quickly to some stimuli, but slowly to others. **Figure 9.7** shows the learning curve of two stimuli: one stimulus readily gains associative strength, while conditioning to the other stimulus occurs slowly. Further, some UCSs produce more rapid learning than other UCSs. Fourth, the level of conditioning on a particular trial is influenced not only by the amount of prior conditioning to the stimulus, but also by the level of previous conditioning to other stimuli also paired with the UCS. A particular UCS can only support a certain amount of conditioning, even when more than one stimulus is paired with the UCS. When two (or more) stimuli are

FIGURE 9.7. The change in associative strength during conditioning for two different stimuli. One stimulus rapidly develops associative strength; the other acquires associative strength more slowly.

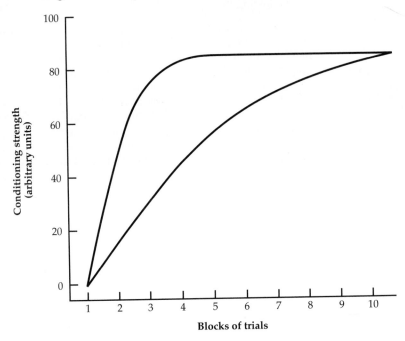

presented, these stimuli must share the associative strength the UCS can support. Thus, associative strength that accrues to one stimulus is not available to be conditioned to the other stimuli. For example, suppose two stimuli are paired with a UCS, and the maximum associative strength that the UCS can support is 10 units. If 7 units are conditioned to one cue paired with the UCS, only 3 units can develop to the other cue.

Rescorla and Wagner (1972) developed a mathematics equation based on the four ideas just outlined. Their mathematics model of Pavlovian conditioning is $\Delta V_A = K (\lambda - V_{AX})$. In this formula, V_A is the associative strength between the conditioned stimulus A and the UCS, and ΔV_A is the change in associative strength that develops on a specific trial when the CS_A and the UCS are paired. The symbol K refers to the rate of conditioning determined by the nature of the CS_A and the intensity of the UCS. (The K value can be separated into α, or alpha, which refers to the power of CS_A, and β, or beta, which reflects the intensity of the UCS.) The symbol λ defines the maximum level of conditioning the UCS supports. The term V_{AX} indicates the level of conditioning that has already accrued to the conditioned stimulus (A) as well as to other stimuli (X) present during conditioning. Thus, $V_{AX} = V_A + V_X$.

To see how this mathematical model works, suppose that a light stimulus is paired with shock on five trials. Prior to training, the value of K is .5, λ is 90 and $V_A = 0$. When we apply these values to the Rescorla-Wagner model, we get:

Trial 1: $\Delta V_A = .5\ (90-0) = 45$

Trial 2: $\Delta V_A = .5\ (90-45) = 22.5$

Trial 3: $\Delta V_A = .5\ (90-67.5) = 11.25$

Trial 4: $\Delta V_A = .5\ (90-78.8) = 5.6$

Trial 5: $\Delta V_A = .5\ (90-84.4) = 2.8$

Total Associative Strength after 5 Trials = 87.2

The data in this example show that conditioning to CS_A occurs rapidly; associative strength grows 45 units on Trial 1, 22.5 units on Trial 2, 11.25 units on Trial 3, 5.6 units on Trial 4, and 2.8 units on Trial 5. Thus, 87.2 units of associative strength accrued to the CS_A after just five trials of conditioning. The rapid development of associative strength indicates that CS_A is an intense and/or a salient stimulus or that the UCS is a strong stimulus, or both.

The Rescorla-Wagner model has been used to explain a number of conditioning phenomena. Let's see how it explains blocking (see Chapter 3). Suppose that we pair a light with a shock for five trials. The K value for the light is .5 and the maximum level of conditioning, or λ, is 90 units of associative strength. As we learned earlier, 87.2 units of associative strength would accrue to the light after five pairings with the shock. Next we pair the light, tone, and shock for five more trials. The K value for the tone is .5, and we would expect that five pairings of the tone and shock would yield strong conditioning. However, only 2.8 units of associative strength are still available to be conditioned, according to the Rescorla-Wagner model. And the tone must share this associative strength with the light cue. Because strong conditioning has already occurred to the light, the Rescorla-Wagner equation predicts little conditioning to the tone. The weak conditioning to the tone due to the prior accrued associative strength to light is illustrated in the calculations below:

Trial 6: $\Delta V_{light} = .5\ (90-87.2) = 1.4$ $\quad$ $\Delta V_{tone} = .5\ (90-87.2) = 1.4$

Trial 7: $\Delta V_{light} = .5\ (90-90) = 0$ $\quad$ $\Delta V_{tone} = .5\ (90-90) = 0$

Trial 8: $\Delta V_{light} = .5\ (90-90) = 0$ $\quad$ $\Delta V_{tone} = .5\ (90-90) = 0$

Trial 9: $\Delta V_{light} = .5\ (90-90) = 0$ $\quad$ $\Delta V_{tone} = .5\ (90-90) = 0$

Trial 10: $\Delta V_{light} = .5\ (90-90) = 0$ $\quad$ $\Delta V_{tone} = .5\ (90-90) = 0$

Total Associative Strength of light = 88.6

Total Associative Strength of tone = 1.4

We learned earlier that blocking occurs when a stimulus previously paired with a UCS is presented with a new stimulus and the UCS. The Rescorla-Wagner model suggests that blocking occurs because the initial CS has already accrued most or all of the associative strength, and little is left to condition to the other stimulus. As the previous equations show, little conditioning occurred to the tone because most of the associative strength had been conditioned to the light prior to the compound pairing of light, tone, and shock. Based on this explanation, the equation the Rescorla-Wagner model generates predicts cue blocking.

AN EVALUATION OF THE RESCORLA-WAGNER MODEL. Many studies have evaluated the validity of the Rescorla-Wagner model of Pavlovian conditioning. While many of these studies have supported this view, other observations have not been consistent with the Rescorla-Wagner model. We will first discuss one area of research—the UCS preexposure effect—that supports the Rescorla-Wagner view. New, we will describe three areas of research—potentiation, CS preexposure, and cue deflation—that provide findings the Rescorla-Wagner model does not predict. Finally, we will discuss several alternative views of Pavlovian conditioning.

Suppose you have had several bouts of the flu recently and again become sick after eating a distinctive food. Would you develop an aversion to this food? Your previous experiences with sickness, independent of the particular food, probably would prevent the conditioning of an association between eating this food and being sick.

This example illustrates the effect of preexposure to the UCS (illness) without the CS (food) on the acquisition of a CR (aversion) when the CS is later presented with the UCS. Psychologists (Baker & Mackintosh, 1979; Randich & Ross, 1985) refer to this phenomenon as the **UCS preexposure effect.** Many studies have consistently observed that preexposure to the UCS impairs subsequent conditioning; for example, several researchers (Domjan & Gemberling, 1980; Mikulka, Leard, & Klein, 1977) have demonstrated that the presentation of a drug that induces illness (UCS) prior to conditioning impairs the subsequent association of a distinctive food (CS) with illness. Similar preexposure interference has been reported with other UCSs (shock: Baker, Mercier, Gabel, & Baker, 1981; and food: Balsam & Schwartz, 1981).

Why does preexposure to the UCS impair subsequent conditioning? The Rescorla-Wagner model provides an explanation: the presentation of the UCS without the CS occurs in a specific environment or context, which results in the development of associative strength to the context. Since the UCS can only support a limited amount of associative strength, conditioning of associative strength to the stimulus context reduces the level of possible conditioning to the CS. Thus, the presence of the stimulus context will block the acquisition of a CR to the CS when the CS is presented with the UCS in the stimulus context. (Referring back to the blocking phenomenon described in Chapter 3, it would be helpful to think of the context as CS_1 and the new stimulus as CS_2.)

How can one validate the context blocking explanation of the UCS preexposure effect? One method is to change the context when the CS is paired with the UCS. A number of studies (Randich & Ross, 1985; Rescorla, Durlach, & Grau, 1985) have shown that the UCS preexposure effect was attenuated when the preexposure context was different from the conditioning context. As a result of the change in context, no stimuli were present during conditioning that could compete with the association of the CS and the UCS. Therefore, the CR was readily conditioned to the CS when paired with the UCS in the next context. We will briefly discuss the Randich and Ross (1985) study to illustrate the effect of context change on the impact of the UCS preexposure effect.

Randich and Ross (1985) placed four groups of rats in context 1 during the first phase of the study. Context 1 was characterized by noise from a fan, but did not have a light, painted walls, or the odor of Pine Sol. Two of these groups— the +C1/C1 and +Cl/C2 experimental groups—received a 10-second unsignaled shock (UCS) in context 1; the other two groups—the −C1/C1 and −C1/C2 control groups—did not receive the shock in context 1. After 10 trials in context 1, animals in the +C1/C1 group were placed again in context 1 and received pairings of a 3-minute noise CS and shock. The −C1/C1 group animals also received noise CS-shock (UCS) pairings in context 1. Randich and Ross observed that the rats that had been preexposed to the shock in context 1 and then conditioned in context 1 showed much less fear of the noise CS than did the control group animals that had not been preexposed to shock. The second experimental group (+C1/C2) received noise CS and shock pairings in context 2. The other control group (−C1/C2) also received noise-shock pairings in context 2. Context 2 was quite different from context 1; it had a light, black-and-white-striped walls, and Pine-Sol odor, but no fan. The animals given UCS preexposure in context 1 and then conditioned in context 2 exhibited strong fear of the noise CS (see **Figure 9.8**). These results suggest that context associations formed during UCS preexposure are responsible for the decrease in the conditioning to the CS when it is paired with the UCS.

FIGURE 9.8. The influence of context change on the UCS preexposure effect. Animals in the +C1/C1 experimental group, which received both preexposure and conditioning in context 1, showed significantly slower acquisition of a conditional emotional response than did animals in the +C1/C2 experimental group (given preexposure in context 1 and conditioning in context 2). Control animals in the −C1/C1 and −C1/C2 groups who did not receive UCS preexposure readily conditioned fear to either context 1 or 2.

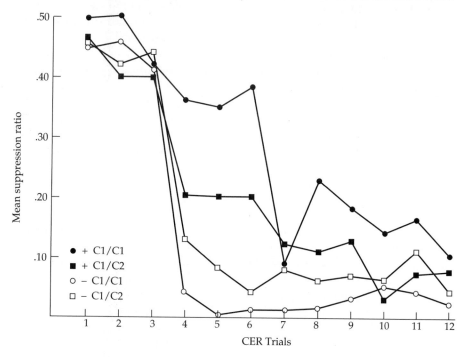

In the next three sections, we will discuss several observations that the Rescorla-Wagner model does not predict. The first problem area is the potentiation effect.

THE POTENTIATION OF A CONDITIONED RESPONSE. The Rescorla-Wagner model predicts that when a salient and a nonsalient cue are presented together with the UCS, the salient cue will accrue more associative strength than the nonsalient cue. This phenomenon, called **overshadowing,** was originally observed by Pavlov (1927). Pavlov found that a more intense tone overshadowed the development of an association between a less intense tone and the UCS. Overshadowing is readily observed in other situations. For example, Lindsey and Best (1973) presented two novel fluids (saccharin and casein hydrosylate) prior to illness. They found that a strong aversion developed to the salient saccharin flavor, but only a weak aversion developed to the less salient casein hydrosylate solution.

Overshadowing does not always occur when two cues of different salience are paired with a UCS; in fact, in some circumstances the presence of a salient cue produces a stronger CR than would have occurred had the less salient cue been presented alone with the UCS. The increased CR to a less salient stimulus because of the simultaneous pairing of a more salient cue during conditioning was first described by John Garcia and his associates (Garcia & Rusiniak, 1980; Rusiniak, Palmerino, & Garcia, 1982). They observed that the presence of a salient flavor cue potentiated rather than overshadowed the establishment of an aversion to a less salient odor cue paired with illness.

Why does the presence of a salient taste cue potentiate rather than overshadow the acquisition of an odor aversion? According to Garcia and Rusiniak (1980), the taste stimulus "indexes" the odor stimulus as a food cue, and thereby mediates the establishment of a strong odor aversion. This indexing process has considerable adaptive significance. The taste cue's **potentiation** of the odor aversion enables an animal to recognize a potentially poisonous food early in the ingestive sequence. Thus, an odor aversion causes animals to avoid dangerous foods before even tasting them.

Rescorla (1982) presents a different view of the potentiation effect, a view consistent with the Rescorla-Wagner model. According to Rescorla, potentiation occurs because the animal perceives the compound stimuli (taste and odor) as a single unitary event and then mistakes each individual element for the compound. If Rescorla's view is accurate, the potentiation effect should depend upon the strength of the taste-illness association. Potentiation should occur with a strong taste aversion, and weakening of the taste-illness association should result in an elimination of the potentiation affect. Rescorla (1981) presented evidence to support his view; that is, he found that extinction of the taste aversion also attenuated the animal's aversion to an odor cue. However, Lett (1982) observed that taste-alone exposure eliminated the taste aversion, but not the odor aversion. The cause of potentiation thus seems unclear; we will discuss this phenomenon again when we look at Rescorla's within-compound view later in the chapter.

THE CS PREEXPOSURE EFFECT. Recall our discussion of Clarence's failure to associate Felicia's drinking and aggression in the chapter opening vignette. The **CS preexposure effect** provides an explanation for his failure to develop apprehension about Felicia's drinking. Many studies (see Lubow, 1989) have reported that preexposure to a specific stimulus (drinking) subsequently retarded the development of a CR (apprehension) to that stimulus when paired with a UCS (hostility). The CS preexposure effect has been reported in a variety of Pavlovian conditioning situations, including conditioned licking of water in rats (Baker & Mackintosh, 1979), conditioned fear in rats (Pearce, Kaye, & Hall, 1982), eyelid conditioning in rabbits (Siegel, 1969), leg-flexion conditioning in sheep and goats (Lubow & Moore, 1959), and flavor aversion learning in rats (Fenwick, Mikulka, & Klein, 1975).

Why is the CS preexposure effect a problem for the Rescorla-Wagner model? According to Rescorla and Wagner (1972) exposure to the CS prior to conditioning should have no effect on the subsequent association of the CS with the UCS. This prediction is based on the assumption that the readiness of a stimulus to be associated with a UCS depends only on the intensity and salience of the CS; the parameter K represents these values in the Rescorla-Wagner model. While neither the intensity nor the salience of the CS is changed as the result of CS preexposure, the subsequent interference with conditioning indicates that the associability of the CS changes when the CS is experienced without the UCS prior to conditioning.

How can we explain the influence of CS preexposure on subsequent conditioning? One explanation involves modifying the Rescorla-Wagner model to allow for a change in the value of K as the result of experience. Yet, the effect of CS preexposure on the acquisition of a CR appears to involve more than just a reduction in the value of K. Instead, Mackintosh (1983) argues that animals learn that a particular stimulus is irrelevant when it predicts no significant event; stimulus irrelevance causes the animal to ignore that stimulus in the future. This failure to attend to the CS and the events that follow it may well be responsible for the interference with conditioning that CS preexposure produces. We will look more closely at this attentional view of CS preexposure when we describe Mackintosh's attentional model of conditioning.

THE CUE DEFLATION EFFECT. The Rescorla-Wagner model suggests that the overshadowing phenomenon involves greater conditioning to a more salient rather than a less salient stimulus; that is, greater associative strength accrues to the more salient rather than less salient cue. What do you suppose would happen to an animal's response to the less salient stimulus if the conditioned response to the more salient stimulus were extinguished? The Rescorla-Wagner model does not suggest any change in the reaction to the less salient cue. However, a number of studies (Kaufman & Bolles, 1981; Matzel, Schachtman, & Miller, 1985) reported that extinction of the more salient (or overshadowing) stimulus increased the response to the less salient (or overshadowed) stimulus. Not all studies find a **cue deflation effect,** or an increased responding to the less salient stimulus, following extinction to a more salient cue; instead, some studies report a decreased response to both the overshadowing and overshadowed stimuli (Durlach, 1989).

An increased response to a CS without additional experience also occurs with the extinction of context associations acquired with UCS preexposure. Recall that exposure to the UCS prior to CS-UCS pairings produces a weaker response to the CS than when no UCS preexposure is given. We learned earlier that context-UCS associations acquired during UCS preexposure block strong conditioning to the CS. Several studies (Matzel, Brown, & Miller, 1987; Timberlake, 1986) show that postconditioning extinction of the response to the training context results in an enhanced response to the CS. Again, not all studies that extinguish the response to the training context have noted an increased responding to the CS (refer to Durlach, 1989). What process is responsible for the change in response to one stimulus following the extinction of a response to another stimulus? Why do some studies report that diminished responding to one stimulus increased the response to the CS, while other studies find that this same procedure decreased the reaction to the CS? The next two sections address both of these questions.

The Importance of Within-Compound Associations

Suppose that a tone and light are paired together with food. According to the Rescorla-Wagner model, the light and tone will compete for associative strength. More recently, Robert Rescorla and his associates (Rescorla & Durlach, 1981; Speers, Gillan, & Rescorla, 1980) have suggested that rather than two stimuli competing for associative strength, a **within-compound association** can be established between the light and tone during conditioning. This within-compound association will result in a single level of conditioning to both stimuli. One procedure facilitating a within-compound association is the simultaneous pairing of both stimuli. As a result of developing a within-compound association, any change in the value of one stimulus will have a similar impact on the other stimulus.

We mentioned earlier that the concept of within-compound associations can explain the potentiation phenomena. Rescorla suggested that the within-compound association of a salient flavor cue and nonsalient odor cue led to a strong aversion (potentiation) when both cues were paired with illness.

The within-compound conditioning view suggests that potentiation is dependent upon the establishment of an association between the odor and flavor cues. According to this view, the failure to form a within-compound association between odor and flavor should eliminate potentiation. One procedure used to prevent within-compound associations is pairing the odor and taste cues sequentially rather than simultaneously. This procedure eliminates the flavor stimulus's potentiation of the odor cue (Holder & Garcia, 1987; Kucharski & Spear, 1985).

While within-compound conditioning may contribute to potentiation, it is not the entire story. As we learned earlier, Lett (1982) did not find that extinction of the flavor aversion eliminated the odor aversion. Further, a number of studies (Bouton, Jones, McPhillips, & Swartzentruber, 1986; Westbrook, Homewood, Horn, & Clarke, 1983) have found that a flavor cue overshadows rather than potentiates an odor aversion. In these studies, overshadowing occurred under conditions that were favorable to within-compound associations.

Recall our discussion of the cue deflation effect, presented in the last section. We learned that several studies showed that the extinction of a response to one component of a compound stimulus enhanced the response to the other component. Yet, other experiments reported that extinction to one component also reduced responding to the other component. The latter result is consistent with the within-compound analysis; that is, a within-compound association is established to both components, so reducing the response to one has a comparable effect on the other. However, the former studies are not consistent with the within-compound analysis. Comparator theory can explain why the extinction of a response to one component would increase the response to the other.

A Comparator Theory of Pavlovian Conditioning

Ralph Miller and his associates (Denniston, Savastano, & Miller, 2001; Miller & Matzel, 1989) have proposed that animals learn about all CS-UCS relationships. However, a particular association may not be evident in the animal's behavior. A strong CS-UCS association may exist but not be expressed in behavior, when compared with another CS even more strongly associated with the UCS. Thus, the ability of a particular stimulus to elicit a CR depends upon its level of conditioning compared to other stimuli. Only when the level of conditioning to that stimulus exceeds that of other stimuli will that CS elicit the CR.

Consider the blocking phenomenon to illustrate **comparator theory.** The comparator approach proposes that an association may exist between CS_2 and the UCS but not be evident in terms of responding because of the stronger CS_1-UCS association. (Recall that the Rescorla-Wagner model assumes that the presence of the CS_1 blocks or prevents the establishment of the CS_2-UCS association.) The comparator theory suggests that there is one condition in which the CS_2 can elicit the CR in a blocking paradigm. The extinction of the conditioned response to the CS_1 can allow the CS_2 to now elicit the CR. The reason that extinction of the response to the CS_1 results in responding to the CS_2 is that the comparison now favors the CS_2-UCS association. Prior to extinction, the CS_1-UCS association was stronger than the CS_2-UCS association. After extinction, the CS_2-UCS association is stronger than CS_1-UCS association.

We learned in an earlier section that extinction of response to the training context eliminated the UCS preexposure effect. These studies (Matzel, Brown, & Miller, 1987; Timberlake, 1986) show that deflation of responding to the training context leads to an increased responding to the CS. This greater responding occurred even though no additional CS-UCS pairings were given. Additional support for the comparator theory comes from experiments in which devaluation of the overshadowing (more salient) stimulus caused an increased responding to the overshadowed (less salient) stimulus (Kaufman & Bolles, 1981; Matzel, Schachtman, & Miller, 1985). This observation suggests that an association between the overshadowed stimulus and the UCS did form, but it was not evident because of its unfavorable comparison with an overshadowing stimulus.

While these observations provide support for the comparator theory, not all studies have found that the deflation of one stimulus increases the response to another stimulus. In fact, many studies have reported that extinguishing the response to one stimulus produces a comparable reduction in the other stimulus, a result that favors the within-compound associative view presented in the previous section.

What is responsible for this discrepancy in results? Durlach (1989) suggested that the presence of strong within-compound associations might overwhelm the comparator effect. In her view, the comparator effect would only be evident when within-compound associations are weak. However, Blaisall, Gunther, & Miller (1999) reported that the amount of posttraining extinction (deflation) is the critical variable that determines whether the CS elicits the CR. These researchers found that extensive extinction trials are needed to eliminate the conditioning to the comparator stimulus and increase responding to the CS.

So what causes the cue deflation effect? Van Hamme and Wasserman (1994) modified the Rescorla-Wagner theory to account for the cue deflation effect within the framework of an associative conditioning framework. In their view, extinguishing the reponse to one conditioned stimulus (the deflated stimulus) changes the value of K to a second conditioned stimulus, which serves to increase the associative strength of the second conditioned stimulus (see Van Hamme & Wasserman, 1994 for the mathematical revision of the Rescorla-Wagner associative model that explains the cue deflation effect). Denniston, Savastano, and Miller (2001) have presented several research findings that this modified associative theory cannot explain, but that the comparator theory can. For example, Denniston, Savastano, and Miller reported that extinction of a second-order comparator stimulus (or a comparator stimulus for the comparator stimulus) increases the response to the first-order comparator stimulus, which then serves to decrease the response to the CS. Future research is needed to clarify the process responsible for the cue deflation effect, as well as establish the validity of the associative and comparator theories of Pavlovian conditioning.

Mackintosh's Attentional View

Nicholas Mackintosh (1975) suggested that animals seek information from the environment that predicts the occurrence of biologically significant events (UCSs). Once an animal has identified a cue that reliably predicts a specific event, it ignores other stimuli that also provide information about the event. According to Mackintosh, animals attend to stimuli that are predictive and ignore those that are not essential. Thus, an animal plays an active role in the conditioning process; that is, conditioning depends not only on the physical characteristics of stimuli, but also on the animal's recognition of the correlation (or lack of correlation) between events (CS & UCS).

Mackintosh's attentional view of Pavlovian conditioning can explain the CS preexposure effect that poses a problem for the Rescorla-Wagner model. We discovered earlier in the chapter that CS preexposure impairs the acquisition of the CR when the CS and UCS are later paired. According to Mackintosh, an animal learns that the CS is irrelevant as a result of preexposure to the CS. In Mackintosh's view, once the animal discovers that a stimulus is irrelevant, it will stop attending to that stimulus, and will therefore have difficulty learning that the CS is correlated with the UCS.

Support for this **learned irrelevance** view of CS preexposure comes from studies in which uncorrelated presentations of the CS and UCS prior to conditioning led to substantial interference with the acquisition of the CR. In fact, Baker and Mackintosh (1977) found that uncorrelated presentations of the CS and the UCS produce significantly greater interference than did CS preexposure or UCS preexposure alone. In their study, the response of water licking to a tone was significantly less evident in animals receiving prior unpaired presentations of the tone (CS) and water (UCS) than either tone alone, water alone, or no preexposure (refer to **Figure 9.9**). This greater impairment of subsequent conditioning when the CS and UCS are unpaired also has been demonstrated in studies of conditioning fear in rats (Baker, 1976) and the eyeblink response in rabbits (Siegel & Domjan, 1971).

Several studies by Geoffrey Hall and his associates (Hall & Channell, 1985; Hall & Honey, 1989) provide additional evidence for an attentional view of the CS preexposure effect. Animals exposed to a novel stimulus exhibit an orienting response to the novel stimulus. Hall and Channell (1985) showed that repeated exposure to light (CS) leads to habituation of the orienting response to that stimulus (see Chapter 2). They also found that later pairings of the light (CS) with milk (UCS) yield a reduced CR compared with control animals who did not experience preexposure to the light CS. These results suggest that habituation of an orienting response to a stimulus is associated with the later failure of conditioning to that stimulus.

What if the orienting response could be reinstated to the conditioned stimulus? Would this procedure restore conditionability to the stimulus? Hall and Channell (1985) reported that the presentation of the conditioned stimulus in a novel context reinstated the orienting response. They also found that pairing the CS and UCS in the new context led to a strong CR. These results indicate that a reinstatement of the orienting response eliminated the CS preexposure effect; that is, the CS now elicited a strong CR.

Why would reinstatement of the orienting response cause CS conditionability to return? An orienting response indicates that an animal is attending to the stimulus, and attention allows the stimulus to be associated with the UCS. These observations provide further support for the view that learned irrelevance is responsible for the CS preexposure effect.

FIGURE 9.9. The amount of licking to a tone (CS) paired with water (UCS) is significantly less in animals preexposed to both the tone and water than to only the water or only the tone, or with no preexposure.

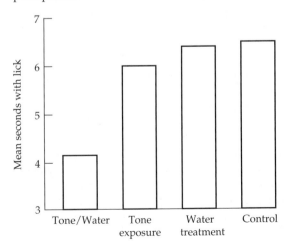

Theories of Pavlovian conditioning have traditionally held that learning occurs at the time of training and that responding is based upon the level of training. Baker and Mercier (1989) refer to these models of Pavlovian conditioning as input-based theories. The Rescorla-Wagner associative theory, Rescorla's within-compound association view, and Mackintosh's attentional perspective are input-based theories of Pavlovian conditioning. In contrast, Miller's comparative theory is an output-based model because it suggests that performance is determined by comparing the level of prior conditioning to each stimulus at the time of testing. However, all of these theories assume that unless further conditioning is provided, the level of learning remains constant after training.

Baker and Mercier present a very different view of Pavlovian conditioning. They contend that the level of conditioning to a CS can change even with no additional CS-UCS pairings. According to Baker and Mercier, animals constantly assess the contingencies between events in their environment. Rather than viewing learning as a static representation of the degree of correlation between events, these researchers suggest that learning changes over time as an animal encounters new information about the degree of contingency between a CS and UCS. For example, what may seem to be two highly correlated events may later be viewed as having little correlation at all. This change in learning would occur if initial CS-UCS pairings were followed by many UCS-alone experiences. Baker and Mercier refer to the constant assessment of contingencies as **retrospective processing.** New data may cause an animal to reassess past experiences and form a new representation of the relationship between the CS and UCS.

Retrospective processing requires the ability to remember past experiences. It also assumes that an animal has a representation of past encounters that it can modify. In this section, we will look at several studies that support retrospective processing.

Suppose that after a tone and light were paired with shock, only the tone was presented prior to shock. How would the animal respond to the light? Baker and Baker (1985) performed such a study and found that fear of the light was reduced compared to a control group that did not receive tone-shock pairings. This study is similar to the blocking paradigm Chapter 3 described. In fact, the only difference between the procedures is the order of tone-light-shock and tone-shock pairings. Baker and Mercier (1989) refer to a procedure in which the tone-shock follows rather than precedes tone-light-shock pairing as **backward blocking.**

What causes backward blocking? Baker and Mercier argue that when animals receive tone-shock after tone-light-shock pairings, they discover that the tone is a better predictor of shock than the light. Through retrospective processing, the animals decide that the light is not an adequate predictor of shock. This decision causes the animal to no longer fear the light.

Recall our discussion of the UCS preexposure effect. We learned that exposure to the UCS impaired later conditioning of the CS and UCS. A similar impairment of conditioning occurs when UCS-alone experiences are intermixed with CS-UCS pairings (Jenkins, Barnes, & Barrera, 1981). According to Baker and Mercier (1989), the animal revises its view of the contingency between the

CS and UCS as a result of UCS-alone experience. In other words, the animal retrospectively examines its earlier view of the CS-UCS contingency and decides that the CS no longer correlates well with the UCS.

Miller and his colleagues (Denniston, Savastano, & Miller, 2001; Savastano, Escobar, & Miller, 1999) have reported that backward blocking does not always occur. These researchers found that if a CS has become able to control "robust responding"—the CS consistently produces an intense CR—the CS appears to become "immune" to backward blocking and additional training to a competing stimulus will not reduce the response to the CS. According to Denniston, Savastano, and Miller (2001), if a CS is "inherently biologically significant" or acquires biological significance, manipulations that increase the response to a competing (comparator) cue will have little effect on responding to the CS. You might wonder what the term *biological significance* means. We will leave you in suspense until the next chapter.

We have described several very different theories of Pavlovian conditioning. In all likelihood, each theory accounts for some aspects of Pavlovian conditioning. Future research will clarify the precise contribution of each theory.

BEFORE YOU GO ON

- How would the Rescorla-Wagner model explain Clarence's failure to develop an association between Felicia's drinking and hostility?
- What prediction would Baker's retrospective processing model make for the development of a drinking-hostility association following Clarence's conversation with his friend Jared?

THEORIES OF OPERANT OR INSTRUMENTAL CONDITIONING

The Nature of Reinforcement

Skinner (1938) defined a reinforcer as an event whose occurrence will increase the frequency of any behavior that produces it. While Skinner was not concerned about when an event would be reinforcing, other psychologists have been interested in specifying the conditions that determine whether an event is reinforcing. Premack's probability-differential theory addresses this issue; we start our discussion of the nature of reinforcement with his view.

Premack's Probability-Differential Theory

We typically assume that reinforcers are things like food or water. However, activities can also be reinforcers. For example, allowing children to watch television or to go to the movies can reinforce studying. Although food and going to the movies appear to be very different types of reinforcers, Premack's (1959, 1965) **probability differential theory** suggests that all reinforcers share a common attribute. According to Premack, a reinforcer is any activity whose probability of occurring is greater than that of the reinforced behavior. Therefore, a movie can be a reinforcer for studying if the likelihood of going to the movie is greater than the probability of studying. In Premack's view, it is the eating response to food, not food per se, that is the reinforcer for a rat. Since eating is a more probable behavior than bar pressing, eating can reinforce bar pressing.

Premack's (1959) study of children illustrates the reinforcing character of high-probability activities. He placed a pinball machine next to a candy dispenser. In the first phase of the study, Premack observed the children's relative rate of responding to each activity. Some children played pinball more frequently than they ate candy and were labeled "manipulators"; other children ate candy more often than they played pinball and were labeled "eaters." During the second phase of the study, manipulators had to eat in order to play the pinball machine, while eaters were required to play the pinball machine in order to get candy. Premack reported that the contingency increased the number of times the "eaters" played the pinball machine and the number of pieces of candy the "manipulators" ate.

Application: The Use of Activity Reinforcers

The use of activities as reinforcers to establish desired modes of behavior has been widespread and quite successful (Allison, 1989). We will examine several studies that are representative of the application of Premack's probability-differential theory to establish desired behaviors. These studies demonstrate that techniques that alter the behavior-reinforcement contingencies of an individual can be used to establish desired, and eliminate undesired, behaviors.

Preschool-aged children have short attention spans and a tendency to become unruly. Homme, de Baca, Devine, Steinhorst, and Rickert (1963) provided an early application of Premack's probability-differential theory to encourage desired behavior in young children. High-probability behaviors such as running around the room and pushing chairs were used as reinforcers for low-probability behaviors like sitting quietly and looking at the blackboard. These researchers reported that in a few days, this procedure produced relatively quiet and attentive children.

In more recent work, Konarski and his associates (Konarski, 1985; Konarski, Johnson, Crowell, & Whitman, 1980) found that activities could be used as reinforcers to increase academic performance in educable mentally retarded students. The academic behaviors involved were reading, coloring, cursive writing, and arithmetic. These researchers found that each of these behaviors could be increased by making performance a contingency for access to another, more preferred activity. For example, if reading activity was a low-frequency behavior, its incidence increased if it was necessary in order to color, which is a higher-frequency behavior.

The applications of Premack's ideas have not been limited to educational settings. The business environment has also proven to be an ideal arena in which to modify behavior using activities as reinforcers. For example, Luthans, Paul, and Baker (1981) reported that total sales increased among department store salesperons when a contingency was established between low-probability sales activity and high-probability time off with pay. In other words, the salespersons increased their sales performance when that activity allowed them time-off with pay. O'Hara, Johnson, and Beehr (1985) noted a similar increase in the sales telephone solicitors made when this contingency was set in place.

Psychologists using activities as reinforcers have made an important discovery. Not only can the use of an activity as a reinforcer increase performance of the target behavior, but it also decreases the level of the activity used as the reinforcer (Allison, 1989). This means that if the activity used as a reinforcer is undesirable, an effective method exists to suppress the inappropriate behavior. To illustrate this application, suppose that a child occasionally screams. Even though screaming may not occur frequently, it can be annoying. A parent could decrease screaming by allowing a child to scream contingent upon the occurrence of the target behavior (for example, reading). This contingency would act to increase a desired activity such as reading and decrease an undesired behavior like screaming.

Premack's probability-differential theory proposes that an activity will be reinforcing if its probability of occurrence is greater than that of the activity being reinforced. Timberlake and Allison's response deprivation theory presents a different view of the nature of reinforcers.

Response Deprivation Theory

William Timberlake and James Allison proposed that response deprivation created by the establishment of a behavior-reinforcer contingency causes an activity to be a reinforcer (Timberlake & Allison, 1974). According to Timberlake and Allison, animals respond at a specific level when given free access to objects important to their survival. For example, a rat given free access to food will consume approximately the same amount of food each day; the rat responds to food at the same level each day because his behavior is adaptive and enhances the rat's chance of survival. When an animal's access to an object is restricted and, therefore, its level of responding is lowered, the animal will be motivated to return to its previous level of responding. Thus, food deprivation will cause a rat to engage in behaviors that will allow it to gain access to food and restore responding to the predeprivation level. Further, Timberlake and Allison assert that a certain activity becomes a reinforcer because the establishment of a behavior-reinforcer contingency restricts the opportunity to participate in that activity. When a contingency is established, the animal increases the level of operant behavior in order to return the performance of the restricted activity to its baseline level.

Timberlake and Allison (1974) conducted a number of studies that support their **response deprivation theory**. Let's briefly examine one of these studies. Animals were deprived of access to a running wheel, and a contingency was established so that the rat was required to drink to gain access to the wheel. Even though the rat's baseline level of responding was higher for drinking than for running, Timberlake and Allison found that the contingency between drinking and running led to an increase in the rat's level of drinking. These results indicate that restricting access to an activity results in that activity becoming a reinforcer. These results also indicate that the relative level of response does not determine whether or not an activity acts as a reinforcer. Instead, restricting access to low-frequency activity, such as running, can increase the response level of another, high-frequency activity, such as drinking, if performing the first activity will provide access to the restricted activity.

The validity of the response deprivation theory has also been demonstrated in an applied setting with human clients (Timberlake & Farmer-Dougan, 1991). The research of Konarski and his colleagues (Konarski, Johnson, Crowell, & Whitman, 1980; Konarski, Crowell, & Duggan, 1985) especially supports the view that restricting access to an activity makes that activity a potential reinforcer. Konarski, Johnson, Crowell, and Whitman (1980) measured the baseline level of coloring and working simple arithmetic problems in grade-school children. Not surprisingly, these young children had a much higher baseline level of coloring than of doing arithmetic problems. The researchers established a contingency so that having access to the lower-probability arithmetic problems was contingent upon doing the higher-probability coloring. Perhaps surprisingly, Konarski, Johnson, Crowell, and Whitman found the children increased their coloring in order to gain the opportunity to complete math problems.

Using a special education population, Konarski, Crowell, and Duggan (1985) assessed the baseline levels of working arithmetic problems and writing. Regardless of which activity was the higher-probability behavior, restricting assess to the lower-probability behavior increased the level of the higher-probability behavior. Konarski, Crowell, and Duggan also found that restricting access to the higher-probability behavior increased the level of the lower-probability behavior.

Principles of Behavioral Economics

We have learned that a contingency restricts an animal's access to an activity. Consider an animal, such as a rat, that cannot eat freely, but instead must bar press to have access to food. How many times will the rat bar press? Intuitively, one might say that the rat would bar press until it was no longer motivated to eat. However, in many circumstances, the contingency would require more response than the animal is willing to emit to satisfy its desire for the food. Under these conditions, the rat will not bar press enough to reach its predeprivation level of food consumption. A number of psychologists (Allison, 1989; Staddon, 1988) have provided some insight into the question of how many times a rat will bar press to obtain reward. We will look at how behavior is allocated next.

Behavioral Allocation

Suppose that an animal could freely engage in two activities. It might not respond equally; instead, its level of responding might be higher for one behavior than the other. As an example, the animal might show 50 A responses and 150 B responses. Allison (1989) referred to the free operant level of two responses as the paired basepoint, or **blisspoint.** The blisspoint would be the unrestricted level of performance of both behaviors.

When a contingency is established, free access to one behavior is restricted, and the animal must emit a second behavior to have access to the first. Returning to our example, the contingency could be that one response A leads to one response B. This contingency means that the animal cannot attain blisspoint; that is, it cannot emit response B three times as often as A.

FIGURE 9.10. This graph shows the blisspoint (open circle) for behaviors A and B. The contingency states that one behavior A is necessary for access to one behavior B. The equilibrium point, or minimum distance to blisspoint, on the contingency line is point 1. Responding at other points takes the animal farther away from blisspoint.

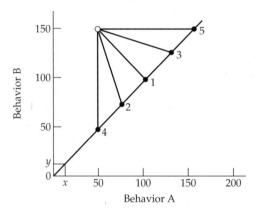

What does an animal do when it cannot attain blisspoint? According to Allison (1989), the animal will respond in a manner that allows it to be as close to the blisspoint as possible. **Figure 9.10** shows how this process works. As this figure shows, blisspoint is 3 B responses to 1 A response, but the contingency specifies 1 B to 1 A. Does the animal emit 50, 100, 150, or 200 A responses? The closest point on the contingency line to the blisspoint is point 1 (see **Figure 9.10**). At this point, the animal would emit 100 A responses to receive 100 B responses (reinforcer). This level of A responding would bring the animal closest to blisspoint.

The concept of blisspoint suggests that an animal does not randomly emit contingent responses. Instead, the animal allocates the number of responses that bring it closest to blisspoint. The concept of blisspoint comes from economic theory and assumes that a person acts to minimize cost and maximize gain. If we think of a contingent behavior as a cost and reinforcing activity as a gain, the **behavioral allocation view** assumes that the animal is emitting the minimal number of contingent responses to obtain the maximum level of reinforcing activities. This approach assumes that the economic principles that apply to purchasing products tell us about the level of response in an operant conditioning setting.

Viken and McFall (1994) have pointed to a potential downside to the use of contingencies. We normally think of contingencies as serving to increase the reponse rate. While this is generally true, it is not always true. Consider the following example from Viken and McFall to illustrate potential pitfalls of using contingencies. Suppose the blisspoint for prosocial behavior and parental rewards in children is 1 to 11; that is, the child's baseline level is one prosocial behavior for every 11 parental rewards (see **Figure 9.11**). What if the parent wants to increase the level of prosocial behavior and establishes a 2:1 contingency, with 1 prosocial behavior producing 2 parental rewards? As **Figure 9.11** indicates, the closest point on the contingency line to blisspoint is 20 prosocial behaviors and 40 parental rewards. Perhaps the parent is not satisfied with this level of prosocial behavior and changes the contingency to 1:1, or one parental reward for every prosocial behavior. Intuitively, this change in contingency should result in a higher level of prosocial behavior. But as **Figure 9.11** shows, blisspoint is now 30 prosocial behaviors for 30 social rewards. Thus, the effect of changing from a 2:1 to 1:1 contingency schedule has the opposite to the desired effect; rather than increasing the level of prosocial behavior, the new contingency actually decreases it. More telling is that establishing an even more stringent 1:2 contingency results in an even further decline in the level of prosocial behavior (see **Figure 9.11**). These observations suggest that the establishment of a contingency must recognize the blisspoint in order for a contingency to have its desired effect.

Choice Behavior

There are many circumstances in which a simple behavior-reinforcement contingency is not operative; instead, the animal or person must choose from two or more contingencies. To illustrate this type of situation, suppose that an operant chamber has two keys instead of one, and the animal receives reinforcement on a VI 1-minute schedule on one key and a VI 3-minute schedule on the other key. How would the animal respond on this task? Richard Herrnstein's **matching law** (Herrnstein, 1961; Herrnstein & Vaughn, 1980) describes how the animal would act in this two-choice situation.

According to Herrnstein's matching law, when an animal has free access to different schedules of reinforcement, the animal allocates its responding in proportion to the level of reinforcement available on each schedule. In terms of our

FIGURE 9.11. This graph shows the blisspoint (open circle) for prosocial behavior and social reward, as well as the contingency lines for the 2:1, 1:1, and 1:2 social rewards-prosocial behavior contingencies. The closed circles show the equilibrium point on each contingency line.

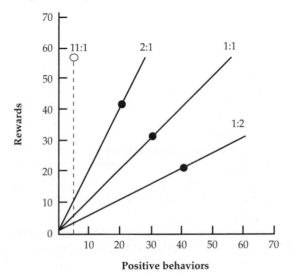

previous example, an animal can obtain three times as much reward on a VI 1-minute schedule than on a VI 3-minute schedule. The matching law predicts that the animal will respond three times as much on the key with the VI 1-minute schedule than it will on the key with the VI 3-minute schedule.

The matching law can be stated mathematically to provide for a precise prediction of the animal's behavior in a choice situation. The mathematical formula for the matching law is:

$$\frac{X}{X + Y} = \frac{R(X)}{R(X) + R(Y)}$$

In the equation, X represents the number of responses on key X, Y is the number of responses on key Y, R(X) represents the number of reinforcements received on key X; and R(Y) is the number of reinforcements on key Y. In our example, the animal can receive three times as many rewards on key X as it can on key Y. The matching law shows that we can expect the animal to key peck three times as much on key X than key Y.

Does the matching law accurately predict the animal's behavior in a choice situation? Herrnstein tested the theory by varying the proportion of reinforcements that the animal could obtain on each key and then determining the pigeon's proportion of key pecks on each key. The data from this study appears in **Figure 9.12.** Herrnstein's results show exceptional matching; that is, the animal's number of responses on each key is a function of the reinforcements available on each key.

Other researchers have shown that the matching also predicts choice behavior in humans (Hantula & Crowell, 1994; Mace, Neef, Shade, & Mauro, 1996). Hantula and Crowell (1994) observed that the matching law predicted the response allocations of college students working on a computerized analogue investment task, while Mace, Neef, Shade, and Mauro (1996) reported that the matching law predicted the behaviors of special education students working on academic tasks.

Our discussion indicates that the matching law assumes that an individual's choice behaviors will be divided proportionally accord to the level of reinforcement available on each schedule. The matching law also predicts behavior when the choice is between two different magnitudes of reinforcement (de Villiers, 1977). For example, suppose a pigeon receives one reinforcer when key pecking on a VI 1-minute schedule and five reinforcers when pecking at a second key on the same VI schedule. How would the pigeon act? While it would seem reasonable to expect the pigeon would only peck the key associated with five reinforcements, the matching law predicts that it would actually respond to the key associated with one reinforcement for 17% of its responses. A real-world example might be having to choose between going to one of two restaurants. While the food at one restaurant may be a greater reinforcer than the food at the other restaurant, the matching law predicts that you will visit both places, and that the frequency of each choice will depend on the difference in reinforcer magnitude between the two restaurants.

The matching law also has been shown to predict the allocation of responses in humans in situations involving differential reinforcer magnitudes. One such situation involves the choice between taking a two-point shot and a three-point

FIGURE 9.12. The proportion of key pecks on X and Y is proportional to the reinforcements available to keys X and Y.

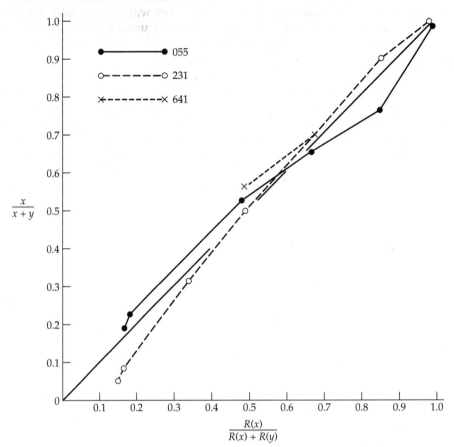

shot in a basketball game. Vollmer and Bourret (2000) determined that the matching law predicted the response allocation of two- and three-point shots male and female basketball players took at a major state university. In their study, they factored into the matching law equation the fact that the magnitude of reinforcement is 1.5 times higher for a three-point shot than for a two-point shot, and they found that the proportion of three-point shots taken matched the percentage of three-point shots made. Notably, the matching law only predicted the response allocation for experienced players, presumably because a basketball player needs to learn the probability of making a two- or a three-point shot before he or she can choose how to allocate his or her shot selection.

Let's return to the restaurant example. Perhaps the quality of food at the two restaurants is similar, but you usually have to wait longer to be seated at one of the two. The matching law also predicts behavior when an individual is faced with a choice between different delays of reinforcement. Again, the matching law states that the level of responding to each choice will be proportional to the delay of reinforcement associated with each choice. For example, a pigeon receives reinforcement after a 1-second delay following pecking one key, while key pecking on the other key produces reinforcement after a 3-second delay. The matching law predicts that 25% of the pigeon's key pecking will be at the key with the 3-second delay and 75% at the key with a 1-second delay. Returning to our restaurant example, suppose that the usual wait is 5 minutes at one restaurant and 60 minutes at the other. The matching law predicts that you will go to the restaurant with only a 5-minute delay 91% of the time.

You might be thinking that the food in the restaurant with a long delay might be much better than the one with a short wait. How would a person behave in this choice situation? Let's suppose that the restaurant with the 60-minute delay is twice as good as the one with a 5-minute wait. Using the matching law, you would go to the restaurant with the 5-minute delay 87 percent of the time even though the food is much better at the other restaurant. This prediction suggests that you will usually choose a small, immediate reinforcer over a large, delayed reinforcer. In fact, pigeons and people typically select small, immediate reinforcers rather than large, delayed ones (Ainslie, 1975). To illustrate this principle, suppose you have to choose between watching a television show or studying for a test. While the reinforcer of a good grade on a test is definitely greater than the temporary enjoyment of a television show, the longer delay of reinforcement for studying will typically lead you to watch television rather than study.

There are many conditions that could lead to a choice of a large, delayed reinforcer instead of a small, immediate one (Mischel, 1974; Rachlin & Green, 1972). The large, delayed reinforcer will be selected if the choice is made well in advance; that is, some time prior to the actual experience of either reinforcer. If people have to choose early in the day between watching television or studying, they are more likely to choose studying; if they make the choice just prior to the beginning of the television show, they are more likely to choose it. Similarly, the large, delayed reinforcer is more likely to be selected if the reinforcers are not visible, or if there is something pleasurable to do until the large, delayed reinforcer becomes available. These techniques have proven useful in developing self-control and in enabling people to resist the temptations of small, immediate rewards (Mischel, 1974).

The matching law is a simple economic principle that predicts an individual's behavior in many choice situations. The student of economics soon discovers that simple principles are not always valid, and more complex processes are needed to accurately describe more complex activities. The same complexity holds true for behavioral economics. While the matching law accurately predicts behavior in a variety of situations, there are some situations in which it is not always valid. Other behavioral economic principles have been applied to explain these more complex choice behavior situations. We will look briefly at one of these principles, called maximizing, next.

Suppose a pigeon has a choice between key pecking on one key on a VI 1-minute schedule and on a second key on a VI 3-minute schedule. As we learned earlier, the matching law predicts that the pigeon will peck at the VI 1-minute key three times as often as it does the VI 3-minute key. The matching law provides one explanation of the pigeon's behavior; that is, the pigeon allocates its responses according to the relative proportion of reinforcements available for each choice. In contrast, the **maximizing law** assumes that the aim of the pigeon's behavior will be to obtain as many reinforcers as possible.

In this example, the maximizing law argues that the pigeon switches responses because it can receive reinforcement on both keys. Instead of the pigeon gaining reinforcement on two VI schedules, suppose that responding on one key is reinforced on a FR-10 schedule and on the other key on an FR-40 schedule. How would the pigeon act in this situation? While the matching law predicts continued responding on both keys, maximizing theory assumes that the pigeon would respond only to the FR-10 key. It is illogical for the pigeon to respond 40 times for a reinforcer when it can obtain the same reinforcer by pecking only 10 times. As expected, research (Rachlin, Battalio, Kagel, & Green, 1981; Staddon & Motheral, 1978) shows that the pigeon's behavior corresponds to the maximizing law rather than the matching law.

You might think that the maximizing law provides a valid explanation for choice behavior. However, not all investigations (Savastano & Fantino, 1994; Vyse & Belke, 1992) have reported results consistent with the maximizing theory. For example, suppose that a pigeon is reinforced on a VR schedule on one key and a VI schedule on a second key. Maximizing theory predicts that the pigeon would make most of the responses on the VR key, since most of the responses on the VI key are wasted. Yet, Vyse and Belke (1992) observed that the pigeon responds more on the VI key than one would predict from the maximizing theory. In an analogous situation with college students, Savastano and Fantino (1994) found that the college students spent more time on the VI schedule than the maximizing schedule predicted. Further, the college students' choices were much closer to the matching law than the maximizing law.

While the concepts of matching and maximizing have advanced our understanding of choice behavior, other behavioral principles are needed to fully explain the economics of choice. Psychologists have proposed a number of alternative theories. For example, **momentary maximization theory** proposes that a specific choice is determined by which alternative is perceived to be best at that moment in time (Silberberg, Warren-Bolton, & Asano, 1988). According to this view, variables such as the size and quality of the reinforcer determine momentary choices, while principles such as matching law determine the overall pattern of responses. An animal may make a momentary choice that does not fit the matching law, but its overall response might. **Delay-reduction theory** suggests that while overall choices are based on the matching law, individual choices depend on which choice produces the shortest delay in receiving the next reinforcer (Fantino, Preston, and Dunn, 1993). Again, an individual choice to produce a shorter delay in reinforcement may not be consistent with the matching law, but the overall pattern of responding is. Research continues to investigate the economics of choice behavior, with the goal of fully understanding both immediate and long-term choices.

BEFORE YOU GO ON

- **What might Premack's probability-differential theory suggest to reduce the amount of Felicia's drinking?**
- **Would Timberlake and Allison's response deprivation hypothesis make the same or a different suggestion?**

CHAPTER SUMMARY

Pavlov suggested that the presentation of the UCS activates the brain area responsible for processing the UCS, which leads to the stimulation of the neural area generating the UCR. The CS also excites a neural area, and if the UCS follows the CS, the brain centers for processing the CS and UCS are active at the same time. This simultaneous activity creates a neural pathway between the CS and UCS brain centers. Following conditioning, the CS elicits the UCR because of its ability to arouse the UCS and UCR brain areas.

Siegel noted that while the unconditioned reaction to morphine is analgesia, or reduced sensitivity to pain, the conditioned response is hyperalgesia, or an increased sensitivity to pain.

Wagner's sometimes opponent-process (SOP) theory suggests that the UCS elicits two unconditioned responses—a primary A1 component and a secondary A2 component. The primary A1 component is elicited rapidly by the UCS and decays quickly after the UCS ends. In contrast, the onset and decay of the secondary A2 component is gradual. Sometimes the A1 and A2 components differ; at other times, the A1 and A2 components are similar reactions. According to Wagner, it is the secondary A2 component that becomes the CR. If the A1 and A2 components differ, the CR will seem different from the UCR, while the CR will appear to be similar to the UCR when the A1 and A2 components are similar.

AESOP proposes that the UCS elicits separate emotive and sensory unconditioned responses. The emotive and sensory UCRs can have different time courses, which can lead to divergent conditioning outcomes for sensory and emotive CRs.

The Rescorla-Wagner model proposes (1) that there is a maximum level of conditioning supported by the UCS; (2) the associative strength increases readily early in training, but more slowly later in conditioning as associative strength approaches asymptote; (3) the rate of conditioning is more rapid with some CSs or UCSs than with others; and (4) the level of conditioning on a particular trial depends upon the level of prior conditioning to the CS and to the other stimuli present during conditioning.

The Rescorla-Wagner theory suggests that blocking occurs as a result of conditioning associative strength to one stimulus, thereby preventing conditioning to a second stimulus due to a lack of available associative strength. Under some conditions, Rescorla suggests that two stimuli paired with a UCS develop a within-compound association instead of competing for associative strength.

The comparator theory argues that animals learn about all CS-UCS relationships. According to the comparator theory, blocking occurs when the animal does not respond to the CS_2 because the CS_2-UCS association is weaker than the CS_1-UCS association. Deflation of the value of the CS_1 by extinction results in an increased response to the CS_2 due to the favorable comparison of the CS_2-UCS association to the CS_1-UCS association.

Mackintosh's attentional view suggests that animals seek information that predicts the occurrence of biologically significant events (UCSs). In Mackintosh's view, the animal learns that the CS is irrelevant as the result of preexposure to the CS. Once an animal discovers that a CS is irrelevant, it has difficulty learning that the CS correlates with the UCS.

Baker's retrospective processing theory proposes that animals are continuously monitoring the contingency between CS and UCS. Subsequent experience with a CS or UCS alone can lead the animal to reevaluate the predictive value of the CS. The backward blocking phenomenon occurs when there is a reduced responding to the CS_2 when CS_1-UCS pairings follow CS_1- CS_2-UCS pairings; this idea provides support for retrospective processing theory.

Premack's probability-differential theory indicates that activities, such as watching television or going to a dance, can serve as reinforcers. According to Premack, high-probability activities reinforce lower-probability activities.

Timberlake and Allison's response deprivation hypothesis states that an activity will serve as a reinforcer if a response contingency limits access to that activity; such a contingency causes an increase in the operant response in order to restore access to the restricted activity.

The behavioral allocation view suggests that an animal emits the number of contingent responses needed to come as close as possible to blisspoint, or the free operant level of two responses.

The matching law states that when two or more operant responses can enable the subject to obtain reinforcement, the rate of responding is in direct proportion to the level of reinforcement available through each response. The maximizing law states that an individual responding in choice situations attempts to obtain as much reinforcement as possible.

Momentary maximization theory argues that a specific choice is determined by the perception of which alternative is best at that moment in time. Delay-reduction theory proposes that while overall choices are based on the matching law, individual choices are determined by which choice produces the shortest delay in gaining the next reinforcer.

CRITICAL THINKING QUESTIONS

1. Yancy initially experienced intense euphoria after injecting heroin. His response to heroin is now much less intense. Using Siegel's research, give an explanation for Yancy's current reaction to heroin. What would happen if Yancy injected heroin while he was in a new place?
2. Dionne becomes ill after drinking several beers, yet she does not develop an aversion to it. Describe the process(es) responsible for these preexposure effects.
3. Nikki is saving her money to buy a car. Vernon goes out every Friday night and never has any money by Saturday morning. How would the matching law explain Nikki's and Vernon's actions? What factors might lead Nikki to spend some of her money on a new dress or Vernon to save his money for a trip to Florida over spring break?

KEY TERMS

affective extension of SOP theory (AESOP)
analgesia
backward blocking
behavioral allocation theory
blisspoint
comparator theory
conditioned emotional reaction
CS preexposure effect
cue deflation effect
delay-reduction theory

hyperalgesia
hypoalgesia
learned irrelevance
Mackintosh's attentional view
matching law
maximizing law
momentary maximization theory
overshadowing
potentiation
probability-differential theory

Rescorla-Wagner associative model
response deprivation theory
retrospective processing theory
sometimes-opponent process (SOP) theory
stimulus-substitution theory
UCS preexposure effect
within-compound association

Biological Influences on Learning

A Nauseating Experience

For weeks, Sean has looked forward to spending the spring semester break in Florida with his roommate Tony and Tony's parents. Since he has never visited Florida, Sean was certain his anticipation would make the eighteen-hour car ride tolerable. When they arrived, Sean felt genuinely welcome; Tony's parents had even planned many sightseeing tours for them during the week's stay. Sean was glad he had come. Tony had often mentioned his mother was a gourmet cook. Sean was certainly relishing the thoughts of her meals, especially since his last enjoyable food had been his own mother's cooking. Sean was also quite tired of the many fast food restaurants they had stopped at during their drive. When Tony's mother called them to dinner, Sean felt very hungry. However, the sight of lasagna on the dining table almost immediately turned Sean's hunger to nausea. As he sat down at the table, the smell of the lasagna intensified his nausea. Sean began to panic; he did not want to offend his hosts, but he hated lasagna. Although he had stopped Tony's mother after she had served him only a small portion, Sean did not know if he could eat even one bite. When he put the lasagna to his mouth, he began to gag and the nausea became unbearable. He quickly asked to be excused and bolted to the bathroom, where he proceeded to vomit everything he had eaten that day. Embarrassed, Sean apologetically explained his aversion to lasagna. Although he liked most Italian food, he had once become intensely ill several hours after eating lasagna, and now he could not stand even the sight or smell of lasagna. Tony's mother said she understood: she herself had a similar aversion to seafood. She offered to make Sean a sandwich, and he readily accepted.

Why did Sean develop this aversion? This chapter explores the learning process that caused Sean to develop his aversion to lasagna, but not to other foods. We will discover that Sean's experience affected his instinctive feeding system, which was modified to become nauseous at the sight of lasagna. This nauseous feeling caused Sean to be no longer able to eat lasagna.

A person's biological character also affects other types of learning. Other examples include drinking during times when reinforcement is unavailable, developing an attachment to one's mother, and learning to avoid aversive events. In this chapter, we will examine several instances in which biological character and the environment join to determine behavior. But before examining these situations, we need to discuss why psychologists initially ignored the influence of biology on learning.

GENERALITY OF THE LAWS OF LEARNING

Why do psychologists train rats or monkeys to press a bar for food, or present a buzzer prior to food presentation for cats or dogs, since these situations bear little resemblance to the real world? (In natural settings, rats and monkeys do not have to bar press for food, and cats and dogs do not usually hear a buzzer before they eat.) The answer to this question lies in the belief that there are some general laws of learning. These laws reveal themselves in the study of any behavior, even behaviors not exhibited in natural settings.

Psychologists investigating operant conditioning use the bar press response because many different species acquire it easily. But the same rules governing the acquisition or extinction of an operant response could be demonstrated by using a maze or alley to study the instrumental conditioning process. Actually, the unnaturalness of bar pressing is thought to be desirable because the animal comes into the conditioning situation without any past experience that may affect its behavior. The following statement by Skinner illustrates the belief that the study of any behavior reveals specific laws governing the operant conditioning: "The general topography of operant behavior is not important, because most if not all specific operants are conditioned. I suggest that the dynamic properties of operant behavior may be studied with a single reflex" (1938, pp. 45–46).

Although Skinner studied operant conditioning using the bar press response, the observations reported in Chapter 4 show that the rules Skinner detailed governing the acquisition and extinction of the bar pressing response control the operant conditioning process with many different behaviors and in many species. Also, research demonstrates that many varied reinforcers can increase the rate of bar pressing and that the rules Skinner described have been found to operate in both laboratory and real-world settings. It is not surprising that psychologists have felt confident that training rats and primates to bar press for food reveals the general laws of operant conditioning.

Similarly, psychologists who present a buzzer prior to food assume that any rules they uncover governing the acquisition or extinction of a conditioned salivation response will represent the general laws of classical conditioning. The choice of a buzzer and food is arbitrary: cats or dogs could be conditioned to salivate as readily to a wide variety of visual, auditory, or tactile stimuli. The following statement by Pavlov illustrates the view that all stimuli are capable of becoming conditioned stimuli: "Any natural phenomenon chosen at will may be converted into a conditioned stimulus . . . any visual stimulus, any desired sound, any odor, and the stimulation of any part of the skin" (1928, p. 86).

The specific UCS used also is arbitrary: any event that can elicit an unconditioned response can become associated with the environmental events that precede it. Thus, Pavlov's buzzer could have as easily been conditioned to elicit fear by pairing it with shock as it was conditioned to elicit salivation by being presented prior to food. Pavlov described the equivalent associability of events in the following statement: "It is obvious that the reflex activity of any effector organ can be chosen for the purpose of investigation, since signaling stimuli can get linked up with any of the inborn reflexes" (1927, p. 17). Pavlov found that many different stimuli can become associated with the UCS of food. Other psychologists documented the conditioning of varied stimuli with a multitude of UCSs. Also, the literature points out that different CSs and UCSs can become associated in both laboratory and natural situations. The idea that any environmental stimulus can become associated with any unconditioned stimulus seemed a reasonable conclusion, based on the research conducted on classical conditioning.

A BEHAVIOR SYSTEMS APPROACH

> All organisms . . . possess the basic behavioral patterns that enable them to survive in their niches, but learning provides the fine tuning necessary for successful adaptation. (Garcia and Garcia y Robertson, 1985)

The "general laws of learning" view we just described assumes that learning is the primary determinant of how an animal acts. According to this approach, learning functions to organize reflexes and random responses so that an animal can effectively interact with the environment. The impact of learning is to allow the animal to adapt to the environment and thereby survive. However, the quote presented at the beginning of this section provides a different perspective on the impact of learning on behavior. Rather than assuming that learning organizes behavior, Garcia and Garcia y Robertson (1985) assume that the organization of behavior already exists within the animal. The function of learning is to enhance already existing organization rather than to create a new organization. Many psychologists (Garcia & Garcia y Robertson, 1985; Hogan, 1989; Timberlake, 2001) have suggested that learning modifies preexisting instinctive systems rather than constructing a new behavioral organization; we will look at this idea next.

William Timberlake's **behavior systems approach** (Timberlake, 2001; Timberlake & Lucas, 1989) offers an alternative to the general laws of learning concept. According to Timberlake, an animal possesses a set of instinctive behavior systems such as feeding, mating, social bonding, care of young, and defense. These instinctive behavior systems are independent and serve a specific function or need within the animal. **Figure 10.1** shows an example of the predatory subsystem of the feeding system in rats. As the figure shows, there are several components of the animal's predatory response. The predatory sequence begins with the rat in a general search mode. The search mode causes the rat to show enhanced general searching, which leads to greater locomotion and increased sensitivity to spatial and social stimuli that are likely to bring the rat closer to food. The increased locomotion and greater sensitivity to the environment lead the rat to notice a small moving object in the distance as its prey. Once the prey is close, the rat shifts from a general search mode to a focal search mode. The focal search mode causes the rat to engage in a set of perceptual-motor modules related to capturing and subduing its prey. Once the prey is captured, the rat shifts to a handle/consume mode, which elicits the biting, manipulating, chewing, and swallowing involved in the consumption of the prey. This complex instinctive predatory behavior system allows the animal to find and consume the nutrients it needs to survive, with the search modes motivating the perceptual-motor modules that allow the rat to locate, approach, and consume its prey.

Timberlake's behavior systems approach suggests that learning evolved as a modifier of already existing behavior systems. According to Timberlake, the impact of learning is to change the integration, tuning, instigation or linkages within a particular behavior system. For example, a new environmental stimulus could become able to release an instinctive motor-response module as a result of a Pavlovian conditioning experience. Learning can also alter the intensity of a simple motor response due to repetition, or improve the efficiency of a complex behavior pattern as a result of the contingent delivery of a reinforcer.

Activation of a mode can also be conditioned to cues that signal the receipt of reinforcers. For example, the search modes that bring the rat into contact with its prey can be conditioned to cues associated with the prey. However, the conditioning of modes is different from the conditioning of perceptual-motor

FIGURE 10.1. Illustration of the basic components of the rat's feeding system. The predatory subsystem can activate one of three modes (general, focal, or handle/consume), which in turn activates one or more modules appropriate to that mode. The arousal of a specific module then leads to one or more specific behaviors, each directed toward the consumption of needed nutrients.

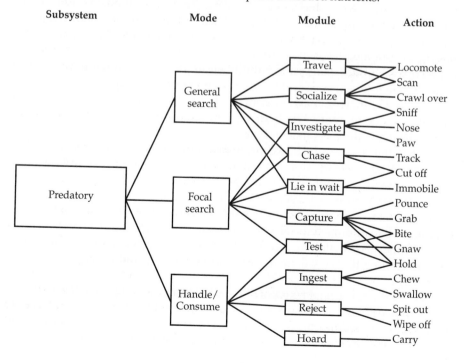

modules (Timberlake, 2001). Specific motor responses are conditioned to specific stimuli as a result of the conditioning of perceptual-motor modules. By contrast, the conditioning of a specific mode produces a general motivational state that sensitizes all of the perceptual-motor modules in that mode. For example, activation of the general search mode of the predatory subsystem sensitizes the rat to engage in the travel, socialize, investigate, chase, and lie in wait perceptual-motor modules (refer to **Figure 10.1**).

One important aspect of Timberlake's behavior systems approach is that different stimuli can be conditioned to different modes. For example, distal cues are relevant to a general search mode—the rat must locate distant prey. By contrast, proximal cues are relevant to a focal search mode—the rat must capture and subdue its prey. Silva, Timberlake, and Gont (1998) evaluated the view that distant cues are conditioned to a general search mode, while proximal cues are conditioned to a focal search mode. In their study, there were two levers on each side of a food tray: one lever was "far" from the food tray; the other "near" to it. Each lever was presented in succession for 4 seconds, followed by food. In the F-N condition, the far lever was presented first, followed by the near lever; in the N-F condition, the near lever was presented first, followed by the far lever. Silva, Timberlake, and Gont found that animals in the F-N condition first attended to the far lever, then transferred their attention to the near lever, and finally nosed the food tray just prior to the presentation of food. In Timberlake's view, the F-N condition resembles the predatory subsystem: the general search mode activated attention to the distal far lever, then the focal search mode activated attention to the proximal near lever. But what about the N-F condition? Silva, Timberlake, and Gont found that the N-F animals attended first to the near lever and then to the food tray, but showed no response to the far lever. The second (far) lever led the rat away from food; since activation of the focal search mode by the first near lever focused attention toward and not away from food, no conditioning occurred to the distal far lever. In fact, rats in the N-F condition spent more time nosing the first near lever than did rats in the F-N condition.

Perhaps another example would illustrate the conditioning of the general search mode to distal cues and the focal search mode to proximal cues. Atkins, Domjan, and Gutierrez (1994) presented a light CS for either 30 seconds or 1,200 seconds to a male quail. The light CS predicted access to a receptive female quail. The male quail approached the alcove where the female quail would appear when the 30-second CS was presented, but not when the 1,200-second CS was presented. Instead, the male quail showed increased locomotion in response to the CS presented for 1,200 seconds. Why the difference in the quail's response to the same CS presented for different durations? The 30-second CS is proximal (near) to the reinforcer (female quail), and thus, a focal search—leading the male to approach the alcove—was conditioned to the 30-second CS. The 1,200-second CS is distal (far) from the reinforcer (female quail); thus, a general search—leading the male to increase locomotion—was conditioned to the 1,200-second CS.

One of the functional features of the behavior system approach is that variations in learning occur between species (Timberlake, 2001). In Timberlake's view, different species of animals learn a particular behavior at different rates. Different species also learn different ways of responding to a particular situation. Considerable variation also occurs within a species. Timberlake suggests that some behaviors are learned more rapidly than others within a given species. Further, there may be different rates of learning of a particular behavior between different members of a species.

What causes these variations between and within animal species? Timberlake suggests that the variations are due either to predispositions or constraints on what an animal or person can learn. A **predisposition** refers to instances in which an animal learns more rapidly or in a different form than expected. Timberlake suggests that predispositions occur when environmental circumstance easily modifies the instinctive behavior system that the animal brings into the situation. Variations in learning also can reflect the impact of a **constraint** on learning; a constraint occurs when an animal learns less rapidly or less completely than expected. According to Timberlake, constraints on learning occur when environmental circumstance is not suited to the animal's instinctive behavior system. In the next five sections, we will examine examples of predispositions and constraints on learning.

ANIMAL MISBEHAVIOR

Several summers ago my family visited Busch Gardens. We observed some unusual behaviors among birds during our visit; they walked on a wire, pedaled a bicycle, pecked certain keys on a piano, and so on. The birds had been trained to exhibit these behaviors using the operant conditioning techniques detailed in Chapter 4. Keller Breland and Marian Breland (Breland & Breland, 1961) initiated the use of operant procedures to teach exotic behaviors to animals. They conducted their research at Animal Behavior Enterprises in Hot Springs, Arkansas to see if the techniques Skinner described could be used in the real world.

The Brelands trained thirty-eight species, including reindeer, cockatoos, raccoons, porpoises, and whales. In fact, they have trained over 6,000 animals to emit a wide range of behaviors, including teaching hens to play a five-note tune on a piano and perform a "tap dance," pigs to turn on a radio and eat breakfast at a table, chicks to run up an inclined platform and slide off, a calf to answer questions in a quiz show by lighting either a yes or no sign, and two turkeys to play hockey. Established by the Brelands and many other individuals, these exotic behaviors have been on display at many municipal zoos and museums of natural history, in department store displays, at fair and trade convention exhibits, tourist attractions, and on television. These demonstrations have not only provided entertainment for millions of people but have also documented the power and generality of the operant conditioning procedures Skinner outlined.

Although Breland and Breland (1961, 1966) were able to condition a wide variety of exotic behaviors using operant conditioning, they noted that some operant responses, although initially performed effectively, deteriorated with continued training despite repeated food reinforcements. According to Breland and Breland, the elicitation of instinctive food-foraging and food-handling behaviors by the presentation of food caused the decline in the effectiveness of an operant response reinforced by food. These instinctive behaviors, strengthened by food reinforcement, eventually dominated the operant behavior. Breland and Breland called the deterioration of an operant behavior with continued reinforcement **instinctive drift,** and the instinctive behavior that prevented the continued effectiveness of the operant response an example of **animal misbehavior.** One example of animal misbehavior is described next.

Breland and Breland attempted to condition pigs to pick up a large wooden coin and deposit it in a piggy bank several feet away. Each pig was required to deposit four or five coins to receive one reinforcement. According to Breland and Breland, "pigs condition very rapidly, they have no trouble taking ratios, they have ravenous appetites (naturally), and in many ways are the most trainable animals we have worked with." However, each pig they conditioned exhibited an interesting pattern of behavior following conditioning (see **Figure 10.2**). At first, the pigs picked up a coin, carried it rapidly to the bank, deposited it, and readily returned for another coin. However, over a period of weeks, the pigs' operant behavior became slower and slower. Each pig still rapidly approached

FIGURE 10.2. Breland and Breland attempted to train this pig to deposit the wooden disk into a piggy bank. Unfortunately, the pig's operant response deteriorated with repeated food reinforcements due to the elicitation of the instinctive foraging and rooting responses.

the coin, but rather than carry it immediately over to the bank, the pigs "would repeatedly drop it, root it, drop it again, root it along the way, pick it up, toss it up in the air, drop it, root it some more, and so on."

Why did the pigs' operant behavior deteriorate after conditioning? According to Breland and Breland, the pigs merely exhibited the instinctive behaviors associated with eating. The presentation of food during conditioning not only reinforces the operant response, but it also elicits instinctive food-related behaviors. The reinforcement of these instinctive food-gathering and food-handling behaviors strengthens the instinctive behaviors, which results in the deterioration of the pigs' operant responses (depositing the coin in the bank). The more dominant the instinctive food-related behaviors become, the longer it takes for the operant response to occur. The slow deterioration of the operant depositing response provides support for Breland and Breland's instinctive drift view of animal misbehavior.

Breland and Breland have reported many other instances of animal misbehavior. For example, they found hamsters that stopped responding in a glass case, porpoises and whales that swallowed balls or inner tubes instead of playing with them to receive reinforcement, cats that refused to leave the area around the food dispenser, and rabbits that refused to approach their feeder. Breland and Breland also reported extreme difficulty in conditioning many bird species to vocalize to obtain food reinforcement. In each case of animal misbehavior, Breland and Breland suggested that the instinctive food-seeking behavior prevented the continued high performance level of an operant response required to receive reinforcement. These findings suggest that the effectiveness of food reinforcement to establish an operant behavior is limited.

Boakes, Poli, Lockwood, and Goodall (1978) established a procedure for producing animal misbehavior in a laboratory. These researchers trained rats to press a flap to obtain a ball bearing and to deposit it in a chute to obtain food reinforcement. They reported that although all the rats initially released the ball bearing readily, the majority of the animals became reluctant to let go of the ball bearing after several training sessions. These rats repeatedly mouthed, pawed, and retrieved the ball bearing before finally depositing it in the chute.

Breland and Breland (1961, 1966) suggested that the elicitation and strengthening of instinctive food-related behaviors during operant conditioning is responsible for animal misbehavior. Boakes, Poli, Lockwood, and Goodall (1978) proposed another explanation. In their view, animal misbehavior is produced by Pavlovian conditioning rather than by operant conditioning. The association of environmental events with food during conditioning causes these environmental events to elicit species-typical foraging and food-handling behaviors; these behaviors then compete with the operant behavior. Consider the misbehavior of the pig detailed earlier. According to Breland and Breland, the pigs rooted the tokens because the reinforcement presented during operant conditioning produced and strengthened the instinctive food-related behavior; in contrast, Boakes, Poll, Lockwood, and Goodall suggested that the association of the token with food caused the token to elicit the rooting behavior.

Timberlake, Wahl, and King (1982) conducted a series of studies to evaluate the validity of each view of animal misbehavior. The results of the experiments Timberlake, Wahl, and King conducted show that both operant and Pavlovian conditioning contribute to producing animal misbehavior. In their **appetitive structure view**, misbehavior represents species-typical foraging and food-handling behaviors that are elicited by pairing food with the natural cues controlling food-gathering activities. Also, the instinctive food-gathering behaviors must be reinforced if the misbehavior is to dominate the operant behavior. Animal misbehavior does not occur in most operant conditioning situations because (1) the cues present during conditioning do not resemble the natural cues eliciting instinctive foraging and food-handling behaviors, and (2) these instinctive behaviors are not reinforced. Let's examine how Timberlake, Wahl, and King validated their appetitive structure view of animal misbehavior.

Timberlake, Wahl, and King used the ball bearing procedure that Boakes, Poli, Lockwood, and Goodall had developed to investigate animal misbehavior. Recall that rats in this situation repeatedly mouth, paw, and retrieve the ball bearing before releasing it down the chute to obtain food reinforcement. Timberlake, Wahl, and King (experiment 1) assessed the contribution of Pavlovian conditioning to animal misbehavior by pairing the ball bearing with food in experimental subjects. Experimental treatment animals received food after the ball bearing had rolled out of the chamber. Also, this study used two control conditions to evaluate the importance of pairing the ball bearing and food: animals in one control condition were given random pairings of the ball bearing and food (random group); subjects in the second control condition received only the ball bearing (CS-only group). They reported that experimental group animals exhibited a significant amount of misbehavior toward the ball bearing: they touched it, carried it about the cage, placed it in their mouths, and bit it while holding it in their forepaws. In contrast, infrequent misbehavior occurred in animals in the two control groups. These observations indicate that the ball bearing and food must be presented together for a high level of misbehavior to occur.

According to Timberlake, Wahl, and King, the pairings of the ball bearing with food are necessary but not sufficient for the development of misbehavior. They also assert that the misbehavior must be reinforced by food presentation for misbehavior to dominate operant responding. Timberlake, Wahl, and King's experiments 3 and 4 evaluated the importance of operant conditioning to the establishment of animal misbehavior. In experiment 3, contact with the ball bearing caused food to be omitted. The researchers assumed that if reinforcement of contact with the ball bearing is necessary for the dominance of animal misbehavior, the contingency that contact with the ball bearing would prevent reinforcement would lead to an absence of animal misbehavior. The results of experiment 3 show that if contact with the ball bearing prevents reinforcement, then the animals did indeed exhibit no contact with the ball bearing. The experimenters then reinforced contact with the ball bearing in experiment 4. If the animal did not touch the ball bearing, it received no food on that trial. Timberlake, Wahl, and King reported that reinforcement of contact with the ball bearing produced a rapid increase in the level of animal misbehavior. These studies suggest that for misbehavior to develop, stimuli (e.g., ball bearings) resembling the natural cues controlling food-gathering activities must be consistently paired with food (Pavlovian conditioning), and the presentation of food must reinforce the occurrence of species-typical foraging and food-handling behaviors elicited by the natural cues (operant conditioning).

Does misbehavior occur in humans? Research needs to be conducted to answer this question. However, a few years ago during the banquet of my middle son's football team, a young girl seated across from me exhibited a pattern of eating behavior definitely resembling the misbehavior Breland and Breland described. The girl spent several minutes playing with her eating utensils before putting a bite of food in her mouth. At the end of the 1½-hour banquet, she had not finished even half her food. Her parents indicated this was typical behavior for their daughter; it was not unusual for her to spend several hours eating, and she had, in fact, spent her entire last birthday party eating rather than playing with her friends. Furthermore, they said that her older brother also took a long time to eat, but not nearly as long as his sister. Surely other children also show excessively long periods of eating behavior; it may be the association of the utensils with food, as well as the reinforcement of the misbehavior, which contributes to this pattern.

BEFORE YOU GO ON

- **What predisposition allowed Sean to develop an aversion to Tony's mother's lasagna?**
- **What constraint prevented him from learning an aversion to his own mother's cooking?**

SCHEDULE-INDUCED BEHAVIOR

B. F. Skinner (1948) described an interesting pattern of behavior that pigeons exhibited when reinforced for key pecking on a fixed-interval schedule. When food reinforcement was delivered to the pigeons on a fixed-interval 15-second schedule, they developed a "ritualistic" stereotyped pattern of behavior during the interval. The pattern of behavior differed from bird to bird: some walked in circles between food presentations; others scratched the floor; still others moved their heads back and forth. Once a particular pattern of behavior emerged, the pigeons repeatedly exhibited it, with the frequency of the behavior increasing as the birds received more reinforcement. Skinner referred to the behaviors of his pigeons on the interval schedule as examples of **superstitious behavior.**

Why do animals exhibit superstitious behavior? One reasonable explanation suggests that animals have associated the superstitious behavior with reinforcement, and this association causes the animals to exhibit high levels of the superstitious behavior. However, Staddon and Simmelhag's (1971) analysis of superstitious behavior indicates it is not an example of the operant behavior Chapter 4 described. They identified two types of behavior produced when reinforcement (for example, food) is programmed to occur on a regular basis: terminal behavior and interim behavior. **Terminal behavior** occurs during the last few seconds of the interval between reinforcer presentations, and it is reinforcer oriented. Staddon and Simmelhag's pigeons pecked on or near the food hopper that delivered food; this is an example of terminal behavior. **Interim behavior,** in contrast, is not reinforcer oriented. Although contiguity influences the development of terminal behavior, interim behavior does not occur contiguously with reinforcement. Terminal behavior falls between interim behavior and reinforcement but does not interfere with the exhibition of interim behavior.

According to Staddon and Simmelhag, terminal behavior occurs in stimulus situations that are highly predictive of the occurrence of reinforcement; that is, terminal behavior is typically emitted just prior to reinforcement on a fixed-interval schedule. In contrast, interim behavior occurs during stimulus conditions that have a low probability of the occurrence of reinforcement; that is, interim behavior is observed most frequently in the period *following* reinforcement.

The strange, superstitious behavior that Skinner initially described is only one example of interim behavior. Animals exhibit a wide variety of other behaviors (i.e. drinking, running, grooming, nest building, aggression) when reinforcement occurs regularly. When fixed-interval schedules of reinforcement elicit high levels of interim behavior, we refer to it as **schedule-induced behavior.**

Schedule-Induced Polydipsia

The most extensively studied form of schedule-induced behavior is the excessive intake of water (polydipsia) when animals are reinforced with food on a fixed-interval schedule. John Falk (1961) was the first investigator to observe **schedule-induced polydipsia.** Falk deprived rats of food until their body weight was approximately 70 to 80% of their initial weight and then trained them to bar press for food reinforcement. When water was available in an operant chamber, Falk found that the rats consumed excessive amounts of water. Even though Falk's rats were not water deprived, they drank large amounts of water; in fact, under certain conditions, animals provided food reinforcement on an interval schedule will consume as much as one-half their weight in water in a few hours. Note that water deprivation, heat stress, or providing a similar amount of food in one meal cannot produce this level of excessive drinking. Apparently, some important aspect of providing food on an interval schedule can elicit excessive drinking.

Is schedule-induced polydipsia an example of interim behavior? Recall Staddon and Simmelhag's definition—interim behavior occurs in stimulus situations that have a low probability of reinforcement occurrence. Schedule-induced drinking does fit their definition: animals reinforced on an interval schedule typically drink during the period *following* food consumption. In contrast, drinking usually does not occur in the period which precedes the availability of food reinforcement.

Researchers have consistently observed schedule-induced polydipsia in rats given food on an interval schedule (Wetherington, 1982). A variety of different interval schedules of reinforcement have been found to produce polydipsia. For example, Falk (1966) observed polydipsia in rats on a fixed-interval schedule, and Jacquet (1972) observed polydipsia on a variety of compound schedules of reinforcement. Schedule-induced polydipsia has also been found in species other than rats. For example, Shanab and Peterson (1969) reported this behavior in pigeons on an interval schedule of food reinforcement, and Schuster and Woods (1966) observed it in primates.

Several factors contribute to the amount of polydipsia (Wetherington, 1982). First, the intensity of food deprivation affects the level of polydipsia observed. Falk (1969) initially established polydipsia in animals of 70 to 80% normal body weight and then decreased the level of deprivation until they reached 95 to 100% of their initial body weight. Falk discovered that the amount the animal drank declined as body weight increased (or motivation decreased).

Second, Falk (1964, 1966) reported that the palatability of the available fluid affects the amount of schedule-induced polydipsia. Falk observed that level of intake declined when animals received an NaCl (salt) solution instead of water. In a similar study, Gilbert (1974) discovered that rats drank less ethanol (alcohol) solution than water. Furthermore, as the concentration of ethanol was increased, the amount of polydipsia declined.

Third, the level of polydipsia depends on the length of time between reinforcements. A number of studies (Falk, 1966; Flory, 1971) show that an inverted-U-shaped relationship exists between the time interval between reinforcements and the level of polydipsia: the amount of polydipsia increases as the interval length increases to asymptote, and then declines with increased interval length. Falk's 1966 study illustrates this effect. He varied the fixed-interval (FI) length from 20 seconds to 300 seconds. As **Figure 10.3** indicates, the level of polydipsia increased as the FI was increased to 180 seconds and then dropped sharply with a 300-second interval.

Other Schedule-Induced Behaviors

Several other instinctive behaviors are observed in animals on interval schedules. A number of psychologists (King, 1974; Staddon & Ayres, 1975) have reported that interval schedules of reinforcement produce high levels of wheel running.

FIGURE 10.3. The amount of water intake as a function of the length of the fixed-interval schedule of food reinforcement. As the graph shows, the amount of water the animals drank first increased as the interreinforcement interval increased up to 180 seconds, then declined with a 300-second interval.

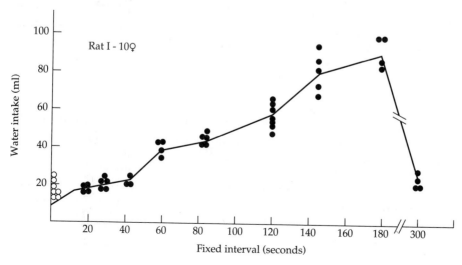

These researchers observed **schedule-induced wheel running** using both food and water reinforcement. Furthermore, Levitsky and Collier (1968) found that the highest rate of wheel running occurs in the time immediately following reinforcement and then decreases as the time for the next reinforcement nears. Moreover, Staddon and Ayres (1975) reported that as the interreinforcement interval increases, the intensity of wheel running initially increases and then declines.

Animals receiving reinforcement on an interval schedule will attack an appropriate target of aggressive behavior. For example, Cohen and Looney (1973) reported that pigeons will attack another bird or a stuffed model of a bird present during key pecking for reinforcement on an interval schedule. Similar **schedule-induced aggression** appears in squirrel monkeys (Hutchinson, Azrin, & Hunt, 1968) and rats (Knutson & Kleinknecht, 1970). Further, Knutson and Kleinknecht (1970) reported that the greatest intensity of aggressive behavior occurred in the immediate postreinforcement period.

The Nature of Schedule-Induced Behavior

Riley and Wetherington (1989) proposed that schedule-induced behavior is an instinctive behavior elicited by periodic reinforcement. The elicited nature of schedule-induced behavior is evident from the fact that animals continue to drink a flavor that was previously paired with illness. (Recall that an aversion to a flavor is established when the flavor is paired with illness.) The relative insensitivity of schedule-induced polydipsia to flavor-aversion learning provides the strongest evidence that reinforcement elicits schedule-induced behavior. Riley, Lotter, and Kulkosky (1979) provide evidence of this insensitivity. They gave two groups of animals spaced food sessions with water available for 13 days. This procedure resulted in schedule-induced polydipsia, or substantial water intake (see **Figure 10.4**). On day 14, animals in group P received an injection of LiCl after experiencing saccharin during the training session; this procedure paired saccharin consumption and illness and led to the establishment of an aversion to saccharin. Evidence of the aversion to saccharin in the group P animals was the significant reduction in saccharin intake on the first test day (day 16). The rats in group S received saline after the training session with saccharin. These animals did not have saccharin paired with illness and developed no aversion to saccharin.

A different result was obtained on the third test day. The saccharin intake in group P was equal to saccharin intake in group S by the third test day (day 20; see **Figure 10.4**). The rapid extinction of a saccharin aversion in group P was much faster than we would generally see with flavor aversions (Elkins, 1973). This rapid extinction suggests an insensitivity of schedule-induced polydipsia to an aversive flavor. It is possible, however, that only a weak aversion was established when saccharin was paired with illness in the schedule-induced polydipsia paradigm.

Hyson, Sickel, Kulkosky, and Riley (1981) evaluated the possibility that the rapid extinction of the saccharin aversion was due to a weak flavor aversion established in a schedule-induced polydipsia situation. These researchers initially established a flavor aversion by pairing saccharin with illness in the animals' home cages. These animals were given either one, two, or four saccharin-illness pairings. After flavor aversion conditioning, animals received either spaced or massed exposure to food in the training situation outside of the home cage. The

FIGURE 10.4. The mean consumption of water during the first 12 days of polydipsia acquisition followed by saccharin and water presentations on alternating days. The animals in group P received a lithium chloride injection following saccharin consumption on day 14, while saline followed saccharin in group S animals. The rapid extinction of the saccharin aversion suggests an insensitivity to an aversive flavor in a schedule-induced polydipsia situation.

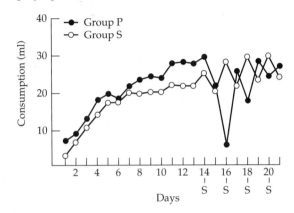

spaced feeding procedure (SIP treatment) produced excessive fluid consumption, while the massed feeding procedure (PD treatment) did not. The researchers found greater suppression of saccharin intake in the massed feeding procedure (PD treatment) than spaced feeding (SIP treatment) during the entire extinction period procedure (see **Figure 10.5**). The suppression over the course of extinction trials in the massed feeding treatment indicates that a strong flavor aversion was established to the saccharin. Yet, the animals in the spaced feeding treatment drank significantly more saccharin than did animals in the massed feeding treatment. This provides strong support for the view that schedule-induced polydipsia is relatively insensitive to a flavor aversion. Further, the continued consumption of saccharin despite its aversion in the spaced feeding paradigm indicates that food elicits drinking.

Hyson, Sickel, Kulkosky, and Riley also observed that the level of suppression of saccharin in the spaced feeding procedure increased with a greater number of saccharin-illness pairings (see **Figure 10.5**). Although continued pairings of saccharin and illness will produce consistently low levels of saccharin consumption (Riley, Wetherington, Wachsman, Fishman, & Kautz 1988), animals who would sip the aversive saccharin flavor after food presentation before, quickly stopped drinking. This cessation of drinking led to the observed suppression of saccharin intake. These results indicate that food elicits drinking, but intake will stop quickly if the flavor is aversive.

Does Schedule-Induced Behavior Occur in Humans?

In many situations in our society, reinforcement is programmed to occur on an interval schedule. Furthermore, excessive levels of instinctive appetitive behaviors

FIGURE 10.5. The mean consumption of saccharin for groups SIP-1, SIP-2, and SIP-4 (top graph) and for groups PD-1, PD-2, and PD-4, (bottom graph). The intake of saccharin was much higher for animals receiving periodic food reinforcements in the training environment (SIP groups) than for animals receiving food in a single meal (PD groups). Also, the greater the number of saccharin-lithium chloride pairings, the stronger the suppression of saccharin intake.

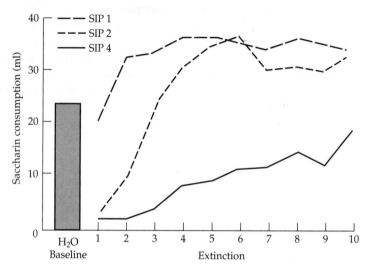

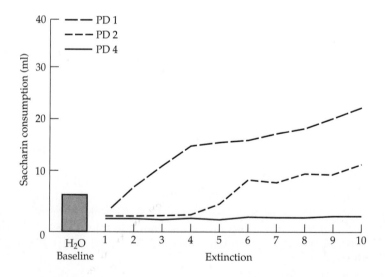

do often occur in humans. Gilbert (1974) suggested that interval schedules could be responsible for the excessive drinking (or alcoholism) in many people. Gilbert's demonstration that rats on an interval schedule consume excessive levels of ethanol supports his view. Animals do not normally drink any ethanol, and the use of an interval schedule of reinforcement is one of the few ways of induc-

313

humans observed that water intake increased when reinforcements (M&Ms) were presented on an interval schedule; the heightened water intake occurred after reinforcement, and, therefore, was a demonstration of schedule-induced behavior in humans. Furthermore, several researchers (Cantor & Wilson, 1984; Cherek, 1982) have observed excessive levels of activities such as eating, smoking, or nail biting in the interval following reinforcement in real-world settings.

While there have been a number of demonstrations of schedule-induced behavior in humans, some important distinctions exist between research with animals and humans (Sanger, 1986). Unlike the consistently powerful demonstration of schedule-induced behavior in animals, evidence indicates that schedule-induced behavior in humans is often weak and variable. Also, schedule-induced behavior develops slowly in animals, but is seen on the first trial in humans. The reasons for differences between animals and humans await future investigation. Further, the real-world relevance of the findings of human schedule-induced behavior is unclear. Schedule-induced behavior in humans decreases even with very short intervals (approximately 240 seconds) between reinforcements. As reinforcers typically occur farther apart in the real world, it is speculative whether reinforcements lead to excessive consummatory behavior in humans.

FLAVOR-AVERSION LEARNING

I have a friend who refuses to walk down an aisle in a supermarket where tomato sauce is displayed; he says that even the sight of cans of tomatoes makes him ill. My oldest son once got sick after eating string beans, and now he refuses to touch them. I once was very nauseated several hours after eating at a local restaurant, and I have not returned since. Almost all of us have some food that we will not eat or a restaurant we avoid. Often the reason for this behavior is that at some time we experienced illness after eating a particular food or in a particular place, and we associated the event with the illness through classical conditioning. Such an experience engenders a flavor aversion to the taste of the food or the place itself. Subsequently, we avoid it.

In Chapter 3, we learned that contiguity plays a critical role in the acquisition of a conditioned response: little conditioning occurs if the CS precedes the UCS by several seconds or minutes. However, animals will develop aversions to taste cues even when the taste stimulus preceded illness by *several hours*. This indicates that, unlike other conditioned responses, the flavor aversion does not depend on contiguity. The association of a flavor with illness is often referred to as **long-delay learning;** this term suggests a difference between flavor-aversion learning and other examples of classical conditioning.

The Selectivity of Flavor-Aversion Learning

We also discovered in Chapter 3 that stimuli differ in salience; that is, some stimuli are more likely than others to become associated with a particular UCS.

Garcia and Koelling's classic study (1966) shows that a taste is more salient when preceding illness than when preceding shock, whereas a light or tone is more salient when preceding shock than when preceding illness. In Garcia and Koelling's study, rats were exposed to either a saccharin taste cue or a light-and-tone compound stimulus. Following exposure to one of these cues, animals received either an electric shock or irradiation-induced illness. **Figure 10.6** presents the results of the study. The animals exhibited an aversion to saccharin when it was paired with illness but not when it was paired with shock. In addition, they developed a fear of the light and tone stimulus when it was paired with shock but not when paired with illness.

On the basis of the Garcia and Koelling study, Seligman (1970) proposed that rats have an evolutionary preparedness to associate tastes with illness. Further support for this view is the observation that adult rats acquire an intense aversion to a flavor after a single taste-illness pairing. Young animals also acquire a strong aversion after one pairing (Klein, Domato, Hallstead, Stephens, & Mikulka, 1975). Apparently, taste cues are very salient in terms of their associability with illness.

Seligman also suggested that rats are contraprepared to become afraid of a light or tone paired with illness. However, other research (Klein, Freda, & Mikulka, 1985) indicates that rats can associate an environmental cue with illness. Klein, Freda, and Mikulka (1985) found that rats avoided a distinctive black compartment previously paired with an illness-inducing apormorphine or lithium chloride injection, while Revusky and Parker (1976) observed that rats did not eat out of a container that had been paired with illness induced by lithium chloride. Although animals can acquire environmental aversions, more trials and careful training procedures are necessary to establish an environmental aversion than a flavor aversion (Riccio & Haroutunian, 1977).

Although rats form flavor aversions more readily than environmental aversions, other species do not show this pattern of stimulus salience. Unlike rats,

FIGURE 10.6. Effects of pairing a gustatory cue or an auditory cue with either external pain or internal illness. In this study, animals readily associated flavor with illness and a click with electric shock, but they did not associate food with electric shock and a click with illness.

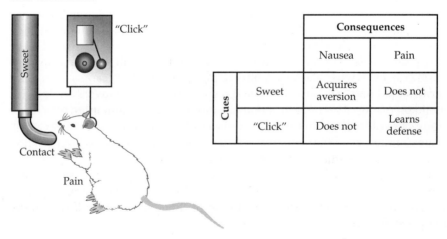

		Consequences	
		Nausea	Pain
Cues	Sweet	Acquires aversion	Does not
	"Click"	Does not	Learns defense

birds acquire visual aversions more rapidly than taste aversions. For example, Wilcoxin, Dragoin, and Kral (1971) induced illness in quail that had consumed sour blue water. They reported that an aversion formed to the blue color, but not to the sour taste. In the same vein, Capretta (1961) found greater salience of visual cues than taste cues in chickens.

Why are visual cues more salient than taste stimuli in birds? According to Garcia, Hankins, and Rusiniak (1974), this salience hierarchy is adaptive. Since birds' seeds are covered by a hard, flavorless shell, they must use visual cues to assess whether food is poisoned; thus, visual cues enable birds to avoid consuming poisonous seeds. Although this view seems reasonable, it does not appear to be completely accurate. According to Braveman, (1974, 1975), the feeding time characteristic of a particular species determines the relative salience of stimuli becoming associated with illness. Rats, which are nocturnal animals, locate their food at night and therefore rely less on visual information than on gustatory information to identify poisoned food. In contrast, birds search for their food during the day, and visual information plays an important role in controlling their food intake. Braveman evaluated this view by examining the salience hierarchies of guinea pigs, which, like birds, seek their food during the day. Braveman found visual cues to be more salient than taste stimuli for guinea pigs.

Flavor-Aversion Learning in Humans

We learned in Chapter 3 that many people report acquiring a flavor aversion as the result of becoming ill after ingesting a particular food or drink. Research has documented the establishment of food aversions in people (see Logue, 1985, for a review of this literature). In one study, Bernstein (1978) found that children in the early stages of cancer acquired an aversion to a distinctively flavored Mapletoff ice cream (maple and black walnut flavor) consumed before toxic chemotherapy that affects the gastrointestinal (GI) tract. Instead of eating Mapletoff ice cream, these children now preferred either to play with a toy or to eat another flavor of ice cream. In contrast, both children who had previously received the toxic therapy to the GI tract without the Mapletoff ice cream and children who had been given the Mapletoff ice cream before toxic chemotherapy that did not involve the GI tract continued to eat the Mapletoff ice cream. Bernstein and Webster (1980) reported similar results in adults.

Both adult and children cancer patients receiving radiation therapy typically lose weight (Bernstein, 1991). These cancer patients also show an aversion to foods eaten prior to chemotherapy (Bernstein & Webster, 1980; Carrell, Cannon, Best, & Stone, 1986). The association of hospital food with illness is a likely cause of the weight loss seen in cancer patients. Can this weight loss be prevented? Experiencing the hospital food without illness prior to the introduction of chemotherapy might work, or experiencing illness without the hospital food might also work. (Refer back to the discussion of the CS preexposure and UCS preexposure effects for an explanation of why these two procedures might reduce the weight loss that occurs with chemotherapy.) Can you think of any other possibilities?

Nature of Flavor-Aversion Learning

Why do animals and people develop aversions to a specific food consumed prior to illness, despite a delay of several hours between consumption of the food and illness? Two very different theories attempt to explain long-delayed flavor-aversion learning: Kalat and Rozin's (1971) learned-safety theory and Revusky's (1977) concurrent interference theory. Research suggests that each process contributes to flavor-aversion learning.

Learned-Safety Theory

James Kalat and Paul Rozin's (1971) **learned-safety theory** suggests that a unique process is responsible for flavor-aversion learning. The contiguity process detailed in Chapter 3 has obvious adaptive significance for most Pavlovian conditioning situations. For example, a child touches a flame and experiences pain. The association of the flame with pain produces the conditioned response of fear; fear elicited on subsequent exposure to the flame motivates this child to avoid pain. However, since the consumption of poisoned food rarely produces immediate illness, the contiguity process characteristic of other classical conditioning situations will not enable an animal to associate food and illness. In Kalat and Rozin's view, a mechanism unique to learning a flavor aversion evolved to allow animals to avoid potentially lethal foods. Kalat and Rozin called this mechanism learned safety.

An animal exposed to a new food consumes only a small portion of it. This low intake of a novel food, called **ingestional neophobia,** has adaptive significance: it prevents animals from consuming large quantities of a potentially poisonous food so that if the food is poisonous, the animals will become sick but not die. According to Kalat and Rozin, if an animal becomes sick within several hours after food consumption, it will associate the food with illness and develop an aversion to that food. However, if illness does not occur, the animal assumes the food is not poisonous and that it can safely consume the food again. Learned safety overcomes an animal's reluctance to eat new foods, enabling it to eat foods which enhance its survival.

Kalat and Rozin (1973), seeking to provide support for their learned-safety view, gave animals one of three treatments. One group of rats received a novel flavor four hours before being made sick (4-P treatment). A second group was made sick half an hour after receiving the novel food (½-P treatment). A third group was given access to the novel flavor and was again exposed to it three and a half hours later; illness followed half an hour later (3½-½-P treatment). A contiguity view of classical conditioning predicts the flavor aversion will be equally strong in the second and third groups, since a half-hour interval separated the flavor and illness in both groups, and the aversion should be weaker in the first group because a four-hour interval separated the flavor and illness. In contrast, the learned-safety view assumes a strong aversion in the second group and a weak aversion in the first and third groups, since the rats in both the first and third groups had four hours after consumption of the novel flavor to learn it was safe. As **Figure 10.7** demonstrates, the results of Kalat and Rozin's study support a learned-safety view of flavor-aversion learning.

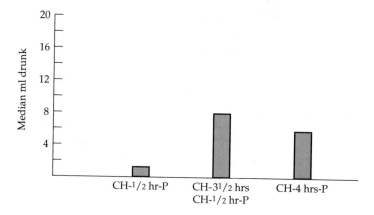

FIGURE 10.7. Mean casein hydrolysate consumption for ½-P, 3½-½-P, and 4-P treatment conditions. The results of this study showed that a significantly stronger aversion to casein hydrolysate developed in the ½-P treatment animals than in either the 3½-½-P or 4-P treatment animals.

Concurrent-Interferrence View

Sam Revusky (1971) argues that the associative processes that influence other forms of classical conditioning also affect flavor-aversion learning. In all cases, Pavlovian conditioning reflects the association of a CS with a UCS. However, since animals often experience several stimuli prior to the UCS, what determines which stimulus becomes associated with the UCS? According to Revusky, proximity is a critical factor in conditioning; the stimulus occurring closest to the UCS will become able to elicit the CR. In this view, a CS will be unable to elicit a CR if other stimuli occur between the CS and UCS. When a stimulus intervenes between the CS and UCS, it will probably produce **concurrent interference.** However, after eating a food, an animal is unlikely to consume another food for several hours. Thus, long-delay learning occurs in flavor-aversion learning as a result of the absence of concurrent interference.

Revusky (1971) conducted a number of studies showing that the presence of other taste cues can interfere with the establishment of a flavor aversion. In a typical study, rats received initial exposure to saccharin (CS) followed by illness 75 minutes later. A second flavor was introduced 15 minutes after the CS and 1 hour before the UCS. For some subjects, tap water was the second solution; for others, it was vinegar. Revusky reported a weaker aversion to saccharin when vinegar rather than water was used as the second solution, indicating that the presentation of vinegar interfered with the establishment of the saccharin aversion. Furthermore, the amount of concurrent interference was related to the intensity of the vinegar: the stronger the vinegar, the weaker the aversion to saccharin. Revusky also found maximum concurrent interference if the second flavor had previously been paired with illness and minimal concurrent interference if the second flavor had previously been experienced without illness.

BEFORE YOU GO ON

- Would the institution of an interval schedule at work cause Sean to eat lasagna at home? At work?
- How would Kalat and Rozin's learned-safety theory explain Sean's aversion to lasagna?

IMPRINTING

Infant Love

You have undoubtedly seen young ducks swimming behind their mother in a lake. What process is responsible for the young birds' attachment to their mother? Konrad Lorenz (1952) investigated this social attachment process, calling it **imprinting.** Lorenz found that a newly hatched bird approaches, follows, and forms a social attachment to the first moving object it encounters. Although typically the first object that the young bird sees is its mother, birds have imprinted to many different and sometimes peculiar objects. In a classic demonstration of imprinting, newly hatched goslings imprinted to Konrad Lorenz and thereafter followed him everywhere. Birds have imprinted to colored boxes and other inanimate objects as well as to animals of different species. After imprinting, the young animal prefers the imprinted object to its real mother; this shows the strength of imprinting.

Although animals have imprinted to a wide variety of objects, certain characteristics of the object affect the likelihood of imprinting. For example, Klopfer (1971) found that ducklings imprinted more readily to a moving object than a stationary object. Also, ducks are more likely to imprint to an object that (1) makes "lifelike" rather than "gliding" movements (Fabricius, 1951); (2) vocalizes rather than remains silent (Collias & Collias, 1956); (3) emits short rhythmic sounds rather than long high-pitched sounds (Weidman, 1956); and (4) measures about 10 cm in diameter (Schulman, Hale, & Graves, 1970).

Harry Harlow (1971) observed that baby primates readily became attached to a soft terry cloth surrogate mother but developed no attachment to a wire mother. Harlow and Suomi (1970) found that infant monkeys preferred a terry cloth mother to a rayon, vinyl, or sandpaper surrogate; liked clinging to a rocking mother rather than to a stationary mother; and chose a warm (temperature) mother over a cold one. Mary Ainsworth and her associates (Ainsworth, 1982; Blehar, Lieberman, & Ainsworth, 1977) reported that human infants also need a warm, responsive mother for social attachment; they found a strong attachment to mothers who were responsive and sensitive to their children's needs. In contrast, infants showed little attachment to anxious or indifferent mothers.

Age plays an important role in the imprinting process. Not only does imprinting occur readily during certain sensitive periods, but also imprinting is less likely to occur following this sensitive period. Illustrating the importance of age in imprinting, Jaynes's (1956) study exposed newly hatched New Hampshire chicks to cardboard cubes at different times. Jaynes reported that five-sixths of the chicks imprinted within 1 to 6 hours after hatching. However, only five-sevenths of the chicks met the criterion for imprinting when exposed to the cardboard cube 6 to 12 hours after hatching. The percentage declined to three-fifths at 24 to 30 hours, two-fifths at 30 to 36 hours, and only one-fifth at 48 to 54 hours.

However, the sensitive period merely reflects a lesser degree of difficulty in forming an attachment; when sufficient experience is given, imprinting will occur after the sensitive period has lapsed. For example, Brown (1975) trained ducklings ranging in age from 20 to 120 hours to follow an object to an equivalent degree. Brown found that although the older the duck, the longer the time required for the duckling to follow the imprinting object, all the ducklings with sufficient training showed an equal degree of attachment to the imprinted object.

The sensitive period for social attachment differs between species; in sheep and goats, it is 2 to 3 hours after birth (Klopfer, Adams, & Klopfer, 1964); in primates, 3 to 6 months and in humans, 6 to 12 months (Harlow, 1971).

Other Examples of Imprinting

A young animal's or person's attachment to "mother" is not the only form of imprinting. We will examine two other instances of imprinting—sexual and food preferences—in this section.

Sexual Preference

Konrad Lorenz (1952) reported an interesting behavior in one of his male jackdaws. The bird attempted courtship feeding with him: it finely minced worms, mixed them with saliva, and attempted to place the worms in Lorenz's mouth. When Lorenz did not open his mouth, he got an earful of worm pulp. Lorenz suggested that the male jackdaw had sexually imprinted to him. The sexual preference of many birds is established during a sensitive period (Eibl-Eibesfeldt, 1970; Lorenz, 1970). Also, the birds' sexual preference does not have to be for their own species; that is, a sexual preference can be established to another species if exposure occurs during the sensitive period. Since sexual preference develops in immature birds when copulation is impossible, the establishment of the birds' sexual preference does not depend upon sexual reinforcement. Further, the imprinted bird's sexual preference is not modified even after sexual experience with another bird species. Perhaps this type of sexual imprinting is a cause of the development and persistence of human sexual preferences.

Food Preference

According to Hess (1962, 1964), an animal's experience with food during a sensitive period of development results in the establishment of a food preference. This preference can develop to a typically nonpreferred food and, once established, is permanent. Consider Hess's (1973) study to illustrate the imprinting of a food preference. Chicks innately prefer to peck at a white circle on a blue background rather than a white triangle on a green background. Hess gave different groups of chicks of various ages experience with the less-preferred stimulus. As **Figure 10.8** indicates, the chicks developed a strong preference for the white-triangle-green-background stimulus if they experienced it

FIGURE 10.8. Percentage of responses to white-triangle-green-background stimulus as a function of age of initial exposure to stimulus. The imprinting to the white-triangle-green-background stimulus developed only during the sensitive period (3 to 5 days old), with imprinting not developing with exposure either before or after the sensitive period.

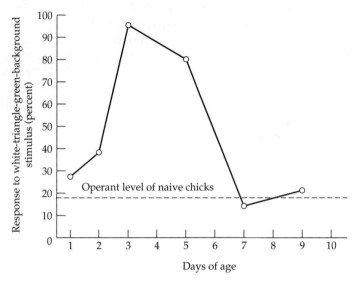

during days 3 to 4 after the chicks had hatched. This preference did not develop if the experience occurred on days 1, 2, 7, or 9 after hatching. These observations indicate that the sensitive period for the establishment of food preference in chicks is 3 to 4 days following hatching. Hess suggests that this time period for the establishment of a food preference is critical because 3-day-old chicks no longer use the yolk sac for nutrients and can peck with maximum accuracy.

Humans differ considerably in their food preferences (Rozin & Zellner, 1985). These preferences may to some degree reflect experience with a specific food during the sensitive period of development. People typically prefer familiar foods, which suggests an imprinting influence in food preference. Food aversions in humans may also be sensitive to a developmental stage; Garb and Stunkard's (1974) observation that people are most apt to develop food aversions between the ages of 6 and 12 years provides additional evidence that imprinting affects the establishment of food preferences and aversions.

Nature of Imprinting

What process allows animals to develop a social attachment (or food preference or sexual preference) during a specific developmental period? Two different views of imprinting have been offered: one suggests that associative learning is responsible for imprinting, and the other proposes that genetic programming produces imprinting. The evidence indicates that both instinctive and associative processes contribute to the imprinting process.

Moltz (1960, 1963) proposed that Pavlovian and operant conditioning are responsible for social imprinting. Consider the imprinting of a chick to its mother to illustrate the **associative learning view of imprinting.** When the chick is old enough to move around in its environment, any large object (for example, mother) in the environment attracts the chick's attention, and it orients toward the object. The chick at this developmental age has little fear of new objects in its environment; therefore, only a low level of arousal will be conditioned to these objects. When the chick's fear system does emerge, new environmental objects will elicit high levels of arousal. Since familiar objects produce only low levels of arousal, their presence elicits relief. This relief reduces the chick's fear and reinforces its approach response, which enables it to reach the familiar object. Thus, the chick develops an attachment to mother (or any other object) because her presence elicits relief and reduces fear. A considerable amount of literature indicates that the imprinted object does have fear-reducing properties. For example, Bateson (1969) and Hoffman (1968) noted that the imprinting object's presence reduced distress vocalizations in birds. Harry Harlow's (1971) classic research with primates clearly shows the fear-reducing properties of "mama."

Harlow (1971) observed that young primates up to 3 months old do not exhibit any fear of new events; after 3 months, a novel object elicits intense fear. Young primates experience a rapid reduction in fear when clinging to their mother. For example, 3-month-old primates are extremely frightened when introduced to a mechanical monster or plastic toy and will run to their mother; clinging to her apparently causes the young primates' fear to dissipate. Human children show a similar development of fear at approximately 6 months of age (Schaffer & Emerson, 1964). Before this time, they exhibit no fear of new objects. After children are 6 months old, an unfamiliar object elicits fear, and children react by running to mother and clinging to her, which causes their fear to subside.

Is this fear reduction responsible for the young primate's or human's attachment to "mother"? Harlow developed two inanimate surrogate mothers to investigate the factors that influence attachment to the mother (see **Figure 10.9**). Each "mother" had a bare body of welded wire; one had only the wire body, and the other was covered with soft terry cloth. In typical studies, primates were raised with both a wire and a cloth-covered surrogate mother. While both the wire and cloth surrogate mothers were equally unresponsive, frightened young primates experienced fear reduction when clinging to the cloth mother but showed no reduction in distress when with their wire mother. When aroused, the infants were extremely motivated to reach their cloth mother, even jumping over a high plexiglass barrier to get to it. In contrast, the frightened young primates showed no desire to approach the wire mother. Also, the young primate preferred to remain with the cloth mother in the presence of a dangerous object rather than to run away alone; however, if the wire mother was present, the frightened primate ran away. These observations indicate that the cloth mother contained the essential components necessary for infant bonding.

Mary Ainsworth and her colleagues (Ainsworth, 1982; Blehar, Lieberman, and Ainsworth (1977) reported a similar reaction in human infants. Consider the Blehar, Lieberman, and Ainsworth (1977) study to illustrate this maternal

FIGURE 10.9. Cloth and wire surrogate mothers.

attraction. They initially observed the maternal behavior of white middle-class Americans feeding their infants from birth to 54 weeks of age. They identified two categories of maternal care: one group of mothers showed responsivity and sensitivity to their children during feeding; the other mothers were indifferent to their infants' needs. During the second stage of their study, Blehar, Lieberman, and Ainsworth examined the behavior of these infants at 1 year of age in a strange environment. In the unfamiliar place, the interested mothers' children occasionally sought their mothers' attention; when left alone in a strange situation, these children were highly motivated to remain with the mother when reunited. In addition, once these children felt secure in the new place, they explored and played with toys. The researchers called this type of mother-infant

bond a **secure relationship.** The behavior of these secure children strikingly resembles the response of Harlow's rhesus monkeys to the cloth mother. In contrast to this secure relationship, children of indifferent mothers frequently cried
and were apparently distressed. Their alarm was not reduced by the presence of
the mother. Also, these children avoided contact with their mothers, either because the mothers were uninterested or because the mothers actually rejected
them. The researchers labeled this mother-infant interaction an **anxious relationship.** The failure of the mothers of these anxious children to induce security
certainly parallels the infant primates' response to the wire surrogate mother.

Moltz's associative learning view suggests that initial conditioning of low
arousal to the imprinting object develops because the object is attention-
provoking, orienting the animal toward the imprinting object. Chicks imprint
more readily to objects moving away than to objects moving toward them. One
would assume that advancing objects would be more attention-provoking than
retreating objects. Chicks' greater imprinting to objects moving away argues
against an explanation of imprinting based only on simple associative learning.
This observation also points to another problem with an associative learning
view: some objects are more likely than others to become imprinting objects. For
example, animals imprint more readily to objects having characteristics of adult
members of their species. A simple associative explanation of imprinting would
not assume that the characteristics of the imprinting object are important: any
object attracting the animal's attention prior to the development of fear should
become able to provide security and, therefore, a strong attachment should en-
sue. The fact that the specific attributes of the object are important in the formation of a social attachment argues against a purely associative explanation of
imprinting.

An Instinctive View of Imprinting

Konrad Lorenz (1935) suggested that imprinting is a genetically programmed form of learning. Imprinting is adaptive because it ensures that environmental events elicit instinctive reactions that enhance the animal's survival.
Hess (1973) also proposed that inheritance governs the imprinting process. Hess
eloquently describes his **instinctive view of imprinting,** or of the role of instinct
in the social attachment of the young mallard to its mother:

> We must consider that young ducks innately possess a schema of the natural
> imprinting object, so that the more a social object fits this schema, the stronger
> the imprinting that occurs to the object. This innate disposition with regard to
> the type of object learned indicates that social imprinting is not just simply an
> extremely powerful effect of the environment upon the behavior of an animal.
> Rather, there has been an evolutionary pressure for the young bird to learn the
> right thing—the natural parent—at the right time—the first day of life—the
> time of the sensitive period that has been genetically provided for. (p. 380)

Several observations indicate that imprinting differs from other forms of associative learning (Graham, 1981). The animal's response to the imprinting object is less susceptible to change than an animal's reaction to events acquired
through conventional associative learning is. For example, conditioned stimuli
that elicit saliva quickly extinguish when food is discontinued. Similarly, the

absence of shock produces a rapid extinction of fear. In contrast, the elimination of reinforcement does not typically lead to a loss of reaction to an imprinting object. Hess (1962, 1964) observed that once a 3- to 4-day-old chick developed a food preference to a less preferred object, this preference remained, despite the subsequent lack of food reinforcement when the chick pecked at this object.

While punishment quickly alters an animal's response to conditioned stimuli associated with reinforcement, animals seem insensitive to punishment from an imprinting object. Kovach and Hess (1963) found that chicks approached the imprinting object despite its administration of electric shock. Harlow's (1971) research shows how powerful the social attachment of the infant primate is to its surrogate mother. Harlow constructed four abusive "monster mothers." One rocked violently from time to time; a second projected an air blast in the infant's face. Primate infants clung to these mothers even as they were abused. The other two monster mothers were even more abusive: one tossed the infant off her, and the other shot brass spikes as the infant approached. Although the infants were unable to cling to these mothers continuously, they resumed clinging as soon as possible when the abuse stopped. Harlow's observations are consistent with observations of many abused children, who typically desire to return to their abusive parent.

THE AVOIDANCE OF AVERSIVE EVENTS

Species-Specific Defense Reactions

We discovered earlier in the chapter that animals possess instinctive responses enabling them to obtain reinforcement (e.g., food, water, mate). Robert Bolles (1970, 1978) suggested that animals also have **species-specific defense reactions (SSDR)** that allow them to avoid dangerous events. According to Bolles, animals have little opportunity to learn to avoid danger: they either possess an instinctive means of keeping out of trouble, or they perish. For example, a deer does not have time to learn to avoid its predator. Unless the deer possesses an instinct for avoiding predators, it will probably wind up as a predator's meal.

The instinctive responses that enable animals to avoid aversive events differ. An animal's evolutionary history determines which behaviors will become SSDRs: responses that enable animals to avoid aversive events will remain in their genetic programming, whereas nonadaptive responses will not be passed on to future generations. According to Bolles, animals experiencing danger narrow their response repertoire to those behaviors that they expect will eliminate the danger. Since evolution has proved the species-specific defense reactions to be effective and other behaviors likely to produce failure, behaviors other than the species-specific defense reactions probably would be nonadaptive. Thus, animals limit their reactions to SSDRs as they attempt to avoid danger.

Rats employ three different species-specific defense reactions: running, freezing, and fighting. They attempt to run from a distant danger; a close danger motivates freezing. When these two responses fail, rats use aggressive behavior to avoid aversive events. Other animals employ different instinctive responses to avoid danger: the mouse, as Bolles suggests in a quote from Robert

Burns's ("To a Mouse"), is "a wee timorous beastie" when experiencing danger, because this is the only way this small and relatively defenseless animal can avoid danger. In contrast, the bird just flies away.

A study by Bolles and Collier (1976) demonstrates that the cues that predict danger not only motivate defensive behavior but also determine which response rats will exhibit when they expect danger. Bolles and Collier's rats received shock in a square or a rectangular box. After they experienced the shock, the rats either remained in the dangerous environment or were placed in another box where no shocks were given. The researchers found that defensive behavior occurred only when the rats remained in the compartment where they had previously been shocked. Also, Bolles and Collier found that a dangerous square compartment produced a freezing response, while a dangerous rectangular box caused the rats to run. These results suggest that the particular SSDR produced depends on the nature of the dangerous environment.

Psychologists have found that animals easily learn to avoid an aversive event when they can use an SSDR. For example, rats readily learn to run to avoid being shocked. Similarly, pigeons easily learn to avoid shock by flying from perch to perch. In contrast, animals have difficulty learning to avoid an aversive event when they must emit a behavior other than an SSDR to avoid the aversive event. D'Amato and Schiff's (1964) study provides an example of this difficulty. Trying to train rats to bar press to avoid electric shock, D'Amato and Schiff reported that over half of their rats, even after having participated in more than 7,000 trials over a 4-month period, failed to learn the avoidance response.

Bolles (1969) provides additional evidence of the importance of instinct in avoidance learning. He reported that rats quickly learned to run in an activity wheel to avoid electric shock, but found no evidence of learning when the rats were required to stand on their hind legs to avoid shock (see **Figure 10.10**). Although Bolles's rats stood on their hind legs in an attempt to escape from the compartment where they were receiving shock, these rats did not learn the same behavior to avoid shock. According to Bolles, the rats' natural response in a small compartment was to freeze, and this innate SSDR prevented them from learning a nonspecies-specific defensive reaction as the avoidance behavior.

Predispositions and Avoidance Learning

Bolles (1978) suggested that sign tracking is responsible for the development of avoidance learning (see Chapter 3). In Bolles's view, aversive events elicit instinctive species-specific defensive responses. The environment present during aversive events becomes able to produce these instinctive defensive reactions as a conditioned response. Whereas instinctive CRs to cues associated with reinforcement elicit approach and contact behavior that enables an animal to obtain reinforcement, stimuli associated with aversive events produce instinctive defensive responses that allow the animal to avoid aversive events.

Bolles's approach suggests that Pavlovian conditioning rather than operant conditioning is responsible for avoidance learning. According to Bolles, the association of environmental stimuli with aversive events rather than reinforcement causes the development of avoidance behavior. Bolles and Riley's (1973) study shows that reinforcement is not responsible for the rapid acquisition of

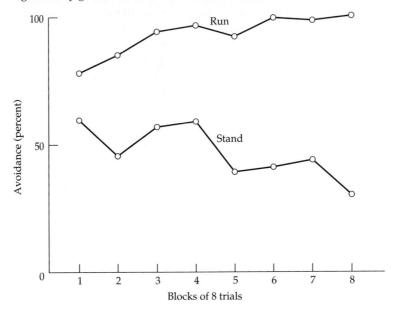

FIGURE 10.10. Percentage of avoidance responses during training in animals that could avoid shock by running or standing on their hind legs. The results of this study show that avoidance learning was significantly greater if the rats could run to avoid shock.

avoidance behavior. In their study, some animals could avoid being shocked by freezing. Bolles and Riley reported that after only a few minutes of training, their animals were freezing most of the time. Two additional groups were included in their study: one group was punished for freezing and could avoid shock by not freezing; the other group was shocked regardless of their behavior. Bolles and Riley observed that the rats punished for freezing still froze much of the time. Furthermore, rats punished for freezing froze as much as the rats shocked regardless of their behavior. Bolles suggested that when an animal is in a small confined area and anticipates an aversive event, it freezes. The animals punished for freezing would still have frozen all the time, in Bolles's view, had frequent shocks not disrupted their freezing. Yet, as soon as the shock ended, the anticipation elicited the instinctive freezing response. Thus, with the exception of shock-induced disruption of freezing in animals punished for freezing, animals either reinforced or punished for freezing showed equivalent levels of freezing behavior. These results suggest that the contingency between the freezing response and the aversive event did not affect these animals' behavior.

BEFORE YOU GO ON

- **Can imprinting explain Sean's preference for his mother's cooking?**
- **Is an SSDR involved in Sean's avoidance of lasagna?**

THE BIOLOGY OF REINFORCEMENT
AND PUNISHMENT

327

CHAPTER 10
Biological Influences
on Learning

People's responses to reinforcement and punishment differ considerably. Some of us are intensely motivated to obtain reinforcement; others show a lack of interest. Similarly, punishment can readily modify some people's behavior; others seem totally oblivious to it. Although psychological factors clearly can affect our sensitivity to reinforcement and punishment, physiological research during the past 40 years demonstrates that several brain systems are significantly involved in our responses to both reinforcers and punishers. Effective functioning of these systems allows us to obtain socially acceptable reinforcers and avoid potential punishments.

Electrical Stimulation of the Brain

James Olds and Peter Milner's research (Olds & Milner, 1954) made a significant contribution to psychology. Olds and Milner found that stimulating some areas of the brain is reinforcing, while stimulating other areas is aversive. It is interesting that they made their classic observations accidentally, while trying to determine the effects of activating the reticular formation. Their electrode placement mistakenly swung forward into the hypothalamus. When this area was aroused, their rats behaved as if the stimulation was reinforcing. For example, the rats strongly preferred the place on the long table where they received the stimulation.

To evaluate their findings further, Olds and Milner made the electrical stimulation contingent on pressing a bar in an operant chamber (see **Figure 10.11**). They found that the rats pressed a bar to receive brain stimulation. The animals' behavior to obtain brain stimulation is called either **electrical stimulation of the brain (ESB)** or intracranial self-stimulation (ICSS). Many species, including pigeons (Goodman & Brown, 1966), rats (Olds & Milner, 1954), cats and dogs (Stark & Boyd, 1963), primates (Brady, 1961), and humans (Heath, 1955) have demonstrated that brain stimulation can be reinforcing.

Although Olds and Milner found that stimulating many brain areas provided reinforcement, activation of other brain areas was aversive. Animals receiving this aversive stimulation learned a new behavior to terminate or avoid it. For example, Delgado, Roberts, and Miller (1954) discovered that cats learned to turn a paddle wheel to terminate brain stimulation, just as they would have done to escape an electrical shock to the feet.

Anatomical Location of Reinforcement and Punishment

Larry Stein and his associates (Stein, 1969) presented evidence indicating that a group of nerve fibers, the **medial forebrain bundle (MFB)** located in the limbic system, is the brain's reinforcement center. Stimulation of the MFB motivates us to approach reinforcement. Another limbic system fiber tract, the **periventricular tract (PVT),** represents the brain's punishment center. Activation of the PVT motivates us to avoid punishment.

FIGURE 10.11. (a) A rat presses a bar for electrical brain stimulation (ESB). (b) A sample cumulative record. Note the extremely high rate of responding (over 2,000 bar presses per hour) that occurred for more than 24 hours and was followed by a period of sleep.

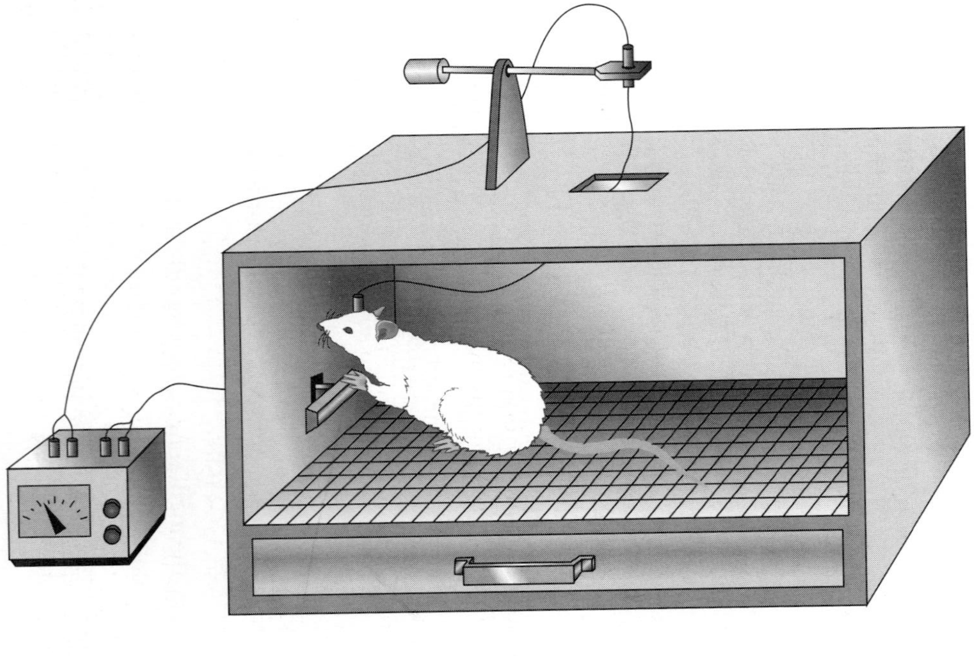

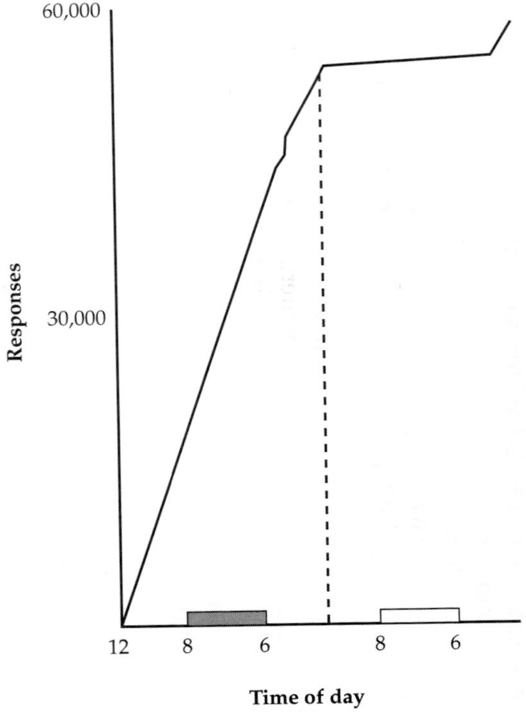

Stein also suggested how the reinforcement (MFB) and punishment (PVT) systems exert control over operant behavior. Activity in the PVT inhibits our tendency to approach events. Stimulation of the MFB—by either internal activation or the presence of a reinforcing event—inhibits the amygdala. The amygdala excites the PVT through the medial thalamus and hypothalamus; inhibiting the amygdala lessens this excitation and thereby suppresses the effectiveness of the PVT punishment system. Stein's theory portrays animals and humans as normally cautious when encountering new events. The MFB reinforcement system inhibits our hesitancy and motivates approach behavior.

The Influence of the Medial Forebrain Bundle

Stimulation of the MFB has four characteristics: (1) it is highly reinforcing; (2) it motivates behavior; (3) its functioning is stimulated by the presence of reinforcers; and (4) its reinforcing effects are enhanced by deprivation. We will discuss each of these characteristics in the following sections.

The Reinforcing Effect of MFB Stimulation

You place a dollar in a video poker machine and pull the lever. When the machine stops spinning, you get four aces and win $200. Not surprisingly, you shout in joy. Why are you so overjoyed after winning $200? The research on MFB stimulation provides a likely answer.

Valenstein and Beer's (1964) study of the reinforcing properties of brain stimulation in rats found that for weeks, rats would press a bar that delivered stimulation of the MFB up to 30 times per minute, stopping for only a short time to eat and groom. These rats responded until exhausted, fell asleep for several hours, and awoke to resume bar pressing. But would electrical stimulation of the brain (ESB) have a more powerful effect on behavior than conventional reinforcers such as food, water, or sex? Routtenberg and Lindy (1965) constructed a situation in which pressing one lever initiated brain stimulation and pressing another lever produced food. The rats in this experiment were placed in this situation for only one hour a day and had no other food source. Still, all of the rats spent the entire hour pressing for brain stimulation, eventually starving themselves to death. Obviously, ESB has greater reinforcing value than food, at least to rats.

The pleasurable aspect of brain stimulation has also been demonstrated in humans. For example, Ervin, Mark, and Stevens (1969) reported that MFB stimulation not only eliminated pain in cancer patients but also produced a euphoric feeling (approximately equivalent to the effect of two strong alcoholic drinks) that lasted several hours. Sem-Jacobson (1968) found that patients suffering intense depression, fear, or physical pain found brain stimulation pleasurable; patients who felt well prior to ESB experienced only mild pleasure.

The Motivational Influence of MFB Stimulation

You go to the bank and cash a $50 check that you received for your birthday. The cashier hands you two $20 and one $10 bill. How does this make you feel? In all likelihood, you would experience a little pleasure from feeling the bills in your palm. Now what might you do next? You could set the money in a drawer for a rainy day, or take it to the music store and buy the latest CD. Perhaps you go to the store. This demonstrates that reinforcers have both pleasurable and motivating properties. The pleasurable property is the feeling that you experience when you receive the reinforcer (money). The motivating property is that, upon receipt of the reinforcer, you are motivated to perform another behavior (spend it).

The research of Elliot Valenstein and his associates (Valenstein, Cox, & Kakolewski, 1969) demonstrated that activation of the medial forebrain bundle motivates behavior. The researchers found that the specific response that brain stimulation motivates depends upon the prevailing environmental conditions: brain stimulation motivates eating when food is available and drinking when water is present. This phenomenon is called **stimulus-bound behavior.**

To this point, we have discussed the reinforcing and motivational effects of direct MFB stimulation. Yet, we do not have electrodes implanted in our MFBs; naturally occurring processes must activate this brain area. The next two sections explain how reinforcement and deprivation naturally stimulate the MFB and increase our search for reinforcement.

The Influence of Reinforcers on MFB Function

Many people report finding sexual intercourse more pleasurable after watching an erotic film. Based on our discussion to this point, do you think it is possible that the movie activates the MFB, which then increases the reinforcing quality of sex? A number of studies have demonstrated that a reinforcing activity (for example, sexual activity) or stimuli associated with a reinforcing activity (for example, an erotic film) enhances the functioning of the MFB.

Mendelson (1967) demonstrated the effect of water on the reinforcement value of ESB. Mendelson compared how often rats in his study pressed a bar to obtain brain stimulation when water was available and when it was not. His results showed that rats exhibited a significantly higher rate of bar-pressing when water was present than when it was absent. Coons and Cruce (1968) found that the presence of food increased the number of attempts to obtain brain stimulation, and Hoebel (1969) reported that a peppermint odor (back to the stimuli associated with reinforcement) or a few drops of sucrose in the mouth had the same effect. These results suggest that the presence of reinforcement enhances the functioning of the MFB. The effect of this enhanced functioning is an increased responding for reinforcers. Further, reinforcers will be more pleasurable due to the higher level of MFB activity. Returning to our example, watching an erotic film activates the MFB, which motivates people to engage in sexual activity, which they find highly reinforcing (pleasurable).

The Influence of Deprivation on the MFB

You go the ball park on a very hot day and drink several beers. It is cold the next time you go to the ball park, and you drink only one beer. Why do you drink more beers on a hot than a cold day? The effect of deprivation on MFB functioning gives us an answer to this question.

Deprivation is a restriction in access to a reinforcer. Drinking ice water is very satisfying on a hot day, yet on a cold day, ice water has little incentive value. This illustrates one characteristic of deprivation: a physiological need increases the incentive value of reinforcers. In this example, thirst on a hot day (a physiological need) enhances the reinforcement value of ice water. Increased activity in the brain's reinforcement system is one probable mechanism behind this enhancement.

Brady (1961) showed that the rate of a rat's self-stimulation varies depending on its level of hunger; the longer the rats were deprived of food, the more intensely they pressed the bar to obtain brain stimulation. Similarly, Olds (1962) found that rats that had been deprived of water valued brain stimulation more than nondeprived rats did.

Mesotelencephalic Reinforcement System

In the late 1980s, Wise and Rompre concluded that the medial forebrain bundle is only part of the brain's reinforcement system. Wise and Rompre (1989) suggest that the **mesotelencephalic reinforcement system** contains two neural pathways. One is the **tegmentostriatal pathway,** which begins in the lateral and preoptic areas of the hypothalamus (see **Figures 10.12 and 10.13**). Neurons in these areas of the hypothalamus detect reinforcement-related stimuli (for example, food or stimuli associated with food) and transmit the information through the MFB to the ventral tegmental area (VTA). Neural impulses from the VTA then move to the nucleus accumbens (NA), septum, and prefrontal cortex, the brain area that plans the response to reinforcement-related stimuli. The second pathway is the **nigrostriatal pathway** (refer to **Figures 10.12 and 10.13**). This pathway begins in the substantia nigra (nigro-) and projects to the neostriatum (-striatal), consisting of the caudate nucleus and putamen.

Function of the Two Reinforcement Systems

Why would the brain have two separate reinforcement systems? It is likely that the two pathways regulate two different aspects of reinforcement (Vaccarino, Schiff, & Glickman, 1989). The tegmentostriatal pathway detects whether sufficient motivation is present for voluntary behavior to occur. For example, a rat will not bar press for food if it is not deprived or if the value of the reinforcer is insufficient. In this context, deprivation and reinforcer value are called motivational variables. Motivational variables also affect the behavioral effects of stimulating structures in the tegmentostriatal pathway other than the MFB (Evans & Vaccarino, 1990). In contrast, motivational variables do not influence the behavioral effects of stimulation of structures in the nigrostriatal pathway (Winn, Williams, & Herberg, 1982).

In addition to motivating behavior, reinforcers facilitate the storage of experiences, commonly known as memory. Memory allows past experiences to influence future behavior—the rat has to be able to remember that it was the bar press that delivered the ESB. While structures in the nigrostriatal pathway are not involved in the motivational aspect of reinforcement, they do play a role in the consolidation, or the permanent storage, of a memory. Evidence for this influence is that memory is significantly enhanced when an animal is exposed to a positive reinforcer for a short time following training (Coulombe & White, 1982; Major & White, 1978). Other studies have shown that stimulation of the nigrostriatal pathway, but not the tegmentostriatal pathway, increases the consolidation of the memory of a reinforcing experience (Carr & White, 1984).

The neurotransmitter dopamine plays a significant role in regulating the behavioral effects of reinforcement (Vaccarino, Schiff, & Glickman, 1989; Wise, 1996). Dopamine regulates only part of the tegmentostriatal system (refer to **Figure 10.13**). The fibers from the lateral hypothalamus to the ventral tegmental area (VTA) are not dopaminergic (Gallistel, Shizgal, & Yeoman, 1981). The neurons in this tract that motivate self-stimulation are heavily myelinated (dopaminergic neurons are not) and thus conduct neural impulses very rapidly (the myelin covering of axons is responsible for the rapid conduction of neural impulses). Dopamine does, however, govern the activity of the neurons that connect the **ventral tegmental area (VTA)** to the nucleus accumbens, septum, and prefrontal cortex, and several lines of evidence indicate that dopamine plays an important role in mediating the effect of reinforcement on behavior.

One indication of dopaminergic influence is the effect of the dopamine agonists amphetamine and cocaine, which have powerful reinforcing properties (see **Figure 10.14**). (A drug agonist stimulates or enhances the activity of a naturally occurring chemical. Thus, cocaine and amphetamine increase the level of dopamine activity at dopaminergic receptors.) Some people are highly motivated to obtain substances such as amphetamine or cocaine. The reinforcing properties of these drugs come in part from their ability to activate the dopaminergic tegmentostriatal pathway. Many researchers have shown that an-

FIGURE 10.12. A view of the mesotelencephalic reinforcement system. The tegmentostriatal pathway begins in the lateral and preoptic area of the hypothalamus and goes through the medial forebrain bundle to the ventral tegmental area. Fibers from the ventral tegmental area then go to the nucleus accumbens, septum, and prefrontal cortex. The nigrostriatal pathway begins in the substantia nigra and projects to the neostriatum.

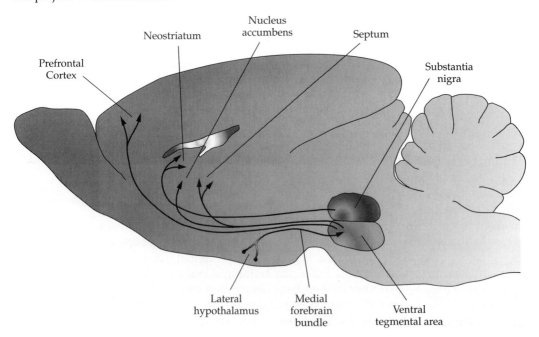

imals will quickly learn a behavior that enables them to self-administer amphetamine and cocaine (Bozarth & Wise, 1983; Koob & Bloom, 1983). They also will learn, and will emit at a high rate, a behavior that triggers injections of cocaine or amphetamine into the **nucleus accumbens (NA)** (Carr & White, 1986). Further, dopamine levels in the nucleus accumbens are elevated after the administration of amphetamine (Hurd & Ungerstedt, 1989) and cocaine (Hurd, Kehr, & Ungerstedt, 1988).

A variety of reinforcers other than cocaine and amphetamine initiate the release of dopamine, providing support for dopaminergic involvement in the neural control of reinforcement. For example, electrical stimulation of the MFB (Blaha & Phillips, 1990) and of the VTA (Phillips, Blaha, & Fibinger, 1989) causes the release of dopamine in the NA. When animals perform a behavior in order to receive stimulation of the MFB or VTA, dopamine is also released. Natural reinforcers, such as food and water, also elicit NA release of dopamine, probably due to the reinforcing properties of drinking or eating in water- or food-deprived animals (Chang, Mark, Hernandez, & Hoebel, 1988). Researchers have also found increased dopamine levels following the administration of alcohol

FIGURE 10.13. The mesotelencephalic reinforcement system consists of two brain pathways. The tegmentostriatal pathway mediates the influence of motivation on reinforcement, and the nigrostriatal pathway is involved in memory consolidation.

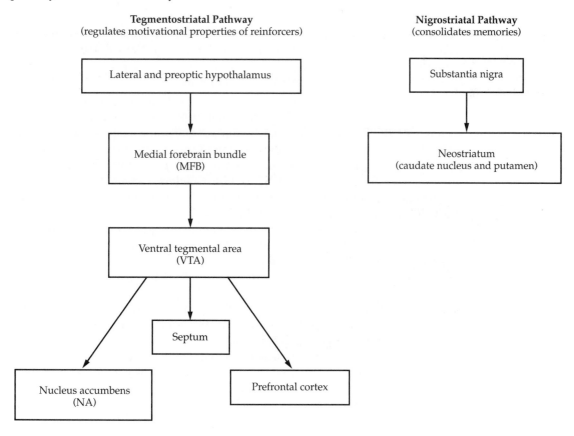

FIGURE 10.14. Diagram showing the separate mechanisms by which heroin and cocaine activate the nucleus accumbens.

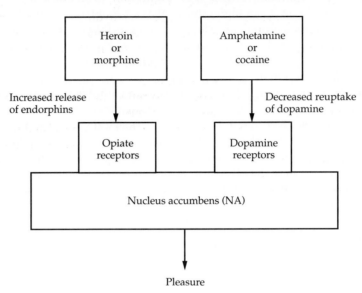

(Gessa, Muntoni, Collu, Vargui, & Mereu, 1985), cannabis (Chen, Paredes, & Gardner, 1994), and nicotine (Mereu, Yoon, Boi, Gessa, Naes, & Westfall, 1986).

Opiate Activation of the Tegmentostriatal Pathway

The opiate drugs also appear to be capable of stimulating the tegmentostriatal pathway (Vaccarino, Schiff, & Glickman, 1989). Animals will learn to self-administer opiate drugs such as heroin or morphine just as they learn to self-administer amphetamine and cocaine (Koob, Pettit, Ettenberg, & Bloom, 1984). Animals will also bar press to receive injections of heroin or morphine into the VTA (Bozarth & Wise, 1981) or NA (Goeders, Lane, & Smith, 1984). Injection of opiate antagonists into the VTA or NA causes rats to stop bar pressing (Britt & Wise, 1983).

Do opiates stimulate the same dopaminergic receptors in the NA and VTA as amphetamine and cocaine? Studies suggest that the opiate drugs activate opiate-sensitive receptors and not dopaminergic receptors (refer to **Figure 10.14**). Drugs that antagonize dopamine receptors reduce the self-administration of amphetamine or cocaine but do not affect self-stimulation for opiate drugs (Ettenberg, Pettit, Bloom, & Koob, 1982). Vaccarino, Bloom, and Koob (1985) reported that the administration of opiate antagonists causes animals to stop self-administering morphine but not cocaine. On the basis of these findings, Koob (1992) suggested that the tegmentostriatal pathway contains two separate types of receptors; dopaminergic agonists activate the dopamine receptors, and opiates stimulate the opiate receptors with the same result—activation of the nucleus accumbens (see **Figure 10.14**).

Some people find gambling highly reinforcing, while others seem totally disinterested. While these differences could be due to differential reinforcement experiences (people who like gambling have been reinforced, and people who dislike gambling have not), individual differences in the functioning of the mesotelencephalic reinforcement system could also influence whether a person finds gambling reinforcing. Individual differences in responding to other reinforcers, both drug and nondrug, could also reflect differences in the level at which the brain's reinforcement system functions.

DeSousa and Vaccarino (2001) suggest that the motivational and reinforcing effects of reinforcers are positively correlated with the level of activity in the mesotelencephalic reinforcement system. How has this positive correlation been documented? One way is to compare animals who respond differently to various reinforcers. For example, some rats consume high levels of sucrose (high sucrose feeders, or HSFs), while other rats consume low levels of sucrose (low sucrose feeders, or LSFs). Sills, Onalaja, and Crawley (1998) found greater dopamine release in the nucleus accumbens when HSFs were given access to sucrose than when LSFs were given access to success. One interpretation of these results is that HSFs find sucrose more reinforcing than do LSFs (and thus consume more sucrose) because their mesotelencephalic reinforcement systems are more responsive to sucrose.

We have suggested that the greater response of HSFs to sucrose is due to the greater response of the mesotelencephalic reinforcement system. If this is a valid interpretation, HSFs should be more responsive to other reinforcers than LSFs are. Amphetamine is a powerful reinforcer that causes the release of dopamine in the nucleus accumbens. And consistent with the prediction, self-administration of amphetamine is significantly higher in HSFs than LSFs (DeSousa, Bush, & Vaccarino, 2000).

Animals also differ in terms of their response to novel environments: low responders (LRs) show much less locomotor response in a novel environment than do high responders (HRs). Perhaps not surprising, HRs self-administer amphetamine more than do LRs (Piazza, Deminiere, LeMoal, & Simon, 1989). Further, dopamine release in response to amphetamine was significantly higher in HRs than LRs (Hooks, Colvin, Juncos, & Justice, 1992).

Reconsider our example of gambling. Our discussion suggests that reinforcement (winning) releases more dopamine in the nucleus accumbens of gamblers than it does in nongamblers. And the greater release of dopamine is one reason why some people gamble and others do not. It also may well be a reason why some people smoke cigarettes and others do not, and why gamblers seem more likely to smoke cigarettes.

The Impact of the PVT Punishment System

Electrical stimulation of the periventricular tract (PVT) produces three effects identical to those that aversive events such as electrical shock induce (Olds, 1962). First, PVT stimulation elicits jumping, biting, and vocalizations, all behaviors that electrical shock and other painful agents can produce. Second, both

PVT stimulation and conventional punishers suppress reinforcement-seeking behavior. Third, animals are motivated to terminate PVT stimulation as well as to acquire behaviors that prevent activation of the PVT. Shock and other aversive events also motivate escape and avoidance behaviors.

Destruction of the PVT produces animals insensitive to aversive events. For example, Margules and Stein (1969) noted that rats with PVT lesions showed large deficits in their ability to avoid electrical shock, suggesting that effective avoidance of and escape from aversive events depends on the effective functioning of the PVT.

The chemical transmitter substance acetylcholine has been implicated in the motivation of escape and avoidance behavior (Carlton, 1969). Injections of drugs that activate cholinergic neurons (those neurons for which acetylcholine is the transmitter substance) increase the influence of punishing agents. In contrast, drugs which block cholinergic activity reduce the effectiveness of punishment.

Margules and Stein (1967) provided evidence of cholinergic transmission in the PVT punishment system. They injected directly into the punishment area drugs that either increase cholinergic activity (for example, carbachol) or decrease it (for example, atropine). Before the injections, rats had been trained to bar press for a reinforcer (milk) and had experienced a tone paired with electrical shocks. Margules and Stein administered the injections while presenting this tone. They reported that drugs that arouse cholinergic neurons increased the effectiveness of the tone in suppressing bar pressing. In contrast, drugs that inhibit cholinergic neurons decreased the suppressive ability of the tone.

One effect of alcohol and similar drugs is to reduce fear and anxiety. Evidence suggests that these drugs can affect the PVT punishment system. For example, Margules and Stein (1967) found that the drug oxazepam not only reduced the suppressive effects of aversive events (for example, electric shock, nonreward, bitter quinine), but also antagonized the punishing effects of brain stimulation.

BEFORE YOU GO ON

- **Describe the influence of the periventricular tract on Sean's aversion to lasagna.**
- **How would cocaine influence Sean's aversion to lasagna?**

CHAPTER SUMMARY

Psychologists have generally assumed that some laws govern the learning of all behaviors. This view has enabled psychologists to study behaviors in the laboratory that animals do not exhibit in natural settings. Further, these psychologists proposed that learning functions to organize reflexes and random responses.

Timberlake's behavior systems approach suggests that animals possess highly organized instinctive behavior systems that serve a specific need or function in the animal. In Timberlake's view, learning evolved as a modifier of instinctive behavior systems and acts to intensify the motivational mode or change the integration or sensitivity in a perceptual-motor module. Variations in learning are due either to predispositions, when an animal learns more rapidly or in a different form than expected, or constraints, when an animal learns less rapidly or completely than expected.

Breland and Breland trained many exotic behaviors in a wide variety of animal species; however, they found that some operant responses, although initially performed effectively, deteriorated with continued training despite repeated food reinforcements. Animal misbehavior occurs when (1) the stimuli present during operant conditioning resemble the natural cues controlling food-gathering activities, (2) these stimuli are paired with food reinforcement, and (3) the instinctive food-gathering behaviors the stimuli elicit during conditioning are reinforced.

Animals receiving an interval schedule of reinforcement exhibit a wide variety of instinctive behaviors (e.g., drinking, running, grooming, nest building, and aggression). Although there is no contingency between these behaviors and reinforcement, these schedule-induced behaviors occur at excessive levels; the highest levels occur in the time period following reinforcement. Schedule-induced behavior appears to reflect the elicitation of instinctive consummatory behavior by periodic reinforcements.

When an animal or person experiences illness after eating a particular food, an association develops between the food and the illness. Subsequently, this association causes the animal or person to avoid that food. Nocturnal animals, like rats, associate flavor more readily with illness than with environmental events. In contrast, visual stimuli are more salient than flavor cues in diurnal animals like birds or guinea pigs.

According to Kalat and Rozin's learned-safety view, when an animal eats a food and no illness results, it learns that the food can be safely consumed in the future; however, if the animal becomes ill after eating, an association forms between the food and illness, and the animal will subsequently avoid that food. Revusky's concurrent interference theory proposes that an aversion may not develop if other foods are experienced between the initial food and the illness.

Young animals develop strong attachments to their mothers through the imprinting process; this attachment has considerable adaptive significance during the young animal's years of dependency. Animals are most likely to imprint during a specified period of development called a sensitive period. The animal's attachment to the imprinted object reflects both associative and instinctive processes. Sexual and food preferences are two other forms of imprinting.

Animals possess instinctive responses called species-specific defense reactions (SSDRs) that allow them to avoid dangerous events. These instinctive means of keeping out of trouble are programmed into animals' genetic structures. Once animals anticipate danger, they will readily learn to avoid it if a species-specific defense reaction is effective.

The mesotelencephalic system mediates the influence of reinforcement on behavior. This system includes the tegmentostriatal pathway, which governs the motivational properties of reinforcers, and the nigrostriatal pathway, which governs memory consolidation.

The pleasurable effects of both amphetamine and cocaine result from the activation of dopaminergic receptors in the tegmentostriatal pathway. The pleasurable effects of opiate agonists such as heroin and morphine result from the stimulation of opiate receptors in the tegmentostriatal pathway. Opiate agonists and dopamine agonists activate different receptors in the tegmentostriatal pathway, with the same end result: activation of the nucleus accumbens. Individual differences in responsivity to reinforcement are very positively correlated with the level of dopamine release in the nucleus accumbens.

Activity in the periventricular tract (PVT), the brain's punishment center, is unpleasant. Punishers activate this system, motivating escape and avoidance behavior.

CRITICAL THINKING QUESTIONS

1. Jeffrey has a drinking problem. He consumes some alcohol every day and often drinks more than he had planned. How would schedule-induced polydipsia explain Jeffrey's problem? Does the schedule-induced polydipsia paradigm suggest an approach to reduce Jeffrey's alcohol consumption?
2. Early social experience has a profound impact on adult emotionality. Discuss the relevance of Harlow's research to human emotional development.
3. Anita finds cocaine extremely pleasurable. In fact, she prefers it to anything else; she says it is even better than a sexual orgasm. Describe the neural system that allows Anita to experience pleasure from cocaine. Explain why cocaine is such a powerful reinforcer.

KEY TERMS

animal misbehavior
anxious relationship
appetitive structure view
associative learning view
behavior systems
   approach
concurrent interference
constraint
electrical stimulation of
   the brain (ESB)
imprinting
ingestional neophobia
instinctive drift
instinctive view of
   imprinting

interim behavior
learned-safety theory
long-delay learning
medial forebrain bundle
   (MFB)
mesotelencephalic
   reinforcement system
nigrostriatal pathway
nucleus accumbens (NA)
periventricular tract
   (PVT)
predisposition
schedule-induced
   aggression

schedule-induced
   behavior
schedule-induced
   polydipsia
schedule-induced wheel
   running
secure relationship
species-specific defense
   reaction (SSDR)
stimulus-bound behavior
superstitious behavior
tegmentostriatal pathway
terminal behavior
ventral tegmental area
   (VTA)

CHAPTER ELEVEN

Complex Learning Tasks

A Day at the Beach

Regina thought it was a lovely summer day. The temperature was about 85 degrees, and the humidity was quite moderate. It would be hard to find a better day to go to the beach. Despite the fact that it was the middle of the summer, Regina had not been to the beach this year. She had always enjoyed the beach, but with a full-time job, Regina had not found the time to go this summer. Her two best friends, Beth and Ivana, had asked her on numerous occasions, but she always seemed to have commitments at work that prevented her from accepting their invitations. When Beth called on Monday, Regina thought she would be able to go to the beach on Saturday. She had just completed a major project and certainly could handle the minor jobs on her desk during the week. On Tuesday, Regina's boss informed her that a report was needed a week earlier than planned, and would have to be on her desk by Monday morning; Regina was devastated. She wanted to go to the beach very badly, but she did not think she could get the report done if she went on Saturday. Beth probably would not ask her again if she backed out this time, but the report had to be done. What could she do? Maybe she could go to her boss, tell her about her commitment to Beth, and ask for an extension on the project. She had always handed in her work on time; maybe the boss would be agreeable. However, Regina decided not to ask for more time: it would look bad, and her boss probably would not agree, anyway. Another option would be to stay up late for the remainder of the week to get the project done. Regina did not function well on little sleep, so she dismissed this option. Could anyone else help her? Her coworker, Heath, was familiar with the project. While he was definitely busy, maybe he would help her. He would understand her social dilemma. She could make it up to him by helping him with his work at some other time. This seemed like a reasonable solution. She would talk with him after lunch.

In this vignette, Regina has a problem. She wants to find a way to go to the beach Saturday while still completing her work project by Monday morning. In the story, Regina recognized the problem, identified her goal, and generated a number of possible solutions. After considering the possibilities and the probable success of each one, she decided on the solution she thought was most likely to be successful.

Each of us faces many problems during our lives. In some instances, we adopt a systematic strategy to solve a problem, while in other cases, we use the first solution that comes to mind. In this chapter, we examine how people solve problems and consider reasons why we might or might not be able to solve a particular problem.

This chapter describes three major complex learning tasks. First, we explore how concepts form. A concept is a symbol that represents a group of objects or events with common characteristics. Recognizing the attributes that define a concept helps us organize our world and respond appropriately to the members of a particular concept. Second, we discuss problem solving. A problem exists when obstacles prevent us from attaining a desired goal. To reach the goal, we must overcome these obstacles by selecting the most effective solution to the problem. Finally, we examine the structure of language and how we learn to use it. Language is a means of communicating our thoughts, feelings, and intentions to other people.

CONCEPT LEARNING

What is an airplane? Webster's International Dictionary defines it as a "fixed-wing aircraft, heavier than air, which is driven by a screw propeller or by a high velocity rearward jet and supported by the dynamic reactions of the air against its wings." The word *airplane* is a concept. A **concept** is a symbol that represents a class or group of objects or events with common properties. Thus, the concept of airplane refers to all objects that (1) have fixed wings, (2) are heavier than air, (3) are driven by a screw propeller or high-velocity rearward jet, and (4) are supported by the dynamic reactions of the air against the wings. Airplanes come in various sizes and shapes, but as long as they have these four properties, we can easily identify them as airplanes. We are all familiar with many concepts. Chair, book, and hat are three such concepts: they stand for groups of objects with common properties.

Concept learning significantly enhances our ability to effectively interact with the environment. Instead of separately labeling and categorizing each new object or event we encounter, we simply incorporate it into our existing concepts. For example, suppose a child sees a large German shepherd. Even though this child may have been exposed only to smaller dogs like poodles and cocker spaniels, he or she will easily identify the barking animal with four legs and a tail as a dog. Thus, concepts enable us to group objects or events that share common properties and to respond in a similar manner to each example of the concept.

You may have noticed the similarity of concept learning to our discussion of generalization and discrimination learning in Chapter 7. If so, you have made a good observation. Concept learning in part involves discriminating between stimuli and then generalizing that discrimination to other stimuli that are similar to the discriminative stimulus. For example, a child may learn the concept of dog and discriminate between dogs and cats. But there are many kinds of dogs. Once the child has learned to discriminate between dogs and cats, the child can generalize the response to different dogs, but not to different cats. We next turn our attention to the process of learning a concept.

The Structure of a Concept

Attributes and Rules

Concepts have two main properties: attributes and rules. An **attribute** is any feature of an object or event that varies from one instance to another. For example, height, weight, and coloring differ from person to person and therefore are attributes of each individual.

An attribute can have a fixed value; for example, the attribute of gender can only be either male or female. In other cases, attributes have continuous values; for instance, the shade of a certain color can vary from light to dark.

Certain properties or attributes are relevant to particular objects or events. For example, the attribute of four legs is relevant for cats, but the attribute of wings is not. To understand a concept, one must learn what attributes are relevant to it.

For each concept, a **rule** defines which objects or events are examples of that particular concept. For the concept of an airplane, the defining rule indicates that to be an airplane, an object must have fixed wings, be heavier than air, be driven by a screw propeller or high-velocity rearward jet, and be supported by the dynamic reactions of the air against its wings.

Types of Rules

A number of different rules may be used to define the attributes of a concept (see **Table 11.1**). In some instances, the rules are simple; in other cases, they are more complex. When the rule is simple, an object or event must possess only one attribute to be an example of that particular concept. Suppose that an object is green. This object belongs to the concept of green whether it is a green car, a green shirt, or a green pea.

The concept *green* is defined by an affirmative rule. An **affirmative rule** specifies that a particular attribute defines a concept. In **Figure 11.1**, the affirmative rule indicates that the concept is *large*. A **negative rule** states that any object or event having a certain attribute is not a member of the concept. **Figure 11.1** shows that any object that is not large is not an example of the concept. Another example of a concept defined by a negative rule is blindness: anyone who can see is not blind.

The rules defining other concepts may be more complex. For example, a **conjunctive rule** defines a concept based on the simultaneous presence of two or more attributes; all the specified attributes must be present for an object or

TABLE 11.1. Rules for Defining Attributes in a Concept

Rule	Symbolic Description	Verbal Description
Affirmation	L	Any large object
Negation	$\overline{L}$	Any object not large
Conjunction	$L \cap C$	Any object both large and a circle
Disjunction	$L \cup C$	Any object either large or a circle or both

Source: Haygood, R. C., Bourne, L. E., Jr. (1965). Attribute and rule-learning aspects of conceptual behavior. *Psychological Review, 72,* 175–195. Copyright 1965 by the American Psychological Association. Reprinted by permission.

FIGURE 11.1. Dashed lines indicate examples of each of the four rules presented in Table 11.1.

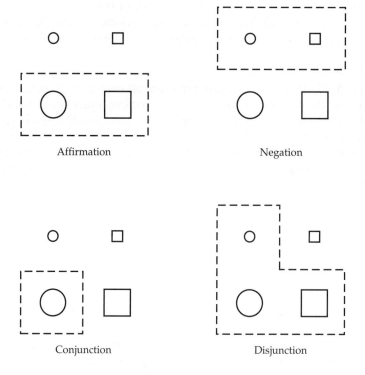

Affirmation

Negation

Conjunction

Disjunction

event to be an example of the concept (see **Figure 11.1**). To illustrate the conjunctive rule, consider the question, "What is poison ivy?" Poison ivy is a *vine* that has *three-leaf clusters;* each leaf is *pointed* and *tooth-edged,* and each vine is *red* at the base of the branch of leaves. To be an example of the concept *poison ivy,* a plant must have all five of these attributes. The Virginia Creeper vine is like poison ivy but has five-leaf clusters; seedlings of the Box Elder also look like poison ivy, but they have straight instead of vinelike stems. Many of us have mistaken other plants for poison ivy because we have not accurately learned the concept of poison ivy.

A disjunctive rule specifies that concepts can be defined by the presence of one of two, or both, common attributes; that is, an example of the concept can possess either of the two common attributes, or it can possess both of them. In **Figure 11.1,** the **disjunctive rule** is *circle* or *large* or both. A large circle is an example of the concept, as are both a large square and a small circle. As another example of a concept defined by a disjunctive rule, consider the question, "What is schizophrenia?" Schizophrenia is characterized by persistent hallucinations and/or delusions. Thus, a person who has either or both of the attributes may suffer from schizophrenia.

Our discussion suggests that for a specific object or event to be an example of a concept, it must have all the attributes characteristic of that concept. Yet, this is not always true. Consider the concept *bird.* We know that birds can fly, are usually relatively small in size, have feathers, build nests, and head for warmer climates during the winter. However, not all birds have all these attributes; a chicken or an ostrich, for example, has only one or two of these characteristics, while a robin has them all. Yet, we classify the chicken, the ostrich, and the robin as birds. Is a robin more of a bird because it has more of the attributes?

The Prototype of a Concept

Rosch (1975, 1978) demonstrated that not all examples of a concept necessarily have all the attributes characteristic of that concept. Consider the concept of furniture. How exemplary of this concept is a desk, a table, or a chair? Rosch found that subjects could rank the degree to which a particular item fit a certain concept. As **Table 11.2** indicates, different pieces vary in the extent to which they are examples of the concept of furniture. *Chair* and *sofa* exemplify the concept to the greatest degree; *bureau* and *end table* to the least.

Why are some objects or events better examples of a concept than are others? Rosch (1975) suggested that the degree to which a member of a concept exemplifies the concept depends on the degree of **family resemblance;** the more attributes a specific object or event shares with other members of a concept, the more the object or event exemplifies the concept. Thus, compared with bureau and end table, sofa and chair are better examples of the concept of furniture because they share more attributes with other members of the concept. Rosch and Mervis (1978) found that the five most typical members of the concept *furniture* had thirteen attributes in common, whereas the five least typical members had only two attributes in common.

When you think of the concept of vegetable, you are most likely to imagine a pea. Why? According to Rosch (1978), the **prototype** of a concept is the object that has the greatest number of attributes in common with other members of the concept and is therefore the most typical member of a category. As **Table 11.2** shows, the pea is the prototype of the concept of *vegetable*. Members of the concept that have many attributes in common with the prototype are considered typical of the concept; thus, carrots and green beans are typical of *vegetable* because they have many of the same attributes as the pea. In contrast, celery, cucumbers, and beets are atypical of the concept because they share only a few attributes with the pea.

The next example provides a very different prototype of a concept. Fehr and Russell (1991) asked subjects to indicate "if maternal love is a type of love?" and "if self-love is a type of love?" Their subjects agreed that maternal love is a type of love more often than they agreed self-love is a type of love, presumably because maternal love better matched their prototype of love.

The degree to which an object or event exemplifies a concept is important. Rosch (1978) asked subjects to indicate whether a particular object or event was a member of a specific concept. For example, subjects were asked if it is true or false that robins and penguins are birds. Rosch reported that subjects took less time to say "true" when the object or event was a good example of the concept (robin) than when it was a poor example (penguin). Thus, the more an object or event differs from the prototype, the more difficult it is to identify it as an example of the concept.

TABLE 11.2. Rankings of Furniture and Vegetable by How Well They Exemplify Their Respective Categories

Furniture		*Vegetables*	
Exemplar	Goodness-of-example rank	Exemplar	Goodness-of-example rank
Chair	1.5	Peas	1
Sofa	1.5	Carrots	2
Couch	3.5	Green beans	3
Table	3.5	String beans	4
Easy chair	5	Spinach	5
Dresser	6.5	Broccoli	6
Rocking chair	6.5	Asparagus	7
Coffee table	8	Corn	8
Rocker	9	Cauliflower	9
Love seat	10	Brussels sprouts	10
Chest of drawers	11	Squash	11
Desk	12	Lettuce	12
Bed	13	Celery	13
Bureau	14	Cucumber	14
End table	15.5	Beets	15

Source: Rosch, E. (1975). Cognitive representations of semantic categories. *Journal of Experimental Psychology: General, 104,* 92–253. Copyright 1975 by the American Psychological Association. Reprinted by permission.

Boundaries of the Concept

Two objects or events may share certain attributes but not be examples of the same concept. For example, although robins and bats both have wings, the robin is a bird and the bat is a mammal. Certain rules define the boundaries of a concept. These rules reveal whether differences between the prototype of a concept and another object or event indicate either that the other object or event is less typical of the concept, or that it is an example of another concept. Thus, even though robins and bats both have wings, the other differences between them mean that the bat and the robin are not members of the same concept.

Sometimes boundaries between concepts are not clearly defined (Zazdeh, Fu, Tanak, & Shimura, 1975). For example, what is the difference between a river and a stream? When the boundary of a concept is vague, it is difficult to know whether an object or event is a member of that concept. Rosch (1978) reported that subjects easily answered that a stone is not a bird, but they had difficulty indicating that a bat is not a bird. In fact, many subjects thought a bat is some kind of bird. This study suggests that we do not always know the boundaries that define certain concepts.

Studying Concept Learning in Humans

Psychologists have conducted numerous experiments examining concept learning in humans. An early study by Smoke (1933) is representative. Smoke presented subjects with a large number of figures that differed in the shape, size,

FIGURE 11.2. Samples of DAX and non-DAX figures. The DAX concept was defined as a circle with one dot inside and one dot outside its boundary. All objects possessing these attributes are examples of the DAX concept.

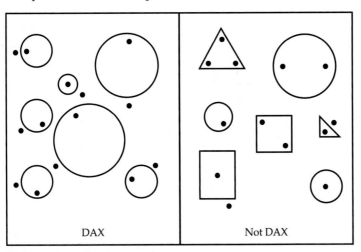

number, and location of their dots. The subjects' task was to learn the concept of DAX, which consisted of a circle with one dot inside and another dot outside (refer to **Figure 11.2**). The DAX concept uses the conjunctive rule; a figure that (1) is a circle, (2) has two dots, and (3) has one dot inside and one outside the circle is an example of the DAX concept. Subjects saw each figure, indicated whether they thought it was an example of the concept, and received feedback about the correctness of their response. Smoke reported that subjects readily learned the concept of DAX.

Studying Concept Learning in Animals

Concept learning involves identification of the properties that characterize a concept as well as those that do not. Can animals learn concepts? The research of Richard Herrnstein and his associates (Herrnstein, 1979; Herrnstein & de Villiers, 1980; Herrnstein, Loveland, & Cable, 1976) clearly shows that animals can learn a concept.

Herrnstein, Loveland, and Cable (1976) presented a series of 80 slides to a group of pigeons. Half of the slides were S^D, and pecking at these slides resulted in a food reinforcement. The other forty slides were S^Δ, and the pigeons did not receive a reinforcer for pecking at them. The S^D slides were examples of natural objects; for example, for some pigeons, the S^D slides were pictures of water, for some they were pictures of trees, and for some they were pictures of a specific woman. The S^Δ slides did not show examples of the appropriate objects. **Figure 11.3** shows positive (S^D) and negative (S^Δ) instances of each concept. During each daily session, the pigeons saw each of the 80 slides briefly. Herrnstein, Loveland, and Cable found that the pigeons quickly learned to respond to the S^D and not to the S^Δ.

FIGURE 11.3. Examples of stimuli Herrnstein, Loveland, and Cable (1976) used in their study. Figures A, C, and E are S^Ds. Figures B, D, and F are S^Δs. The concept of *water* is present in Figure A, but not in Figure B. The concept of *trees* is present in Figure C, but not in Figure D. The particular woman present in Figure E is not present in Figure F.

Did these pigeons really learn a concept? Did they discover which stimuli contained examples of the concept and which did not? Or did they merely learn to respond to some particular stimuli but not to others? Herrnstein and de Villiers (1980) evaluated whether the pigeons had actually learned a concept in two ways. First, they presented the same 80 slides to the pigeons, but this time not just the S^D slides contained examples of the concept; that is, the example slides were randomly assigned to S^D and S^Δ. If the pigeons were just learning to respond to some stimuli but not to others, then the random assignment of slides should not affect how fast the pigeons learned the discrimination. Although the pigeons did learn the discrimination when the slides were randomly presented as S^D and S^Δ, Herrnstein and de Villiers reported that learning was much slower when no concept defined S^D and S^Δ.

Herrnstein and de Villiers also used a positive-transfer test to show that the pigeons did learn a concept. After the pigeons had learned the discrimination in which S^D contained an example of the concept and S^Δ did not, they viewed two new slides of S^D and S^Δ. According to Herrnstein and de Villiers, if the pigeons had only learned to respond to certain stimuli, then learning to discriminate new slides of S^D and S^Δ should proceed at the same rate as original learning. However, if the pigeons had learned the concept, positive transfer should occur, and the pigeons should readily learn how to respond to the new slides. Herrnstein and de Villiers observed considerable positive transfer to the new slides; the pigeons responded differentially to the new examples of S^D and S^Δ almost as effectively as they had to the original slides.

Pigeons have shown the ability to learn many different concepts since Herrnstein's classic studies. In Chapter 7, we described a study by Watanabe, Sakamoto, and Wakita (1995) showing that pigeons could learn to discriminate between paintings of Monet and those of Picasso. The pigeons appeared to learn the concept of a Monet painting, as distinguished from a Picasso painting, because the pigeons responded to new Monet paintings during testing as they had to Monet paintings (S^Ds) experienced during training. Pigeons also have learned to discriminate between the music of Bach and the music of Stravinsky (Porter & Neuringer, 1984) and between line drawings of different objects (Kirkpatrick-Steger, Wasserman, & Biederman, 1996). Monkeys also have been able to learn concepts (Schrier & Brady, 1987). Schrier and Brady (1987) found that monkeys could learn the concept of *humans*. In their study, monkeys were shown pictures of scenes with humans (S^D) and pictures of scenes without humans (S^Δ) in a simultaneous two-choice discrimination procedure. Schrier and Brady reported that the monkeys rapidly learned to choose the pictures that featured humans.

The preceding concept learning studies in pigeons used two-dimensional pictures. Pigeons can also learn to discriminate between three-dimensional objects. For example, Delius (1992) used three-dimensional objects that were either spherical (e.g., marbles, ball bearings) or nonspherical (e.g., buttons, dice) as S^Ds and S^Δs. Delius reported that pigeons rapidly learned to discriminate between spherical and nonspherical objects. After the pigeons had learned the concepts of *spherical* and *nonspherical*, Delius presented two-dimensional pictures of the spherical and nonspherical objects and reported that the pigeons were able to respond with a high degree of accuracy to the two-dimensional pictures of these objects.

Dolphins also are able to discriminate between three-dimensional objects (Helweg, Roitblat, Nachigall, & Hautus, 1996). Objects such as a cube, rectangle, and pyramid were presented to dolphins, who used echolocation to respond to the object associated with reinforcement and not to the object associated with an absence of reinforcement. Helweg, Roitblat, Nachigall, and Hautus (1996) found that the dolphins were able to respond effectively, even when the objects were free to rotate and sway.

Our discussion indicates that pigeons can learn which stimuli are examples of a particular concept and which are not. Thus, animals can organize their environments according to events that are examples of concepts and events that are not. However, the stimuli used in the preceding studies involved natural concepts; that is, the stimuli represented concrete aspects of the natural environment. Can animals also learn abstract concepts such as *same* or *different?* D'Amato and his associates (D'Amato & Salmon, 1984; D'Amato, Salmon, & Colombo, 1985) used a procedure called **matching to sample** to investigate whether primates can learn abstract concepts. The matching-to-sample procedure involves first presenting a stimulus item (e.g., a square) and then presenting two stimuli (e.g., a square and a dot). The subjects are reinforced if they chose the matching stimulus on the second presentation. To evaluate whether monkeys can learn the abstract concepts of *same* and *different,* a series of sample and test stimuli were presented. If the monkey is learning the abstract concept, the level of performance should improve with each trial. Further, if the monkey has learned to choose on the basis of sameness (or differentness), presentation of a new test stimulus should not affect performance. D'Amato and his associates reported that the monkey's level of performance improved with each trial and that monkeys did perform well when presented with new stimuli. These studies suggest that monkeys can learn abstract concepts. Wasserman (1995) found that pigeons can also acquire abstract concepts such as *same* and *different.*

Theories of Concept Learning

There are two main theories of concept learning. One view argues that concept learning is an associative process; the other argues that concept learning is a cognitive process.

Associative Theory

Clark Hull (1920) envisioned concept learning as a form of discrimination learning (see Chapter 7). In his view, concepts have both relevant and irrelevant attributes. On each trial of a concept-learning study, a subject determines whether the object or event shown is characteristic of the concept. A subject who responds correctly receives reinforcement by feedback (the researcher tells the subject the response was correct). As a result of reinforcement, response strength increases to the attributes characteristic of the concept.

Consider the Smoke study described earlier. The subjects received reinforcement when they recognized DAX figures (figures of a circle with one dot on the inside of the circle and another on the outside). As the result of reinforcement, the stimulus (figure) and response (DAX) were associated. In contrast, subjects that identified figures that were not examples of the DAX concept did not receive reinforcement. The result of nonreinforcement was a diminished response to nonexamples of the concept of DAX.

Hull's classic study (1920) provides evidence for an associative view of concept learning. In this study, adult subjects learned 6 lists of 12 paired associates. The stimuli were Chinese letters containing 12 different features. The stimuli changed from task to task, but the features did not. (Six of the features appear in **Figure 11.4.**) Nonsense syllables paired with each feature were the responses.

The same feature-nonsense syllable pairs were used in all of the lists. Hull found that the subjects learned each successive list more rapidly than the preceding one. According to Hull, the subjects were able to learn later lists more quickly because they had learned the common feature of each stimulus in the category. Hull believed that subjects were not consciously aware of the association, but instead had become trained to respond to a specific stimulus event.

Hull's associative theory assumes that people associate a feature with the concept name. People recognize that a stimulus is a member of a concept by determining whether it possesses that feature. We learned earlier that a concept may possess several features, and the stimulus with the most features is the prototype of that concept. Suppose a person is asked whether a nonprototype stimulus is a member of a particular concept. Will the person be able to recognize that the stimulus is a member of that concept? Prototype theory (Rosch, 1978) suggests that a person compares the new stimulus to the prototype. If there is sufficient commonality, the person recognizes that the stimulus is a member of that concept. A lack of commonality causes a person to respond slowly or even fail to recognize that the new stimulus is a member of the concept. For example, people are slow to perceive an illness when the symptoms do not match one of our disease prototypes. Bishop (1991) found that a person may be slow to seek help for a heart attack if his or her symptoms do not fit the prototype of this disease.

FIGURE 11.4. The stimuli used in Hull's concept-learning study. Notice that each of the features on the left is part of the corresponding feature in each list on the right.

A second associative view, called exemplar theory, suggests that a person associates specific stimuli or exemplars with the concept (Posner, 1973). For example, robin and bluejay are examples of the concept *bird*. When exposed to a new stimulus, the person compares the new stimulus with memories of previously observed stimuli. If the new stimulus closely resembles the exemplars of a specific concept, the person recognizes the new stimulus as a member of that concept. Exemplar theory recognizes that people generalize from an exemplar to a new stimulus when that new stimulus is similar to the exemplar. For the concept of *bird*, for example, a person will recognize that a cardinal is a bird because the cardinal resembles a robin and a bluejay.

Which associative theory is valid? Evidences exists to support both views. For example, Franks and Bransford (1971) presented subjects with a series of stimuli and later asked them whether they had previously seen the stimuli. During testing, subjects saw many stimuli. Some of these stimuli had been presented previously, while others had not. Some of the new stimuli were prototypes of previously viewed stimuli. Franks and Bransford found that their subjects were more likely to recognize the prototypes that they had never seen than the nonprototypes that they had actually seen. Yet other research supports exemplar theory. For example, Posner and Keele (1968) had subjects associate various patterns of dots to specific categories. They then presented new patterns and asked subjects to indicate to which category each pattern belonged. The subjects classified a particular pattern based on the resemblance of that pattern to patterns previously associated with that category.

Evidence supporting both theories is not surprising. When people learn concepts, they not only establish prototypes, but they associate exemplars with the concept. Recognition that a new stimulus is a member of a specific concept can be based on its similarity to either the prototype or to exemplars.

Most psychologists supported Hull's view that associative processes alone control concept learning until the late 1950s, when further research revealed that cognitive processes also are involved in concept learning.

Cognitive Process in Concept Learning

How does a person learn a concept? According to Bruner, Goodnow, and Austin (1956), a concept is learned by testing hypotheses about the correct solution. If the first hypothesis is correct, the individual has learned the concept. However, if the hypothesis is incorrect, another hypothesis will be generated and tested. Hypothesis testing continues until a correct solution is discovered.

Consider the DAX concept. Suppose that on the first trial (see **Figure 11.5**), the individual saw a figure of a circle and a dot, and his or her first guess or hypothesis was that this figure was an example of the concept DAX. Since DAX is a figure with a circle and two dots, the response "DAX" to the first figure was wrong. Thus, the initial hypothesis was incorrect, and the subject needed to generate a new one. On trial 2, the subject hypothesized that DAX was a single dot inside the circle, so his or her response was "Not DAX." The subject learned that this response was also wrong, and on trial 3, he or she hypothesized that two dots represent the concept. Again the subject learned that this guess was wrong. The subject's next hypothesis was that the concept was any two dots and a circle. Although trial 4 suggests that this is a possibility, trial 5 proves it to

FIGURE 11.5. A hypothetical series of eight trials of the DAX problem. Successive rows show, trial by trial, the stimulus presented, the response given, and the feedback the experimenter provided.

Trial	Figure presented	Response	Feedback
1	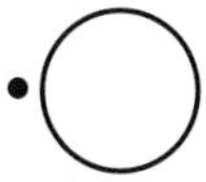	"DAX"	Wrong
2	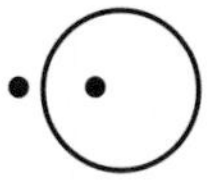	"Not DAX"	Wrong
3	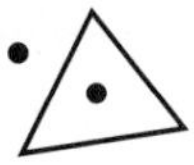	"DAX"	Wrong
4		"DAX"	Right
5	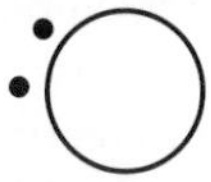	"DAX"	Wrong
6		"DAX"	Right
7		"Not DAX"	Right
8	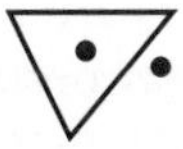	"Not DAX"	Right

be incorrect. The subject then hypothesized that the concept of DAX is one dot inside a circle and one dot outside. The subject tested this hypothesis on trials 6, 7, and 8 and finally concluded that it was correct. Our example suggests that, in addition to forming hypotheses to learn concepts, individuals adopt a win-stay, lose-shift strategy; that is, they will stick with a hypothesis as long as it works and will generate a new one when evidence indicates that the old hypothesis is not valid. What evidence demonstrates that concept learning involves testing hypotheses? Levine's classic study (1966) provides support for a hypothesis-testing view of concept learning.

Levine (1966) developed a blank-trials procedure to evaluate the theory that people learn concepts by testing hypotheses. On each trial, subjects were shown two letters. The letters differed in terms of color (black or white), identity (X or

FIGURE 11.6. The stimuli Levine used in his blank trials are in the middle of the figure. The eight possible hypotheses are to the left and right of the stimuli. The column below each hypothesis shows the pattern of choices that test the hypothesis.

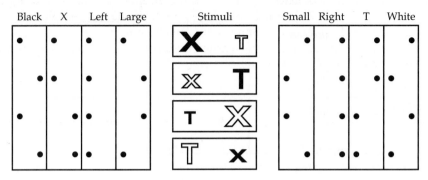

T), size (large or small) and position (left or right). One attribute (for example, white) Levine chose as the concept; the subjects' task was to learn which attribute had been chosen. On each trial, the subjects chose one of the two stimuli and were told whether their response contained the correct attribute. After each study trial, subjects were given four blank trials. On each blank trial, two stimuli were presented and the subjects again tried to choose the one that represented the concept. However, the subjects received no feedback on these trials. The subjects' responses on the blank trials indicated whether they were testing a hypothesis about the correct attribute. If they were, a particular pattern of responses would appear. **Figure 11.6** presents a pattern of responses. Suppose that a subject hypothesized that black was the correct attribute. This subject's responses should match those depicted in the first column of **Figure 11.6**. In contrast, the responses of a subject who thought that large was correct should match those in the fourth column, while a random pattern of responses would develop if subjects had not been testing hypotheses to learn the concept.

Levine found that subjects engaged in hypothesis testing on over 95% of the trials. Furthermore, he found that subjects adopted a win-stay, lose-shift strategy. When a hypothesis was confirmed on a feedback trial, subjects retained this hypothesis throughout the blank trials and continued to use it until they received feedback that the attribute was incorrect. When a hypothesis was found to be incorrect on a study trial, they generated and used a new hypothesis on the four subsequent blank trials and then on study trials until it was discontinued.

Two additional aspects of Levine's research are important. First, subjects typically do not use a specific hypothesis more than once while learning a concept. Once a hypothesis has proven incorrect, that hypothesis will not be evaluated again during the study. Apparently, people remember past hypotheses that have proven invalid and test different hypotheses until they find the correct one. Second, Levine showed that subjects can test more than one hypothesis at a time. Consider the subjects' responses on the first study trial. Suppose that a subject chose a large black X, thinking that either black or X was the correct concept. The subject was told that the response was incorrect. This information indicates that neither black nor X is the correct attribute. Levine's results showed that when subjects learned that both attributes were incorrect, they remembered that information and did not guess either black or X on blank trials.

Do not assume that associative learning and hypothesis testing are mutually exclusive means of learning a concept. A concept can be learned using either method, but it is learned best when both means are employed. For example, Reber, Kassin, Lewis, and Cantor (1980) found that subjects acquired a concept most rapidly when they learned both the rules defining the concept and specific instances of the concept.

BEFORE YOU GO ON

- **What concept had Regina learned about the beach?**
- **How can associative and cognitive theories explain Regina's concept of beach?**

PROBLEM SOLVING

The Missionaries-and-Cannibals Problem

On one side of a river there are three missionaries and three cannibals. They have a boat on their side that is capable of carrying two people at a time across the river. The goal is to transport all six people across to the other side of the river. At no point can the cannibals on either side of the river outnumber the missionaries on that side of the river (or the cannibals would eat the outnumbered missionaries). This constraint only holds when there is at least one missionary on the side of the river where there are more cannibals. That is, it is all right to have one, two or three cannibals on the same side of the river with zero missionaries, because they would have no missionaries to eat. (Wickelgren, 1974)

Can you solve this problem? (Remember that someone will have to row the boat back after each trip across.) Spend several minutes trying to find a solution.

Were you able to transport the missionaries and cannibals without losing any missionaries? If you are like most people, you had great difficulty solving this problem. **Figure 11.7** provides the series of trips necessary to move all the cannibals and missionaries to the other side of the river. Each box indicates where the missionaries, cannibals, and boat are after each trip. The arrows between the boxes show which people take the boat ride on each trip. The trips (arrows) following the odd numbers take the missionaries and cannibals across; the trips following the even numbers are to return the boat to the original side.

Why is this problem so difficult to solve? The difficulty lies on trip 6. On this trip, it is *necessary* to have both a cannibal and missionary return across the river; otherwise, the cannibals will outnumber the missionaries on one side or the other. People usually pause for a long time at this point and are very likely to make an error. Why? The reason is that this choice (and the solution to the problem) appears to lead away from the solution to the problem; that is, this choice takes some of the missionaries and cannibals back to the original side of the river. Like this problem, solutions to many real-life problems do not

FIGURE 11.7. Solution to the missionaries-and-cannibals problem. At the starting point, the three missionaries and cannibals are on the left side of the river. On each boat ride, two people can travel across. The problem is that at no point can the cannibals outnumber missionaries on either side. The odd-numbered trips are across the river and the even numbers are return trips. The key to the solution of this problem is on trip 6: only by returning both a cannibal and a missionary to the original side of the river can the problem be solved.

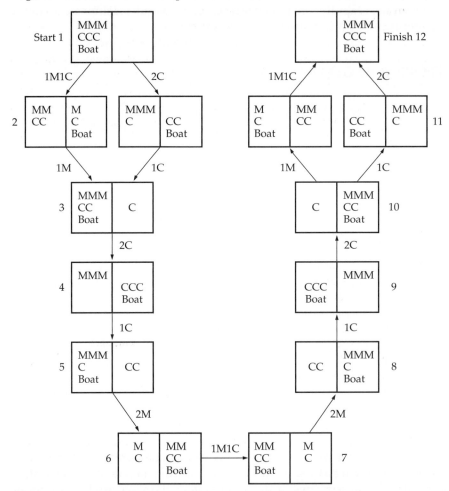

necessarily follow a straight line toward the goal. We will now examine how problems are solved, as well as suggest some ideas that might enhance your problem-solving ability.

The Nature of the Problem

What is a problem? A **problem** is a situation in which a person is motivated to reach a goal, but some obstacle or obstacles blocks the attainment of the goal. The person's task is to find a solution to the problem; that is, to discover a way to overcome the obstacles.

Edward Thorndike (1898) proposed that animals and people solve problems by trial and error (see Chapter 1). For example, Thorndike did not believe that the cats in his famous puzzle box study were able to figure out how to open the latch to escape from the box. Instead, the cats performed a large number of responses, and those that enabled them to reach the goal were reinforced. Wolfgang Kohler (1925) suggested a different view of problem solving. According to Kohler, an animal internally or mentally explores the problem before exhibiting a specific response. The exploration involves considering and rejecting possible solutions and finally developing insight as to the correct solution.

Consider Kohler's classic primate studies. Kohler presented several chimpanzees with the problem of reaching a piece of fruit that was suspended over their heads in their play area. The problem was structured so that the chimps could not reach the fruit even by jumping. Kohler randomly placed several boxes and sticks throughout the play area. According to Kohler, the chimpanzees initially attempted to reach the fruit by jumping. When that failed, they stopped jumping and paced back and forth. Kohler then observed that the chimps abruptly stopped pacing and, looking quite resolute, used the boxes and sticks to reach the fruit. One chimp obtained the fruit by gathering several boxes, stacking them on top of each other, and climbing up the boxes to reach the fruit. Another chimp climbed on one box and used a stick to knock down the fruit. A third chimp collected two hollow sticks and made one long stick by inserting the end of one stick into the other.

Several critical observations led Kohler to suggest that **insight** was responsible for the chimpanzees' solutions to the problem. First, the chimps solved the problem with few or no mistakes. Second, once they had solved the problem, the chimps were able to quickly solve other similar problems.

Chimpanzees are not the only animals to insightfully solve problems. Epstein (1981) observed a similar phenomenon in pigeons. In his study, Epstein initially trained pigeons to peck at a model banana to obtain food reinforcement. The pigeons were also taught to move a box across the floor of a compartment by pecking at the box. Finally, the pigeons were placed in the compartment with the movable box at one end and the model banana suspended out of reach at the other end. The pigeons' feathers had been clipped so they could not fly to reach the banana. Epstein reported that the pigeons initially looked back and forth from the box to the banana. Finally, they stopped looking, moved the box under the banana, and climbed onto the box to peck at the banana. What cognitive processes enabled Kohler's chimpanzees and Epstein's pigeons to solve their problems? We will look at possible answers to this question next.

Defining the Problem

Developing a definition of a problem entails identifying both the starting point, or **initial state,** of the problem and the end point, or **goal state,** of the problem. Consider the following example to illustrate this aspect of problem solving. How can you get from the store to your car without getting wet in the rain when you have no umbrella? The initial state of this problem is that you are in the store and it is raining. The goal state of this problem is getting to the car without becoming wet.

A representation of the problem involves two additional processes: First, you need to identify the operations that solve the problem. In our example, you want to get to your car without getting wet. Some operations that would help you avoid getting wet include bringing along an umbrella to the store, not losing the umbrella in the store, knowing how to open the umbrella when you leave the store, or using some other item to cover your head. Second, restrictions limit what you can do to solve a problem. In our example, stealing another person's umbrella or parking at the door of the store are not acceptable solutions to the problem.

Well-Defined versus Ill-Defined Problems

Some problems are well-defined: both the initial state and the goal state of the problem are clear. Our example of getting to your car without becoming wet is a well-defined problem; a **well-defined problem** has an initial state and a goal state that is obvious. However, some problems are ill-defined: an **ill-defined problem** has no clear starting point or end point. Consider the problem of an instructor who wants to teach a good class. How does the instructor determine whether a class is good? Since there are not inherent definite standards to measure the success of a course, how can the instructor know that he or she has reached the goal state? In this example, the end point is unclear. In some cases, the starting point is unclear. For example, a person may recognize that a car must be in good working order to run smoothly, but the individual may not be able to check the condition of the car and therefore cannot identify the starting point of the problem.

Solving Ill-Defined Problems

Reitman (1965) suggested that identifying the starting point and end point is the key to bringing an ill-defined problem closer to a well-defined one and that this objective can be accomplished by generating additional structures (subproblems). Consider the following example. Suppose you are asked to write a term paper for a biology class. How can you best accomplish this goal? The starting point is gathering and analyzing a large body of literature. The end point is a finished term paper that has a beginning, a middle, and an end, is sufficient in length and depth, and accurately discusses the topic. To narrow the definition of the problem, you must first choose a specific topic, such as genetics. You can further define the problem by identifying several subtopics of genetics, and then break these subtopics down into even more specific groups. In Reitman's view, the subtopics establish a series of subproblems that you can then solve one at a time.

Simon (1973) suggested that creating a set of manageable subproblems provides the structure for converting an ill-defined problem into a well-defined one. Wessels (1982) asserted that creating a hierarchy of clearly stated subproblems makes an ill-defined problem easier to solve. Several studies have found that using subproblems facilitates the solving of such ill-defined problems as designing a shop (Hayes, 1978), writing a fugue (Reitman, 1965), and building a warship (Simon, 1973).

After the problem has been defined, the next step is to develop a plan of attack. There are two major strategies—algorithms and heuristics—that can be used to solve problems.

Algorithms

An **algorithm** is a precise set of rules used to solve a particular type of problem. To illustrate, consider the algorithm for subtracting: one number is deducted from another to obtain the correct answer. If the algorithm is applied correctly, the solution will be accurate; in this case, following the rules of subtraction will produce a correct calculation.

In some cases, a simple algorithm is all you need to solve the problem. The application of the subtraction algorithm, for instance, quickly leads to a correct answer. However, in many cases, the set of rules that will solve the problem is not easy to identify. In these situations, many alternatives must be tried before the correct solution is found. This process of trial and error often uses an enormous amount of time to solve a problem, as illustrated by Samuel's (1963) analysis of the application of this strategy to the game of checkers. Using an algorithm to develop a plan to win a checker game would involve (1) identifying all possible opening moves, (2) predicting an opponent's response to each of these moves, and (3) anticipating all the further responses of both players until all the possible outcomes of the game had been analyzed. Samuel calculated that discovering a series of moves that would guarantee a win would involve considering 10^{40} moves and take 10^{21} centuries to complete. Obviously, using an algorithm to play checkers is not very practical.

Heuristics

A **heuristic** is a "best guess" or "rule of thumb" solution to a problem. The use of a heuristic is an alternative to the exhaustive search that the algorithm strategy usually entails. Heuristics increase the likelihood but do not guarantee the problem will be solved. Suppose you are playing chess. Using an algorithm to discover a winning solution is not practical. You could decide to use a heuristic strategy such as maximizing the protection of the queen. You may not always be able to protect your queen and win (for example, when the only way to win is to sacrifice your queen), but usually heuristics will help you find a winning approach.

Consider the following real-world example of a problem that both an algorithm and a heuristic could solve. You need a special tool to fix your car, but you do not have the tool, nor do you know which hardware store carries that tool. One way to solve your problem is to call every hardware store in the telephone book—using an algorithm to solve the problem. However, you might find this strategy time-consuming, especially if there are hundreds of hardware stores in the telephone book. An alternative would be to call the hardware stores that have large ads in the phone book, since these stores would be more likely to stock the desired tool. Solving the problem this way uses a heuristic strategy.

Many heuristics can be used to solve various problems (Medin & Ross, 1997). Some of these heuristic strategies provide a systematic method of arriving at a solution without taking as long as an algorithm. Other heuristic strategies represent cognitive shortcuts to problem solving and often lead to incorrect solutions. Two of them, working backward and means-end analysis, entail the systematic evaluation of a problem. Two other heuristics, representativeness and availability, are affected by bias from past experience and therefore sometimes lead to ineffective solutions.

WORKING-BACKWARD HEURISTIC. Best (1995) likened many problems to a tree with many branches. The trunk of the tree is the starting point, and one of the twigs is the end point. The logical approach to solving a problem is to work forward from the starting point toward the end point. Unfortunately, this approach can lead a person to branch off in the wrong direction. Going off on a wrong branch will make it difficult, and sometimes impossible, to solve the problem. One widely used heuristic that avoids this problem is the **working-backward heuristic.** In the working-backward heuristic, the person starts at the end point and works backward to the starting point.

The working-backward heuristic is commonly used in mathematics and other formal systems of analysis. In an elegant analysis of this type of heuristic, Newell, Shaw, and Simon (1958) found that computers programmed to use the working-backward heuristic rapidly generated proofs for mathematical theorems. In contrast, the computers programmed to work forward from the axioms required a great deal of time to prove even simple theorems.

The failure to use the working-backward heuristic can even be fatal. Six climbers died trying to ascend the summit of Mount Everest in 1996 in part because of the failure to have sufficient oxygen supplies at the highest camp. The failure to apply the working-backward heuristic contributed to these climbers' deaths. The best strategy for reaching the summit of a tall mountain is to start by determining the equipment and supplies needed at the highest camp on the night before the attempt on the summit (Krakauer, 1997). The number of people who need to be at the highest camp on the night before the summit attempt is determined next, followed by the number of people needed to supply the highest camp. This process of working backward is continued until the logistics are completed for the entire expedition. Had the working-backward heuristic been followed, the climbers would have had sufficient supplies at the highest camp and likely would have survived (Krakauer, 1997).

MEANS-END ANALYSIS. Another systematic heuristic used for solving problems is the **means-end analysis,** which breaks down a particular problem into a series of subproblems that are solved. These solutions, in turn, may make it possible to solve the original problem.

Newell and Simon (1972) provide a real-world example of the means-end heuristic:

> I want to take my son to nursery school. What's the difference between what I have and what I want? One of distance. What changes distance? My automobile. My automobile won't work. What is needed to make it work? A new battery. What has new batteries? An auto repair shop. I want the repair shop to put in a new battery; but the shop doesn't know I need one. What is the difficulty? One of communication. A telephone . . . and so on. (p. 416)

In this example, the starting point is an automobile that does not work; the end point is getting the child to the nursery school; the problem is how to take the child in the car to the nursery school. Creating an initial subproblem of why the automobile does not work helps solve the larger problem. Recognizing that the car needs a new battery not only solves the subproblem but also increases the probability that the overall problem will be solved.

The means-end analysis heuristic places substantial demand on the short-term store, or our memory of recent events (see Chapter 12). Each subproblem must be kept in memory until the subproblem following it is solved. Although this heuristic is demanding of memory; it is also effective. In fact, this method can be used to solve problems that cannot be accurately solved with other heuristics (Medin & Ross, 1997).

Working backward and means-end analysis both represent systematic heuristic problem-solving strategies. They seek all available information and, under most circumstances, provide accurate solutions. Other heuristics do not consider all the available information in solving a problem; instead, they use only a limited amount of information. Using cognitive shortcuts that fail to use all available information can cause errors in judgment and lead to inaccurate solutions. Amos Kahneman and Daniel Tversky (Kahneman & Tversky, 1972, 1973; Kahneman, Slovic, & Tversky, 1982) have identified two types of heuristics—representatives and availability—as cognitive shortcuts to problem solving.

REPRESENTATIVENESS STRATEGY. Representativeness is a heuristic that makes judgments based only on the obvious characteristics of the problem. Consider the following example. You are presented the problem, "What occupation should John pursue in college?" You are told that John is shy, helpful, good with figures, and has a passion for detail. You may ask for and receive further details needed to solve this problem; however, if you use the **representativeness strategy,** you will not seek additional information but will choose John's career based only on the facts initially given—facts that prompt you to decide that John should become an accountant. Although this strategy allows for faster choices, you may be ignoring salient information (for example, John's preferences, his previous school grades, or the job opportunities in this field).

Kahneman and Tversky (1972, 1973) reported that the representativeness strategy is frequently used, even when it leads to illogical solutions. In one study, Kahneman and Tversky presented their subjects with a problem similar to the last example. In addition to being given the personality sketch, subjects were told that the information was based on a psychologist's projective test given at the beginning of John's senior year of high school. Although the subjects expressed little faith in personality tests, they still based their selections on information provided by John's test results.

If, as suggested, use of the representative strategy may lead to error, why do people use it? There are two reasons. First, this strategy often does work. Second, the strategy provides a quick way to make a decision. For example, suppose you are managing a convenience store and have been robbed at gunpoint several times late at night. It is now 2:00 A.M.; someone enters the store alone. This person seems anxious and nervous—just like the previous robbers. The present conditions are similar to those that existed at the time of the previous robberies. You decide that this person is a robber and call the police. Although you may have behaved differently had you waited to gather further information, this choice is definitely the safest one. Thus, when using the representativeness strategy, we base our solutions entirely on similarities between available information and past experience.

AVAILABILITY STRATEGY. Solutions selected using the **availability strategy** are based only on information that can be readily brought to mind (Levi & Pryor, 1987). According to Levi and Pryor, people usually select the solution that is more mentally "available," much as a person chooses a sweater because it is at the top of the dresser drawer. The availability heuristic means that solutions are usually based on recent experiences, which are most likely to be on our minds. Suppose you are trying to choose whether to drive or fly to college. If you have just read about a horrible airplane crash, your fears about the dangers of flying will be greater than if you did not have this information. Employing an availability strategy may prompt you to choose to drive, even though this solution may entail much more time and effort.

Execution of the Strategy

Once someone has chosen a strategy, the next step is to decide how to execute it. In many instances, the execution of the strategy is straightforward. Simple, well-defined strategies can be executed in a short time. For example, suppose you need a hammer to repair a chair. This problem can be quickly solved by going to the hardware store and buying a hammer. However, if you need a more sophisticated tool, you may have problems fixing the chair. The chosen strategy usually requires more time and effort to execute when the problem is ill-defined. Some of this difficulty may stem back to the first stage in the problem-solving process, identifying the problem. Failing to make a precise identification of (1) the initial and goal states of an ill-defined problem, (2) the operations that can solve the problem, or (3) the restrictions to the solution can result in complications in executing the strategy and solving the problem.

The Problem Solved

The final stage of problem solving is determining the accuracy of the solution. Although we may not always know if we have solved a problem correctly, feedback often indicates whether our solution was effective. This information about the accuracy of the solution is important for two reasons. First, when we know we have chosen the right solution, we can then overcome the obstacles and reach our goals. If our solution is not accurate, this feedback lets us know that we need to find another way to solve the problem. At this point, we will start over at the beginning of the problem-solving process. Second, the success or failure of our attempt to solve a problem can influence future problem solving by prompting us to continue to use effective approaches and to abandon ineffective ones. However, in some cases, present problem solving can negatively affect future decisions by causing us to retain previously effective problem-solving approaches that are no longer effective, and to overlook approaches that may have been ineffective in one situation but might be effective in another. We look at these effects of experience next.

The Consequences of Past Experience

Functional Fixedness

After shopping at a local mall, you walk back to your car and notice that your license plate is loose. You know that it will probably fall off if you don't tighten the screws holding the plate to the frame, but how do you tighten the screws without a screwdriver? Although you might think of using a coin as a screwdriver, many other people might fail to recognize that a coin can be used other than to buy things. Solving a problem often requires that we use a familiar object in a novel way. However, it is often hard to recognize these solutions.

Functional fixedness refers to the difficulty involved in recognizing novel uses for an object. In our example, because of functional fixedness, many people would not think to use a coin as a screwdriver. Prior experience using an object to solve one problem makes it difficult to recognize that the same object can be used in a different manner to solve another problem.

Maier first discussed the concept of functional fixedness in 1931, and many studies have since demonstrated this phenomenon (see Weisberg, DiCamillo, & Phillips, 1979, for a review of this literature). To study functional fixedness, Birch and Rabinowitz (1951) gave their subjects in the experimental groups two problems to solve. For the first problem, subjects were asked to complete an electrical circuit. Some of the subjects received a switch to use; others had a relay. Control subjects did not participate in this initial problem. In the second problem, subjects were then shown two strings hanging from the ceiling and told to tie the ends of the strings together. The problem was that the two strings were too far apart to hold one and reach the other. To solve this problem, subjects were given access to two heavy objects, a switch and a relay. The subjects could then tie a heavy object to the end of one string, swing that string like a pendulum, grab the end of the other string, catch the first string when it swung back to them, and then tie the two strings together. Birch and Rabinowitz reported that subjects who had used the relay to complete the circuit in the first problem chose the switch as the weight in the pendulum problem. In contrast, subjects who had used the switch to solve the first problem chose the relay as the weight in the second problem. Control subjects used the relay and switch equally often. These results indicate that once the experimental group subjects had established a function for an object (relay or switch) during the first problem, they did not think of using that object in a different manner to solve the second problem. Because control subjects had no prior experience with either object, the function of the objects had not been fixed, and these subjects chose either one to solve the pendulum problem.

Functional fixedness reflects an inability to perceive objects as having more than one function. This rigidity can impair problem solving; however, there are ways to overcome functional fixedness. One way is to learn that objects can function in many ways. To illustrate this concept, Flavell, Cooper, and Loiselle (1958) asked subjects to use objects such as a switch and pliers in various ways before exposing them to the pendulum problem. Flavell, Cooper, and Liselle reported that using one of these objects in several different ways prompted subjects to use that object again as a weight in the pendulum problem. However, if a subject had used the object in only one way, the subject did not tend to use that object to solve the pendulum problem.

Set

Functional fixedness is not the only source of negative transfer in problem solving. People also have a tendency to attack new problems in the same way they have solved earlier problems: The tendency to continue to use an established problem-solving method for future tasks is referred to as a **set.** A set is a source of negative transfer only if a new problem-solving approach is needed. In fact, if the habitual approach will effectively solve the new problem, the set will actually be a source of positive transfer; that is, the set will enhance the solving of the new problem.

Luchins's classic study (1942) showed the impact of set on problem solving. Subjects were given a series of problems that involved measuring out a given amount of water by using a water tap and three jars of different sizes. **Table 11.3** presents the sizes of the jars and the amount of water needed to solve the eleven problems. All subjects received problem 1, which could be solved by filling Jar A and pouring three times the water into Jar B. Subjects in the experimental group received problems 2 through 11; control-group subjects were only given problems 7 through 11. Most of the subjects in the experimental group learned that a single approach, $B - A - 2C$, could solve problems 2 through 6. Although problems

TABLE 11.3. Luchins's Water Measurement Problem

| Problem | Given Jars of the Following Sizes | | | Obtain the amount |
	A	B	C	
1.	29	3		20
2. E1	21	127	3	100
3. E2	14	163	25	99
4. E3	18	43	10	5
5. E4	9	42	6	21
6. E5	20	59	4	31
7. C1	23	49	3	20
8. C2	15	39	3	18
9.	28	76	3	25
10. C3	18	48	4	22
11. C4	14	36	8	6

Note: E = Experimental group; C = Control group.
Source: Luchins, A. S. (1942). Mechanization in problem solving. *Psychological Monographs, 54,* whole no. 24B. Copyright 1942 by the American Psychological Association. Reprinted by permission.

7 through 11 could also be solved using this approach, a simpler strategy, A + C or A − C, could be used to solve these problems. Control subjects used the shorter solution for problems 7 through 11; in contrast, experimental subjects continued to use the longer method. This study demonstrated that the experimental group subjects established a set, or a habitual method of problem solving, as they solved problems 2 through 6, and they continued to use this approach for the remaining problems. Why did they continue to use the less efficient strategy? The reason is that the first strategy was still successful in solving the problem. According to Luchins, a set "blinded people to fresh ways of exploring problems," which is unproductive when other solutions are more efficient.

The Nature of Expertise

People differ in terms of their ability to solve problems: some are extremely good at solving problems; others are not. Researchers have examined why by comparing chess masters with novice players (see Charness, 1991, for a review of this literature). This research has shown that, because of repeated practice, the chess master has learned thousands of different patterns, perhaps as many as 50,000 in some cases, and can therefore predict the effectiveness of all possible moves before choosing a particular one. In contrast, the novice player, before every move, must generate from scratch several possible responses to the opponent's last move and then try to anticipate the consequences of each possible reaction before deciding which move to choose. Thus, an expert has more knowledge than the novice. But expertise involves more than greater knowledge; an expert also possesses more abstractions and uses more general concepts than does the novice, who is more concrete and employs specific bits of information. In terms of chess, experts have a general understanding of the utility of each piece and how each piece can move to the greatest advantage, whereas the novice has memorized some moves that in the past have been successful.

Other researchers have provided additional insight into the nature of expertise. Experts are more able to extract information from a problem than are novices (Shanteau, 1992). The greater perceptiveness allows the expert to recognize important information that the novice misses. Experts also are better able to perceive the similarity between new and old problems than are novices (Hardimann, Dufresne, & Mestre, 1989). The ability to recognize similarities enables the expert to use principles gained from previous experience to solve new problems. Further, experts are able to perceive the whole problem, which allows them to go forward from the initial goal state (Bedard & Chi, 1992). In contrast, the novice sees only the initial and goal states and must use a slower heuristic.

Expertise is not without its drawbacks. Experts are more likely to show functional fixedness or mental sets than are novices. The reliance on past experiences can cause the expert to be less likely than the novice to learn from mistakes (Camerer & Johnson, 1991; Hawkins & Hastie, 1990). Heuristic biases can lead the expert to choose solutions that are no more effective than those chosen by a novice. While experience may lead experts to be more confident than novices, their choices are not always more successful in such areas as accounting (Bedard, 1989) and pilot judgment (Wickens, Stokes, Barnett, & Hyman, 1992).

BEFORE YOU GO ON

- What strategy did Regina use to solve her problem of getting her work done and going to the beach?
- Did past experience help or hinder Regina's search for a solution to her problem?

LANGUAGE

The Nature of Language

Language serves three very important functions in our lives. First, language allows us to communicate with other people. Just imagine how difficult life would be if we could not express our ideas to family and friends. We could not, for example, complain to our friends about how much schoolwork we have this weekend, or call home to ask for money. Second, language facilitates the learning process. The first two sections of this chapter discussed concept learning and problem solving. Although these two processes can occur without language, language facilitates them by providing a system of interrelated symbols and rules. Third, language allows us to recall information beyond the limits of our memory stores.

A subdiscipline of psychology, psycholinguistics, has been developed to study language. At its most elemental level, psycholinguistics describes the nature of speech sounds, called phonemes, and how phonemes combine to form words. A higher level of analysis, called grammar, discusses the rules by which words combine to form phrases and sentences. The highest level of study deals with semantics. Semantics is the study of the meaning of language. Psycholinguists have studied how we learn language as well as whether primates can also communicate with language.

The Structure of Language

Phonemes

A **phoneme** is the simplest functional speech sound. For example, consider the words *pin* and *bin*. These two words have different meanings and can be distinguished only because their initial sounds, /p/ and /b/, are different phonemes. Note that these distinguishing sounds can occur anywhere in the word. The word pairs *but, bet* and *top, ton* illustrate that the different phonemes occurring at various places in words enable us to distinguish the meanings of different words.

Every language has a limited number of different sounds or phonemes. English is comprised of 45 basic sounds, but some languages have as few as 15 basic sounds or as many as 85 (Mills, 1980). Also, phonemes differ from one language to the next. For example, English contains the /l/-/r/ distinction (as in the words *late* and *rate*), but no such sound difference exists in Japanese. In fact, Miyawaki, Strange, Verbugge, Liberman, Jenkins, and Fujimura (1975) reported that the Japanese do not hear the difference between the two sounds. When they are learning to speak English, they have difficulty mastering the phoneme distinction between /l/ and /r/. This research indicates that we only distinguish the phonemes that exist in the languages we are familiar with. No wonder we have such difficulty learning a new language.

How do we learn to recognize phonemes? Eimas and Corbit (1973) discovered that phonemes have distinctive psychological meanings; that is, each sound has its own categorical boundaries and can be distinguished from other sounds. Consider the two syllables *ba* and *pa*. Using a speech synthesizer, Eimas and Corbit slowly changed the sound from the phoneme /b/ to the phoneme /p/, thus changing the syllable *ba* to the syllable *pa*. Although the synthesizer changed the speech sound gradually, the subjects did not respond to the subtle changes. Instead, they reported hearing an abrupt change in the syllable. This finding indicates that sharp physical boundaries delineate different phonemes.

Interestingly, Eimas, Siqueland, Jusczyk, and Vigorito (1971) used habituation (see Chapter 2) to show that even one-month-old babies make similar categorical distinctions between phonemes. Infants from Spanish-speaking homes who had never been exposed to English (Lasky, Syrdal-Lasky, & Klein, 1975) react the same way as infants from English-speaking homes. These observations suggest an innate ability to detect specific phonemes. However, experience determines which sounds gain significance. The finding that different languages use different phonemes indicates that cultural experience governs which phonemes adults will be able to recognize. Additional support for this view comes from studies in which subjects are trained to make phoneme distinctions they normally do not make. For example, Streeter and Landauer (1976) reported that Spanish children could be taught to distinguish between *ba* and *pa*, a discrimination that is not part of the Spanish language.

Morphemes

A **morpheme** is the smallest meaningful unit of language. Whereas phonemes are single sounds that enable us to distinguish the meanings of different words, morphemes are the simplest combinations of phonemes that can be formed and still have meaning. Some morphemes are single phonemes, such as the words *A* and *I*. Other morphemes contain two or more phonemes; the words *fun, joy,* and *car,* for example. A morpheme does not have to be a word; prefixes (e.g., *un-* and *re-*) and suffixes (*-er* and *-able*) are also morphemes. Similarly, parts of words that make a noun plural (leaf to leaves) or indicate that a verb is present or past (catch, caught) are also morphemes. Consider the words *pill* and *pillow*. Adding *ow* to the word *pill* creates a word with a different meaning. The word *pill* is a **free morpheme,** because it can stand alone; *-ow* is a **bound morpheme** because it must be bound to a free morpheme to have meaning.

Sentences

Words can be combined into a **phrase,** a group of two or more related words that express a single thought, and phrases can connect to form a sentence. A **sentence** consists of two or more phrases and conveys assertion, question, command, wish, or exclamation. For example, the sentence, *The couple bought the house,* consists of two major phrases: the noun phrase *the couple* and the verb phrase *bought the house.*

How do we construct a sentence? Phrases cannot be randomly combined to form a sentence. Rules govern the formation of sentences, and rules determine how phonemes are grouped to form words and how words are combined to express various ideas. The rules that govern language are called **syntax.**

Syntax: The Rules of Language

Syntax is the system of rules for combining the various units of speech. These rules can form an infinite number of morphemes, phrases, and sentences. Thus, human language is generative: syntax enables us to create an infinite number of meaningful expressions. Every language has its own syntax and, therefore, its own unique way of communicating ideas.

Phonology

Languages do not use every possible phoneme combination. For example, the two phonemes /p/ and /z/ cannot be combined to begin a word in the English language. Each language restricts the way in which phonemes can combine to produce meaningful morphemes. **Phonology** refers to the rules that dictate how phonemes can be combined into morphemes.

Grammar

Grammar rules establish the ways that words can be combined into meaningful phrases, clauses, and sentences. Words must be arranged to indicate mutual relations; they cannot be grouped haphazardly, Consider the following example provided by the noted psycholinguist Noam Chomsky (1957): *Colorless green ideas sleep furiously* is a meaningful sentence, although somewhat ridiculous, whereas the same five words arranged as *Furiously sleep ideas green colorless* is not even a sentence. When words are organized according to the rules of grammar, the resulting sentence conveys some kind of meaning. However, words strung together randomly do not express a coherent thought or idea.

Linguists have studied the structure of the sentence in terms of phrases. This analysis of the constituents of a sentence is called **phrase-structure grammar.** The analysis begins by dividing a sentence into a noun phrase and a verb phrase. **Figure 11.8** presents a diagram of the phrase-structure grammar for the sentence *The couple bought the house.* As the diagram illustrates, the noun and verb phrase can then be divided further. This detailed linguistic analysis identifies all of the constituent structures of the sentence. The phrase-structure analysis of a simple sentence can be easy; obviously, complex sentences are more difficult to diagram. I still remember my seventh-grade English class and the considerable frustration I experienced trying to construct "grammar trees." Perhaps you have similar memories.

The rules of grammar are elaborate, and we do not always follow them. However, because they are generally accepted, using these rules of grammar allows us to communicate effectively with each other.

FIGURE 11.8. The phrase-structure grammar of the sentence
The couple bought the house.

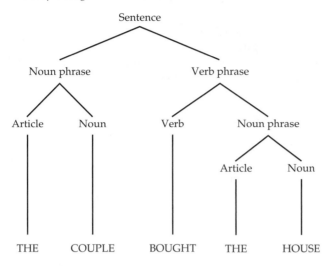

Semantics: The Meaning of Language

Consider the following two sentences: *The boy hit the ball. The ball was hit by the boy.* As **Figure 11.9** shows, the grammar trees for these two sentences are quite different, but the sentences convey the same meaning. According to Houston (1986), the fact that different sentences may have the same meaning points to one important problem of the phrase-structure grammar approach to language. Also, according to Houston, there is a second difficulty with this approach: one sentence may have two different meanings. For example, the sentence "They are growing trees" can mean either that a group of people are in the business of growing trees, or that certain trees are in the process of growing. **Figure 11.10** presents the phrase-structure analyses of this ambiguous sentence.

Analyzing the grammar of a sentence is not the same as analyzing the meaning or the study of **semantics.** Noam Chomsky (1965) recognized this difference. In Chomsky's view, the arrangement of the words in a sentence represents the sentence's **surface structure.** The meaning or idea conveyed by the sentence is its **deep structure.** Only by determining the deep structure can we understand the meaning of a sentence.

How do we figure out the meaning of a sentence? A number of psycholinguists have described this process (Forster, 1979; Wanner & Maratsos, 1978). The first step in the comprehension of a sentence is to divide it into **clauses.** For example, the sentence, *The pitcher threw the ball, and the batter hit it,* expresses two complete thoughts or propositions; these two thoughts are clauses. Evidence of the application of clause analysis comes from a study by Foder, Bever, and Garrett (1974) in which subjects heard a clicking sound either in the middle of the first clause or between the two clauses. Regardless of when the click was actually presented, subjects reported hearing a click between the two clauses. This study indicates that a clause is a cognitive unit that resists disruption. Thus, the click presented in the middle of the first clause "migrated" to the end of the

FIGURE 11.9. The phrase-structure grammar of the two sentences *The boy hit the ball* and *The ball was hit by the boy.*

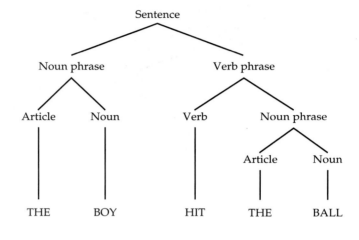

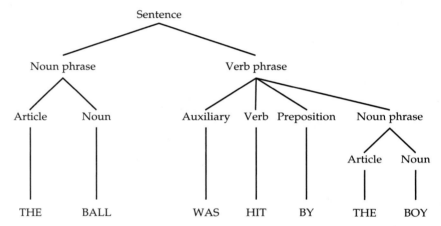

clause, and a click presented at either point in the sentence represented a "mental comma" between the two clauses.

After we have divided a sentence into clauses, we can then determine its meaning. Let's use the sentence *The cat chased the mouse* to illustrate this process. To understand the sentence, the reader must determine who is the "doer" and who is "done-to." One approach is to use the "first-noun-phrase-did-it" strategy (Bever, 1970). Using this strategy, we assume the sentence is in the active voice, and we tentatively identify the first noun clause as the doer and the second noun clause as the done-to. This strategy can convey the meaning of the sentence, and of most sentences, since we use the active voice much more frequently than the passive voice. However, it will communicate an incorrect meaning if the sentence is in the passive voice. Several clues indicate the use of the passive voice; for example, the words *was* and *by* in the sentence *The mouse was chased by the cat.* These cue words indicate that the first-noun-phrase-did-it strategy is invalid.

FIGURE 11.10. Two different phrase-structure grammar trees for the ambiguous sentence *They are growing trees.*

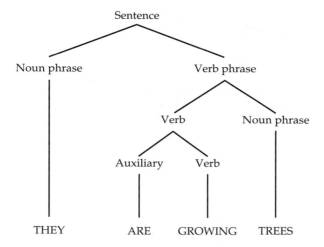

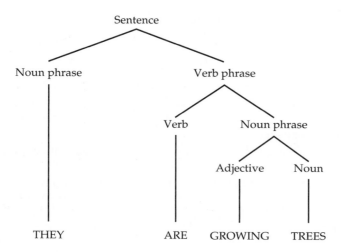

Slobin (1966) suggested that an elaborate grammatical analysis is often used to determine the deep structure of passive-voice sentences. To provide evidence for this view, Slobin asked his subjects to listen to a sentence, look at a picture, and then decide whether the sentence described the picture. Slobin reported that subjects took longer to react to passive-voice sentences than to active-voice sentences. Because the grammatical analysis was more elaborate, subjects had longer reaction times for passive-voice sentences than for active-voice ones.

Note that we sometimes can use shortcuts to determine meaning (Slobin, 1966). For example, consider the sentence: *The flowers are watered by the girl.* Even though the sentence is in the passive voice, we can quickly determine its logical meaning. It is plausible that girls water flowers; flowers do not water girls. However, this shortcut will not work for sentences with reversible meanings, for example, *The cat is chased by the dog.*

Not only do we receive and interpret language, we also generate it. According to Chomsky (1965), we can express ideas in a number of ways; that is, deep structures can be transmitted through various surface structures. Chomsky suggested that transformational rules enable the same deep structure to generate many different surface structures. Each language has its own acceptable rules of transformational grammar. Individuals in particular cultures must learn these rules so that their use of language complies with accepted grammatical principles and is thus understood by other members of that culture.

Acquisition of Language

There are two major views of how humans acquire the ability to use language. A learning view, first proposed by B. F. Skinner in 1957, proposed that we acquire language through the operant conditioning process (see Chapter 4). According to this approach, children learn to use language because their parents and other people in their environment reinforce it. The psycholinguistic theory, initially described by Noam Chomsky in 1965, proposed that language acquisition is innate. In this view, humans are born with certain mechanisms that enable them to learn to communicate with only a minimal amount of linguistic experience.

A Reinforcement View

Suppose that a mother hears her young child say "Mama." In all likelihood, the mother will be pleased, and she will give the child a hug and kiss. This affection reinforces the child's behavior and thus increases the frequency of the child's use of language.

Skinner (1957) argued that humans acquire responses, including language, according to the laws of operant conditioning (see Chapter 4). In Skinner's view, shaping is used to encourage children to learn to communicate with words. Initially, adults reinforce approximations of a desired verbal response, but eventually they expect a closer resemblance to the final behavior before providing reinforcement. Consider Anne, a baby learning to talk. When Anne first makes any sound resembling a real word, such as the *m* sound for *mama*, Anne's parents are delighted and reinforce her with praise and affection. However, as Anne continues to make nonsense sounds, her parents gradually stop responding to them. To again receive reinforcement, Anne must learn to say something closer to an actual word, such as "mama."

Words are not the only language units that we can acquire through reinforcement. Skinner argued that phrases and sentences can also be learned by the process of shaping; initially, nongrammatical phrases and sentences may be reinforced, but eventually only correct language use will be reinforced.

Psycholinguists have been extremely critical of Skinner's reinforcement view of language acquisition (see Lenneberg, 1969, for a discussion of these criticisms). There are three major aspects of this criticism. The first problem is that

Skinner's view assumes that parents reinforce the correct use of language and ignore or penalize incorrect use, but observations (McNeill, 1966) show that parents reinforce and punish only the content, not the grammatical correctness, of their children's language. Thus, a parent will allow a grammatically incorrect sentence to be used as long as the content is accurate. Brown, Cazden, and Bellugi's (1969) description of the language of two children, Eve and Adam, provides an excellent illustration of the influence of parental approval and disapproval on a child's use of language:

> Gross errors of word choice were sometimes corrected, as when Eve said, "What the guy idea." Once in a while an error of pronunciation was noticed and corrected. More commonly, however, the grounds on which an utterance was approved or disapproved . . . were not strictly linguistic at all. When Eve expressed the opinion that her mother was a girl by saying, "She a girl," the mother answered, "That's right." The child's utterance was ungrammatical but the mother did not respond to that fact; instead she responded to the truth . . . of the proposition the child intended to express . . . Adam's "Walt Disney comes on Tuesday" was disapproved because Walt Disney came on some other day. It seems then to be truth value rather than syntactic well-formedness that chiefly governs explicit verbal reinforcement by parents—which renders mildly paradoxical the fact that the usual product of such (training) is an adult whose speech is highly grammatical but not notably truthful. (pp. 70–71)

A second problem that psycholinguists have cited with the reinforcement view concerns the creative aspect of language. Children (as well as adults) frequently use original combinations of words to convey an idea. The fact that people can generate new but grammatically accurate language is difficult to explain in terms of operant conditioning principles: how can children (or adults) use a combination of words that they have never said nor heard before and that therefore has never been reinforced? Consider Miller's (1965) statement to illustrate this criticism of the reinforcement theory:

> By a rough, but conservative, calculation there are 10^{20} sentences 20 words long, and if a child were to learn only these it would take him something on the order of 1000 times the estimated age of the earth just to learn them. . . . Any attempt to account for language acquisition that does not have a generative character will encounter this difficulty . . . Since the variety of admissible word combinations is so great, no child could learn all of them. Instead of learning specific combinations of words, he learns rules for generating admissible combinations. (pp. 176, 178)

The final and perhaps strongest criticism comes from Lenneberg's research showing that despite widely varying social conditions, most children acquire language in a relatively constant pattern. It seems reasonable to expect that children living in different cultures would show various patterns of language acquisition. Yet, Lenneberg found that nonsense sounds are always followed by one-word speech, which then develops into the use of two-word sentences, followed by telegraphic speech, and then the use of complex sentences. The observation that even children raised by deaf parents follow the same pattern of language development suggests that social reinforcement is not a critical determinant of language acquisition.

A Psycholinguistic View

Noam Chomsky (1965, 1975, 1987) was very impressed with how easily young children learn their native language. He described the universal sequence of language development from nonsense sounds to the generation of complex sentences and, on the basis of these observations, suggested that children are born with a language-generating mechanism called the **language acquisition device (LAD).** The LAD "knows" the universal aspects of language. This knowledge allows children to readily grasp the syntax relevant to their native language. In Chomsky's view, however, this biological preparedness does not result in automatic language acquisition; a child must still be exposed to language to learn it. Usually, though, parents eager for their child to start talking provide more than adequate stimulation.

Chomsky's view that children are inherently prepared to learn language has received a considerable amount of support from psycholinguists (Dodd & White, 1980). For example, Lenneberg (1967, 1969) argued that language acquisition is an innate, species-specific characteristic and that its expression depends only on physical maturation and minimal exposure to language. According to Lenneberg, language is acquired in a fixed order and at a particular rate. Even when maturation is abnormally slow, as in the case of children with Down syndrome, language is still learned in the same sequence, but at a slower rate.

While only minimal exposure is necessary for language to be acquired, the earlier the experience, the better. Johnson and Newport (1989) evaluated the ability of Korean and Chinese immigrants to accurately identify 276 sentences as being grammatically correct or incorrect. Each immigrant had been living in the United States for approximately 10 years. Even though all the immigrants had the same length of exposure to English, Johnson and Newport found that those immigrants who arrived before age 8 understood grammar as well as native speakers. The accuracy declined to approximately 80% when age at immigration was 11 to 15 years of age and approximately 75% when age at immigration was 17 to 39 years of age. While individuals who immigrate to the United States after age 8 can master basic words and how to use them, the results of Johnson and Newport's study suggest that these immigrants are unlikely to become as fluent as individuals born in the United States in producing and comprehending subtle grammatical differences.

Deaf children also appear to need only minimal exposure to learn sign language. Petitto and Marentette (1991) reported that deaf children with deaf-signing parents learn to sign at the same age that hearing children with hearing-speaking parents learn to speak. However, deaf children who are not exposed to sign language early never become as fluent in signing as do deaf children exposed at an early age. The deaf children who are not exposed to sign language at an early age also have a difficult time producing and comprehending the subtle aspects of language. These results support the view that early exposure to language is necessary for a person to become proficient in a language. Failure to get this early language experience—either sign language in deaf children or English in immigrants—has permanent effects.

Our discussion suggests that human language acquisition is a biologically based form of learning that occurs during a sensitive period of development.

Some psychologists (Elkind, 1981; Rice, 1989) argue that language acquisition is not a unique form of learning, but instead merely reflects cognitive strategies that are translated into language. If language acquisition merely reflects an extension of our cognitive abilities, then we should see a high level of correspondence between cognitive abilities and language proficiency. While a high correspondence usually does exist between cognitive and linguistic abilities, as Pinker (1999) points out, cognitive development and linguistic development can be decoupled. Consider two case studies described by Cromer (1981). In one case history, a 20-year-old woman was deprived of language until the age of 12. Despite extensive training, the woman's language ability never progressed beyond that of a typical two-year-old. However, the woman did show a general cognitive ability of a 7- to 12-year-old child. The second case history involves a child who had poor cognitive ability. This child could create highly complex, grammatically correct language. Unfortunately, the content of the child's language was often nonsensical, presumably because language content depends upon cognitive ability. It would seem that humans are biologically prepared to learn language, but need some cognitive ability to use it effectively.

Application: Teaching Chimpanzees Language

Monkeys use sounds to communicate with each other. A primate can express a variety of different emotional states in a manner that other primates understand and respond to. Observations of vervet monkeys in Kenya (Seyfarth, Cheney, & Marler, 1980) reveal both the sophistication of primates' vocalizations as well as the reactions of other primates to these vocalizations. For example, the vervet monkeys made distinctive alarm calls when they spotted predators. The sight of a leopard caused them to emit a series of short, tonal calls. The sight of an eagle elicited a low-pitched grunt. The reaction to a snake consisted of a series of high-pitched "chutters." Each of these calls elicited a different response from vervet monkeys nearby: they ran for cover when hearing the eagle alarm call; and they looked down when hearing the snake alarm call. These observations indicate that primates can communicate through vocalizations; however, these vocalizations are not language. Can primates learn to use language to communicate?

Early investigations suggested that primates could not learn language. Winthrop and Luella Kellogg (1933) raised the baby chimpanzee Gua in their home with their infant son Donald. Despite many attempts to teach Gua to speak, the chimp never uttered any English words, although she did learn to obey certain commands. Cathy and Keith Hayes (1951) were somewhat more successful in teaching the chimpanzee Vicki to speak. Vicki learned to say three words—*papa, mama,* and *cup.* Yet she acquired these words only after a long period of training, which included manipulating the chimp's lips.

Beatrice and Allen Gardner (1971) were much more successful in teaching language to their chimp, Washoe. The Gardners believed that intellectual impairment was not responsible for earlier failures to teach chimpanzees language; instead, these failures were caused by the chimpanzees' physical inability to produce the complex vocalizations necessary for speech. So instead of trying to teach Washoe to speak English, they taught her American Sign Language. Washoe lived in a trailer in the Gardners' backyard and had the companionship of one or two people who talked to her only in sign language during all her waking hours. After four years of training, Washoe had learned over 200 signs and was able to combine them into sentences, such as *Please tickle more* or *Give me sweet drink.*

Did Washoe learn to use language to communicate? The Gardners thought so. Washoe's "language" certainly had many of the characteristics of human language. First, it made sense. For example, Washoe used the sign for *cat* to point out a cat, and the sign for *dog* to identify a dog. Second, Washoe's verbalizations were in sentence form. Third, Washoe's sentences were structured according to the rules of grammar; the sentence *Please tickle more* illustrates Washoe's mastery of syntax. Finally, Washoe responded to questions. For example, if the Gardners asked in sign language the question, "Who pretty?", Washoe answered, "Washoe."

Researchers have used techniques other than sign language to teach primates to communicate. Duane Rumbaugh and his colleagues (Rumbaugh & Gill, 1976; Savage-Rumbaugh, Rumbaugh, & Boysen, 1980) taught chimpanzees language with the aid of a computer. To obtain what they wanted, the chimpanzees had to press the keys that corresponded to specific words. For example, their chimpanzee Lana learned to send the following message, "Please machine make movie period." Two other chimpanzees, Austin and Sherman, even learned to communicate with each other through the computer. For example, Rumbaugh and his colleagues sometimes gave either Austin or Sherman food; the "unfed" chimpanzee had to ask the "fed" chimpanzee for food. Austin and Sherman learned to ask each other for food and for many other things.

Despite the fact that primates appear to use language to communicate, many psychologists do not believe that primates are capable of learning language. Herbert Terrace (1979), for example, teaching American Sign Language to a chimpanzee named Nim Chimpsky, noted some important differences between Nim's signing and human language. An intense, directed effort was required to teach Nim even very simple signs, whereas children do not need to be taught language; they learn to talk simply by being in an environment where language is used. Also, Terrace found no evidence that Nim could create unique grammatically correct sentences. According to Terrace, the chimpanzee did not learn the creative aspect of language; that is, she did not know how to use rules to create an infinite number of new and complex sentences. Instead, Terrace argued that the chimpanzee's multiword sentences merely imitated the order the trainer used. Reviewing the transcripts of the communications of Washoe and several other chimpanzees, Terrace concluded that these animals were unable to generate syntactically correct, novel combinations of signs. Terrace also noted that few of Nim's statements were spontaneous; most of them came in response to a human's statement. This lack of spontaneous speech is quite different from human speech.

Other psychologists (Marx, 1980; Pate & Rumbaugh, 1983; Thompson & Church, 1980) have supported Terrace's view. They report that while their chimpanzees were able to learn the meanings of many symbols, the chimps were unable to link them together into a meaningful sentence. Further, Rumbaugh (1990) reported that while his chimpanzees would respond when symbols were arranged in a familiar order, the chimps were unable to respond correctly to a new symbol order. These observations suggest that chimpanzees, unlike humans, are unable to generate or understand new linguistic units.

You might conclude that the research shows that primates are unable to learn language. However, recent studies by Sue Savage-Rumbaugh and Duane Rumbaugh (Savage-Rumbaugh, Sevcik, Brakke, & Rumbaugh, 1992; Savage-Rumbaugh, Shanker, & Taylor, 1996) suggest that the *Pan paniscus* chimpanzee may be able to learn language. The *Pan paniscus* chimpanzee, while related to the common (*Pan troglodytes*) chimpanzee, shows social behavior more typical of humans than other chimpanzees. For example, the *Pan paniscus* chimpanzee, also known as the pygmy chimpanzee or the bonobo chimpanzee, forms long-lasting attachments. Further, the female bonobo is sexually responsive throughout her menstrual cycle, and a male bonobo shares responsibility for infant care with its female mate. By contrast, for most other chimpanzee species, females are promiscuous and only responsive during estrus, and males contribute little to child-rearing.

The Rumbaughs first tried to teach a female bonobo, Mata, to respond by pressing symbols representing specific words on a board. While Mata was unable to learn to use the symbols, her infant son Kanzi quickly mastered the task (see **Figure 11.11**). Both Kanzi and his sister Panbanisha were able to use the symbols to request objects and to describe past events. Perhaps most importantly, Savage-Rumbaugh, Sevcik, Brakke, and Rumbaugh (1992) reported that Kanzi and Panbanisha were able to construct new requests using original combinations of symbols. Interestingly, Kanzi also has shown an ability to understand spoken English. He can respond even to original commands, such as "Go to the refrigerator and get out a tomato."

FIGURE 11.11. Photograph of Panbanisha, a bonobo chimpanzee, pressing symbols that represent specific words. Panbanisha has learned to press appropriate symbols to answer a question.

Why might Kanzi and Panbanisha have been able to master language when other chimpanzees apparently were not able to do so? Savage-Rumbaugh, Sevcik, Brakke, and Rumbaugh (1992) suggest several reasons. First, bonobos may have better language capabilities than other chimpanzees, although Kanzi and Panbanisha 's mother was not able to learn to use the symbols. Second, Kanzi and Panbanisha were exposed to language early in life, observing and then imitating language. Perhaps this early observational and imitation experience promotes better language acquisition than does the formal training researchers used with other chimpanzees. While the behavior of Kanzi and Panbanisha seems to suggest that some primates can learn language, earlier research generated the same kind of optimism. Some researchers (Kako, 1999; Wallman, 1992) continue to express skepticism that Kanzi's and Panbanisha 's communications demonstrate all of the properties of language, although Kako (1999) acknowledges that Kanzi appears to comprehend both the meaning of words and the relations between words contained in the structure of language. The final answer to the question of whether primates truly learn language awaits future research.

BEFORE YOU GO ON

- **How did language assist Regina in solving her problem?**
- **Could she have solved her problem without the use of language?**

CHAPTER SUMMARY

A concept is a symbol that represents a class or group of objects or events that have common characteristics. The prototype best exemplifies the concept because it possesses more attributes of the concept than the other members of the concept do. Boundaries specify the point at which a particular object or event is not a member of a specific concept.

The affirmative rule states that the presence of a particular attribute defines the concept. The negative rule states that a member of the concept cannot possess a specific attribute. The presence of two or more attributes defines a concept by the conjunctive rule. The disjunctive rule states that the presence of one of two or both attributes defines the concept.

We learn concepts by associating the concept name with specific instances of the concept. A concept can also be learned by testing hypotheses about the attributes of the concept or about the rules defining the concept.

A problem exists when an obstacle or obstacles blocks attainment of a desired goal. Thorndike argued that problems are solved by trial and error. Kohler argued that a problem is first explored internally. Possible solutions are then tested, and, finally, insight into the correct solution is gained. Insight enables the problem to be solved.

Defining the problem—identifying both the starting point, or initial state, and the end point, or goal state, of the problem—is the first step. In some cases, the problem is well-defined, with clear starting and end points; however, some problems are ill-defined. The key to solving an ill-defined problem is generating subproblems.

The initial step in problem solving also involves identifying the operations one can use to solve the problem as well as restrictions that will not help to solve the problem. The second step in problem solving is developing a strategy. There are two types of strategies: algorithms, which are precise rules, and heuristics, which are best-guess strategies.

Some heuristics are systematic problem-solving methods. Using the working-backward strategy, the problem solver begins at the end point and works back to the starting point. This means-end strategy breaks the problem down into a series of subproblems. Other heuristic strategies are cognitive shortcuts, which are usually effective but sometimes lead to extreme errors. With the representative strategy, solutions are based only on the obvious characteristics of the problem; with the availability strategy, only information that one can remember is used to solve problems.

Executing the strategy is the third step, and solving the problem is the final step. Difficulties are common in solving a problem. These difficulties are sometimes caused by the influence of past experiences. In the case of functional fixedness, inability to recognize new uses for familiar objects impairs problem solving. Solving problems may also be impaired by a set, which motivates a person to approach new problems with strategies that solved earlier problems, even when the old strategies are no longer effective.

Experts are generally able to solve problems more readily than novices, in part due to greater knowledge and understanding, which enables the expert to use principles gained from previous experience to solve new problems.

Language allows us to communicate with others; it facilitates the learning process and enables us to recall information beyond the limits of our memory stores. The phoneme is the simplest speech sound. Phonemes combine to form a morpheme, the smallest meaningful unit of language. Morphemes are words (free morphemes) as well as prefixes and suffixes (bound morphemes). Words can be combined into a phrase, which expresses a single thought, and phrases can be grouped to form a sentence, which conveys an assertion, question, command, wish, or exclamation.

Syntax is the system of rules that govern how various units of speech can be combined. Phonology refers to the rules specifying how phonemes can be combined into words, whereas the rules of grammar establish how words are combined into meaningful phrases and sentences. Grammar refers to the surface structure of a sentence; the meaning conveyed by the sentence is called the deep structure. The study of the meaning of language, called semantics, has shown that the same sentence can have different meanings, and different sentences can have the same meaning.

Skinner argued that children acquire language because they are reinforced for appropriate language use. Chomsky argued that humans have an innate ability to learn language and that language can be used to communicate after only a minimal amount of linguistic experience.

Primates have been taught sign language and can use signs in sentences. Some psycholinguists believe that these primates communicate with language, and therefore argue that language is not limited to humans. However, other psycholinguists believe that primates are not actually using language, but are merely imitating behavior that their trainers have reinforced.

CRITICAL THINKING QUESTIONS

1. Dana Carvey is Paula's favorite comedian. Explain what process allows Paula to identify Carvey as a comedian. Why does she view Carvey as a great comedian?
2. Benita does not have sufficient funds for the remainder of the month. How might she obtain, in a legal fashion, enough money to pay her bills? Explain the process that allows Benita to decide how to obtain more money.
3. Lawrence read about psychologists training primates to use sign language. He is skeptical that primates use language to communicate. Discuss the basis of this skepticism. What evidence supports the claims that primates can acquire language? Does the most recent evidence in the area provide important new information? What do you think is the likely outcome of this controversy?

KEY TERMS

affirmative rule	heuristic	problem
algorithm	ill-defined problem	prototype
attribute	initial state	representativeness
availability strategy	insight	strategy
bound morpheme	language	rule
clause	language acquisition	semantics
concept	device (LAD)	sentence
conjunctive rule	matching to sample	set
deep structure	means-end analysis	surface structure
disjunctive rule	morpheme	syntax
family resemblance	negative rule	well-defined problem
free morpheme	phoneme	working-backward
functional fixedness	phonology	heuristic
goal state	phrase	
grammar	phrase-structure grammar	

CHAPTER 12

The Storage of Our Experiences

A Fleeting Experience

While working at a construction site last year, Donald was hit in the head by a piece of wood. Although the accident only left Donald unconscious for several minutes, it completely altered his life. Donald can still recall events that occurred prior to the injury, but once new thoughts leave his consciousness, they are lost. Two experiences occurred today that demonstrate Donald's memory problem. Donald and his wife were shopping when a man whom Donald could not recall ever meeting approached them with a friendly greeting: "Hello, Helen and Don." The man commented it was a beautiful day to go shopping. He was looking for a sweater for his daughter's birthday, but so far had had no luck finding the right sweater. Helen mentioned that the clothing store at the other end of the mall had nice sweaters and the man said that he would try that store. After the man had walked away, Helen identified the "stranger" as a neighbor, Bill Jones, who had moved into a house down the block several months ago. Don became frustrated when Helen told him he frequently talked with this neighbor. Helen, too, was frustrated; she often wished that Don would remember what she told him. She knew Don would ask her again about Bill Jones the next time they met. When they arrived home, Don received a telephone call from his aunt, informing him of his uncle's death. Don, immediately struck with an intense grief, cried for almost an hour over the loss of his favorite uncle. Yet, after another phone call, Donald no longer recalled his uncle's death. Helen told him again, and he experienced the intense grief all over again.

Donald suffers from a disorder called anterograde amnesia. His memory problems are the direct result of his accident, which caused an injury to an area of the brain called the hippocampus. The hippocampus is involved in the storage of recent experiences in a permanent, or relatively permanent, way. As the result of brain damage, Donald cannot store the experiences that have occurred since the accident.

For a person to recall an event, the brain must go through three processes. First, it must store the experience as a memory. Second, it must encode or organize the memory into a meaningful form. Third, the brain must retrieve the memory. This chapter describes the storage and encoding of our experiences, and Chapter 13 looks at the retrieval of memory. Chapter 13 also discusses forgetting as a result of retrieval failure. We examine memory losses that result from storage failure in this chapter, and we also describe the biological basis of memory storage.

MEASURES OF MEMORY

How do psychologists measure the memory of past events? There are two primary ways to test memory. Explicit methods involve overt (observable) measures of memory. Implicit methods assess memory indirectly.

There are two **explicit measures of memory:** recall and recognition. **Recall measures** require a subject to access a memory. With **free recall,** no cues are available to assist recall. An example of free recall might be the question "What did you have for dinner last night?" With **cued recall,** signals are presented that can help with the recall of a past experience. The question "What did you have at the Mexican restaurant?" would be an example of a cued recall test. In this example, the reference to the type of restaurant helps you remember what you had for dinner last night. Under most circumstances, recall is higher with cued recall than free recall. The reason for this will be evident shortly.

There are some occasions when information is presented, and the subject's task is to judge whether the information accurately reflects a previous experience. When the memory measure is a judgment of the accuracy of a memory, it is a **recognition measure** of memory. With yes-no recognition, the memory task involves a decision as to whether or not the information is accurate. A forced-choice recognition task involves the selection of the correct information among incorrect information. Performance on recognition tasks is a function of several factors. One is the strength of the memory; another is punishment for false recognition. Recognition is better with a strong memory but poorer when a person is penalized for selecting an incorrect alternative.

Do recognition measures yield better retention than recall measures? Most students would claim that they do better on a recognition measure than on a free recall test. Yet the presence of certain distractors can actually yield rather poor recognition performance (Watkins & Tulving, 1975).

There are also several **implicit measures of memory.** Ebbinghaus (1885) used the **savings score** to measure memory. To obtain a savings score, one subtracts the number of trials it takes to relearn a task from the number of trials the original learning required. Needing fewer relearning trials probably reflects that the memory was retained from original learning. **Reaction time** is another implicit measure of memory. A subject is presented with a stimulus, and the time it takes to react to that stimulus is recorded. If the subject reacts more readily on the second encounter than on the first, the faster reaction time is thought to be due to the memory of the prior experience. Both explicit and implicit measures have yielded significant information about the nature of memory.

Richard Atkinson and Richard Shiffrin (1971) suggested that there are three stages in the storage of information: sensory register, short-term store, and long-term store. As **Figure 12.1** shows, external input is initially stored in the **sensory register** for a very brief time, usually 0.25 to 2 seconds. The information contained in the sensory register is an initial impression of the external environment; this impression decays rapidly after leaving the sensory register and will be lost unless it is processed into the short-term store. The **short-term store** is a temporary, limited-capacity facility for our experiences. Memories can remain in the short-term store for 5, 10, 15 seconds, or even longer. The length of time information remains in short-term store depends upon whether the experience is being rehearsed or repeated. Without rehearsal, information can be lost from the short-term store before it is stored in a meaningful way. Since the short-term store can retain only a limited amount of information, old information will be "bumped out" when new information enters the short-term store, unless there is enough room for both the old and the new information. Most information contained in the short-term store is transferred into the **long-term store,** the site of permanent memory storage.

Storage of a memory in the long-term store does not guarantee the ability to recall that particular memory. The presence of other memories may interfere with the recollection of a particular experience; this failure to recall a specific memory because of the presence of other memories is called **interference.** The failure to recall a memory also may result from the absence of a specific stimulus that can retrieve the memory. People can use salient aspects of an

FIGURE 12.1. A diagram illustrating the Atkinson-Shiffrin three-stage model of memory storage. Initially, experiences are stored in the sensory register. In the second stage of memory storage, or the short-term store, experiences are interpreted and organized. The final stage, or long-term store, represents the site of permanent (or almost permanent) memory storage.

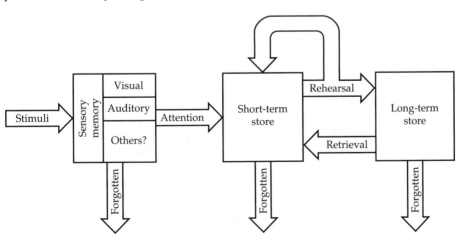

event, called **memory attributes,** to remember the event. The absence of these environmental events can cause a memory failure.

Atkinson and Shiffrin suggest that the short-term store organizes experiences in meaningful ways, facilitating later retrieval. The organization of experience can occur even after a memory moves to long-term store, where it can receive additional processing. This processing may facilitate later recall. It can also alter the memory, making the memory more logical or appealing.

We will use the Atkinson-Schiffrin model to organize our discussion of the storage of an experience. We will address alternatives to this view of memory storage later in this chapter.

SENSORY REGISTER

How are memories stored? Several lines of evidence suggest that a copy of an experience is stored in the sensory register. However, the copy lasts for only a very short time (usually 0.25 to 2 seconds). Research on the sensory store has focused on two sensory systems: the visual system and the auditory system. The visual copy contained in the sensory store is referred to as an **icon,** and the copy is stored in **iconic memory.** The auditory experience contained in the sensory store is referred to as an **echo,** and the copy is stored in **echoic memory.**

Iconic Memory

In Search of an Icon

The classic research of George Sperling (1960, 1963) examined the storage of visual information in the sensory register. Sperling's findings demonstrated that (1) an icon is a copy of a visual experience and (2) an iconic memory lasts for only a very brief time following the event. Sperling presented to subjects an array of letters arranged in three horizontal rows of four letters each (see **Figure 12.2**). An apparatus called a tachistoscope was used to present the letters on a screen for 0.05 seconds. The screen was then blank for a specified retention interval of 0 to 1 second. Some of Sperling's subjects received a **partial report technique;** they were asked at the end of the interval to recall all the letters in one of the three rows. The subjects were not informed before the end of the retention interval which line they were to recall. A tone presented at the end of the retention interval indicated which line should be recalled: a high pitch indicated the top row; a medium-pitched tone, the middle row; and a low-pitched tone, the bottom row. Presenting the tone very soon after the presentation of the array of letters enabled the subjects to remember most of the letters. However, if the retention interval was greater than 0.25 seconds, the subjects' performance declined significantly, and they could remember only about one letter per line (refer to **Figure 12.3**). The fact that retention is high on an immediate but not on a delayed retention test indicates that even though subjects have access to all information contained in the sensory store, the visual copy fades quickly following entry into the sensory register.

FIGURE 12.2. Sperling's procedure for investigating the visual sensory memory. This illustration shows one trial using the partial report technique. In this procedure, subjects see 12 letters for ½₀ second. A tone is presented at the appropriate time to indicate which row of letters the subjects should attempt to recall. A high-pitched tone means the top row; a medium-pitched tone, the middle row; and a low-pitched tone, the bottom row.

Phase 1 Experimenter presents array for ¹⁄₂₀ second	**Phase 2** Tone signals which row subject is to recall	**Phase 3** Subject tries to recall correct row

X G O B T M L R V A S F	High tone means recall top row. Medium tone means recall middle row. Low tone means recall bottom row.	For example: high tone signals subject to recall X G O B

FIGURE 12.3. Performance level in Sperling's investigation of visual sensory memory. The solid line on the graph shows the number of letters recalled (left axis) and the percentage recalled (right axis) for subjects given the partial report technique as a function of the delay between signal and recall. The bar at the right presents the number and percentage correct for the whole report technique. As the graph indicates, a subject can report all the letters immediately after the stimulus ends; however, the recall of letters declines rapidly following stimulus presentation.

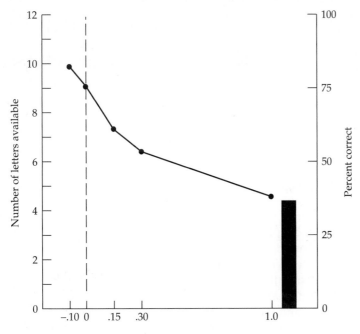

Delay of the partial report cue (seconds)

Sperling asked some of his subjects to recall as many of the 12 letters in the array as possible. When recall occurred immediately after the stimulus presentation had ended, this procedure, referred to as a **whole report technique,** resulted in subjects remembering only about 4.5 letters (see **Figure 12.3**). Sperling's observations with the partial report technique indicated that all 12 letters were encoded into the sensory store; why, then, could subjects receiving the whole report technique remember only about one-third of them? Since experiences stored in the sensory register decay rapidly, the image fades before the subjects can recall more than 4 or 5 of the letters.

Note that when the retention interval was longer than 0.25 seconds, subjects were able to recall approximately 4.5 of the letters, or 1.5 of the letters in a particular row. As we learned earlier in this chapter, only a limited amount of information can be transferred from the sensory register to short-term memory. The ability of Sperling's subjects to recall only 4.5 of all 12 letters, or 1.5 of the 4 letters in a particular row, after a 0.5- or 1-second delay suggests that only these letters were transferred from the sensory store to short-term memory, and that decay caused the rest to be lost.

The Duration of an Icon

Sperling's study (1960) suggests that visual images are stored in the sensory register for 0.25 seconds. However, depending on conditions, icons may persist for as long as a second or for less than 0.25 seconds. The intensity of the visual events appears to affect the duration of an icon. For example, Keele and Chase (1967) reported that iconic memory is longer when a bright rather than dim display of letters is used. Similarly, if the preletter and postletter exposure displays are very bright, Averbach and Sperling (1961) observed that the icon may last less than 0.25 seconds, whereas the icon may persist for more than a second when the displays following a visual event are very dark. These results suggest that an intense stimulus produces a long-duration iconic memory, and a strong second visual experience can reduce the duration of the visual image of the first stimulus.

Echoic Memory

In Search of an Echo

The sensory register can also contain a record of an auditory experience. Neisser (1967) called the memory of an auditory experience in the sensory register echoic memory, or an "echo" of a recent event. Moray, Bates, and Barnett (1965) conducted an evaluation of echoic memory comparable to Sperling's study of iconic memory. Each subject sat alone in a room containing four high-fidelity loudspeakers placed far enough apart so that subjects could discriminate the sounds coming from each speaker. At various times during the study, each speaker emitted a list of spoken letters. The list ranged from one to four letters, transmitted simultaneously from each loudspeaker. For example, at the same instant, loudspeaker 1 produced letter *e;* loudspeaker 2, letter *k;* loudspeaker 3, letter *g;* and loudspeaker 4, letter *t.*

For some trials, each subject was required to report as many letters as possible, a procedure analogous to Sperling's whole report technique. Moray, Bates, and Barnett reported that subjects remembered only a small proportion of the letters presented from the four loudspeakers. On other trials, subjects were asked to recall the letters coming from only one of the four loudspeakers. In this procedure, analogous to Sperling's partial report technique, subjects recalled the letters on most of the trials.

Darwin, Turvey, and Crowder's (1972) results also show that an echo lasts a very short time. Their experiment was similar to the Moray, Bates, and Barnett study, with two exceptions: first, subjects heard simultaneous lists of letters from three rather than four locations; second, after the termination of the list, the time delay before the subjects were required to recall the letters varied. Darwin, Turvey, and Crowder used four delay intervals: 0 seconds (immediately after the letters were presented) and 1, 2, or 4 seconds later. As **Figure 12.4** indicates, using the partial report technique, the level of recall declined as the interval between the auditory event and the testing increased. In fact, using a 4-second retention interval, recall with the partial report technique was similar to recall with the whole report technique. These results point out that the copy of an auditory experience stored in echoic memory is only temporary. We learned in our discussion of iconic memory that the typical duration of an icon is approximately 0.25 seconds. **Figure 12.4** suggests that an echo lasts several seconds. Why does the representation of an auditory experience stored in sensory memory decay more slowly than the trace of a visual event?

FIGURE 12.4. Performance level in Darwin, Turvey, and Crowder's study of the auditory sensory system. The graph presents the number of items available as a function of the delay between signal offset and recall test. The bar at the right shows performance with the whole report technique. The results of this study show rapid forgetting of auditory stimuli stored in the sensory register.

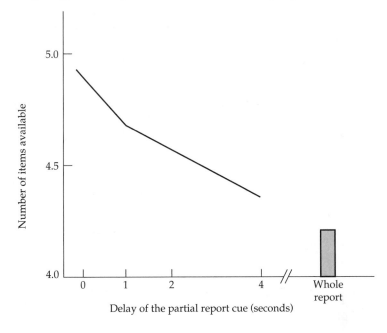

Although you might anticipate that an echo would have the same duration as an icon, Wingfield and Byrnes (1981) suggest that the typical duration of an echo is 2 seconds. To examine why the sensory register stores an auditory event for a longer period than a visual event, consider this example. Suppose you look at a chair. All the information needed to detect that the object is a chair is contained in your visual snapshot of the chair. Thus, salient physical characteristics of visual events can be detected by examining a single visual image of an event from a particular moment. However, suppose that someone says the word *chair* to you. Five separate sounds, or phonemes, are contained in this word (see Chapter 11 for a discussion of phonemes). To detect that the word is *chair*, you must combine the five sounds into one word. Although this combining of sounds into a word takes place in the short-term store, the detection of each of the phonemes occurs in the sensory register.

Crowder and Morton (1969) used a serial learning procedure to estimate the duration of echoic memory. (In the typical serial learning study, subjects are presented a list of items to learn. Each subject's task is to learn the items in the exact order in which they are presented. Experiments on serial learning demonstrate that subjects do not learn each item on the list at the same rate. Instead, they learn items at the beginning and at the end of the list more readily than items in the middle of the list. This difference in the rate of learning is called the **serial position effect.**) Crowder and Morton presented to subjects several lists of random digits; each list contained seven digits presented at a rate of 100 milliseconds per digit. After each list, a brief, 400-millisecond delay ensued. Subjects then recalled as many of the seven digits as possible. Although all the digits were presented visually, some subjects were told to look at the digits and remain silent until the time for recall. Other subjects were instructed to say the name of each digit aloud when it was presented. As **Figure 12.5** shows, although the rate of recall did not differ for items early in the list using either the visual (silent) or auditory (aloud) presentations, the retention of the last few digits was greater with auditory than with visual presentation. Thus, more errors were made on the last few digits when the subject remained silent, relying on visual presentation alone.

One explanation for this difference is that iconic and echoic memory have different durations. According to Crowder and Morton, with visual presentation, subjects have poor recall of the last items on the list because the visual trace of these digits fades before the end of the 400-millisecond retention interval. In contrast, recall of the last digits is higher with the auditory presentation because the echo of the last few digits remains through the 400-millisecond delay. If it is assumed that several hundred milliseconds are required to present the last few items of the list and 400 milliseconds intervene between the last digit and recall, then the duration of echoic memory is close to the 2-second estimate Darwin, Turvey, and Crowder (1972) suggested.

The Nature of a Sensory Memory

Psychologists initially thought that a sensory memory is an exact replica of an event; that is, an icon is an exact copy of a visual stimulus and an echo is an exact duplicate of a sound (Posner, 1982). However, more recent research suggests

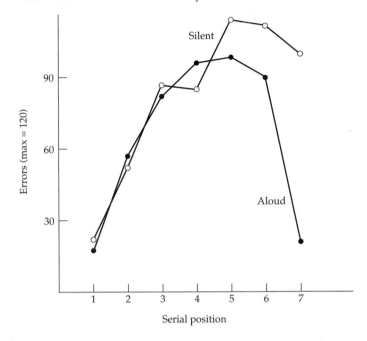

FIGURE 12.5. The number of errors as a function of the serial position of the letters for subjects who received stimuli that were either silent or aloud. The recall of the letters at the end of the list was significantly better (there were fewer errors) when the letters were read aloud rather than silently.

that some processing of an event occurs in the sensory register (Leahey & Harris, 2001). For example, Merikle (1980) modified Sperling's partial report procedure by presenting mixed arrays of numbers and letters. Recall that Sperling presented different pitches to indicate the specific line of letters to be recalled. Merikle found that a cue to recall a specific set of numbers, which requires some processing of the stimulus array, was as effective as a cue to recall a particular line. These results support the view that some categorization occurs in the sensory register and that a sensory memory may not be an exact copy of a sensory experience.

We have examined the nature of iconic and echoic sensory memories. While auditory and visual memories are quite important, memories exist for all the senses. The memory of the fragrance of perfume certainly lingers after the odor is gone. Similarly, taste and tactile experiences last beyond the end of stimulation. Thus, the memory of spicy food remains after the food is swallowed and the memory of stepping on a pebble while walking barefoot on the beach definitely lasts for a while. As we will discover in Chapter 13, all types of sensory experiences play a central role in the retrieval of past experiences.

BEFORE YOU GO ON

- **Can Don store his experiences in his sensory register?**
- **If so, do his immediate recollections differ from those of his wife Helen?**

SHORT-TERM STORE

The short-term store is thought to have five major characteristics: (1) it has a brief storage span; (2) the memories it contains are easily disrupted by new experiences; (3) its storage capacity is limited—it can maintain only a small amount of information; (4) its main function is to organize and analyze information; and (5) it also has a rehearsal function; that is, the short-term store can rehearse or replay memories of prior experiences. We next examine these five characteristics of the short-term store.

The Span of Short-Term Memory

Say the nonsense syllable TXZ, and then start counting backward by threes, beginning with the number 632 and continuing with 629, 626, 623, 620, 617, 614, 611, 608, 605, 602, 599, 596, 593, 590, 587, 584, 581, 578, and 575. Do you remember the nonsense syllable? In all likelihood, you do not. The sensory receptors detected the nonsense syllable, and the memory of the syllable was registered in the sensory register and entered into the short-term store. Yet, the memory of the nonsense syllable was lost as the result of the counting-backward task. Because this task required only approximately 20 seconds to complete, it appears that the memory of the nonsense syllable is rapidly forgotten after entering the short-term store.

This example was modeled after the classic Peterson and Peterson study (1959). In this study, subjects were presented a number of three-consonant trigrams. After saying the three letters of each trigram, the subjects were given a number and required to start counting backward by threes. The numbers used were different following each trigram. The subjects were given a signal to designate when to stop counting backward and to recall the trigram; the signal was presented at different retention intervals varying from 3 to 18 seconds. **Figure 12.6** presents the level of recall of a trigram as a function of the interval between presentation of a trigram and testing. As the figure shows, recall declines rapidly: the likelihood that a subject can remember the trigram is about 54% with a 3-second recall interval, compared with only about a 6% recall of the trigrams with an 18-second interval. Peterson and Peterson's study illustrates the brief retention of an item after leaving the short-term store.

The brief retention span of a short-term memory has adaptive significance—it allows us to quickly shift attention from one event to the next. As Gleitman (1987) points out, imagine how difficult a long-distance telephone operator would find it to remember one telephone number while dialing the next.

Disrupting Short-Term Memory

Consider the following series of events to illustrate how easily a memory contained in the short-term store can be disrupted. After locating a number in the telephone book, you begin dialing; then your roommate says something to you, and you stop dialing to respond. After responding, you begin to dial the number again, but now you cannot remember it.

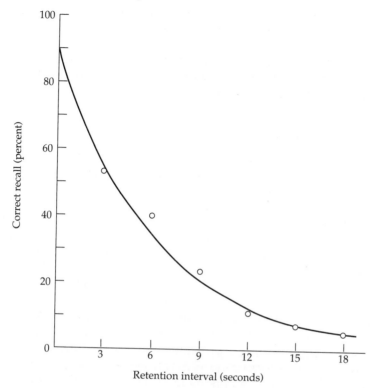

FIGURE 12.6. The percentage of correct recall of CCC trigram as a function of the interval between trigram presentation and recall test. The results of this study indicated a rapid decline in recall of the trigrams after stimulus presentation.

Evidence of the disruption of short-term memories comes from the memory-span studies discussed earlier. Recall that Peterson and Peterson (1959) found that subjects asked to count backward after the presentation of a trigram were unable to recall the trigram just 18 seconds after it was presented. Waugh and Norman (1965) suggested that the numbers had replaced the trigram in the short-term store and, thus, Peterson and Peterson's subjects were unable to recall the trigram.

Memories in the short-term store are easily disrupted because the storage capacity of this store is so limited. As the capacity is reached, new memories automatically replace older ones. And unless they are stored in a meaningful way, the events will be lost forever. Thus, you forget a telephone number when your roommate distracts you; your roommate's words displace the memory of the number. You must look up the number again because it has not been stored in a retrievable way in the long-term store.

Limited Storage Capacity

Repeat the following list of nonsense syllables.

SYX	GXL	TRZ	QNW
BGC	RDH	KDM	HCX
NFQ	FZJ	PHY	YPC
JBD	GBX	LCN	CQT
OTS	DZP	TBR	LKC

Now repeat as many of the nonsense syllables as you can remember. If your memory is like that of most college students, you will only be able to remember four or five or even six or seven of the nonsense syllables. Your inability to recall most or all of the nonsense syllables reflects the limited storage capacity of the short-term store.

In 1956, George Miller published a classic paper entitled "The Magic Number Seven, Plus or Minus Two: Some Limits on Our Capacity for Processing Information." Miller presented evidence that people can hold approximately five to nine items at a time in short-term store. An item may be a single letter or number; it can also be a word or an idea. A number of studies suggests that the capacity of the short-term store is seven plus or minus two items of information. For example, Kaufman, Lord, Reese, and Volkmann (1949) reported that subjects could accurately estimate the number of dots when six or fewer dots were presented on a screen for 0.2 seconds; however, subjects could only guess when more than six dots appeared in the pattern. Pollack (1953) found that listeners recalled only six or seven items from a list of words, letters, or digits read at a fast, constant rate. Based on this and other information, Miller (1956) concluded that the short-term store is limited to seven plus or minus two items.

However, Watkins (1974) suggested that the true capacity of the short-term store may be only three to four items. According to Watkins, although the capacity of the short-term store appears to be seven plus or minus two items, some recall actually reflects information stored in the long-term store; that is, Watkins argued that information presented early in an experience has already been permanently stored. Thus, the capacity of the short-term store is actually three to four items. We will look at evidence to support this view shortly.

The Organization of Our Experiences

The main function of the short-term store is to organize information arriving from the sensory register. The experience then is retained in the long-term store until it is recalled in the organized form. One type of organization the short-term store accomplishes is chunking. A second type of organization is coding. The formation of associations is a third organizational process the short-term store carries out.

The short-term store's organization of information provides some significant advantages. People can reduce the impact of the limited storage capacity of the short-term store by organizing incoming information from the sensory register. As a result of this organization, an event can become more significant or meaningful and thus become more likely to be remembered. The recall of our experiences from the long-term store is greatly enhanced by these organizational processes. We will look more closely at the short-term store's organizational processes (chunking, coding, and forming associations) next.

Suppose you hear the three letters B A T. You undoubtedly will "hear" the word *bat*. The combining of the three letters into a single word reflects a short-term store process called **chunking**. Chunking is an automatic organizational process of the short-term store. It also significantly enhances our ability to recall past experiences. Let's look at these two aspects of chunking.

THE SHORT-TERM STORE AND CHUNKING. People automatically chunk information contained in the short-term store. For example, in presenting six-digit numbers for subjects to memorize, Bower and Springston (1970) found that most people chunked the six digits into groups of three digits, separated by a pause and in a distinct melodic pattern. Thus, the six-digit number 427316 became 427-316. The division of a seven-digit telephone number into two separate chunks is another example of chunking. Norman (1976) describes an example of the natural use of chunking by the short-term store: Children learn the twenty-six letters of the alphabet by using rhyming and melodic rhythm to create three chunks; each chunk contains two elements, and each element has two units of one to four letters. Norman diagrammed the chunking of the alphabet: [(ab-cd) (ef-g)] [(hi-jk) (lmno-p)] [(qrs-tuv) (w-xyz)].

Does chunking increase the amount of information the short-term store can retain? Simon (1974) evaluated the view that the short-term store can retain seven chunks of information, regardless of the absolute amount of information contained in each chunk. Using himself as a subject, Simon found that he could immediately recall seven 1-syllable words, about seven 2-syllable words, and about six 3-syllable words. However, Simon found he could only remember four 2-word phrases (for example, *milky way, criminal lawyer*) and only about three longer phrases (for example, *All's fair in love and war*). Although Simon's observations indicate that chunking can increase the absolute amount of information retained in the short-term store, they also indicate that the short-term store does not consistently contain seven chunks. Recall that Watkins (1974) suggested that the true capacity of the short-term store is three to four chunks. Watkins reported that when only a small amount of information is contained in each chunk, the capacity of the short-term store appears to be five to nine chunks; however, some of the subjects' recall actually reflects information stored in the long-term store.

THE EFFECT OF CHUNKING ON RECALL. We have learned that more information can be retained in the short-term store through chunking. There are two additional issues related to the impact of chunking. First, does chunking improve the short-term recall of our experiences? Second, are memories recalled from the long-term store in an organized fashion? We next will address these two questions.

Murdock's 1961 study evaluated the role of chunking in the short-term recall of our experiences. Murdock presented his subjects a three-consonant trigram, a three-letter word, or three three-letter words and then required them to count backward for 0, 3, 6, 9, 12, 15, or 18 seconds. As **Figure 12.7** indicates, the retention of the three-consonant trigram was identical to that Peterson and Peterson (1959) observed; recall of the trigram declined dramatically over the

FIGURE 12.7. The percentage of correct recall as a function of the type of stimulus material and the length of the retention interval. The results show that the recall of a three-letter word is greater on an 18-second test than the recall of either three consonants or three words.

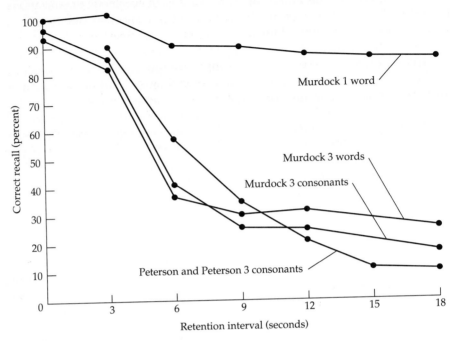

18-second retention interval. However, Murdock's subjects after 18 seconds exhibited a high level of recall of the three-letter, one-word unit. Furthermore, on the 18-second recall test, the retention of the three-word unit containing nine total letters equaled the lower level of the three-letter trigram.

Chunking does not merely improve recall; instead, it causes the information to be recalled from the long-term store in a specific order. Suppose that a subject receives the following list of items:

tea	cabbage	lion	coffee
milk	seal	potato	orange
cow	spinach	lemon	elephant
apple	pear	soda	carrot

This list contains four categories of items: beverages, animals, vegetables, and fruit. How would subjects recall the items on the list? Subjects receiving the above list will recall the items in each category together, even though the items were presented separately. The recall of material in terms of categories is called **clustering** (Tulving & Donaldson, 1972). The organization of material allows us to relate similar events and contributes to a structured and meaningful world. Organization is a very important aspect of the learning process; its significance should be apparent throughout the text.

We have discovered that the short-term store combines information into smaller units. The short-term store can also code information; that is, transform an event into a totally new form. For example, visual experiences can be coded into an acoustic (auditory) code, and words or ideas can become an image, or a visual code. While the transformation, or **coding,** of experiences is a natural property of the short-term store, most people do not use the coding properties of the short-term store effectively. Yet, people can learn to effectively transform their experiences; we will discuss the use of coding systems in mnemonic or memory enhancement techniques later in this chapter.

ACOUSTIC CODES. Suppose you see the word *car* on a sign. In all likelihood, your short-term store will transform the visual image of the word *car* into the sound of the word. This observation suggests that we encode a visual experience as a sound or as an **acoustic code.**

Conrad's study (1964) illustrates the acoustical coding of visual information. He presented a set of letters to his subjects visually and then asked them to recall all the letters. Analyzing the types of errors subjects made on the recall test, Conrad found that errors were made based on the sounds of the letters rather than on their physical appearance. For example, subjects were very likely to recall the letter P as the similar sounding T, but they were unlikely to recall it as the visually similar F.

Why does the short-term store transform visual events into an acoustic representation? According to Howard (1983), the short-term store not only retains specific information but also represents a space for thinking. Since language plays a central role in thinking, it seems logical that visual events would be acoustically coded to aid the thinking process.

VISUAL CODES. Look at, but do not name, the objects in **Figure 12.8** for 30 seconds. Now close your book and see how many of these objects you can name. How many were you able to remember? If you have a good visual memory, you probably were able to recall most of the objects. In fact, most people would be able to recall more of the objects seen in a picture than objects presented verbally (Paivio, 1986). This indicates that encoding objects as images in **visual codes** can be more effective than storing them as words.

People differ in their ability to store experiences as images. About 1% of adults have excellent visual memories (Haber, 1969). These individuals are able to recall a sharp image of previous experiences. This visual memory, or **eidetic image,** lasts about four minutes and provides excellent retention of prior events. An eidetic image, or photographic memory, is more common in children than adults, although adults can learn to make greater use of visual codes; we will examine this topic in our discussion of mnemonics later in this chapter.

The memory of some experiences can be quite vivid. I remember quite clearly where I was and what I was doing when my aunt called to tell me that my father had died. I often remember that experience and still feel its pain. My memory of the circumstances that existed when I learned of my father's death is an example of a flashbulb memory. A **flashbulb memory** is the vivid, detailed, and long-lasting memory of a very intense emotional experience (Brown & Kulik, 1977).

FIGURE 12.8. How good is your memory? Look at this photograph for 30 seconds, but do not name the objects. Close the book and try to recall as many of the objects as you can.

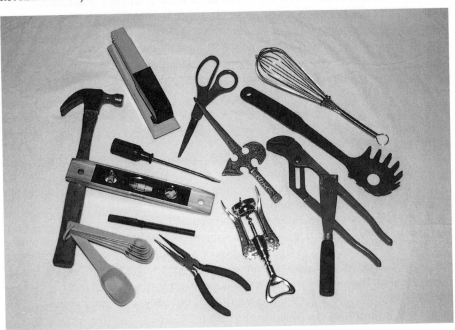

Research has suggested that three separate elements make up a flashbulb memory (Burke, Heuer, & Reisburg, 1992). First, information is stored that is central to the event (for example, learning that my father had died). Second, peripheral details are associated with the event (for example, my aunt calling me to tell me of my father's death). Finally, personal circumstances surrounding the event are stored as part of the memory (for example, I was watching a football game on a Sunday afternoon when my aunt called). Not all our experiences are recalled in such vivid detail. Flashbulb memories occur primarily when an event has many consequences for the person (McCloskey, Wible, & Cohen, 1988), such as when a parent dies.

Some questions have been raised about the accuracy of flashbulb memories (Neisser, 1982). Many people believe they have a vivid memory of the Challenger explosion. Do they have an accurate memory? McCloskey, Wible, and Cohen (1988) interviewed 29 subjects both one week and nine months after the Challenger accident. While their subjects still believed they had a vivid memory of the explosion nine months later, they had forgotten much of the detail of the event, and their recollections were distorted. Pillimer (1984) reported a similar forgetting following the assassination attempt of President Reagan. Palmer, Schreiber, and Fox (1991) suggest that firsthand knowledge of the event is critical to accurate flashbulb memory. They compared people's recollections of the 1989 San Francisco earthquake for those who had actually experienced the earthquake with the memories of those who merely learned about it on television. Persons who directly experienced the earthquake had more accurate knowledge of the earthquake than did persons who merely watched it on television.

If someone asks you to respond to the word *day*, in all likelihood you will think of the word *night*. Recall from Chapter 1 that your response indicates you have learned an association between the words *day* and *night*. One organizational function of the short-term store is to form associations between concepts or events. Two basic kinds of associations, episodic and semantic, are formed by the short-term store. Episodic associations are based on temporal contiguity. For example, if someone insults you, you will associate this person with the verbal abuse. Semantic associations are based on the similarity of the meanings of events. For example, the association of *day* and *night* is a semantic association because both represent times of day.

Does the short-term store randomly associate concepts? Some associations appear to be made in a logical, organized fashion. Episodic associations are organized temporally. Consider our encoding of the 12 months of the year. We do not merely associate the months, but rather learn the months in temporal order. However, we do not associate the months in alphabetical order. While recall of the months in temporal order is easy, you would have difficulty remembering the months in alphabetical order.

Semantic memories seem to be organized hierarchically. This hierarchical structure is from general to specific concepts. Examine the hierarchy of the concept of *minerals* presented in **Figure 12.9**. As the illustration shows, there are four levels in the hierarchy. The concept of minerals contains two types: metals and stones. Similarly, there are three types of metals: rare, common, and alloys. A

FIGURE 12.9. Illustration showing four levels of the hierarchy of the concept *minerals*. Minerals can be grouped into two types: metals and stones. In turn, metals can be classified as rare, common, and alloys; stones as precious or masonry. In the fourth level, *platinum* is an example of a rare metal, *diamond* of a precious stone.

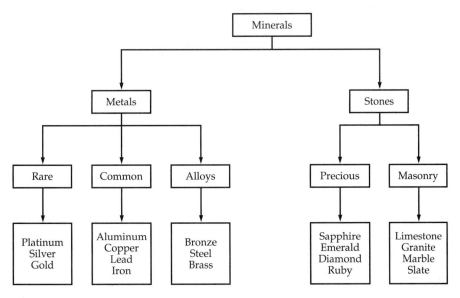

number of psychologists have discussed the organizational structure of semantic memories; we begin with Collins and Quillian's hierarchical approach.

A HIERARCHICAL APPROACH. Collins and Quillian (1969) suggested that semantic memory consists of hierarchical networks of interconnected concepts. According to Collins and Quillian's **hierarchical approach,** each concept is represented by a node, and two nodes or concepts are connected by an associative link. At each node are paths to information about that concept. **Figure 12.10** presents one of these associative networks. The superordinate concept *animal* is connected to its subordinate network *bird*, which then is linked to its subordinate, *canary*. The illustration also shows that each node has associated concept information; for example, the node *canary* contains the information that the canary can sing and is yellow.

How did Collins and Quillian verify that semantic memory contains networks of interconnected associations? They reasoned that the response time for accessing information contained in a network would depend upon the number of links separating the information. According to Collins and Quillian, the greater the separation, the longer the reaction time. Consider these two questions: Can a canary sing? or Does a canary have skin? The first question you probably answered more readily, since the information about singing is contained in the node *canary*. The information about skin is located in the animal node, which is separated from the node *canary* by two associative links. Verifying that a canary has skin should take longer than verifying that a canary can

FIGURE 12.10. Illustration of the Collins and Quillian hierarchical model of semantic memory for the concept *animal*. The animal concept node contains four properties and is associated with the nodes of bird and fish, which also have associated properties.

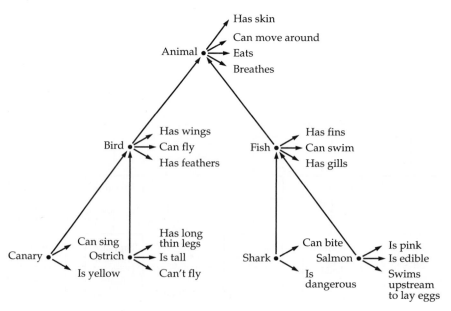

sing due to the greater separation of information between the node and the links in the former than in the latter statement.

Collins and Quillian investigated how the number of linkages separating the information affects the reaction time to verify statements. They observed that reaction time to verify statements was positively related to the number of nodes separating information (see **Figure 12.11**). As the figure shows, subjects could respond more rapidly to the statement that a canary can sing than a canary has skin.

Our discussion suggests that concepts are stored in a hierarchy of interconnected nodes. While considerable evidence supports this view, some researchers have found it too simplistic. Three main problems have been identified with the Collins and Quillian hierarchical approach (Glass & Holyoak, 1986). First, this theory assumes that concepts are stored in semantic memory in a logical hierarchy. Yet, research suggests that this may not always be true. Consider the two statements: *The collie is an animal* and *The collie is a mammal.* Quillian and

FIGURE 12.11. Reaction time and the levels separating associated concepts. This study showed that a person's reaction time to verify a statement was positively related to the number of nodes separating the information; that is, the greater the separation of the nodes, the longer the period needed to verify the concept.

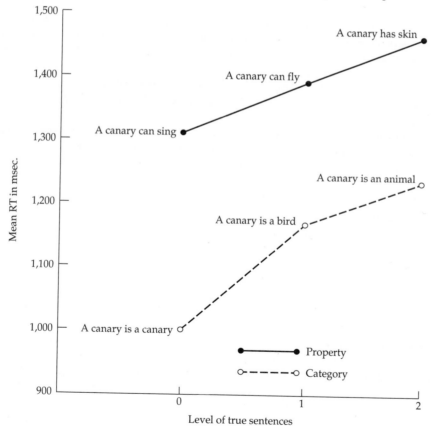

Collins's view would suggest that reaction time would be longer for the first than the second statement. The reason is that the concept node *mammal* is closer than the concept node *animal* to the node *collie* (the concept *animal* is superordinate to the concept *mammal*). Yet, Rips, Shoben, and Smith (1973) observed that subjects could verify the statement *The collie is an animal* more readily than *The collie is a mammal*. Thus, the speed of reaction time does not always relate to the number of levels of concepts separating information.

A second problem involves the idea that information is stored at only one node. For example, the information that animals breathe is only stored at the concept node for *animal*. If this assumption is valid, it should take longer to verify the statement *An ostrich can breathe* than *An animal can breathe*. Yet, Conrad (1972) reported no difference in reaction time for these types of sentences. This result suggests that information is stored at more than one node.

Finally, the Collins and Quillian view assumes that all subordinates of a concept are equally representative of that concept. This approach assumes that a canary and an ostrich are equally representative of the concept *bird*. We discovered in Chapter 11 that all members of a particular concept are not equally representative of the concept; that is, members vary in how closely they resemble the prototype of the concept. A canary is more representative than an ostrich of the concept *bird*. This means a person can verify that *a canary is a bird* more readily than *an ostrich is a bird* (Roth & Shoben, 1983).

SPREADING ACTIVATION THEORY. Collins and Loftus (1975) revised two main aspects of the Collins and Quillian model. First, they suggested that properties can be associated with more than one concept. For example, the property *red* can be associated with a number of concepts like *fire engine, apple, roses,* and *sunsets* (see **Figure 12.12**). Second, a particular property can be more closely associated with some concepts than with others. As **Figure 12.12** demonstrates, the property red is more closely associated with a fire engine than a sunset.

The **spreading activation theory** proposes that once a concept or property is activated, activation spreads to associated concepts or properties. For example, if you heard the word *red*, you would think of associated concepts such as *fire engines* and *sunsets*. According to Collins and Loftus (1975), the activation spreads until even more distant associations can be recalled. For example, the activation of the *fire engine* concept could activate the associated concept of *vehicle*.

The difference in the lengths of association between properties and concepts explains the differences in reaction time needed to verify various statements. The greater length of association between *red* and *sunset* than *red* and *fire engine* means most people can more rapidly verify the statement *Fire engines are red* than *Sunsets are red*.

The spreading activation theory can also explain the priming phenomenon, or the facilitation of recall of specific information following exposure to closely related information. To show the effect of **priming**, Meyer and Schvaneveldt (1971) asked subjects to indicate as rapidly as possible when two items were both words (e.g., *first-truck*) or were not both words (e.g., *roast-brive*). Some of the word pairs were related (e.g., *bread-butter*) and other word pairs were not related (e.g., *rope-crystal*). Meyer and Schvaneveldt observed that subjects were able to identify the pairs as both being words more quickly if the words were

FIGURE 12.12. Illustration of spreading activation theory. According to Collins and Loftus, a property such as red can be associated with several concepts. Also, each concept can have associated properties. A particular property may be more closely associated with some concepts than others.

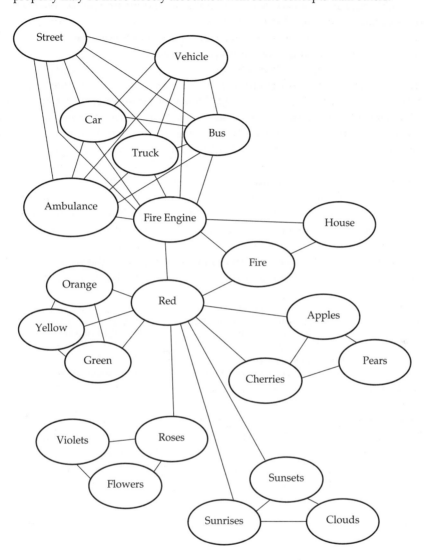

related than if they were not related. According to the spreading activation theory, the prime word activates related words, which leads to a rapid identification of both as words. The lack of priming slows the identification of the second string of letters as a word.

The spreading activation model suggests that semantic memory is organized in terms of associations between concepts and properties of concepts. Rumelhart and McClelland proposed a different theory of encoding in 1986; we will next examine their parallel distributed processing model.

PARALLEL DISTRIBUTED PROCESSING MODEL. David Rumelhart and James McClelland (1986) suggested that memory is composed of a series of interconnected associative networks. Their **parallel distributed processing model** proposes that memory consists of a wide range of different connections that are simultaneously active. According to their theory, thousands of connections are possible. A connection can either be excitatory or inhibitory. Experience can alter the strength of either an excitatory or inhibitory connection.

The parallel distributed processing model assumes that "knowledge" is not located in any particular connection. Instead, knowledge is distributed throughout the entire system; that is, the total pattern and strength of connections represents the influence of an experience. With each individual training experience, the strength of individual connections changes. With continued training, the strength of the connections changes until the desired pattern is reached.

Suppose a person sees and smells a rose. How is this experience encoded? According to Rumelhart and McClelland (1986), the sight of the rose (visual input) arouses a certain pattern of neural units, and the smell of the rose (olfaction input) activates a different pattern of neural units. **Figure 12.13** presents a hypothetical pattern in which a rose activates four neural visual units and four neural olfactory units.

As the figure shows, the pattern of neural A units that the sight of a rose activates is +1, −1, −1, and +1, and the pattern of neural B units activated by the

FIGURE 12.13. Hypothetical illustration of pattern associator matrix of visual and olfactory units activated by the sight and smell of a rose. The sight of a rose activates four A units in a +1, −1, −1, and +1 pattern, whereas the smell of a rose activates four B units in a −1, −1, +1, and +1 pattern. The interconnection of all visual A units with all olfactory B units allows the presence of the sight of a rose to elicit the recall of a rose's smell.

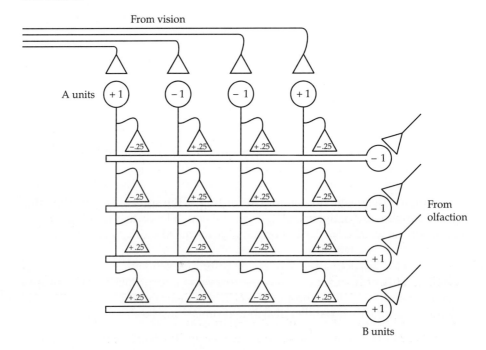

smell of a rose is -1, -1, $+1$, and $+1$. (A positive value indicates excitation of a neural unit, and a negative value indicates inhibition of a neural unit.) Rumelhart and McClelland proposed that the neural A units stimulated by the sight of a rose become associated with the neural B units activated by the smell of a rose.

Perhaps you see a rose in a vase on a table. This visual image is likely to cause you to recall the smell of a rose. Rumelhart and McClelland's parallel distributed processing model can explain how the sight of a rose causes you to remember the smell of the rose. According to Rumelhart and McClelland, each neural unit activated by the sight of a rose is associated with each neural unit activated by the smell of a rose. They suggest that the specific neural units stimulated by the sight of the rose will arouse the pattern of neural units normally activated by smell of a rose. Stimulation of these olfactory neural units will produce the perception of the smell of a rose.

How does activating the visual units arouse the memory of a rose's smell? Using matrix algebra methods, Rumelhart and McClelland were able to construct a matrix of interconnected elements, or a pattern associator. This pattern associator matrix forms during the associations of two events and enables the presentation of one event to elicit the recall of the other event. The pattern associator matrix in **Figure 12.13** is established by the association of the sight and smell of a rose and allows the sight of the rose to activate the pattern of neural activity produced by the smell of a rose. Similarly, the smell of the rose can activate the pattern produced by the sight of the rose and cause us to remember the visual image of a rose.

The main idea of the parallel distributed processing approach is that knowledge is derived from the connections rather than from the nodes. The extensive synaptic connections in the nervous system are consistent with a parallel rather than serial processing model of memory. Karl Lashley's (1950) classic examination of the location of memory provides additional support for a parallel distributed processing view. Lashley trained rats in a simple discrimination and then destroyed a small part of each animal's brain. The intent of this destruction was to locate the site of the animal's memory of the discrimination. Lashley discovered that the animals still showed retention of the discrimination despite the absence of the brain tissue. He continued the search for the engram by destroying other brain areas, but the rats remained able to recall their past learning. On the basis of his observations, Lashley stated:

> It is not possible to demonstrate the isolated localization of a memory trace anywhere within the nervous system. Limited regions may be essential for learning or retention of a particular activity, but within such regions the parts are functionally equivalent. The engram is represented throughout the region. (p. 733)

Lashley's statement suggests that knowledge is distributed throughout an entire region of the nervous system. Interestingly, the parallel distributed processing model came to the same conclusion almost a half a century later.

BEFORE YOU GO ON

- **What is the span of Donald's short-term store?**
- **Does his short-term store seem more susceptible to disruption?**

The Rehearsal Function of the Short-Term Store

Suppose you are trying to learn the French word for *door*. To learn that the French phrase for door is *la porte,* you must form an association between the words *door* and *la porte.* In an attempt to learn the association, you repeat the two words to yourself several times. This process, called **rehearsal,** keeps the memories in the short-term store. Rehearsal has two main functions (Eich, 1985). First, it keeps information in the short-term store so that you don't forget it. Second, rehearsal can provide the opportunity to make information more meaningful.

There is an important difference between these two functions of rehearsal. We can merely repeat information contained in the short-term store. When we are simply repeating material we have experienced, we are using **mainte-nance rehearsal.** This form of rehearsal will keep information in the short-term store and can lead to establishment of some associations. However, the likelihood of later recall of our experiences is greatly enhanced by **elaborative rehearsal.** With elaborative rehearsal, we alter information to create a more meaningful memory. We may attempt to relate the experience to other information, form a mental image of the experience, or organize the experience in some new way.

Consider the following example to illustrate the difference between maintenance and elaborative rehearsal. You have an exam tomorrow, and the material is quite complex. Attempts at trying to memorize the information by repeating the information has not helped. You simply cannot recall the material for the exam, and you are quite worried. A friend suggests that instead of merely repeating the words, you relate this new information to concepts presented earlier in the class. The friend indicates several ways of relating current and previous concepts. You think about the relationships between the concepts, and now you understand the material for the test.

Does rehearsal increase the strength of a memory in the long-term store? A series of studies by Rundus (Rundus, 1971; Rundus & Atkinson, 1970) suggests that rehearsal does enhance the recall of an event by increasing the strength of a memory stored in the long-term store. In one of Rundus's studies, subjects received a list of words to recall; the words were presented at a rate of one word every 5 seconds. Subjects were instructed to study the list by repeating the words during the 5-second interval between the presentation of the words. After the entire list had been presented, the subjects were required to recall as many words as possible from the list. The level of recall of a particular word was compared to the number of times it was rehearsed during the interval between the word presentations. Rundus observed that the more times a word is rehearsed, the higher the likelihood a subject will be able to recall the word. In other words, the more a memory is rehearsed, the greater the chances are that the memory will be recalled at a later time.

You may think that rehearsal always increases the level of recall. However, evidence indicates that this is not so (Craik & Watkins, 1973); in fact, unless rehearsal leads to the organization of an event, rehearsal will not improve recall. Craik and Watkins (1973) presented subjects with a list of 21 words and instructed them to repeat the last word that began with a given letter until the next word beginning with that letter was presented, then rehearse the second word until another word beginning with that letter was presented, and so on. For example, suppose the given letter was G and the list of words was: daughter, oil, rifle, garden, grain, table, football, anchor, and giraffe. The subjects rehearsed *garden* until the word *grain* was presented, and then *grain* until *giraffe* was presented. Using this procedure, Craik and Watkins varied the amount of time words were rehearsed. Thus, in this list, *garden* was rehearsed for less time than *grain*. Each subject received 27 lists, and the number of words between critical words varied in each list. After completing the 27 lists, each subject was asked to recall as many words as possible from any of the lists. Craik and Watkins found that the amount of time a word was held in the short-term store had no impact on the level of recall, and thus the amount of rehearsal did not affect the recall of the critical word.

Why did rehearsal affect recall in the Rundus study but not in the Craik and Watkins study? The answer may lie in one of the differences between their studies: subjects in the Craik and Watkins experiment rehearsed only a single word (the last word beginning with a specific letter); whereas subjects in Rundus's study rehearsed several words. Thus, subjects could organize the information in the Rundus study, but not in the Craik and Watkins study. This suggests that rehearsal enhances recall only if the subject organizes the information during rehearsal.

BEFORE YOU GO ON

- **Could Donald have a problem with maintenance rehearsal?**
- **Or could Donald have a problem with elaborative rehearsal?**

Alternatives to the Atkinson-Shiffrin Multistage Model

The **Atkinson-Shiffrin three-stage model** argues that memories are held for a brief time in the short-term store prior to being transferred to the permanent or long-term store. While in the short-term store, the memory is rehearsed, which acts to increase its organization and enhance the likelihood that it will be retrieved. Several alternatives have been offered to the Atkinson-Shiffrin model. One alternative is a revised multistage storage model. Another alternative assumes that recall differences reflect differing levels of processing. We will describe an alternative stage model, followed by a discussion of a levels of processing approach.

A Rehearsal Systems Approach

Alan Baddeley (Baddeley, 1990; Gathercole & Baddeley, 1993) proposed an alternative to the Atkinson-Shiffrin multistage model. Baddeley's **rehearsal systems approach** argued that while memories are retained in the sensory systems, those memories are analyzed by a process that he called **working memory** (see **Figure 12.14**). According to Baddeley, working memory possesses the attributes of the short-term store; that is, it has a limited capacity and duration, and rehearsal acts to enhance organization and increase retrieval.

FIGURE 12.14. An illustration of Baddeley's memory system. The central executive coordinates rehearsal systems such as the phonological loop and the visuospatial sketch pad.

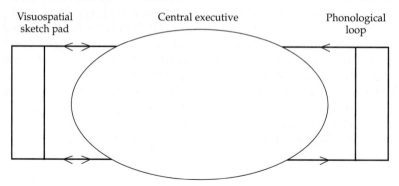

Baddeley suggested that several sensory systems hold information for rehearsal in working memory. One rehearsal system is the phonological loop. The **phonological loop** retains information in the verbal sensory system for a brief time, while the information is rehearsed. According to Baddeley, there are two components of the phonological loop: one component holds speech-based information; the other contains subvocal speech, or speech to oneself. The phonological loop does not require acoustic input and can be activated by visual events or by internal processes. Baddeley argues that the phonological loop is capable of holding information for approximately 2 seconds, unless rehearsal keeps the input in working memory.

In Baddeley's view, the phonological loop works in a manner analogous to a circus performer spinning plates on reeds. The performer spins one plate, then spins another plate, and then a third plate. Only a certain number of plates can be spun before the performer must return to the first plate and respin it. Failure to respin the first plate will cause it to stop and fall off the reed. The phonological loop can only hold information for a brief time before it must be spun (rehearsed) again.

The **visuospatial sketch pad** is a second rehearsal system. According to Baddeley, this system rehearses visual or spatial experiences, maintaining visual or spatial information by creating a mental image of an experience. For example, while listening to a radio announcer describe a basketball game, a person can visualize the action taking place.

According to Baddeley, a **central executive** coordinates the phonological loop, visuospatial sketch pad, and other rehearsal systems. The central executive determines which rehearsal system a specific event is placed in. It also can retrieve information from any rehearsal system as well as transfer information among rehearsal systems or between permanent memory and rehearsal systems.

Baddeley envisions working memory as a collection of organizational processes that extract information from several independent sensory registers. Not all psychologists have accepted the idea that there is no separate short-term store. Cowan (Cowan, 1994; Cowan, Day, Saults, Keller, Johnson, & Flores, 1992) advocated a separate facility to store immediate memories; that is, a short-term store that is separate from the sensory register and the long-term store. Let's briefly examine the evidence that supports this view.

The word-list effect is one finding that is not consistent with Baddeley's concept of working memory. The word-list effect refers to the finding that memory span, or the number of words recalled, will be greater for words that are shorter and easier to pronounce than for longer words that are more difficult to pronounce. A working memory interpretation of the word-list effect is that shorter words can be rehearsed more extensively because they do not require as much time to rehearse as longer words. However, Cowan (1994) argued that the word-list effect was not merely due to increased rehearsal. Instead, Cowan asserted that subjects recall longer words more poorly because more memory content is lost reporting a longer word than a shorter word.

The Cowan, Day, Saults, Keller, Johnson, and Flores (1992) study provides support for the existence of a short-term store. In their study, subjects were shown two lists of words: some subjects saw a list of printed words that began with shorter words and ended with longer words, while other subjects saw a list that started with longer words and ended with shorter words. At the end of each list, the subjects saw a cue indicating whether to report the words in forward or backward order. These investigators found that the recall of the shorter words was low when the shorter words appeared early in the list and the cue called for backward recall. Similarly, the recall of the shorter words was low when the shorter words appeared late in the list and the cue called for forward recall. In contrast, recall of the shorter words was high when the shorter words were recalled first. As rehearsal time for the shorter words was constant in both lists, the order of recall seemed to determine the level of recall of the shorter words; that is, recall of the shorter words was high if they were recalled first and poor if they were reported later. Cowan and his colleagues interpreted these results to mean that since time was needed to report the longer words, the shorter words were lost from the short-term store during the time used to recall the longer words. Therefore, the shorter words were unavailable for recall.

A Levels of Processing View

Fergus Craik and Robert Lockhart (1972) offer a very different alternative to the Atkinson-Shiffrin three-stage model of memory storage. Craik and Lockhart suggest that memories differ in the extent to which they have been processed. Their **levels of processing view** assumes that a memory can be processed at many different levels (see **Table 12.1**). An event can receive only shallow, superficial analysis, or it can be interpreted at a deeper level. Consider the various levels at which you might process the word *car*. The initial processing involves an analysis of the physical characteristics of the word, determining the lines and angles of the individual letters. A deeper level of processing involves identifying the three letters. A still deeper level of processing leads you to identify the word, and then to determine its meaning at an even deeper level of memory processing.

The level of processing an event receives has an effect on recall of the event, according to Craik and Lockhart's view. They propose that all experiences result in a permanent memory trace, but that the strength of the trace depends on the level of processing the memory receives. Craik and Lockhart propose that the

TABLE 12.1. The Depth of Processing View of the Memory of a Beautiful Automobile

Depth of Processing	Example of Level of Processing
Shallow processing (physical and perceptual aspects)	The person detects the lines, angles, and contour of an automobile.
Intermediate processing (object is recognized and labeled)	The person recognizes that the object he or she sees is an automobile.
Deep processing (semantic meaning)	The person compares the attributes of a beautiful automobile (styling, color) to this automobile; he or she identifies this automobile as beautiful.

more we process an event, the more durable its memory trace will be and the greater the likelihood that we will recall it.

Craik and Tulving (1975) discuss how the analysis or **elaboration** of experiences influences the recall of those events. According to Craik and Tulving, the elaborateness of memory encoding refers to the extent to which we organize or relate events with other events. For example, suppose you learn a list containing the words *grief, love, forgotten,* and *spinster.* You could encode the words in the list in an elaborative fashion by relating them to each other—perhaps by using them together in a sentence. A less elaborate encoding would be to analyze the meaning of each word without attempting to relate the words to each other.

According to Craik and Tulving, there are also differences in the extent to which we analyze an event independent of its relation to other events. We can interpret an experience phonetically in terms of its physical characteristics and semantically in terms of its meaning. Craik and Tulving suggest that although we analyze both the physical and semantic features of an event, events differ in the levels of phonetic and semantic elaboration. Some events may receive little semantic or physical elaboration, and other experiences undergo substantial physical or semantic elaboration.

Consider the following two examples to illustrate how semantic and phonetic elaboration may vary. In the first case, you are reading about the predatory behavior of lions. While reading, you concentrate on the meaning of the words rather than the physical attributes of the words. In the second case, you are attempting to evaluate the rhythm of a poem. In this case, you need to analyze the physical features of the words rather than their semantic aspects.

We have discovered that experiences undergo varying degrees of elaboration prior to storage. Craik and Tulving (1975) performed an experiment to demonstrate that the level of elaboration determines our ability to recall previously experienced events. In this study, they presented several words and asked subjects whether each word made sense in various sentences. For example, one word was *watch,* and two sentences that different subjects received for the word *watch* were: *He dropped the _____* and *An old man hobbled across the room and picked up the valuable _____ from the mahogany table.* According to Craik and Tulving, semantic analysis is required to determine whether the insertion of the word *watch* makes sense in each case, but subjects exposed to the second sentence had to use greater elaboration than did subjects receiving the first sentence. An unannounced memory test showed that the level of recall was affected by the degree of elaboration: The greater the elaboration, the higher the level of retention of the word.

Craik and Lockhart (1972) proposed that we have only one memory system and that the ability to remember a past experience depends on how deeply we process that event. In their view, we will remember deeply processed information better than we will experiences that we process only shallowly. However, a number of researchers (Morris, Bransford, & Franks, 1977; Stein, 1978) have reported that in some instances an event that undergoes shallower processing is retained better than another experience that undergoes a deeper level of processing. These results indicate that the depth of information processing does not completely control the recall of previous experiences.

Many studies show that in certain situations shallowly processed information can be recalled well. For example, Kolers (1979) found that people can remember for long periods the type of print that they read. Other experiments indicate that reexperiencing an event can lead to improved recall even when the level of processing does not increase. Nelson's (1979) study illustrates this observation. He found that asking a question such as "Does the word *train* have an *n* sound?" twice leads to better recall of the question. According to Nelson, the second presentation of the question does not lead to any deeper processing of the information, yet it does result in better retention.

At this point you might be confused. Is there a short-term store or not? Is the levels of processing view valid or not? While future research will undoubtedly clarify the nature of memory storage, it is possible that the short-term store has the functionality of working memory; that is, the short-term store may be able to extract information from relevant sensory registers. It is also likely that while a shallowly processed event can be recalled, the more an event is processed, the more likely the event will be recalled.

BEFORE YOU GO ON

- **Does Don's poor recall reflect a deficit in his working memory?**
- **How would the levels of processing view explain Don's poor recall of recent events?**

LONG-TERM STORE

Memories are permanently (or relatively permanently) encoded in the long-term store. We will explore two aspects of the long-term storage of experiences. First, we will examine evidence that there are several different types of long-term memories. Second, we will discuss the physiological processes governing the long-term storage of an event, as well as the psychological and physiological circumstances that can result in the failure to store an experience. A memory may be permanently stored yet still not be recalled; Chapter 13 describes the processes that result in the failure to recall a prior event.

Episodic versus Semantic Memories

We distinguished earlier between episodic and semantic associations. Endel Tulving (1972, 1983) suggested that there are two types of long-term memories: episodic and semantic memories. An **episodic memory** consists of information about events associated with a particular time and place, whereas a **semantic memory** contains knowledge associated with the use of language. For example, remembering that you had bacon and eggs for breakfast at the local diner is an example of an episodic memory, while remembering that a sentence contains a noun phrase and a verb phrase is an example of a semantic memory. Tulving emphasized that the difference between episodic and semantic memory is greater than just the different types of information stored in each memory; he argued that the episodic memory system is functionally distinct from the semantic memory system. **Table 12.2** presents a list of the informational and operational differences between episodic and semantic memory. The interested reader should refer to Tulving's 1983 book *Elements of Episodic Memory* for a detailed discussion of episodic and semantic memory.

TABLE 12.2. Characteristics of Episodic and Semantic Memory

Diagnostic Feature	Episodic	Semantic
Information		
Source	Sensation	Comprehension
Units	Events; episodes	Fact; ideas; concepts
Organization	Temporal	Conceptual
Reference	Self	Universe
Veridicality	Personal belief	Social agreement
Operations		
Registration	Experiential	Symbolic
Temporal coding	Present; direct	Absent; indirect
Affect	More important	Less important
Inferential capability	Limited	Rich
Context dependency	More pronounced	Less pronounced
Vulnerability	Great	Small
Access	Deliberate	Automatic
Retrieval queries	Time? Place?	What?
Retrieval consequences	Change system	System unchanged
Retrieval mechanisms	Synergy	Unfolding
Recollective experience	Remembered past	Actualized knowledge
Retrieval report	Remember	Know
Developmental sequence	Late	Early
Childhood amnesia	Affected	Unaffected

Source: Tulving, E. (1983). Elements of episodic memory. Oxford: Clarendon Press/Oxford University Press. By permission of the Oxford University Press.

The processes involved in the storage and retrieval of episodic and semantic memories differ. According to Tulving, the episodic memory system registers immediate sensory experiences, while the semantic memory system records knowledge conveyed by language. The episodic memory system detects the temporal order of events; problems of temporal order can be solved only by inference in the semantic memory system. Tulving reports that the episodic memory system has limited inferential capacity; that is, information stored in the episodic memory system is based mainly on direct sensory impressions. In contrast, the semantic memory system has a rich inferential capacity and can therefore discover the rules of a language merely from experience with that language.

Tulving has found that the recollection of memories from the episodic system is deliberate and often requires conscious effort, whereas recall of information contained in the semantic system is automatic and can occur without conscious knowledge. Although we can be aware of knowledge contained in both memory systems, we interpret episodic memories as part of our personal past and semantic memories as part of the impersonal present. Thus, we use the term *remember* when referring to episodic memories and the term *know* to describe semantic memories. According to Tulving, when we retrieve information from episodic memory, it is often changed, but memories we recall from the semantic memory are not altered. Thus, the episodic memory system is much more vulnerable to distortion than are memories contained in the semantic system.

Two Functionally Different Memory Systems

Tulving (1983) detailed the results of many experiments documenting the existence of separate episodic and semantic memory systems. Let's briefly examine one study supporting the distinction.

A study by Wood, Taylor, Penny, and Stump (1980) provides strong support for separate episodic and semantic memory systems. These researchers compared the regional cerebral blood flow of two groups of subjects; one group was involved in a semantic memory task, the other in an episodic memory task. The authors observed differences in the regional cerebral blood flow in each of the two groups and suggested that their results indicate "an anatomical basis for the distinction between episodic and semantic memory."

A number of psychologists (Kintsch, 1980; Naus & Halasz, 1979) disagree with the idea that the episodic and semantic memory systems represent two separate systems. Instead, they suggest that there is a single memory system and that its content varies from highly context-specific episodes to abstract generalizations. Tulving (1983) asserts that the dissociation studies provide convincing evidence that there are in fact two separate memory systems. However, Tulving does recognize that the episodic and semantic memory systems are highly interdependent. Thus, an event takes on more meaning if both semantic and episodic knowledge are involved in its storage. Yet, Tulving believes that these two memory systems can also operate independently. For example, a person can store information about a particular temporal event that is both novel and meaningless, a result which can occur only if the episodic memory system is independent of the semantic memory system.

Procedural versus Declarative Memories

I have not been on a bicycle in several years. Yet, I would certainly remember how to ride a bicycle. As a child, I had many experiences riding bicycles. The storage of these past experiences of riding bicycles would allow me to ride a bicycle. My storage of memories of bicycle riding is an example of a procedural memory.

According to Squire (1986), **procedural memory** is skill memory (see **Table 12.3**). Procedural memories are not accessible to conscious awareness; instead, evidence of a procedural memory can only be gained through observations of performance. These memories represent knowledge of how to do things like tie shoelaces or play the piano. These behaviors are stored as a result of instrumental or operant conditioning experiences. Procedural memories can also represent emotional reactions to environmental events such as becoming hungry when arriving at the movie theater or feeling fearful before driving over a high bridge. These emotional reactions are stored as a result of Pavlovian conditioning.

Procedural memories are acquired slowly, through repeated experience. The extensive practice required to learn how to play the piano is one example of the importance of repeated experience for the storage of procedural memories. Evidence of the existence of a procedural memory lies in how well or poorly the human or nonhuman animal responds. For example, the intensity of a person's fear when driving over a high bridge indicates the strength of the person's procedural memory. Similarly, the quality of piano playing documents the strength of this procedural memory.

Suppose your favorite television show is on at 8:30 P.M. on Tuesday evenings. Remembering the day and time that your favorite show airs is an example of **declarative memory** (see **Table 12.3**). Squire refers to declarative memory as factual memory. The time and day of the television show is a fact, and you stored this information as a declarative memory. Other examples of declarative memory include remembering the route to school or recognizing a familiar face.

We are consciously aware of declarative memories. According to Squire, a declarative memory can exist as a verbal thought or a nonverbal image. Thus, you are verbally aware of the time when your favorite television show will be

TABLE 12.3. Characteristics of Procedural and Declarative Memory

Procedural Memory	Declarative Memory
Stores skills and procedures	Stores faces, episodes, and data
Is learned over many trials	Can be learned in a single trial
Contained within processing systems	Available to many processing systems
Information is modality-specific	Information is modality-general
Develops early	Develops late
Preserved in amnesia	Impaired in amnesia
Inaccessible to conscious recollection	Accessible to conscious recollection

on, while your knowledge of the route to school may exist as a nonverbal image. A declarative memory can be formed in a single experience; however, practice can enhance the ability to recall a declarative memory.

Recall our discussion of the interdependence of episodic and semantic memories. A similar interdependence exists between procedural and declarative memory. For example, tying a shoe can be a declarative memory; that is, you can have knowledge of how a shoe is tied, which is a declarative memory. Yet, tying one's shoe also exists as a procedural memory. Similarly, repeated practice can transform the conscious knowledge (or declarative memory) of the route to school into an unconscious habit (or procedural memory).

We have been discussing several types of long-term memories. But what physical changes provide the basis for the permanent record of an event? We will address this question next.

In Search of the Engram

Many scientists (Lynch, 1986; Rosenzweig, 1984) have proposed that permanent memory represents changes in neural responsiveness. This view, referred to as **cellular modification theory,** suggests that learning permanently alters the functioning of specific neural systems. This change can reflect either the enhanced functioning of existing neural circuits or the establishment of new neural connections. We will briefly examine the cellular modification view next.

Learning in the Aplysia Californica

Eric Kandel and his associates (Abrams, Karl, & Kandel, 1991; Eliot, Blumenfeld, Edmonds, Kandel, & Siegelbaum, 1991; Hawkins, Kandel, & Siegelbaum, 1993) have investigated changes in synaptic responsivity following learning in the sea snail *Aplysia californica* (see **Figure 12.15**). This simple, shellless marine mollusk has three external organs—the gill, the mantle, and the siphon—that retract or withdraw when either the mantle or the siphon is touched. This defensive withdrawal response can be either increased or decreased as a result of experience.

Hawkins, Kandel, and Siegelbaum (1993) found that the habituation of the defensive reaction is caused by a depression of synaptic responsivity in the sensorimotor neurons in the defensive reflex of *Aplysia*. This decreased synaptic responsivity reflects a decreased calcium ion influx into the cell and a reduced neurotransmitter release from the presynaptic membrane. In contrast, sensitization results from an increased synaptic responsivity in the sensorimotor neurons of the defensive reflex. The increased responsivity reflects the greater neurotransmitter release that presynaptic facilitation causes. The consequences of presynaptic facilitation are enhanced neurotransmitter release from the sensory neuron and increased activity in the motor neuron.

The defensive reaction of the *Aplysia* also can be conditioned. For example, Carew, Hawkins, and Kandel (1983) paired a light touch to the mantle or siphon (CS) with a strong electric shock to the tail (UCS). These investigators reported that following repeated pairings of the light touch (CS) with electric shock (UCS), the light touch alone elicited the withdrawal response (CR). Hawkins, Kandel, and Siegelbaum (1993) found that the CS produces the same increase in

FIGURE 12.15. *Aplysia californica.* In this shell-less marine mollusk, touching either the siphon or the mantle elicits a defensive retraction of the three external organs—the gill, the mantle, and the siphon (*a*). The external organs are relaxed and (*b*) withdrawn.

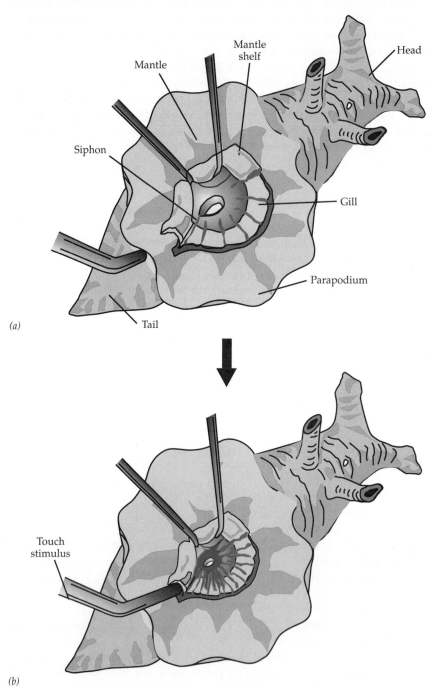

(a)

(b)

synaptic responsivity as a sensitizing stimulus does. The increased synaptic responsivity produced by the CS causes an increased neurotransmitter release and the elicitation of the defensive conditioned response.

Conditioning can lead not only to increased neurotransmitter release, but also to an increased number of synaptic connections. The research of Gary Lynch (Lynch, 1986) looks at the structural changes that conditioning produces; we will look at his work next.

Structural Changes and Experience

Lynch found that experience enhances the level of calcium ion entry into the cell. This influx of calcium ions into the cell activates a dormant enzyme called Calpain. The effect of Calpain is to break down the protein fodrin, a major component of neural dendrites, as well as acting as the coating around the dendrites (see **Figure 12.16**). The breakdown of the dendrite's coating exposes

FIGURE 12.16. Diagram illustrating the chemical communication of information between neurons. When a neural impulse reaches the axon's terminal button, chemical transmitter substances stored in the synaptic vesicles are released into the synaptic gap. The neurotransmitter substances migrate from the presynaptic membrane of the transmitting neuron to the postsynaptic membrane. The neurotransmitter substances either depolarize (excite) or hyperpolarize (inhibit) the postsynaptic membrane.

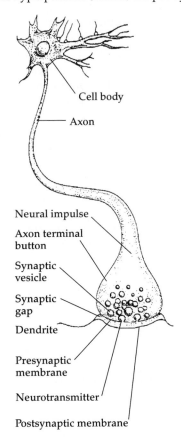

FIGURE 12.17. Aborization of dendrites. Continued experience increases the number of neural connections because of the breakdown of the dendritic coating.

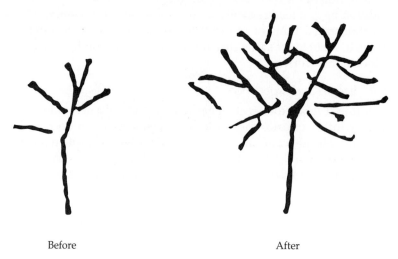

Before   After

more of the dendrite to stimulation from other neurons; that is, as the coating breaks down, the neuron becomes more sensitive. With continued experience the breakdown process continues, resulting in even greater neural sensitivity.

Lynch (1986) also suggested that the breakdown of cellular coating allows the dendrites to change shape and spread out, leading to the establishment of new neural connections (see **Figure 12.17**). In Lynch's view, this arborization of the dendrites results in the establishment of new neural connections, which represents the biological basis of learning.

These neuronal changes are also the neural basis of memory. Lynch and Baudry (1984) trained rats to find food in an eight-arm radial maze (see **Figure 12.18**). The procedure used in this study involved placing food reinforcement in all eight arms. The rats' task on each trial was to visit each of the arms only once. When a rat returned to a previously visited arm, it received no food. The rats quickly learned the task; they remembered which arms they had visited and which arms they still could visit to receive reinforcement. Lynch and Baudry then implanted a pump in the rat's brain that could infuse a chemical called leupeptin into the lateral ventricle. This chemical inhibits the breakdown of fodrin, thereby preventing the establishment of new neural connections. These researchers found that the animals that received leupeptin entered the arms of the radial maze randomly, recalling nothing of their past learning experience, whereas control animals that did not receive leupeptin showed good recall of the prior experiences.

Anatomical Basis of Memory Formation

Research has indicated that two brain structures—the **medial temporal lobe** and the **mediodorsal thalamus**—are critical to the storage of information. Larry Squire and his colleagues (Squire, 1987; Squire & Zola-Morgan, 1988;

FIGURE 12.18. Eight-arm radial maze used to study spatial memory. In studies of spatial memory, the researchers place reinforcement (food) in the arms of the maze, and rats are required to visit each of these arms without returning to a previously visited arm.

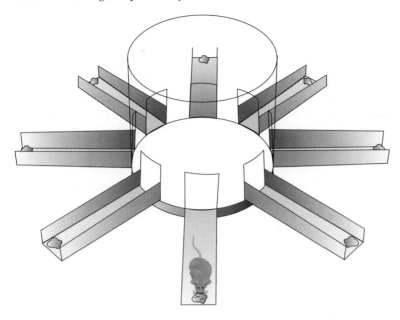

Zola-Morgan & Squire, 1993) provided a model detailing the biological structures involved in memory (see **Figure 12.19**). According to Zola-Morgan and Squire (1993), information is first processed in the sensory areas of the cortex and then sent to structures in the medial temporal lobe for further processing. Key structures in the medial temporal lobe include the hippocampus and surrounding cortical areas. Projections from these medial temporal lobe structures then convey information to the mediodorsal thalamus, where the information receives still further processing. Following analysis by the mediodorsal thalamus, information is relayed to the frontal lobe.

The frontal lobe appears to play a crucial role in the planning, execution, and control of behavior. Zola-Morgan and Squire (1993) suggest that the medial temporal lobe structures and the mediodorsal thalamus jointly establish long-term memory and that connections between these brain areas and the frontal lobe provide a route for memories to use to influence behavior. According to this model, the structures in the medial temporal lobe and the mediodorsal thalamus are involved in memory storage. Our discussion begins with evidence of the role of the medial temporal lobe, followed by an examination of the role of the mediodorsal thalamus.

Medial Temporal Lobe

The Case of H. M.

In 1953, patient H. M. had his medial temporal lobe (including the hippocampus, amygdala, and surrounding cortical tissue) removed as a treatment for epilepsy. Although the operation successfully treated his severe epilepsy, this success proved costly. While H. M. remained pleasant and good-humored after the operation, he suffered from a severe memory deficit. H. M. was very cooperative, and many researchers (Gabrieli, Cohen, & Corkin, 1988; Milner, 1970; Scoville & Milner, 1957) have examined the details of his memory disorder.

The most profound deficit is H. M.'s **anterograde amnesia,** or the inability to recall events that have occurred since the operation. For example, on each visit to the hospital, H. M. has to be reintroduced to his doctors. His inability to recall events that occurred following his surgery results from his failure to permanently store those experiences. H. M. also shows **retrograde amnesia** for events that took place only a few years prior to his operation. He can recall memories more than several years old, though, and he can carry on a conversation about those events. H. M. is fully aware of the extent of his memory impairment:

> Every day is alone in itself, whatever enjoyment I've had, and whatever sorrow I've had . . . Right now, I'm wondering. Have I done or said anything amiss? You see, at this moment everything looks clear to me, but what happened just before? That's what worries me. It's like waking from a dream; I just don't remember. (Milner, 1970, p. 37)

While H. M. has suffered severe memory impairment, some areas of his memory did remain intact. Squire (1987) suggested that although H. M. cannot store declarative memories, he can store and recall procedural memories. Fur-

FIGURE 12.19. A view of the key structures for memory storage and retrieval. Information is sent from sensory areas of the cortex to the medial temporal lobe (hippocampus and adjacent areas), then to the mediodorsal thalamus for further analysis. Connections from the medial temporal lobe and the mediodorsal thalamus to the frontal lobe allow memory to influence behavior.

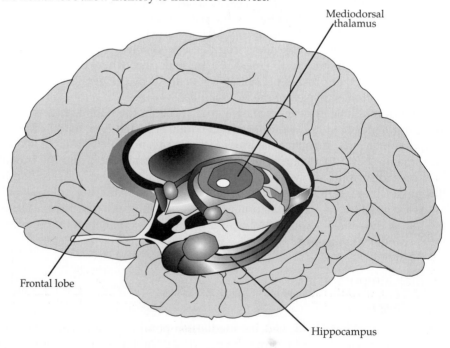

ther, while he has lost recent episodic memories, his semantic memories are not affected by medial temporal lobe damage. Although H. M.'s language ability was not affected by the operation, and he can still read and write, his speech contains no words introduced into the English language since his surgery (Gabrieli, Cohen, & Corkin, 1988).

Brenda Milner (1965) has conducted many studies to evaluate H. M.'s memory. Her work clearly shows that H. M. can acquire new skills (procedural memories). In one study, H. M. participated in a mirror drawing task (see **Figure 12.20a**). The task involves tracing an object while looking at it in a mirror. This task is difficult and requires practice. On this task, H. M.'s performance improved over a series of trials; he made fewer errors as he learned the task (see **Figure 12.20b**). Further, his improvement was maintained over several days of

FIGURE 12.20. The mirror drawing task. (*a*) In this illustration, H. M. traces a star seen in a mirror. (*b*) H. M. made fewer errors each day of training, and his improvement was retained over 3 days of training.

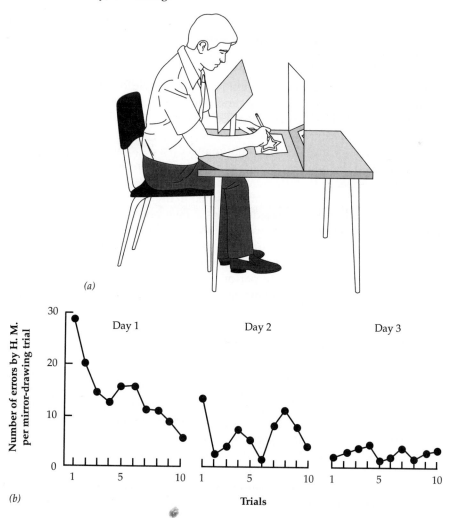

training. This indicates that a memory of the task has formed. While H. M.'s performance did improve, he could not remember having participated in the task from day to day (episodic memory).

How could H. M. become increasingly adept at tracing the figure but have no recollection of having previously drawn it? Tracing the figure is a visuomotor skill and involves procedural memory. Procedural memories appear to be unaffected by damage to the medial temporal lobe. In contrast, awareness of having traced the figure is the recollection of an event and, therefore, is an episodic memory. Damage to the medial temporal lobe does appear to adversely affect the storage of episodic memories. Another example should clarify the kind of memory loss H. M. experienced. After his father died, H. M. could not remember it (an episodic memory), but he felt a little sad when he thought about his father (a procedural memory).

The Importance of the Hippocampus

Removal of the medial temporal lobe damages a number of structures, including the hippocampus, amygdala, and surrounding cortical areas. Recent evidence (Zola-Morgan & Squire, 1993) indicates that the **hippocampus,** and not the amygdala, is the key memory structure in the medial temporal lobe. Studies using nonhuman animals as subjects have shown that lesions to the hippocampus and surrounding areas (perirhinal, entorhinal, and parahippocampal cortices) produce deficits in the retention of a simple object discrimination (Squire, Zola-Morgan, & Chen, 1988) and performance on a delayed matching to sample task (Alvarez-Royo, Clower, Zola-Morgan, & Squire, 1991).

Damage to the hippocampus has also been shown to produce profound and long-lasting memory impairments in humans. Zola-Morgan, Squire, and Amaral (1986) studied the memory of patient R. B., a 52-year-old man with a history of coronary disease. R. B. suffered a cardiac arrest, which caused a temporary loss of blood to the brain (anoxia) and resulted in brain damage. The brain damage produced profound anterograde amnesia. Five years after his cardiac arrest, patient R. B. died. Histological examination of his brain revealed a significant amount of degeneration of the hippocampal tissue (see **Figure 12.21**). Damage to the hippocampus has also been linked to memory deficits in other patients. Squire, Amaral, and Press (1990) performed a high-resolution MRI on several patients with severe memory impairments and observed a significant reduction in the size of the hippocampus in each case. Recent MRI scans on H. M. also show the bilateral absence of most of the hippocampus and all of the entorhinal and parahippocampal cortices (Corkin, Amaral, Gonzalez, Johnson, & Hyman, 1997; see **Figure 12.22**).

While the amygdala of patient H. M. was removed with the hippocampus, it is likely that removal of the amygdala was not significantly involved in producing his amnesia (Zola-Morgan & Squire, 1993). One line of evidence for this lack of involvement is the observation that damage limited to the amygdala produces no memory deficit in primates (Zola-Morgan, Squire, & Amaral, 1989).

H. M. was unable to store new declarative memories, but he was able to retrieve declarative memories acquired prior to his surgery, an observation that supports the idea that the hippocampus is involved in the storage of declarative memories, but is not the site where those memories are stored. Several researchers (Gabrieli, 1998; Tulving, 1998) point to the frontal and temporal lobes as the storage site for declarative memories. Gabrieli (1998) suggests that "knowledge in a domain (e.g., for pictures or words, living or manufactured objects) is distributed over a specific, but extensive neural network." Activation of a specific neural network allows us to remember a past experience. In support of this view, PET scan studies (Tulving & Markowitsch, 1997) reveal that the frontal and temporal lobes become active during the retrieval of past events.

Mediodorsal Thalamus

Damage to the mediodorsal thalamus also has been associated with profound memory impairment (Aggleton & Mishkin, 1985; Horel & Misantone, 1976). Horel and Misantone (1976) observed that destruction of the mediodorsal thalamus affected the ability of primates to distinguish new from familiar objects. However, mediodorsal thalamic lesions had no influence on the retention of a simple visual discrimination. These observations suggest that, like medial temporal lobe damage, lesions of the mediodorsal thalamus affect declarative but not procedural memories. Damage limited to the mediodorsal thalamus produces mild memory deficits compared to the amnesia observed following hippocampal damage (Aggleton & Mishkin, 1985). However, more severe memory loss occurs when the surrounding structures as well as the mediodorsal thalamic nuclei undergo damage.

Memory impairments have also been observed in humans following damage to the mediodorsal thalamic nuclei. For example, Von Cramon, Hebel, and Schuri (1985) studied seven patients who had severe memory impairments following medial thalamic infarctions, or anoxia to this area of the brain. These researchers used a CT scan to identify common areas damaged by the loss of blood supply to the brain. As expected, all of these patients showed considerable damage to the mediodorsal thalamus and surrounding tissue.

FIGURE 12.21. Two different photographs of the hippocampus. Normal hippocampal structures are visible in the left photograph; the degeneration of hippocampal pyramidal cells of field CA1 caused by anoxia in patient R. B. is evident in the right photograph.

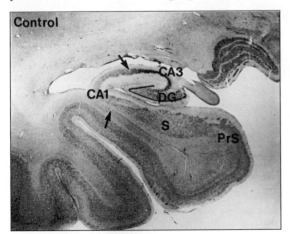
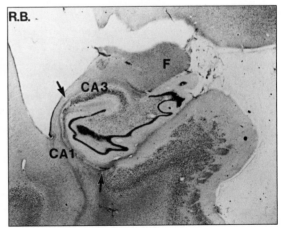

FIGURE 12.22. The hippocampus (H) and entorhinal cortex (EC) are present in the brain of a normal subject (right), but absent bilaterally in the brain of H. M. (left).

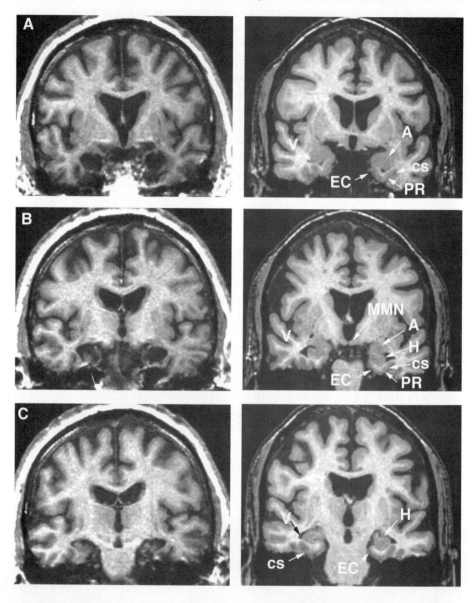

We have learned that anoxia can damage the brain and lead to memory loss. Severe memory impairment is also seen in chronic alcoholics. This memory loss was first described by the Russian neurologist Sergei Korsakoff in 1889. His alcoholic patients were unable to recall past events; if an event recurred, these individuals showed no evidence of having previously experienced it. This disorder is now called **Korsakoff's syndrome.** The memory loss characteristic of Korsakoff's syndrome appears to be associated with damage to the mediodorsal thalamus (Victor, Adams, & Collins, 1989).

The memory impairment in Korsakoff's syndrome, like the impairment following damage to the hippocampus and mediodorsal thalamus, is selective; it involves a loss of declarative but not procedural memory. For example, Sidman, Stoddard, and Mohr (1968) trained a patient with Korsakoff's syndrome to press a square containing the image of a circle from among seven other squares containing ellipses of various sizes. Even after several minutes of working on other tasks, the patient could select the appropriate stimulus. These observations indicate that this particular patient could remember the correct response. However, although the patient continued to respond appropriately, he soon forgot the words for what he had learned. When asked during training what he was doing, he replied he was choosing the circle. However, after several minutes, he could no longer verbally describe his actions. These results indicate that the patient retained knowledge of the contingency between behavior and reinforcement (procedural memory), but forgot exactly what he was doing (declarative memory).

Although patients with damage to the mediodorsal thalamic nuclei show memory deficits similar to those seen in medial temporal lobe patients, individuals with damage to the medial temporal lobe differ in some ways. Patients like H. M., with medial temporal lobe damage, are aware of their memory deficits. In contrast, Korsakoff's syndrome patients, and others with mediodorsal thalamic nuclei damage, are unaware of their memory loss. These individuals will confabulate, or make up stories, to fill in the gaps in their memories. Further, emotion is intact following medial temporal lobe damage, whereas patients tend to be emotionally flat and apathetic after damage to the mediodorsal thalamus. The confabulation and lack of insight in patients with Korsakoff's syndrome are probably due to damage to the prefrontal cortex (Mosocovitch, 1992). The mediodorsal thalamus projects to the prefrontal cortex, and individuals with Korsakoff's syndrome show impairments like those seen following damage to the prefrontal cortex.

APPLICATION: MNEMONICS

When my middle son was in high school, he requested that I ask him some questions for his science test. One question required him to list five items. As he recalled the list to me, it was evident that he had a system for remembering the list. He had memorized the first letter of each item and was using these letters to recall each item on the list. Although he was unaware of it, he was using a **mnemonic technique** to recall the list of items. People often unknowingly use mnemonic techniques to increase recall. For example, medical students trying to remember the bones in a person's hand often use a mnemonic device; they take the first letter of each bone, construct a word from the letters, and use the word to recall the bones when taking a test.

You may have noted that the two cases just described are examples of the coding process detailed earlier in the chapter. Your observation is accurate. There is nothing mystical about mnemonics. Mnemonic techniques merely use the short-term store efficiently. You have undoubtedly seen memory experts on television. Although they seem to possess extraordinary memories, their ability to recall information stems from their use of mnemonic techniques. There are a number of these techniques, each with the ability to take unorganized material and store it in a meaningful way.

The remainder of this chapter discusses several mnemonic techniques. Students in my classes using these techniques have found them an effective means of enhancing recall. Because this chapter provides only a brief discussion, interested readers should refer to the *Memory Book* by Lorayne and Lucas (2000) to master the use of mnemonics.

Method of Loci

Suppose you need to give a memorized speech in one of your classes. Trying to remember the words by rote memorization would be a time-consuming process, and you would be likely to make many mistakes. The **method of loci** is one mnemonic technique you might use to recall the speech. This method, which the Greeks developed to memorize speeches, first involves establishing an ordered series of known locations. For example, the person can take "a mental walk" through his or her home, entering the house through the living room, and so on. The individual would then separate the speech into several key thoughts, associating the key thoughts in the order corresponding to the walk through the house. Perhaps your speech will be on Pavlov's research on the classical conditioning process. The first key thought may be to remember that Pavlov used dogs to investigate conditioning. You need to associate this thought with your living room. To do this, you might form a mental image of Pavlov and a dog in your living room. When you give the speech, you need only imagine going into the living room and seeing Pavlov and his dog there. This mental image will enable you to tell your class that Pavlov investigated conditioning processes using dogs. Perhaps you can see from our discussion that the method of loci represents a structured technique for using the associative capacities of the short-term store to remember a speech. The use of imagery increases the meaningfulness of the material and thus acts to enhance your recall of the speech.

The method of loci can be used to remember any list, in either a specific or a random order. For example, you need to buy six items at the grocery store (see **Figure 12.23**). You could write the items on a piece of paper or use the method of loci to remember them. Perhaps one item you need is dog food. You could associate a container of dog food with your living room. Using this method to recall lists of items will help you improve your memory and will document the power of mnemonic techniques.

Peg Word System

Another popular mnemonic technique used to enhance recall of a list is the **peg word system.** An example of a popular peg word system is:

One is a bun.

Two is a shoe.

Three is a tree.

Four is a door.

Five is a hive.

Six is sticks.

Seven is heaven.

Eight is a gate.

Nine is wine.

Ten is a hen.

Let's see how this peg word mnemonic system works. Suppose you wanted to learn the following list of words: table, candle, firewood, glass, cigar, picture, book, ashtray, car, and lamp. To use the peg word system to remember the list, first associate the word *table* with the first peg word, *bun.* To do this, perhaps imagine a bun sitting on a table. Next, associate the word *candle* with the second peg word, *shoe.* To do this, imagine a candle burning a hole in a shoe. Associate each word in the list with the appropriate peg word. The peg word system works like the method of loci: both efficiently use the associative capacity of the short-term store. This system is also effective because a person can recall any item without having to start at the beginning of the list.

FIGURE 12.23. A mental trip through the house provides an illustration of how one could use the method of loci to remember a shopping list of six items: butter, bread, flour, thumbtacks, sugar, and dog food. This method involves associating the mental image of the item with a familiar place, such as a room in your house.

Remembering Names

Why do many people have such a hard time remembering other people's names? To recall a name, an individual must associate the person with his or her name, store this association, and then be able to retrieve the person's name. The main problem with remembering a person's name lies in the storage process: the association of a person's name with that individual is a difficult one to form. As is true with many recall problems, the association will eventually be formed with enough repetition and, therefore, eventually will be recalled. Mnemonics offer a technique for enhancing the association between a name and a person; the enhanced storage of this association enables a person to recall a name after a single experience.

Lorayne and Lucas (2000) provide many examples of the use of mnemonics to recall people's names. Let's examine several of them. Suppose that you meet a person named Bill Gordon. Perhaps Bill Gordon has very bushy eyebrows. Lorayne and Lucas suggest that when you first meet him, you might visualize his eyebrows as being a *garden* with dollar *bills* growing there. The mental image you form when you first meet someone and then elicit when you see this person again will thus provide you with the information needed to recall the person's name.

What if you meet a woman named Ms. Pukcyva? How can you possibly use the mnemonic technique to recall her name? Perhaps she has a tall hairdo; you could see hockey *pucks shivering* as they fly out of her hair. After you have formed this association, the next time you meet Ms. Pukcyva you will remember her name.

This mnemonic technique can create a mental image that contains not only a person's name, but also other bits of information about the individual. For example, suppose that Mr. Gordon works for U.S. Steel. You can add this information into your mental image by seeing an American flag (*U.S.*) made of *steel* growing out of the garden. Practice is required before you will be able to rapidly form a mental image of a person's name and then remember the name. The more you practice, the more efficient you will become at remembering names.

Do mnemonics work? The empirical evidence (Harris & Morris, 1984) indicates that they are effective. Bugelski's study (1968) provides one example of the effectiveness of mnemonic techniques. Bugelski had an experimental group learn a list of words using the "one is a bun" peg word system, and control subjects learn the list without the aid of the mnemonic technique. Bugelski then asked subjects to recall specific words; for example, he asked them, "What is the seventh word?" Bugelski reported that experimental subjects recalled significantly more words than control subjects did.

Crovitz (1971) demonstrated the effectiveness of the method of loci. He had subjects learn a list of 32 words using either the method of loci or no special techniques. Crovitz reported that experimental subjects who learned the list with the method of loci recalled 26 of the words, compared to 7 words for the control subjects who did not have the benefit of this mnemonic technique.

Several points are important in making effective use of mnemonics. First, Kline and Groninger (1991) reported that it is especially important to create vivid mental images. For example, imaging a person throwing a cheese hat across the living room will make the method of loci more effective. Second, the individual needs to rely on a well-learned body of knowledge (Hilton, 1986). Not knowing the rooms in a house would make using the method of loci difficult. But when used appropriately, mnemonics is an effective way to improve recall. It has even proved to be effective in brain-damaged persons like Donald in our chapter vignette (Wilson, 1987).

BEFORE YOU GO ON

- **What area of Donald's brain was probably damaged in his accident?**
- **How could mnemonics help Donald improve his memory?**

CHAPTER SUMMARY

The Atkinson-Shiffrin three-stage model proposes that memory is stored in three successive stages. The sensory register is the first stage. A visual copy contained in the sensory store is referred to as an icon and is stored in the iconic memory. An auditory experience in the sensory store is called an echo and is stored in the echoic memory. Echoes last longer than icons because while a visual experience conveys all the information needed to detect salient characteristics, recognition of an auditory event requires that individual sounds be retained in the sensory store until the whole event is detected. Information in the sensory register decays rapidly and is lost unless it is transferred to the short-term store.

According to the Atkinson-Shiffrin model, the short-term store serves as a temporary storage facility. Information remains in the short-term store for approximately 15 to 20 seconds, and during this time an experience is interpreted and organized to produce a more meaningful memory. The short-term store is thought to have a limited storage capacity; it can retain only three or four units of information at one time. New information can easily disrupt and replace memories contained in this holding store.

Chunking combines units or bits of information. Information is recalled in categories or clusters of chunked material. Coding transfers information into a new form; for example, visual experiences can be coded into an acoustic code, and words or ideas can become an image or visual code. Another organizational function of the short-term store is the association of events.

Collins and Quillian suggest that semantic memory consists of interconnected concepts and properties associated to each concept node. According to Collins and Quillian, the response time needed to access information from semantic memory is determined by the number of linkages separating concept nodes.

Spreading activation theory assumes that a property can be associated with more than one concept, but any particular property will be more closely associated with some concepts. Once a concept or property is activated, the activation spreads to associated concepts or properties.

The parallel distributed model assumes that knowledge is not contained in any particular location, but instead is distributed throughout the entire system. According to this view, a memory consists of a series of interconnected associated networks with either excitatory or inhibitory properties.

According to the Atkinson-Shiffrin model, the short-term store can rehearse or replay prior experiences. This rehearsal can help retain information in the short-term store for a longer period (maintenance rehearsal). This increased rehearsal also enhances the interpretation and organization of the memory (elaborative rehearsal), improving the likelihood that the memory will later be available for recall.

Baddeley's rehearsal systems approach argues that information is retained in several sensory registers for analysis by the working memory. Rehearsal systems hold information in working memory so that it can be processed into a more organized memory. The central executive places information into a rehearsal system, transfers information among rehearsal systems and between permanent memory and rehearsal systems, and retrieves information from any rehearsal systems.

The Craik-Lockhart levels of processing view assumes that a memory can be processed at many different levels. In their view, the more an event is processed, the greater the likelihood it will be recalled. The level of elaboration affects retrieval presumably by enhancing the identification of the important aspects of an experience.

The long-term store is the site of permanent memory. An episodic memory consists of information associated with a particular time and place, whereas a semantic memory contains knowledge necessary for language use. An episodic memory is easy to store but difficult to retrieve; in contrast, a semantic memory is difficult to store but easy to retrieve. Procedural memories contain information about the performance of specific skills, while declarative memories contain knowledge about the environment.

The cellular modification theory argues that learning can modify the responsivity of specific neurons as well as produce structural changes in neurons. Work with *Aplysia californica* has demonstrated that habituation decreases neurotransmitter release, whereas both sensitization and conditioning increase neurotransmitter release. Experience causes the coatings of dendrites to break down, resulting in arborization, or the establishment of new connections between neurons. This structural change appears to underlie the permanent storage of experience.

Information is first processed in the sensory areas of the cortex and then sent to the medial temporal lobe for further processing. Projections from the medial temporal lobe convey information to the mediodorsal thalamus for additional processing. Damage to the medial temporal lobe causes anterograde amnesia, or an inability to recall events subsequent to the damage, limited to episodic and declarative memory. Damage to the mediodorsal thalamus is also associated with anterograde amnesia and with Korsakoff's syndrome. The mediodorsal thalamus projects to the prefrontal cortex, and individuals with damage to the mediodorsal thalamus, like those with prefrontal lobe damage, confabulate and show a lack of insight.

Memory can be improved by the use of techniques called mnemonics. There are a number of mnemonic techniques, and the effectiveness of each stems from enhanced organization of information during the storage process.

CRITICAL THINKING QUESTIONS

1. Vikas is about to write down the exam date his professor just announced when the student next to him asks for a pen. When Vikas returns to writing the exam date, he can no longer remember the date and now has to ask the professor. Why did Vikas forget the date of the exam? How common is this type of forgetting? What might Vikas do to remember the date in the future?

2. In his American literature class, Salman learned that William Faulkner was an important twentieth-century American writer. Salman will need to remember that Faulkner was a twentieth- and not a nineteenth-century author on his next test. Using spreading activation theory, explain how he will store the information and how he will identify Faulkner as a twentieth-century writer.

3. Jondrea was in an automobile accident but has no recollection of it. What process is likely to be responsible for Jondrea's inability to recall the accident?

KEY TERMS

acoustic code
anterograde amnesia
Atkinson-Shiffrin three-
    stage model
cellular modification
    theory
central executive
chunking
clustering
coding
cued recall
declarative memory
echo
echoic memory
eidetic image
elaboration
elaborative rehearsal
episodic memory
explicit measure of
    memory
flashbulb memory

free recall
hierarchical approach
hippocampus
icon
iconic memory
implicit measure of
    memory
interference
Korsakoff's syndrome
levels of processing view
long-term store
maintenance rehearsal
medial temporal lobe
mediodorsal thalamus
memory attribute
method of loci
mnemonic techniques
parallel distributed
    processing model
partial report technique
peg word system

phonological loop
priming
procedural memory
reaction time
recall measure
recognition measure
rehearsal
rehearsal systems
    approach
retrograde amnesia
savings score
semantic memory
sensory register
serial position effect
short-term store
spreading activation
    theory
visual code
visuospatial sketch pad
whole report technique
working memory

CHAPTER 13

Memory Retrieval and Forgetting

A Look Into the Past

Steve's grandfather died yesterday. He was very surprised to learn that his grandfather had died. Although he was 90 when he died, Steve's grandfather had been in relatively good health. He was riding in Steve's mother's automobile when he had a massive coronary. He died immediately, and Steve was glad he did not suffer. The plane ride home to his grandfather's funeral was long, and during the trip, Steve had a lot of time to reminisce about childhood experiences with his grandfather. His grandparents lived in Brooklyn when he was young, and Steve would stay with them for one week every summer. He remembered those visits with his grandparents as being quite wonderful. His grandfather would take him to see the Dodgers play at Ebbets Field at least twice during each visit. He could still remember seeing Jackie Robinson, Roy Campanilla, and Duke Snider play for the Dodgers. Steve was sure that his passion for baseball began during those trips to see the Dodgers play. Steve also went to Coney Island with his grandparents. He remembered fondly the arcade where his grandfather would give him money to play the games. Visits to Coney Island meant eating at Nathan's restaurant. Steve can still taste one of Nathan's hotdogs and is sure they are one of life's greatest treats. Remembering Nathan's hotdogs also reminded him of becoming very ill after riding a roller coaster at Coney Island. Not surprisingly, Steve no longer enjoys riding on roller coasters. He continued to remember his childhood experiences with his grandfather throughout the plane ride. Toward the end of the flight, Steve realized that his grandfather would always be with him. His survival past death was possible because of his grandson's ability to remember the past.

Remembering is a very important part of all of our lives. It allows us to recall a first love, or a special vacation with our parents. Yet we do not remember all of the events that happen to us. People often forget where they left their car in the parking lot of a large shopping mall, or where they put the car keys when they are late for an appointment. In this chapter, we will discuss why sometimes we are able to recall events from the past, but at other times we are unable to remember past experiences.

Benton Underwood (1983) suggested that memory can be conceptualized as a collection of different types of information. Each type of information is called a **memory attribute.** For example, the memory of an event contains information regarding the place where the event occurred. This is referred to as the spatial attribute of that memory. A memory also contains information about the temporal characteristics of an event; Underwood calls this the temporal attribute. According to Underwood, there are 10 memory attributes: acoustic, orthographic, frequency, spatial, temporal, modality, context, affective, verbal associative, and transformational.

The Function of an Attribute

Before discussing each type of memory attribute, let us first look at the two basic functions of attributes as described by Underwood. First, when a specific aspect of an experience is established as a memory attribute, forgetting can increase. Interference, a major cause of forgetting, often occurs as a result of the failure to differentiate between memories. Information contained in a memory attribute provides a basis for distinguishing memories and thus can prevent forgetting. Second, the presence of the stimulus contained in the memory attribute can act to retrieve a memory. When we encounter a stimulus that is a salient aspect of a past event, the presence of that stimulus causes us to recall the memory of that event. We will discuss memory attributes and their role in the recall of past experiences in more detail later.

Although there are 10 attributes of memory, not every memory will contain information about each attribute. Even though a stimulus may characterize a particular aspect of a past experience, if it is not a memory attribute of that experience, it will not lead to the recall of the event. For example, you have a traffic accident on a particular day. If the day of the accident is not an attribute of the memory, the anniversary of the accident will not remind you of this misfortune. The one or two most salient aspects of an experience generally will become memory attributes of the event, and retrieval will be based solely on the presence of these stimuli.

Types of Attributes

Acoustic Attribute

Recall from Chapter 12 that experiences are acoustically coded by the short-term store. Underwood suggested that one attribute of a memory provides information about the acoustical properties of an event. Because speech communication would be impossible if people could not discriminate between verbal signals, acoustical properties of an event are clearly important.

Long and Allen's (1973) study illustrates the important influence of the **acoustic attribute** on the recall of an experience. Long and Allen presented to their subjects a list of 18 words organized in one of two ways: six groups of three rhyming words (e.g., Ted, red, head; Jack, black, back) or six groups of three conceptually related words (e.g., Ted, Jack, Jean; red, black, green). After the list was presented, the subjects were asked to recall as many words as they could. Remember that while the list is being presented, subjects organize the words into clusters (see Chapter 12). Long and Allen, interested in whether their subjects would cluster the words based on the acoustic attribute or the conceptual attribute, found that the words were clustered according to the way they sounded rather than according to their meaning. These observations indicate that the influence of the acoustic attribute was dominant in the recall of the words.

Orthographic Attribute

Events differ in terms of structural characteristics. For example, different letters have different shapes. Words differ in length, in number of syllables, in number of repeated letters, and in terms of unusual or infrequently appearing sequences. Underwood referred to the structural characteristics of events as their **orthographic attribute.**

To differentiate items, for example to distinguish an A from a K, a person must recognize the feature characteristics of each item. Evidence indicates people are able to do so. For example, Zechmeister (1969) reported that subjects rated words based on their orthographic distinctiveness. Furthermore, people can use the orthographic attribute to recall a particular event. To illustrate the influence of orthographic attribute on the retrieval of a memory, Hintzman, Block, and Inskeep (1972) presented to subjects eight successive 18-word lists. Half of the words on each list were presented in uppercase block letters; the other half, in lowercase script letters. Hintzman, Block, and Inskeep found that, on a free recall task (a task in which subjects can recall items in any order), some subjects reported words in the script type in one group and words in the block type in another group. These results indicate that some subjects used the orthographic attribute of type style to retrieve the words from memory. (They also used other attributes to recall the words, because not all subjects clustered the words based on type style.)

Frequency Attribute

According to Underwood, a counting mechanism that registers every experience provides a record of the number of times a person experiences a specific event. In Underwood's view, the frequency of an event's occurrence, or the **frequency attribute,** can be used to recall the memory of that event.

Ekstrand, Wallace, and Underwood (1966) presented to subjects a list of eight four-letter words and asked them to guess how frequently each of the words appeared in everyday print such as books and newspapers. The results showed that these estimates corresponded well to the actual frequency that the words did appear (**Figure 13.1**). Thus, people do store information about how frequently certain events occur.

Can this information about frequency be used to recall a specific memory? Ekstrand, Wallace, and Underwood (1966) also evaluated this aspect of memory attribute theory. Subjects in this study received a list of 75 words; 40 were presented only once; 20 were presented twice; 10, three times; and 5, four times.

FIGURE 13.1. The subjects' mean judgments of the frequency with which words occur in printed discourse were highly related to the actual frequency of occurrence; the more often the words appeared, the higher the subjects' estimate of their occurrence in print.

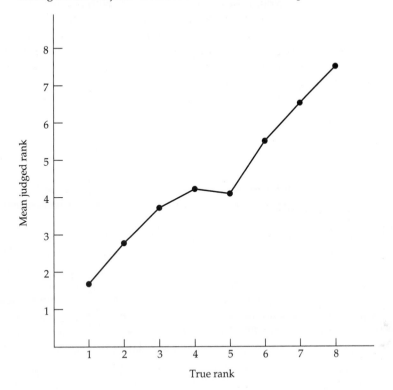

After the list had been presented, the subjects were shown pairs of the words from the list and asked to indicate which of the two words had occurred more frequently. If frequency is an attribute of memory, then the subjects should be able to recognize the word that had appeared more frequently. Ekstrand, Wallace, and Underwood reported that their subjects did use the frequency information and identified the correct word. Identification was not perfect, but a greater difference in how frequently the two words appeared was correlated with greater accuracy of recall. For example, subjects were better able to identify the correct word if one word had been presented one time and the other word presented four times than if the words had been presented two and three times.

Spatial Attribute

Students will occasionally tell me that they can remember the location on the page (for example, it was on a left hand page close to the bottom) where a particular study is described in a textbook. These people have stored information about the spatial location of a certain item, which represents the **spatial attribute** of a memory.

According to Underwood (1983), spatial information can become part of a person's memory of an event. A study by Weeks (1975) shows that the stimulus contained in the spatial attribute can prompt retrieval of a memory. In Weeks's study, subjects received five successive lists of trigrams presented through either a single speaker or two speakers placed 120 degrees apart. When all five lists were presented through the same speaker, interference developed, and subjects had difficulty remembering words from later lists. However, if the first four lists were presented through one speaker and the fifth through the second speaker, the subjects could readily remember the words presented in the last list. These results suggest that the spatial location of the speaker became an attribute that helped subjects remember the last list.

Temporal Attribute

On September 15th, I know it's my birthday. The knowledge of my birth date is the **temporal attribute** of that event. Almost everyone knows the date of his or her birthday as well as the dates of other significant events. These observations indicate that time can be a very important part of a memory. Even so, research shows that only *significant* temporal information is used to recall an experience.

Underwood (1977) presented to college students a list of eight events; the events occurred approximately a year apart, and Underwood made certain the subjects were familiar with the details of these events. The students were asked to rank the events in the order they had taken place. Underwood reported that of 108 students, only 2 did so correctly. Apparently, the temporal attribute does not always contain sufficient information for retrieval; a person may know that an event occurred but may not know exactly when. For example, you may have received an excellent grade on a test on a particular date last year, but that date this year does not remind you of the test or grade. Only when the date becomes associated with the event will the temporal attribute enhance retrieval of the memory of the event.

Modality Attribute

Underwood (1983) asserts that memories may also contain information regarding the sensory modality through which the event was experienced. Thus, one attribute of a memory is knowledge of whether the event was seen, heard, or felt. What is the function of this **modality attribute** of a memory? In Underwood's view, the modality attribute serves the same purpose as any other attribute: it is used to differentiate among memories, and to prompt retrieval of a particular memory. Hintzman, Block, and Inskeep's 1972 study provides support for this view.

Hintzman, Block, and Inskeep (1972) presented several lists of words visually and other lists of words orally. Subjects were then asked to identify which words they had heard and which they had viewed. The authors reported that their subjects identified the words correctly 74% of the time, indicating that the memory of each word contained information regarding the sensory modality that had registered the word. Hintzman, Block, and Inskeep also asked subjects to recall as many words as possible and found that subjects had clustered the words based on the method of presentation, again indicating that subjects used the modality attribute to remember the words.

Underwood notes that although the input modality is an attribute of a memory, there is a high level of interchange among memories established through different modalities. To understand an experience often requires information received through other modalities. Underwood presents the following example to illustrate this cross-modality interchange. Suppose you use your index finger to write letters of the alphabet on the back of another person. Can this person tell which letters you have drawn? Evidence indicates the answer is yes. According to Underwood, the correct detection occurs because the tactile stimulation was translated into a memory system that has access to visual information about the letters. This visual information is used to identify the letters that the person experienced tactilely.

Context Attribute

The event's background can become an attribute of memory, and reexposure to that background context can prompt the retrieval of the memory of that event. For example, in the beginning of the classic movie *Casablanca*, Ingrid Bergman did not recognize Humphrey Bogart, even though they had had a love affair many years earlier. However, the song "As Time Goes By" reminded her of past experiences with the male character. The song was part of the context in which their love affair had taken place, and thus the song was a memory attribute of the affair. Hearing the song retrieved the memory of their romance and caused her to remember the events surrounding her affair. The experience Ingrid Bergman's character had is not unique. You have undoubtedly been reminded of a past event by reexperiencing some aspect of the context in which that event occurred.

Underwood's view suggests that context is a memory attribute. A considerable amount of research has been conducted to investigate the **context attribute.** Some of this research has involved human subjects (Smith, Glenberg, & Bjork, 1978; Underwood, 1983); other studies have used nonhuman animals as subjects (Gordon, 1983; Spear & Riccio, 1994). Both types of research show that context is an important memory attribute. We will briefly examine some of this research next.

How can we know whether context has become a memory attribute? One way to demonstrate the influence of context on memory retrieval is to learn a response in one context and then see if a change in context produces a memory loss. In 1975, Gooden and Baddeley conducted an interesting study showing the importance of context on memory. These investigators had scuba divers listen to a list of words. The divers were either 10 feet underwater or were sitting on the beach when they heard the words. The divers were either tested in the same context or in the other context. Gooden and Baddeley observed better recall when the scuba divers were tested in the same context than when they were tested in the opposite context (see **Figure 13.2**). In other words, the scuba divers who heard the words underwater remembered the words better when tested underwater than when on the beach, and the divers who heard the words on the beach remembered them better on the beach than underwater.

The influence of context in animals' memory retrieval was demonstrated by Gordon, McCracken, Dess-Beech, and Mowrer (1981). Animals in this study were trained in a distinctive environment to actively respond to avoid shock in

FIGURE 13.2. Illustration of the effect of a change in context on recall. Scuba divers remembered a list of words better in the training context than they did in a new context.

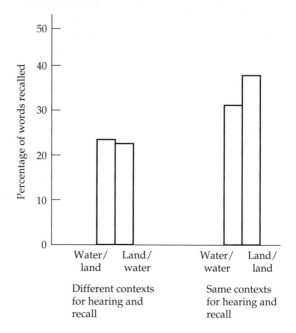

a shuttle box. Forty-eight hours later, the rats were placed either in the shuttle box in the original training room or in an identical shuttle box located in another room that differed in terms of size, lighting, odor, ambient noise level, and holding cage. Gordon, McCracken, Dess-Beech, and Mowrer reported high retention when the rats were tested in the training context and significantly poorer performance when testing occurred in a novel context (refer to **Figure 13.3**).

Perhaps you are now concerned about taking an examination in a new context. Not all studies have shown that a change in context leads to forgetting. For example, Saufley, Otaka, and Bavaresco (1985) told approximately 5,000 college students during the semester that some would be taking their final exams in other rooms both to relieve overcrowded classrooms and to assist in the proctoring of exams. Saufley, Otaka, and Bavaresco reported that the average examination grades did not differ for students taking their exam in a different classroom than for those students taking the exam in their regular classroom.

Underwood (1983) argues that although context is one attribute of memory, a memory also contains information about other characteristics of an event. The significance and availability of other attributes influence whether a memory is recalled in another context. If the context is the most unique or significant aspect of a memory, retrieval will depend on the presence of the context; however, if other attributes are important and available, retrieval will occur even in a new context.

The reminder-treatment studies (Gordon, 1983) demonstrate that retrieval can occur in a new context when other attributes are able to produce recall. The

FIGURE 13.3. The mean latencies to cross to the black chamber on the retention test for groups A-A and B-B (trained and tested in the same environment) and groups A-B and B-A (trained in one environment and tested in another). The results show that retention of past avoidance training is greater when rats are tested in the original rather than in the new context.

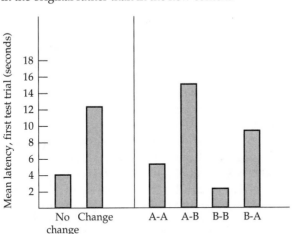

reminder treatment involves presenting subjects during testing with a subset of the stimuli that were present in training. Although this reminder treatment is insufficient to produce learning, it can induce retrieval of a past experience, even in a novel context. The Gordon, McCracken, Dess-Beech, and Mowrer (1981) study shows this influence of the reminder treatment. Recall that in this study, changing the context caused rats to forget their prior active-avoidance responses. Another group of animals in the study received the reminder treatment 4 minutes before they were placed in the novel environment. The reminder treatment involved placing animals for 15 seconds in a cueing chamber—a white, translucent box identical to the white chamber of the avoidance apparatus where they had received shock during training. Following the reminder treatment, the rats were placed in a holding cage for 3.5 minutes and then transferred to the shuttle box in the novel context. Gordon, McCracken, Dess-Beech, and Mowrer found that animals receiving the reminder treatment performed as well as the animals that had been tested in the training context. Exposure to the cueing chamber prevented the forgetting that normally occurs in a novel context.

Smith (1982) discovered that a reminder treatment could be used with human subjects to reduce the forgetting that occurs when the context is changed from training to testing. In Smith's studies, one group of subjects received a list of 32 words to learn in one context and then was asked to recall the list in the same context; a second group was asked to recall the list in a new context. A third group of subjects was exposed to a context-recall technique prior to testing in a new context. The context-recall technique involved instructing subjects to think of the original training context and ignore the new context when trying to recall the list of words. Smith reported that subjects in the context-recall technique group remembered as many words in a new room as did subjects tested in their original learning room. In contrast, subjects who were tested in a new context but did not receive the reminder treatment showed poor recall of their prior training.

Affective Attribute

Underwood (1983) asserted that the emotional responses produced by various events can be effective attributes of memories. Some events are pleasant; others unpleasant. The memory of an event contains much information regarding the emotional character of that event. This **affective attribute** enables a person to distinguish among various memories as well as to retrieve the memory of a particular event.

Underwood theorized that the affective attribute could be viewed as an internal contextual attribute; that is, it contains information about the internal consequences of an event. Events not only produce internal changes, they also occur during a particular internal state. Suppose you are intoxicated at a party. The next day a friend asks you if you had an enjoyable time, but you do not remember. This situation is an example of **state-dependent learning** (Overton, 1982). In a state-dependent learning study, an experience encountered during one internal state will not be recalled when the internal state changes. According to our memory attribute framework, internal state is an attribute of memory; that is, our memory of an event contains knowledge of the internal state. A change in internal state eliminates an attribute of memory, which can lead to a failure to recall the event. We will next examine evidence that internal state is a memory attribute.

STATE-DEPENDENT LEARNING. Donald Overton (1964) trained rats to obtain food in a T-maze. Half the animals were trained after receiving pentobarbital (a drug that depresses central nervous system activity); the remaining half were trained after receiving saline. The two groups of animals were subdivided again during testing: half of each group was tested after receiving pentobarbital; the other half, after saline. As **Table 13.1** shows, half the animals were tested when they were in the same internal state as they had been during training; the other half were tested during a state different from that experienced during

TABLE 13.1. Retention of Response as a Function of Training and Testing Conditions

Training	Testing	
	Drug	No Drug
Drug	Good retention	Poor retention
No drug	Poor retention	Good retention

Note: The high level of retention occurred in the groups experiencing the same conditions during both training and testing.

training. Overton found a high recall of the instrumental response if rats had received pentobarbital or saline prior to both training and testing. In contrast, retention was impaired if animals had been given pentobarbital before training and saline prior to testing, or saline before training and pentobarbital prior to testing. Thus, a previously learned response can be forgotten when the internal state changes.

State-dependent learning has been reported for a variety of behaviors, including approach in the T-maze (Overton, 1964), escape and avoidance responding in a shuttle box (Holmgren, 1964), and bar pressing in an operant chamber (Kubena & Barry, 1969). Researchers have observed state-dependent learning in rats, monkeys, cats, dogs, goldfish, and humans. The studies with humans have used alcohol (Goodwin, Powell, Bremer, Hoine, & Stein, 1969), amphetamine (Swanson & Kinsbourne, 1979), and marijuana (Eich, Weingartner, Stillman, & Gillin, 1975).

Events can also be experienced during a particular internal emotional state, and a change in this emotional state can lead to forgetting. Using hypnosis, Gordon Bower (1981) manipulated mood state (either happy or sad) before training and again prior to testing. Some subjects experienced the same mood prior to both training and testing, and other subjects experienced one mood state before training and the other before testing. Bower found significantly better recall when the emotional state induced before testing matched the emotional state present during training. Thus, a change in mood state, as well as drug state, can lead to forgetting.

THE KAMIN EFFECT. Changes in internal state can occur naturally; these changes can also lead to forgetting because of the absence of the internal attributes of a memory. In 1957, Kamin reported that rats were unable to perform a previously learned active-avoidance response on an intermediate retention test (1 to 3 hours after original training), whereas avoidance performance was excellent both immediately and 24 hours after the initial aversive experience (see **Figure 13.4**). This U-shaped retention function, the **Kamin effect,** has been consistently replicated (Brush, 1971), and the poor performance on the intermediate retention interval has been attributed to retrieval failure. A number of studies (Bintz, 1970; Klein, 1972; Seybert, McClanahan, & Gilliland, 1982; Spear, Klein, & Riley, 1971) support a retrieval-failure explanation of the Kamin effect. When the memory of original training is available (both immediately and 24 hours after training), subjects show a high level of performance in the original training situation (Klein & Spear, 1970). However, when the memory of a prior avoidance response is unavailable (on an intermediate retention test), subjects do not respond according to prior training in the original situation; that is, they act like untrained rats in a new situation.

Why are animals unable to recall the memory of a prior response on an intermediate retention test? The answer is that the animal experiences different internal states immediately after training (and 24 hours later) and 1 to 3 hours after training. Because avoidance training is aversive, a number of physiological changes take place during the acquisition of the avoidance response. One physiological response that occurs during avoidance training is the release of adrenocorticotrophic hormone (ACTH) from the pituitary gland, and one effect

FIGURE 13.4. The mean number of active avoidance responses as a function of the time between training and testing. The animals in this study showed better performance of a previously learned avoidance response when tested either immediately after training or 24 hours after training. Performance declined on tests during the intermediate retention interval (1 hour) after training.

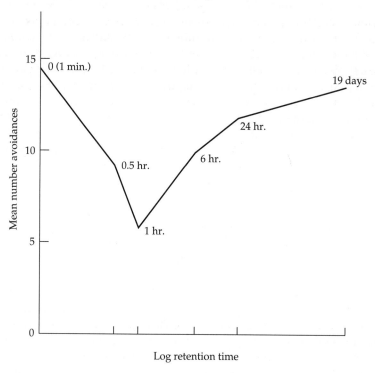

of ACTH is the excitement of specific neural systems. This excitement produces the motivational and emotional arousal characteristic of stressful experiences (Grossman, 1967). Approximately 1 hour after a stressful experience, the presence of adrenal corticotrophic hormones released by the adrenal cortex causes the inhibition of the ACTH release. This inhibition lasts several hours and results in a lowered responsivity to stressful experiences. Thus, performance of the avoidance response on the intermediate retention test is poor. The corticoid inhibition is no longer present on the 24-hour test; the internal responsivity, and thus response performance, has returned to the normal state.

Several studies support the theory that ACTH inhibition is responsible for poor performance on an intermediate retention test. First, Spear, Klein, and Riley (1971) found that animals forgot avoidance learning acquired during the intermediate interval state when they also were tested at the 24-hour interval. Second, Klein (1972) observed that direct injection of ACTH into the lateral anterior hypothalamus at the intermediate retention test resulted in a high level of performance of the learned response. These treatments are assumed to reestablish the internal state that was present during training, and thus eliminate the forgetting usually observed on an intermediate retention test.

The internal state experienced during training is one attribute of memory.

Although a change in internal state can lead to retrieval failure, in some circumstances forgetting does not occur despite a change in internal state. For example, although intoxicated people do forget some events, they can clearly remember others. The attribute model of memory suggests that the presence of other memory attributes can lead to retrieval, despite the change in internal state.

Eich, Weingartner, Stillman, and Gillin (1975) examined the state-dependent effects of the drug marijuana. With the permission of appropriate government agencies, subjects smoked either a marijuana cigarette (drug condition) or a cigarette with the active ingredient THC removed (nondrug condition). Some subjects smoked the marijuana 20 minutes before learning a list of words and again before testing 4 hours after training. Other subjects were given the marijuana prior to training and the nondrug before testing; still other subjects received the nondrug before training and the marijuana before testing. A final group of subjects smoked the nondrug before both training and testing. Eich, Weingartner, Stillman, and Gillin evaluated the influence of marijuana by measuring heart rate (marijuana increases heart rate) and the subjective experience of being "high." They found that compared with the nondrug condition, marijuana produced a strong physiological and psychological effect.

The researchers tested half of the subjects using a free-recall task; the other half using category names of the words given in training as retrieval cues. In the free-recall testing, the subjects showed state-dependent learning; they remembered more words when the same state was present during both training and testing than when the states differed (see **Table 13.2**). This lower recall on the free-recall test was observed whether the subjects were in a drug state during training and a nondrug state in testing or in a nondrug state during training and a drug state during testing. In contrast to the state-dependent effects with the free-recall test, subjects receiving the cued-recall test did not demonstrate state-dependent effects. When the subjects received the category words at testing, they showed a high level of recall in all four treatment conditions.

Why didn't a change in internal state cause the subjects to forget the words in the cued-recall testing procedure? Eich (1980) suggested that people typically rely on external cues. If these cues are unavailable, they will use subtle cues associated with their physiological or mental state to retrieve memories. The

TABLE 13.2. Treatment Conditions and Results of a State-Dependent Learning Study

Condition		Average Number of Words Recalled	
Study	Test	Free Recall	Cued Recall
Nondrug	Nondrug	11.5	24.0
Nondrug	Drug	9.9	23.7
Drug	Nondrug	6.7	22.6
Drug	Drug	10.5	22.3

Source: Eich, J. E., Weingartner, H., Stillman, R. C., & Gillin, J. C. (1975). State-dependent accessibility of retrieval cues in the retention of a categorized list. *Journal of Verbal Learning and Verbal Behavior, 14,* 408–417.

cued-recall procedure provided verbal cues that eliminated the need to use internal retrieval cues for recall.

Verbal Associative Attribute

According to Underwood (1983), when a person hears or sees a word, the word may produce a variety of verbal associates. For example, the word *cat* may elicit the associative response *animal*. The category word *animal* is a **verbal associative attribute** of the memory of *cat*, and its presence may help retrieve the word *cat* on a retrieval test. Verbal associative attributes are responsible for the enhanced recall that occurs as the result of associative learning. Underwood suggested that there are two types of verbal associative attributes: parallel associates and class associates.

PARALLEL ASSOCIATIVE ATTRIBUTE. Underwood (1983) proposed three major types of **parallel associative attributes:** antonyms, synonyms, and functional associates. Functional associates are formed because of functional contiguity; they include pairs such as cup-saucer, table-chair, and key-lock. The presence of a parallel associate during testing can result in the retrieval of a memory which would otherwise not have been recalled.

The influence of parallel associates on retrieval was demonstrated by a study by Jenkins, Mink, and Russell (1958). They constructed four lists of words, with each list consisting of twelve pairs of words. Thus, the four lists combined contained 48 pairs, all of which differed in terms of the strength of the individual associates. Some had high associative strength (e.g., man-woman); others had low associative strength (e.g., comfort-chair). Four different associative strengths were used—76, 43, 32, and 12; the strengths varied according to the number of subjects producing the same associative responses. Each list contained three pairs of each associative strength. As **Figure 13.5** indicates, the higher the associate strength of a pair, the higher the recall of the words, indicating that the presence of a parallel associate increased the recall of the associated word.

CLASS ASSOCIATIVE ATTRIBUTE. Underwood (1983) proposed that when a word elicits the category name that includes that word, the category name is a **class associative attribute** of the word. The presence of the category name can then act to retrieve the word during testing. For example, the category name *animal* can serve as a memory attribute of the word *cat.*

Wood and Underwood (1967) found that the presence of the word *black* on a list of words enhanced the retrieval of three apparently unrelated words: *derby, coffee,* and *skunk. Black* was a class associate of each word; that is, it has conceptual similarity to each of the other three words. Thus, *black* was a memory attribute of each word: if subjects remembered the word *black,* they would also remember the other three words. The observation that the inclusion of the word *black* facilitated the recall of its class associates, but not of the other words on the list, supports Underwood's view.

Transformational Attribute

The final class of memory attributes Underwood (1983) proposed is the **transformational attribute.** People sometimes transform information to make it

FIGURE 13.5. The mean recall of 12 pairs of words in a 24-word list as a function of the associative strength of word pairs. Subjects in this study recalled items better when the pairs of words were highly related than when they were unrelated.

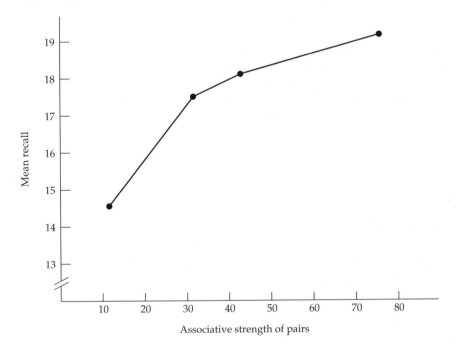

easier to learn and recall. For example, the nonsense syllable *tfx* can be changed into the word *tax*. During testing, the word *tax* must be decoded into the non-sense syllable *tfx*. According to Underwood, a part of the memory of the non-sense syllable must consist of the information for decoding. This decoding information constitutes the transformational attribute. This section discusses three major types of transformational attributes: images, natural language me-diators, and order transformations.

IMAGES. Many words or ideas can be transformed into images. For exam-ple, the word *car* can be transformed into the image of a car. According to Un-derwood (1983), the image is a transformational attribute of the word or idea. Remembering the image will enable a person to recall the word or idea. Recall our discussion of mnemonic techniques in the last chapter. Mnemonics make great use of imagery in information storage, and the use of these techniques en-hances recall of past events.

NATURAL LANGUAGE MEDIATORS. Consider the following example. In a paired-associate learning task, a subject is learning the associate "dog-car." If a subject injects the word *chase* between *dog* and *car*, the natural language media-tor is *dog-chase-car*. According to Underwood (1983), the **natural language me-diator** produces a meaningful link between the two words. Underwood reports that subjects attempting to learn verbal material often use natural language mediators. For example, subjects learning a serial list of words often will add a word or two to the list to create a story. Underwood has found that the use of natural language mediators can enhance the recall of past verbal experiences, as long as the memory contains decoding information, or knowledge of the words to be deleted.

ORDER TRANSFORMATIONS. Underwood (1983) suggests that relatively meaningless nonsense syllables can be recoded to create more meaningful verbal units. For example, the nonsense syllable *rac* can become the word *car*. As was true for images and natural language mediators, order transformations can increase the recall of verbal units. However, this is true only if people have during recall a rule for rearranging the verbal units into their original forms. As we learned in the last chapter, one of the advantages of the mnemonic techniques is that they provide a simple rule for coding experiences and then decoding them during testing.

BEFORE YOU GO ON

- **What memory attribute might remind Steve of his visit to Ebbets Field with his grandfather?**
- **Would the anniversary of a trip to Ebbets Field be likely to remind Steve of his grandfather?**

FORGETTING

How Quickly We Forget

Left to itself every mental content gradually loses its capacity for being retrieved, or at least suffers loss in this regard under the influence of time. Facts crammed at examination time soon vanish, if they were not sufficiently grounded by other study and later subjected to sufficient review. (Hermann Ebbinghaus, 1885, page 4)

This quote characterizes Ebbinghaus's view of forgetting. His work contributed to our current attention to the **forgetting** of past events. Our discussion of forgetting begins with a description of his research.

Ebbinghaus (1885) conducted an extensive study of memory, using himself as the only subject, in the latter part of the nineteenth century. To study memory, Ebbinghaus invented the nonsense syllable—two consonants separated by a vowel (e.g., BAF or XOF). He memorized relatively meaningless nonsense syllables because he felt that these verbal units would be uncontaminated by his prior experience. He assumed that any difference in the recall of specific nonsense syllables would be due to forgetting and not to differential familiarity with the nonsense syllables.

After memorizing a list of 10 to 12 nonsense syllables, Ebbinghaus relearned the list of nonsense syllables. (In Ebbinghaus's study, savings in relearning the lists was used to indicate how much of the list was retained; the greater the savings, the higher the recall.) He memorized over 150 lists of nonsense syllables at various retention intervals. As **Figure 13.6** shows, Ebbinghaus forgot almost half of a prior list after 24 hours, and six days later recalled only one-fourth of the prior learning. Ebbinghaus's results show a rapid forgetting following acquisition of a list of nonsense syllables.

Why did Ebbinghaus forget so much of his prior learning? Psychologists have proposed three theories to explain why we forget previous experiences. First, some psychologists (McGeoch, 1932) have suggested that memories decay, a view which assumes that memory is lost through disuse; that is, memories that are not recalled will not survive. Second, some have proposed that interference among memories causes forgetting (McGeoch, 1932; Underwood, 1957). Interference refers to the inability to recall a specific event as the result of having experienced another event. The third theory is that the absence of a specific stimulus can lead to forgetting (Underwood, 1969, 1983). This view holds

FIGURE 13.6. Percentage of prior learning retained as a function of the interval between training and testing. Ebbinghaus found that the recall of nonsense syllables declined rapidly as the interval between training and testing increased.

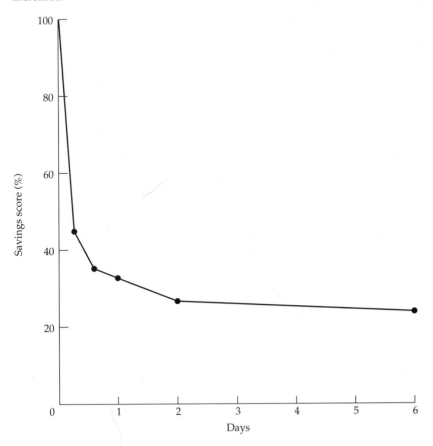

FIGURE 13.7. The number of syllables recalled as a function of time between training and testing in subjects who were either asleep or awake during the retention interval. The results show that recall was higher in subjects who slept during the retention interval than in subjects who spent the interval awake.

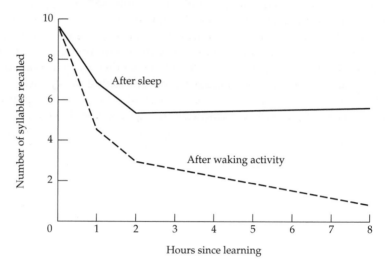

Decay of a Memory

It is generally assumed that specific physical changes take place when an event is experienced (see Chapter 12). The **engram,** or physical representation of an event, enables a person to recall the experience at a later time. A few psychologists (McGeoch, 1932) have proposed that the engram fades with disuse; that is, that the physiological changes that took place during learning and that represent the record of the experience will diminish unless the memory is retrieved from time to time. Retrieval may prevent decay or strengthen a decaying memory.

In a classic study, Jenkins and Dallenbach (1924) evaluated the **decay of forgetting view** by teaching subjects a list of nonsense syllables to a criterion of one trial without errors. The retention of the nonsense syllables was evaluated one, two, four, or eight hours later. Half the subjects spent their retention interval awake; the other half of the subjects slept during the interval. If the decay view is accurate and the time between learning and recall determines the level of forgetting, an equal amount of forgetting should occur regardless of whether the subjects were asleep or awake during the retention interval. As **Figure 13.7** shows, subjects who were awake actually forgot more than those asleep during the retention interval, suggesting that activities that occurred while the subjects were awake contributed to the amount of forgetting.

Note that subjects who slept during the interval still forgot a considerable amount during that time. Is this forgetting the result of decay? According to

Underwood (1957), the methods Jenkins and Dallenbach (1924) employed were inadequate by contemporary standards. In addition, Jenkins and Dallenbach's subjects had been in other studies; this previous participation may have produced high levels of interference, which in turn may have caused the forgetting seen in the asleep condition.

Conducting a more controlled investigation of the effects of sleep on retention, Ekstrand (1967) used subjects who had not experienced prior paired-associate tasks. One group of subjects slept during the eight-hour retention interval after learning a list of paired associates; the other group was awake during the retention interval. Ekstrand observed that subjects in the awake condition forgot 23% of the paired associates, whereas subjects in the sleep condition forgot only 11%. These observations suggest that interference, which resulted from prior experience with paired associates, caused much of the forgetting that Jenkins and Dallenbach reported in the asleep condition subjects. However, subjects in the asleep condition in the Ekstrand study did forget some material. Decay of memory may have been responsible for this forgetting. It is also feasible that extraexperimental sources of interference (interference from verbal material learned outside the laboratory) contributed to the forgetting that occurred in the asleep condition. We will next examine some research supporting a decay view; we will discuss interference as a cause of forgetting later in the chapter.

Rozin and Gleitman (cited in Gleitman, 1971) used fish as their subjects and trained them to avoid shock in a shuttle box. The fish spent either a four-week or an eight-week retention interval in either the training temperature (25–26°C) or in a hot tank (33°C). Rozin and Gleitman reasoned that since fish are cold-blooded, heating the fish tank would accelerate their metabolic processes, thereby increasing the rate of memory decay. Rozin and Gleitman reported that the fish kept in the hot tank forgot more during the retention interval than did the fish in the training tank.

Other investigators have attempted to slow down metabolic rate to decrease the decay of memory and thereby reduce the amount of forgetting. Rensch and Ducker (1966) observed that goldfish treated with chlorpromazine, a drug that suppresses central nervous system activity, during the retention interval exhibited greater retention of a visual discrimination than did goldfish not given chlorpromazine. Ducker and Rensch (1968) observed a similar decrease in forgetting in goldfish kept in the dark during the retention interval, as did Alloway (1969) in grain beetles kept in a cold environment after training.

Gleitman (1971) points to one problem in concluding that decay is a source of forgetting. Studies evaluating the decay view have inferred that treatments such as heat or sleep affect forgetting by altering the metabolic processes that govern erosion of the memory trace. Unfortunately, no study has proved that this relationship exists; thus, decay remains only a possible source of forgetting. In contrast, considerable evidence indicates that interference is a cause of forgetting.

Interference

You are warmly greeted by someone who looks familiar, and you respond, "Hello, Bill." Unfortunately, the man's name is not Bill, but Sam. Why did you incorrectly apply the wrong name to the familiar face? Interference is one possible cause.

There are two types of **interference:** proactive and retroactive. **Proactive interference (PI)** involves an inability to recall recent experiences because of the memory of earlier experiences. For example, a group of subjects learns one list of paired associates (A-B list) and then learns a second list of paired associates (A-C list). (In a paired-associates learning task, subjects are presented a list of stimuli and responses. The list usually consists of 10 to 15 pairs, and subjects are required to learn the correct response to each stimulus. In some cases, the associates are nonsense syllables; in other cases, words. An example of one set of pairs would be the words book-shoe in the A-B list and book-window in the A-C list.) When subjects are asked to recall the associates from the second list, they are unable to do so because the memory of the first list interferes. How do we know that these subjects would not have forgotten the response to the second list even if they had not learned the first? To show that it is the memory of the first list that caused the forgetting of the second list, a control group of subjects learned only the second list (see **Table 13.3** to compare the treatments given to experimental and control subjects). Any poorer recall of the second list by the experimental subjects as compared to the control subjects is assumed to reflect proactive interference. Returning to our incorrect naming example, you may have known someone named Bill in the past who looked like the more-recently-met Sam. The memory of the facial attributes associated with Bill caused you to identify Sam as Bill.

Retroactive interference (RI) occurs when people cannot remember distant events because the memory of more recent events intervenes. Retroactive interference can be observed with the following paradigm: experimental subjects learn two lists of paired associates (A-B, A-C) and then take a retention test that asks them to recall the responses from the first list. The retention of the first list of responses among experimental subjects is compared with the retention of the list among a control group required to learn only the first list (refer to **Table 13.4** to see the treatments given the experimental and control subjects). If the recall of the first list is poorer for experimental subjects than for the control group subjects, retroactive interference is the likely cause of the difference. The incorrect naming of Sam as Bill could also have been due to retroactive interference. You could have recently met a man named Bill, and the memory of the facial characteristics associated with Bill caused you to be unable to name longtime acquaintance Sam.

Why does interference occur? In 1940, Melton and Irwin offered a two-factor theory of interference; we will look at their view next.

TABLE 13.3. Design of a Proactive Interference Study

Group	Stage of Experiment		
	I	II	III
Experimental	Learn first materials	Learn materials to be remembered	Test for recall
Control	Unrelated activity	Learn materials to be remembered	Test for recall

Group	Stage of Experiment		
	I	II	III
Experimental	Learn materials to be remembered	Learn new materials	Test for recall
Control	Learn materials to be remembered	Unrelated activity	Test for recall

Melton and Irwin's Two-Factor Theory of Interference

According to Melton and Irwin's **two-factor theory of interference** (1940), competition between memories is a source of both proactive and retroactive interference. Consider the A-B, A-C paradigm, in which the same stimulus (A) has been associated with two responses (B and C). Since the task requires subjects to recall only one response, Melton and Irwin suggested that the response with the strongest association to the stimulus will be elicited. Thus, a subject may forget response C because of competition from response B if response B has a stronger association to stimulus A. However, if the stimulus response association A-C is stronger than that of A-B, the subject will be unable to recall the responses from task A-B.

Melton and Irwin proposed that although competition is the only cause of proactive interference, a second factor, unlearning, can also produce retroactive interference. According to Melton and Irwin, for subjects to learn the second list (A-C), they must unlearn or extinguish the first list (A-B). They do not view unlearning as an erasure of A-B associations. Instead, they suggest that subjects suppress A-B associations in order to learn the second list. Unlearning of the first list causes subjects to forget these responses when they take a retention test given immediately after second-list acquisition.

Melton and Irwin suggested that the suppression of first-list responses is only temporary and that the association will spontaneously recover during the interval after second-list learning. The recovery of the strength of first-task associations may lead to a recall of the first-list responses. As the memory of first-list responses becomes available, response competition becomes the sole determinant of which memory the subject will recall.

Underwood's List Differentiation View

Underwood (1983) suggested that interference is caused not by response competition, but instead by a failure of task differentiation. According to Underwood, subjects do remember responses from both tasks but are unable to remember which task a particular response was associated with. Thus, subjects asked to recall the response learned from the first task can remember the response from both tasks, but will appear to have forgotten them because the subjects cannot remember which response came from the first list. A considerable amount of research indicates that the failure of **list differentiation,** rather than competition, is a source of forgetting. Let's briefly look at the evidence.

We learned earlier that subjects who learned one task in one environment and another task in a different environment do not display interference.

According to Underwood, learning in different environments enables subjects to differentiate between memories. Although responses from the two tasks are still in associative competition, interference will not occur because the subjects are able to differentiate between the two tasks. In Underwood's view, interference occurs when a subject cannot differentiate between memories.

According to Underwood, any treatment that increases the distinctiveness of memories will reduce the level of interference. We know that interference is reduced when the distribution of practice on the first list differs from that of the second list (Underwood & Ekstrand, 1966). Furthermore, Underwood and Freund (1968) observed less interference when original-list and interpolated-list learning were separated by three days, even when the two lists were acquired with the same distribution of practice. Underwood argues that each of these treatments (different distributions of practice, different times, different environments) increased the distinctiveness of the memories, and this increased list differentiation was responsible for the reduced interference.

Postman's Generalized Competition View

Barnes and Underwood (1959) noted that the level of proactive interference (PI) increases following interpolated list learning, whereas the amount of retroactive interference (RI) declines. These researchers argued that the changes in interference were due to the spontaneous recovery of the original-list responses. However, while some studies have observed spontaneous recovery, others have not (Postman, Stark, & Fraser, 1968). Based on this conflicting evidence, Postman, Stark, and Fraser (1968) suggested that "it is clear that long-term spontaneous recovery is not a dependable phenomenon."

These observations suggest that spontaneous recovery cannot be responsible for the predictable changes in interference that follow interpolated-list learning. They also imply that unlearning is not responsible for the unavailability of original-list responses during interpolated-list acquisition. Postman and his associates (Postman, 1967; Postman, Stark, & Fraser, 1968) suggest that **generalized competition,** rather than unlearning, is responsible for both an inability to recall first-list responses as the second list is acquired, and the changes in interference after interpolated-list learning.

According to Postman, generalized competition is a "set" or disposition to continue to respond in the manner learned most recently. A selector mechanism excludes from subjects' response repertoire all responses except those being learned. It is this selector mechanism, not unlearning, that prevents a subject from being able to remember original-list responses. Postman suggests that following interpolated-list acquisition, the "set" to respond dissipates, or generalized competition declines; the reduced disposition to respond according to recency is responsible for the increased PI and decreased RI. Throughout the text, we have seen that recency plays an important role in determining behavior. Postman's generalized competition proposes a mechanism that ensures that recency will have a significant impact on behavior.

What evidence indicates that generalized competition exists? Melton and Irwin (1940) argued that the relative strength of competing responses determines the level of interference. Yet, it is the relative degree of learning of each list, not individual response strength, that determines the amount of interference (Runquist, 1957). The observation that the learning of the entire task, rather than the memory of individual responses, is a function of interference supports the view that a selector mechanism acts to limit responses to the most recent task for a short time following learning.

Forgetting and Short-Term Memory

What causes us to forget information in the short-term store? Peterson and Peterson (1959) suggested that memories fade within a few seconds after leaving the short-term store. They believed that the decay of a short-term memory is an automatic process, and that future recall of that memory will occur only if the memory has been transferred to the long-term store. Furthermore, these researchers argued that rehearsal postpones the onset of the decay of a short-term memory but that the memory begins to fade as soon as rehearsal stops.

Melton (1963), offering another interpretation of the rapid forgetting that Peterson and Peterson observed, claimed that interference was responsible for the rapid forgetting of the trigrams. In Melton's view, subjects recalling a specific trigram encounter two sources of interference. First, the backward-counting task is a source of retroactive interference; the memory of the numbers interferes with recall of the trigrams. Second, the memory of trigrams presented at the beginning of the study may proactively interfere with the recall of trigrams presented later in the study. Since Peterson and Peterson reported only the average recall of all trigrams, Melton argued that the recall of the trigrams presented early in the study may have been greater than the reported average.

Gleitman (1987) offers an analogy that may help illustrate the difference between the decay and interference theories. Suppose that some packages are on a loading dock, ready to be stored in a warehouse. Packages may be lost, and therefore not stored in the warehouse, if they either rot (decay) or are shoved off by other packages (interference). Which of the processes, decay or interference, causes the forgetting of short-term memories? The evidence (Wessels, 1982) indicates that in the Petersons' study, both decay and interference were responsible for an inability to recall a trigram presented 18 seconds earlier.

Keppel and Underwood (1962) provided evidence that proactive interference caused most of the retention loss the Petersons observed. In the Keppel and Underwood study, three trigrams were presented on each of three trials. Three retention intervals (3, 9, and 18 seconds) were used on each trial. Keppel and Underwood reported that on the first trial, subjects showed no decline in recall with the 3- to 18-second interval. In contrast, on the second trial, a loss of recall of the trigram occurred with the 18-second interval, and an even greater loss of retention was seen on the third trial (refer to **Figure 13.8**). Thus, as subjects learned more trigrams, they became less able to remember them after 18 seconds. Keppel and Underwood argue that the memories of trigrams acquired on the earlier trials interfered with the recall of trigrams experienced on later trials.

Waugh and Norman (1965) evaluated the influence of retroactive interference on short-term memory. In this study, subjects received a list of digits (for example, 1, 7, 8, 3, 4, 2, 5, 6, 3, 4, 8, 2, 9, 7 *) followed by the presentation of a tone, which is indicated by the *. The number that appeared before the tone is the probe digit, and subjects were asked to recall the digit that followed the probe digit the *first time* it was presented. Thus, in our example, the correct digit to recall is 8. Waugh and Norman varied the number of digits that intervened between the correct response and the probe digit. According to Waugh and Norman, the more digits that intervened, the greater the retroactive interference and the lower recall a subject should have of the correct digit. However, more time is required when the number of intervening units increases, and because of this time lapse between the correct digit and recall, decay, not retroactive interference, would be responsible for the low recall. To control for the influence of time, Waugh and Norman used two rates of presentation: four digits per second (fast rate) and only one digit per second (slow rate). If interference is responsible for forgetting, then recall of a 12-item presentation, for example, should be the same, regardless of whether the items were presented in 3 seconds or in 12 seconds. However, if decay is responsible for forgetting, then recall should be affected by the rate of presentation; that is, more forgetting should occur when it takes 12 seconds rather than 3 to present the 12 digits. **Figure 13.9** shows the results of Waugh and Norman's study. The number of intervening digits affected the level of recall; the percentage of correct responses declined from almost 100% with one intervening digit to less than 10% with 12 intervening digits. In contrast, the rate of presentation did not affect recall of the correct digit. These observations support the view that retroactive interference, not decay, affects the recall of memories from the short-term store.

Some evidence suggests that decay does occur, but it is simply not apparent because interference is a more powerful and common cause of forgetting. A

FIGURE 13.8. The proportion of correct responses as a function of the number of previous items and the length of the retention interval. This study shows that the amount of forgetting on the 18-second retention test increased with greater prior training.

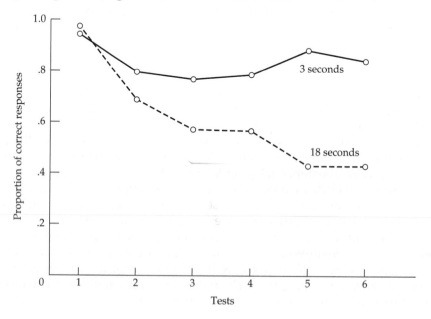

FIGURE 13.9. The probability of recall as a function of the rate of stimulus presentation and the number of intervening items. These results showed that the level of retroactive interference was affected by the number of intervening items; that is, the greater the number of intervening items, the poorer the recall. However, researchers found that rate of stimulus presentation did not influence recall.

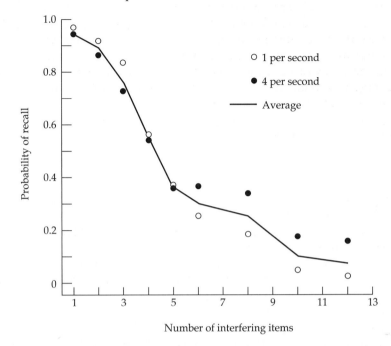

number of studies (Baddeley & Scott, 1971; Shiffrin & Cook, 1978) indicate that decay can be observed under certain conditions. For example, Shiffrin and Cook (1978) told their subjects that they were studying how well people forget information, not how well people can remember—a procedure which Shiffrin and Cook believed would minimize rehearsal and enhance the detection of decay. Their subjects participated in a tone-detection task. In this task, a tone was presented against a background of white noise many times during a 40-second trial. Also, in each 40-second trial, five consonants were presented for 2.5 seconds each. The subjects were instructed to repeat the five consonants, then put them out of their minds and continue with the tone-detection task. At the end of each trial, subjects were asked to recall the letters.

Shiffrin and Cook used two kinds of trials: on long-delay trials, the letters were presented early in the trial (32.5 seconds prior to the end of the trial); on short-delay trials, the letters were presented late in the trial (12.5 seconds before the end of the trial). According to Shiffrin and Cook, if decay is a cause of forgetting, more forgetting should occur with a long-delay trial than with a short-delay trial. Shiffrin and Cook reported that subjects forgot 20% of the letters on the short-delay trials, and forgot 30% on the long-delay trials. This result is consistent with the decay theory.

Increased forgetting on long-delay trials may be caused by processes other than decay. Retroactive interference from events occurring during the retention interval may explain the greater incidence of forgetting observed on long-delay trials; yet the subjects' experiences during the interval were not similar to the letters and should thus have caused a minimal amount of interference. The recall differences may have been caused by proactive interference; however, Baddeley and Scott (1971), using a task similar to Shiffrin and Cook's, tested subjects after only one trial, a procedure designed to minimize the development of proactive interference. These experimenters also observed greater forgetting with a long-delay test than with a short-delay test. The results of these two studies suggest that decay accounts for some forgetting of previously learned material.

BEFORE YOU GO ON

- **Could interference cause Steve to forget that his grandmother sometimes went to the baseball games?**
- **Might decay be an alternate explanation for the forgetting that his grand-mother went?**

RECONSTRUCTION OF THE PAST

How accurate is a person's recollection of an experience? Sir Fredrick Bartlett (1932) argued that a memory of an experience is often inaccurate. Sometimes details of an event are forgotten, creating an imperfect memory. To create a logical and realistic experience, people may add information to the memory during recall. Or an experience may not make sense to an individual, and some information will be deleted or new information added to establish a memory consistent with the individual's view of the world. The alteration of a memory to correspond to the individual's expectations is called **memory reconstruction.** Bartlett first studied this memory reconstruction process years ago.

Memory Reconstruction Studies

Bartlett examined the alteration of a memory during recall. In one of his classic studies, he had subjects read the folktale "The War of the Ghosts." This story contains a number of details about the experiences and eventual death of a warrior who was engaged in combat with ghosts (see **Figure 13.10**). The students were tested for recall of the story immediately after reading it and then several hours or days later. Bartlett noted that the subjects' memory of the stories, when tested at both time intervals, often differed from the original story. He found that some aspects of the stories were deleted, some were overemphasized, and in other cases, new information was added. According to Bartlett, the content and structure of the folktale was quite different from actual events that the subjects had experienced. Because of their unfamiliarity with the story, the subjects reconstructed their memory of it to be more consistent with their own cultural expectations. Bartlett reported that each subject retained some key facts about the story and then used these key ideas to reconstruct the story. He found that subjects retained the main features of the story, but since each subject was using personal knowledge to reconstruct the story, each subject's story differed. An example of a reconstructed story also appears in **Figure 13.10.**

To demonstrate how extensively a memory can be altered by reconstruction, Bartlett presented a figure to a subject, and then told the subject to reproduce it for a second subject. In some cases, the transmission of information continued through 10 subjects. Bartlett noted that not only did the final drawing differ from the original, but the changes were quite extensive. Also, the figure changed from subject to subject. **Figure 13.11** shows the change in each subject's recollection of the figure presented.

Bartlett's research suggests that we reconstruct memories based on inferences of what "must have happened." A study of Brewer and Treyens (1981) demonstrates the inferential quality of memory reconstruction. In their study, subjects waited in a room prior to participating in an "active study." After leaving, subjects were asked to describe the waiting room. In addition to indicating that the waiting room contained a desk, chair, and walls, a third of the subjects said that a bookcase was in the room, which was untrue. For these subjects, a bookcase "should" have been in the room and they "remembered" it to be there.

When are memories reconstructed? Bartlett argued that memories are reconstructed when the event is stored. Some research (Kintsch, 1974) does show that experiences can be altered during storage, while other experiments (Hasher & Griffin, 1978) indicate that memories can be altered at the time of retrieval.

Some memories may in fact reflect what "actually happened." According to Maki (1990), when an event seems confusing or contains irrelevant details, people reconstruct the memory to conform to what "must have happened." In contrast, when the event is easily understood or is distinctive or surprising, the memory will be what "actually happened."

Can information received from others influence our recollections of the past? We next turn our attention to this question.

The Accuracy of Eyewitness Testimony

Elizabeth Loftus (1980, 1992) recognized a significant relationship between the memory reconstruction process and the accuracy of eyewitness testimony. According to Loftus, trial witnesses recall what they think they saw or heard. The literature on memory reconstruction suggests that their recollections may not always be accurate. In all likelihood, the incident they are recalling occurred months or years earlier, and the witnesses may have forgotten some aspects of the event. To create a logical and realistic account, the witnesses will fill in information consistent with the aspects they actually remember.

Loftus (1980, 1992) contends that information received from others can also alter a memory. Because of this information, the memory of the past event is inaccurate, and the memory is subsequently changed to conform to the information received from other people. Consider Loftus's 1975 study to illustrate this process. In her study, subjects first were shown a series of slides showing a red sports car headed for a collision. Two groups of subjects saw the same sequence

FIGURE 13.10. Bartlett had subjects read stories such as "The War of the Ghosts." Subject recollections of these stories varied significantly from the original tales. An example of a reconstructed version appears here.

The War of the Ghosts

Original story

One night two young men from Egulac went down to the river to hunt seals, and while they were there it became foggy and calm. Then they heard warcries, and they thought: "Maybe this is a war-party." They escaped to the shore, and hid behind a log. Now canoes came up, and they heard the noise of paddles, and saw one canoe coming up to them. There were five men in the canoe, and they said:

"What do you think? We wish to take you along. We are going up the river to make war on the people."

One of the young men said: "I have no arrows."

"Arrows are in the canoe," they said.

"I will not go along. I might be killed. My relatives do not know where I have gone. But you," he said, turning to the other, "may go with them."

So one of the young men went, but the other returned home.

And the warriors went on up the river to a town on the other side of Kalama. The people came down to the water, and they began to fight, and many were killed. But presently the young man heard one of the warriors say: "Quick, let us go home; that Indian has been hit." Now he thought: "Oh, they are ghosts." He did not feel sick, but they said he had been shot.

So the canoes went back to Egulac, and the young man went ashore to his house, and made a fire. And he told everybody and said: "Behold I accompanied the ghosts, and we went to fight. Many of our fellows were killed, and many of those who attacked us were killed. They said I was hit, and I did not feel sick."

He told it all, and then he became quiet. When the sun rose he fell down. Something black came out of his mouth. His face became contorted. The people jumped up and cried.

He was dead.

Remembered story

Two men from Edulac went fishing. While thus occupied by the river they heard a noise in the distance.

"It sounds like a cry," said one, and presently there appeared some in canoes who invited them to join the party on their adventure. One of the young men refused to go, on the ground of family ties, but the other offered to go.

"But there are no arrows," he said.

"The arrows are in the boat," was the reply.

He thereupon took his place, while his friend returned home. The party paddled up the river to Kaloma, and began to land on the banks of the river. The enemy came rushing upon them, and some sharp fighting ensued. Presently someone was injured, and the cry was raised that the enemy were ghosts.

The party returned down the stream, and the young man arrived home feeling none the worse for his experience. The next morning at dawn he endeavored to recount his adventures. While he was talking, something black issued from his mouth. Suddenly he uttered a cry and fell down. His friends gathered around him.

But he was dead.

of slides except for one difference: some subjects saw the car approaching a stop sign, while the other subjects saw a yield sign in the slide (see **Figure 13.12**). After seeing the slides, the subjects were asked a series of questions about the accident. One question was "Did you see the stop sign?" For half of these subjects, this question was consistent with the slides; that is, they actually saw the stop sign. For the other subjects, this question was inconsistent with their experiences, since they did not see a stop sign. The other half of the subjects had the question "Did you see the yield sign?"

A week later, all subjects were asked to recall the accident. Testing involved showing subjects pairs of slides and then asking them to identify which slide they actually saw. Loftus reported that subjects who were asked the question consistent with their actual experience correctly identified the actual slide (either stop sign or yield sign) that they had seen 75% of the time. Subjects who were asked the inconsistent question identified the correct slide only 40% of the time.

Why did the inconsistent question cause many subjects to think that the other sign was actually in the scene? According to Loftus, the wording of the question implied that the other sign was present during the accident, and thus the subjects altered their memories of the accident to include the unseen sign. These results show that information received during recall can alter a memory.

The results of Loftus's study have special relevance to the reliability of eyewitness testimony. They demonstrate that a clever attorney may be able to change a witness's memory of a crime by asking leading questions, thereby altering the outcome of a trial. Other psychologists have also found that suggestion can alter the content of memory; see Ayers & Reder, 1998 for a review of this literature.

FIGURE 13.11. Subject 1 was shown the original drawing and asked to reproduce it after half an hour. The reproduction of the original drawing was shown to subject 2, whose reproduction was presented to subject 3, and so on through subject 10. This figure presents the original drawing and the 10 reproductions. Note that the drawing changes with each successive reproduction.

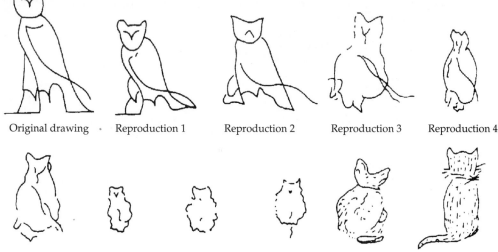

Original drawing · Reproduction 1   Reproduction 2   Reproduction 3   Reproduction 4

Reproduction 5 Reproduction 6   Reproduction 7   Reproduction 8 Reproduction 9   Reproduction 10

FIGURE 13.12. Did You See the Stop Sign? The top photo shows the car approaching a yield sign, while the bottom depicts the car approaching a stop sign. Subjects who saw the top slide sometimes altered their memories, believing they had seen the bottom one.

Even very subtle wording of a question may change a witness's memory. Loftus and Zanni (1975) asked subjects one of two questions about a car accident. Some subjects were asked, "Did you see the broken headlight?" Others were questioned, "Did you see a broken headlight?" Subjects who heard the word *the* were much more likely to say that they did see a broken headlight in the film. On the basis of the Loftus and Zanni study, as well as similar studies, it is no wonder that many psychologists and legal scholars question the accuracy of eyewitness testimony.

Does the memory reconstruction process permanently change the memory? The evidence (Zaragoza, McCloskey, & Jamis, 1987) suggests that the original memory still exists, but that the person is uncertain whether the original or the reconstructed memory is accurate. Research on eyewitness testimony (Chandler, 1991; Schooler, Gerhard, & Loftus, 1986) also indicates that an individual witnessing an accident and then receiving misleading information cannot discriminate between the real and suggested events.

One topic of recent investigation is whether all people are equally susceptible to memory reconstruction. Loftus, Levidow, and Duensing (1992) investigated the influence of misinformation on the accuracy of memory in 2,000 persons between the ages of 5 and 75. Their study involved the use of an interactive video at a science museum in San Francisco. All of the subjects were asked questions after watching the video. Some subjects were exposed to misleading information, while others were not. Loftus and her colleagues found that the youngest (up to 20) and oldest (over 65) subjects were most susceptible to memory alteration; that is, misinformation had the greatest influence on the youngest and oldest subjects.

False Memory Syndrome

A depressed young woman seeks psychological help. Her therapist, discussing her past, comes to believe that her depression is caused by sexual abuse that occurred during her childhood. The therapist suggests that the depression is a result of her father's sexual abuse. The woman at first denies that she was abused, but the therapist keeps questioning her about childhood experiences. After a while, the woman begins to remember experiences of being sexually abused by her father. The therapist explains that she has repressed these painful memories and that therapy has allowed her to recall them. The young woman stops seeing and talking to her father and publicly accuses him of sexual abuse. The father is arrested and imprisoned. Has justice been served? The answer depends on the accuracy of repressed memories.

The vignette just described could be any one of many **repressed memory** cases that have led to litigation over the last decade. Literally hundreds of lawsuits have been filed by adults who claim to have been victimized as children by parents, teachers, and neighbors. The legal system has often found these claims to be valid (Toufexis, 1991). For example, in 1991 a woman won $1.4 million from a church-run school in Washington. She claimed to have been repeatedly raped by a teacher at the school, to have repressed her memory of the rapes, and two decades later to have remembered the incidents. In the same year, a woman in Ohio won a $5 million settlement from her uncle, whom she claimed had sexually abused her as a child.

Can a person repress painful memories and then recall them many years later? Many psychologists (Briere & Conte, 1993; Whitfield, 1995) believe that individuals can repress the memory of extremely painful childhood experiences, even if the abuse is long-lasting. It is assumed that these events are buried in the person's unconscious and are revealed only through the process of therapy. While the publicity over repressed memories suggests a real phenomenon, other psychologists (Kihlstrom, 1998; Lindsay & Poole, 1995; Loftus, 1997, 1998) are skeptical about the accuracy of most, if not all, of these cases. Loftus (1997, 1998) argues that highly suggestible people with extreme emotional problems may be persuaded that their emotional problems are the result of repressed memories of sexual abuse. The therapists' suggestive questions are thought to reconstruct the patients' memories of the past and convince the patients that they have been abused as children. In the last section, we learned that misinformation can create an inaccurate record of an event. Continued prodding by therapists could certainly create false memories of child abuse.

Perhaps one case history would illustrate why many psychologists doubt the authenticity of repressed memories of sexual abuse. Loftus (1997) described a case history of a young woman who accused her minister father of sexual abuse. The woman recalled during the course of therapy with her church counselor that she was repeatedly raped by her father, who got her pregnant and then aborted the pregnancy with a coat hanger. As it turned out, subsequent evidence revealed that the woman was still a virgin and that her father had had a vasectomy years before the sexual abuse supposedly occurred.

The creation of an inaccurate record of childhood sexual abuse is now called the **false memory syndrome.** Many individuals have reported realizing that their therapists have created inaccurate memories; they often feel that they have been victimized by their therapists. These individuals have formed a support group, called the False Memory Syndrome Foundation, to help with their recovery.

Can a suggestion create a false memory of a childhood event? Loftus and Coan (1994) provide compelling evidence that it can. These researchers contacted a family member of each of the teenage subjects in their study. These family members were instructed to "remind" the subject of an incident in which the subject was lost in a shopping mall. Loftus and Coan later questioned their subjects and found that each of the subjects had created an emotionally laden memory of that event. For example, one subject named Chris was told by his older brother James that he had been lost in the mall when he was 5 years old and found by a tall older man in a flannel shirt. When questioned about the incident a few days later, Chris recalled being scared, being asked by the older man if he was lost, and being scolded later by his mother. Chris's description became even more detailed over the next few weeks when he recalled the incident in this way: "I was with you guys for a second and I think I went over to look at the toy store . . . I thought I was never going to see my family again. I was really scared, you know. And then this old man, I think he was wearing blue flannel, came up to me . . . he had like a ring of gray hair . . . he had glasses."

Loftus and Coan's study shows how easy it is to create a false memory. It is not hard to imagine that a therapist's suggestive questions and consistent prodding could lead a person to create a false memory of childhood abuse. While it is clear that people can forget past experiences, there are doubts about the accuracy of memories of childhood sexual abuse that have been "recovered" as a result of therapy. We will have more to say about repressed memories when we discuss motivated forgetting in the next section.

Motivated Forgetting

Sigmund Freud suggested that people can repress extremely painful memories. Repression is viewed as a process that minimizes anxiety and protects self-concept. The repressed memory is not erased, but rather is submerged in the unconscious. Painful memories that have been repressed can be retrieved during therapy.

We have learned in this chapter that people can forget previous experiences and that retrieval cues can help people access forgotten memories. Yet we have not examined whether people can deliberately forget previous experiences. Psychologists have investigated this kind of motivated forgetting using a procedure called **directed forgetting.** In this procedure, subjects are instructed to forget some information but not other information. We will first describe the directed forgetting procedure and then comment again on the issue of repressed memories.

A pigeon is presented a sample stimulus; sometime later, two stimuli are presented. The pigeon is reinforced for selecting the previously viewed stimulus. You should recall that, with this procedure, the pigeon is on a delayed-matching-to-sample procedure. Suppose that during the interval, the pigeon is presented one of two cues: On some trials, the pigeon receives a "remember cue," while on other trials, a "forget cue" is presented. The "remember cue" informs the pigeon that it should remember the sample because a test will follow, and it must select the sample to receive reinforcement. The "forget cue" informs the pigeon that it can forget the sample because there will be no test on this trial. Will the pigeon "forget" the sample after receiving a "forget cue"? To assess directed forgetting, the pigeon receives infrequent probe trials. On a probe trial, the comparison stimuli are presented after the "forget cue." A failure to respond more often to the sample than to the other stimulus presumably reflects forgetting caused by the "forget cue." **Figure 13.13** presents a diagram of the directed forgetting procedure.

Research (Maki & Hegvik, 1980; Stonebraker & Rilling, 1981) has consistently reported that a pigeon's performance is significantly impaired following a "forget cue" when compared to performance following a "remember cue." In other words, the pigeon is more likely to select the sample than the other stimulus after a "remember cue" than following a "forget cue." Directed forgetting has also been observed using the delayed-matching-to-sample procedure in primates (Roberts, Mazmanian, & Kraemer, 1984).

What causes directed forgetting? Researchers have proposed several theories (Roper & Zentall, 1993). One theory argues that the "forget cue" stops the rehearsal process and thereby prevents memory elaboration. A second view holds that directed forgetting is caused by retrieval rather than elaboration failure. According to the retrieval explanation, the memory of the sample is available, but the "forget cue" is a poor retrieval cue, while the "remember cue" is an effective retrieval cue. Many studies have attempted to evaluate the rehearsal

FIGURE 13.13. A diagram showing the procedure used in a directed forgetting study. During training, the pigeon sees a specific stimulus, followed by either a "remembering cue" (r) or a "forget cue" (f) and then two sample stimuli. During testing, the pigeon is presented the stimulus and the sample after the "forget cue" to determine if the pigeon has forgotten the previously presented stimulus.

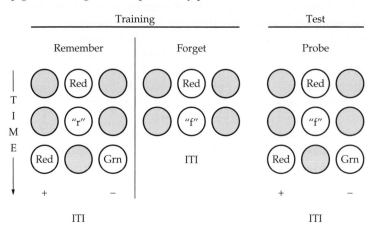

versus retrieval theories, but they have not provided conclusive evidence for either theory (see Roper & Zentall, 1993, for a complete discussion of this issue).

Studies have also investigated directed forgetting in humans (Bjork, 1989; Geiselman, Bjork, & Fishman, 1983). Directed forgetting studies with humans involve the use of either a recall measure, in which subjects are required to name either to-be-forgotten or to-be-remembered items, or a recognition task, in which subjects are merely asked to indicate whether an item has been presented. Some studies (Elmes, Adams, & Roediger, 1970; Geiselman, Bjork, & Fishman, 1983) have compared recall versus recognition measures of directed forgetting and have found that directed forgetting occurs with recall but not with recognition. This suggests that directed forgetting is caused by retrieval failure, because recognition but not recall would provide a retrieval cue to prevent forgetting. However, other studies (Archer & Margolin, 1970; Davis & Okada, 1971) have observed directed forgetting with recognition tests, a result that points to encoding failure as a cause of directed forgetting. Thus, the human studies, like the nonhuman animal studies, have not provided definitive evidence for a cause of directed forgetting; it is certainly possible that both encoding and retrieval processes contribute to this phenomenon.

We have learned that humans and nonhuman animals can be directed to forget experiences. Whether people can initiate their own forgetting remains to be documented. The concept of repression requires willful forgetting of disturbing information. No convincing evidence has yet been offered that humans can repress such information for years and then remember it accurately (Holmes, 1990). In fact, most extremely negative experiences are remembered well. For example, Helmreich (1992) reported that Holocaust survivors have vivid memories of their experiences. Similarly, Malmquist (1986) found that in a group of 5-to-10-year-old children who witnessed a parent's murder, not one of the children repressed this memory. Instead, all of the children were haunted by the memory of the murder.

Can a person repress the memory of abuse and than recall it many years later? Directed memory studies suggest that voluntary processes can cause forgetting. Furthermore, retrieval cues can lead the person to recall previously forgotten information. These two findings would suggest that people could repress disturbing memories and then recall them much later. Yet extremely emotional experiences appear to be remembered, not forgotten, and memories can easily be altered at the time of retrieval. Whether repressed memories of abuse actually exist awaits future verification.

ANATOMICAL BASIS OF MEMORY RETRIEVAL

In Chapter 12, we learned that several brain areas, including the temporal lobe, the hippocampus, and the dorsomedial thalamus, are involved in memory storage. Several psychologists (Malamut, Saunders, & Mishkin, 1984; Warrington, 1985; Zola-Morgan & Squire, 1986) have suggested that damage to the hippocampus also can lead to an inability to recall past events. We next examine evidence that amnesia is caused by retrieval failure and then look at studies showing that hippocampal damage can lead to difficulty retrieving stored information.

Warrington and Weiskrantz (Warrington & Weiskrantz, 1968, 1970; Weiskrantz & Warrington, 1975) conducted a number of studies comparing the memories of amnesics with the memories of individuals who were able to recall prior events. In one study (refer to Warrington & Weiskrantz, 1968), human subjects were given a list of words to remember. The amnesics were unable to remember the words even after several repetitions; however, Warrington and Weiskrantz noted that as the amnesics had been given several lists, they began to give responses from earlier lists. In contrast, fewer prior-list intrusions were observed in nonamnesic subjects. These results indicate that the amnesics had stored the responses from earlier lists but were unable to retrieve the appropriate responses. These observations further suggest that amnesics are more susceptible to interference than are nonamnesics and that interference was responsible for the higher level of retrieval failure in amnesic subjects.

Further evidence that amnesic patients suffer from a retrieval deficit comes from Warrington and Weiskrantz's 1970 study. They used three testing procedures: recall, recognition, and fragmented words. With the recall procedure, subjects were asked to recall as many words as they could from a previously learned list. With the recognition procedure, subjects were asked to identify the words they had previously learned from an equal number of alternative words. With the fragmented words procedure, subjects were presented five-letter words in a partial form by omitting two or three of the letters. As **Figure 13.14** shows, the percentage of correct responses for both amnesic and nonamnesic subjects was greater for the recognition than for the recall procedure. Further, the level of recall was equal for the amnesic and nonamnesic subjects with the fragmented words procedure. These results indicate that the amnesic subjects had stored the words but were unable to retrieve them on the recall test. According to Warrington and Weiskrantz, the recognition and fragmented word treatments provided the subjects with the cues they needed for retrieval and, therefore, enabled the amnesic to remember the words. Other studies by Weiskrantz and Warrington (1975) also showed that providing cues to amnesics at the time of testing significantly increased recall.

Our discussion suggests that retrieval failure caused the memory deficits of the amnesic subjects in Warrington and Weiskrantz's studies. Let's examine evidence that this retrieval failure results from hippocampal malfunctions; see Squire (1987) for a review of this literature.

Malamut, Saunders, and Mishkin (1984) evaluated the effect of damage to the hippocampus on the retention of a visual discrimination task in monkeys. They found that primates with hippocampal lesions required significantly more trials to relearn the task than did nonlesioned animals. In fact, hippocampal-lesioned animals required almost as many trials to relearn the task as they did to learn the task during original training. Also, Zola-Morgan and Squire (1986) found that destruction of the hippocampus produced poor recall on a matching-to-sample task. Lesions did not affect learning but did disrupt recall of a response. These observations show that the hippocampus plays an important role in the retrieval of memories.

FIGURE 13.14. The percentage of correct responses for amnesic and control subjects on either a free recall test, a recognition test, or a fragmented word test. The level of recall in amnesics was equal to control subjects with the fragmented word test, but poorer than controls with either a free recall or a recognition test.

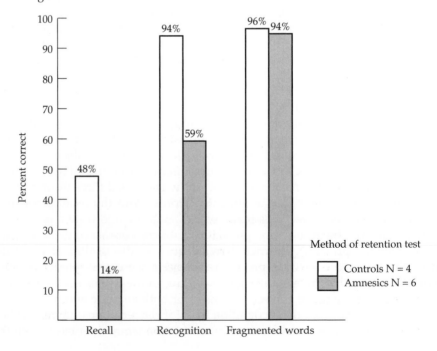

Zola-Morgan and Squire (1993) suggest that memories are stored by the medial temporal lobe and mediodorsal thalamus. Memories are retrieved by the hippocampus, and projections from the hippocampus to the frontal lobes provide a "route by which recollections are translated into action." The frontal lobes serve an important function in guiding behavior, and information from memory stores is critical to the effective functioning of the frontal lobes. The projections from the hippocampus to the frontal lobes enable us to remember the past and to use our memories to perform effectively in the present.

BEFORE YOU GO ON

- **Why might Steve be motivated to forget that he rode a roller coaster at Coney Island? What mechanism(s) might enable him to do so?**
- **How would damage to his hippocampus affect Steve's recollections of things he did with his grandfather?**

CHAPTER SUMMARY

According to Underwood, a memory contains a collection of different types of information, called memory attributes. A memory attribute can decrease interference by providing a basis for distinguishing memories. When one aspect of an event is reexperienced, the attribute of that event prompts the recall of the entire memory.

The acoustic attribute stores information about the auditory properties of an event. The physical characteristics of an event are contained in the orthographic attribute. In the frequency attribute, the memory stores a record of the number of times an event is experienced. The time that an event occurred is recorded in the temporal attribute, and the place where it occurred is contained in the spatial attribute of the memory. The modality attribute provides information about the sensory modality through which the human or nonhuman animal experienced the event.

The background in which an event took place is stored in the context attribute. The affective attribute of a memory provides information about the emotional condition surrounding an event. The affective attribute can be viewed as an internal contextual attribute: it registers internal changes in affect, changes that may either be natural reactions to the event or may be drug-induced.

The associates of verbal items are also attributes of a memory. There are two types of verbal associative attributes: parallel attributes (antonyms, synonyms, and functional associates of the verbal item) and class attributes (the category name of the verbal item). The transformational attribute contains information about how to decode items that were coded during learning. The three types of transformational attributes are images, natural language mediators, and order transformations.

One cause of the failure to remember is the absence of a stimulus associated with memory. Another cause of forgetting is decay. Memories decay when the physiological changes that took place during memory formation, and that represent the record of the event, diminish with time.

Interference is the third cause of forgetting. Interference occurs when the memory of one experience prevents the retrieval of the memory of another event. There are two types of interference: proactive interference is the inability to recall recent events because of the memory of a past experience; retroactive interference is the inability to remember distant events because of the memory of recent events.

Melton and Irwin's two-factor theory assumes that interference is caused by competition and unlearning. According to Melton and Irwin, competition among memories produces both proactive and retroactive interference, whereas unlearning, or the temporary suppression of distant memories during current learning, causes only retroactive interference. As the effect of unlearning diminishes, competition alone determines which type of interference occurs.

According to Underwood, the failure to distinguish memories is one cause of interference. Postman suggests that generalized competition, a "set" to continue to respond in the manner most recently learned, is another source of interference.

The memory of an experience is not always accurate. Sometimes details of an event are forgotten, creating an imperfect memory. To produce a logical, realistic memory of an event, people add information to the memory during recall. If an experience does not make sense, some information may be deleted, new information may be added, or both, to establish a memory of an event that is consistent with the individual's perception of the world. Misleading information or questions can alter a person's recollection of a witnessed event. The original memory is not erased altogether, but the person cannot discriminate between the real and suggested events.

Some psychologists believe that individuals can repress extremely disturbing childhood memories. Other psychologists argue that suggestions create a false memory of childhood experiences that did not really occur.

Humans and nonhuman animals can be directed to forget an event. The presentation of a "forget cue" following a stimulus leads the subject to forget that stimulus. Encoding or retrieval failure are thought to contribute to directed forgetting. Repression may result in voluntary forgetting, with therapy or some other process later retrieving the memory of the event. Or a recovered memory may reflect memory alteration that leads to the "remembrance" of an event that never happened.

The hippocampus has been shown to govern memory retrieval. Hippocampal damage leads to amnesia because of an inability to retrieve stored memories. Memories are retrieved by the hippocampus and then routed to the frontal lobes, which act to guide behavior.

CRITICAL THINKING QUESTIONS

1. Keisha had a great time at the party last night, but awoke unable to recall anything that took place. Describe state-dependent learning and how it might explain Keisha's memory loss.

2. Angela often confuses the names of acquaintances. Discuss how interference theory would explain Angela's memory problem.

3. John recently suffered a stroke and now has trouble remembering recent events. He can remember an event for a brief time, but he quickly forgets it. What areas were damaged by his stroke? What are the functions of these areas, and why did damage to them cause his memory deficits?

KEY TERMS

acoustic attribute
affective attribute
class associative attribute
context attribute
decay of forgetting view
directed forgetting
engram
false memory syndrome
forgetting
frequency attribute
generalized competition
interference

Kamin effect
list differentiation
memory attribute
memory reconstruction
modality attribute
natural language
 mediator
orthographic attribute
parallel associative
 attribute
proactive interference (PI)
repressed memory

retroactive interference
 (RI)
spatial attribute
state-dependent learning
temporal attribute
transformational attribute
two-factor theory of
 interference
verbal associative
 attribute

Glossary

Acoustic attribute   The acoustic properties of an event, which serve as a retrieval cue for that experience.

Acoustic code   The transformation of visual experiences into an auditory message.

Acquired drive   An internal drive state produced when an environmental stimulus is paired with an unconditioned source of drive.

Action-specific energy   An internal force that motivates a specific action.

Active avoidance response   An overt response to a feared stimulus that prevents an aversive event.

Affective attribute   The mood state present during an event, which can serve as a memory attribute of that experience.

Affective Extension of SOP theory (AESOP)   Wagner's view that a UCS elicits separate affective and sensory unconditioned response sequences.

Affirmative rule   When a concept is defined by the rule that a particular attribute defines the concept.

Algorithm   A precise set of rules to solve a particular problem.

Analgesia   A reduced sensitivity to painful events.

Analyzer   An internal mechanism that detects the presence of the salient aspect of a stimulus.

Animal misbehavior   Operant behavior that deteriorates rather than improves with continued reinforcement.

Anterograde amnesia   An inability to recall events that occur after some disturbance to the brain.

Anticipatory contrast   The long-lasting change in responding due to an anticipated change in the reinforcement contingency.

Anticipatory frustration response (r_F)   Stimuli associated with nonreward produce a frustration state, which motivates escape from the nonrewarding environment.

Anticipatory goal response (r_G)   Stimuli associated with reward produce a conditioned arousal response, which motivates an approach to the reward.

Anticipatory pain response (r_P)   Stimuli associated with painful events produce a fear response, which motivates escape from the painful environment.

Anticipatory relief response (r_R)   Stimuli associated with termination of an aversive event produces relief, which motivates approach behavior.

Anxious relationship   The relationship developed between a mother and her infant when the mother is indifferent to her infant.

Appetitive behavior   Instinctive or learned response motivated by action-specific energy and attracted to a sign stimulus.

Appetitive structure view   Idea that animal misbehavior represents species-typical foraging and food-handling behaviors, which are elicited by pairing food with the natural cues controlling feeding.

Association   The linkage of two events, usually as the result of a specific experience.

Associative learning view of imprinting   The idea that attraction to the imprinting object develops because of its arousal-reducing properties.

Associative-link expectancy   A representation containing knowledge of the association of two events that occur together.

Associative shifting   The transfer of a response from one stimulus to a second stimulus when the second stimulus is gradually introduced and then the first stimulus removed.

A state   The initial affective reaction to an environmental stimulus in opponent-process theory.

Asymptotic level   The maximum level of conditioning.

Atkinson-Shiffrin three-stage model   The view that an experience is sequentially stored in the sensory register, short-term store, and long-term store.

Attribute   A feature of an object or event that varies from one instance to another.

Autoshaping   A key-peck or bar-press response established by periodic reinforcements.

Availability strategy   A heuristic where problems are solved based only on the information that can be readily remembered.

Avoidance response   A behavioral response that prevents an aversive event.

Backward blocking   Reduced conditioned response to the second stimulus (CS_2) caused when two stimuli (CS_1 and CS_2) are paired with a UCS, followed by the presentation of only the first stimulus (CS_1) with the UCS.

Backward conditioning   A paradigm in which the UCS is presented and terminated prior to the CS.

Behavioral allocation theory   The idea that an animal emits the minimum number of contingent responses in order to obtain the maximum number of reinforcing activities.

Behavioral autonomy   A situation in which the continued reinforcement of a specific behavior leads to the occurrence of the response despite a devalued reinforcer.

Behavioral contrast   In a two-choice discrimination task, the increase in response to S^D that occurs at the same time as responding to S^Δ declines.

Behaviorism   A school of thought that emphasizes the role of experience in determining actions.

Behavior modification   Techniques for changing behavior that rely on the use of Pavlovian conditioning or instrumental or operant conditioning principles.

Behavior-reinforcer-belief   A type of declarative knowledge that causes an animal or person to perform a specific behavior in the expectation of a specific consequence.

Behavior systems approach   Timberlake's idea that learning evolved as a modifier of innate behavior systems and functions to change the integration, tuning, instigation, or linkages within a particular system.

Blisspoint   The free operant level of two responses.

Blocking   The prevention of the acquisition of a CR to a second stimulus (CS_2) when two stimuli are paired with a UCS and conditioning has already occurred to the first stimulus (CS_1).

Bound morpheme   A morpheme that must be attached to a free morpheme to have meaning.

B state   The opposite affective response that is elicited by the initial affective reaction, or A state, in opponent-process theory.

Cathexis   Tolman's idea that the ability of deprivation states to motivate behavior transfers to the stimuli present during the deprivation state.

Causal attribution   The perceived cause of a specific event.

Cause and effect   When one event produces a second event.

Cellular modification theory   The view that learning permanently alters the functioning of specific neural systems.

Central executive   Baddeley's concept of the process that coordinates rehearsal systems and retrieves memory from and transfers information to permanent memory.

Chunking   The combining of several units of information into a single unit.

Class associative attribute   The category name of a word that can serve as the memory attribute for the word.

Clause   A group of words containing a noun phrase and a verb phrase.

Clustering   The recall of information in specific categories.

Coding   The transformation of an experience into a totally new form.

Cognition   An understanding or knowledge of the structure of the psychological environment.

Cognitive map   Spatial knowledge of the physical environment gained through experience.

Cognitive theories of learning   The view that learning involves a recognition of when events will occur and an understanding of how to influence those events.

Comparator theory   The theory that the ability of a particular stimulus to elicit a CR depends upon a comparison of the level of conditioning to that stimulus and to other stimuli paired with the UCS.

Complex idea   The association of sensory impressions or simple ideas.

Compound schedule   A complex contingency where two or more schedules of reinforcement are combined.

Concept   A symbol that represents a class of objects or events with common characteristics.

Concurrent interference   The prevention of learning when a stimulus intervenes between the conditioned and unconditioned stimuli or when a behavior occurs between the operant response and reinforcement.

Conditional discrimination   A situation in which the availability of reinforcement to a particular stimulus depends upon the presence of a second stimulus.

Conditioned emotional reaction   The ability of a CS to elicit emotional reactions as a result of the association of the CS with a painful event.

Conditioned immune system enhancement   The ability of a CS to elicit enhanced immune system functioning as a CR.

Conditioned immune system suppression   The suppression of immune system functioning as a CR elicited by a CS.

Conditioned inhibition   The permanent inhibition of a specific behavior as a result of the continued failure of that response to reduce the drive state. Alternatively, a stimulus (CS−) may develop the ability to suppress the response to another stimulus (CS+) when the CS+ is paired with a UCS and the CS− is presented without UCS.

Conditioned reflex   The acquisition of a new S-R association as a result of experience.

Conditioned response (CR)   A learned reaction to a conditioned stimulus.

Conditioned stimulus (CS)   A stimulus that becomes able to elicit a learned response as a result of being paired with an unconditioned stimulus.

Conditioned withdrawal reaction   When environmental cues associated with withdrawal produce a conditioned craving and motivation to resume drug use.

Conditioning of opponent response   When a CS develops the ability to elicit a conditioned response opposite to the UCR.

Conjunctive rule   The simultaneous presence of two or more attributes that define a concept.

Constraint   When learning occurs less rapidly or less completely than expected.

Context attribute   The context in which an event occurred, which can be a retrieval cue.

Context blocking   The idea that conditioning to the context can prevent acquisition of a CR to a stimulus paired with the UCS in that context.

Contiguity   The temporal pairing of CS and UCS.

Contingency   The specified relationship between a specific behavior and reinforcement.

Contingency management   The use of contingent reinforcement and nonreinforcement to increase the frequency of appropriate behavior and eliminate inappropriate behaviors.

Continuity theory of discrimination learning   The idea that the development of a discrimination is a continuous and gradual acquisition of excitation to S^D and inhibition to S^Δ.

Contrapreparedness   An inability to associate a specific conditioned stimulus and a specific unconditioned stimulus despite repeated conditioning experiences.

Counterconditioning   The elimination of a conditioned response when the conditioned stimulus is paired with an opponent or antagonistic unconditioned stimulus.

CS preexposure effect   When the presentation of a CS prior to conditioning impairs the acquisition of the conditioned response once the CS is paired with UCS.

CS-UCS interval   The interval between the termination of the CS and the onset of the UCS.

Cue-controlled relaxation   The conditioning of relaxation to a CS as a result of the association of that stimulus with exercises that elicit relaxation as a UCR.

Cue deflation effect   When the extinction of a response to one cue leads to an increased reaction to the other conditioned stimulus.

Cue predictiveness   The consistency with which the CS is experienced with the UCS, which influences the strength of conditioning.

Cued recall   A memory task that provides a stimulus that is part of the learned experience.

Debriefing   An experimenter informing a subject about the nature of a study after the subject finishes participating in the study.

Decay of forgetting view   The view that forgetting is due to the fading or erasure of a memory.

Declarative memory   Factual memory, or the memory of specific events.

Deep structure (of a sentence)   The meaning or idea conveyed by a sentence.

Delayed conditioning   A paradigm in which the CS onset precedes the UCS, and CS termination occurs either with UCS onset or during UCS presentation.

Delay-reduction theory   The behavior economic theory that states that overall behavior in a choice task is based on the matching law, while individual choices are determined by which choice produces the shortest delay in the next reinforcer.

Depression effect   An effect in which a shift from high to low reward magnitude produces a lower level of responding than if the reward magnitude had always been low.

Differential reinforcement of high responding (DRH) schedule   A schedule of reinforcement in which a specific high number of responses must occur with a specified time in order for reinforcement to occur.

Differential reinforcement of low responding (DRL) schedule   A schedule of reinforcement in which a certain amount of time must elapse without responding, with reinforcement following the first response after the interval.

Differential reinforcement of other behaviors (DRO)   A schedule of reinforcement in which the absence of a specific response within a specified time leads to reinforcement.

Differential reinforcement schedule   A schedule of reinforcement in which a specific number of behaviors must occur within a specified time in order for reinforcement to occur.

Directed forgetting   The forgetting of an event following the presentation of the "forget cue."

Discrimination learning   Responding in different ways to different stimuli.

Discriminative operant   An operant behavior that is under the control of a discriminative stimulus.

Discriminative stimulus   A stimulus that signals the availability or unavailability of reinforcement.

Dishabituation   The recovery of a habituated response as the result of the presentation of a sensitizing stimulus.

Disinhibition   When the conditioned stimulus elicits a conditioned response after a novel stimulus is presented during extinction.

Disjunctive rule   When the concept is defined by the rule that the concept can possess either or both of two attributes.

Displacement   In a conflict situation, the occurrence of a behavior unrelated to that conflict.

Drive   An intense internal force that motivates behavior.

Echo   The auditory record of an event contained in the sensory register.

Echoic memory   The auditory memory of an event stored in the sensory register.

Efficacy expectancy   A feeling that one can or cannot execute a particular behavior.

Eidetic image   The recall of a sharp visual image of an event, which lasts for about four minutes.

Elaboration   The extent to which an event is analyzed.

Elaborative rehearsal   The organization of experiences while information is maintained in the short-term store.

Elation effect   An effect in which a shift from low to high reward magnitude produces a greater level of responding than if the reward magnitude had always been high.

Electrical stimulation of the brain (ESB)   The high levels of instrumental or operant behavior exhibited when responding leads to activation of reinforcement areas of the brain.

Engram   The physical representation of an event in a person's memory.

Episodic memory   The memory of temporally related events, or the time and place of an experience.

Equivalence belief principle   Tolman's idea that the reaction to a secondary reward is the same as the original goal.

Errorless discrimination learning   A training procedure in which the gradual introduction of S^Δ leads to responding S^D without any errors to S^Δ.

Escape response   A behavioral response to an aversive event that is reinforced by the termination of the aversive event.

Evolution   The changes in the physical and behavioral characteristics that occur over many generations when the environment of that species slowly changes.

Excitatory generalization gradient   A graph showing the level of generalization from an excitatory conditioned stimulus (CS+) to other stimuli.

Expectancy   A mental representation of event contingencies.

Expectancy-value theory   Rotter's suggestion that the likelihood of behavior is determined by the perceived value of reward times the value of that reward.

Explicit measure of memory   An observable measure of the strength of a memory.

External attribution   A belief that events are beyond one's control.

External expectancy   The belief that there is little connection between your behavior and reward.

External inhibition   The presentation of a novel stimulus during conditioning suppresses response to the conditioned stimulus.

Extinction   The elimination or suppression of a response caused by the discontinuation of reinforcement or the removal of the unconditioned stimulus.

Extinction of conditioned response   When the conditioned stimulus does not elicit the conditioned response because the unconditioned stimulus no longer follows the conditioned stimulus.

Extinction of instrumental or operant response   When the discontinuance of reinforcement leads to response suppression.

Eyeblink conditioning   When a CS becomes able to elicit a conditioned eyeblink as a result of being paired with a puff of air or a brief electrical shock below the eye.

False memory syndrome   The creation of an inaccurate record of childhood sexual abuse.

Family resemblance   Occurs when an object or event shares many attributes with other members of the concept.

Fear   Conditioned response to stimuli associated with painful events; motivates avoidance of aversive events.

Fear conditioning   The conditioning of fear to a CS as a result of the association of that CS with a painful event.

Fixed action pattern (FAP)   An instinctive response that is released by the presence of an effective sign stimulus.

Fixed-interval schedule   A contingency in which reinforcement is available only after a specified period of time, and the first response emitted after the interval has elapsed is reinforced.

Fixed-ratio schedule   A contingency in which a specific number of responses is needed to produce reinforcement.

Flashbulb memory   A vivid, detailed, and long-lasting memory of a very intense experience.

Flavor-aversion learning   Avoidance of a flavor that precedes an illness experience.

Flooding (or response prevention)   A behavior therapy in which a phobia is eliminated by forced exposure to the feared stimulus without an aversive consequence.

Forgetting   The inability to recall a past experience.

Free morpheme   A morpheme that can stand alone and still have meaning.

Free recall   A memory task that requires recall with no cues available.

Frequency attribute   The frequency of an event, which can be a retrieval cue.

Functional fixedness   Difficulty recognizing novel uses for an object.

Functionalism   Early school of psychology that emphasized the instinctive origins and adaptive functions of behavior.

Generalization   Responding in the same manner to similar stimuli.

Generalization gradient   A visual representation of the response strength produced by stimuli of varying degrees of similarity to the training stimulus.

Generalized competition   A temporary tendency (or set) to respond with most recent learning.

Goal state   The desired end point of a problem.

Global attribution   The assumption that a specific outcome will be repeated in many situations.

Grammar   The rules that define the ways words can be combined into meaningful phrases, clauses, and sentences.

Habit   Hull's concept that a specific environmental stimulus becomes associated with a particular response when that response produces drive reduction.

Habit hierarchy   The varying level of associative strengths between a stimulus environment and the behaviors associated with that environment.

Habit strength   The strength of the connection between a particular environmental stimulus and a specific response.

Habituation   A decrease in responsiveness to a specific stimulus as a result of repeated experience with it.

Heuristic   A "best guess" solution to problem solving.

Hierarchial approach   Collins and Quillian's idea that memory consists of hierarchical networks of interconnected concepts.

Higher-order conditioning   The phenomenon that a stimulus (CS_2) can elicit a CR even without being paired with the UCS if the CS_2 is paired with another conditioned stimulus (CS_1).

Hippocampus   A brain structure in the limbic system that plays a central role in memory storage and retrieval.

Hopelessness   The belief that positive events will not occur or that negative events cannot be controlled.

Hopelessness depression   A form of clinical depression that is produced by the belief that positive events will not occur or that negative events cannot be controlled.

Hull-Spence theory of discrimination learning   The idea that conditioned excitation first develops to S^D, followed by the conditioning of inhibition to S^Δ.

Hyperalgesia   An increased sensitivity to a painful event.

Hypoalgesia   Lessened sensitivity to a painful event.

Icon   The visual copy of an event contained in the sensory register.

Iconic memory   The visual memory of an event stored in the sensory register.

Ill-defined problem   A problem with no clear starting or goal state.

Implicit measure of memory   A measure that provides an indirect assessment of the strength of a memory.

Imprinting   The development of a social attachment to stimuli experienced during a sensitive period of development.

Incentive motivation (K)   The idea that the level of motivation is affected by magnitude of reward: the greater the reward magnitude, the higher the motivation to obtain that reward.

Informed consent   A written agreement indicating that a subject is willing to participate in a psychological study.

Ingestional neophobia   The avoidance of novel foods.

Inhibition   Pavlov's idea that presentation of the CS without the UCS activates a central inhibitory state that suppresses the CR.

Inhibition of delay   The prevention of a response to the CS until just prior to the UCS in a trace conditioning paradigm.

Inhibitory generalization gradient   A graph showing the level of generalization from an inhibitory conditioned stimulus (CS−) to other stimuli.

Innate releasing mechanism (IRM)   A hypothetical process by which a sign stimulus removes the block on the release of the fixed action pattern.

Insight   A sudden realization of how to solve a problem.

Instinct   An inherited pattern of behavior common to members of a particular species.

Instinctive drift   When operant behavior deteriorates despite continued reinforcement due to the elicitation of instinctive behaviors.

Instinctive view of imprinting   The view that imprinting is a genetically programmed form of learning.

Instrumental conditioning procedure   A conditioning procedure in which the environment constrains the opportunity for reward and a specific behavior can obtain reward.

Interference   An inability to recall a specific memory due to the presence of other memories.

Interim behavior   The behavior that follows reinforcement when an animal is reinforced on an interval schedule of reinforcement.

Internal attribution   The assumption that personal factors lead to a particular outcome.

Internal expectancy   The belief that one's actions determine whether a goal is reached.

Interval schedule of reinforcement   A contingency that specifies that reinforcement becomes available at a certain period of time after the last reinforcement.

Irrelevant incentive effect   The acquisition of an excitatory link expectancy that a particular stimulus is associated with a specific reinforcer under an irrelevant drive state.

Kamin effect   The poor retention of a prior aversive experience or an intermediate retention test (1 to 4 hours after training) but good recall either immediately or 24 hours later.

Korsakoff's syndrome   The inability of alcoholics to recall past events due to a failure to permanently store experiences.

Language   A system of words and word meanings, and a set of rules for combining the words.

Language acquisition device (LAD)   Chomsky's idea of an innate mechanism that allows children to grasp the syntax of their language with minimal experience.

Lashley-Wade theory of generalization   The idea that generalization occurs when animals are unable to distinguish between the test stimulus and the conditioning stimulus.

Latent inhibition   The idea that exposure to neutral stimuli establishes an inhibitory state that later impairs excitatory conditioning to that stimulus.

Latent learning   Knowledge of the environment gained through experience but not evident under current conditions.

Law of effect   The process when a reward strengthens an S-R association.

Law of exercise   Thorndike's idea that the strength of a stimulus-response connection can be increased with use.

Law of readiness   Sufficient motivation must exist in order to develop an association or exhibit a previously established habit.

Learned helplessness   The belief that events are independent of behavior and are uncontrollable, which results in emotional trauma as well as motivational and cognitive deficits.

Learned irrelevance   The presentation of a stimulus without a UCS leads to the recognition that the stimulus is irrelevant, stops attention to that stimulus, and impairs conditioning when the stimulus is later paired with the UCS.

Learned-safety theory   The recognition that a food can be safely consumed.

Learning   A relatively permanent change in the ability to exhibit a specific behavior that occurs as a result of experience.

Levels of processing view   The idea that an experience can be processed at many levels and that the deeper the experience is processed, the more likely it will be remembered.

List differentiation   An ability to distinguish between memories, reducing the level of interference.

Local contrast   A change in behavior that occurs following a change in reinforcement contingency. The change in behavior fades with extended training.

Locus of control   The generalized expectation that either internal or external factors may control behavior.

Long-delay learning   The association of a flavor with an illness that occurred even several hours after the flavor was consumed.

Long-term store   The site of permanent memory storage.

Mackintosh's attentional view   The idea that animals attend to stimuli that are predictive of biologically significant events (UCS_s) and ignore stimuli that are irrelevant.

Maintenance rehearsal   The mere repetition of information in the short-term store.

Matching law   When an animal has free access to two different schedules of reinforcement, its response is proportional to the level of reinforcement available on each schedule.

Maximizing law   The goal of behavior in a choice task is to obtain as many reinforcements as possible.

Means-end analysis   Breaking a particular problem into a series of solvable subproblems.

Medial forebrain bundle (MFB)   The area of the limbic system that is part of the brain's reinforcement center.

Medial temporal lobe   A central nervous system structure, containing the hippocampus and surrounding cortical areas, that is involved in the storage and retrieval of experiences.

Mediodorsal thalamus   A central nervous system structure involved in the storage of experiences.

Memory attribute   A salient aspect of an event whose presence can lead to retrieval of the past event.

Memory reconstruction   The alteration of a memory to provide a consistent view of the world.

Mesotelencephalic reinforcement system   A central nervous system structure that mediates the influence of reinforcement on behavior.

Method of loci   A mnemonic technique in which items are stored in an ordered series of known locations and a specific item is recalled by visualizing that item in an appropriate location.

Mnemonic techniques   A set of techniques to enhance the storage and retrieval of information.

Modality attribute   Information about the sensory modality through which an event was experienced.

Modeling   The acquisition of behavior as a result of observing the experiences of others.

Momentary maximization theory   The view that the behavior in a choice task is determined by which alternative is perceived as best at that moment in time.

Morpheme   The smallest meaningful amount of language.

Motivated forgetting   The deliberate forgetting of an experience.

Natural language mediator   The use of a word to mediate the association of two unrelated verbal units.

Negative contrast (or depression) effect   An effect in which a shift from high to low reward magnitude produces a lower level of responding than if the reward magnitude had always been low.

Negative punishment   Loss or unavailability of reinforcement because of inappropriate behavior.

Negative reinforcement   The termination of an aversive event, which reinforces the behavior that preceded it.

Negative reinforcer   The termination of an aversive event, which reinforces the behavior that terminated the aversive event.

Negative rule   A concept is defined by the rule that any object or event having a certain attribute is not a member of the concept.

Nigrostriatal pathway   A neural pathway that begins in the substantia nigra and projects to the neostriatum and that serves to facilitate reinforcement-induced enhancement of memory consolidation.

Noncontinuity theory of discrimination learning   The idea that discrimination is learned rapidly once an animal discovers the relevant dimension and attends to relevant stimuli.

Nucleus accumbens (NA)   A basal forebrain structure that plays a significant role in the influence of reinforcement on behavior.

Occasion setting   The ability of one stimulus to enhance the response to another stimulus.

Omission training   A schedule of reinforcement in which the absence of responding leads to reinforcement.

Operant chamber   An apparatus that creates an enclosed environment, used for the study of operant behavior within it.

Operant conditioning   When a specific response produces reinforcement, and the frequency of the response determines the amount of reinforcement obtained.

Operant response   A behavior that controls the rate at which specific consequences occur.

Opponent-process theory   The theory that an event produces an initial instinctive affective response, which is followed by an opposite affective reaction.

Orthographic attribute   The feature properties of an event, which serve as a memory attribute.

Outcome expectancy   The perceived consequences of either a behavior or an event.

Overshadowing   In a compound conditioning situation, the prevention of conditioning to one stimulus due to the presence of a more salient or intense stimulus.

Pain-induced aggression   Anger and aggressive behavior elicited by punishment.

Parallel associative attribute   Associations that are based on equality (synonyms), opposition (antonyms), or functional contiguity.

Parallel distributed processing model   The idea that memory is composed of a series of interconnected associative networks and that knowledge is distributed throughout the entire system.

Partial reinforcement effect (PRE)   The greater resistance to extinction of an instrumental or operant response following intermittent rather than continuous reinforcement during acquisition.

Partial report technique   A procedure that requires subjects to remember and report part of the information they learned.

Passive avoidance response   A contingency in which the absence of responding leads to the prevention of an aversive event.

Peak shift   The shift in the maximum response, which occurs to a stimulus other than S^D and in the stimulus direction opposite that of the S$^\Delta$.

Peg word system   A mnemonic technique in which items are associated with the peg words appropriate to a particular system.

Periventricular tract (PVT)   The area of the limbic system that represents the brain's punishment center.

Personal attribution   A belief that internal characteristics cause a particular outcome.

Personal helplessness   A perceived incompetency that leads to failure and feelings of helplessness.

Phobia   An unrealistic fear of a specific environmental event.

Phoneme   The simplest functional speech sound.

Phonological loop   A rehearsal system that holds and analyzes verbal information.

Phonology   The rules that dictate how phonemes can be combined into morphemes.

Phrase   A group of two or more related words that expresses a single thought.

Phrase-structure grammar   The analysis of the constituent elements of a sentence.

Positive contrast (or elation) effect   An effect in which a shift from low to high reward magnitude produces a greater level of responding than if the reward magnitude had always been high.

Positive punishment   The use of a physically or psychologically painful event as the punisher.

Positive reinforcer   An event whose occurrence increases the frequency of the behavior that precedes it.

Postreinforcement pause   A cessation of behavior following reinforcement on a ratio schedule, which is followed by resumption of responding at the intensity characteristic of that ratio schedule.

Potentiation   The enhancement of an aversion to a nonsalient stimulus when a salient stimulus is also paired with the UCS.

Predisposition   Instances where learning occurs more rapidly or in a different form than expected.

Preparedness   An evolutionary predisposition to associate a specific conditioned stimulus and a specific unconditioned stimulus.

Primary reinforcer   An activity whose reinforcing properties are innate.

Priming   The facilitation of recall of specific information following exposure to closely related information.

Proactive interference (PI)   The inability to recall recent experiences as a result of the memory of earlier experiences.

Probability-differential theory   Premack's idea that an activity will have reinforcing properties when its probability of occurrence is greater than that of the reinforced behavior.

Problem   An obstacle that prevents the attainment of a desired goal.

Procedural memory   A skill memory or the memory of a highly practiced behavior.

Prototype   The object that has the greatest number of attributes characteristic of the concept and that is therefore the most typical member of that concept.

Punishment   A means of eliminating undesired behavior by using an aversive event that is contingent upon the occurrence of the inappropriate behavior.

Ratio schedule of reinforcement   A contingency that specifies that a certain number of behaviors are necessary to produce reinforcement.

Reaction time   The time it takes to react to a stimulus, which provides an implicit measure of the strength of a memory.

Reactive inhibition   In Hull's theory, the temporary suppression of behavior due to the persistence of a drive state after unsuccessful behavior.

Recall measure   An explicit measure of memory requiring access to an experience.

Reciprocal inhibition   Wolpe's term for the idea that only one emotional state can be experienced at a time.

Recognition measure   An explicit measure of memory requiring identification of a previous experience.

Rehearsal   The repetition of an event that keeps the memory of an event in the short-term store.

Rehearsal systems approach   Baddeley's theory that information is retained in several sensory registers for analysis by working memory.

Reinforcement   An event (or termination of an aversive event) that increases the frequency of the behavior that preceded it.

Reinforcer   An event (or termination of an event) that increases the frequency of the behavior that preceded it.

Reinforcer devaluation effect   The association of a reinforcer with an aversive event, which reduces the behavioral control that reinforcer exerts.

Representative strategy   A heuristic that solves problems based only on the obvious characteristics of the problem.

Repressed memory   A process that submerges a memory into the unconscious to minimize anxiety and protect the self-concept.

Rescorla-Wagner associative theory   The view that a particular UCS can support only a specific level of conditioning and that when two or more stimuli are paired with a UCS, each stimulus must compete for the associative strength available for conditioning.

Resemblance   The similarity in appearance of two or more events.

Response cost   A negative punishment technique in which an undesired response results in either the withdrawal of or failure to obtain reinforcement.

Response deprivation theory   Timberlake and Allison's idea that when a contingency restricts access to an activity, it causes that activity to become a reinforcer.

Response-outcome expectancy   The belief that a particular response leads to a specific consequence or outcome.

Response prevention (or flooding)   A behavior therapy where a phobia is eliminated by forced exposure to the feared stimulus without an aversive consequence.

Retrieval   The ability to access a memory and recall a past experience.

Retroactive interference (RI)   The inability to recall distant events because of the memory of more recent events.

Retrograde amnesia   The inability to recall events that occurred prior to a traumatic event.

Retrospective processing theory   The continual assessment of contingencies, which leads to a reevaluation of prior conditioning of a CS with a UCS.

Rule   A rule defines the objects or events that are examples of a particular concept.

Salience   The property of a specific stimulus that allows it to become readily associated with a particular UCS.

Savings score   The number of trials needed to relearn a task, a score that provides an implicit measure of the strength of a memory.

Scallop effect   A pattern of behavior characteristic of a fixed-interval schedule, where responding stops after reinforcement and then slowly increases as the time approaches when reinforcement will be available.

Schedule-induced aggression   The high levels of aggressive behavior exhibited following reinforcement on an interval schedule.

Schedule-induced behavior   The high levels of instinctive behavior that occur following reinforcement on an interval schedule.

Schedule-induced polydipsia   The high levels of water consumption following food reinforcement on an interval schedule.

Schedule-induced wheel running   The high levels of wheel running following reinforcement on an interval schedule.

Schedule of reinforcement   A contingency that specifies how often or when we must act to receive reinforcement.

S^D   A stimulus that indicates the availability of reinforcement contingent upon the occurrence of an appropriate response.

S^Δ   A stimulus that indicates that reinforcement is unavailable and that the operant response will be ineffective.

Secondary reinforcer   An activity that has developed its reinforcing properties through its association with primary reinforcers.

Secure relationship   The establishment of a strong bond between a mother who is sensitive and responsive to her infant and that infant.

Semantic memory   The memory of knowledge concerning the use of language, and the rules for the solution of problems or acquisition of concepts.

Semantics   The meaning of language.

Sensitization   An increased reactivity to all environmental events following exposure to an intense stimulus.

Sensory preconditioning   The initial pairing of two stimuli, which will enable one of the stimuli (CS_2) to elicit the CR without being paired with a UCS if the other stimulus (CS_1) is paired with UCS.

Sensory register   The initial storage of memory for a very brief time as an exact duplicate of the event.

Sentence   Two or more phrases that convey an assertion, question, command, wish, or exclamation.

Serial position effect   The faster learning and greater recall of items at the beginning and end of a list rather than at the middle of the list.

Set   The tendency to use an established method for solving problems.

Shaping (or successive approximation procedure)   A technique of acquiring a desired behavior by first selecting a highly occurring operant behavior, then slowly changing the contingency until the desired behavior is learned.

Short-term store   A temporary storage facility where information is modified to create a more meaningful experience.

Sidman avoidance task   A procedure in which an animal experiences periodic aversive events unless it responds to prevent them, with the occurrence of the avoidance response delaying the occurrence of the aversive event for a specific period of time.

Sign stimulus   A distinctive environmental event that can activate the IRM and release stored energy.

Sign tracking   The orientation toward stimuli that enables animals to approach and contact reinforcers.

Simple idea   The mind's representation of a sensory impression.

Simultaneous conditioning   A paradigm in which the CS and UCS are presented together.

Sometimes opponent-process (SOP) theory   Wagner's idea that the CS becomes able to elicit the secondary A2 component of the UCS as the CR, and the A2 component is sometimes the opposite of and sometimes the same as the A1 component.

Spatial attribute   The spatial location of an item, which can serve as a memory attribute.

Spatial-temporal hierarchy   A hierarchy where phobic scenes are related to distance (either physical or temporal) to the phobic object.

Species-specific defensive reaction (SSDR)   An instinctive reaction, elicited by signals of danger, that allows the avoidance of an aversive event.

Specific attribution   The belief that a particular outcome is limited to a specific situation.

Spontaneous recovery   The return of a CR when an interval intervenes between extinction and testing without additional CS-UCS pairings, or when the instrumental or operant response returns without additional reinforced experience.

Spreading activation theory   The idea that once a concept or property of a concept is activated, the activation spreads to associated concepts or properties.

S-R (stimulus-response) associative theories   The view that learning involves the association of a specific stimulus with a specific response.

Stable attribution   The assumption that the factors that resulted in a particular outcome will not change.

State-dependent learning   Learning based on events experienced in one state; the events will not be recalled if the subject is tested in a different state.

Stimulus-bound behavior   Behavior tied to the prevailing environmental conditions and elicited by stimulation of the brain's reinforcement center.

Stimulus narrowing   The restriction of a response to a limited number of situations.

Stimulus-outcome expectancy   The belief that a particular consequence or outcome will follow a specific stimulus.

Stimulus-substitution theory   Pavlov's view that the pairing of the CS and UCS allows the CS to elicit the UCR as the CR.

Successive approximation procedure (or shaping) A technique for acquiring a desired behavior by first selecting a behavior with a high operant rate, then slowly changing the contingency until the desired behavior is learned.

Superstitious behavior A "ritualistic" stereotyped pattern of behavior exhibited during the interval between reinforcements.

Suppression ratio A measure of the fear produced by a specific conditioned stimulus obtained by dividing the number of operant responses during that CS by the number of responses during the CS and without the CS.

Surface structure (of a sentence) The arrangement of the words in a sentence.

Sustained contrast The long-lasting change in responding due to the anticipated change in the reinforcement contingency.

Sutherland-Mackintosh attentional theory The theory that attention to the relevant dimension is strengthened in the first stage, and association of a particular response to the relevant stimulus occurs in the second stage of discrimination learning.

Syntax The system of rules for combining the various units of speech.

Systematic desensitization A graduated counterconditioning treatment for phobias in which the relaxation state is associated with the phobic object.

Tegmentostriatal pathway A neural pathway that begins in the lateral hypothalamus, goes through the medial forebrain bundle and ventral tegmental area, terminates in the nucleus accumbens, and governs the motivational properties of reinforcers.

Temporal attribute The time that an event occurred, which can be a retrieval cue for that experience.

Temporal conditioning A technique in which the presentation of the UCS at regular intervals causes the time of the UCS to become able to elicit the CR.

Terminal behavior The behavior that just precedes reinforcement when an animal is reinforced on an interval schedule of reinforcement.

Thematic hierarchy A hierarchy in which phobic scenes are related to a basic theme.

Time-out from reinforcement A negative punishment technique in which an inappropriate behavior leads to a period of time during which reinforcement is unavailable.

Tolerance Reduced reactivity to an event with repeated experience.

Trace conditioning The CS is presented and terminated prior to UCS onset with this conditioning paradigm.

Transformational attribute A transformed or altered event that can serve as a memory attribute for that experience.

Transposition Kohler's idea that animals learn relationships between stimuli, and that they respond to different stimuli based on the same relationship as the original training stimuli.

Two-choice discrimination learning A task when the S^D and S^Δ are on the same stimulus dimension.

Two-factor theory of avoidance learning Mowrer's view that in the first stage, fear is conditioned through the classical conditioning process, and in the second stage, an instrumental or operant response is acquired that terminates the feared stimulus.

Two-factor theory of interference Melton and Irwin's idea that competition between memories causes PI and RI and that unlearning leads to RI.

UCS preexposure effect   The effect caused by exposure to the UCS prior to conditioning; it impairs later conditioning when a CS is paired with that UCS.

Unconditioned reflex   An instinctual response to an environmental event.

Unconditioned response (UCR)   An innate reaction to an unconditioned stimulus.

Unconditioned stimulus (UCS)   An environmental event that can elicit an instinctive reaction without any experience.

Universal helplessness   A belief that environmental forces produce failure and result in helplessness.

Unstable attribution   The belief that other factors may affect outcomes in the future.

Variable-interval schedule   A contingency in which there is an average interval of time between available reinforcements, but the interval varies from one reinforcement to the next contingency.

Variable-ratio schedule   A contingency in which an average number of behaviors produces reinforcement, but the actual number of responses required to produce reinforcement varies over the course of training.

Ventral tegmental area (VTA)   A structure in the tegmentostriatal reinforcement system that projects to the nucleus accumbens.

Verbal associative attribute   An attribute of a word that can act as a retrieval cue.

Vicarious conditioning   The development of the CR to a stimulus after observation of the pairing of CS and UCS.

Vicious-circle behavior   An escape response that continues despite punishment, due to a failure to recognize that the absence of the escape behavior will not be punished.

Visual code   The transformation of a word into an image.

Visuospatial sketch pad   A rehearsal system that holds and analyzes visual and spatial information.

Well-defined problem   A problem with clear initial and goal states.

Whole report technique   A procedure that requires the subject to remember and report all the information they learned, if they can.

Withdrawal   An increase in the intensity of the effective opponent B state following the termination of the event.

Within-comprehend association   The association of two stimuli, both paired with a UCS, which leads both to elicit the CR.

Working-backward heuristic   A technique for finding the solution to a problem by starting with the end point and working back to the start point.

Working memory   Information being actively processed by rehearsal systems.

References

Abramowitz, A. J., & O'Leary, S. G. (1990). Effectiveness of delayed punishment in an applied setting. *Behavior Therapy, 21*, 231–239.

Abramowitz, J. S. (1997). Effectiveness of psychological and pharmacological treatments for obsessive-compulsive disorder: A quantitative review. *Journal of Consulting and Clinical Psychology, 65*, 44–52.

Abrams, T. W., Karl, K. A., & Kandel, E. R. (1991). Biochemical studies of stimulus convergence during classical conditioning in *Aplysia:* Dual regulation of adenylate cyclase by Ca^{2+}/calmodulin and transmitter. *Journal of Neuroscience, 11*, 2655–2665.

Abramson, L. Y. (1977). Universal versus personal helplessness: An experimental test of the reformulated theory of learned helplessness and depression. Unpublished doctoral dissertation, University of Pennsylvania, Philadelphia.

Abramson, L. Y., Garber, J., & Seligman, M. E. P. (1980). Learned helplessness in humans: An attributional analysis. In J. Garber & M. E. P. Seligman (Eds.), *Human helplessness: Theory and applications.* New York: Academic.

Abramson, L. Y., Metalsky, G. I., & Alloy, L. B. (1989). Hopelessness depression: A theory-based subtype of depression. *Psychological Review, 96*, 358–372.

Abramson, L. Y., & Sackeim, H. A. (1977). A paradox in depression: Uncontrollability and self-blame. *Psychological Bulletin, 84*, 838–851.

Abramson, L. Y., Seligman, M. E. P., & Teasdale, J. D. (1978). Learned helplessness in humans: Critique and reformulation. *Journal of Abnormal Psychology, 87*, 49–74.

Adams, C. D. (1982). Variations in the sensitivity of instrumental responding to reinforcer devaluation. *Quarterly Journal of Experimental Psychology, 34B*, 77–98.

Adams, C. D., & Dickinson, A. (1981). Instrumental responding following reinforcer devaluation. *Quarterly Journal of Experimental Psychology, 33B*, 109–122.

Adelman, H. M., & Maatsch, J. L. (1956). Learning and extinction based upon frustration, food reward, and exploratory tendency. *Journal of Experimental Psychology, 52*, 311–315.

Ader, R., & Cohen, N. (1981). Conditioned immunopharmacologic responses. In R. Ader (Ed.), *Psychoneuroimmunology.* New York: Academic Press.

Ader, R., & Cohen, N. (1982). Behaviorally conditioned immunosuppression and murine systemic lupus erythematosus. *Science, 215*, 1534–1536.

Ader, R., & Cohen, N. (1985). CNS-immune system interactions: Conditioning phenomena. *Behavior and Brain Science, 8*, 379–394.

Ader, R., & Cohen, N. (1993). Psychoneuroimmunology: Conditioning and stress. *Annual Review of Psychology, 44*, 53–85.

Aggleton, J. P., & Mishkin, M. (1985). Mammillary-body lesions and visual recognition in monkeys. *Experimental Brain Research, 58*, 190–197.

Ainslie, G. (1975). Specious reward: A behavioral theory of impulsiveness and impulse control. *Psychological Bulletin, 82*, 485–489.

Ainsworth, M. D. S. (1982). Attachment: Retrospect and prospect. In C. M. Parkes & J. Sevenson-Hinde (Eds.), *The place of attachment in human behavior.* New York: Basic Books.

Akins, C. A., Domjan, M., & Gutierrez, G. (1994). Topography of sexually conditioned behavior in male Japanese quail *(Coturnix japonica)* depends on the CS-US interval. *Journal of Experimental Psychology: Animal Behavior Processes, 20*, 199–209.

Alavarez-Royo, P., Clower, R. P., Zola-Morgan, S., & Squire, L. R. (1991). Stereotaxic lesions of the hippocampus in monkeys: Determination of surgical coordinates and analysis of lesions using magnetic resonance imaging. *Journal of Neuroscience Methods, 38*, 223–232.

Allison, J. (1989). The nature of reinforcement. In S. B. Klein & R. R. Mowrer (Eds.), *Contemporary learning theories: Instrumental conditional theory and the impact of biological constraints in learning* (pp. 13–39). Hillsdale, N.J.: Erlbaum.

Alloway, T. M. (1969). Effects of low temperature upon acquisition and retention in the grain beetle *(Tenebrio molitor). Journal of Comparative and Physiological Psychology, 69*, 1–8.

Alloy, L. B., Kelly, K. A., Mineka, S., & Clements, C. M. (1990). Comorbidity in anxiety and depressive disorders: A helplessness/hopelessness perspective. In J. D. Maser & C. R. Cloniger (Eds.), *Comorbidity in anxiety and mood disorders.* Washington, D.C.: American Psychiatric Press.

American Psychological Association. (1992). Ethical principles of psychologists and code of conduct. *American Psychologist, 47*, 1597–1611.

Amsel, A. (1958). The role of frustrative nonreward in noncontinuous reward situations. *Psychological Bulletin, 55*, 102–119.

Amsel, A. (1967). Partial reinforcement effects on vigor and persistence. In K. W. Spence & J. T. Spence (Eds.), *The psychology of learning and motivation* (Vol. 1). New York: Academic Press.

Amsel, A. (1972). Behavior habituation, counterconditioning, and a general theory of persistence. In A. H. Black & W. F. Prokasy (Eds.), *Classical conditioning II: Current research and theory.* New York: Appleton-Century-Crofts.

Amsel, A. (1994). Precis of frustration theory: An analysis of dispositional learning and memory. *Psychonomic Bulletin and Review, 1*, 280–296.

Annau, Z., & Kamin, L. J. (1961). The conditioned emotional response as a function of intensity of the US. *Journal of Comparative and Physiological Psychology, 54*, 428–432.

Archer, B. U., & Margolin, R. R. (1970). Arousal effects in intentional recall and forgetting. *Journal of Experimental Psychology, 86*, 8–12.

Armus, H. L. (1959). Effect of magnitude of reinforcement on acquisition and extinction of a running response. *Journal of Experimental Psychology, 58*, 61–63.

Arnold, H. M., Grahame, N. J., & Miller, R. R. (1991). Higher-order occasion setting. *Animal Learning & Behavior, 19*, 58–64.

Aronson, L., Balsam, P. D., & Gibbon, J. (1993). Temporal comparator rules and responding in multiple schedules. *Animal Learning & Behavior, 21*, 293–302.

Atkinson, J. W. (1958). *Motives in fantasy, action, and society.* Princeton, N.J.: Van Nostrand.

Atkinson, J. W. (1964). *An introduction to motivation.* Princeton, N.J.: Van Nostrand.

Atkinson, R. C., & Shiffrin, R. M. (1971). The control of short-term memory. *Scientific American, 225,* 82–90.

Averbach, E., & Sperling, G. (1961). Short-term storage of information in vision. In C. Cherry (Ed.), *Fourth London symposium on information theory.* London and Washington, D.C.: Butterworth.

Ayers, M. S., & Reder, L. M. (1998). A theoretical review of the misinformation effect: Predictions from an activation-based memory model. *Psychonomic Bulletin and Review, 5,* 1–21.

Ayllon, T., & Azrin, N. H. (1965). The measurement and reinforcement of behavior of psychotics. *Journal of the Experimental Analysis of Behavior, 8,* 357–383.

Ayllon, T., & Azrin, N. H. (1968). *The token economy: A motivation system for therapy and rehabilitation.* New York: Appleton-Century-Crofts.

Azrin, N. H. (1964, September). Aggression. Paper presented at the meeting of the American Psychological Association, Los Angeles.

Azrin, N. H., Hake, D. F., Holz, W. C., & Hutchinson, R. R. (1965). Motivational aspects of escape from punishment. *Journal of the Experimental Analysis of Behavior, 8,* 31–44.

Azrin, N. H., & Holz, W. C. (1966). Punishment. In W. K. Honeg (Ed.), *Operant behavior: Areas of research and application* (pp. 380–447). New York: Appleton-Century-Crofts.

Azrin, N. H., Holz, W. C., & Hake, D. F. (1963). Fixed-ratio punishment. *Journal of the Experimental Analysis of Behavior, 6,* 141–148.

Azrin, N. H., Hutchinson, R. R., & McLaughlin, R. (1965). The opportunity for aggression as an operant reinforcer during aversive stimulation. *Journal of the Experimental Analysis of Behavior, 8,* 171–180.

Azrin, N. H., Hutchinson, R. R., & Sallery, R. D. (1964). Pain aggression toward inanimate objects. *Journal of the Experimental Analysis of Behavior, 7,* 223–228.

Azrin, N. H., Sneed, T. J., & Foxx, R. M. (1973). A rapid method of eliminating bedwetting (enuresis) of the retarded. *Behavior Research and Therapy, 11,* 427–434.

Baddeley, A. (1990). *Human memory: Theory and practice.* Boston: Allyn & Bacon.

Baddeley, A. D., & Scott, D. (1971). Short-term forgetting in the absence of proactive inhibition. *Quarterly Journal of Experimental Psychology, 23,* 275–283.

Baer, D. M. (1962). Laboratory control of thumb sucking by withdrawal and representation of reinforcement. *Journal of the Experimental Analysis of Behavior, 5,* 525–528.

Baerends, G. P., Brouwer, R., & Waterbolk, H. T. (1955). Ethological studies of *Lebistes reticulatus (Peters):* I. An analysis of the male courtship pattern. *Behaviour, 8,* 249–334.

Baker, A. G. (1976). Learned irrelevance and learned helplessness: Rats learn that stimuli, reinforcers, and responses are uncorrelated. *Journal of Experimental Psychology: Animal Behavior Processes, 2,* 131–141.

Baker, A. G., & Baker, P. A. (1985). Does inhibition differ from excitation? Proactive interference, contextual conditioning, and extinction. In R. R. Miller & N. S. Spear (Eds.), *Information processing in animals: Conditioned inhibition* (pp. 151–184). Hillsdale, N.J.: Erlbaum.

Baker, A. G., & Mackintosh, N. J. (1977). Excitatory and inhibitory conditioning following uncorrelated presentations of CS and US. *Animal Learning and Behavior, 5,* 315–319.

Baker, A. G., & Mackintosh, N. J. (1979). Preexposure to the CS alone, US alone, or CS and US uncorrelated: Latent inhibition, blocking by context, or learned irrelevance? *Learning and Motivation, 10,* 278–294.

Baker, A. G., & Mercier, P. (1989). Attention, retrospective processing, and cognitive representations. In S. B. Klein & R. R. Mowrer (Eds.), *Contemporary learning theories:*

Pavlovian conditioning and the status of traditional learning theory (pp. 85–101). Hillsdale, N.J.: Erlbaum.

Baker, A. G., Mercier, P., Gabel, J., & Baker, P. A. (1981). Contextual conditioning and the US preexposure effect in conditioned fear. *Journal of Experimental Psychology: Animal Behavior Processes, 7*, 109–128.

Balleine, B. W. (2001). Incentive process in instrumental conditioning. In R. R. Mowrer & S. B. Klein (Eds.), *Handbook of contemporary learning theories* (pp. 307–366). Mahrah, N.J.: Erlbaum.

Balleine, B. W., & Dickinson, A. (1991). Instrumental performance following reinforcer devaluation depends upon incentive learning. *Quarterly Journal of Experimental Psychology, 43B*, 279–296.

Balleine, B. W., & Dickinson, A. (1992). Signalling and incentive processes in instrumental reinforcer devaluation. *Quarterly Journal of Experimental Psychology, 45B*, 285–301.

Balleine, B. W., Garner, C., & Dickinson, A. (1995). Instrumental outcome devaluation is attenuated by the antiemetic ondansetron. *Quarterly Journal of Experimental Psychology, 48B*, 235–251.

Balsam, P. D., & Schwartz, A. L. (1981). Rapid contextual conditioning in autoshaping. *Journal of Experimental Psychology: Animal Behavior Processes, 7*, 382–393.

Bandura, A. (1971). *Social learning theory.* Morristown, N.J.: General Learning.

Bandura, A. (1977). Self-efficacy: Toward a unifying theory of behavior change. *Psychological Review, 84*, 191–215.

Bandura, A. (1982). The self and mechanisms of agency. In J. Suls (Ed.), *Psychological perspectives on the self* (Vol. 1, pp. 3–39). Hillsdale, N.J.: Erlbaum.

Bandura, A. (1986). *Social foundations of thought and action: A social cognition theory.* Englewood Cliffs, N.J.: Prentice-Hall.

Bandura, A., & Adams, N. E. (1977). Analysis of the self-efficacy theory of behavioral change. *Journal of Personality and Social Psychology, 1*, 287–310.

Bandura, A., Adams, N. E., & Beyer, J. (1977). Cognitive processes mediating behavioral change. *Journal of Personality and Social Psychology, 35*, 125–129.

Bandura, A., Blanchard, E. B., & Ritter, R. (1969). The relative efficacy of desensitization and modeling approaches for inducing behavioral, affective, and attitudinal changes. *Journal of Personality and Social Psychology, 13*, 173–199.

Bandura, A., Grusec, J. E., & Menlove, F. L. (1967). Vicarious extinction of avoidance behavior. *Journal of Personality and Social Psychology, 5*, 16–23.

Bandura, A., Jeffrey, R. W., & Gajdos, F. (1975). Generalizing change through participant modeling with self-directed mastery. *Behavior Research and Therapy, 13*, 141–152.

Bandura, A., & Perloff, B. (1967). Relative efficacy of self-monitored and externally imposed reinforcement systems. *Journal of Personality and Social Psychology, 7*, 11–16.

Bandura, A., & Rosenthal, T. L. (1966). Vicarious classical conditioning as a function of arousal level. *Journal of Personality and Social Psychology, 3*, 54–62.

Bandura, A., Ross, D., & Ross, D. A. (1963). Imitation of film-mediated aggressive models. *Journal of Abnormal and Social Psychology, 66*, 3–11.

Banks, R. K., & Vogel-Sprott, M. (1965). Effect of delayed punishment on an immediately rewarded response in humans. *Journal of Experimental Psychology, 70*, 357–359.

Barnes, G. W. (1956). Conditioned stimulus intensity and temporal factors in spaced-trial classical conditioning. *Journal of Experimental Psychology, 51*, 192–198.

Barnes, J. M., & Underwood, B. J. (1959). "Fate" of first-list associations in transfer theory. *Journal of Experimental Psychology, 58*, 97–105.

Baron, A. (1965). Delayed punishment of a runway response. *Journal of Comparative and Physiological Psychology, 60*, 131–134.

Bartlett, F. C. (1932). *Remembering: A study in experimental and social psychology.* London: Cambridge University Press.

Barton, E. S., Guess, D., Garcia, E., & Baer, D. M. (1970). Improvement of retardates' mealtime behaviors by time-out procedures using multiple baseline techniques. *Journal of Applied Behavior Analysis, 3,* 77–84.

Bass, M. J., & Hull, C. L. (1934). The irradiation of a tactile conditioned reflex in man. *Journal of Comparative Psychology, 17,* 47–65.

Bateson, P. P. G. (1969). Imprinting and the development of preferences. In A. Ambrose (Ed.), *Stimulation in early infancy* (pp. 109–132). New York: Academic.

Baum, M. (1970). Extinction of avoidance responding through response prevention (flooding). *Psychological Bulletin, 74,* 276–284.

Bechterev, V. M. (1913). *La psychologie objective.* Paris: Alcan.

Becker, H. C., & Flaherty, C. F. (1982). Influence of ethanol on contrast in consummatory behavior. *Psychopharmacology, 77,* 253–258.

Becker, H. C., & Flaherty, C. F. (1983). Chlordiazepoxide and ethanol additively reduce gustatory negative contrast. *Psychopharmacology, 80,* 35–37.

Bedard, J. (1989). Expertise in auditing: Myth or reality? *Accounting, Organizations and Society, 14,* 113–131.

Bedard, J., & Chi, M. T. H. (1992). Expertise. *Current Directions in Psychological Science, 1,* 135–139.

Berger, S. M. (1962). Conditioning through vicarious instigation. *Psychological Review, 69,* 450–466.

Berkowitz, L. (1971). The contagion of violence: An S-R mediational analysis of some effects of observed aggression. In M. Page (Ed.), *Nebraska Symposium on Motivation,* 95–135, Lincoln: University of Nebraska Press.

Berkowitz, L. (1978). Do we have to believe we are angry with someone in order to display "angry" aggression toward that person? In L. Berkowitz (Ed.), *Cognitive theories in social psychology: Papers reprinted from the advances in Experimental Social Psychology* (pp. 455–463). New York: Academic.

Berkowitz, L., & LePage, A. (1967). Weapons as aggression-eliciting stimuli. *Journal of Personality and Social Psychology, 7,* 202–207.

Bernard, L. L. (1924). *Instinct: A study in social psychology.* New York: Henry Holt.

Bernstein, I. L. (1978). Learned taste aversions in children receiving chemotherapy. *Science, 200,* 1302–1303.

Bernstein, I. L. (1991). Aversion conditioning in response to cancer and cancer treatment. *Clinical Psychology Review, 11,* 185–191.

Bernstein, I. L., & Webster, M. M. (1980). Learned taste aversions in humans. *Physiology and Behavior, 25,* 363–366.

Bersh, P. J. (1951). The influence of two variables upon the establishment of a secondary reinforcer for operant responses. *Journal of Experimental Psychology, 41,* 62–73.

Best, J. B. (1995). *Cognitive Psychology* (4th ed.). Minneapolis, Minn.: West Publishing Company.

Betts, S. L., Brandon, S. E., & Wagner, A. R. (1996). Differential blocking of the acquisition of conditioned eyeblink responding and conditioned fear with a shift in UCS locus. *Animal Learning and Behavior, 24,* 459–470.

Bever, T. G. (1970). The cognitive basis for linguistic structures. In J. R. Hayes (Ed.), *Cognition and development of language.* New York: Wiley.

Biederman, G. B., D'Amato, M. R., & Keller, D. M. (1964). Facilitation of discriminated avoidance learning by dissociation of CS and manipulandum. *Psychonomic Science, 1,* 229–230.

Bintz, J. (1970). Time-dependent memory deficits of aversively motivated behavior. *Learning and Motivation, 1,* 405–406.

Birch, H. G., & Rabinowitz, H. S. (1951). The negative effect of previous experience on productive thinking. *Journal of Experimental Psychology, 41,* 121–125.

Bishop, G. D. (1991). Understanding the understanding of illness: Lay disease representations. In J. A. Skelton & R. T. Croyle (Eds.), *Mental representation in health and illness*. New York: Springer-Verlag.

Bjork, R. A. (1989). Retrieval inhibition as an adaptive mechanism in human memory. In H. L. Roediger & F. I. M. Craik (Eds.), *Variety of memory and consciousness*, (pp. 309–330). Hillsdale, N.J.: Erlbaum.

Black, R. W. (1968). Shifts in magnitude of reward and contrast effects in instrumental selective learning: A reinterpretation. *Psychological Review, 75*, 114–126.

Blaha, C. D., & Phillips, A. G. (1990). Application of in vivo electrochemistry to the measurement of changes in dopamine release during intracranial self-stimulation. *Journal of Neuroscience Methods, 34*, 125–133.

Blaisdell, A. P., Gunther, L. M., & Miller, R. R. (1999). Recovery from blocking through deflation of the block stimulus. *Animal Learning and Behavior, 27*, 63–76.

Blanchard, R. J., & Blanchard, D. C. (1969). Crouching as an index of fear. *Journal of Comparative and Physiological Psychology, 67*, 370–375.

Blehar, M. C., Lieberman, A. F., & Ainsworth, M. D. S. (1977). Early face-to-face interaction and its relation to later infant-mother attachment. *Child Development, 48*, 182–194.

Blodgett, H. C., & McCutchan, K. (1947). Place versus response learning in a simple T-maze. *Journal of Experimental Psychology, 37*, 412–422.

Blodgett, H. C., & McCutchan, K. (1948). The relative strength of place and response learning in the T-maze. *Journal of Comparative and Physiological Psychology, 41*, 17–24.

Bloomfield, T. M. (1972). Contrast and inhibition in discrimination learning by the pigeon: Analysis through drug effects. *Learning and Motivation, 3*, 162–178.

Boakes, R. A., Poli, M., Lockwood, M. J., & Goodall, G. (1978). A study of misbehavior: Token reinforcement in the rat. *Journal of the Experimental Analysis of Behavior, 29*, 115–134.

Bolles, R. C. (1969). Avoidance and escape learning: Simultaneous acquisition of different responses. *Journal of Comparative and Physiological Psychology, 68*, 355–358.

Bolles, R. C. (1970). Species-specific defense reactions and avoidance learning. *Psychological Review, 77*, 32–48.

Bolles, R. C. (1972). Reinforcement, expectancy and learning. *Psychological Review, 79*, 394–409.

Bolles, R. C. (1978). The role of stimulus learning in defensive behavior. In S. H. Hulse, H. Fowler, & W. K. Honig (Eds.), *Cognitive processes in animal behavior* (pp. 89–108). Hillsdale, N.J.: Erlbaum.

Bolles, R. C. (1979). *Learning theory* (2nd ed.). New York: Holt, Rinehart & Winston.

Bolles, R. C., & Collier, A. C. (1976). The effect of predictive cues on freezing in rats. *Animal Learning and Behavior, 4*, 6–8.

Bolles, R. C., & Riley, A. (1973). Freezing as an avoidance response: Another look at the operant-respondent distinction. *Learning and Motivation, 4*, 268–275.

Bolles, R. C., & Tuttle, A. V. (1967). A failure to reinforce instrumental behavior by terminating a stimulus that had been paired with shock. *Psychonomic Science, 9*, 255–256.

Booth, N. P. (1980). An opponent-process theory of motivation for jogging. Cited in R. L. Solomon, The opponent-process theory of motivation. *American Psychologist, 35*, 691–712.

Borkovec, T. D. (1976). Physiological and cognitive processes in the regulation of fear. In G. E. Schwartz & D. Shapiro (Eds.), *Consciousness and self-regulation: Advances in research* (pp. 261–312). New York: Plenum.

Boudewyns, P. A., Fry, T. J., & Nightingale, E. J. (1986). Token economy programs in VA medical centers: Where are they today? *The Behavior Therapist, 9*, 126–127.

Bouton, M. E., Jones, D. L., McPhillips, S. A., & Swartzentruber, D. (1986). Potentiation and overshadowing in odor-aversion learning: Role of method of odor presentation, the distal-proximal area distinction, and the conditionality of odor. *Learning and Motivation, 17,* 115–138.

Bower, G. H. (1981). Mood and memory. *American Psychologist, 36,* 129–148.

Bower, G. H., Fowler, H., & Trapold, M. A. (1959). Escape learning as a function of amount of shock reduction. *Journal of Experimental Psychology, 48,* 482–484.

Bower, G. H., Hilgard, E. R. (1981). *Theories of learning* (5th ed.). Englewood Cliffs, N.J.: Prentice-Hall.

Bower, G. H., & Springston, F. (1970). Pauses as recording points in letter sequences. *Journal of Experimental Psychology, 83,* 421–430.

Bower, G. H., Starr, R., & Lazarovitz, L. (1965). Amount of response-produced change in the CS and avoidance learning. *Journal of Comparative and Physiological Psychology, 59,* 13–17.

Bozarth, M. A., & Wise, R. A. (1981). Heroin reward is dependent on a dopaminergic substrate. *Life Science, 29,* 1881–1886.

Bozarth, M. A., & Wise, R. A. (1983). Neural substrates of opiate reinforcement. *Progress in Neuropharmacology and Biological Psychiatry, 7,* 569–575.

Brady, J. V. (1961). Motivational-emotional factors and intracranial self-stimulation. In D. E. Sheer (Ed.), *Electrical stimulation of the brain.* Austin: University of Texas Press.

Brandon, S. E., & Wagner, A. R. (1991). Modulation of a discrete Pavlovian conditioned reflex by a putative emotive Pavlovian conditioned stimulus. *Journal of Experimental Psychology: Animal Behavior Process, 17,* 299–311.

Braud, W., Wepman, B., & Russo, D. (1969). Task and species generality of the "helplessness" phenomenon. *Psychonomic Science, 16,* 154–155.

Braveman, N. S. (1974). Poison-based avoidance learning with flavored or colored water in guinea pigs. *Learning and Motivation, 5,* 182–194.

Braveman, N. S. (1975). Formation of taste aversions in rats following prior exposure to sickness. *Learning and Motivation, 6,* 512–534.

Breland, K., & Breland, M. (1961). The misbehavior of organisms. *American Psychologist, 61,* 681–684.

Breland, K., & Breland, M. (1966). *Animal behavior.* New York: Macmillan.

Brewer, W. F., & Treyens, J. C. (1981). Role of schemata in memory for places. *Cognitive Psychology, 13,* 207–230.

Briere, J., & Conte, J. R. (1993). Self-reported amnesia for abuse in adults molested as children. *Journal of Traumatic Stress, 6,* 21–31.

Bright, R. A., & Everitt, D. E. (1992). Beta-blockers and depression. Evidence against an association. *Journal of the American Medical Association, 267,* 1783–1787.

Bristol, M. M., & Sloane, H. N., Jr. (1974). Effects of contingency contracting on study rate and test performance. *Journal of Applied Behavior Analysis, 7,* 271–285.

Britt, M. D., & Wise, R. A. (1983). Ventral tegmental site of opiate reward: Antagonism by a hydrophilic opiate receptor blocker. *Brain Research, 258,* 105–108.

Brogden, W. J. (1939). Sensory preconditioning. *Journal of Experimental Psychology, 25,* 323–332.

Brooks, C. I. (1980). Effect of prior nonreward on subsequent incentive growth during brief acquisition. *Animal Learning and Behavior, 8,* 143–151.

Brown, J. L. (1975). *The evolution of behavior.* New York: Norton.

Brown, J. S. (1948). Gradients of approach and avoidance responses and their relation to level of motivation. *Journal of Comparative and Physiological Psychology, 41,* 450–465.

Brown, J. S., & Jacobs, A. (1949). The role of fear in the motivation and acquisition of responses. *Journal of Experimental Psychology, 39,* 747–759.

Brown, J. S., Martin, R. C., & Morrow, M. W. (1964). Self-punitive behavior in the rat: Facilitative effects of punishment on resistance to extinction. *Journal of Comparative and Physiological Psychology, 57,* 127–133.

Brown, P. L., & Jenkins, H. M. (1968). Autoshaping of the pigeon's key peck. *Journal of the Experimental Analysis of Behavior, 11,* 1–8.

Brown, R., Cazden, C., & Bellugi, U. (1969). The child's grammar from I to III. In J. P. Hill (Ed.), *Minnesota symposium on child psychology* (Vol. 2). Minneapolis: University of Minnesota Press.

Brown, R., & Kulik, J. (1977). Flashbulb memories. *Cognition, 5,* 73–99.

Brucke, E. (1874). *Lectures on physiology.* Vienna: University of Vienna.

Bruner, J. S., Goodnow, J. J., & Austin, G. A. (1956). *A study of thinking.* New York: Wiley.

Brush, F. R. (Ed.). (1970). *Aversive conditioning and learning.* New York: Academic.

Brush, F. R. (1971). Retention of aversively motivated behavior. In F. R. Bush (Ed.), *Aversive conditioning and learning.* New York: Academic.

Bugelski, B. R. (1968). Images as mediators in one-trial paired-associated learning: II. Self-timing in successive lists. *Journal of Experimental Psychology, 77,* 328–334.

Burke, A., Heuer, F., & Reisberg, D. (1992). Remembering emotional events. *Memory and Cognition, 20,* 277–290.

Buske-Kirschbaum, A., Kirschbaum, C., Stierle, H., Jabij, L., & Hellhammer, D. (1994). Conditioned manipulation of natural killer (NK) cells in humans using a discriminative learning protocol. *Biological Psychology, 38,* 143–155.

Butler, R. A., & Harlow, H. F. (1954). Persistence of visual exploration in monkeys. *Journal of Comparative and Physiological Psychology, 47,* 257–263.

Butter, C. M., & Thomas, D. R. (1958). Secondary reinforcement as a function of the amount of primary reinforcement. *Journal of the Experimental Analysis of Behavior, 51,* 346–348.

Caldwell, W. E., & Jones, H. B. (1954). Some positive results on a modified Tolman and Honzik insight maze. *Journal of Comparative and Physiological Psychology, 47,* 416–418.

Camerer, C., & Johnson, E. J. (1991). The process-performance paradox in expert judgment: How can experts know so much and predict so badly? In K. M. Ericsson & J. Smith (Eds.), *Toward a theory of expertise: Prospects and limits.* Cambridge: Cambridge University Press.

Camp, D. S., Raymond, G. A., & Church, R. M. (1967). Temporal relationship between response and punishment. *Journal of Experimental Psychology, 74,* 114–123.

Campbell, B. A., & Church, P. M. (1969). *Punishment and aversive behavior.* New York: Appleton-Century-Crofts.

Campbell, B. A., & Kraeling, D. (1953). Response strength as a function of drive level and amount of drive reduction. *Journal of Experimental Psychology, 45,* 97–101.

Cantor, M. B., & Wilson, J. F. (1984). Feeding the face: New directions in adjunctive behavior research. In F. R. Brush & J. B. Overmier (Eds.), *Affect, conditioning, and cognition.* Hillsdale, N.J.: Erlbaum.

Capaldi, E. J. (1971). Memory and learning: A sequential viewpoint. In W. K. Honig & P. H. R. James (Eds.), *Animal memory* (pp. 115–154). New York: Academic.

Capaldi, E. J. (1994). The relation between memory and expectancy as revealed by percentage and sequence of reward investigations. *Psychonomic Bulletin and Review, 1,* 303–310.

Capaldi, E. J., Hart, D., & Stanley, L. R. (1963). Effect of intertrial reinforcement on the aftereffect of nonreinforcement and resistance to extinction. *Journal of Experimental Psychology, 65,* 70–74.

Capaldi, E. J., & Spivey, J. E. (1964). Stimulus consequences of reinforcement and nonreinforcement: Stimulus traces or memory. *Psychonomic Science, 1,* 403–404.

Capretta, P. J. (1961). An experimental modification of food preference in chickens. *Journal of Comparative and Physiological Psychology, 54,* 238–242.

Carew, T. J., Hawkins, R. D., & Kandel, E. R. (1983). Differential classical conditioning of a defensive withdrawal reflex in *Aplysia californica. Science, 219,* 397–420.

Carlin, A. S., Hoffman, H. G., & Weghorst, S. (1997). Virtual reality and tactile augmentation in the treatment of spider phobia: A case report. *Behaviour Research and Therapy, 35,* 153–158.

Carlton, P. L. (1969). Brain-acetylcholine and inhibition. In J. T. Tapp (Ed.), *Reinforcement and behavior* (pp. 288–325). New York: Academic.

Carr, G. D., & White, N. (1984). The relationship between stereotype and memory improvement produced by amphetamine. *Psychopharmacology, 82,* 203–209.

Carr, G. D., & White, N. (1986). Anatomical dissociation of amphetamine's rewarding and aversive effects: An intracranial microinjection study. *Psychopharmacology, 39,* 340–346.

Carrell, L. E., Cannon, D. S., Best, M. R., & Stone, M. J. (1986). Nausea and radiation-induced taste aversions in cancer patients. *Appetite, 7,* 203–208.

Carter, L. F. (1941). Intensity of conditioned stimulus and rate of conditioning. *Journal of Experimental Psychology, 28,* 481–490.

Catania, A. C. (1979). *Learning.* Englewood Cliffs, N.J.: Prentice-Hall.

Catania, A. C., & Reynolds, G. S. (1968). A quantitative analysis of the responding maintained by interval schedules of reinforcement. *Journal of Experimental Analysis of Behavior, 11,* 327–383.

Chandler, C. C. (1991). How memory for an event is influenced by related events: Interference in modified recognition tests. *Journal of Experimental Psychology: Learning, Memory, and Cognition, 17,* 115–125.

Chang, V. C., Mark, G. P., Hernandez, L., & Hoebel, B. G. (1988). Extracellular dopamine increases in the nucleus accumbens following rehydration or sodium repletion. *Society for Neuroscience Abstracts, 14,* 527.

Charness, N. (1991). Expertise in chess: The balance between knowledge and search. In K. A. Ericsson & J. Smith (Eds.), *Toward a general theory of expertise* (pp. 39–63). Cambridge, England: Cambridge University Press.

Chen, J., Paredes, W., & Gardner, E. L. (1994). Delta^9-Tetrahydrocannabinol's enhancement of nucleus accumbens dopamine resembles that of reuptake blockers rather than releasers—Evidence from in vivo microdialysis experiments with 3-methoxytyramine. Paper presented at the annual meeting of College Problems in Drug Dependence, Palm Beach, Fla.

Cherek, D. R. (1982). Schedule-induced cigarette self-administration. *Pharmacology, Biochemistry, and Behavior, 17,* 523–527.

Cheyne, J. A., Goyeche, J. R., & Walters, R. H. (1969). Attention, anxiety, and rules in resistance-to-deviation in children. *Journal of Experimental Child Psychology, 8,* 127–139.

Childress, A. R., Ehrman, R., McLellan, T. A., & O'Brien, C. P. (1986). Extinguishing conditioned responses during opiate dependence treatment. Turning laboratory findings into clinical procedures. *Journal of Substance Abuse Treatment, 3,* 33–40.

Chomsky, N. (1957). *Syntactic structures.* The Hague: Mouton.

Chomsky, N. (1965). *Aspects of the theory of syntax.* Cambridge, Mass.: M.I.T. Press.

Chomsky, N. (1975). *Reflections on language.* New York: Pantheon.

Chomsky, N. (1987). Language in a psychological setting. *Sophia Linguistic Working Papers in Linguistics, No. 22* (pp. 322–323). Tokyo: Sophia University.

Church, R. M. (1969). Response suppression. In B. A. Campbell & R. M. Church (Eds.), *Punishment and aversive behavior* (pp. 111–156). New York: Appleton-Century-Crofts.

Church, R. M., & Black, A. H. (1958). Latency of the conditioned heart rate as a function of the CS-UCS interval. *Journal of Comparative and Physiological Psychology, 51,* 478–482.

Clark, L. A., Watson, D., & Mineka, S. (1994). Temperament, personality, and the mood and anxiety disorders. *Journal of Abnormal Psychology, 103,* 103–116.

Cohen, P. S., & Looney, T. A. (1973). Schedule-induced mirror responding in the pigeon. *Journal of the Experimental Analysis of Behavior, 19*, 395–408.

Collias, N. E., & Collias, E. C. (1956). Some mechanisms of family integration in ducks. *Auk, 73*, 378–400.

Collier, G., Hirsch, E., & Hamlin, P. H. (1972). The ecological determinants of reinforcement in the rat. *Physiology & Behavior, 9*, 705–716.

Collins, A. M., & Loftus, E. F. (1975). A spreading activation theory of semantic processing. *Psychological Review, 82*, 407–428.

Collins, A. M., & Quillian, M. R. (1969). Retrieval time from semantic memory. *Journal of Verbal Learning and Verbal Behavior, 8*, 240–247.

Colwill, R. C., & Rescorla, R. A. (1985). Instrumental conditioning remains sensitive to reinforcer devaluation after extensive training. *Journal of Experimental Psychology: Animal Behavior Processes, 11*, 520–536.

Conners, F. A. (1992). Reading instruction for students with moderate mental retardation: Review and analysis of research. *American Journal of Mental Retardation, 96*, 577–597.

Conrad, C. (1972). Cognitive economy in semantic memory. *Journal of Experimental Psychology, 92*, 149–154.

Conrad, R. (1964). Acoustic confusions in immediate memory. *British Journal of Psychology, 55*, 75–84.

Coons, E. E., & Cruce, J. A. F. (1968). Lateral hypothalamus: Food and current intensity in maintaining self-stimulation of hunger. *Science, 159*, 1117–1119.

Corey, J. R., & Shamov, J. (1972). The effects of fading on the acquisition and retention of oral reading. *Journal of Applied Behavior Analysis, 5*, 311–315.

Corkin, S., Amaral, D. G., Gonzalez, R. G., Johnson, K. A., & Hyman, B. T. (1997). H. M.'s medial temporal lobe lesion: Findings from magnetic resonance imaging. *Journal of Neuroscience, 17*, 3964–3979.

Coulombe, D., & White, N. (1982). The effect of posttraining hypothalamic self-stimulation on sensory preconditioning in rats. *Canadian Journal of Psychology, 36*, 57–66.

Coulter, X., Riccio, D. C., & Page, H. A. (1969). Effects of blocking an instrumental avoidance response: Facilitated extinction but persistence of "fear." *Journal of Comparative and Physiological Psychology, 68*, 377–381.

Coussons, M. E., Dykstra, L. A., & Lysle, D. T. (1992). Pavlovian conditioning of morphine-induced alterations in immune function. *Journal of Neuroimmunology, 39*, 219–230.

Cowan, N. (1994). Mechanisms of verbal short-term memory. *Current Directions in Psychological Science, 6*, 185–189.

Cowan, N., Day, L., Saults, J. S., Keller, T. A., Johnson, T., & Flores, L. (1992). The role of verbal output time in the effects of word length on immediate memory. *Journal of Memory and Language, 31*, 1–17.

Coyne, J. C., & Whiffen, V. E. (1995). Issues in personality as diathesis for depression: The case of sociotrophy-dependency and autonomy-self-criticism. *Psychological Bulletin, 4*, 278–287.

Craig, K. D., & Weinstein, M. S. (1965). Conditioning vicarious affective arousal. *Psychological Reports, 17*, 955–963.

Craig, R. L., & Siegel, P. S. (1980). Does negative affect beget positive effect? A test of opponent–process theory. *Bulletin of the Psychonomic Society, 14*, 404–406.

Craik, F. I. M., & Lockhart, R. S. (1972). Levels of processing: A framework for memory research. *Journal of Verbal Learning and Behavior, 11*, 671–684.

Craik, F. I. M., & Tulving, E. (1975). Depth of processing and the retention of words in episodic memory. *Journal of Experimental Psychology: General, 104*, 268–294.

Craik, F. I. M., & Watkins, M. J. (1973). The role of rehearsal in short-term memory. *Journal of Verbal Learning and Verbal Behavior, 12,* 599–607.

Creer, T. L., Chai, H., & Hoffman, A. (1977). A single application of an aversive stimulus to eliminate chronic cough. *Journal of Behavior Research and Experimental Psychiatry, 8,* 107–109.

Crespi, L. P. (1942). Quantitative variation of incentive and performance in the white rat. *American Journal of Psychology, 55,* 467–517.

Cromer, R. F. (1981). Reconceptualizing language acquisition and cognitive development. In R. L. Schiefelbusch & D. D. Brinker (Eds.), *Early language: Acquisition and Intervention.* Baltimore: University Park Press.

Crooks, J. L. (1967). Observational learning of fear in monkeys. Unpublished manuscript, University of Pennsylvania, Philadelphia.

Crovitz, H. F. (1971). The capacity of memory loci in artificial memory. *Psychonomic Science, 24,* 187–188.

Crowder, R. G., & Morton, J. (1969). Precategorical acoustic storage (PAS). *Perception and Psychophysics, 5,* 365–373.

Crowell, C. R., Hinson, R. E., & Siegel, S. (1981). The role of conditional drug responses in tolerance to the hypothermic effects of ethanol. *Psychopharmacology, 73,* 51–54.

Cruser, L., & Klein, S. B. (1984). The role of schedule-induced polydipsia on temporal discrimination learning. *Psychological Reports, 58,* 443–452.

Cunningham, C. E., & Linscheid, T. R. (1976). Elimination of chronic infant ruminating by electric shock. *Behavior Therapy, 1,* 231–234.

Daly, H. B. (1974). Reinforcing properties of escape from frustration aroused in various learning situations. In G. H. Bower (Ed.), *The psychology of learning and motivation* (Vol. 8, pp. 87–231). New York: Academic.

D'Amato, M. R. (1970). *Experimental psychology: Methodology, psychophysics, and learning.* New York: McGraw-Hill.

D'Amato, M. R., Fazzaro, J., & Etkin, M. (1968). Anticipatory responding and avoidance discrimination as factors in avoidance conditioning. *Journal of Experimental Psychology, 77,* 41–47.

D'Amato, M. R., & Salmon, D. P. (1984). Cognitive processes in cebus monkeys. In H. L. Roitblat, R. G. Berver, & H. S. Terrace (Eds.), *Animal cognition* (pp. 149–168). Hillsdale, N.J.: Erlbaum.

D'Amato, M. R., Salmon, D. P., & Colombo, M. (1985). Extent and limits of the matching concept in monkeys. (*Cebus apella*). *Journal of Experimental Psychology: Animal Behavior Processes, 11,* 35–51.

D'Amato, M. R., & Schiff, E. (1964). Further studies of overlearning and position reversal learning. *Psychological Reports, 14,* 380–382.

Darwin, C. J., Turvey, M. T., & Crowder, R. B. (1972). An auditory analogue of the Sperling partial report procedure: Evidence for brief auditory storage. *Cognitive Psychology, 3,* 255–267.

Davidson, G. C., & Neale, J. M. (1994). *Abnormal Psychology* (6th ed.). New York: Wiley.

Davidson, R. S. (1972). Aversive modification of alcoholic behavior: Punishment of an alcohol-reinforced operant. Unpublished manuscript, U.S. Veterans Administration Hospital, Miami, Florida.

Davidson, T. L., Aparicio, J., & Rescorla, R. R. (1988). Transfer between Pavlovian facilitators and instrumental discriminative stimuli. *Animal Learning and Behavior, 16,* 285–291.

Davis, H. (1968). Conditioned suppression: A survey of the literature. *Psychonomic Monograph Supplements, 2* (14, 38), 283–291.

Davis, J. C., & Okada, R. (1971). Recognition and recall of positively forgotten words. *Journal of Experimental Psychology, 89,* 181–186.

Davis, M. (1974). Sensitization of the rat startle response by noise. *Journal of Comparative and Physiological Psychology, 87*, 571–581.

Delgado, J. M. R., Roberts, W. W., & Miller, N. E. (1954). Learning motivated by electric stimulation of the brain. *American Journal of Physiology, 179*, 587–593.

Delius, J. D. (1992). Categorical discrimination of objects and pictures by pigeons. *Animal Learning and Behavior, 20*, 301–311.

Denniston, J. C., Savastano, H. I., & Miller, R. R. (2001). The extended comparator hypothesis: Learning by contiguity, responding by relative strength. In R. R. Mowrer & S. B. Klein (Eds.), *Handbook of contemporary learning theories* (pp. 65–117). Mawrah, N.J.: Erlbaum.

Denny, M. R. (1971). Relaxation theory and experiments. In F. R. Brush (Ed.), *Aversive conditioning and learning* (pp. 235–299). New York: Academic.

Denny, M. R., & Weisman, R. G. (1964). Avoidance behavior as a function of the length of nonshock confinement. *Journal of Comparative and Physiological Psychology, 58*, 252–257.

DeSousa, N. J., & Vaccarino, F. J. (2001). Neurobiology of reinforcement: Interaction between dopamine and cholecystokinin systems. In R. R. Mowrer and S. B. Klein (Eds.), *Handbook of Contemporary Learning Theories* (pp. 441–468). Mawrah, N.J.: Erlbaum.

DeSousa, N. J., Bush, D. E. A., & Vaccarino, F. J. (2000). Self-administration of intravenous amphetamine is predicted by individual differences in sucrose feeding in rats. *Pharmacology, Biochemistry, and Behavior, 148*, 52–58.

de Villiers, P. A. (1977). Choice in concurrent schedules and a quantitative formulation of the law of effect. In W. K. Honig & J. E. R. Staddon (Eds.), *Handbook of operant conditioning*. Englewood Cliffs, N.J.: Prentice-Hall.

Dewey, J. (1886). *Psychology*. New York: Harper & Row.

Dickinson, A. (1989). Expectancy theory in animal conditioning. In S. B. Klein & R. R. Mowrer (Eds.), *Contemporary learning theories: Pavlovian conditioning and the states of traditional learning theory* (pp. 279–308). Hillsdale, N.J.: Erlbaum.

Dickinson, A., & Balleine, B. W. (1994). Motivational control of goal-directed action. *Animal Learning and Behavior, 22*, 1–18.

Dickinson, A., & Balleine, B. W. (1995). Motivational control of instrumental action. *Current Directions in Psychological Science, 4*, 162–167.

Dickinson, A., & Dawson, G. R. (1987). Pavlovian processes in the motivation control of instrumental performance. *Quarterly Journal of Experimental Psychology, 39B*, 201–213.

Dickinson, A., & Nicholas, D. J. (1983). Irrelevant incentive learning during instrumental conditioning: The role of drive-reinforcer and response-reinforcer relationships. *Quarterly Journal of Experimental Psychology, 35B*, 249–263.

Dodd, D. H., & White, R. M. (1980). *Cognition: Mental structures and processes*. Boston: Allyn & Bacon.

Domjan, M. (1976). Determinants of the enhancement of flavor-water intake by prior exposure. *Journal of Experimental Psychology: Animal Behavior Processes, 2*, 17–27.

Domjan, M. (1977). Selective suppression of drinking during a limited period following aversive drug treatment in rats. *Journal of Experimental Psychology: Animal Behavior Processes, 3*, 66–76.

Domjan, M., & Gemberling, G. A. (1980). Effects of expected vs. unexpected proximal US preexposure on taste-aversion learning. *Animal Learning and Behavior, 8*, 204–210.

Donegan, N. H., & Wagner, A. R. (1987). Conditioned diminution and facilitation of the UR: A sometimes opponent-process interpretation. In I. Gormezano, W. F. Prokasy, & R. F. Thompson (Eds.), *Classical conditioning III* (pp. 339–369). Hillsdale, N.J.: Erlbaum.

Dorry, G. W., & Zeaman, D. (1975). The use of a fading technique in paired-associate teaching of a reading vocabulary with retardates. *Mental Retardation, 11*, 3–6.

Dorry, G. W., & Zeaman, D. (1976). Teaching a simple reading vocabulary to retarded: Effectiveness of fading and on fading procedures. *American Journal of Mental Deficiency, 79,* 711–716.

Drabman, R., & Spitalnik, R. (1973). Social isolation as a punishment procedure: A controlled study. *Journal of Experimental Child Psychology, 16,* 236–249.

Ducker, G., & Rensch, B. (1968). Verzogerung des Vergessens erlernter visuellen Aufgaben bei Fischen durch Dunkelhaltung. *Pfluegers Archiv fur die Gesamte Physiologie des Menschen und der Tiere, 301,* 1–6.

Du Nann, D. G., & Weber, S. J. (1976). Short- and long-term effects of contingency managed instruction on low, medium, and high GPA students. *Journal of Applied Behavior Analysis, 9,* 375–376.

Durlach, P. (1989). Learning and performance in Pavlovian conditioning: Are failures of contiguity failures of learning or performance? In S. B. Klein & R. R. Mowrer (Eds.), *Contemporary learning theories: Pavlovian conditioning and the status of traditional learning theory* (pp. 19–69). Hillsdale, N.J.: Erlbaum.

Ebbinghaus, H. (1885). *Memory: A contribution to experimental psychology,* H. A. Ruger & C. E. Bussenius (Trans.). New York: Dover.

Ehrman, R. N., Robbins, S. J., Childress, A. R., & O'Brien, C. P. (1992). Conditioned responses to cocaine-related stimuli in cocaine abuse patients. *Psychopharmacology, 107,* 523–529.

Eibl-Eibesfeldt, I. (1961). The fighting behavior of animals. *Scientific American, 205,* 112–122.

Eibl-Eibesfeldt, I. (1970). *Ethology: The biology of behavior.* New York: Holt.

Eich, J. E. (1980). The cue-dependent nature of state-dependent retrieval. *Memory and Cognition, 8,* 157–173.

Eich, J. E. (1985). Levels of processing, encoding specificity elaboration, and CHARM. *Psychological Review, 92,* 1–38.

Eich, J. E., Weingartner, H., Stillman, R. C., & Gillin, J. C. (1975). State-dependent accessibility of retrieval cues in the retention of a categorized list. *Journal of Verbal Learning and Verbal Behavior, 14,* 408–417.

Eimas, P. D., & Corbit, J. D. (1973). Selective adaptation of linguistic feature detectors. *Cognitive Psychology, 4,* 99–109.

Eimas, P. D., Siqueland, E. R., Jusczyk, P., & Vigorito, J. (1971). Speech perception in infants. *Science, 171,* 303–306.

Ekstrand, B. R. (1967). Effect of sleep on memory. *Journal of Experimental Psychology, 75,* 64–72.

Ekstrand, B. R., Wallace, W. P., & Underwood, B. J. (1966). A frequency theory of verbal-discrimination learning. *Psychological Review, 73,* 566–578.

Eliot, L. S., Blumenfeld, H., Edmonds, B. W., Kandel, E. R., & Siegelbaum, S. A. (1991). Imaging [Ca] transients at *Aplysia* sensorimotor synapses: Contribution of direct and indirect modulation to presynaptic facilitation. *Society of Neuroscience Abstracts, 17,* 1485.

Elkind, D. (1981). Recent research in cognitive and language development. In L. T. Benjamin (Ed.), *The G. Stanley Hall lecture series* (Vol. 1). Washington, D.C.: American Psychological Association.

Elkins, R. L. (1973). Attenuation of drug-induced bait shyness to a palatable solution as an increasing function of its availability prior to conditioning. *Behavioral Biology, 9,* 221–226.

Elmes, D. G., Adams, C., & Roediger, H. (1970). Cued forgetting in short-term memory. *Journal of Experimental Psychology, 86,* 103–107.

Emmelkamp, P. M. G., & Scholing, A. (1990). Behavioral treatment for simple and social phobias. In R. Noyes, Jr., M. Roth, & G. D. Burrows (Eds.), *Handbook of anxiety: The treatment of anxiety* (Vol. 4). Amsterdam: Elsevier.

Emmelkamp, P. M. G., Van Der Helm, M., Van Zanten, B. L., & Plochg, I. (1980). Treatment of obsessive-compulsive patients: The contribution of self-instructional training to the effectiveness of exposure. *Behavior Research and Therapy, 18*, 61–66.

Emshoff, J. G., Redd, W. H., & Davidson, W. S. (1976). Generalization training and the transfer of prosocial behavior in delinquent adolescents. *Journal of Behavior Therapy and Experimental Psychiatry, 7*, 141–144.

Epstein, D. M. (1967). Toward a unified theory of anxiety. In B. A. Maher (Ed.), *Progress in experimental personality research.* New York: Academic.

Epstein, R. (1981). On pigeons and people: A preliminary look at the Columbian Simulation Project. *The Behavior Analyst, 4*, 43–55.

Ervin, F. R., Mark, V. H., & Stevens, J. R. (1969). Behavioral and affective responses to brain stimulation in man. In J. Zubin & C. Shagass (Eds.), *Neurological aspects of psychopathology.* New York: Grune & Stratton.

Estes, W. K., & Skinner, B. F. (1941). Some quantitative properties of anxiety. *Journal of Experimental Psychology, 29*, 390–400.

Ettenberg, A., Pettit, H. O., Bloom, F. E., & Koob, G. F. (1982). Heroin and cocaine intravenous self-administration in rats: Mediation by separate neural systems. *Psychopharmacology, 78*, 204–209.

Evans, K. R., & Vaccarino, F. J. (1990). Amphetamine- and morphine-induced feeding: Evidence for involvement of reward mechanisms. *Neuroscience, Biobehavioral Reviews, 14*, 9–22.

Eysenck, M. W. (1978). Levels of processing: A critique. *British Journal of Psychology, 68*, 157–169.

Fabricius, E. (1951). Zur Ethologie Junger Anatiden. *Acta Zoologica Fennica, 68*, 1–175.

Fairweather, G. W., Sanders, D. H., Maynard, H., & Cressler, D. C. (1969). *Community life for the mortally ill: An alternative to institutional care.* Chicago: Aldine.

Falk, J. L. (1961). Production of polydipsia in normal rats by an intermittent food schedule. *Science, 133*, 195–196.

Falk, J. L. (1964). Studies on schedule-induced polydipsia. In M. H. Wayner (Ed.), *Thirst.* Oxford: Pergamon.

Falk, J. L. (1966). The motivational properties of schedule-induced polydipsia. *Journal of the Experimental Analysis of Behavior, 9*, 19–25.

Falk, J. L. (1969). Conditions producing psychogenic polydipsia in animals. *Annals of the New York Academy of Sciences, 157*, 569–593.

Fanselow, M. E., & Baackes, M. P. (1982). Conditioned fear-induced opiate analgesia on the formalin test: Evidence for two aversive motivational systems. *Learning and Motivation, 13*, 200–221.

Fanselow, M. S., & Bolles, R. C. (1979). Naloxone and shock-elicited freezing the rat. *Journal of Comparative and Physiological Psychology, 93*, 736–744.

Fantino, E., Preston, R. A., & Dunn, R. (1993). Delay reduction: Current status. *Journal of the Experimental Analysis of Behavior, 60*, 159–169.

Fazzaro, J., & D'Amato, M. R. (1969). Resistance to extinction after varying amounts of nondiscriminative or cue-correlated escape training. *Journal of Comparative and Physiological Psychology, 68*, 373–376.

Feather, B. W. (1967). Human salivary conditioning: A methodological study. In G. A. Kimble (Ed.), *Foundations of conditioning and learning.* New York: Appleton-Century-Crofts.

Feeney, D. M. (1987). Human rights and animal welfare. *American Psychologist, 42*, 593–599.

Fehr, B., & Russell, J. A. (1991). The concept of love viewed from a prototype perspective. *Journal of Personality and Social Psychology, 60*, 425–438.

Felton, J., & Lyon, D. O. (1966). The postreinforcement pause. *Journal of the Experimental Analysis of Behavior, 9*, 131–134.

Feltz, D. L. (1982). The analysis of the causal elements in Bandura's theory of self-efficacy and an anxiety-based model of avoidance behavior. *Journal of Personality and Social Psychology, 42,* 764–781.

Fenwick, S., Mikulka, P. J., & Klein, S. B. (1975). The effect of different levels of preexposure to sucrose on acquisition and extinction of conditioned aversion. *Behavioral Biology, 14,* 231–235.

Ferster, C. B., & Skinner, B. F. (1957). *Schedules of reinforcement.* New York: Appleton-Century-Crofts.

Flaherty, C. F. (1982). Incentive contrast: A review of behavioral changes following shifts in reward. *Animal Learning and Behavior, 10,* 409–440.

Flaherty, C. F. (1985). *Animal learning and cognition.* New York: Knopf.

Flaherty, C. F. (1996). *Incentive relativity.* New York: Cambridge University Press.

Flaherty, C. F., & Davenport, J. W. (1972). Successive brightness discrimination in rats following regular versus random intermittent reinforcement. *Journal of Experimental Psychology, 96,* 1–9.

Flaherty, C. F., & Driscoll, C. (1980). Amobarbital sodium reduces successive gustatory contrast. *Psychopharmacology, 69,* 161–162.

Flakus. W. J., & Steinbrecher, B. C. (1964). Avoidance conditioning in the rabbit. *Psychological Reports, 14,* 140.

Flavell, J. H., Cooper, A., & Loiselle, R. H. (1958). Effect of the number of preutilization functions on functional fixedness in problem solving. *Psychological Reports, 4,* 343–350.

Flory, R. K. (1971). The control of schedule-induced polydipsia: Frequency and magnitude of reinforcement. *Learning and Motivation, 2,* 215–227.

Foder, J. A., Bever, T. G., & Garrett, M. F. (1974). *The psychology of language: An introduction to psycholinguistics and generative grammar.* New York: McGraw-Hill.

Forster, K. I. (1979). Levels of processing and the structure of the language processor. In W. E. Cooper & T. Walker (Eds.), *Sentence processing.* Hillsdale, N.J.: Erlbaum.

Fowler, H., & Trapold, M. A. (1962). Escape performance as a function of delay of reinforcement. *Journal of Experimental Psychology, 63,* 464–467.

Fox, M. W. (1969). Ontogeny of prey-killing behavior in canidae. *Behavior, 35,* 259–272.

Franks, J. J., & Bransford, J. D. (1971). Abstraction of visual patterns. *Journal of Experimental Psychology, 90,* 65–74.

Freedman, P. E., Hennessy, J. W., & Groner, D. (1974). Effects of varying active/passive shock levels in shuttle box avoidance in rats. *Journal of Comparative and Physiological Psychology, 86,* 79–84.

Frey, P. W. (1969). Within- and between-session CS intensity performance effects in rabbit eyelid conditioning. *Psychonomic Science, 17,* 1–2.

Friesen. W. O. (1989). Neuronal coding of leech swimming movements. In J. W. Jacklet (Ed.), *Neuronal and cellular oscillators* (pp. 269–316). New York: Dekker.

Fuchs, C. Z., & Rehm, L. P. (1977). Self-control depression program. *Journal of Consulting and Clinical Psychology, 45,* 206–215.

Gabrieli, J. D. E. (1998). Cognitive neuroscience of human memory. *Annual Review of Psychology, 49,* 87–115.

Gabrieli, J. D. E., Cohen, N. J., & Corkin, S. (1988). The impaired learning of semantic knowledge following bilateral medial temporal-lobe resection. *Brain and Cognition, 7,* 157–177.

Galbraith, D. A., Byrick, R. J., & Rutledge, J. T. (1970). An aversive conditioning approach to the inhibition of chronic vomiting. *Canadian Psychiatric Association Journal, 15,* 311–313.

Gallistel, C. R., Shizgal, P., & Yeomans, J. (1981). A portrait of the substrate for self-stimulation. *Psychological Review, 88,* 228–273.

Ganz, L. (1968). An analysis of generalization behavior in the stimulus-deprived organism. In G. Newton & S. Levine (Eds.), *Early experience and behavior* (pp. 365–411). Springfield, Ill.: Charles C. Thomas.

Ganz, L., & Riesen, A. H. (1962). Stimulus generalization to hue in the dark-reared macaque. *Journal of Comparative and Physiological Psychology, 55*, 92–99.

Garb, J. J., & Stunkard, A. J. (1974). Taste aversions in man. *American Journal of Psychiatry, 131*, 1204–1207.

Garcia, J. (1988). Food for Tolman: Cognitions and cathexis in concert. In T. Archer & L. G. Nilsson (Eds.), *Aversion, avoidance and anxiety: Perspectives on aversively motivated behavior.* (pp. 45–85). Hillsdale, N.J.: Erlbaum.

Garcia, J., Brett, L. P., & Rusiniak, K. W. (1989). Limits of Darwinian conditioning. In S. B. Klein & R. R. Mowrer (Eds.), *Contemporary learning theories: Instrumental conditioning theory and the impact of biological constraints on learning* (pp. 181–203). Hillsdale, N.J.: Erlbaum.

Garcia, J., Clark, J. C., & Hankins, W. G. (1973). Natural responses to scheduled rewards. In P. P. G. Bateson & P. H. Klopfer (Eds.), *Perspectives in ethology* (pp. 1–41). New York: Plenum.

Garcia, J., & Garcia y Robertson, R. (1985). Evolution of learning mechanisms. In B. L. Hammonds (Ed.), *Psychology and learning.* Washington, D.C.: American Psychological Association.

Garcia, J., Hankins, W. G., & Rusiniak, K. W. (1974). Behavioral regulation of the milieu interne in man and rat. *Science, 185*, 824–831.

Garcia, J., Kimeldorf, D. J., & Hunt, E. L. (1957). Spatial avoidance in the rat as a result of exposure to ionizing radiation. *British Journal of Radiology, 30*, 318–322.

Garcia, J., Kimeldorf, D. J., & Koelling, R. A. (1955). Conditioned aversion to saccharin resulting from exposure to gamma radiation. *Science, 122*, 157–158.

Garcia, J., & Koelling, R. A. (1966). Relation of cue to consequence in avoidance learning. *Psychonomic Science, 4*, 123–124.

Garcia, J., & Rusiniak, K. W. (1980). What the nose learns from the mouth. In D. Muller-Schwarze & R. M. Silverskin (Eds.), *Chemical senses.* New York: Plenum.

Gardner, B. J., & Gardner, R. A. (1971). Two-way communication with an infant chimpanzee. In A. M. Schrier & F. Stolnitz (Eds.), *Behavior of nonhuman primates: Modern research trends.* New York: Academic.

Gardner, B. T., & Gardner, R. A. (1980). Two comparative psychologists look at language acquisition. In K. E. Nelson (Ed.), *Children's language.* New York: Halsted.

Gatchel, R. J., & Proctor, J. D. (1976). Physiological correlates of learned helplessness in man. *Journal of Abnormal Psychology, 85*, 27–34.

Gathercole, S. E., & Baddeley, A. D. (1993). Working memory and language. Hove, England: Erlbaum.

Geiselman, R. E., Bjork, R. A., & Fishman, D. (1983). Disrupted retrieval in directed forgetting: A link with posthypnotic retrieval. *Journal of Experimental Psychology: General, 112*, 58–72.

Gelder, M. (1991). Psychological treatment for anxiety disorders: Adjustment disorder with anxious mood, generalized anxiety disorders, panic disorder, agoraphobia, and avoidant personality disorder. In W. Coryell & G. Winokur (Eds.), *The clinical management of anxiety disorders* (pp. 10–27). New York: Oxford University Press.

Gelfand, D. M., Hartmann, D. P., Lamb, A. K., Smith, C. L., Mahan, M. A., & Paul, S. C. (1974). The effects of adult models and described alternatives on children's choice of behavior management techniques. *Child Development, 45*, 585–593.

Geller, E. S., & Hahn, H. A. (1984). Promoting safety belt use at industrial sites: An effective program for blue collar employees. *Professional Psychology: Research and Practice, 15*, 553–564.

Gentry, G. D., Weiss, B., & Laties, V. G. (1983). The microanalysis of fixed-interval responding. *Journal of the Experimental Analysis of Behavior, 39,* 327–343.

Gessa, G. L., Muntoni, F., Collu, M., Vargiu, L., & Mereu, G. (1985). Low doses of ethanol activate dopaminergic neurons in the ventral tegmental area. *Brain Research, 348,* 201–204.

Gilbert, R. M. (1974). Ubiquity of schedule-induced polydipsia. *Journal of the Experimental Analysis of Behavior, 21,* 277–284.

Girodo, M. (1974). Yoga meditation and flooding in the treatment of anxiety neurosis. *Journal of Behavior Therapy and Experimental Psychiatry, 5,* 157–160.

Glass, A. L., & Holyoak, K. J. (1975). Alternative conceptions of semantic memory. *Cognition, 3,* 313–339.

Glass, A. L., & Holyoak, K. J. (1986). *Cognition.* New York: Random House.

Glasscock, S. G., Friman, P. C., O'Brien, S., & Christopherson, E. F. (1986). Varied citrus treatment of ruminant gagging in a teenager with Batten's disease. *Journal of Behavior Therapy and Experimental Psychiatry, 17,* 129–133.

Gleitman, H. (1971). Forgetting of long-term memories in animals. In W. K. Honig & P. H. R. James (Eds.), *Animal memory* (pp. 2–46). New York: Academic.

Gleitman, H. (1987). *Psychology* (3rd ed.). New York: Norton.

Glueck, S., & Glueck, E. (1950). *Unraveling juvenile delinquency.* Cambridge, Mass.: Harvard University Press.

Goeders, N. E., Lane, J. D., & Smith, J. E. (1984). Self-administration of methionine enkephalin into the nucleus accumbens. *Pharmacology, Biochemistry and Behavior, 20,* 451–455.

Gollin, E. S., & Savoy, P. (1968). Fading procedures and conditional discrimination in children. *Journal of the Experimental Analysis of Behavior, 48,* 371–388.

Gooden, D. R., & Baddeley, A. D. (1975). Context-dependent memory in two natural environments: On land and underwater. *British Journal of Psychology, 66,* 325–331.

Goodman, I. J., & Brown, J. L. (1966). Stimulation of positively and negatively reinforcing sites in the avian brain. *Life Sciences, 5,* 693–704.

Goodwin, D. W., Powell, B., Bremer, D., Hoine, H., & Stein, J. (1969). Alcohol and recall: State-dependent effects in man. *Science, 163,* 1358–1360.

Gorczynski, R. M. (1987). Analysis of lymphocytes in, and host environment of, mice showing conditioned immunosuppression to cyclophosphamide. *Brain, Behavior, and Immunity, 1,* 21–35.

Gordon, W. C. (1983). Malleability of memory in animals. In R. L. Mellgren (Ed.), *Animal cognition and behavior* (pp. 399–426). New York: North Holland.

Gordon, W. C., McCracken, K. M., Dess-Beech, N., & Mowrer, R. R. (1981). Mechanisms for the cueing phenomenon: The addition of the cueing context to the training memory. *Learning and Motivation, 12,* 196–211.

Gormezano, I. (1972). Investigations of defense and reward conditioning in the rabbit. In A. H. Black & W. F. Prokasy (Eds.), *Classical conditioning II: Current theory and research* (pp. 151–181). New York: Academic.

Gormezano, I., Kehoe, E. J., & Marshall, B. S. (1983). Twenty years of classical conditioning research with the rabbit. In J. M. Prague & A. N. Epstein (Eds.), *Progress in psychobiology and physiological psychology* (Vol. 10, pp. 198–265). New York: Academic.

Graham, D. (1989). *Ecological learning theory.* Florence, KY: Taylor & Francis/Routledge.

Granger, R. G., Porter, J. H., & Christoph, N. L. (1983). Adjunctive behavior in children as a function of interreinforcement interval length. Paper presented at Southeastern Psychological Association Convention, Atlanta, Georgia.

Grant, D. A., & Schneider, D. E. (1948). Intensity of the conditioned stimulus and strength of conditioning: I. The conditioned eyelid response to light. *Journal of Experimental Psychology, 38,* 690–696.

Grant, D. A., & Schneider, D. E. (1949). Intensity of the conditioned stimulus and strength of conditioning: II. The conditioned galvanic skin response to an auditory stimulus. *Journal of Experimental Psychology, 39,* 35–40.

Grau, J. W. (1987). The central representation of an aversive event maintains opioid and nonopioid forms of analgesia. *Behavioral Neuroscience, 101,* 272–288.

Greiner, J. M., & Karoly, P. (1976). Effects of self-control training on study activity and academic performance: An analysis of self-monitoring, self-reward, and systematic planning components. *Journal of Counseling Psychology, 23,* 495–502.

Grice, G. R. (1948). The relation of secondary reinforcement to delayed reward in visual discrimination learning. *Journal of Experimental Psychology, 38,* 1–16.

Grice, G. R., & Hunter, J. J. (1964). Stimulus intensity effects depend upon the type of experimental design. *Psychological Review, 71,* 247–256.

Grossen, N. E., Kostensek, D. J., & Bolles, R. C. (1969). Effects of appetitive discriminative stimuli on avoidance behavior. *Journal of Experimental Psychology, 81,* 340–343.

Grossman, S. P. (1967). *A textbook of physiological psychology.* New York: Wiley.

Groves, P. M., Lee, D., & Thompson, R. F. (1969). Effects of stimulus frequency and intensity on habituation and sensitization in acute spinal rat. *Physiology and Behavior, 4,* 383–388.

Groves, P. M., & Thompson, R. F. (1970). Habituation: A dual-process theory. *Psychological Review, 77,* 419–450.

Guthrie, E. R. (1935). *The psychology of learning.* New York: Harper.

Guthrie, E. R. (1942). Conditioning: A theory of learning in terms of stimulus, response, and association. In N. B. Henry (Ed.), *The forty-first year book of the National Society of Education: II. The psychology of learning* (pp. 17–60). Chicago: University of Chicago Press.

Guthrie, E. R. (1959). Association by contiguity. In S. Koch (Ed.), *Psychology: A study of a science,* (vol. 2, pp. 158–195). New York: McGraw-Hill.

Gutman, A., Sutterer, J. R., & Brush, R. (1975). Positive and negative behavioral contrast in the rat. *Journal of the Experimental Analysis of Behavior, 23,* 377–384.

Guttman, N. (1953). Operant conditioning, extinction, and periodic reinforcement in relation to concentration of sucrose used as reinforcing agent. *Journal of Experimental Psychology, 46,* 213–224.

Guttman, N., & Kalish, H. I. (1956). Discriminability and stimulus generalization. *Journal of Experimental Psychology, 51,* 79–88.

Haaga, D. A. F. (1995). Metatraits and cognitive assessment. Application to attributional style and depressive symptoms. *Cognitive Therapy and Research, 19,* 121–142.

Haber, R. N. (1969). Eidetic images, with biographical sketches. *Scientific American, 220,* 36–44.

Hake, D. F., Azrin, N. H., & Oxford, R. (1967). The effects of punishment intensity on squirrel monkeys. *Journal of the Experimental Analysis of Behavior, 10,* 95–107.

Hall, G. (1979). Exposure learning in young and adult laboratory rats. *Animal Behavior, 27,* 586–591.

Hall, G., & Channell, S. (1985). Differential effects of contextual change on latent inhibition and on the habituation of an orienting response. *Journal of Experimental Psychology: Animal Behavior Processes, 11,* 470–481.

Hall, G., & Honey, R. (1989). Perceptual and associative learning. In S. B. Klein & R. R. Mowrer (Eds.), *Contemporary learning theories: Pavlovian conditioning and the status of traditional learning theory* (pp. 117–147). Hillsdale, N.J.: Erlbaum.

Hall, J. F. (1976). *Classical conditioning and instrumental learning: A contemporary approach.* Philadelphia: Lippincott.

Hall, J. F. (1982). *An invitation to learning and memory.* Boston: Allyn & Bacon.

Hammen, C. L., & Krantz, S. (1976). Effect of success and failure on depressive cognitions. *Journal of Abnormal Psychology, 85,* 577–586.

Hammond, L. J. (1966). Increased responding to CS− in differential CER. *Psychonomic Science, 5,* 337–338.

Hanratty, M. A., Liebert, R. M., Morris, L. W., & Fernandez, L. E. (1969). Imitation of film-mediated aggression against live and inanimate victims. *Proceedings of the 77th Annual Convention of the American Psychological Association,* 457–458.

Hanson, H. M. (1959). Effects of discrimination training on stimulus generalization. *Journal of Experimental Psychology, 58,* 321–334.

Hantula, D. A., & Crowell, C. R. (1994). Behavioral contrast in a two-option analogue task of financial decision making. *Journal of Applied Behavior Analysis, 27,* 607–617.

Hardimann, P. T., Dufresne, R., & Mestre, J. (1989). The relation between problem categorization and problem solving among experts and novices. *Memory and Cognition, 17,* 627–638.

Harlow, H. F. (1971). *Learning to love.* San Francisco: Albion.

Harlow, H. F., & Suomi, S. J. (1970). Nature of love—Simplified. *American Psychologist, 25,* 161–168.

Harris, J. E., & Morris, P. E. (1984). *Everyday memory, actions, and absent-mindedness.* London: Academic.

Harris. V. W., & Sherman, J. A. (1973). Use and analysis of the "Good Behavior Game" to reduce disruptive classroom behavior. *Journal of Applied Behavior Analysis, 6,* 405–417.

Hartman, T. F., & Grant, D. A. (1960). Effect of intermittent reinforcement on acquisition, extinction, and spontaneous recovery of the conditioned eyelid response. *Journal of Experimental Psychology, 60,* 89–96.

Hasher, L., & Griffin, M. (1978). Reconstruction and reproductive processes in memory. *Journal of Experimental Psychology: Human Learning and Memory, 4,* 318–330.

Hawkins, R. D., Kandel, E. R., & Seigelbaum, S. A. (1993). Learning to modulate transmitter release: Themes and variations in synaptic plasticity. *Annual Review of Neuroscience, 16,* 625–665.

Hawkins, S. A., & Hastie, R. (1990). Hindsight: Biased judgments of past events after the outcomes are known. *Psychological Bulletin, 107,* 311–327.

Hayes, J. R. (1978). *Cognitive psychology.* Homewood, Ill.: Dorsey.

Hayes, K. J., & Hayes, C. (1951). The intellectual development of a home-raised chimpanzee. *Proceedings of the American Philosophical Society, 95,* 105–109.

Hayes, S. C., & Cone, J. D. (1977). Reducing residential energy use: Payments, information, and feedback. *Journal of Applied Behavior Analysis, 10,* 425–435.

Haygood, R. C., & Bourne, L. E., Jr. (1965). Attribute and rule-learning aspects of conceptual behavior. *Psychological Review, 72,* 175–195.

Heath, R. G. (1955). Correlations between levels of psychological awareness and physiological activity in the central nervous system. *Psychosomatic Medicine, 17,* 383–395.

Helmreich, W. B. (1992). *Against all odds: Holocaust survivors and the successful lives they made in America.* New York: Simon and Schuster.

Helweg, D. A., Roitblat, H. L., Nachtigall, P., & Hautus, M. J. (1996). Recognition of aspect-dependent three-dimensional objects by an echolocating Atlantic Bottleneck dolphin. *Journal of Experimental Psychology: Animal Behavior Processes 22,* 19–31.

Herrnstein, R. J. (1961). Relative and absolute strength of response as a function of frequency of reinforcement. *Journal of the Experimental Analysis of Behavior, 4,* 267–272.

Herrnstein, R. J. (1979). Acquisition, generalization, and discrimination reversal of a natural concept. *Journal of Experimental Psychology: Animal Behavior Processes, 5,* 116–129.

Herrnstein, R. J., & de Villiers, P. A. (1980). Fish as a natural category for people and pigeons. In G. H. Bower (Ed.), *Psychology of learning and motivation* (Vol. 14, pp. 60–97). New York: Academic.

Herrnstein, R. J., Loveland, D. H., & Cable, C. (1976). Natural concepts in pigeons. *Journal of Experimental Psychology: Animal Behavior Processes, 2*, 285–302.

Herrnstein, R. J., & Vaughn, W. (1980). Melioration and behavioral allocation. In J. E. R. Staddon (Ed.), *Limits to action: The allocation of individual behavior* (pp. 143–176). New York: Academic.

Hess, E. H. (1962). Ethology: An approach toward the complete analysis of behavior. In R. Brown, E. Galanter, E. H. Hess, and G. Mandler (Eds.), *New directions in psychology.* New York: Holt.

Hess. E. H. (1964). Imprinting in birds. *Science, 146*, 1128–1139.

Hess, E. H. (1973). *Imprinting.* Princeton, N.J.: Van Nostrand Reinhold.

Hilgard, E. R., & Marquis, D. G. (1940). *Conditioning and learning.* New York: Appleton-Century-Crofts.

Hill, W. F., & Spear, N. E. (1963). Extinction in a runway as a function of acquisition level and reinforcement percentage. *Journal of Experimental Psychology, 65*, 495–500.

Hilton, H. (1986). *The executive memory guide.* New York: Simon and Schuster.

Hines, B., & Paolino, R. M. (1970). Retrograde amnesia: Production of skeletal but not cardiac response gradient by electroconvulsive shock. *Science, 169*, 1224–1226.

Hintzman, D. L., Block, R. A., & Inskeep, N. R. (1972). Memory for mode of input. *Journal of Verbal Learning and Verbal Behavior, 11*, 741–749.

Hiramoto, R. M., Hiramoto, N. S., Solvason, H. B., & Ghanta, V. K. (1987). Regulation of natural immunity (NK activity) by conditioning. *Annals of the New York Academy of Sciences, 496*, 545–552.

Hiroto, D. S. (1974). Locus of control and learned helplessness. *Journal of Experimental Psychology, 102*, 187–193.

Hiroto, D. S., & Seligman, M. E. P. (1975). Generality of learned helplessness in man. *Journal of Personality and Social Psychology, 31*, 311–327.

Hoebel, B. G. (1969). Feeding and self-stimulation: Neural regulation of food and water intake. *Annals of the New York Academy of Sciences, 157*, 758–778.

Hoffman, H. S. (1968). The control of stress vocalization by an imprinting stimulus. *Behavior, 30*, 175–191.

Hoffman, H. S. (1969). Stimulus factors in conditioned suppression. In B. A. Campbell & R. M. Church (Eds.), *Punishment and aversive behavior* (pp. 185–234). New York: Appleton-Century-Crofts.

Hogan, J. A. (1989). Cause and function in the development of behavior systems. In E. M. Blass (Ed.), *Handbook of behavioral and neurobiology* (Vol. 8, pp. 129–174). New York: Plenum Press.

Hokanson, J. E. (1970). Psychophysiological evaluation of the catharsis hypothesis. In E. I. Megargee & J. E. Hokanson (Eds.), *The dynamics of aggression.* New York: Harper & Row.

Holder, H. D., & Garcia, J. (1987). Role of temporal order and odor intensity in taste-potentiated odor aversions. *Behavioral Neuroscience, 101*, 158–163.

Holland, P. C. (1983). Occasion setting in Pavlovian feature discriminations. In M. L. Commons, R. J. Herrnstein, & A. R. Wagner (Eds.), *Quantitative analysis of behavior: Discrimination processes* (Vol. 4, pp. 182–206). New York: Ballinger.

Holland, P. C. (1986). Temporal determinants of occasion setting in feature-positive discriminations. *Animal Learning and Behavior, 14*, 111–120.

Holland, P. C. (1992). Occasion setting in Pavlovian conditioning. In D. L. Medin (Ed.), *The psychology of learning and motivation.* (Vol. 28, pp. 69–125). San Diego, Calif.: Academic Press.

Holland, P. C., & Rescorla, R. A. (1975). The effects of two ways of devaluing the unconditioned stimulus after first- and second-order appetitive conditioning. *Journal of Experimental Psychology: Animal Behavior Processes, 1*, 355–363.

Hollon, S. D., Evans, M. D., & DeRubeis, R. J. (1990). Cognitive mediation of relapse prevention following treatment for depression: Implications of differential risk. In R. E. Ingram (Ed.), *Contemporary psychological approaches to depression: Theory, research, and treatment* (pp. 117–136). New York: Plenum Press.

Holmes, D. (1990). The evidence for repression: An examination of sixty years of research. J. Singer (Ed.), *Repression and dissociation: Implications for personality theory, psychopathology, and health.* Chicago: University of Chicago Press.

Holmgren, B. (1964). Nivel de vigilia y reflecjos condicionados. *Boletin del Instituto de Investigaciones de la Actividad Nerviosa Superior (Havana), 1,* 33–50.

Homel, R., McKay, P., & Henstridge, J. (1995). The impact on accidents of random breath testing in New South Wales; 1982–1992. In C. N. Kloeden & A. J. Mclean (Eds.), *Proceedings of the 13th International Conference on Alcohol, Drugs and Traffic Safety, Adelaide,* 13 August–19 August 1995 (Vol. 2, pp. 849–855). Adelaide, Australia: NHMRC Road Accident Research Unit. The University of Adelaide 5005.

Homme, L. W., de Baca, P. C., Devine, J. V., Steinhorst, R., & Rickert, E. J. (1963). Use of the Premack principle in controlling the behavior of nursery-school children. *Journal of the Experimental Analysis of Behavior, 6,* 544.

Honig, W. K., & Stewart, J. E. (1988). Pigeons can discriminate locations presented in pictures. *Journal of the Experimental Analysis of Behavior, 50,* 541–551.

Honig, W. K., & Stewart, K. E. (1993). Relative numerosity as a dimension of stimulus control: The peak shift. *Animal Learning and Behavior, 21,* 346–354.

Hooks, M. S., Colvin, A. C., Juncos, J. L., & Justice, J. B., Jr. (1992). Individual differences in basal and cocaine-stimulated extracellular dopamine in the nucleus accumbens using quantitative microdialysis. *Brain Research, 587,* 306–312.

Horel, J. A., & Misantone, L. G. (1976). Visual discrimination impaired by cutting temporal lobe connections. *Science, 193,* 336–338.

Horner, R. D., & Keilitz, I. (1975). Training mentally retarded adolescents to brush their teeth. *Journal of Applied Behavior Analysis, 8,* 301–310.

Houston, J. P. (1986). *Fundamentals of learning and memory* (3rd ed.). Orlando, Fla.: Harcourt Brace Jovanovich.

Hoveland, C. I. (1937). The generalization of conditioned responses: IV. The effects of varying amounts of reinforcement upon the degree of generalization of conditioned responses. *Journal of Experimental Psychology, 21,* 261–276.

Howard, D. V. (1983). *Cognitive psychology: Memory, language, and thought.* New York: Macmillan.

Hughes, C. W., Kent, T. A., Campbell, J., Oke, A., Croskill, H., & Preskorn, S. H. (1984). Central blood flow and cerebrovascular permeability in an inescapable shock (learned helplessness) animal model of depression. *Pharmacology, Biochemistry, and Behavior, 21,* 891–894.

Hull, C. L. (1920). Quantitative aspects of the evolution of concepts: An experimental study. *Psychological Monographs, 28,* Whole No. 123.

Hull, C. L. (1943). *Principles of behavior.* New York: Appleton.

Hull, C. L. (1952). *A behavior system.* New Haven, Conn.: Yale University Press.

Hulse, S. H., Jr. (1958). Amount and percentage of reinforcement and duration of goal confinement in conditioning and extinction. *Journal of Experimental Psychology, 56,* 48–57.

Hume, D. (1955). *An inquiry concerning human understanding.* Indianapolis, Ind.: Bobbs-Merrill. (Original work published 1748; "My own life," a brief autobiographical sketch, was originally published 1776.)

Humphreys, L. G. (1939). Acquisition and extinction of verbal expectations in a situation analogous to conditioning. *Journal of Experimental Psychology, 25,* 294–301.

Hurd, Y. L., Keyr, J., & Ungerstedt, U. (1988). In vivo microdialysis as a technique to monitor drug transport: Correlation of extracellular cocaine levels and dopamine overflow in the rat brain. *Journal of Neurochemistry, 51,* 1314–1316.

Hurd, Y. L., & Ungerstedt, U. (1989). Cocaine: An in vivo microdialysis evaluation of its acute action on dopamine transmission in rat striatum. *Synapse, 3,* 48–54.

Hutchinson, R. R., Azrin, N. H., & Hunt, G. M. (1968). Attack produced by intermittent reinforcement of a concurrent operant response. *Journal of the Experimental Analysis of Behavior, 11,* 498–495.

Hyson, R. L., Sickel, J. L., Kulkosky, P. J., & Riley, A. L. (1981). The insensitivity of schedule-induced polydipsia to conditioned taste aversions: Effect of amount consumed during conditioning. *Animal Learning and Behavior, 9,* 281–286.

Innis, N. K. (1979). Stimulus control of behavior during postreinforcement pause of FI schedules. *Animal Learning and Behavior, 7,* 203–210.

Jackson, R. L., Alexander, J. H., & Maier, S. F. (1980). Learned helplessness, inactivity, and associative deficits: Effects of inescapable shock on response choice escape learning. *Journal of Experimental Psychology: Animal Behavior Processes, 6,* 1–20.

Jacobson, E. (1938). *Progressive relaxation.* Chicago: University of Chicago Press.

Jacquet, Y. F. (1972). Schedule-induced licking during multiple schedules. *Journal of the Experimental Analysis of Behavior, 17,* 413–423.

Jaffe, P. G., & Carlson, P. M. (1972). Modelling therapy for text anxiety: The role of affect and consequences. *Behavior Research and Therapy, 10,* 329–339.

James, W. A. (1890). *The principles of psychology, I and II.* New York: Holt.

Jason, L. A., Ji, P. Y., Anes, M. D., & Birkhead, S. H. (1991). Active enforcement of cigarette control laws in the prevention of cigarette sales to minors. *Journal of the American Medical Association, 266* (22), 3159–3161.

Jason, L. A., Ji, P. Y., Anes, M. D., & Xaverius, P. (1992). Assessing cigarette sales rates to minors. *Evaluation and the Health Professions, 15,* 375–384.

Jaynes, J. (1956). Imprinting: The interaction of learned and innate behavior: I. Development and generalization. *Journal of Comparative and Physiological Psychology, 49,* 201–206.

Jenkins, H. M., Barnes, R. A., & Barrera, F. J. (1981). Why autoshaping depends on trial spacing. In C. M. Locurto, H. S. Terrace, & J. Gibbon (Eds.), *Autoshaping and conditioning theory* (pp. 255–284). New York: Academic.

Jenkins, H. M., & Harrison, R. H. (1960). Effect of discrimination training on auditory generalization. *Journal of Experimental Psychology, 59,* 246–273.

Jenkins, H. M., & Moore, B. R. (1973). The form of the autoshaped response with food or water reinforcers. *Journal of the Experimental Analysis of Behavior, 20,* 163–181.

Jenkins, J. G., & Dallenbach, K. M. (1924). Obliviscence during sleep and waking. *American Journal of Psychology, 35,* 605–612.

Jenkins, J. J., Mink, W. D., & Russell, W. A. (1958). Associative clustering as a function of verbal association strength. *Psychological Reports, 4,* 127–136.

Jenkins, W. O., McFann, H., & Clayton, F. L. (1950). A methodological study of extinction following aperiodic and continuous reinforcement. *Journal of Comparative and Physiological Psychology, 43,* 155–167.

Johnson, E. E. (1952). The role of motivational strength in latent learning. *Journal of Comparative and Physiological Psychology, 45,* 526–530.

Johnson, J. S., & Newport, E. L. (1989). Critical period effects in second language learning: The influence of maturational state on the acquisition of English as a second language. *Cognitive Psychology, 21,* 60–99.

Jones, M. C. (1924). The elimination of children's fears. *Journal of Experimental Psychology, 7,* 383–390.

Jones, R. S., & Eayrs, C. B. (1992). The use of errorless learning procedures in teaching people with a learning disability: A critical review. *Mental Handicap Research, 5,* 204–212.

Kahneman, D., Slovic, P., & Tversky, A. (Eds.). (1982). *Judgment under uncertainty: Heuristics and biases.* New York: Cambridge University Press.

Kahneman, D., & Tversky, A. (1972). Subjective probability: A judgment of representativeness. *Cognitive Psychology, 3,* 430–454.

Kahneman, D., & Tversky, A. (1973). On the psychology of prediction. *Psychological Review, 80,* 237–251.

Kako, E. (1999). Elements of syntax in the systems of three language–trained animals. *Animal Learning and Behavior, 27,* 1–14.

Kalat, J. W., & Rozin, P. (1971). Role of interference in taste-aversion learning. *Journal of Comparative and Physiological Psychology, 77,* 53–58.

Kalat, J. W., & Rozin, P. (1973). "Learned safety" as a mechanism in long-delay learning in rats. *Journal of Comparative and Physiological Psychology, 83,* 198–207.

Kalish, H. I. (1969). Stimulus generalization. In M. H. Mary (Ed.), *Learning: processes.* London: Macmillan.

Kalish, H. I. (1981). *From behavioral science to behavior modification.* New York: McGraw-Hill.

Kallman, W. M., Hersen, M., & O'Toole, D. H. (1975). The use of social reinforcement in a case of conversion reaction. *Behavior Therapy, 6,* 411–413.

Kamin, L. J. (1954). Traumatic avoidance learning: The effects of CS-UCS interval with a trace-conditioning procedure. *Journal of Comparative and Physiological Psychology, 47,* 65–72.

Kamin, L. J. (1956). The effects of termination of the CS and avoidance of the US on avoidance learning. *Journal of Comparative and Physiological Psychology, 49,* 420–424.

Kamin, L. J. (1957). The retention of an incompletely learned avoidance response. *Journal of Comparative and Physiological Psychology, 50,* 457–460.

Kamin, L. J. (1968). "Attention-like" processes in classical conditioning. In M. R. Jones (Ed.), *Miami symposium on the prediction of behavior: Aversive stimulation* (pp. 9–31). Miami: University of Miami Press.

Kamin, L. J., Brimer, C. J., & Black, A. H. (1963). Conditioned suppression as a monitor of fear of the CS in the course of avoidance training. *Journal of Comparative and Physiological Psychology, 56,* 497–501.

Kamin, L. J., & Schaub, R. E. (1963). Effects of conditioned stimulus intensity on the conditioned emotional response. *Journal of Comparative and Physiological Psychology, 56,* 502–507.

Kanarek, R. B. (1974). The energetics of meal patterns. Unpublished doctoral dissertation, Rutgers—The State University, New Brunswick.

Kaplan, M., Jackson, B., & Sparer, R. (1965). Escape behavior under continuous reinforcement as a function of aversive light intensity. *Journal of the Experimental Analysis of Behavior, 8,* 321–323.

Katcher, A. H., Solomon, R. L., Turner, L. H., LoLordo, V. M., Overmeir, J. B., & Rescorla, R. A. (1969). Heart-rate and blood pressure responses to signaled and unsignaled shocks: Effects of cardiac sympathetomy. *Journal of Comparative and Physiological Psychology, 42,* 163–174.

Kaufman, E. L., Lord, M. W., Reese, T. W., & Volkmann, Jr. (1949). The discrimination of visual number. *American Journal of Psychology, 62,* 498–525.

Kaufman, M. A., & Bolles, R. C. (1981). A nonassociative aspect of overshadowing. *Bulletin of the Psychonomic Society, 18,* 318–320.

Kazdin, A. E. (1972). Response cost: The removal of conditioned reinforcers for therapeutic change. *Behavior Therapy, 3,* 533–546.

Kazdin, A. E. (1974a). Covert modeling, modeling similarity, and reduction of avoidance behavior. *Behavior Therapy, 5,* 325–340.

Kazdin, A. E. (1974b). Effects of covert modeling, multiple models, and model reinforcement on assertive behavior. *Behavior Therapy 7,* 211–222.

Kazdin, A. E. (1982). History of behavior modification. In A. S. Bellack, M. Hersen, & A. E. Kazdin (Eds.), *International handbook of behavior modification and behavior therapy.* New York: Plenum.

Keele, S. W., & Chase, W. G. (1967). Short-term visual storage. *Perception and Psychophysics, 2,* 383–385.

Keith-Lucas, T., & Guttman, N. (1975). Robust-single-trial delayed backward conditioning. *Journal of Comparative and Physiological Psychology, 88,* 468–476.

Keller, F. S., & Hull, L. M. (1936). Another "insight" experiment. *Journal of Genetic Psychology, 48,* 484–489.

Kellogg, W. N., & Kellogg, L. A. (1933). *The ape and the child.* New York: McGraw-Hill.

Kendler, H. H., & Gasser, W. P. (1948). Variables in spatial learning: I. Number of reinforcements during training. *Journal of Comparative and Physiological Psychology, 41,* 178–187.

Kenny, F. T., Solyom, L., & Solyom, C. (1973). Faradic disruption of obsessive ideation in the treatment of obsessive neurosis. *Behavior Therapy, 4,* 448–457.

Keppel, G., & Underwood, B. J. (1962). Proactive inhibition in short-term retention of single items. *Journal of Verbal Learning and Verbal Behavior, 1,* 153–161.

Kihlstrom, J. F. (1998). Exhumed memory. In S. J. Lynn & K. M. McConkey (Eds.), *Truth in memory* (pp. 3–31). New York: Guilford.

Kimble, G. A. (1961). *Hilgard and Marguis's conditioning and learning* (2nd ed.). New York: Appleton-Century-Crofts.

Kimble, G. A., & Reynolds, B. (1967). Eyelid conditioning as a function of the interval between conditioned and unconditioned stimuli. In G. A. Kimble (Ed.), *Foundations of conditioning and learning.* New York: Appleton-Century-Crofts.

Kimmel, H. D. (1965). Instrumental inhibitory factors in classical conditioning. In W. F. Prokasy (Ed.), *Classical conditioning: A symposium* (pp. 148–171). New York: Appleton-Century-Crofts.

King, G. D. (1974). Wheel running in the rat induced by a fixed-time presentation of water. *Animal Learning and Behavior, 2,* 325–328.

King, M. G., Husband, A. J., & Kusnecov, A. W. (1987). Behaviorally conditioned immunosuppression using antilymphocyte serum: Duration of effect and role of corticosteriods. *Medical Science Research, 15,* 407–408.

Kintsch, W. (1974). *The representation of meaning in memory.* Hillsdale, N.J.: Erlbaum.

Kintsch, W. (1980). Semantic memory: A tutorial. In T. D. Nickerson (Ed.), *Attention and performance VIII,* (pp. 595–620). Hillsdale, N.J.: Erlbaum.

Kintsch, W., & Witte, R. S. (1962). Concurrent conditioning of bar-press and salivation responses. *Journal of Comparative and Physiological Psychology, 55,* 963–968.

Kirkpatrick-Steger, J., Wasserman, E. A., & Biederman, I. (1996). Effects of spatial rearrangement of object components on picture recognition in pigeons. *Journal of the Experimental Analysis of Behavior, 65,* 465–475.

Klein, D. C., & Seligman, M. E. P. (1976). Reversal of performance deficits and perceptual deficits in learned helplessness and depression. *Journal of Abnormal Psychology, 85,* 11–26.

Klein, S. B. (1972). Adrenal-pituitary influence in reaction of avoidance-learning memory in the rat after intermediate intervals. *Journal of Comparative and Physiological Psychology, 79,* 341–359.

Klein, S. B. (2000). *Biological psychology,* Upper Saddle River, N.J.: Prentice-Hall.

Klein, S. B., Domato, G. C., Hallstead, C., Stephens, I., & Mikulka, P. J. (1975). Acquisition of a conditioned aversion as a function of age and measurement technique. *Physiological Psychology, 3*, 379–384.

Klein, S. B., Freda, J. S., Mikulka, P. J. (1985). The influence of a taste cue on an environmental aversion: Potentiation or overshadowing? *Psychological Record, 35*, 101–112.

Klein, S. B., & Spear, N. E. (1970). Forgetting by the rat after intermediate intervals ("Kamin effect") as retrieval failure. *Journal of Comparative and Physiological Psychology, 71*, 165–170.

Kline, S., & Groninger, L. D. (1991). The imagery bizarreness effect as a function of sentence complexity and presentation time. *Bulletin of the Psychonomic Society, 29*, 25–27.

Klopfer, P. H. (1971). Imprinting: Determining its perceptual basis in ducklings. *Journal of Comparative and Physiological Psychology, 75*, 378–385.

Klopfer, P. H., Adams, D. K., & Klopfer, M. S. (1964). Maternal "imprinting" in goats. *National Academy of Science Proceedings, 52*, 911–914.

Knecht v. Gillman, 488 F. 2nd 1136 (8th Cir. 1973).

Knutson, J. F., & Kleinknecht, R. A. (1970). Attack during differential reinforcement of low rate of responding. *Psychonomic Science, 19*, 289–290.

Kohlenberg, R. J. (1970). The punishment of persistent vomiting: A case study. *Journal of Applied Behavior Analysis, 3*, 241–245.

Kohler, W. (1925). *The mentality of apes.* London: Routledge & Kegan Paul.

Kohler, W. (1939). Simple structural functions in the chimpanzee and the chicken. In W. D. Ellis (Ed.), *A source book of gestalt psychology* (pp. 217–227). New York: Harcourt Brace.

Kolers, F. A. (1979). A pattern-analyzing basis of recognition. In L. S. Cermak and F. I. M. Craik (Eds.), *Levels of processing human memory.* Hillsdale, N.J.: Erlbaum.

Konarski, E. A., Jr. (1985). The use of response deprivation to increase the academic performance of EMR students. *The Behavior Therapist, 8*, 61.

Konarski, E. A., Jr., Crowell, C. R., & Duggan, L. M. (1985). The use of response deprivation to the academic performance of EMR students. *Applied Research in Mental Retardation, 6*, 15–31.

Konarski, E. A., Jr., Johnson, M. R., Crowell, C. R., & Whitman, T. L. (1980). Response deprivation, reinforcement, and instrumental academic performance in an EMR classroom. *Behavior Therapy, 13*, 94–102.

Koob, G. F. (1992). Drugs of abuse: Anatomy, pharmacology, and function of reward pathways. *Trends in Pharmacological Science, 13*, 177–184.

Koob, G. F., & Bloom, F. E. (1983). Behavioral effects of opioid peptides. *British Medical Bulletin, 39*, 89–94.

Koob, G. F., Pettit, H. O., Ettenberg, A., & Bloom, F. E. (1984). Effects of opiate antagonist and their quaternary derivatives on heroin self-administration in the rat. *Journal of Pharmacology and Experimental Therapeutics, 229*, 481–486.

Korsakoff, S. S. (1889). Etude médico-psychologique sur une forme des maladies de la mémoire. *Revue philosophique, 5*, 501–530.

Kovach, J. K., & Hess, E. H. (1963). Imprinting: Effects of painful stimulation upon the following response. *Journal of Comparative and Physiological Psychology, 56*, 461–464.

Krakauer, J. (1997). *Into thin air.* New York: Villard.

Krank, M. D., & MacQueen, G. M. (1988). Conditioned compensatory responses elicited by environmental signals for cyclophosphamide-induced suppression of antibody production in mice. *Psychobiology, 16*, 229–235.

Krechevsky, I. (1932). "Hypotheses" in rats. *Psychological Review, 39*, 516–532.

Kubena, R. K., & Barry, H. (1969). Generalization by rats of alcohol and atropine stimulus characteristics to other drugs. *Psychopharmalogia, 15*, 196–206.

Kucharski, D., & Spear, N. E. (1985). Potentiation and overshadowing in preweanling and adult rats. *Journal of Experimental Psychology: Animal Behavior Processes, 11*, 15–34.

Kusnecov, A. V., Sivyer, M., King, M. G., Husband, A. J., Cripps, A. W., & Clancy, R. L. (1983). Behaviorally conditioned suppression of the immune response by antilymphocyte serum. *Journal of Immunology, 130*, 2117–2120.

Lang, P. J. (1978). Self-efficacy theory: Thoughts on cognition and unification. In S. Rachman (Ed.), *Advances in behaviour research and therapy* (Vol. 1, pp. 187–192). Oxford: Pergamon.

Lang, P. J., & Melamed, B. G. (1969). Avoidance conditioning of an infant with chronic ruminative vomiting. *Journal of Abnormal Psychology, 74*, 1–8.

Langer, E. J. (1983). *The psychology of control.* Beverly Hills, Calif.: Sage.

Larew, M. B. (1986). Inhibitory learning in Pavlovian backward conditioning procedures involving a small number of US-CS trials. Unpublished doctoral dissertation, Yale University, New Haven, Conn.

Larzelere, R. E. (1996). A review of the outcomes of parental use of nonabusive or customary physical punishment. *Pediatrics, 98*, 824–828.

Larzelere, R. E., Schneider, W. N., Larson, D. B., & Pike, L. (1996). The effects of discipline responses in delaying toddler misbehavior recurrences. *Child and Family Behavior Therapy, 18*, 35–57.

Lashley, K. S. (1929). *Brain mechanisms and intelligence.* Chicago: University of Chicago Press.

Lashley, K. S. (1950). In search of the engram. *Symposia of the Society for Experimental Biology, 4*, 454–482.

Lashley, K. S., & Wade, M. (1946). The Pavlovian theory of generalization. *Psychological Review, 53*, 72–87.

Lasky, R. E., Syrdal-Lasky, A., & Klein, R. E. (1975). VOT discrimination by four- to six-and-a-half-month-old infants from Spanish environments. *Journal of Experimental Child Psychology, 20*, 215–225.

Lawrence, D. H., & DeRivera, J. (1954). Evidence for relational transposition. *Journal of Comparative and Physiological Psychology, 47*, 465–471.

Lazarus, A. A. (1971). *Behavior therapy and beyond.* New York: McGraw-Hill.

Le, A. D., Poulos, C. X., & Cappell, H. (1979). Conditioned tolerance to the hypothermic effect of ethyl alcohol. *Science, 206*, 1109–1110.

Leahey, T. H., & Harris, R. J. (2001). *Learning and cognition* (5th ed.). Upper Saddle River, N.J.: Prentice-Hall.

Leff, R. (1969). Effects of punishment intensity and consistency on the internalization of behavioral suppression in children. *Developmental Psychology, 1*, 345–356.

Lefkowitz, M. M., Walder, L. O., & Eron, L. D. (1963). Punishment, identification, and aggression. *Merill-Palmer Quarterly, 9*, 159–174.

Lehnert, H., Reinstein, D. K., Strowbridge, B. W., & Wurtman, R. J. (1984). Neurochemical and behavioral consequences of acute, uncontrollable stress: Effects of dietary tyrosine. *Brain Research, 303*, 215–223.

Lenneberg, E. H. (1967). *Biological foundations of language.* New York: Wiley.

Lenneberg, E. H. (1969). On explaining language. *Science, 164*, 635–643.

Lett, B. T. (1982). Taste potentiation in poison-avoidance learning. In R. Herrnstein (Ed.), *Harvard symposium on quantitative analysis of behavior* (Vol. 4). Hillsdale, N.J.: Erlbaum.

Levi, A. S., & Pryor, J. B. (1987). Use of the availability heuristic in probability estimates of future events. *Organizational Behavior and Human Decision Processes, 40*, 219–234.

Levine, M. (1966). Hypothesis behavior by humans during discrimination learning. *Journal of Experimental Psychology, 71*, 331–338.

Levis, D. J. (1976). Learned helplessness: A reply and an alternative S-R interpretation. *Journal of Experimental Psychology: General, 105,* 47–65.

Levis, D. J. (1989). The case for a return to a two-factor theory of avoidance: The failure of nonfear interpretations. From S. B. Klein and R. R. Mowrer (Eds.), *Contemporary learning theories: Pavlovian conditioning and the status of traditional learning theory* (pp. 227–277). Hillsdale, N.J.: Erlbaum.

Levis, D. J., & Boyd, T. L. (1979). Symptom maintenance: An intrahuman analysis and extension of the conservation of anxiety principle. *Journal of Abnormal Psychology, 88,* 107–120.

Levitsky, D., & Collier, G. (1968). Schedule-induced wheel running. *Physiology and Behavior, 3,* 571–573.

Lewis, D. J. (1952). Partial reinforcement in the gambling situation. *Journal of Experimental Psychology, 43,* 447–450.

Lewis, D. J. (1959). A control for the direct manipulation of the fractional anticipatory goal response. *Psychological Reports, 5,* 753–756.

Lewis, D. J. (1960). Partial reinforcement: A selective review of the literature since 1950. *Psychological Bulletin, 57,* 1–28.

Lewis, D. J., & Duncan, C. P. (1958). Expectation and resistance to extinction of a lever-pulling response as a function of percentage of reinforcement and amount of reward. *Journal of Experimental Psychology, 55,* 121–128.

Liberman, R. P., & Raskin, D. E. (1971). Depression: A Behavioral formulation. *Archives of General Psychiatry, 24,* 515–523.

Lindsay, D. S., & Poole, D. A. (Fall 1995). Remembering childhood sexual abuse in therapy: Psychotherapists' self-reports, beliefs, practices, and experiences. *Journal of Psychiatry and Law,* 461–476.

Lindsey, G., & Best, P. (1973). Overshadowing of the less salient of two novel fluids in a taste-aversion paradigm. *Physiological Psychology, 1,* 13–15.

Locke, J. (1964). *An essay concerning human understanding.* New York: New American Library. (Original work published 1690.)

Loftus, E. F. (1975). Leading questions and the eyewitness report. *Cognitive Psychology, 7,* 560—572.

Loftus, E. F. (1980). *Memory.* Reading, Mass.: Addison-Wesley.

Loftus, E. F. (1992). When a lie becomes memory's truth: Memory distortion after exposure to misinformation. *Psychological Science, 3,* 121–123.

Loftus, E. F. (1997). Repressed memory accusations: Devastated families and devastated patients. *Applied Cognitive Psychology, 11,* 25–30.

Loftus, E. F. (1998). The price of bad memories. *Skeptical Inquirer, 22,* 23–24.

Loftus, E. F., & Coan, D. (1994). The construction of childhood memories. In D. Peters (Ed.), *The child witness in context: Cognitive, social and legal perspectives.* New York: Kluwer.

Loftus, E. F., Levidow, B., & Duensing, S. (1992). Who remembers best? Individual differences in memory for events that occurred in a science museum. *Applied Cognitive Psychology, 6,* 93–107.

Loftus, E. F., & Zanni, G. (1975). Eyewitness testimony: The influence of the wording of a question. *Bulletin of the Psychonomic Society, 15,* 86–88.

Logan, F. A. (1952). The role of delay of reinforcement in determining reaction potential. *Journal of Experimental Psychology, 43,* 393–399.

Logan, F. A. (1960). *Incentive.* New Haven, Conn: Yale University Press.

Logue, A. W. (1985). Conditioned food aversion learning in humans. In N. S. Braveman & P. Bronstein (Eds.), Experimental assessment and clinical applications of conditioned food aversions. *Annals of the New York Academy of Sciences, 443,* 316–329.

Logue, A. W., Ophir, I., & Strauss, K. E. (1981). The acquisition of taste aversions in humans. *Behaviour Research and Therapy, 19,* 319–333.

Long, D., & Allen, G. A. (1973). Relative effects of acoustic and semantic relatedness on clustering free recall. *Bulletin of the Psychonomic Society, 1,* 316–318.

Lorayne, H., & Lucas, J. (2000). *The memory book.* New York: Ballantine.

Lorenz, K. (1935). Der Kumpan in der Umwelt des Vogels. *Journal of Ornithology, 83,* 137–213, 289–413.

Lorenz, K. (1950). The comparative method of studying innate behavior patterns. In Society for Experimental Biology, Symposium No. 4, *Physiological mechanisms in animal behaviour.* New York: Academic.

Lorenz, K. (1952). The past twelve years in the comparative study of behavior. In C. H. Schiller (Ed.), *Instinctive behavior* (pp. 288–317). New York: International Universities Press.

Lorenz, K. (1969). Innate bases of learning. In K. H. Pibram (Ed.), *On the biology of learning.* New York: Harcourt, Brace, & World.

Lorenz, K. (1970). Companions as factors in the bird's environment. In R. Martin (Trans.), *Studies in animal and human behaviour* (Vol. 1). Cambridge, Mass.: Harvard University Press.

Lorenz, K., & Tinbergen, N. (1938). Taxis und Instinkhandlung in der Eirollbewegung der Graigrans. *Zeitschrift fur Tierpsychologie, 2,* 1–29.

Lovaas, O. I., Koegel, R., Simmons, J. Q., & Long, J. S. (1973). Some generalization and follow-up measures on autistic children in behavior therapy. *Journal of Applied Behavior Analysis, 6,* 131–166.

Lovaas, O. I., & Simmons, J. Q. (1969). Manipulation of self-destruction in three retarded children. *Journal of Applied Behavior Analysis, 2,* 143–157.

Lovitt, T. C., Guppy, T. E., & Blattner, J. E. (1969). The use of free-time contingency with fourth graders to increase spelling accuracy. *Behaviour Research and Therapy, 7,* 151–156.

Lubow, R. E. (1989). *Latent inhibition and conditioned attention theory.* Cambridge, England: Cambridge University Press.

Lubow, R. E., & Moore, A. U. (1959). Latent inhibition: The effect of nonreinforced preexposure to the conditioned stimulus. *Journal of Comparative and Physiological Psychology, 52,* 415–419.

Luchins, A. S. (1942). Mechanization in problem solving. *Psychological Monographs, 54,* Whole No. 248.

Luthans, F., Paul, R., & Baker, D. (1981). An experimental analysis of the impact of contingent reinforcement of salespersons' performance behavior. *Journal of Applied Psychology, 66,* 314–323.

Lynch, G. (1986). *Synapses, circuits, and the beginnings of memory.* Cambridge: MIT Press.

Lynch, G., & Baudry, M. (1984). The biochemistry of memory: A new and specific hypothesis. *Science, 224,* 1057–1063.

Lysle, D. T., & Maslonek, K. A. (1991). Immune alterations induced by a conditioned aversive stimulus: Evidence for a time-dependent effect. *Psychobiology, 19,* 339–344.

MacCorquodale, K., & Meehl, P. E. (1954). Edward C. Tolman. In W. K. Estes, et al. (Eds.), *Modern learning theory* (pp. 177–266). New York: Appleton-Century-Crofts.

Mace, F. C., Neef, N. A., Shade, D., & Mauro, B. C. (1996). Effects of problem difficulty and reinforcer quality on time allocated to concurrent arithmetic problems. *Journal of Applied Behavior Analysis, 27,* 585–596.

Mackintosh, N. J. (1975). A theory of attention: Variations in the associability of stimuli with reinforcement. *Psychological Review, 82,* 276–298.

Mackintosh, N. J. (1983). *Conditioning and associative learning.* Oxford: Oxford University Press.

MacPherson, E. M., Candee, B. L., & Hohman, R. J. (1974). A comparison of three methods for eliminating disruptive lunchroom behavior. *Journal of Applied Behavior Analysis, 7*, 287–297.

Maddux, J. E., & Stanley, M. A. (1986). Self-efficacy theory in contemporary psychology: An overview. *Journal of Social and Clinical Psychology, 4*, 249–255.

Madsen, C. H., Madsen, C. K., Saudargas, R. A., Hammond, W. R., & Edgar, D. E. (1970). Classroom RAID (Rules, Approval, Ignore, Disapproval): A cooperative approach for professionals and volunteers. *Journal of School Psychology, 8*, 180.

Maier, N. R. F. (1931). Reasoning in humans: II. The solution of a problem and its appearance in consciousness. *Journal of Comparative Psychology, 12*, 181–194.

Maier, S. F., & Seligman, M. E. P. (1976). Learned helplessness: Theory and evidence. *Journal of Experimental Psychology: General, 105*, 3–46.

Major, R., & White, N. (1978). Memory facilitation by self-stimulation reinforcement mediated by nigrostriatal bundle. *Physiology and Behavior, 20*, 723–733.

Maki, R. (1990). Memory for script actions: Effects of relevance and detail expectancy. *Memory and Cognition, 18*, 5–14.

Maki, W. S., & Hegvik, D. K. (1980). Directed forgetting in pigeons. *Animal Learning and Behavior, 8*, 567–574.

Malamut, B. L., Saunders, R. C., & Mishkin, M. (1984). Monkeys with combined amygdalo-lesions succeed in object discriminations learning despite 24-hour interval. *Behavioral Neuroscience, 98*, 759–769.

Malleson, N. (1959). Panic and phobia. *Lancet, 1*, 225–227.

Malmo, R. B. (1965). Finger sweat prints in differentiation of low and high incentive. *Psychophysiology, 1*, 231–240.

Malmquist, C. P. (1986). Children who witness parental murder. Posttraumatic aspects. *Journal of the American Academy of Child Psychiatry, 25*, 320–325.

Maloney, D. M., Harper, T. M., Braukmann, C. M., Fixsen, D. L., Phillips, E. L., & Wolf, M. M. (1976). Teaching conversation-related skills to predelinquent girls. *Journal of Applied Behavior Analysis, 9*, 371.

Margules, D. L., & Stein, L. (1967). Neuroleptics versus tranquilizers: Evidence from animal behavior studies of mode and site of action. In H. Brill, et al., (Eds.), *Neuropsychopharmacology.* Amsterdam: Elsevier.

Margules, D. L., & Stein, L. (1969). Cholinergic synapses of a periventricular punishment system in the medial hypothalamus. *American Journal of Physiology, 217*, 475–480.

Marks, J. M. (1987). *Fears, phobias, and rituals: Panic, anxiety, and their disorders.* New York: Oxford University Press.

Marshall, W. L., Boutilier, J., & Minnes, P. (1974). The modification of phobic behavior by covert reinforcement. *Behavior Therapy, 5*, 469–480.

Martin, G., & Pear, J. (1992). *Behavior modification: What it is and how to do it.* Englewood Cliffs, N.J.: Prentice-Hall.

Martin, L. K., & Riess, D. (1969). Effects of US intensity during previous discrete delay conditioning on conditioned acceleration during avoidance extinction. *Journal of Comparative and Physiological Psychology, 69*, 196–200.

Marx, J. L. (1980). Ape-language controversy flares up. *Science, 207*, 1330–1333.

Masters, J. C., Burish, T. G., Hollon, S. D., & Rimm, D. C. (1987). *Behavior therapy: Techniques and empirical findings* (3rd ed.). San Diego, Calif.: Harcourt, Brace, Jovanovich.

Masterson, F. A. (1969). Escape from noise. *Psychological Reports, 24*, 484–486.

Matzel, L. D., Brown, A. M., & Miller, R. R. (1987). Associative effects of US preexposure: Modulation of conditioned responding by an excitatory training context. *Journal of Experimental Psychology: Animal Behavior Processes, 13*, 65–72.

Matzel, L. D., Schachtman, T. R., & Miller, R. R. (1985). Recovery of an overshadowed association achieved by extinction of the overshadowing stimulus. *Learning and Motivation, 16,* 398–412.

Mayer, J. (1953). Genetic, traumatic, and environmental factors in the etiology of obesity. *Psychological Review, 33,* 472–508.

McAllister, W. R., McAllister, D. E., & Douglass, W. K. (1971). The inverse relationship between shock intensity and shuttle-box avoidance learning in rats. *Journal of Comparative and Physiological Psychology, 74,* 426–433.

McCalden, M., & Davis, C. (1972). *Report on priority lane experiment on the San Francisco-Oakland Bay Bridge.* Sacramento, Calif.: Department of Public Works.

McCarron, L. R. (1973). Psychophysiological discriminants of reactive depression. *Psychophysiology, 10,* 223–230.

McCloskey, M., Wible, C. G., & Cohen, N. J. (1988). Is there a special flashbulb-memory mechanism? *Journal of Experimental Psychology: General, 117,* 171–181.

McCord, W., McCord, J., & Zola, I. K. (1959). *Origins of crime: A new evaluation of the Cambridge-Somerville Youth Study.* New York: Columbia University Press.

McGaugh, J. L., & Landfield, P. W. (1970). Delayed development of amnesia following electroconvulsive shock. *Physiology and Behavior, 5,* 1109–1113.

McGeoch, J. A. (1932). Forgetting and the law of disuse. *Psychological Review 39,* 352–370.

McIlvane, W. J., Kledaras, J. B., Iennaco, F. M., McDonald, S. J., & Stoddard, L. T. (1995). Some possible limits on errorless discrimination reversals in individuals with severe mental retardation. *American Journal of Mental Retardation, 99,* 430–436.

McNeill, D. (1966). Developmental psycholinguistics. In F. Smith & G. A. Miller (Eds.), *The genesis of language* (pp. 15–84). Cambridge, Mass.: MIT Press.

McSweeney, F. K., & Melville, C. L. (1988). Positive contrast as a function of component duration using a within-session procedure. *Behavioural Processes, 16,* 21–41.

Medin, D. L., & Ross, B. H. (1992). *Cognitive psychology* (2nd ed.). Fort Worth, Tex.: Harcourt Brace Jovanovich.

Meichenbaum, D. H. (1972). Examination of model characteristics in reducing avoidance behavior. *Journal of Behavior Therapy and Experimental Psychiatry, 3,* 225–227.

Melamed, B. G., & Siegel, L. J. (1975). Reduction of anxiety in children facing hospitalization and surgery by use of filmed modeling. *Journal of Consulting and Clinical Psychology, 43,* 511–521.

Mellgren, R. L. (1972). Positive and negative contrast effects using delayed reinforcement. *Learning and Motivation, 3,* 185–193.

Melton, A. W. (1963). Implications of short-term memory for a general theory of memory. *Journal of Verbal Learning and Verbal Behavior, 2,* 1–21.

Melton, A. W., & Irwin, J. M. (1940). The influence of degree of interpolated learning on retroactive inhibition and the overt transfer of specific responses. *American Journal of Psychology, 53,* 173–203.

Mendelson, J. (1967). Lateral hypothalamic stimulation in satiated rats: The rewarding effects of self-induced drinking. *Science, 157,* 1077–1979.

Mendelson, J., & Chorover, S. L. (1965). Lateral hypothalamic stimulation in satiated rats: T-maze learning for food. *Science, 149,* 559–561.

Mereu, G., Yoon, K-W-P., Boi, V., Gessa, G. L., Naes, L., & Westfall, T. C. (1987). Preferential stimulation of ventral tegmental area dopaminergic neurons by nicotine. *European Journal of Pharmacology, 141,* 395–400.

Merikle, P. M. (1980). Selection from visual persistence by perceptual groups and category membership. *Journal of Experimental Psychology: General, 109,* 279–295.

Merzenich, M. M., Jenkins, W. M., William, M., Johnston, P., Schreiner, C., Miller, S. L., & Tallal, P. (1996). Temporal processing deficits of language-learning impaired children ameliorated by training. *Science, 271,* 77–81.

Metalsky, G. I., Abramson, L. Y., Seligman, M. E. P., Semmel, A., & Peterson, C. (1982). Attributional styles and life events in the classroom: Vulnerability and invulnerability to depressive mood reactions. *Journal of Personality and Social Psychology, 43,* 612–617.

Meyer, D. E., & Schvaneveldt, R. W. (1971). Facilitation in recognizing pairs of words: Evidence of a dependence between retrieval operations. *Journal of Experimental Psychology, 90,* 227–234.

Meyer, V., Robertson, J., & Tatlovy, A. (1975). Home treatment of an obsessive-compulsive disorder by response prevention. *Journal of Behavior Therapy and Experimental Psychiatry, 6,* 37–38.

Mikulka, P. J., Leard, B., & Klein, S. B. (1977). The effect of illness (US) exposure as a source of interference with the acquisition and retention of a taste aversion. *Journal of Experimental Psychology: Animal Behavior Processes, 3,* 189–210.

Miles, R. C. (1956). The relative effectiveness of secondary reinforcers throughout deprivation and habit-strength parameters. *Journal of Comparative and Physiological Psychology, 49,* 126–130.

Miller, G. A. (1956). The magical number seven, plus or minus two: Some limits on our capacity for processing information. *Psychology Review, 63,* 81–97.

Miller, G. A. (1965). Some preliminaries to psycholinguistics. *American Psychologist, 20,* 15–20.

Miller, N. E. (1941). The frustration-aggression hypothesis. *Psychological Review, 48,* 337–342.

Miller, N. E. (1948). Studies of fear as an acquirable drive: I. Fear as motivation and fear-reduction as reinforcement in learning of new responses. *Journal of Experimental Psychology, 38,* 89–101.

Miller, N. E. (1951). Comments on multiple-process conceptions of learning. *Psychological Review, 58,* 375–381.

Miller, N. E. (1985). The value of behavioral research on animals. *American Psychologist, 40,* 423–440.

Miller, R. R., & Matzel, L. D. (1989). Contingency and relative associative strength. In S. B. Klein & R. R. Mowrer (Eds.), *Contemporary learning theories: Pavlovian conditioning and the status of traditional learning theory* (pp. 61–84). Hillsdale, N.J.: Erlbaum.

Miller, W. R., & Seligman, M. E. P. (1973). Depression and the perception of reinforcement. *Journal of Abnormal Psychology, 82,* 62–73.

Miller, W. R., & Seligman, M. E. P. (1975). Depression and learned helplessness in man. *Journal of Abnormal Psychology, 84,* 228–238.

Mills, C. B. (1980). Effects of context on reaction time to phonemes. *Journal of Verbal Learning and Verbal Behavior, 19,* 75–83.

Milner, B. (1965). Memory disturbance after bilateral hippocampal lesions. In P. Milner & S. Glickman (Eds.), *Cognitive processes and the brain.* Princeton, N.J.: Van Nostrand.

Milner, B. (1970). Memory and the temporal regions of the brain. In K. H. Pribram & D. E. Broadbent (Eds.), *Biology of memory* (pp. 29–50). New York: Academic.

Milvy, P. (Ed.). (1977). *The marathon: Physiological, medical, epidemiological, and psychological studies* (Annals, Vol. 301). New York: New York Academy of Sciences.

Mineka, S., Davidson, M., Cook, M., & Keir, R. (1984). Observational conditioning of snake fear in rhesus monkeys. *Journal of Abnormal Psychology, 93,* 355–372.

Mischel, W. (1974). Processes in delay of gratification. In L. Berkowitz (Ed.), *Advances in experimental social psychology* (Vol. 7). New York: Academic Press.

Mischel, W., & Grusec, J. E. (1966). Determinants of the rehearsal and transmission of neutral and aversive behaviors. *Journal of Personality and Social Psychology, 3,* 197–205.

Miyawaki, K., Strange, W., Verbugge, R. R., Liberman, A. M., Jenkins, J. J., & Fujimura, O. (1975). An effect of linguistic experience: The discrimination of r and l by native speakers of Japanese and English. *Perception and Psychophysics, 18,* 331–340.

Moltz, H. (1960). Imprinting: Empirical basis and theoretical significance. *Psychological Bulletin, 57*, 291–314.

Moltz, H. (1963). Imprinting: An epigenetic approach. *Psychological Review, 70*, 123–138.

Monti, P. M., & Smith, N. F. (1976). Residual fear of the conditioned stimulus as a function of response prevention after avoidance or classical defensive conditioning in the rat. *Journal of Experimental Psychology: General, 105*, 148–162.

Moore, J. W. (1972). Stimulus control: Studies of auditory generalization in rabbits. In A. H. Black & W. F. Prokasy (Eds.), *Classical conditioning II* (pp. 206–230). New York: Appleton-Century-Crofts.

Moore, R., & Goldiamond, I. (1964). Errorless establishment of visual discrimination using fading procedures. *Journal of the Experimental Analysis of Behavior, 7*, 269–272.

Moray, N., Bates, A., & Barnett, R. (1965). Experiments on the four-eared man. *Journal of the Acoustical Society of America, 38*, 196–201.

Morris, C. D., Bransford, J. D., & Franks, J. J. (1977). Levels of processing versus transfer-appropriate processing. *Journal of Verbal Learning and Verbal Behavior, 16*, 519–533.

Moscovitch, A., & LoLordo, V. M. (1968). Role of safety in the Pavlovian backward fear conditioning procedure. *Journal of Comparative and Psychological Psychology, 66*, 673–678.

Moscovitch, M. (1992). Memory and working-with-memory: A component-process model based on modules and central systems. *Journal of Cognitive Neuroscience, 4*, 257–267.

Mowrer, O. H. (1938). Preparatory set (Expectancy): A determinant in motivation and learning. *Psychological Review, 45*, 62–91.

Mowrer, O. H. (1939). A stimulus-response analysis and its role as a reinforcing agent. *Psychological Review, 46*, 553–565.

Mowrer, O. H. (1947). On the dual nature of learning—A reinterpretation of "conditioning" and "problem solving." *Harvard Educational Review, 17*, 102–148.

Mowrer, O. H. (1956). Two-factor learning theory reconsidered, with special reference to secondary reinforcement and the concept of habit. *Psychological Review, 63*, 114–128.

Mowrer, O. H. (1960). *Learning theory and behavior.* New York: Wiley.

Mowrer, R. R., & Klein, S. B. (2001). The transitive nature of contemporary learning theory. In R. R. Mowrer & S. B. Klein (Eds.), *Handbook of contemporary learning theories* (pp. 1–21). Mawrah, N.J.: Erlbaum.

Moyer, K. E. (1972, March). A physiological model of aggression: Does it have different implications? Presented at the Houston Neurological Symposium on neural basis of violence and aggression.

Moyer, K. E., & Korn, J. H. (1964). Effects of UCS intensity on the acquisition and extinction of an avoidance response. *Journal of Experimental Psychology, 67*, 352–359.

Moyer, K. E., & Korn, J. H. (1966). Effect of UCS intensity on the acquisition and extinction of a one-way avoidance response. *Psychonomic Science, 4*, 121–122.

Murdock, B. B., Jr. (1961). The retention of individual items. *Journal of Experimental Psychology, 62*, 618–625.

National Transportation Safety Board, 2000. *Actions to Reduce Fatalities, Injuries, and Crashes Involving the Hard Core Drinking Driver.* Safety Report NTSB/SR-00/01. Washington, DC.

Naus, M. J., & Halasz, F. G. (1979). Developmental perspectives on cognitive processing and semantic memory. In L. S. Cermak & F. I. M. Craik (Eds.), *Levels of processing in human memory* (pp. 259–288). Hillsdale, N.J.: Erlbaum.

Neisser, U. (1967). *Cognitive psychology.* New York: Appleton-Century-Crofts.

Neisser, U. (1982). *Memory observed.* San Francisco: W. H. Freeman.

Nelson, D. L. (1979). Remembering pictures and words: Appearance, significance, and name. In L. S. Cermak & F. I. M. Craik (Eds.), *Levels of processing in human memory.* Hillsdale, N.J.: Erlbaum.

Nelson v. Heyne 491, F. 2nd 352 (1974).

Nevin, J. A. (1973). The maintenance of behavior. In J. A. Nevin (Ed.), *The study of behavior: Learning, motivation, emotion, and instinct,* Glenview, Ill.: Scott, Foresman.

Newell, A., Shaw, J. C., & Simon, H. A. (1958). Elements of a theory of human problem solving. *Psychological Review, 65,* 151–166.

Newell, A., & Simon, H. A. (1972). *Human problem solving.* Englewood Cliffs, N.J.: Prentice-Hall.

Newsweek, September 13, 1982.

Nichols, C. S., & Russell, S. M. (1990). Analysis of animal rights literature reveals the underlying motives of the movement: Ammunition for counter offensive by scientists. *Endocrinology, 127,* 985–989.

Nietzel, M. T., Bernstein, D. A., & Milich, R. (1994). *Clinical psychology* (4th ed.). Upper Saddle River, N.J.: Prentice-Hall.

Nissen, H. W. (1951). Analysis of a complex conditional reaction in chimpanzees. *Journal of Comparative and Physiological Psychology, 44,* 9–16.

Noble, C. E. (1966). S-O-R and the psychology of human learning. *Psychological Reports, 18,* 923–943.

Noble, M., & Harding, G. E. (1963). Conditioning of rhesus monkeys as a function of the interval between CS and US. *Journal of Comparative and Physiological Psychology, 56,* 220–224.

Nolen-Hoeksema, S., Morrow, J., & Fredrickson, B. L. (1993). Response styles and the duration of episodes of depressed mood. *Journal of Abnormal Psychology, 102,* 20–28.

Norman, D. A. (1976). *Memory and attention* (2nd ed.). New York: Wiley.

O'Hara, K., Johnson, C. M., & Beehr, T. A. (1985). Organizational behavioral management: A review of empirical research and recommendations for further investigations. *Academy of Management Review, 10,* 848–864.

Ohio Rev. Code Ann, (1977). Sec 5122.271 (E).

Olds, J. (1962). Hypothalamic substrates of reward. *Psychological Review, 42,* 554–604.

Olds, J., & Milner, P. (1954). Positive reinforcement produced by electrical stimulation of septal area and other regions of rat brain. *Journal of Comparative and Physiological Psychology, 47,* 419–427.

Olness, K., & Ader, R. (1992). Conditioning as an adjunct in the pharmacotherapy of lupus erythematosus. *Journal of Developmental and Behavioral Pediatrics, 13,* 124–125.

O'Reilly, C. A., & Exon, J. H. (1986). Cyclophosphamide-conditioned suppression of the natural killer cell response in rats. *Physiology and Behavior, 37,* 759–764.

Ost, L.-G. (1989). One-session treatment for specific phobias. *Behaviour Research and Therapy, 27,* 1–7.

Overmier, J. B., & Seligman, M. E. P. (1967). Effects of inescapable shock upon subsequent escape and avoidance learning. *Journal of Comparative and Physiological Psychology, 63,* 28–33.

Overton, D. A. (1964). State-dependent or "dissociated" learning produced with pentobarbitol. *Journal of Comparative and Physiological Psychology, 57,* 3–12.

Overton, D. A. (1982). Memory retrieval failures produced by changes in drug state. In R. L. Isaacson & N. E. Spear (Eds.), *The expression of knowledge* (pp. 113–140). New York: Plenum Press.

Paivio, A. (1986). *Mental representation: A dual-coding approach.* New York: Oxford University Press.

Paletta, M. S., & Wagner, A. R. (1986). Development of context-specific tolerance to morphine: Support for a dual-process interpretation. *Behavioral Neuroscience, 100,* 611–623.

Palmer, S., Schreiber, G., & Fox, C. (1991, November 22–24). *Remembering the earthquake: "Flashbulb" memory of experienced versus reported events.* Paper presented at the 32nd annual meeting of the Psychonomic Society, San Francisco.

Parke, R. D., & Deur, J. L. (1972). Schedule of punishment and inhibition of aggression in children. *Developmental Psychology, 7,* 266–269.

Parke, R. D., & Walters, R. H. (1967). Some factors determining the efficacy of punishment for inducing response inhibition. *Monograph of the Society for Research in Child Development, 32* (Whole No. 19).

Pate, J. L., & Rumbaugh, D. M. (1983). The language-like behavior of Lana Chimpanzee: Is it merely discrimination learning and paired-associate learning? *Animal Learning and Behavior, 11,* 134–138.

Paul, G. L. (1969). Behavior modification research: Design and tactics. In C. M. Franks (Ed.), *Behavior therapy: Appraisal and status* (pp. 29–62). New York: McGraw-Hill.

Paul G. L., & Menditto, A. A. (1992). Effectiveness of inpatient treatment programs for mentally ill adults in public psychiatric facilities. *Applied and Preventive Psychology: Current Scientific Perspectives, 1,* 41–63.

Paul, G. P., & Lentz, R. J. (1977). *Psychosocial treatment of chronic mental patients (Milieu vs. social learning programs).* Cambridge, Mass.: Harvard University Press.

Paulson, K., Rimm, D. C., Woodburn, L. T., & Rimm, S. A. (1977). A self-control approach to inefficient spending. *Journal of Consulting and Clinical Psychology, 45,* 433–435.

Pavlov, I. (1927). *Conditioned reflexes.* Oxford: Oxford University Press.

Pavlov, I. (1928). *Lectures on conditioned reflexes: The higher nervous activity of animals, 1,* H. Gantt (Trans.). London: Lawrence and Wishart.

Pearce, J. M., Kaye, H., & Hall, G. (1982). Predictive accuracy and stimulus associability: Development of a model for Pavlovian learning. In M. L. Commons, R. J. Herrnstein, & A. R. Wagner (Eds.), *Quantitative analyses of behavior, III* (pp. 241–255). Cambridge, Mass.: Ballinger.

Pearce, J. M., Nicholas, D. J., & Dickinson, A. (1981). The potentiation effect during serial conditioning. *Quarterly Journal of Experimental Psychology, 33,* 159–179.

Penney, R. K. (1967). Children's escape performance as a function of schedules of delay of reinforcement. *Journal of Experimental Psychology, 73,* 109–112.

Penney, R. K., & Kirwin, P. M. (1965). Differential adaptation of anxious and nonanxious children in instrumental escape conditioning. *Journal of Experimental Psychology, 70,* 539–549.

Perin, C. T. (1942). Behavior potentiality as a joint function of the amount of training and the degree of hunger at the time of extinction. *Journal of Experimental Psychology, 30,* 93–113.

Perin, C. T. (1943). A quantitative investigation of the delay-of-reinforcement gradient. *Journal of Experimental Psychology, 32,* 37–51.

Peterson, C., & Seligman, M. E. P. (1984). Causal explanations as a risk factor in depression: Theory and evidence. *Psychological Review, 91,* 347–374.

Peterson, L. R., & Peterson, M. J. (1959). Short-term retention of individual verbal items. *Journal of Experimental Psychology, 58,* 193–198.

Peterson, N. (1962). The effect of monochromatic rearing on the control of responding by wavelength. *Science, 136,* 774–775.

Peterson, R. F., & Peterson, L. R. (1968). The use of positive reinforcement in the control of self-destructive behavior in a retarded boy. *Journal of Experimental Child Psychology, 6,* 351–360.

Petitto, L. A., & Marentette, P. F. (1991). Babbling in the manual mode: Evidence for the ontogency of language. *Science, 251,* 1493–1496.

Phillips, A. G., Blaha, C. D., & Fibinger, H. C. (1989). Neurochemical correlates of brain-stimulation reward measured by ex vivo and in vivo analyses. *Neuroscience and Biobehavioral Reviews, 13,* 99–104.

Piazza, P. V., Deminiere, J. M., LeMoal, M., & Simon, H. (1989). Factors that predict individual vulnerability to AMPH self-administration. *Science, 245,* 1511–1513.

Piliavin, I. M., Piliavin, J. A., & Rodin, J. (1975). Costs, diffusion, and the stigmatized victim. *Journal of Personality and Social Psychology, 32,* 429–438.

Piliavin, J. A., Dovidio, J. F., Gaertner, S. L., & Clark, R. D., III. (1981). Responsive bystanders: The process of intervention. In J. Grzelak & V. Derlega (Eds.), *Living with other people: Theory and research on cooperation and helping.* New York: Academic.

Pillimer, D. B. (1984). Flashbulb memories of the assassination attempt on President Reagan, *Cognition, 16,* 63–80.

Pinker, S. (1999). *Words and rules: The ingredients of language.* New York: Basic Books.

Plotnick, R., Mir, D., & Delgado, J. M. R. (1971). Aggression, noxiousness, and brain stimulation in unrestrained rhesus monkeys. In B. E. Eleftheriou & J. P. Scott (Eds.), *The physiology of aggression and defeat.* New York: Plenum.

Plummer, S., Baer, D. M., & LeBlanc, J. M. (1977). Functional considerations in the use of procedural time out and an effective alternative. *Journal of Applied Behavior Analysis, 10,* 689–706.

Pollack, I. (1953). The information in elementary auditory displays: II. *Journal of the Acoustical Society of America, 25,* 765–769.

Porter, D., & Neuringer, A. (1984). Music discrimination by pigeons. *Journal of Experimental Psychology: Animal Behavior Processes, 10,* 138–148.

Posner, M. I. (1973). *Cognition: An introduction.* Glenview, Ill.: Scott, Foresman.

Posner, M. I. (1982). Cumulative development of attentional theory. *American Psychologist, 37,* 168–179.

Posner, M. I., & Keele, S. W. (1968). On the genesis of abstract ideas. *Journal of Experimental Psychology, 77,* 353–363.

Postman, L. (1967). Mechanisms of interference in forgetting. Vice-presidential address given at the annual meeting of the American Association for Advancement of Science, New York.

Postman, L., Stark, K., & Fraser, J. (1968). Temporal changes in interference. *Verbal Learning and Verbal Behavior, 7,* 672–694.

Powell, J., & Azrin, N. (1968). The effects of shock as a punisher for cigarette smoking. *Journal of Applied Behavior Analysis, 1,* 63–71.

Powley, R. L. (1977). The ventromedial hypothalamic syndrome, satiety, and a cephalic phase hypothesis. *Psychological Review, 84,* 89–126.

Premack, D. (1959). Toward empirical behavior laws: I. Positive reinforcement. *Psychological Review, 66,* 219–233.

Premack, D. (1965). Reinforcement theory. In D. Levine (Ed.), *Nebraska symposium on motivation* (pp. 123–180). Lincoln: University of Nebraska.

Prokasy, W. F., Jr., Grant, D. A., & Myers, N. A. (1958). Eyelid conditioning as a function of unconditional stimulus intensity and intertrial intervention. *Journal of Experimental Psychology, 55,* 242–246.

Prokasy, W. F., Jr., & Hall, J. F. (1963). Primary stimulus generalization. *Psychological Review, 70,* 310–322.

Pubols, B. H., Fr. (1960). Incentive magnitude, learning, and performance in animals. *Psychological Bulletin, 51,* 89–115.

Rachlin, H., Battalio, R. C., Kagel, J. H., & Green, L. (1981). Maximization theory in behavioral psychology. *The Behavioral and Brain Sciences, 4,* 371–388.

Rachlin, H., & Green, L. (1972). Commitment, choice and self-control. *Journal of the Experimental Analysis of Behavior, 17,* 15–22.

Rachman, S. J. (1990). *Fear and courage.* New York: W. H. Freeman.

Rackham, D. (1971). *Conditioning of the pigeon's courtship and aggressive behavior.* Master's thesis, Dalhousie University, Halifax, Nova Scotia. Cited in E. Hearst & H. M.

Jenkins, *Sign-tracking: The stimulus-reinforcer relation and directed action*. Austin, Tex.: The Psychonomic Society, 1974.

Randich, A., & Ross, R. T. (1985). Contextual stimuli mediate the effects of pre- and postexposure to the unconditioned stimulus on conditioned suppression. In P. D. Balsam & A. Tomie (Eds.), *Context and learning* (pp. 105–132). Hillsdale, N.J.: Erlbaum.

Rapport, M. D., & Bostow, D. E. (1976). The effects of access to special activities on the performance in four categories of academic tasks with third-grade students. *Journal of Applied Behavior Analysis, 9,* 372.

Razran, G. H. S. (1949). Stimulus generalization of conditioned responses. *Psychological Bulletin, 46,* 337–365.

Redd, W. H., Morris, E. K., & Martin, J. A. (1975). Effects of positive and negative adult-child interactions on children's social preference. *Journal of Behavior Therapy and Experimental Psychiatry, 19,* 153–164.

Reichle, J., Brubakken, D., & Tetrault, G. (1976). Eliminating perseverative speech by positive reinforcement and time-out in a psychotic child. *Journal of Behavior Therapy and Experimental Psychiatry, 1,* 179–183.

Reitman, W. R. (1965). *Cognition and thought: An information processing approach.* New York: Wiley.

Renner, K. E., & Tinsley, J. B. (1976). Self-punitive behavior. In G. Bower (Ed.), *The psychology of learning and motivation* (Vol. 10). New York: Academic.

Rensch, B., & Ducker, G. (1966). Verzogerung des Vergessens erlernter visuellen Aufgaben bei Tieren durch Chlorpromazin. *Pfluegers Archiv Fur die Gesamte Physiologie des Menschen und der Tiere, 289,* 200–214.

Rescorla, R. A. (1968). Probability of shock in presence and absence of CS in fear conditioning. *Journal of Comparative and Physiological Psychology, 66,* 1–5.

Rescorla, R. A. (1971). Summation and retardation tests of latent inhibition. *Journal of Comparative and Physiological Psychology, 75,* 77–81.

Rescorla, R. A. (1973). Effects of US habituation following conditioning. *Journal of Comparative and Physiological Psychology, 82,* 137–143.

Rescorla, R. A. (1978). Some implications of a cognitive perspective on Pavlovian conditioning. In S. H. Hulse, H. Fowler, & W. K. Honig (Eds.), *Cognitive processes in animal behavior* (pp. 15–50). Hillsdale, N.J.: Erlbaum.

Rescorla, R. A. (1981). Simultaneous associations. In P. Harzum & M. D. Zeiler (Eds.), *Predictability, correlation and contiguity* (pp. 47–80). New York: Wiley.

Rescorla, R. A. (1982). Effect of a stimulus intervening between CS and US in autoshaping. *Journal of Experimental Psychology: Animal Behavior Processes, 8,* 131–141.

Rescorla, R. A. (1985). Conditioned inhibition and facilitation. In R. R. Miller & N. E. Spear (Eds.), *Information processing in animals: Conditioned inhibition.* Hillsdale, N.J.: Erlbaum.

Rescorla, R. A. (1986). Facilitation and excitation. *Journal of Experimental Psychology: Animal Behavior Processes, 12,* 325–332.

Rescorla, R. A. (1990). Evidence for an association between the discriminative stimulus and the response-outcome association in instrumental learning. *Journal of Experimental Psychology: Animal Behavior Processes, 16,* 326–334.

Rescorla, R. A., & Durlach, P. J. (1981). Within-event learning in Pavlovian conditioning. In N. E. Spear & R. R. Miller (Eds.), *Information processing in animals: Memory mechanisms* (pp. 81–112). Hillsdale, N.J.: Erlbaum.

Rescorla, R. A., Durlach, P. J., & Grau, J. W. (1985). Contextual learning in Pavlovian conditioning. In P. D. Balsam & A. Tomie (Eds.), *Context and learning* (pp. 23–56). Hillsdale, N.J.: Erlbaum.

Rescorla, R. A., & LoLordo, V. M. (1965). Inhibition of avoidance behavior. *Journal of Comparative and Physiological Psychology, 59,* 406–412.

Rescorla, R. A., & Solomon, R. L. (1967). Two-process learning theory: Relations between Pavlovian conditioning and instrumental learning. *Psychological Review, 74,* 151–182.

Rescorla, R. A., & Wagner, A. R. (1972). A theory of Pavlovian conditioning: Variations in the effectiveness of reinforcement and nonreinforcement. In A. H. Black & W. F. Prokasy (Eds.), *Classical conditioning II* (pp. 64–99). New York: Appleton-Century-Crofts.

Revusky, S. (1971). The role of interference in association over a delay. In W. K. Honig & P. H. R. James (Eds.), *Animal memory* (pp. 155–214). New York: Academic.

Revusky, S. (1977). The concurrent interference approach to delay learning. In L. J. Barker, M. R. Best, & M. Domjan (Eds.), *Learning mechanisms in food selection* (pp. 319–363). Waco, Tex.: Baylor University Press.

Revusky, S., & Parker, L. A. (1976). Aversions to drinking out of a cup and to unflavored water produced by delayed sickness. *Journal of Experimental Psychology: Animal Behavior Processes, 2,* 342–353.

Reynolds, G. S. (1961a). Behavioral contrast. *Journal of the Experimental Analysis of Behavior, 4,* 57–71.

Reynolds, G. S. (1961b). Attention in the pigeon. *Journal of the Experimental Analysis of Behavior, 4,* 203–208.

Reynolds, G. S. (1968). *A primer of operant conditioning.* Glenview, Ill.: Scott, Foresman.

Riccio, D. C., & Haroutunian, V. (1977). Failure to learn in a taste-aversion paradigm: Associative or performance deficit? *Bulletin of the Psychonomic Society, 10,* 219–222.

Rice, J. R. (1989). Children's language acquisition. *American Psychologist, 44,* 149–156.

Riggs, D. S., & Foa, E. B. (1993). Obsessive-compulsive disorder. In D. H. Barlow (Ed.), *Clinical handbook of psychological disorders* (2nd ed., pp. 189–239). New York: Guilford Press.

Riley, A. L., Lotter, E. C., & Kulkosky, P. J. (1979). The effects of conditioned taste aversions on the acquisition and maintenance of schedule-induced polydipsia. *Animal Learning and Behavior, 7,* 3–12.

Riley, A. L., & Wetherington, C. L. (1989). Schedule-induced polydipsia: Is the rat a small furry human? (An analysis of an animal model of alcoholism). In S. B. Klein & R. R. Mowrer (Eds.), *Contemporary learning theories: Instrumental conditioning theory and the impact of biological constraints on learning* (pp. 205–233). Hillsdale, N.J.: Erlbaum.

Riley, A. L., Wetherington, C. L., Wachsman, A. M., Fishman, H. S., & Kautz, M. A. (1988). The effects of conditioned taste aversions on schedule-induced polydipsia: An analysis of the initiation and postpellet temporal distribution of licking. *Animal Learning and Behavior, 16,* 292–298.

Rips, L. J., Shoben, E. J., & Smith, E. E. (1973). Semantic distance and the verification of semantic relationships. *Journal of Verbal Learning and Verbal Behavior, 12,* 1–20.

Risley, T. R. (1968). The effects and side effects of punishing the autistic behaviors of a deviant child. *Journal of Applied Behavior Analysis, 1,* 21–34.

Ritter, B. (1969). The use of contact desensitization, demonstration-plus-participation, and demonstration alone in the treatment of acrophobia. *Behavior Research and Therapy, 7,* 157–164.

Rizley, R. C. (1978). Depression and distortion in the attribution of causality. *Journal of Abnormal Psychology, 87,* 32–48.

Rizley, R. C., & Rescorla, R. A. (1972). Associations in higher-order conditioning and sensory preconditioning. *Journal of Comparative and Physiological Psychology, 81,* 1–11.

Robbins, D. (1971). Partial reinforcement: A selective review of the alleyway literature since 1960. *Psychological Bulletin, 76,* 415–431.

Roberts, W. A., Mazmanian, D. S., & Kraemer, P. J. (1984). Directed forgetting in monkeys. *Animal Learning and Behavior, 12,* 29–40.

Robins, C. J. (1988). Attributions and depression: Why is the literature so inconsistent? *Journal of Personality and Social Psychology, 54,* 880–889.

Robinson, N. M., & Robinson, H. B. (1961). A method for the study of instrumental avoidance conditioning with children. *Journal of Comparative and Physiological Psychology, 54,* 20–23.

Rohde, P., Lewinsohn, P. M., & Seeley, J. R. (1991). Comorbidity of unipolar depression: II. Comorbidity with other mental disorders in adolescents and adults. *Journal of Abnormal Psychology, 100,* 214–222.

Rohner, R. P. (1986). *The warmth dimension: foundations of parental acceptance rejection theory.* Thousand Oaks, CA: Sage Publications.

Roper, K. L., & Zantall, T. R. (1993). Directed forgetting in animals. *Psychological Review, 113,* 513–532.

Rosch, E. (1975). Cognitive representations of semantic categories. *Journal of Experimental Psychology: General, 104,* 192–253.

Rosch, E. (1978). Principles of categorization. In E. Rosch & B. Lloyd (Eds.), *Cognition and categorization* (pp. 28–48). Hillsdale, N.J.: Erlbaum.

Rosch, E., & Mervis, C. B. (1978). Family resemblances: Studies in the internal structure of categories. *Cognitive Psychology, 7,* 573–605.

Rosellini, L. (1998, April 13). When to spank. *U.S. News & World Report,* pp. 52–58.

Rosellini, R., & Seligman, M. E. P. (1975). Learned helplessness and escape from frustration. *Journal of Experimental Psychology: Animal Behavior Processes, 1,* 149–158.

Rosenzweig, M. R. (1984). Experience, memory, and the brain. *American Psychologist, 39,* 365–376.

Ross, H. L. (1981). Deterring the drinking driver: Legal policy and social control (2nd ed.). Lexington, MA: Lexington Books.

Roth, E. M., & Shoben, E. E. (1983). The effect of context on the structure of categories. *Cognitive Psychology, 15,* 346–379.

Roth, S., & Kubal, L. (1975). The effects of noncontingent reinforcement on tasks of differing importance: Facilitation and learned helplessness effects. *Journal of Personality and Social Psychology, 32,* 680–691.

Rothbaum, B. O., Hodges, L. F., Kooper, R., & Opdyke, D. (1995). Effectiveness of computer-generated (virtual reality) graded exposure in the treatment of acrophobia. *American Journal of Psychiatry, 152,* 626–628.

Rotter, J. B. (1954). *Social learning and clinical psychology.* Englewood Cliffs, N.J.: Prentice-Hall.

Rotter, J. B. (1966). Generalized expectancies for internal versus external control of reinforcement. *Psychological Monographs, 80* (Whole No. 609).

Routtenberg, A., & Lindy, J. (1965). Effects of the availability of rewarding septal and hypothalamic stimulation on bar-pressing for food under conditions of deprivation. *Journal of Comparative and Physiological Psychology, 60,* 158–161.

Rozin, P., & Zellner, D. (1985). The role of Pavlovian conditioning in the acquisition of food likes and dislikes. *Annals of the New York Academy of Sciences, 443,* 189–202.

Rumbaugh, D. M. (1990). Comparative psychology and the great apes: Their competency in learning, language, and numbers. *Psychological Record, 40,* 15–39.

Rumbaugh, D. M., & Gill, R. V. (1976). The mastery of language-type skills by the chimpanzee (*Pan*). *Annals of the New York Academy of Sciences, 280,* 562–578.

Rumelhart, D. E., McClelland, J. L., & The PDP Research Group. (1986). *Parallel distributed processing: Explorations in the microstructure of cognition: Vol. 1. Foundations.* Cambridge, Mass.: Bradford Books/MIT Press.

Rundus, D. (1971). Analysis of rehearsal processes in free recall. *Journal of Experimental Psychology, 89,* 63–77.

Rundus, D., & Atkinson, R. C. (1970). Rehearsal processes in free recall: A procedure for direct observation. *Journal of Verbal Learning and Verbal Behavior, 9,* 99–105.

Runquist, W. N. (1957). Retention of verbal associates as function of strength. *Journal of Experimental Psychology, 54,* 369–375.

Rusiniak, K. W., Palmerino, C. C., & Garcia, J. (1982). Potentiation of odor by taste in rats: Tests of some nonassociative factors. *Journal of Comparative and Physiological Psychology, 96,* 775–780.

Russell, R. K., & Sipich, J. F. (1973). Cue-controlled relaxation in the treatment of test anxiety. *Journal of Behavior Therapy and Experimental Psychiatry, 4,* 47–49.

Samuel, A. L. (1963). Some studies in machine learning using the game of checkers. In E. A. Feigenbaum & J. Feldman (Eds.), *Computers and thought.* New York: McGraw-Hill.

Sanger, D. J. (1986). Drug taking as adjunctive behavior. In S. R. Goldberg & I. P. Stolerman (Eds.), *Behavioral analysis of drug dependence.* New York: Academic.

Saufley, W. H., Otaka, S. R., & Bavaresco, J. L. (1985). Context effects: Classroom tests and context independence. *Memory and Cognition, 13,* 522–528.

Savage-Rumbaugh, E. S., Rumbaugh, D. M., & Boysen, S. (1980). Do apes use language? *American Scientist, 68,* 49–61.

Savage-Rumbaugh, E. S., Sevcik, R. A., Brakke, K. E., & Rumbaugh, D. M. (1992). Symbols: Their communicative use, communication, and combination by bonobos (*Pan panicus*). In L. P. Lipsitt & C. Rovee-Collier (Eds.), *Advances in infancy research* (Vol. 7, pp. 221–278). Norwood, N.J.: Ablex.

Savage-Rumbaugh, E. S., Shanker, S., & Taylor, T. T. (1996). Apes with language. *Critical Quarterly, 38,* 45–57.

Savastano, H. I., Escobar, M., & Miller, R. R. (2001). *A comparative hypothesis account of the CS-preexposure effects.* Cited in Denniston, J. C., Savastano, H. I., & Miller, R. R. The extended comparative hypothesis. In R. R. Mowrer & S. B. Klein (Eds.), *Handbook of Learning Theories.* Mawrah, N.J.: Erlbaum.

Savastano, H. I., & Fantino, E. (1994). Human choice in concurrent ratio-interval schedules of reinforcement. *Journal of the Experimental Analysis of Behavior, 61,* 453–463.

Schaffer, H. R., & Emerson, P. E. (1964). The development of social attachments in infancy. *Monographs Social Research in Child Development, 29,* 1–77.

Schleidt, W. (1961). Reaktionen von Truthuhnern auf fliegende Rauvogel and Versuche zur Analyse inhrer AAM's. *Zeitschrift fur Tierpsychologie, 18,* 534–560.

Schlosberg, H., & Solomon, R. L. (1943). Latency of response in a choice discrimination. *Journal of the Experimental Psychology, 33,* 22–39.

Schooler, J. W., Gerhard, D., & Loftus, E. F. (1986). Quantities of the unreal. *Journal of Experimental Psychology: Learning, Memory and Cognition, 12,* 171–181.

Schrier, A. M., & Brady, P. M. (1987). Categorization of natural stimuli by monkeys (*Macaca mulatta*): Effects of stimulus set size and modification of exemplars. *Journal of Experimental Psychology: Animal Behavior Processes, 13,* 136–143.

Schulman, A. H., Hale, E. B., & Graves, H. B. (1970). Visual stimulus characteristics of initial approach response in chicks (*Gallus domesticus*). *Animal Behavior, 18,* 461–466.

Schuster, C. R., & Woods, J. H. (1966). Schedule-induced polydipsia in the rhesus monkey. *Psychological Reports, 19,* 823–828.

Schwartz, B., & Reisberg, D. (1991). *Learning and memory.* New York: Norton.

Schwitzgebel, R. K., & Schwitzgebel, R. K. (1980). *Law and psychological practice.* New York: Wiley.

Scoville, W. B., & Milner, B. (1957). Loss of recent memory after bilateral hippocampal lesions. *Journal of Neurology, Neurosurgery and Psychiatry, 20,* 11–21.

Sears, R. R., Maccoby, E. E., & Levin, H. (1957). *Patterns of child rearing.* Evanston, Ill.: Row Peterson.

Seaver, W. B., & Patterson, A. H. (1976). Decreasing fuel-oil consumption through feedback and social commendation. *Journal of Applied Behavior Analysis, 9,* 147–152.

Seligman, M. E. P. (1970). On the generality of laws of learning. *Psychological Review, 77,* 406–418.

Seligman, M. E. P. (1975). *Helplessness: On depression, development, and death.* San Francisco: W. H. Freeman.

Seligman, M. E. P., & Campbell, B. A. (1965). Effects of intensity and duration of punishment on extinction of an avoidance response. *Journal of Comparative and Physiological Psychology, 59,* 295–297.

Seligman, M. E. P., & Maier, S. F. (1967). Failure to escape traumatic shock. *Journal of Experimental Psychology, 74,* 1–9.

Seligman, M. E. P., & Schulman, P. (1986). Explanatory style as a predictor of productivity and quitting among life insurance agents. *Journal of Personality and Social Psychology, 50,* 832–838.

Sem-Jacobson, C. W. (1968). *Depth-electrographic stimulation of the human brain and behavior: From fourteen years of studies and treatment of Parkinson's disease and mental disorders with implanted electrodes.* Springfield, Ill.: Thomas.

Senkowski, P. C. (1978). Variables affecting the overtraining extinction effect in discrete-trial lever pressing. *Journal of Experimental Psychology: Animal Behavior Processes, 4,* 131–143.

Seybert, J. A., McClanahan, L. G., & Gilliland, J. S. (1982). Retention following appetitive discrimination training: The Kamin effect. *Bulletin of the Psychonomic Society, 19,* 37–40.

Seyfarth, R. M., Cheney, D. L., & Marler, P. (1980). Monkey responses to three different alarm calls: Evidence of predator classification and semantic communication. *Science, 210,* 801–803.

Shanab, M. E., & Birnbaum, D. W. (1974). Durability of the partial reinforcement and partial delay of reinforcement extinction effects after minimal acquisition training. *Animal Learning and Behavior, 2,* 81–85.

Shanab, M. E., & Peterson, J. L. (1969). Polydipsia in the pigeon. *Psychonomic Science, 15,* 51–52.

Shanab, M. E., Sanders, R., & Premack, D. (1969). Positive contrast in the runway obtained with delay of reward. *Science, 164,* 724–725.

Shanteau, J. (1992). The psychology of experts: An alternative view. In G. Wright & F. Bolger (Eds.), *Expertise and decision support* (pp. 11–23). New York: Plenum Press.

Shaw, D. W., & Thoresen, C. E. (1974). Effects of modeling and desensitization in reducing dentist phobia. *Journal of Counseling Psychology, 21,* 415–420.

Sheffield, F. D. (1965). Relation between classical conditioning and instrumental learning. In W. F. Prokasy (Ed.), *Classical conditioning.* New York: Appleton-Century-Crofts.

Sheffield, F. D. (1966). New evidence on the drive-induction theory of reinforcement. In R. N. Haber (Ed.), *Current research in motivation* (pp. 98–111). New York: Holt.

Sheffield, F. D., & Roby, T. B. (1950). Reward value of a nonnutritive sweet taste. *Journal of Comparative and Physiological Psychology, 43,* 471–481.

Sherrington, C. S. (1906). *Integrative action of the nervous system.* New Haven, Conn.: Yale University Press.

Shiffrin, R. M., & Cook, J. R. (1978). Short-term forgetting of item and order information. *Journal of Verbal Learning and Verbal Behavior, 17,* 189–218.

Shimoff, E., Catania, A. C., & Matthews, B. A. (1981). Uninstructed human responding: Sensitivity of low-rate performance to schedule contingencies. *Journal of the Experimental Analysis of Behavior, 36,* 207–220.

Shipley, R. H. (1974). Extinction of conditioned fear in rats as a function of several parameters of CS exposure. *Journal of Comparative and Physiological Psychology, 87*, 699–707.

Sidman, M. (1953). Avoidance conditioning with brief shock and no exteroceptive warning signal. *Science, 118*, 157–158.

Sidman, M., & Stebbins, W. C. (1954). Satiation effects under fixed-ratio schedules of reinforcement. *Journal of Comparative and Physiological Psychology, 47*, 114–116.

Sidman, M., & Stoddard, L. T. (1967). The effectiveness of fading in programming and simultaneous form discrimination for retarded children. *Journal of the Experimental Analysis of Behavior, 10*, 3–15.

Sidman, M., Stoddard, L. T., & Mohr, J. P. (1968). Some additional quantitative observations of immediate memory in a patient with bilateral hippocampal lesions. *Neuropsychologia, 6*, 245–254.

Siegel, S. (1969). Effect of CS habituation on eyelid conditioning. *Journal of Comparative and Physiological Psychology, 69*, 157–159.

Siegel, S. (1975). Evidence from rats that morphine tolerance is a learned response. *Journal of Comparative and Physiological Psychology, 89*, 498–506.

Siegel, S. (1976). Morphine analgesic tolerance: Its situation specificity supports a Pavlovian conditioning model. *Science, 193*, 323–325.

Siegel, S. (1977). Morphine tolerance acquisition as an associative process. *Journal of Experimental Psychology: Animal Behavior Processes, 3*, 1–13.

Siegel, S. (1978). A Pavlovian conditioning analysis of morphine tolerance. In N. A. Krasnegor (Ed.), *Behavioral tolerance: Research and treatment implications* (NIDA Research Monograph No. 18). Washington, D.C.: U.S. Government Printing Office.

Siegel, S. (1984). Pavlovian conditioning and heroin overdose: Reports by overdose victims. *Bulletin of the Psychonomic Society, 22*, 428–430.

Siegel, S. (1989). Pharmacological conditioning and drug effects. In J. A. Goudie & M. W. Emmett-Oglesby (Eds.), *Psychoactive drugs: Tolerance and sensitization* (pp. 115–180). Clifton, N.J.: Humana Press.

Siegel, S. (1991). Feedforward processes in drug tolerance and dependence. In R. G. Lister & H. J. Weingartner (Eds.), *Perspectives in cognitive neuroscience* (pp. 405–416). New York: Oxford University Press.

Siegel, S., & Andrews, J. M. (1962). Magnitude of reinforcement and choice behavior in children. *Journal of Experimental Psychology, 63*, 337–341.

Siegel, S., & Domjan, M. (1971). Backward conditioning as an inhibitory procedure. *Learning and Motivation, 2*, 1–11.

Siegel, S., Hinson, R. E., & Krank, M. D. (1978). The role of predrug signals in morphine analgesic tolerance: Support for a Pavlovian conditioning model of tolerance. *Journal of Experimental Psychology: Animal Behavior Processes, 4*, 188–196.

Siegel, S., Hinson, R. E., Krank, M. D., & McCully, J. (1982). Heroin "overdose" death: Contribution of drug-associated environmental cues. *Science, 216*, 436–437.

Siegel, S., Sherman, J. E., & Mitchell, D. (1980). Extinction of morphine analgesic tolerance. *Learning and Motivation, 11*, 289–301.

Silberberg, A., Warren-Boulton, F. R., & Asano, T. (1988). Maximizing present value: A model to explain why moderate response rates obtain on variable-interval schedules. *Journal of the Experimental Analysis of Behavior, 49*, 331–338.

Sills, T. L., Onalaja, A. O., & Crawley, J. N. (1998). Mesolimbic dopamine mechanisms underlying individual differences in sugar consumption and amphetamine hypolocomotion in Wistrar rats. *European Journal of Neuroscience, 10*, 1895–1902.

Silva, F. J., Timberlake, W., & Gont, R. S. (1998). Spatiotemporal characteristics of serial CSs and their relation to search modes and response form. *Animal Learning and Behavior, 26*, 299–312.

Simon, G. A. (1973). The structure of ill-structured problems. *Artificial Intelligence, 4*, 181–202.

Simon, G. A. (1974). How big is a chunk? *Science, 183*, 482–488.

Skinner, B. F. (1938). *The behavior of organisms: An experimental analysis.* New York: Appleton-Century-Crofts.

Skinner, B. F. (1948). Superstition in the pigeon. *Journal of Experimental Psychology, 38*, 168–172.

Skinner, B. F. (1953). *Science and human behavior.* New York: Macmillan.

Skinner, B. F. (1957). *Verbal behavior.* New York: Appleton-Century-Crofts.

Slobin, D. I. (1966). Grammatical transformations and sentence comprehension in childhood and adulthood. *Journal of Verbal Learning and Verbal Behavior, 5*, 219–227.

Smith, M. C., Coleman, S. R., & Gormezano, I. (1969). Classical conditioning of the rabbit's nictitating membrane response at backward, simultaneous, and forward CS-US intervals. *Journal of Comparative and Physiological Psychology, 69*, 226–231.

Smith, S. M. (1982). Enhancement of recall using multiple environmental contexts during learning. *Memory and Cognition, 19*, 405–412.

Smith, S. M., Glenberg, A., & Bjork, R. A. (1978). Environmental context and human memory. *Memory and Cognition, 6*, 342–353.

Smoke, K. L. (1933). Negative instances in concept learning. *Journal of Experimental Psychology, 16*, 583–588.

Solnick, J. V., Rincover, A., & Peterson, C. R. (1977). Some determinants of the reinforcing and punishing effects of time-out. *Journal of Applied Behavior Analysis, 10*, 415–424.

Solomon, R. L. (1977). An opponent-process theory of acquired motivation: The affective dynamics of addiction. In J. D. Maser & M. E. P. Seligman (Eds.), *Psychopathology: Experimental models* (pp. 66–103). San Francisco: W. H. Freeman.

Solomon, R. L. (1980). The opponent-process therapy of acquired motivation: The costs of pleasure and the benefits of pain. *American Psychologist, 35*, 691–712.

Solomon, R. L., & Corbit, J. D. (1974). An opponent-process theory of motivation: Temporal dynamics of affect. *Psychological Review, 81*, 119–145.

Solomon, R. L., & Wynne, L. C. (1953). Traumatic avoidance learning: Acquisition in normal dogs. *Psychological Monographs, 67* (Whole No. 354).

Solovason, H. B., Ghanta, V. K., & Hiramoto, R. N. (1988). Conditioned augmentation of natural killer cell activity. Independence from nociceptive and dependence on interferon. *Journal of Immunology, 140*, 661–665.

Spear, N. E., Klein, S. B., & Riley, E. P. (1971). The Kamin effect as "state-dependent learning": Memory-retrieval failure in the rat. *Journal of Comparative and Physiological Psychology, 74*, 416–425.

Spear, N. E., & Riccio, D. C. (1994). *Memory: Phenomena and principles.* Needham Heights, Mass.: Allyn and Bacon.

Speers, M. J., Gillan, D. J., & Rescorla, R. A. (1980). Within-compound associations in a variety of compound conditioning procedures. *Learning and Motivation, 11*, 135–149.

Spence, K. W. (1936). The nature of discrimination learning in animals. *Psychological Review, 43*, 427–449.

Spence, K. W. (1956). *Behavior theory and conditioning.* New Haven, Conn.: Yale University.

Sperling, G. (1960). The information available in brief visual presentations. *Psychological Monographs, 74* (Whole No. 498).

Sperling, G. (1963). A model for visual memory task. *Human Factors, 5*, 19–31.

Squire, L. R. (1986). Mechanisms of memory. *Science, 232*, 1612–1619.

Squire, L. R. (1987). *Memory and brain.* New York: Oxford University Press.

Squire, L. R., Amaral, D. G., & Press, G. A. (1990). Magnetic resonance measurements of hippocampal formation and mammillary nuclei distinguish medial temporal lobe and diencephalic amnesia. *Journal of Neuroscience, 10,* 3106–3117.

Squire, L. R., & Zola-Morgan, S. (1988). Memory: Brain systems and behavior. *Trends in Neuroscience, 11,* 170–175.

Squire, L. R., Zola-Morgan, S., & Chen, K. (1988). Human amnesia and animal models of amnesia: Performance of amnesic patients on tests designed for the monkey. *Behavioral Neuroscience, 11,* 210–221.

Staats, C. K., & Staats, A. W. (1957). Meaning established by classical conditioning. *Journal of Experimental Psychology, 54,* 74–80.

Staddon, J. E. R. (1988). Quasi-dynamic choice models: Melioration and ratio invariance. *Journal of the Experimental Analysis of Behavior, 49,* 303–320.

Staddon, J. E. R., & Ayres, S. L. (1975). Sequential and temporal properties of behavior induced by a schedule of periodic food delivery. *Behavior, 54,* 26–49.

Staddon, J. E. R., & Motheral, S. (1978). On matching and maximizing in operant choice situations. *Psychological Review, 85,* 436–444.

Staddon, J. E. R., & Simmelhag, V. L. (1971). The "Superstition" experiment: A reexamination of its implications for the principles of adaptive behavior. *Psychological Review, 78,* 3–43.

Stapleton, J. V. (1975). Legal issues confronting behavior modification. *Behavioral Engineering, 2,* 35.

Stark, P., & Boyd, E. S. (1963). Effects of cholinergic drugs on hypothalamic self-stimulation response rates of dogs. *American Journal of Physiology, 205,* 745–748.

Starr, M. D. (1978). An opponent process theory of motivation: VI. Time and intensity variables in the development of separation–induced distress calling in ducklings. *Journal of Experimental Psychology: Animal Behavior Processes, 4,* 338–355.

Stein, B. S. (1978). Depth of processing reexamined: The effects of the precision of encoding and test appropriateness. *Journal of Verbal Learning and Verbal Behavior, 17,* 165–174.

Stein, L. (1969). Chemistry of purposive behavior. In J. T. Tapp (Ed.), *Reinforcement and behavior.* New York: Academic.

Steinbrecher, C. D., & Lockhart, R. A. (1966). Temporal avoidance conditioning in the cat. *Psychonomic Science, 5,* 441–442.

Steketee, G. S. (1993). *Treatment of obsessive-compulsive disorder.* New York: Guilford Press.

Stephens, C. E., Pear, J. J., Wray, L. D., & Jackson, G. C. (1975). Some effects of reinforcement schedules in teaching picture names to retarded children. *Journal of Applied Behavior Analysis, 8,* 435–447.

Steur, F. B., Applefield, J. M., & Smith, R. (1971). Televised aggression and the interpersonal aggression of preschool children. *Journal of Experimental Child Psychology, 11,* 442–447.

Stonebraker, T. B., & Rilling, M. (1981). Control of delayed matching-to-sample performance using directed forgetting techniques. *Animal Learning and Behavior, 9,* 196–220.

Storms, L. H., Boroczi, G., & Broen, W. E., Jr. (1962). Punishment inhibits an instrumental response in hooded rats. *Science, 135,* 1133–1134.

Straus, M. A., & Kantor, G. K. (1994). Corporal punishment of adolescents by parents: A risk factor in the epidemiology of depression, suicide, alcohol abuse, child abuse, and wife beating. *Adolescence, 29,* 543–561.

Streeter, L. A., & Landauer, J. K. (1976). Effects of learning English as a second language on the acquisition of new phonetic contrast. *Journal of the Acoustical Society of America, 59,* 448–451.

Stuart, R. B. (1971). A three-dimensional program for the treatment of obesity. *Behavior Research and Therapy, 9,* 177–186.

Sutherland, N. S., & Mackintosh, N. J. (1971). *Mechanisms of animal discrimination learning.* New York: Academic.

Swanson, J. M., & Kinsbourne, M. (1979). State-dependent learning and retrieval: Methodological cautions against theoretical considerations. In J. F. Kihlstrom & F. J. Evans (Eds.), *Functional disorders of memory.* Hillsdale, N.J.: Erlbaum.

Sweeney, P. D., Anderson, K., & Bailey, S. (1986). Attributional style in depression: A meta-analytic review. *Journal of Personality and Social Psychology, 50,* 974–991.

Tait, R. W., Marquis, H. A., Williams, R., Weinstein, L., & Suboski, M. S. (1969). Extinction of sensory preconditioning using CER training. *Journal of Comparative and Physiological Psychology, 69,* 170–172.

Tait, R. W., & Saladin, M. E. (1986). Concurrent development of excitatory and inhibitory associations during backward conditioning. *Animal Learning and Behavior, 14,* 133–137.

Tarpy, R. M., & Koster, E. D. (1970). Stimulus facilitation of delayed-reward learning in the rat. *Journal of Comparative and Physiological Psychology, 71,* 147–151.

Tarpy, R. M., & Mayer, R. E. (1978). *Foundations of learning and memory.* Glenview, Ill.: Scott, Foresman.

Tarpy, R. M., & Sawabini, F. L. (1974). Reinforcement delay: A selective review of the last decade. *Psychological Bulletin, 81,* 984–987.

Tennen, H., & Eller, S. J. (1977). Attributional components of learned helplessness and facilitation. *Journal of Personality and Social Psychology, 35,* 265–271.

Terrace, H. S. (1963a). Errorless discrimination learning in the pigeon: Effects of chlorpromazine and imipramine. *Science, 140,* 318–319.

Terrace, H. S. (1963b). Errorless transfer of a discrimination across two continents. *Journal of the Experimental Analysis of Behavior, 6,* 223–232.

Terrace, H. S. (1963c). Discrimination learning with and without "errors." *Journal of the Experimental Analysis of Behavior, 6,* 1–27.

Terrace, H. S. (1964). Wavelength generalization after discrimination learning with and without errors. *Science, 144,* 78–80.

Terrace, H. S. (1966). Stimulus control. In W. K. Honig (Ed.), *Operant behavior: Areas of research and application.* New York: Appleton-Century-Crofts.

Terrace, H. S. (1979). *Nim.* New York: Knopf.

Terrell, G., & Ware, R. (1961). Role of delay of reward in speed of size and form discrimination learning in childhood. *Child Development, 32,* 409–415.

Tharp, R. G., & Wetzel, R. J. (1969). *Behavior modification in the natural environment.* New York: Academic.

Theios, J., Lynch, A. D., & Lowe, W. F., Jr. (1966). Differential effects of shock intensity on one-way and shuttle avoidance conditioning. *Journal of Experimental Psychology, 72,* 294–299.

Thomas, D. R., Mood, K., Morrison, S., & Wiertelak, E. (1991). Peak shift revisited: A test of alternative interpretations. *Journal of Experimental Psychology: Animal Behavior Processes, 17,* 130–140.

Thomas, E., & DeWald, L. (1977). Experimental neurosis: Neuropsychological analysis. In J. D. Master & M. E. P. Seligman (Eds.), *Psychopathology: Experimental models.* San Francisco: W. H. Freeman.

Thompson, C. R., & Church, R. M. (1980). An explanation of the language of a chimpanzee. *Science, 208,* 313–314.

Thompson. R. F., Clark, G. A., Donegan, N. H., Lavond, D. G., Lincoln, J. S., Madden, J., Mamounas, L. A., Mauk, M. D., McCormick, D. A., & Thompson, J. K. (1984). Neuronal substrates of learning and memory: A "multiple-trace" view. In G. Lynch,

J. L. McGaugh, & N. M. Weinberger (Eds.), *Neurobiology of learning and memory,* (pp. 137–164). New York: Guilford.

Thompson, R. F., Hicks, L. H., & Shvyrok, V. B. (1980). *Neural mechanisms of goal-directed behavior and learning.* New York: Academic.

Thompson, R. F., & Spencer, W. A. (1966). Habituation: A model phenomenon for the study of neural substrates of behavior. *Psychological Review, 73,* 16–43.

Thorndike, E. L. (1898). Animal intelligence: An experimental study of the associative processes in animals. *Psychological Review Monograph Supplement, 2,* 1–109.

Thorndike, E. L. (1913). *Educational psychology, vol. II: The psychology of learning.* New York: Teachers College, Columbia University.

Thorndike, E. L. (1932). *Fundamentals of learning.* New York: Teachers College, Columbia University.

Tiffany, S. T., & Baker, T. B. (1981). Morphine tolerance in rats: Congruence with a Pavlovian paradigm. *Journal of Comparative and Physiological Psychology, 95,* 747–762.

Timberlake, W. (1986). Unpredicted food produces a mode of behavior that affects rats' subsequent reactions to a conditioned stimulus: A behavior-system approach to context blocking. *Animal Learning and Behavior, 14,* 276–286.

Timberlake, W. (2001). Motivated modes in behavior systems. In R. R. Mowrer & S. B. Klein (Eds.), *Handbook of contemporary learning theories* (pp. 155–209). Mawrah, N.J.: Erlbaum.

Timberlake, W., & Allison, J. (1974). Response deprivation: An empirical approach to instrumental performance. *Psychological Review, 81,* 146–164.

Timberlake, W., & Farmer-Dougan, V. A. (1991). Reinforcement in applied settings: Figuring out ahead of time what will work. *Psychological Bulletin, 110,* 379–391.

Timberlake, W., & Lucas, G. A. (1989). Behavior systems and learning: From misbehavior to general principles. In S. B. Klein & R. R. Mowrer (Eds.), *Contemporary learning theory: Instrumental conditioning theory and the impact of biological constraints on learning* (pp. 237–275). Hillsdale, N.J.: Erlbaum.

Timberlake, W., Wahl, G., & King, D. (1982). Stimulus and response contingencies in the misbehavior of rats. *Journal of Experimental Psychology: Animal Behavior Processes, 8,* 62–85.

Tinbergen, N. (1951). *The study of instinct.* Oxford: Clarendon.

Tinbergen, N., & Van Iersel, J. J. A. (1947). Displacement reactions in the three-spined stickleback. *Behavior, 1,* 56–63.

Todd, G. E., & Cogan, D. C. (1978). Selected schedules of reinforcement in the black-tailed prairie dog (*Cynomys ludovicianus*). *Animal Learning and Behavior, 6,* 429–434.

Toister, R. P., Condron, C. J., Worley, L., & Arthur, D. (1975). Faradic therapy of chronic vomiting in infancy: A case study. *Journal of Behavior Therapy and Experimental Psychiatry, 6,* 55–59.

Tolman, E. C. (1932). *Purposive behavior in animals and men.* New York: Century.

Tolman, E. C. (1959). Principles of purposive behavior. In S. Koch (Ed.), *Psychology: A study of a science,* (Vol. 2, pp. 92–157). New York: McGraw-Hill.

Tolman, E. C., & Honzik, C. H. (1930a). "Insight" in rats. *University of California Publications in Psychology, 4,* 215–232.

Tolman, E. C., & Honzik, C. H. (1930b). Degrees of hunger; reward and nonreward; and maze learning in rats. *University of California Publications in Psychology, 4,* 241–256.

Tolman, E. C., Ritchie, B. F., & Kalish, D. (1946). Studies of spatial learning: II. Place learning versus response learning. *Journal of Experimental Psychology, 36,* 221–229.

Tombaugh, T. N. (1966). Resistance to extinction as a function of the interaction between training and extinction delays. *Psychological Review, 19,* 791–798.

Touchette, P. E. (1969). Tilted lines as complex stimuli. *Journal of the Experimental Analysis of Behavior, 12,* 211–214.

Toufexis, A. (1991, October 28). When can memories be trusted? *Time,* pp. 86–88.

Trapold, M. A., & Fowler, H. (1960). Instrumental escape performance as a function of the intensity of noxious stimulation. *Journal of Experimental Psychology, 60,* 323–326.

Trapold, M.A., & Winokur, S. (1967). Transfer from classical conditioning and extinction to acquisition, extinction, and stimulus generalization of a positively reinforced instrumental response. *Journal of Experimental Psychology, 73,* 517–525.

Traupmann, K. L. (1972). Drive, reward, and training parameters and the overlearning-extinction effect (OEE). *Learning and Motivation, 3,* 359–368.

Trenholme, I. A., & Baron, A. (1975). Intermediate and delayed punishment of human behavior by loss of reinforcement. *Learning and Motivation, 6,* 62–79.

Troland, L. T. (1928). *The fundamentals of human motivation.* New York: Van Nostrand.

Tulving, E. (1972). Episodic and semantic memory. In E. Tulving & W. Donaldson (Eds.), *Organization of memory* (pp. 381–403). New York: Academic.

Tulving, E. (1983). *Elements of episodic memory.* Oxford: Clarendon Press/Oxford University Press.

Tulving, E. (1998). Brain/mind correlates of human memory. In M. Sabourin, F. Craik, & M. Robert (Eds.), *Advances in psychological science: Vol. 2. Biological and cognitive aspects* (pp. 441–460). Hove, East Sussex, England: Psychology Press.

Tulving, E., & Donaldson, W. (1972). *Organization of memory.* New York: Academic.

Tulving, E., & Markowitsch, H. J. (1997). Memory beyond the hippocampus. *Current Opinion in Neurobiology, 7,* 209–216.

Ullman, L. P., & Krasner, L. (1965). *Case studies in behavior modification.* New York: Holt, Rinehart & Winston.

Ulrich, R. E., Wolff, P. C., & Azrin, N. H. (1964). Shock as an elicitor of intra- and inter-species fighting behavior. *Animal Behavior, 12,* 14–15.

Underwood, B. J. (1957). Interference and forgetting. *Psychological Review, 64,* 48–60.

Underwood, B. J. (1969). Attributes of memory. *Psychological Review, 76,* 559–573.

Underwood, B. J. (1977). *Temporal codes for memories: Issues and problems.* Hillsdale, N.J.: Erlbaum.

Underwood, B. J. (1983). *Attributes of memory.* Glenview, Ill.: Scott, Foresman.

Underwood, B. J., & Ekstrand, B. R. (1966). An analysis of some shortcomings in the interference theory of forgetting. *Psychological Review, 73,* 540–549.

Underwood, B. J., & Freund, J. S. (1968). Effect of temporal separation of two tasks on proactive inhibition. *Journal of Experimental Psychology, 78,* 50–54.

U.S. Department of Justice. *Special Report: Drunk Driving,* February 1988.

Vaccarino, F. J., Bloom, R. E., & Koob, G. F. (1985). Blockade of nucleus accumbens opiate receptors attenuates intravenous heroin reward in the rat. *Psychopharmacology, 86,* 37–42.

Vaccarino, F. J., Schiff, B. B., & Glickman, S. E. (1989). Biological view of reinforcement. In S. B. Klein & R. R. Mowrer (Eds.), *Contemporary learning theories: Instrumental conditioning and the impact of biological constraints on learning* (pp. 111–142). Hillsdale, N.J.: Erlbaum.

Valenstein, E. S., & Beer, B. (1964). Continuous opportunities for reinforcing brain stimulation. *Journal of Experimental Analysis of Behavior, 7,* 183–184.

Valenstein, E. S., Cox, V. C., & Kakolewski, J. W. (1969). The hypothalamus and motivated behavior. In J. T. Tapp (Ed.), *Reinforcement and behavior.* New York: Academic.

Vandercar, D. H., & Schneiderman, N. (1967). Interstimulus interval functions in different response systems during classical discrimination conditioning of rabbits. *Psychonomic Science, 9,* 9–10.

Van Hamme, L. J., & Wasserman, E. A. (1994). Cue competition in causality judgments: The role of nonpresentation of compound stimulus elements. *Learning and Motivation, 25,* 127–151.

Victor, M., Adams, R. D., & Collins, G. H. (1989). *The Wernicke-Korsakoff syndrome and related neurological disorders due to alcoholism and malnutrition* (2nd ed.). Philadelphia: Davis.

Viken, R. J., & McFall, R. M. (1994). Paradox lost: Implications of contemporary reinforcement theory for behavior therapy. *Current Directions in Psychological Science, 3,* 121–125.

Voeks, V. W. (1954). Acquisition of S-R connections: A test of Hull's and Guthrie's theories. *Journal of Experimental Psychology, 47,* 137–147.

Vollmer, T. R., & Bourret, J. (2000). An application of the matching law to evaluate the allocation of two- and three-point shots by college basketball players. *Journal of Applied Behavior Analysis, 33,* 137–150.

Von Cramon, D. Y., Hebel, N., & Schuri, U. (1985). A contribution to the anatomical basis of thalamic amnesia. *Brain, 108,* 993–1008.

Von Holst, E., & Von St. Paul, U. (1962). Electrically controlled behavior. *Scientific American, 206,* 50–59.

Vyse, S. A., & Belke, T. W. (1992). Maximizing versus matching on concurrent variable-interval schedules. *Journal of the Experimental Analysis of Behavior, 58,* 325–334.

Wagner, A. R. (1981). SOP: A model of automatic memory processing in animal behavior. In N. E. Spear & R. R. Miller (Eds.), *Information processing in animals: Memory mechanisms* (pp. 5–47). Hillsdale, N.J.: Erlbaum.

Wagner, A. R., & Brandon, S. E. (1989). Evolution of a structured connectionist model of Pavlovian conditioning (AESOP). In S. B. Klein & R. R. Mowrer (Eds.), *Contemporary learning theories: Pavlovian conditioning and the status of traditional learning theory* (pp. 149–189). Hillsdale, N.J.: Erlbaum.

Wagner, A. R., Logan, F. A., Haberlandt, K., & Price, T. (1968). Stimulus selection in animal discrimination learning. *Journal of Experimental Psychology, 76,* 171–180.

Wahler, R. G., Winkel, G. H., Peterson, R. F., & Morrison, D. C. (1965). Mothers as behavior therapists for their own children. *Behaviour Research and Therapy, 3,* 113–124.

Walk, R. D., & Walters, C. P. (1973). Effect of visual deprivation on depth discrimination of hooded rats. *Journal of Comparative and Physiological Psychology, 85,* 559–563.

Wallman, J. (1992). *Aping language.* Cambridge, England: Cambridge University Press.

Walters, G. C., & Grusec, J. F. (1977). *Punishment.* San Francisco: W. H. Freeman.

Wanner, E., & Maratsos, M. (1978). An ATN approach to comprehension. In M. Halle, J. Bresnan, & G. A. Miller (Eds.), *Linguistic theory and psychological reality.* Cambridge, Mass.: MIT Press.

Warner, L. H. (1932). An experimental search for the "conditioned response." *Journal of Genetic Psychology, 41,* 91–115.

Warrington, E. K. (1985). A disconnection analysis of amnesia. *Annals of the New York Academy of Sciences, 444,* 72–77.

Warrington, E. K., & Weiskrantz, L. (1968). A study of learning and retention in amnesic patients. *Neuropsychologia, 6,* 283–291.

Warrington, E. K., & Weiskrantz, L. (1970). Amnesic syndrome: Consolidation or retrieval? *Nature, 228,* 628–630.

Wasserman, E. A. (1993). Comparative cognition: Beginning the second century of the animal intelligence. *Psychological Bulletin, 113,* 211–228.

Wasserman, E. A. (1995). The conceptual abilities of pigeons. *American Scientist, 83,* 246–250.

Watanabe, S., Sakamoto, J., & Wakita, M. (1995). Pigeons' discrimination of paintings by Monet and Picasso. *Journal of the Experimental Analysis of Behavior, 63,* 165–174.

Watkins, M. H., & Tulving, E. (1975). Episodic memory: When recognition fails. *Journal of Experimental Psychology: General, 104,* 5–29.

Watkins, M. J. (1974). When is recall spectacularly higher than recognition? *Journal of Experimental Psychology, 102,* 161–163.

Watson, J. B. (1916). The place of the conditioned reflex in psychology. *Psychological Review, 23,* 89–116.

Watson, J. B., & Morgan, J. J. B. (1917). Emotional reactions and psychological experimentation. *American Journal of Psychology, 28,* 163–174.

Watson, J. B., & Rayner, R. (1920). Conditional emotional reactions. *Journal of Experimental Psychology, 3,* 1–14.

Waugh, N. C., & Norman, D. A. (1965). Primary memory. *Psychological Review, 72,* 89–104.

Weeks, R. A. (1975). Auditory location as an encoding dimension. *Journal of Experimental Psychology: Human Learning and Memory, 104,* 316–318.

Weidman, U. (1956). Some experiments on the following and the flocking reaction of mallard ducklings. *British Journal of Animal Behavior, 4,* 78–79.

Weinstock, S. (1958). Acquisition and extinction of a partially reinforced running response at a 24-hour intertrial interval. *Journal of Experimental Psychology, 56,* 151–158.

Weisberg, R., DiCamillo, M., & Phillips, D. (1979). Transferring old associations to new situations: A nonautomatic process. *Journal of Verbal Learning and Verbal Behavior, 17,* 219–228.

Weiskrantz, L., & Warrington, E. K. (1975). The problem of the amnesic syndrome in man and animals. In R. L. Isaacson & K. H. Pribram (Eds.), *The hippocampus* (pp. 411–428). New York: Plenum.

Weisman, R. G., & Litner, J. S. (1972). The role of Pavlovian events in avoidance training. In R. A. Boakes & M. S. Halliday (Eds.), *Inhibition and learning.* London: Academic Press.

Weisman, R. G., & Palmer, J. A. (1969). Factors influencing inhibitory stimulus control: Discrimination training and prior nondifferential reinforcement. *Journal of the Experimental Analysis of Behavior, 12,* 229–237.

Weiss, B., Dodge, K. A., Bates, J. E., & Pettit, G. S. (1992). Some consequences of early harsh discipline: Child aggression and a maladaptive social information. *Child Development, 63,* 1321–1335.

Weiss, J. M., Goodman, P. A., Losito, P. G., Corrigan, S., Charry, J., & Bailey, W. (1981). Behavioral depression produced by an uncontrolled stressor: Relation to norepinephrine, dopamine, and serotonin levels in various regions of the rat brain. *Brain Research Review, 3,* 167–205.

Weiss, J. M., & Simpson, P. G. (1986). Depression in an animal model: Focus on the locus coeruleus in antidepressants and receptor function. In D. L. Murphy (Ed.), *Antidepressant and receptor functions* (pp. 191–209). Chichester: John Wiley.

Weiss, J. M., Simpson, P. G., Ambrose, M. J., Webster, A., & Hoffman, L. J. (1985). Chemical basis of behavioral depression. In: E. Katkin & S. Manuck (Eds.), *Advances in behavioral medicine* (Vol. 1, pp. 233–275). Greenwich: JAI Press.

Weiss, J. M., Simpson, P. G., Hoffman, L. J., Ambrose, M. G., Cooper, S., & Webster, A. (1986). Infusion of adrenergic receptor agonist and antagonists into the locus coeruleus and ventricular system of the brain: Effects on swim-motivated and spontaneous motor activity. *Neuropharmacology, 25,* 367–384.

Weiss, S. J., & Schindler, C. W. (1981). Generalization peak shift in rats under conditions of positive reinforcement and avoidance. *Journal of the Experimental Analysis of Behavior, 35,* 175–185.

Wells, U. C., Forehand, R., Hickey, K., & Green, K. D. (1977). Effects of a procedure derived from the overcorrection principle on manipulated and nonmanipulated behavior. *Journal of Applied Behavior Analysis, 10,* 679–688.

Wessels, M. G. (1982). *Cognitive psychology.* New York: Harper & Row.

Westbrook, R. F., Homewood, J., Horn, K., & Clarke, J. C. (1983). Flavor-odor compound conditioning: Odor potentiation and flavor-attenuation. *Quarterly Journal of Experimental Psychology, 35B,* 13–33.

Wetherington, C. L. (1982). Is adjunctive behavior a third class of behavior? *Neuroscience and Biobehavioral Reviews, 6,* 329–350.

White, A. G., & Bailey, J. S. (1990). Reducing disruptive behaviors of elementary physical education students with Sit and Watch. *Journal of Applied Behavior Analysis, 23,* 353–359.

White, M. A. (1975). Natural rates of teacher approval and disapproval in the classroom. *Journal of Applied Behavior Analysis, 8,* 367–372.

Whitfield, C. L. (1995). *Memory and abuse: Remembering and healing the effects of trauma.* Deerfield Beach, FL: Health Communications.

Wickelgren, W. A. (1974). *How to solve problems.* San Francisco: W. H. Freeman.

Wickens, C. D., Strokes, A., Barnett, B., & Hyman, F. (1992). The effects of stress on pilot judgment in a MIDIS simulator. In O. Svenson & J. Maule (Eds.), *Time pressure and stress in human judgment and decision making.* New York: Plenum.

Wikler, A., & Pescor, F. T. (1967). Classical conditioning of a morphine abstinence phenomenon, reinforcement of opioid-drinking behavior and "relapse" in morphine-addicted rats. *Psychopharmacologia, 10,* 255–284.

Wilcott, R. C. (1953). A search for subthreshold conditioning at four different auditory frequencies. *Journal of Experimental Psychology, 46,* 271–277.

Wilcoxon, H. C., Dragoin, W. B., & Kral, P. A. (1971). Illness-induced aversions in rat and quail: Relative salience of visual and gustatory cues. *Science, 7,* 489–493.

Williams, B. A. (1983). Another look at contrast in multiple schedules. *Journal of the Experimental Analysis of Behavior, 39,* 345–384.

Williams, B. A. (1989). Component duration efforts in multiple schedules. *Animal Learning and Behavior, 17,* 223–233.

Williams, B. A. (1991a). Marking and bridging versus conditioned reinforcement. *Animal Learning and Behavior, 19,* 264–269.

Williams, B. A. (1991b). Choice as a function of local versus molar contingencies of reinforcement. *Journal of the Experimental Analysis of Behavior, 56,* 455–473.

Williams, S. B. (1938). Resistance to extinction as a function of the number of reinforcements. *Journal of Experimental Psychology, 23,* 506–522.

Willows, A. O. D., & Hoyle, G. (1969). Neuronal network triggering a fixed action pattern. *Science, 166,* 1549–1551.

Wilson, B. A. (1987). *Rehabilitation of memory.* New York: Guilford Press.

Wilson, P. N., & Pearce, J. M. (1990). Selective transfer of responding in conditional discriminations. *Quarterly Journal of Experimental Psychology, 42B,* 41–58.

Wine, J. J., & Krasne, T. B. (1982). The cellular organization of crayfish escape behavior. In D. C. Sandman & H. Atwood (Eds.), *The biology of crustacea:* Vol. 4 (pp. 241–292). New York: Academic Press.

Wingfield, A., & Byrnes, D. L. (1981). *The psychology of human memory.* New York: Academic.

Winn, P., Williams, S. F., & Herberg, L. J. (1982). Feeding stimulated by very low doses of d-amphetamine administered systemically or by microinjection into the striatum. *Psychopharmacology, 78,* 336–341.

Wise, R. A. (1996). Addictive drugs and brain stimulation reward. *Annual Review of Neuroscience, 19,* 319–340.

Wise, R. A., & Rompre, P. O. (1989). Brain dopamine and reward. *Annual Review of Psychology, 40,* 191–225.

Wolf, M. M., Hanley, E. L., King, L. A., Lachowicz, J., & Giles, D. K. (1970). The timer game: A variable-interval contingency for the management of out-of-seat behavior. *Exceptional Children, 37,* 113–117.

Wolf, M. M., Risley, T., & Mees, H. L. (1964). Application of operant conditioning procedures to the behavior problems of an autistic child. *Behavior Research and Therapy, 1,* 305–312.

Wolpe, J. (1958). *Psychotherapy by reciprocal inhibition.* Stanford, Calif.: Stanford University Press.

Wolpe, J. (1976). *Theme and variations: A behavior therapy casebook.* Elmsford, N.J.: Pergamon.

Wolpe, J. (1978). Self-efficacy theory and psychotherapeutic change: A square peg for a round hole. In S. Rachman (Ed.), *Advances in behavior research and therapy* (Vol. 1, pp. 231–236). Oxford: Pergamon.

Wood, F., Taylor, B., Penny, R., & Stump, D. (1980). Regional cerebral blood flow response to recognition memory versus semantic classification tasks. *Brain and Language, 9,* 113–122.

Wood, G., & Underwood, B. J. (1967). Implicit responses and conceptual similarity. *Journal of Verbal Learning and Verbal Behavior, 6,* 1–10.

Woods, P. J., Davidson, E. H., & Peters, R. J. (1964). Instrumental escape conditioning in a water tank: Effects of variations in drive stimulus intensity and reinforcement magnitude. *Journal of Comparative and Physiological Psychology, 57,* 466–470.

Woodworth, R. S. (1918). *Dynamic psychology.* New York: Columbia University Press.

Wright v. McMann, 460 F. 2d 126 (2d Cir. 1972).

Yule, W., Sacks, B., & Hersov, L. (1974). Successful flooding treatment of a noise phobia in an eleven-year-old. *Journal of Behavior Therapy and Experimental Psychiatry, 5,* 209–211.

Zalcman, S., Irwin, J., & Anisman, H. (1991). Stressor-induced alterations of natural killer cell activity and central catecholamines in mice. *Pharmacology, Biochemistry and Behavior, 39,* 361–366.

Zaragoza, M. S., McCloskey, M., & Jamis, M. (1987). Misleading post-event information and recall of the original event: Further evidence against the memory impairment hypothesis. *Journal of Experimental Psychology: Learning, Memory, and Cognition, 13,* 36–44.

Zazdeh, L. A., Fu, K. S., Tanak, K., & Shimura, M. (Eds.). 1975. *Fuzzy sets and their applications to cognitive and decision processes.* New York: Academic.

Zeaman, D. (1949). Response latency as a function of the amount of reinforcement. *Journal of Experimental Psychology, 39,* 466–483.

Zechmeister, E. B. (1969). Orthographic distinctiveness. *Journal of Verbal Learning and Verbal Behavior, 8,* 754–761.

Zola-Morgan, S., & Squire, L. R. (1986). Memory impairment in monkeys following lesions limited to the hippocampus. *Behavioral Neuroscience, 100,* 155–160.

Zola-Morgan, S., & Squire, L. R. (1993). Neuroanatomy of memory. *Annual Review of Neuroscience, 16,* 547–563.

Zola-Morgan, S., Squire, L. R., & Amaral, D. G. (1986). Human amnesia and the medial temporal region: Enduring memory impairment following a bilateral lesion limited to field CA1 of the hippocampus. *Journal of Neuroscience, 6,* 2950–2967.

Zola-Morgan, S., Squire, L. R., & Amaral, D. G. (1989). Lesions of the hippocampal formation but not lesions of the fornix or the mammillary nuclei produce long-lasting memory impairment in monkey. *Journal of Neuroscience, 9,* 897–912.

Zygmont, D. M., Lazar, R. M., Dube, W. V., & McIlvane, W. J. (1992). Teaching arbitrary matching via sample stimulus-control shaping to young children and mentally retarded individuals: A methodological note. *Journal of the Experimental Analysis of Behavior, 57,* 109–117.

Credits

Figure 1.1. Adapted from Swenson, L. C. (1980). *Theories of learning*. Belmont, Calif.: Wadsworth.

Figure 1.2. Adapted from Imada, H., & Imada, S. (1983). Thorndike's (1898) puzzle-box experimental revisited, *Kwansie University Annual Studies, 32,* 167–184.

Figure 1.3. Adapted from Yerkes, R. M., & Margulis, S. (1909). The method of Pavlov in animal psychology. *Psychological Bulletin, 6,* 257–273. Copyright 1909 by the American Psychological Association. Reprinted by permission.

Figure 1.4. Adapted from Davidoff, L. (1980). *Introduction to psychology* (2nd ed.). New York: McGraw-Hill.

Figure 1.5. Adapted from Swenson, L. C. (1980). *Theories of learning*. Belmont, Calif.: Wadsworth.

Figure 2.1. Adapted from Lorenz, K. (1950). The comparative method of studying innate behavior patterns. In J. F. Danelli & R. Brown, *Symposia of the Society for Experimental Biology: Physiological mechanisms in animal behavior.* New York: Academic Press.

Figure 2.2. Adapted from Tinbergen, N. (1951). *The study of instinct.* Oxford: Clarendon.

Figure 2.3. From *Motivation: Theory, research, and applications* by H. Petri. Copyright 1991 by Wadsworth Publishing Company, a division of Thompson Learning. Fax 800-730- 2215.

Figure 2.4. From Domjan, M. (1976). Determinants of the enhancement of flavor-water intake by prior exposure. *Journal of Experimental Psychology: Animal Behavior Processes, 2,* 17–27. Copyright 1976 by the American Psychological Association. Reprinted by permission.

Figure 2.5. From Davis, M. (1974). Sensitization of the rat startle response by noise. *Journal of Comparative and Physiological Psychology, 87,* 571–581. Copyright 1974 by the American Psychological Association. Reprinted by permission.

Figure 2.6. Adapted from Solomon, R. L., & Corbit, J. D. (1974). An opponent-process theory of motivation: Temporal dynamics of affect. *Psychological Review, 81,*

119–145. Copyright 1974 by the American Psychological Association. Reprinted by permission.

Figure 2.7. Adapted from Solomon, R. L., & Corbit, J. D. (1974). An opponent-process theory of motivation: Temporal dynamics of affect. *Psychological Review, 81,* 119–145. Copyright 1974 by the American Psychological Association. Reprinted by permission.

Figure 3.2. Adapted from Swenson, L. C. (1980). *Theories of learning.* Belmont-Calif.: Wadsworth.

Figure 3.3. From Gormezano, I. (1969). Classical conditioning. In J. B. Sidowski (Ed.), *Experimental methods of instrumentation in psychology.* New York: McGraw-Hill.

Figure 3.5. Data from Kimble, G. A., & Reynolds, B. (1967). Eyelid conditioning as a function of the interval between conditioned and unconditioned stimuli. In G. A. Kimble (Ed.), *Foundations of conditioning and learning.* New York: Appleton-Century- Crofts.

Figure 3.6. From Grice, G. R., & Hunter, J. J. (1964). Stimulus intensity effects depends upon the type of experimental design. *Psychological Review, 71,* 247–256. Copyright 1964 by the American Psychological Association. Reprinted by permission.

Figure 3.7. Adapted from Prokasy, W. P., Jr., Grant, D. A., & Myers, N. A. (1958). Eyelid conditioning as a function of unconditioned stimulus intensity and intertrial interval. *Journal of Experimental Psychology, 55,* 242–246. Copyright 1958 by the American Psychological Association. Reprinted by permission.

Figure 3.8. Adapted from Rescorla, R. A. (1968). Probability of shock in the presence and absence of CS in fear conditioning. *Journal of Comparative and Physiological Psychology, 68,* 1–5. Copyright 1968 by the American Psychological Association. Reprinted by permission.

Figure 3.9. Adapted from Hartman, T. F., & Grant, D. A. (1960). Effect of intermittent reinforcement on acquisition, extinction, and spontaneous recovery of the conditioned eyelid response. *Journal of Experimental Psychology, 60,* 89–96. Copyright 1960 by the American Psychological Association. Reprinted by permission.

Figure 3.11. Adapted from Humphreys, L. G. (1939). The effect of random alternation of reinforcement on the acquisition and extinction of conditioned eyelid reactions. *Journal of Experimental Psychology, 25,* 141–158. Copyright 1939 by the American Psychological Association. Reprinted by permission.

Figure 3.12. Adapted from Shipley, R. H. (1974). Extinction of conditioned fear in rats as a function of several parameters of CS exposure. *Journal of Comparative and Physiological Psychology, 87,* 669–707. Copyright 1974 by the American Psychological Association. Reprinted by permission.

Figure 3.13. From Kimmel, H. D. (1965). Instrumental inhibitory factors in classical conditioning. In W. F. Prokasy (Ed.), *Classical conditioning: A symposium.* New York: Irvington.

Figure 3.17. Reprinted with permission from Ader, R., & Cohen, N. (1982). Behaviorally conditioned immunosuppression and murine systemic lupus erythematosus. *Science, 215,* 1534–1536. Copyright 1982 by the American Association for the Advancement of Science.

Figure 4.1. By Edmund Fantino and Cheryl A. Logan. *The experimental analysis of behavior. A biological perspective.* Copyright 1979 by W. H. Freeman and Company. Reprinted by permission.

Figure 4.2. Adapted from Swenson, L. C. (1980). *Theories of learning.* Belmont, Calif.: Wadsworth.

Figure 4.3. Adapted from Bersh, P. J. (1951). The influence of two variables upon the establishment of a secondary reinforcer for operant responses. *Journal of Experimental Psychology, 41,* 62–73. Copyright 1951 by the American Psychological Association. Reprinted by permission.

Figure 4.6. From *Physiology and Behavior, 9,* Collier, G., Hirsch, E., & Hamlin, P. H. The ecological determinants of reinforcement in the rat, 705–716. Copyright 1972, with permission from Elsevier Science.

Figure 4.7. Adapted from Reynold, G. S. (1968). *A primer of operant conditioning.* Glenview, Ill.: Scott, Foresman, and Company.

Figure 4.8. From Grice, G. R. (1948). The relation of secondary reinforcement to delayed reward in visual discrimination learning. *Journal of Experimental Psychology, 38,* 1–16. Copyright 1948 by the American Psychological Association. Reprinted by permission.

Figure 4.9. Adapted from Guttman, N. (1954). Equal reinforcing values for sucrose and glucose solutions compared with sweetness values. *Journal of Comparative and Physiological Psychology, 47,* 358–361. Copyright 1954 by the American Psychological Association. Reprinted by permission.

Figure 4.12. From D'Amato, M. R. (1970). *Experimental psychology: Methodology, psychophysics, and learning.* New York: McGraw-Hill.

Figure 4.13. From Jenkins, W. O., McFann, H., & Clayton, F. L. (1950). A methodological study of extinction following a periodic and continuous reinforcement. *Journal of Comparative and Physiological Psychology, 43,* 155–167. Copyright 1950 by the American Psychological Association. Reprinted by permission.

Figure 4.14. From Hulse, S. H., Jr. (1958). Amount and percentage of reinforcement and duration of goal confinement in conditioning and extinction. *Journal of Experimental Psychology, 56,* 48–57. Copyright 1958 by the American Psychological Association. Reprinted by permission.

Figure 4.15. From Ayllon, T., & Arzin, N. H. (1965). The measurement and reinforcement of behavior of psychotics. *Journal of the Experimental Analysis of Behavior, 8,* 357–383. Copyright 1965 by the Society for the Experimental Analysis of Behavior, Inc. Reprinted by permission.

Figure 5.1. Adapted from Trapold, M. A., & Fowler, H. (1960). Instrumental escape performance as a function of the intensity of noxious stimulation. *Journal of Experimental Psychology, 60,* 323–326. Copyright 1960 by the American Psychological Association. Reprinted by permission.

Figure 5.2. Adapted from Fowler, H., & Trapold, M. A. (1962). Escape performance as a function of delay of reinforcement. *Journal of Experimental Psychology, 63,* 464–467. Copyright 1962 by the American Psychological Association. Reprinted by permission.

Figure 5.3. From Fazzaro, J., & D'Amato, M. R. (1969). Resistance to extinction after varying amounts of nondiscriminative or cue-correlated escape training. *Journal of Comparative and Physiological Psychology, 68,* 373–376. Copyright 1969 by the American Psychological Association. Reprinted by permission.

Figure 5.4. From Brown, J. S., Martin, R. C., & Morrow, M. W. (1964). Self-punitive behavior in the rat: Facilitative effects of punishment on resistance to extinction. *Journal of Comparative and Physiological Psychology, 57,* 127–133. Copyright 1964 by the American Psychological Association. Reprinted by permission.

Figure 5.6. From Flaherty, C. F., Hamilton, L. W., Gandelman, R. J., & Spear, N. E. (1977). *Learning and memory.* Chicago: Rand McNally.

Figure 5.7. From Emmelkanp, van der Helm, van Zanten, and Plochg, 1980. Reprinted with permission from *Behavior Research and Therapy.* Copyright 1980, Pergamon Journals, Ltd.

Figure 5.8. Adapted from Skinner, B. F. (1938). *The behavior of organisms: An experimental analysis*. New York: Appleton-Century-Crofts.

Figure 5.9. Adapted from Camp, D. S., Raymond, G. A., & Church, R. M. (1967). Temporal relationship between response and punishment. *Journal of Experimental Psychology, 74,* 114–123. Copyright 1967 by the American Psychological Association. Reprinted by permission.

Figure 5.10. From Azrin, N. H., Holz, W. C., & Hake, D. F. (1963). Fixed-ratio punishment. *Journal for the Experimental Analysis of Behavior, 6,* 141–148. Copyright 1963 by the Society for the Experimental Analysis of Behavior, Inc.

Figure 5.11. Adapted from Camp, D. S., Raymond, G. A., & Church, R. M. (1967). Temporal relationship between response and punishment. *Journal of Experimental Psychology, 74,* 114–123. Copyright 1967 by the American Psychological Association. Reprinted by permission.

Figure 5.12. Photo courtesy of Albert Bandura, Stanford University.

Figure 5.13. Photo courtesy of Peter Lang.

Figure 6.1. From Klein, S. B. (1982). *Motivation: Biosocial approaches*. New York: McGraw-Hill.

Figure 6.2. Adapted from Crespi, L. P. (1942). Quantitative variation of incentive and performance in white rats. *American Journal of Psychology, 55,* 467–517. Copyright 1942 by the Board of Trustees of the University of Illinois. Used with permission of the University of Illinois Press.

Figure 6.3. From Kamin, L. J. (1956). The effects of termination of the CS and the avoidance of the UCS on avoidance learning. *Journal of Comparative and Physiological Psychology, 49,* 420–424. Copyright 1956 by the American Psychological Association. Reprinted by permission.

Figure 6.4. From D'Amato, M. R., Fazzaro, J., & Etkin, M. (1968). Anticipatory responding and avoidance discrimination as factors in avoidance conditioning. *Journal of Experimental Psychology, 77,* 41–47. Copyright 1968 by the American Psychological Association. Reprinted by permission.

Figure 6.5. From Bolles, R. C. (1979). *Learning Theory* (2nd ed.). New York: Holt, Rinehart, and Winston.

Figure 7.1. Adapted from Guttman, N., & Kalish, H. I. (1956). Discriminability and stimulus generalization. *Journal of Experimental Psychology, 51,* 79–88. Copyright 1956 by the American Psychological Association. Reprinted by permission.

Figure 7.2. From Hoveland, C. I. (1937). The generalization of conditioned responses: II. The sensory generalization of conditioned responses with varying frequencies of tones. *Journal of General Psychology, 17,* 125–148. Published by Heldref Publications, 4000 Albemarle St., N. W., Washington, D.C. 20016.

Figure 7.3. From Jenkins, H. M., & Harrison, R. H. (1960). Effect of discrimination training on auditory generalization. *Journal of Experimental Psychology, 59,* 246–253. Copyright 1960 by the American Psychological Association. Reprinted by permission.

Figure 7.4. From Weisman, R. G., & Palmer, J. A. (1969). Factors influencing inhibitory stimulus control: Discrimination training and prior non-differential reinforcement. *Journal of the Experimental Analysis of Behavior, 12,* 229–337. Copyright 1969 by the Society for the Experimental Analysis of Behavior, Inc.

Figure 7.5. Reprinted with permission from Peterson, N. (1962). Effect of monochromatic rearing on the control of responding by wavelength. *Science, 136,* 774–775. Copyright 1962 by the American Association for the Advancement of Science.

Figure 7.6. From Reynolds, G. S. (1968). *A primer of operant conditioning*. Glenview, Ill.: Scott, Foresman and Company.

Figure 7.8. From Davidson, T. L., Aparicio, J., & Rescorla, R. A. (1988). Transfer between Pavlovian facilitators and instrumental discriminative stimuli. *Animal Learning and Behavior, 16,* 285–291. Reprinted by permission of Psychonomic Society, Inc.

Figure 7.9. Adapted from Rescorla, R. A., & Solomon, R. L. (1967). Two-process theory: Relationships between Pavlovian conditioning and instrumental learning. *Psychological Review, 74,* 151–182. Copyright 1967 by the American Psychological Association. Reprinted by permission.

Figure 7.10. From Spence, K. W. (1937). The difference response in animals to stimuli varying within a single dimension. *Psychological Review, 44,* 430–444. Copyright 1937 by the American Psychological Association. Reprinted by permission.

Figure 7.11. From Hanson, H. (1959). Effects of discrimination training on stimulus generalization. *Journal of Experimental Psychology, 58,* 321–324. Copyright 1959 by the American Psychological Association. Reprinted by permission.

Figure 7.12. Reproduced from *The psychology of learning and memory* by Barry Schwartz and Daniel Reisberg, by permission of W. W. Norton Company, Inc. Copyright 1991 by W. W. Norton & Company, Inc.

Figure 7.13. Adapted from Terrace, H. S. (1963). Discrimination training with and without "errors." *Journal of the Experimental Analysis of Behavior, 6,* 1–27. Copyright 1963 by the Society for the Experimental Analysis of Behavior. Reprinted by permission.

Figure 7.14. From *Principles of learning and behavior,* 2nd edition, by M. Domjan and B. Burkhard. Copyright 1986. Reprinted with permission of Brooks/Cole, an imprint of the Wadsworth Group, a division of Thompson Learning. Fax 800-730-2215.

Figure 8.1. From Tolman, E. C., Ritchie, B. F., & Kalish, D. (1946). Studies of spatial learning: II. Place learning versus response learning. *Journal of Experimental Psychology, 36,* 221–229. Copyright 1946 by the American Psychological Association. Reprinted by permission.

Figure 8.2. From Tolman, E. C., & Honzik, C. H. (1930). "Insight" in rats. *University of California Publications in Psychology, 4,* 215–232. Copyright 1930 by The Regents of the University of California.

Figure 8.3. From Tolman, E. C., & Honzik, C. H. (1930). Degrees of hunger, reward and nonreward; and maze learning in rats. *University of California Publications in Psychology, 4,* 241–256. Copyright 1930 by The Regents of the University of California.

Figure 8.4. Adapted from Dickinson, A., & Nicholas, D. J. (1983). Irrelevant incentive learning during instructional conditioning: The role of drive-reinforcer and response-reinforcer relationships. *Quarterly Journal of Experimental Psychology, 35B,* 249–263. Reprinted by permission of The Experimental Psychology Society.

Figure 8.5. Adapted from Dickinson, A., & Dawson, G. R. (1987). Pavlovian processes in the motivation control of instrumental performance. *Quarterly Journal of Experimental Psychology, 39B,* 201–213. Reprinted by permission of The Experimental Psychology Society.

Figure 8.6. From Seligman, M. E. P., & Maier, S. F. (1967). Failure to escape traumatic shock. *Journal of Experimental Psychology, 74,* 1–9. Copyright 1967 by the American Psychological Association. Reprinted by permission.

Figure 8.7. From Klein, D. C., & Seligman, M. E. P. (1976). Reversal of performance deficits and perceptible deficits in learned helplessness and depression. *Journal of Abnormal Psychology, 85,* 11–26. Copyright 1976 by the American Psychological Association. Reprinted by permission.

Figure 8.8. From Miller, W. R., & Seligman, M.E. P. (1973). Depression and the perception of reinforcement. *Journal of Abnormal Psychology, 82,* 62–73. Copyright 1973 by the American Psychological Association. Reprinted by permission.

Figure 8.9. From Bandura, A., & Adams, N. E. (1977). Analysis of self-efficacy theory of behavioral change. *Cognitive Therapy and Research, 1*, 287–310.

Figure 9.2. From Siegel, S. (1977). Morphine tolerance acquisition as an associative process. *Journal of Experimental Psychology: Animal Behavior Processes, 3*, 1–13. Copyright 1977 by the American Psychological Association. Reprinted by permission.

Figure 9.3. Adapted from Wagner, A. R., & Brandon, S. E. (1989). Evolution of a structured connectionist model of Pavlovian condition (AESOP). In S. B. Klein & R. R. Mowrer (Eds.), *Contemporary learning theory: Pavlovian conditioning and the status of traditional learning theory* (pp.149–189). Hillsdale, N.J.: Erlbaum.

Figure 9.4. From Paletta, M. S., & Wagner, A. R. (1986). Development of context-specific tolerance to morphine: Support for a dual-process interpretation. *Behavioral Neuroscience, 100*, 611–623. Copyright 1986 by the American Psychological Association. Reprinted by permission.

Figure 9.5. Adapted from Thompson, R. F., & Krupa, D. J. (1994). Organization of memory traces in the mammalian brain. *Annual Review of Neuroscience, 17*, 519–549.

Figure 9.6. From Wagner, A. R., & Brandon, S. E. (1989). Evolution of a structured connectionist model of Pavlovian condition (AESOP). In S. B. Klein & R. R. Mowrer (Eds.), *Contemporary learning and the status of traditional learning theory* (pp. 149–189). Hillsdale, N.J.: Erlbaum.

Figure 9.8. From Randich, A., & Ross, R. T. (1985). Contextual stimuli mediate the effects of pre- and postexposure to the unconditioned stimulus on conditioned suppression. In P. D. Balsam & A. Tomie (Eds.), *Context and learning.* Hillsdale, N.J.: Erlbaum.

Figure 9.9. Adapted from Baker, A. G., & Mackintosh, N. J. (1972). Excitatory and inhibitory conditioning following uncorrelated precentations of CS and UCS. *Animal Learning and Behavior, 5*, 315–319. Reprinted by permission of Psychonomic Society, Inc.

Figure 9.10. From Allison, J. (1989). The nature of reinforcement. In S. B. Klein & R. R. Mowrer (Eds.), *Contemporary learning theories: Instrumental conditioning theory and the impact of biological constraints on learning* (pp. 13–39). Hillsdale, N.J.: Erlbaum.

Figure 9.11. From Viken, R. J., & McFall, R. M. (1994). Paradox lost: Implications of contemporary reinforcement theory for behavior therapy. *Current Directions in Psychological Science, 3*, 121–124.

Figure 9.12. From Herrnstein, R. J. (1961). Relative and absolute strength of response as a function of frequency of reinforcement. *Journal of the Experimental Analysis of Behavior, 4*, 267–272. Copyright 1961 by the Society for the Experimental Analysis of Behavior, Inc.

Figure 10.1. From Timberlake, W. (2001). Motivational modes in behavior systems. In R. R. Mowrer & S. B. Klein (Eds.). *Handbook of contemporary learning theories.* Mawrah, N.J.: Erlbaum.

Figure 10.2. Photo Courtesy of Animal Behavior Enterprises, Inc. Hot Springs, Arkansas. Used by permission of Marian Breland.

Figure 10.3. Adapted from Falk, J. L. (1966). Schedule-indicated polydipsia as a function of fixed-interval length. *Journal of the Experimental Analysis of Behavior, 9*, 37–39. Copyright 1966 by the Society for the Experimental Analysis of Behavior.

Figure 10.4. From Riley, A. L., Lotter, E. C., & Kulkosky, P. J. (1979). The effects of conditioned taste aversions on the acquisition and maintenance of schedule-induced polydipsia. *Animal Learning and Behavior, 7*, 3–12. Reprinted by permission of Psychonomic Society, Inc.

Figure 10.5. From Hyson, R. L., Sickel, J. L., Kulkosky, P. J., & Riley, A. C. (1981). The insensitivity of schedule-induced polydipsia to conditioned taste aversions: Effect of amount consumed during conditioning. *Animal Learning and Behavior, 9,* 281–286. Reprinted by permission of Psychonomic Society, Inc.

Figure 10.6. Adapted from Garcia, J., Clark, J. C., & Hankins, W. G. (1973). Natural responses to scheduled rewards. In P. P. G. Bateson & P. H. Klopfer (Eds.). *Perspectives in Ethology* (vol. 1). New York: Plenum.

Figure 10.7. From Kalat, J. W., & Rozin, P. (1973). "Learned safety" as a mechanism in long-delay taste-aversion learning in rats. *Journal of Comparative and Physiological Psychology, 83,* 198–207. Copyright 1973 by the American Psychological Association. Reprinted by permission.

Figure 10.8. Reprinted with permission from Hess, E. H. (1964). Imprinting in birds, *Science, 113,* 1132–1139. Copyright 1964 American Association for the Advancement of Science.

Figure 10.9. Courtesy of Harlow Primate Laboratory, University of Wisconsin.

Figure 10.10. From Bolles, R. C. (1969). Avoidance and escape learning. *Journal of Comparative and Physiological Psychology, 68,* 355–358. Copyright 1969 by the American Psychological Association. Reprinted by permission.

Figure 10.11. In H. H. Jasper, L. D. Proctor, R. S. Knighton, W. C. Noshav, & R. T. Costello (Eds.). *Reticular formation of the brain.* Boston: Little, Brown. Copyright 1958 by Little, Brown, and Company.

Figure 10.12. From Klein, S. B. (2000). *Biological psychology.* Upper Saddle River, N.J.: Prentice-Hall.

Figure 10.13. From Klein, S. B. (2000). *Biological psychology.* Upper Saddle River, N.J.: Prentice-Hall.

Figure 10.14. From Klein, S. B. (2000). *Biological psychology.* Upper Saddle River, N.J.: Prentice-Hall.

Figure 11.2. From Smoke, K. L. (1932). An objective study of concept formation. *Psychological Monographs, 42,* whole no. 191. Copyright 1932 by the American Psychological Association. Reprinted by permission.

Figure 11.3. Photographs provided by Richard Herrnstein.

Figure 11.4. From Hull, C. L. (1920). Quantitative aspect of the evolution of concepts: An experimental study. *Psychological Monographs, 28,* whole no. 123. Copyright 1920 by the American Psychological Association. Reprinted by permission.

Figure 11.5. From Kimble, G. A., Garmezy, N., & Zigler, E. (1984). *Psychology* (6th ed.). New York: Wiley.

Figure 11.6. From Levine, M. (1966). Hypothesis behavior by humans during discrimination learning. *Journal of Experimental Psychology, 71,* 331–338. Copyright 1966 by the American Psychological Association. Reprinted by permission.

Figure 11.11. Photograph courtesy of Yerkes Primate Center. Copyright by Georgia State University Language Research Center.

Figure 12.1. Figure from "Human Memory: A Proposed System and Its Control Processes." By Atkinson, R. C., & Shiffrin, R. M. *The Psychology of Learning and Motivation, Advances in Research and Theory,* Volume 2, edited by Spence, K. W., & Spence, J. T. Copyright © 1965 by Academic Press, reproduced by permission of the publisher.

Figure 12.3. From Sperling, G. (1960). The information available in brief visual presentations. *Psychological Monographs, 74,* whole no. 498. Copyright 1960 by the American Psychological Association. Reprinted by permission.

Figure 12.4. Figure from *"An Auditory Analogue of the Sperling Partial Report Procedure: Evidence for Brief Auditory Storage,"* by Darwin, C. T., Tuvey, M. T., & Crowder, R. G. in *Cognitive Psychology,* Volume 3: 255–267. Copyright © 1972 by Academic Press, reproduced by permission of the publisher.

Figure 12.5. From Crowder, R. G., & Morton, J. (1969). Precategorical acoustic storage (PAS). *Perception and Psychophysics, 5,* 365–373.

Figure 12.6. From Peterson, L. R., & Petersen, M. J. (1959). Short-term retention of individual verbal items. *Journal of Experimental Psychology, 58,* 193–198. Copyright © 1959 by the American Psychological Association. Reprinted by permission.

Figure 12.7. Figure from "Implications of Short-Term Memory for a General Theory of Memory." By Melton, A. W. in *Journal of Verbal Learning and Verbal Behavior,* Volume 2: 1–21. Copyright 1963 by Academic Press, reproduced by permission of the publisher.

Figure 12.10. Figure from "Retrieval Time from Semantic Memory." By Collins, A. M., & Quillian, M. R. in *Journal of Verbal Learning and Verbal Behavior,* Volume 8: 247. Copyright 1969 by Academic Press, reproduced by permission of the publisher.

Figure 12.11. From "Retrieval Time from Semantic Memory" by Collins, A. M., & Quillian, M. R. in *Journal of Verbal Learning and Verbal Behavior, 8:* 247. Copyright © 1969 by Academic Press, reproduced by permission of the publisher.

Figure 12.12. From Collins, A. M., & Loftus, E. F. (1975). A spreading activating theory of semantic memory. *Psychological Review, 82,* 407–428. Copyright 1975 by the American Psychological Association. Reprinted by permission.

Figure 12.13. From McClelland, J. L., Rumelhart, D. E., & Hinton, G. E. (1986). The appeal of parallel distributed processing. In Rumelhart, D. E., McClelland, J. L., and the PDP Research Group (Eds.). *Parallel distributed processing: Explorations in the microstructure of cognition* (Vol. 1). Cambridge, Mass.: MIT Press.

Figure 12.14. From Baddeley, A. D. (1986). *Working memory: Oxford Psychology Series* No. 11. Copyright 1986. Reprinted by permission Oxford University Press.

Figure 12.15. From Klein, S. B. (2000). *Biological psychology.* Upper Saddle River, N.J.: Prentice-Hall.

Figure 12.17. From Klein, S. B. (2000). *Biological psychology.* Upper Saddle River, N.J.: Prentice-Hall.

Figure 12.19. Adapted from Squire, L. R. (1986). The neuropsychology of memory. In P. Marler and H. Terrace (Eds.). *The Biology of learning.* Berlin: Springer-Verlag.

Figure 12.21. Reprinted with permission from Squire, L. R. (1986). Mechanisms of memory. *Science, 232,* 1612–1619. Copyright 1986 by the American Association for the Advancement of Science.

Figure 12.22. From Corkin, S., Amaral, D. G., Gonzalez, R. G., Johnson, K. A., & Hyman, B. T. (1997). H. M.'s medial temporal lobe lesion: Findings from magnetic resonance imaging. *Journal of Neuroscience, 17,* 3964–3979. Copyright 1997 by the Society of Neuroscience.

Figure 13.1. From Underwood, B. J. (1983). *Attributes of memory.* Glenview, Ill.: Scott, Foresman and Company.

Figure 13.2. Adapted from Gooden, D. R., & Baddeley, A. D. (1975). Context-dependent memory in two natural environments: On land and underwater. *British Journal of Psychology, 66,* 325–331.

Figure 13.3. Figure from "Mechanisms for the Cueing Phenomenon: The Addition of the Cueing Context to the Training Memory." By Gordon, W. C., McCracken, K. M., Dess Beech, N., & Mowrer, R. R. in *Learning and motivation,* Volume 12: 196–211. Copyright © 1981 by Academic Press, reproduced by permission of the publisher.

Figure 13.4. From Kamin, L. J. (1957). Retention of an incompletely learned avoidance response. *Journal of Comparative and Physiological Psychology, 50,* 457–460. Copyright 1957 by the American Psychological Association. Reprinted by permission.

Figure 13.5. Adapted and reproduced with permission of authors and publishers from Jenkins, J. J., Mink, W. P., & Russell, W. A. Associative clustering as a function of

Author Index

Subject Index

561